Professional XNA Programming

Introduction xxiii

Part I: XNA Framework Basics

Chapter 1: Introducing XNA 3
Chapter 2: Creating Your First Game: Pong. 29
Chapter 3: Helper Classes 61
Chapter 4: Game Components 91

Part II: Basic Graphics Engine

Chapter 5: Writing Your Own XNA Graphics Engine 115
Chapter 6: Shader Management. 145
Chapter 7: Realism Through Normal Mapping 173
Chapter 8: Post-Screen Shaders and the Rocket Commander Game. 207

Part III: Improving Your Game Engine

Chapter 9: Adding Sound with XACT. 243
Chapter 10: Player Input and the User Interface 267
Chapter 11: Creating XNA Shooter. 295

Part IV: Writing a Racing Game

Chapter 12: Generating Landscapes and Tracks 333
Chapter 13: Physics 369
Chapter 14: Fine-Tuning and "Modding" the Racing Game 401

Part V: Writing Multiplayer Games

Chapter 15: Multiplayer and Xbox Live 447
Chapter 16: Role-Playing Games 485
Chapter 17: Dungeon Quest. 517
Appendix A: Resources 545

Index 557

Professional

XNA™ Programming

Building Games for Xbox 360™ and Windows®
with XNA Game Studio 2.0, Second Edition

Professional

XNA™ Programming

**Building Games for Xbox 360™ and Windows®
with XNA Game Studio 2.0, Second Edition**

Benjamin Nitschke

WILEY

Wiley Publishing, Inc.

Professional XNA™ Programming

Published by
Wiley Publishing, Inc.
10475 Crosspoint Boulevard
Indianapolis, IN 46256
www.wiley.com

Manufactured in the United States of America

10 9 8 7 6 5 4 3 2 1

ISBN-13: 978-0-470-26128-6

This book is dedicated to all the people that helped me become a game programmer, especially all the programmers out there creating engines and libraries, sharing knowledge, and writing reusable code to help out fellow programmers.

About the Author

Benjamin Nitschke is the founder, lead programmer, and game designer at exDream entertainment. He is 26 years old, and lives in Hannover, Germany. He became a DirectX MVP of Microsoft in 2006 for his outstanding work in the DirectX community, especially with the free game Rocket Commander.

He started young — at the age of 9 he bought his first computer, a C64. He did not have many games, but he was very eager to type in commands on the C64, and from that to writing the first applications and games in Basic was not a big step. A few years later, he finally got a PC (386) and started some small game projects (Tetris clones, shoot-em-up games, and so on). exDream entertainment was founded 10 years ago, and it released a couple of smaller games before the first RTS game, Arena Wars, was created. Arena Wars was the first commercial .NET game ever and was released in 2004, where it received more than 20 awards worldwide, especially for the great multiplayer modes.

Recently, Benjamin has developed a couple of free open source games such as Rocket Commander and the XNA Racing Game Starter Kit, along with many game modifications. These games feature many video tutorials and a good documentation and code style to help beginners create their first video games. The video tutorials have been viewed more than 100,000 times and the games were downloaded and played even more often than that.

About the Technical Editor

Michael Morton has been a hobby game developer for over 16 years, covering a gamut of graphics technologies and implementations. He is the administrator of the popular XNA website, ziggyware.com, and was recently awarded the Microsoft MVP for his consistent dedication to helping the community learn XNA and DirectX.

Credits

Executive Editor
Chris Webb

Development Editor
Kenyon Brown

Technical Editor
Michael Morton

Production Editor
Christine O'Connor

Copy Editor
Nancy Rapoport

Editorial Manager
Mary Beth Wakefield

Production Manager
Tim Tate

Vice President and Executive Group Publisher
Richard Swadley

Vice President and Executive Publisher
Joseph B. Wikert

Project Coordinator, Cover
Lynsey Stanford

Compositor
Simmy Cover, Happenstance Type-O-Rama

Proofreader
Christopher M. Jones

Indexer
Johnna VanHoose Dinse

Acknowledgments

First and foremost, I would like to thank my parents for not supporting my childhood interest in computers at first. Only in this way did I become insanely interested and motivated in programming even without knowing anyone else that had a computer.

I want to thank Chris Webb for giving me the opportunity to become an author. I also want to thank Kenyon Brown, Michael Morton, and everyone else at Wiley. It was an absolute pleasure to work with all of you.

I would also like to thank my colleagues and friends for supporting me in my game projects. Thanks to Enrico Ciesiek for helping me out with the chapters and thanks to Christoph Rienaecker for giving me so many cool 3D models for my games. Thanks also fly out to Boje Holtz, Leif Griga, and Manuel Nitschke for testing and feedback.

Without the hard work of the XNA team, and also the .NET, DirectX, and Xbox 360 teams at Microsoft, this book would not have been possible. They are not only responsible for creating XNA, DirectX, .NET, and many other frameworks that made this book and the games in it as useful as they are, but they are also incredibly cool guys, who are easy to talk to and very supportive. I especially want to thank Christina Storm, Tom Miller, Mitch Walker, Dave Mitchell, Dirk Primbs, and Uwe Baumann at Microsoft.

Finally, I want to thank my family and friends for supporting me while I was writing the book. I'm sure it couldn't have been easy to see me go for days without sleep. In a way, this is my gift to all of you.

Contents

Acknowledgments xi
Introduction xxiii

Part I: XNA Framework Basics 1

Chapter 1: Introducing XNA 3

Introduction to the XNA Framework 3
XNA Game Studio Express 4
Application Model 5
Content Pipeline 8
Get the Free XNA Game Studio Express 9
Requirements 10
Installing 10
What About Visual Studio 2005 Professional? 12
Configuring Your Xbox 360 13
Getting Started 15
Your First Project 15
F5 and Go 16
Changing the Code 17
Notes about XNA 21
Important Links 21
Is C# Good for Game Development? 22
Getting Used to the Content Pipeline 23
Differences with MDX 24
Additional Tools and Tips 24
Changes in XNA 2.0 25
Troubleshooting 27
Summary 28

Chapter 2: Creating Your First Game: Pong 29

Game Ideas 30
Write Down Your Ideas! 30
Agile Methodology 32
Solving Initial Difficulties 33
Creating Some Textures 34

Let's Write Pong   **35**
  Sprites   35
  Unit Testing in Games   37
  Adding the Ball and Paddles   41
  Handling Player Input   44
  Collision Testing   47
  Adding Sound   53
How This Looks on the Xbox 360   **56**
Challenge: Improve the Pong Game   **57**
Troubleshooting   **58**
Summary   **59**

Chapter 3: Helper Classes   **61**

Managing the Content Pipeline   **62**
  Supported File Formats   63
  Advantages and Disadvantages   64
  Handling Content Directories   65
  Importing and Accessing Content   66
Logging Error Messages   **68**
Unit Testing in XNA   **69**
  NUnit and TestDriven.Net   70
  Starting Unit Tests   71
  Golden Rules   73
RandomHelper Class   **73**
  Generate Random Vectors   74
StringHelper Class   **74**
  Extracting Filenames   75
  Writing Lists   76
Other Helpers   **77**
  SpriteHelper Class   77
  EnumHelper Class   79
  ColorHelper Class   80
The Breakout Game   **80**
  Unit Testing in Breakout   82
  Breakout Levels   83
  The Game Loop   85
  Drawing Breakout   86
  Collision Testing   88
Challenge: Improve the Breakout Game   **89**
Summary   **90**

Contents

Chapter 4: Game Components   **91**

The Game Class   **92**
Game Components   **93**
More Helper Classes   **95**
  TextureFont Class   95
  Input Class   97
  Sound Class   98
Tetris, Tetris, Tetris!   **99**
  Rendering the Background   100
  Handling the Grid   101
  Block Types   102
  Gravity   105
  Handling Input   107
  Testing   110
Challenge: Create the NextBlock Game Component   **111**
Summary   **111**

Part II: Basic Graphics Engine   **113**

Chapter 5: Writing Your Own XNA Graphics Engine   **115**

What Should Your Engine Be Able to Do?   **116**
  The Engine Unit Test   117
  3D Models   119
  Rendering of Textures   121
  Line Rendering   123
3D Programming   **127**
  Model Unit Test   131
  Testing Other Models   135
Plugging in More Game Components   **136**
  Simple Camera Class   137
  ScreenshotCapturer Class   139
Making Sure Games Run on the Xbox 360   **140**
  Downloading the XNA Game Launcher   140
  Xbox 360 Setup and Deploying Games   141
  Console Debugging and Tools   142
Challenge: Write a Game Component   **143**
Summary   **143**

Contents

Chapter 6: Shader Management   **145**

Shader Overview   **146**

History   146

Shaders Everywhere in XNA   147

Example Games   148

Step-by-Step Shader Tutorial   **150**

FX Composer   151

FX File Layout   153

Parameters   155

Vertex Input Format   158

Vertex Shader   159

Pixel Shader   162

Importing the Shader into Your Engine   **164**

Compiling Shaders   165

Using Parameters   166

Vertex Formats   167

Rendering with Shaders   167

Testing the Shader   169

Challenge   **170**

Summary   **170**

Chapter 7: Realism Through Normal Mapping   **173**

Adding Detail to Objects   **174**

Problems   177

Asteroids! Wrong Game or What?   178

So How Do Shaders Work?   **182**

Vertex Shaders and Matrices   185

Pixel Shader and Optimizations   187

ShaderEffect Class   **189**

TangentVertex Format   191

Normal Mapping Unit Test   193

Adding Tangent Data with a Custom Processor   195

Final Asteroid Unit Test   199

More Shaders   **201**

Offset Mapping   201

Glass Shader   202

Reflection and Water   203

Challenge: Add Parallax Mapping   **204**

Summary   **205**

Contents

Chapter 8: Post-Screen Shaders and the Rocket Commander Game   207

Handling Post-Screen Shaders   **208**
Pre-Screen Sky Cube Mapping   208
Writing a Simple Post-Screen Shader   214
Improvements   217
Implementing Post-Screen Shaders   **219**
RenderToTexture Class   220
PostScreenDarkenBorder Class   221
Unit Test Result   224
More Post-Screen Shaders   **225**
Motion Blur   227
Color Correction   228
Menu Effects   231
Rocket Commander Game   **232**
Performance in XNA   232
Moving from MDX to XNA   234
Using Threads to Improve Performance   235
Result and Screenshots   235
Challenge: Write an Edge Detection Shader   **237**
Summary   **239**

Part III: Improving Your Game Engine   **241**

Chapter 9: Adding Sound with XACT   **243**

No DirectSound   **244**
Handling .wav Files   245
Using XACT   **248**
Creating Projects   249
Creating Your Wave Bank   250
Compressing Music Data   252
Sound Banks   254
Cue Variables   256
Other Effects   257
Changes in XNA 2.0   259
Sound Class   **260**
Rocket Motor Sound   263
Whoosh, What Was That?   264
Menu Sounds   265
Challenge: Create Your XACT Project   **265**
Summary   **266**

Contents

Chapter 10: Player Input and the User Interface   **267**

Input Class   **268**

The Update Method in the Input Class   271

Mouse Rectangles   272

Entering Text in XNA   275

Game Screens   **277**

Help Screen   280

In-Game User Interface   281

Tips   286

Cameras   **287**

Space Camera   **289**

Challenge: Write a Free Camera Class   **292**

Summary   **293**

Chapter 11: Creating XNA Shooter   **295**

Putting It All Together   **296**

Sounds   297

User Interface   298

Textures   300

3D Models   301

Animated Textures   303

Billboards   305

Landscape Rendering   **308**

Base Texture and Normal Map   308

Height Map   310

Adding Objects   312

XNA Shooter Game   **315**

Game Logic   317

3D Effects   319

Unit Class   320

Projectile Class   323

Item Class   325

Final Screenshot   327

Challenge: Write a Game with Your Engine   **327**

Summary   **329**

Part IV: Writing a Racing Game   331

Chapter 12: Generating Landscapes and Tracks   333

Game Comparisons   334
Gran Tourismo   335
Need for Speed   335
Trackmania   336
XNA Racing Game   337
Landscape Rendering   338
Textures   339
Rendering   340
Optimizing Tips   345
Tracks   349
Unit Testing to the Rescue   349
Interpolating Splines   352
More Complex Tracks   354
Importing the Track Data   356
Generating Vertices from the Track Data   358
Final Result   363
Challenge: Create a New Unit Test Track   365
Summary   366

Chapter 13: Physics   369

Newton's Laws of Motion   370
Keep It Simple   372
Gravitation   376
Physics Engines   379
Ageia PhysX   381
Havok   382
ODE   383
Other   383
Implementing Physics   385
Handling Loopings   385
Spring Physics   388
Collision Detection   391
PhysicsAsteroidManager   392
Car Collision   395
Challenge: Figure Out the Road Collision   398
Summary   400

xx

Contents

Chapter 14: Fine-Tuning and "Modding" the Racing Game **401**

Game Concept **403**
Game Idea 405
Additional Features 407
Game Screens **409**
Splash Screen 410
Main Menu 413
Game Screen 414
Highscores 417
Final Unit Testing and Tweaking **418**
Tweaking the Track 421
Shadow Mapping 422
Final Testing on Windows 428
Final Testing on the Xbox 360 430
Additional Ideas **433**
More Cars 433
Online Highscore List 433
More Shaders and Effects 434
More Game Modes 435
Multiplayer Mode 436
Challenge: Write Your Own Mod! **437**
Example Game: Speedy Racer 438
Summary **442**

Part V: Writing Multiplayer Games **445**

Chapter 15: Multiplayer and Xbox Live **447**

What's New in XNA 2.0 **448**
Overview About Networking in XNA 2.0 449
TCP Versus UDP 450
Firewalls and Punching Through NATs 453
Network Architecture **455**
Sending UDP Data 458
Connecting Two Players 462
Network Messages 464
Server Game List 470
Writing a Chat Application **474**
Game Screens 474
Handling Chat Messages 479
The Final Chat Application 482

Challenge: Write a Multiplayer Application **483**

Summary **484**

Chapter 16: Role-Playing Games **485**

Types of Role-Playing Games **486**

"Hack and Slash" Role-Playing Games 487

Massively Multiplayer Role-Playing Games 491

Designing Dungeon Quest **493**

Ideas **494**

Scenario **494**

Story **496**

Characters **498**

Enemies **501**

Weapons and Items **506**

Abilities and Spells **506**

Abilities 507

Spells 508

Leveling System 510

Challenge: Improve the Leveling System **513**

Summary **514**

Chapter 17: Dungeon Quest **517**

Creating the Engine **518**

Changes to the Graphic Engine 519

Using Collada Model Files 522

Handling Many Point Lights 526

Adding AI 530

Path-Finding 530

Alert-System via Cries 531

Multiplayer Support **532**

Network Messages 533

Xbox LIVE Support 535

The Dungeon Quest Editor **539**

Summary **544**

Appendix A: Resources **545**

Index **557**

Introduction

Up until recently, the concept for the Xbox 360 as a platform for creating homebrew games was not even thinkable. For most people creating console games was just a pure impossibility, not just because SDKs (Software Development Kit) are expensive, but because you won't even get a SDK. Access to any development information to create console games is often prohibited only to big development studios and game publishers, not independent game developers and beginners.

This has all changed. Microsoft's new XNA Framework makes homebrew, cross-platform games for Windows and the Xbox 360 possible. XNA is not only just a new framework, but it is also the best framework available today to create games. With no other language or tool, you will be able to create powerful games with little effort. I would never have been able to create a great game like the Racing Game in such a short time frame if not for XNA.

Whom This Book Is For

This book is aimed at a variety of audiences. You should have knowledge of the programming language C#, but if you already know C++ or Java, it will be very easy to switch. If you have not worked with any high-level programming language before, I suggest you pick up a C# book first. Even without knowledge of programming, this book has many tips and tricks in it for upcoming game programmers. For a more practical use of this book, you should follow along with the examples and code. Most of the chapters are organized in a way that is equally useful to both beginners and experienced game programmers. All you need to write successful games is your willingness to learn the game programming techniques presented in this book and the desire to explore the world of computer games and keep improving over and over again.

What This Book Covers and How It's Structured

Part I, "XNA Framework Basics," covers the basics of XNA. You will learn all about the XNA Framework and XNA Game Studio Express. Even if you already know some of the basics, there are many useful tips and tricks in the first chapter. The second chapter explains the creation process of your first game; it is a simple one, but the lessons learned here will help you out later. In Chapters 3 and 4, two more games are created, but more important, the foundation for your game engine is built.

Thanks to the many helper classes of Part I, writing the game engine in Part II, "Basic Graphics Engine," is much easier so you can focus on the hard parts of getting 3D models and shaders to work. Everything in XNA is based on shaders because there is no more fixed function rendering so I spend most of my time discussing shaders, normal mapping, post-screen effects, and more. At the end of Part II, the Rocket Commander XNA game appears as an example of a game that combines all the shaders and the game engine from the previous chapters.

Part III, "Improving Your Game Engine," goes back to the basics and talks about audio, UI, input handling, and managing your game engine in a meaningful way. You create a new game called XNA Shooter based on the XNA Graphics Engine and the Rocket Commander game. XNA Shooter is a really fun, old-school shoot-'em-up game with cool 3D graphics and advanced shader effects.

In Part IV, "Writing a Racing Game," you pull in all the knowledge you've gained to create a full-blown racing game in XNA. This part features the most advanced topics such as landscape and 3D track rendering, creating and handling physics engines, and many new shader technologies such as shadow mapping, detail mapping, and rendering in an optimized way for optimal performance.

Part V (Chapters 15-17) is about Dungeon Quest, a role playing game with multiplayer support. Chapter 15 starts with an explanation of the networking basics and a simple chat application, which also works on Windows, even in XNA 1.0 if you like. Then Chapter 16 talks a little bit about role playing games and Chapter 17 finally shows the Dungeon Quest game with some really cool tricks and tips on creating your own full-blown role playing game.

If you are ready to begin learning XNA game development, I suggest you read on and start with Chapter 1, "Introducing XNA." Good luck creating your first XNA games and, above all, have fun! I hope you enjoy reading this book as much as I enjoyed writing it.

Source Code

As you work through the examples in this book, you may choose either to type in all the code manually or to use the source code files that accompany the book. All of the source code used in this book, including all the code to create a full racing game in XNA, is available for download at http://www.wrox.com. Once at the site, simply locate the book's title (either by using the Search box or by using one of the title lists) and click the Download Code link on the book's detail page to obtain all the source code for the book.

Because many books have similar titles, you may find it easiest to search by ISBN; this book's ISBN is 978-0-470-26128-6.

Once you download the code, just decompress it with your favorite compression tool. Alternatively, you can go to the main Wrox code download page at http://www.wrox.com/dynamic/books/download.aspx to see the code available for this book and all other Wrox books.

Errata

We make every effort to ensure that there are no errors in the text or in the code. However, no one is perfect, and mistakes do occur. If you find an error in one of our books, like a spelling mistake or faulty piece of code, we would be very grateful for your feedback. By sending in errata you may save another reader hours of frustration and at the same time you will be helping us provide even higher-quality information.

To find the errata page for this book, go to `http://www.wrox.com` and locate the title using the Search box or one of the title lists. Then, on the book details page, click the Book Errata link. On this page you can view all errata that has been submitted for this book and posted by Wrox editors. A complete book list including links to each book's errata is also available at `www.wrox.com/misc-pages/booklist.shtml`.

If you don't spot "your" error on the Book Errata page, go to `www.wrox.com/contact/techsupport` `.shtml` and complete the form there to send us the error you have found. We'll check the information and, if appropriate, post a message to the book's errata page and fix the problem in subsequent editions of the book.

Part I: XNA Framework Basics

Chapter 1: Introducing XNA

Chapter 2: Creating Your First Game: Pong

Chapter 3: Helper Classes

Chapter 4: Game Components

1

Introducing XNA

Welcome to the world of XNA. As a game programmer you probably know about DirectX and maybe even the basics of the XNA Framework. This chapter explains how to install XNA Game Studio Express and how to use it in a productive way. It also contains quite a lot of tips that might even be useful for anyone who already knows the basics.

In the next few chapters you start developing some cool smaller games. Part I contains the basic foundation and information about the helper classes you will use later in this book to develop a full-blown graphics engine for more advanced game projects. To keep things simple you start with 2D programming in Part I and then advance to 3D in Part II.

Let's get started.

Introduction to the XNA Framework

XNA, developed by Microsoft, was started a few years ago, but kept very secret. At the GDC (the biggest annual Game Developers Conference) in 2004, Microsoft announced XNA for the first time. XNA is not just a framework like DirectX; it also contains a lot of tools and even a custom IDE derived from Visual Studio to make the game programmer's life easier. Because no tools or bits were released until 2006, DirectX developers saw only the "XNA" logo in the upper-right corner of the DirectX SDK documentation from 2004 to 2006 (see Figure 1-1). (XNA just means "XNAs Not Acronymed.")

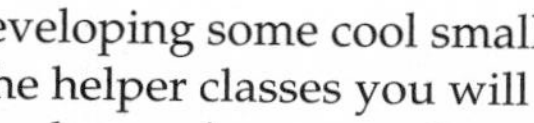

Figure 1-1

This means Microsoft was working on the XNA Framework for quite a while, but the developers did not really know what to expect. It could be a successor to the DirectX Framework, they thought, but when Direct3D 10 Beta for Windows Vista was released in the end of 2005, it seemed that DirectX was still the preferred graphics framework even for this new operating system. Then early in 2006, at the GDC, the Microsoft XNA Build March 2006 CTP was released. XNA Build is a tool that allows you to manage complex build processes, similar to Ms-build and tools like Ants, but more complex and powerful. Because Microsoft's MechCommander 2 was also released as a Shared Source Release, a lot of people downloaded it and tried to rebuild the MechCommander 2 game. But after a while, not much happened, and small to mid-sized teams, in particular, don't really need a complex build management tool.

Then it was quiet for a while and only Microsoft personnel and DirectX MVPs (I am lucky to be one) received information about the upcoming XNA Framework and XNA Game Studio releases. The rest of the world found out about that at the Gamefest conference in August (a new game developer conference by Microsoft), where Microsoft announced the XNA Game Studio Express beta 1 release on August 30, 2006. The first beta contained only one starter kit, "Space Wars," and XNA did not include much 3D functionality. Many developers and hobbyists tried out XNA and wrote many small 2D games with the help of the Sprite classes in XNA. Although you could quickly create your Pong clone or some simple shoot-'em-up game, it was very hard to write your own 3D model importer and render code.

XNA Game Studio Express was initially targeted at beginners, hobbyists, and students to allow them to quickly develop their own games for the Windows and Xbox 360 platform. But this does not mean professional game studios cannot use XNA. A special XNA Game Studio Professional version targeted to professional game studios was planned to be released in 2007, but plans have changed quite a lot. Instead of having two separate versions, one for professional game developers and one for hobbyists, Microsoft's XNA team decided that it made more sense to have only one version, namely XNA 2.0, that can do everything. To publish a game on the Xbox 360, even if using the Xbox Live Arcade system, you need a publishing deal anyway and have to submit your game to Xbox Live. New with XNA 2.0 comes the support of Visual Studio 2005 Professional, but if you want to develop with XNA 1.0 (first four parts of the book) and want to use Visual Studio 2005 or 2008, follow the tricks I describe later in this chapter on how to work with VS and XNA productively.

Microsoft released another beta of XNA 1.0 a few months later in November 2006, before the final release of XNA Game Studio Express in December 2006. The final version included the content pipeline and many new features you will learn about in Chapters 2 and 3.

XNA is completely free and, for the first time, allows developers to create games for both the Windows platform and for the Xbox 360 platform simultaneously. But if you want to run your XNA game on the Xbox 360 console, you have to join the "Creators Club" for an annual fee of $99.

XNA Game Studio Express

Figure 1-2 shows you XNA Game Studio Express. The information provided here is for XNA Game Studio Express 1.0, but installing version 2.0 should be identical.

The screen does not just look similar to Visual C# 2005 Express; it actually is Visual C# 2005. There are only some minor changes to your project settings if you create an XNA project. Also, an extra option in Tools ➪ Options allows you to select your Xbox 360 device and enter the encryption key. Additionally, there are some new features inside the IDE — for example, the content pipeline that allows you to import textures, models, and shaders very quickly into your project. More about all that in a little bit.

Chapter 1: Introducing XNA

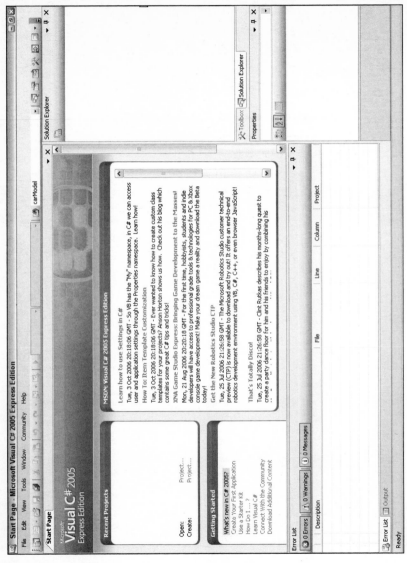

Figure 1-2

XNA Game Studio Express is currently the only available IDE for developing games with the XNA Framework, but once Microsoft ships XNA Game Studio 2.0 (end of 2007) you can also develop with Visual Studio 2005 Standard or Professional. If you have Visual Studio 2005, but try to use XNA 1.0 with it to create an XNA project, there will be no templates in it. Even worse: If you try to open a .csproj file you created with XNA Game Studio Express, Visual Studio cannot open the project. It is not supported in XNA 1.0. Read on for a few tips on how to get XNA 1.0 working with Visual Studio 2005 in the section "What About Visual Studio 2005 Professional?" If you start with XNA 2.0, you don't have to worry about this; Visual Studio 2005 will be supported out-of-the-box.

Application Model

The XNA Framework is divided into three essential parts (see Figure 1-3):

- ❑ **XNA Graphic Engine** in the Microsoft.Xna.Framework.dll
- ❑ **XNA Game Application Model** in the Microsoft.Xna.Framework.Game.dll
- ❑ **XNA Content Pipeline** in the Microsoft.Xna.Framework.Content.Pipeline.dll

All of these dlls are written in C# and are completely managed. This means you can open them up with a tool like Reflector (available from www.aisto.com/roeder/dotnet/) and see directly how they work (see Figure 1-4). Most internal functionality just calls to the DirectX dlls and simplifies things a little bit. The content pipeline is discussed shortly.

Figure 1-3

Application Model in XNA

Graphic Engine
Microsoft.Xna.Framework.Pipeline.dll

Game Application Model
Microsoft.Xna.Framework.Pipeline.dll

Content Pipeline
Microsoft.Xna.Framework.Pipeline.dll

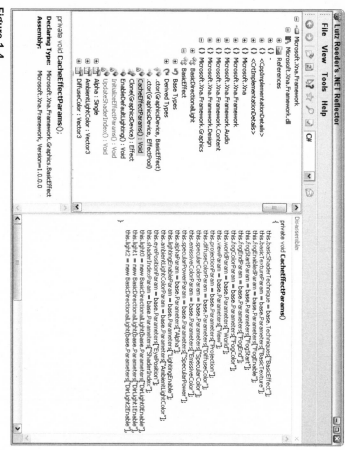

Figure 1-4

Take a look at the Application Model. Each XNA project uses a Game class, which contains all the important game components, the graphics device, the window settings, and the content manager. You can also add the input and sound handling here. Basically everything that your game does on a very high level somehow roots in the game class or at least is in some component that can be accessed from the game class.

The following are the three most important methods in the game class (see Figure 1-5). For the final release, Microsoft also added the `LoadGraphicsContent` and `UnloadGraphicsContent` helper methods by default to the `Game1.cs` class, which is created automatically for you when you create a new XNA project, but in most samples of this book these methods are not used because it is much simpler to have all initialization and loading code at one place in the `Initialize` function.

- `Initialize ()`
- `Update (GameTime time)`
- `Draw (GameTime time)`

Figure 1-5

You can probably already guess what all these do. `Initialize` loads all your game content, sets all your startup settings, and initializes everything you need. If you want to follow the design patterns Microsoft provides for XNA, you would do all the loading in the `LoadGraphicsContent` method. `Update` is called before each frame is drawn to update your game time, input, sound, and everything else that is not visible on the screen. If your game is GPU-limited, it can very well happen that `Update` is called more often than `Draw`, but your update code should run independent of the drawing code anyway. None of the samples in this book will need special care for the number of times `Update` and `Draw` are called. And finally, `Draw` is called each frame to draw everything to the screen. The separation of `Update` and `Draw` might not always be important and can almost always be ignored for unit tests, but for the final game it is important to make sure the game logic runs independent of the draw code. For example, on the Windows platform, the user could press Alt and Tab or minimize the game, in which case `Draw` does not need to be called anymore. Even with `Draw` not called anymore you may still want the game to continue to run in the background via the `Update` method. This is especially important for network games to make sure the player is still synchronized.

Additionally, you can add `GameComponent` classes to your game class, which again have an `Update` and a `Draw` method. Both of these methods are automatically called from your game `Update` and `Draw` methods. The initialization can happen directly in the constructor there. Initially Microsoft wanted the developers to create and add game components with the designer of Visual Studio, which can be seen in the first beta of XNA Game Studio Express (released August 30, 2006). The designer feature was later removed because it did not work well, was not supported for the Xbox 360 platform, and because not many developers used it anyway.

The idea with the game components is to reuse parts of your code and make it very easy to just plug them into your games. Examples of game components include a frame counter or maybe a sky cube mapping renderer for the 3D background. In my opinion, there are two major drawbacks: No standard game components are shipped with XNA, and it is not really hard to code such an application model yourself and even extend it. I do not use many `GameComponent` classes in this book, but feel free to plug them in on your own. Read Chapter 4 for more details of the `GameComponent` class and learn about its advantages and disadvantages. Because the game class has a `Components` property, it is very easy to add more components.

Don't get me wrong — the basic idea of game components is really great. There was a small webcast from Mitch Walker, the Program Manager of the XNA Framework at Microsoft, at the time the first XNA beta was released about the game components and how to combine them. At first I was not very sure what to think of the content pipeline and the game components idea; it looked cool in the webcasts, but when I started coding my first game projects in XNA I did not find it very useful to work with the designer that was presented in the first beta. In the second beta and the final release, most of the initial game component code was removed as well as the graphical designer component in XNA Game Studio. This happened because Microsoft was not able to find a way to implement the designer and game components idea in a useful way for the Xbox 360 console. (It had only worked on the Windows platform before.) See Chapter 4 for more details about game components..

While it can be a hassle to implement the UI and menu logic yourself, it makes game menus more unique. Almost every game implements its own UI. But if you think about it, a standard menu system, as Windows uses for every app, is boring; it is always nice to see the ways in which menus are presented in new games. You can still extract code very easily and create your own game components if you want to create a new game, and then you can just reuse the code (for example, the SkyCubeMapping class). Some game components, such as the camera and screenshot capturer classes from Chapter 4, are good examples for components that can be reused in many other games, but almost everything else in the games from this book is implemented without using game components.

One of Microsoft's goals with this application model is for the community of game developers to create and share their game components quite easily and improve the community aspect of XNA. As you can see from the many XNA game development sites and the projects on open source sites such as www.codeplex.com, the community is very active and willing to share, but it might not have much to do with the application model. Check out the links later in this chapter for more information.

Content Pipeline

The content pipeline is used to import, compile, and load game assets such as textures, 3D models, shaders, and sound files to your game project (see Figure 1-6). It greatly reduces the amount of custom code you have to do to get graphics, 3D data, and shaders into your game. For example, if you drop a model file into your project and it uses two textures and a specific shader, the content pipeline will process your model file and automatically find and add the required textures and shaders. You don't have to do this for yourself; the content importer "compiles" the data into a binary format and, in the process, it picks up everything you need.

Say the shader you added through the model you dropped into your project contains an error. In the past you would have to start your game project, and then get an exception telling you that the shader could not be compiled and the game would crash. Now the shader is compiled in the build process and you don't have to start your game to see that it does not work yet. You can quickly fix the error through the line and error message from the build output in XNA Game Studio Express and then rebuild.

The content pipeline does not just consist of one dll; there are five different dlls:

❑ **Microsoft.Xna.Framework.Content.Pipeline.dll** contains the basic functions for the content pipeline.

❑ **Microsoft.Xna.Framework.Content.Pipeline.EffectImporter.dll** is used to compile and import shaders.

❑ **Microsoft.Xna.Framework.Content.Pipeline.FBXImporter.dll** is the biggest of all dlls and contains a lot of code to import .fbx 3D model files and supports many features — for example, skinning and bones.

❑ **Microsoft.Xna.Framework.Content.Pipeline.TextureImporter.dll** is used to import texture files to your game. These files can be .dds files already in the DirectX format (which is the best format for textures and supports hardware compression), but .png, .jpg, .bmp, and .tga files are also supported. 2D sprites are just textures, too, and usually use the uncompressed 32-bit format.

❑ **Microsoft.Xna.Framework.Content.Pipeline.XImporter.dll** allows you to import .x 3D model files, a format that was used by many DirectX applications and samples.

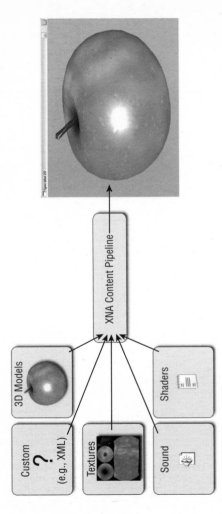

Figure 1-6

Your game itself will never require any of these dlls; they are just used to build and compile the content into .xnb (XNA Binary) files in your build process. This makes the distribution easier because you don't have to worry about the game content files anymore; it is easier to make sure all the content files are there when you start your game. Don't modify the .xnb files; they are just the output format (such as .exe) and should not be modified directly. You also can't convert the data back to textures, models, or shaders (well it might be possible, but it is hard to find working tools for that). The .xnb files are also very different on the Windows platform and the Xbox 360 platform, whereas the game source code and the content files might be exactly the same.

Additionally, you can create your own custom content processors, which allow you to compile any other game asset you have (for example, another model format) into .xnb files. You explore that in Part II when you have to make sure all your 3D models have tangent data for the normal mapping shaders.

Okay, that's all the basics you need for now. It is time to get going and code your first game.

Get the Free XNA Game Studio Express

To start coding right away, you have to make sure that you have the correct tools installed; the IDE is an especially important tool to get started quickly. If you already have XNA Game Studio Express installed and configured, you can skip this chapter. This part was written just in case anyone needs additional tips and tricks, such as how to get XNA running in Visual Studio 2005 Professional, which is not supported out of the box, but quite useful if you use Visual Studio plug-ins or tools such as SourceSafe or Team Foundation (to work better in a team, for example).

Requirements

XNA Game Studio Express targets Windows XP SP2 (SP means Service Pack) and Windows Vista. SP2 is important because of the requirements of the .NET 2.0 Framework. Other platforms such as Windows 2003 or older Windows platforms that support .NET 2.0 are not officially supported, but run fine, too. XNA is also tested only on 32-bit platforms, but it works fine on Windows XP x64 and Windows Vista, too, even as a development platform.

Because XNA Game Studio Express is based on Visual C# Express, it has the same basic requirements. You basically need a computer, nothing fancy. But for game development, you have much higher basic requirements anyway, which I discuss shortly. Visual C# Express runs on Windows 2000 SP4, Windows XP SP2, Windows 2003 SP1, Windows XP x64, and Windows Vista. As you can see, the older the operating system, the more service packs you need.

And finally, you also need the most current DirectX runtimes, and if you are serious about game development, better get the full DirectX SDK. The DirectX SDK is not required by XNA Game Studio Express because the dlls just call the underlying DirectX dlls, but it is always useful to have some more documentation on your system, and DirectX contains many samples and tutorials, which are useful if you run into trouble. For example, the DirectX SDK contains tools to help you generate DDS texture files, which are optimized for the best graphic card texture formats available today.

Because XNA does not support the fixed function pipeline anymore, as DirectX or Managed DirectX do, it is important that you have a graphic card that supports at least Shader Model 1.1 or even better, Shader Model 2.0. The first graphic cards with shader support were shipped back in 2001 (GeForce 3 and ATI 7000); Model 2.0 (GeForce 5x, ATI 9x00 Series) was introduced in 2003 and made the next generation with Shader Model 2.0 (GeForce 5x, ATI 9x00 Series) was introduced in 2003 and made popular by the many games in 2004 that made good use of shaders (Far Cry, Doom 3, Half-Life 2). Shader Model 3.0 (GeForce 6x, ATI x1000 Series) was the standard in 2006 and new cards with Shader Model 4.0 (GeForce 8x) were shipped late 2006/early 2007. The Xbox 360 uses an extended version of Shader Model 3.0.

So this is what you need at a minimum before attempting to install XNA Game Studio Express:

❑ Windows XP SP2 or Windows Vista

❑ 512MB RAM, but better to have more — 1 or 2 GB

❑ 1 GHz CPU, the faster the better, using the IDE and compiling your projects is faster and more fun

❑ Shader Model 1.1 graphic card (Nvidia GeForce 3 or 4, ATI Radeon 7x) or Shader Model 2.0 (GeForce 5/FX or ATI Radeon 9x00)

Installing

Get the latest version of XNA Game Studio Express for free at http://msdn.microsoft.com/directx/xna/.

The beta versions and XNA 1.0 still required that you install Visual C# Express and the latest version of DirectX 9.0c first; maybe this will change when the final version of XNA 2.0 is shipped. All of these downloads are completely free and it is really a nice thing to have all these tools available without any costs involved. This enables many more people, especially students, hobbyists, and normal players, to check out the development environment and maybe get even more excited about game development than they already are.

Start with installing XNA Game Studio Express (see Figure 1-7). There are no special options you have to select; the installer will do everything for you (for example, adding firewall rules for Xbox 360 testing). The installer also adds the XNA help, the starter kits, and the project templates to get you started.

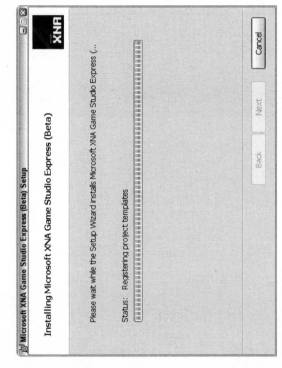

Figure 1-7

You will not really need the DirectX SDK, but I recommend that you install it. You will have additional documentation available and a great repertoire of tutorials and samples in case you need more information about common techniques for your graphic engine.

You can download DirectX from the Microsoft DirectX Developer Center page on http://msdn.microsoft.com/directx/.

When installing it, you should select to install the Redistributable in the custom setup step, too. You will need it if you want to install your game on other computers. When DirectX is installed, you can check out the newest features by taking a look at the samples with the DirectX Sample Browser. If you haven't worked much with Managed DirectX before and are interested, check out the documentation and tutorials.

If you want to use an Xbox 360 controller on your Windows machine (which works just fine thanks to the fact that the controller uses USB) you can just plug it into your PC and it should work fine on Windows XP and Vista after it automatically installs all required drivers. If that does not work automatically, you can also download the drivers yourself and follow the instructions from the official hardware site of Microsoft products at www.microsoft.com/hardware/gaming/download.mspx.

Last but not least, you will do a lot of unit testing in this book, and for that I usually recommend NUnit and TestDriven.NET (and later even xUnit, a newer unit testing framework released in late 2007). NUnit is an external dll and TestDriven.NET is not supported in the Visual Studio Express Editions anymore. It does not matter for this book because all source code will use its own kind of unit testing with a special class later on.

If you use Visual Studio 2005, I suggest using TestDriven.NET, and if you are using Visual Studio 2005 Team System, you can also use the Unit Testing features implemented directly in VS there. Alternatively there are also other Unit Testing Frameworks around (for example, MbUnit, csUnit, and so on). Most of the samples in this book keep things simple and use only very basic features of unit testing and make it look like many little test programs.

You can certainly do all your work inside the XNA Game Studio Express IDE, and Microsoft encourages you to do so. All samples in this book work fine with the Express editions and I did not use any external dlls (which was also one of the requirements for the XNA Starter Kits). However, some people already have Visual Studio 2005 and may feel more comfortable doing their coding over there. Read on for a couple of tricks on how to get XNA working with Visual Studio 2005 Professional.

What About Visual Studio 2005 Professional?

XNA Game Studio Express 1.0 is fine and a nice environment to work in. However, if you are used to tools like SourceSafe or any other CMS (Content Management System) or plug-ins like CodeRush, TestDriven.NET, and other productivity tools, you will run into a bunch of problems. As I said earlier, it is not even possible to open your XNA 1.0 projects from Visual Studio 2005. If you are using XNA 2.0 where Visual Studio 2005 is supported out-of-the-box or do not care about Visual Studio 2005 or Visual Studio 2008, you can skip this section.

The XNA Framework uses the .NET 2.0 Framework and DirectX 9.0c. To run games on any Windows PC, it needs the .NET 2.0 Framework, DirectX 9.0c, and the XNA dlls. If you are a game developer you will have the latest DirectX SDK anyway and if you have Visual Studio 2005, you will have the .NET 2.0 Framework, too, so the only thing you need for running and even compiling XNA applications are the two XNA dlls:

☐ Microsoft.Xna.Framework.dll

☐ Microsoft.Xna.Framework.Game.dll

These dlls are referenced in all XNA projects, so if you just add them to a project in Visual Studio 2005, you can directly start coding. To get started, just copy over the Game1.cs and Program.cs files from an empty XNA project you created with XNA Game Studio Express.

Another problem could arise if you work on a 64-bit operating system such as Windows XP x64 or Windows Vista x64. Although DirectX 9.0c has had 64-bit dlls for some time now and the .NET Framework runs fine on 64 bit, too, the problem lies in the XNA Framework, which is available only in a 32-bit version (called x86, by the way). People using the 64-bit operating systems of Windows had the same problem in the past with Managed DirectX, which is available only for 32 bit, too. Using a 64-bit operating system does not mean you cannot use 32-bit applications anymore; quite the contrary. Almost all applications that exist today are written for 32-bit operating systems, but they run fine in the 32-bit mode of Windows XP x64 or Windows Vista x64.

Why do I even bring this up if you can run 32-bit and 64-bit applications on 64-bit operating systems? Well, you cannot use 64-bit assemblies (dlls) from 32-bit applications or vice versa. The reason for that is that a Windows process has to be run either in 64 bit or 32 bit; emulating 32 bit from 64 bit would be too slow and is not even supported. Now how do you get XNA working in 64-bit mode? You don't, it is just not supported. Instead, you have to make sure that the .NET Framework and your application run in 32-bit mode; then Windows will start the whole process in 32-bit mode and you can load the XNA dlls just fine. If you don't do that, your game cannot even be started on any x64-bit platform.

In Visual Studio 2005, you can just select x86 platform instead of All CPUs in the Project Properties Build screen. In XNA Game Studio Express there is no such option and if you want the same setting you have to add a line to your .csproj file in each PropertyGroup section:

```
<PlatformTarget>x86</PlatformTarget>
```

I also wrote a little tool that converts XNA Game Studio Express projects to Visual Studio 2005 projects and back, and it handles the x64-bit issue. The newest version of the tool also supports Visual Studio 2008. You can download it from my blog at http://exdream.no-ip.info/blog/2007/07/19/XnaProjectChangerToolvsVS2008Support.aspx.

Configuring Your Xbox 360

To connect your Xbox 360 to your PC, you have to install the XNA Framework on your Xbox 360 first via the Xbox Live Service. Unlike the Windows platform, the download of the XNA Framework for the Xbox 360 is not free. You will have to join the "Creator's Club" subscription on the Xbox 360 through the Xbox Live Marketplace for $99 a year or $49 for four months. Microsoft does this to have a little control over the developers. Console development is usually very closed off and there is no open source thinking as in the Windows or Linux world. We can all just hope this is going to change.

First of all, make sure your PC and the Xbox 360 are connected to the same network. You don't have to connect the Xbox 360 directly to your PC; just plug it into the same network (router or modem). It is important that you always have access to the Internet from the console and not just to your PC because XNA requires an Xbox Live connection on your console. Once you have installed the XNA Framework on the Xbox 360, which also includes a custom version of the .NET 2.0 Compact Framework to make it run on the console, you can start the XNA Game Launcher (see Figure 1-8).

In the XNA Game Launcher you can now start your game projects or copy over XNA games from your friends or the Internet and start them on your console. Before you can connect to the PC, you will have to make an encryption key first by clicking Settings and then "Create Encryption Key." You will now see the encryption key; don't close this window. On your PC, open XNA Game Studio Express and go to ToolsOptions and scroll down. You will see the new XNA Game Studio option. Here you can add your Xbox 360 and enter your encryption key; then just click Add (see Figure 1-9).

13

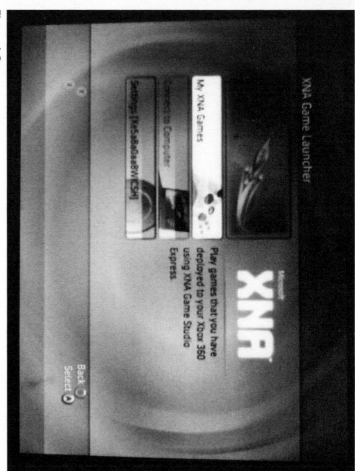

Figure 1-8

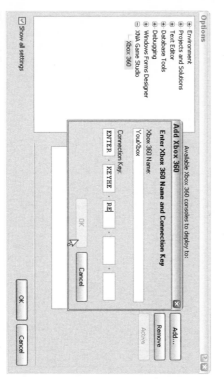

Figure 1-9

After you have successfully entered the encryption key, you can click OK on both the PC and the console. If this fails or you reinstall XNA Game Studio, you can always get a new encryption key and enter it again here.

From now on you can create Xbox 360 projects and deploy them to your console, which can be done in the XNA Studio build menu. If you start to debug a project with F5 it will get deployed, too, and you can directly debug it on your console, which is pretty cool because you can step through code on your PC and immediately see the results on your Xbox 360 (kind of multi-monitor developing for free). Read more about running your first game in Chapter 2.

Getting Started

You have everything set up now and it is time to finally do some coding and get your hands dirty. In this chapter you will just create a simple project with the help of the XNA Studio templates. Then you will change the code a little and add a little functionality to the Update and Draw methods. In the next chapter, you create your first game after you learn about the SpriteBatch class.

Your First Project

Create a new XNA project in XNA Studio by clicking File ↔ New Project. Now select Windows Game and enter a name for your first project — for example, "Hello World" — or just leave it as "WindowsGame1" (see Figure 1-10). As you can see, you can also create games based on the starter kits quite easily from here, too.

You can see now that a new project was created and it contains two source files: Game1.cs and Program.cs. The Program file basically just contains the following three lines of code:

```
using (Game1 game = new Game1())
{
    ..game.Run();
} // using
```

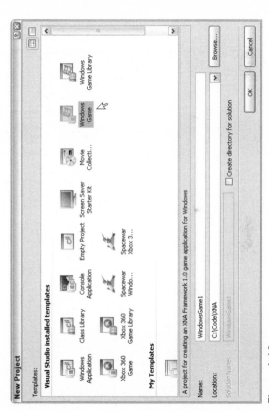

Figure 1-10

The Game1 class contains the Initialize, Update, and Draw methods mentioned a little bit earlier. Initialize does nothing for now and Update just checks if the Back button on the first connected gamepad was pressed.

For now you are just interested in the Draw method, which basically just executes the following line to clear the background to a specific color:

```
graphics.GraphicsDevice.Clear(Color.CornflowerBlue);
```

F5 and Go

If you press F5, the project starts (same as Debug-Start Debugging) and you see the screen shown in Figure 1-11, which shows the blue color on a blank boring window that is specified in the Draw method.

To feel like you are actually doing something, change the Color to Color.Green and press F5 again. The window now has a green background. The Clear method of the graphics device has other overloads that can be used to clear the depth and stencil buffers, which will be done automatically if you just set the color. For example, later in this book you will just need to clear the depth buffer, but not the color of the background. To do that you just write the following line:

```
graphics.GraphicsDevice.Clear(ClearOptions.DepthBuffer,
   Color.Green, 1, 0);
```

By default, the ClearOptions are set to ClearOptions.Target | ClearOptions.DepthBuffer, which means both the background color and the depth buffer are cleared. By the way, if you don't know it already, the | operator between the ClearOptions flags will combine both settings.

Figure 1-11

Changing the Code

Instead of giving up here, think about some ways you can modify the code in a useful manner. First of all, you should be able to quit your program by pressing Esc. By default, XNA just adds the following lines to the Update method, which quits the program when the Xbox 360 controller's Back button is being pressed:

```
// Allows the default game to exit on Xbox 360 and Windows
if (GamePad.GetState(PlayerIndex.One).Buttons.Back ==
ButtonState.Pressed)
    this.Exit();
```

To learn more about the Input classes, see Chapter 3, "Helper Classes." For now, you will just use a quick and dirty way to access the keyboard. If you modify the code in the following way, you can also press Escape now to quit the application:

```
// Get current gamepad and keyboard states
GamePadState gamePad = GamePad.GetState(PlayerIndex.One);
KeyboardState keyboard = Keyboard.GetState();
// Back or Escape exits our game on Xbox 360 and Windows
if (gamePad.Buttons.Back == ButtonState.Pressed ||
    keyboard.IsKeyDown(Keys.Escape))
    this.Exit();
```

As you can see, you put the gamepad and keyboard states in extra variables to have easier access. If you press F5 again, you can quit the game with Escape now.

Next you are going to jump a little bit ahead and load a graphic into your game. More details about sprites are discussed in Chapter 2. The idea is to display a small background texture and tile it over the whole screen. Then you implement some simple keyboard and gamepad controls to move the background as in a top-down racing game or a tile engine, which is often used in 2D role playing games. For a more complex tile engine you would need more textures like stones, grass, water, mud, and so on, and then even transition textures you can put between grass and water, for example. This requires more textures and custom code, but overall this is not a very hard topic. You can also find a lot of information about this topic on the Internet if you are really interested in tile engines.

For your simple first project, you just add the texture shown in Figure 1-12.

Figure 1-12

17

To load this texture (`CityGroundSmall.jpg`) into your game, just drag it into your project on the Solution Explorer. Then click the file in the project and select Properties. You should now see the screen shown in Figure 1-13.

Normally you would just see the build action and some options for copying the content file to the output directory (e.g., if you want to include a .dll or .xml file). But if XNA Studio detects one of the supported content file formats, you will see the advanced XNA properties. There are three important new settings: Asset Name, Content Importer, and Content Processor. The Asset Name is used to load the content later; each content file must have a unique Asset Name. For the Content Importer you can select a Texture, as in this case, or a Model Importer for .x files or an Effect Importer for .fx files.

The Content Processor contains more options; for example, you could select DXT, DXT mip-mapped, or Sprite 32bpp for your texture here. DXT is a compression format, which is also used in .dds files and it is very good for textures in games because they get compressed down in a 1:6 ratio (or 1:4 if they contain transparent pixels). This means you can have up to six times as many textures for the same space on the hard disk and graphic memory. For 2D sprites it is usually better not to compress them, because you see them in their full size, and using 32 bpp (bits per pixel) guarantees the best possible sprite quality. For more information about the content pipeline, read the next part of this chapter.

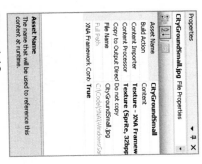

Figure 1-13

If you press F5 or build the project (F6) the content is processed and a new file, `CityGroundSmall.xnb`, will be created in your output directory. The build output window also shows the following new line:

```
Building CityGroundSmall.jpg -> bin\x86\Debug\CityGroundSmall.xnb
```

The final thing you have to do is load the imported texture. You do that in the `Initialize` method and use a new variable, `backgroundTexture`, in your class. To load the texture, you use the asset name you specified earlier (it was actually generated automatically from the filename of the file you dragged into your project). To render the texture on the screen, you need a `SpriteBatch`, which is discussed in the next chapter. Basically it sets up the alpha blending, then draws textures into the sprite and finally draws everything on the screen:

```
Texture2D backgroundTexture;
SpriteBatch sprites;
```

```
protected override void Initialize()
{
    backgroundTexture = content.Load<Texture2D>("CityGroundSmall");
    sprites = new SpriteBatch(graphics.GraphicsDevice);
    base.Initialize();
} // Initialize()
```

To display the background texture, you have to start the sprite batch and render the texture to your sprites in the Draw method:

```
protected override void Draw(GameTime gameTime)
{
    graphics.GraphicsDevice.Clear(Color.Green);

    sprites.Begin();
    sprites.Draw(backgroundTexture, Vector2.Zero, Color.White);
    sprites.End();
    base.Draw(gameTime);
} // Draw(gameTime)
```

This renders the background texture at the location (0, 0) on top of your green background. With the color parameter, you can also recolor a sprite, but for now this is not important.

If you press F5, you will now see the result shown in Figure 1-14.

Figure 1-14

One final thing you are going to add for this first project is the capability to scroll the background with the cursor keys or a gamepad, and then you render the scrollable tiles to the whole background. To capture the gamepad and keyboard input, you modify the Update method a little:

```
float scrollPosition = 0;
protected override void Update(GameTime gameTime)
{
    // Get current gamepad and keyboard states
    GamePadState gamePad = GamePad.GetState(PlayerIndex.One);
    KeyboardState keyboard = Keyboard.GetState();
    // Back or Escape exits our game on Xbox 360 and Windows
    if (gamePad.Buttons.Back == ButtonState.Pressed ||
        keyboard.IsKeyDown(Keys.Escape))
        this.Exit();

    // Move 400 pixels each second
    float moveFactorPerSecond = 400 *
    (float)gameTime.ElapsedRealTime.TotalMilliseconds / 1000.0f;
    // Move up and down if we press the cursor or gamepad keys.
    if (gamePad.DPad.Up == ButtonState.Pressed ||
        keyboard.IsKeyDown(Keys.Up))
        scrollPosition += moveFactorPerSecond;
    if (gamePad.DPad.Down == ButtonState.Pressed ||
        keyboard.IsKeyDown(Keys.Down))
        scrollPosition -= moveFactorPerSecond;

    base.Update(gameTime);
} // Update(gameTime)
```

The first few lines are the same as before. Then you calculate how many pixels you would move this frame. If a frame would take 1 second, moveFactorPerSecond would be 400; for 60 frames it would be 400/60. Because you use floats here instead of just integers, you can have a couple of thousand frames and the movement is still 400 pixels per second if you press up or down.

The variable scrollPosition is changed if the user presses up or down. In your draw method, you can now render each tile and add the scrollPosition to the y position to move the background up and down:

```
protected override void Draw(GameTime gameTime)
{
    graphics.GraphicsDevice.Clear(Color.Green);

    sprites.Begin();
    int resolutionWidth = graphics.GraphicsDevice.Viewport.Width;
    int resolutionHeight = graphics.GraphicsDevice.Viewport.Height;
    for (int x = 0; x <= resolutionWidth / backgroundTexture.Width;
        x++)
    for (int y = -1; y <= resolutionHeight / backgroundTexture.Height;
        y++)
    {
        Vector2 position = new Vector2(
            x * backgroundTexture.Width,
            y * backgroundTexture.Height +
            ((int)scrollPosition) % backgroundTexture.Height);
        sprites.Draw(backgroundTexture, position, Color.White);
```

```
    } // for for
    sprites.End();
    base.Draw(gameTime);
} // Draw(gameTime)
```

Now you can start your project and move around with up and down. This is pretty good for your first little application, isn't it?

Notes about XNA

To finish this chapter, here are some additional tips and tricks about the XNA Framework and XNA Game Studio Express 1.0 and 2.0. As you saw, you can just start coding and it works great, but it is always good to have a couple of bookmarks for your browser you will find on the Internet. You can also rely on when you run into problems or don't know how to solve a specific issue. Additionally, this section discusses the advantages of .NET and C# a little and checks out the differences between XNA and Managed DirectX.

Important Links

Here are a few links for your bookmarks:

❑ `http://msdn.microsoft.com/directx/xna/` — XNA Developer Center on Microsoft's MSDN page with the XNA Game Studio Forum and the XNA Framework Forum, which are the most active XNA forums you will find on the Internet. You can also download the latest XNA version here, read the FAQ, and see what's new.

❑ `http://en.wikipedia.org/wiki/Microsoft_XNA` — Entry on Wikipedia about XNA, constantly updated and contains many links to other topics. A few useful external links are listed on the bottom of the page.

❑ `www.thezbuffer.com` — One of the first Managed DirectX sites with a lot of articles, links to blogs and people. Andy Dunn, the creator of the site, always keeps it up-to-date, shows you the newest XNA projects, and knows a lot about Managed DirectX and XNA.

❑ `www.ziggyware.com` — An XNA community website founded by Michael "Ziggy" Morton. It has grown a lot in the last years and contains hundreds of articles and news posts, and has a very active community behind it. Make sure to check out the active discussion forum; the site also features XNA Image of the day, polls, and other cool stuff.

❑ `www.riemers.net` — A very old and solid DirectX site with tons of information about DirectX. Recently switched to XNA and has great information on that, too. There is also an active forum on this site.

❑ `http://xnadevelopment.com` — One of the first XNA sites with many links, tutorials, and tips to get you started in the XNA world. Not many updates here, however.

❑ `http://xnaresources.com` — Another site that had a lot of news and some really useful tutorials on tile engines for XNA 1.0, but not much updates recently either.

❑ `http://abi.exdream.com` — Official website of the author. You can find more games I made here, as well as Rocket Commander XNA, the XNA Shooter, or the Racing Game from this book, and all the documentation and video tutorials I made for them. Additionally, I suggest checking out the Rocket Commander Video Tutorials, which were pretty popular on Coding4Fun.

❑ http://XnaProjects.net — Another website created by the author just for hosting XNA games like the ones in this book. It is a completely open website for everyone to use, upload games, and to add your own links to, but there are no articles or tutorials on this site, just the games with installers, source code, screenshots, and videos.

Is C# Good for Game Development?

There are constantly forum threads on sites like www.GameDev.net discussing the differences between C++ and C#. Usually after a few posts, they all end in a senseless language war. Back in the early days of .NET (2002) I discussed quite a lot in those threads, but it was way too depressing when 99.9 percent of the programmers were on the C++ side and there was no way to convince anyone because they didn't even take you seriously. The language war does not really have anything to do with C# as a language, but the constant language battles gave newer languages like Java or C# a bad start. For example Java failed as a game programming platform except for cell phone games. But if you think about it, the same kind of wars happened in the days when C replaced Assembler and C++ replaced C. Even to this day, more than 20 years after C++ was developed by Bjarne Stroustrup, some game programmers still use C and do not really take full advantage of C++. If you take a look at the source code for popular game engines such as Quake or Half-Life, it looks more like C than C++.

This is something really strange in the game programming world; everyone is afraid of losing too much performance by switching to a new language, and additionally, they fear that they might also lose their old code base or have a lot of work converting it to a new language. However, game programmers quickly adopt new techniques and scripting languages, and are always on the very latest hardware developments. One year before Shader Model 4 cards were even available, we game developers had Direct3D 10 available and many people checked this out without even having the hardware to run it.

I adopted .NET and C# pretty quickly in the beginning of 2002 after checking out the early betas at the end of 2001. I had just started a new game engine and our team had a new project we wanted to do. There were absolutely no graphic engines or anything but some simple 2D games around in the early years of .NET. This made it very hard to use OpenGL or DirectX directly in C#. It required a lot of calls to unmanaged dlls and involved a lot of nasty pointer logic, which is available only in the unsafe mode of C#. In 2003, Microsoft finally released the first beta of Managed DirectX, which made it possible to program new DirectX applications quite easily in .NET. It proved that using Managed DirectX instead of the native DirectX dlls has only a performance impact of 1–2 percent, which is really not important if you think about it (just the CPU has a little more work; most games are GPU bound anyway).

However, this did not mean that game developers were jumping on C#; everyone was still very skeptical and even after I released the first commercial .NET game ever, *Arena Wars*, in 2004, it took another year until more and more developers finally gave .NET another chance. Students and beginners especially really appreciate the simplicity of C#, and more and more people started to develop games in .NET. C++ versus C# discussions still exist and the discussion points are still the same, but the result is more balanced right now. (I stopped looking at any topic that has "vs" in the name a long time ago; it is just a waste of time reading the same arguments over and over again.)

Always remember this when you run into someone who tells you that C++ is superior and that C# is only for newbies. The same thing happened with Assembler and C++ a few years ago. In the future, there will be new languages that make our life easier and there will still be people hesitant to adopt them right away. Most big game studios also can't just adopt every new technology right away. The studio might be in the middle of a big project and also might have a very big code base, which is not easy to port. In the long run, however, code will get converted and we will move up the ladder of high-level languages.

Figure 1-15 is an old picture I did to show the differences between DirectX with C++ and Managed DirectX in C#. As you can see, MDX code can be half the size of unmanaged code. For XNA, the code would even be shorter and it gets much easier to load textures and show them on the screen, but the comparison to MDX gets harder because the concepts are different.

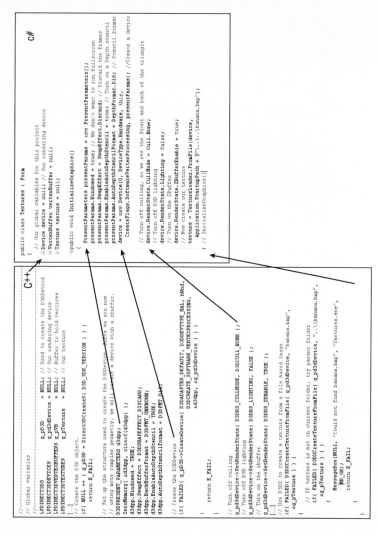

Figure 1-15

Getting Used to the Content Pipeline

As you saw earlier with your first XNA project, it is quite easy to just drag and drop a texture into your game project inside XNA Studio. Although it is nice to have all your game content in one place and side by side with the code, there are a couple of things you have to remember. Most of the projects I have seen throughout my career have not put the textures, models, or shaders directly in the Visual Studio project. The reason for that is that it is much easier to just copy a few files over and then let the game load them directly. By default, Visual Studio will also not copy any content files to your output directory; you have to change the Build Action from None to Content and set the Copy to Output Directory setting to Copy if newer. This is quite a hassle and XNA makes it a little easier.

You might even ask why you should change the way you loaded textures before. If you just want your game to run on the Windows platform, you can certainly load textures and shaders dynamically and without importing them first into your project as XNA content files. This has the advantage that you can change textures or shaders while the game is running (a feature that is not supported by the XNA content pipeline). However, for model files this will not work because there are no load methods other than from the ContentManager class, which only loads compiled .xnb content files.

On the Xbox 360, you can load content files only; there is no support to load textures or shaders directly. If you use direct texture or shader loading, make sure you exclude that code from the Xbox 360 platform; the dlls for the Xbox will not support loading anything but the content files.

For more details about important model files, read the chapters in Part II of this book. Handling 3D models is not as easy as just using textures for 2D games. For that reason this part of the book sticks with sprites and 2D textures and keeps things simple. For simple 2D games it is nice and easy, but to write a serious game you will need 3D models and many cool shader effects. I also suggest that you get an artist to do the textures and 3D models for you. It is a quite complex topic and you might waste a lot of time doing all this yourself. Other people might also be more talented doing textures and 3D models; take advantage of your coding skills and let other people do the painting. If you don't have any artists available, try to use some of the models and textures from this book and the XNA starter kits.

Differences with MDX

If you are coming from MDX (Managed DirectX) and want to migrate your game to the XNA Framework, there is a great guide on the official XNA pages at http://msdn2.microsoft.com/en-us/directx/Aa937797.aspx.

You can find the same help in the XNA documentation. I won't repeat all that here, but basically you have to remember that XNA uses right-handed matrices and MDX was left handed by default. Also, there are some new classes and structures to make sure you don't need the Windows.Forms namespace anymore. Because there is no fixed-function pipeline support, the old way of working with Windows Forms and handles and thinking of supporting older PC configurations is no longer necessary. Graphics and shaders are discussed in Part II of this book.

Additional Tools and Tips

Additionally you should take a look at the Getting Started help topics in the XNA documentation, which can be accessed from XNA Studio-Help-Contents-XNA Game Studio Express. You can find more information about connecting to your Xbox 360, writing your first project, and using all the starter kits.

As I mentioned before, TestDriven.NET is a nice tool for Visual Studio, and test-driven development is a very important methodology in this book (see Chapter 3). Another great tool for .NET development is the Ants Profiler. Unlike all other tools and programs I mentioned so far, it is not free, but there are alternatives available on the Internet, which might help you as well. The Ants Profiler can be used to directly see how much time every single line of your project takes. In my opinion, this is much more useful than using some high-level application performance tool such as NvPerf from Nvidia, PIX from the DirectX SDK, or the Performance Counters of Windows. You can quickly figure out why parts of your render code get slow, and you can detect bugs that call slow methods way too often. By using a profiler tool and by investigating you and others source code, you not only get a lot of interesting information, but you also learn more about the structure of an application and why some things work so well and others take so much time.

For more links on the Internet, check out the great collection of XNA links at http://xnadevelopment.com/links.shtml.

There are many more sites about XNA and it seems every day you see a couple of new community sites and more resources. Do a Google search to find out which site is the most popular.

Changes in XNA 2.0

This book was originally written with XNA Game Studio Express (1.0) in mind. While Parts I through IV were originally written when only XNA 1.0 was available, Part V , "Writing Multiplayer Games," focuses more on XNA 2.0 and the added networking capabilities. But all changes required to make the older code run on XNA 2.0 were implemented and additions were made to the chapters where something new happened in XNA 2.0. Please note that if you just want to develop on the Windows platform, you can already write network games in XNA 1.0 with help of the System.Net namespace.

This section states the changes that are coming in XNA 2.0 and known at the time of this writing. Most information about XNA 2.0 was first announced on the Gamefest in August 2007.

First and foremost, XNA 2.0 supports Visual Studio 2005 out-of-the-box, both the standard editions and the professional editions, including the Team System version. In XNA 1.0, you could only use Visual C# Express, and while C# is still the only officially supported language for XNA you can use other languages such as Visual Basic, IronPython, F#, or even C++, which will work on Windows, but might not work on the Xbox 360 because of some restrictions. Only the Compact .NET 2.0 Framework runs on the Xbox 360 and some languages such as IronPython make use of language features such as Reflect.Emit, which are just not available on the Xbox 360 at this time.

Aside from other improvements to the project management and framework, the most important addition to XNA is the new networking API, which allows you to write multiplayer games and using Xbox Live on the Xbox 360 and Windows System Link on Windows XP and Vista. All the new networking capabilities will be discussed in Part V of this book. These are the key points about XNA networking in XNA 2.0:

❑ Enables you to write networked multiplayer games on the Xbox 360 and Windows.

❑ Matchmaking system via Xbox LIVE on the Xbox 360 and System Link on Windows.

❑ No need to create or host your own servers, which really makes creating multiplayer games a lot easier than it used to be. All the server management will be hosted for you on the Xbox Live and Windows for Games Live services.

❑ Easy to create game sessions and search for them.

❑ Game flow management, Host Migration, and an integrated messaging system keeps you focused on developing the game, not the networking APIs required.

As described in more detail in Chapter 14, all data in the XNA 2.0 networking APIs is transmitted through UDP, which is normally unreliable, but the XNA team has built a reliable framework on top of it, similar to DirectPlay. You basically just use the SendData and ReceiveData methods to send and receive network messages. You can implement client-server-style games as first person shooters usually use, or peer-to-peer games as role playing or strategy games usually use. It is totally up to you; you could even use a hybrid approach.

Because XNA makes great use of the Xbox Live system, you get all the features in there for free, which includes your gamer card, friend management, and chat system (you can even show the keyboard and messages boxes on the Xbox 360 now). You can even enable voice support for your games. There are also nice tools to support the development of multiplayer games on the Xbox 360 and the built-in latency and packet loss simulation tools help you prepare for problems that can occur when playing your game over the Internet.

This all sounds similar to DirectPlay of the DirectX Framework, which was not very successful and was depreciated a few years ago because game developers would not use it. Instead, most games would just use Windows sockets directly or use another networking API. But in XNA, it will be the only way to write network games (at least on the Xbox 360), which gives me hope that XNA networking will be a lot more successful than DirectPlay was.

It is very easy to enable multiplayer support in XNA with just one single line of code:

```
Components.Add(new GamerServicesComponent(this));
```

But writing network games themselves is not that easy. It is great to have all that built-in support and, as you will see in Chapter 14, it gets you up and running quickly — but to write a full-blown network game and to understand all multiplayer components, you have a long road ahead. For this reason, the networking APIs are discussed at the end of this book with the most complex game Dungeon Quest, which is a full-blown multiplayer role playing game that has a great replay value and allows users to create new worlds easily.

Other new features of XNA 2.0 include simplified model rendering such as helping you to render models quickly via the new EnableDefaultLighting method in the BasicEffect class. There were also improvements made to the game components classes; not only are more game components available, but you can also nest game components now. You can learn more about game components in Chapter 4.

Most of the XNA 2.0 Framework has not changed and is still compatible with XNA 1.0 code. Even in parts where performance improvements were made, the calling code is still the same. You will just enjoy the new capabilities and you can extend your game easier or add one of the new features in the rendering engine. For example, occlusion querying and multiple render targets are now supported. Another improvement is the project templates for content importers and processors to help you writing content processors, which was very hard to do previously. Working on your own content processors is still hard work, but at least there is some help to get you started now.

I also want to mention the many samples that are available on the XNA Creators Club. When the first edition of this book was written, the website was non-existent, but now, only 9 months later, many more community sites are available, and you can find many very active XNA forums. On XNA Creators Club at http://creators.xna.com, you can find a lot of useful samples beyond the scope of this book such as Generated Geometry, Aiming, 3d Audio, 3D Picking, Billboards and 3D particles, Distortion Effects, Normal Mapping, Non Photorealistic rendering, Bloom post process, and other samples. Several mini-games and the very popular XNA Starter kits can also be found on the XNA Creators club, including Space Wars (Asteroids clone), Marblets (puzzle game), Ship Game (Descent-style game), and the Racing Game (see Part IV of this book).

Another notable feature in XNA 2.0 is the ability to use XNA inside a window control, which is useful for level editors such as the Dungeon Quest Editor discussed at the very end of this book. The Input classes in XNA now support more devices like the Chatpad, the Big button pad, guitars, drums, or flight sticks. See Chapter 10 for more information.

Last but not least, there are improvements to the Audio framework, too, which are discussed in Chapter 9. XNA 2.0 features better cue management and a new and easier XACT editor, which is important to create and manage sound effect files in XNA.

Other changes to the XNA Framework will be mentioned when they are relevant to the discussion in the book, such as the Content Pipeline, which is a little bit simpler to use in XNA 2.0. You can more easily load and unload assets, and you no longer have to handle device loss or device reset events. To get the most recent version of the source codes for the samples in this book go to the official book site or XnaProjects.net.

Troubleshooting

You have now read everything you need to know to get started with your first XNA project. If you just read through this chapter, I highly recommend that you at least open up the project for this chapter (download it from `www.wrox.com/WileyCDA/WroxTitle/productCd-0470126779.html`) and run it.

If you run into problems installing DirectX, .NET 2.0, or XNA, try to search for help on the XNA Forums at `http://forums.xna.com/`. If the tips in this book do not help you with a particular problem you should always do a Google search and check out the XNA Forums. This way you can get more current help about some problems. For .NET 2.0 it is important that you have the most recent service pack for your operating system. For DirectX make sure you have the most recent graphics driver and a decent graphics card to even work on 3D graphics. Finally, for XNA, make sure you have everything correctly installed before starting the XNA setup.

Getting XNA to work on Windows isn't very hard. On the Xbox 360, a lot of things can go wrong. Here are a couple of tips to make sure you meet the requirements for running XNA games on your 360:

❑ You need an Xbox 360 Live Account on your Xbox 360, which must be connected at all times when you develop and test your XNA games.

❑ Make sure your PC and the Xbox 360 are on the same network and that they can "see" each other. You can test ping-ing the Xbox 360 IP from your PC or connecting to your PC as a media center from the Xbox 360.

❑ If the Xbox 360 XNA Framework could not be installed, search for more help on the Internet to see if your Xbox 360 meets the minimum requirements (you need a hard disk, for example).

❑ When you create an encryption key in Settings of the XNA Game Launcher and it is not accepted by your PC because you maybe mistyped it or it contained 0 (the number zero) and O letters, which almost look the same, just try it again; you can always create a new encryption key. See the section "Configuring Your Xbox 360" earlier in this chapter for details.

❑ If the XNA Game Launcher does not start, or all buttons are grayed out, or if you receive some error like 0xffffffff, it means that your profile is not connected to Xbox Live or it has some wrong settings. If you had an older version of the XNA Framework installed before, uninstall it, delete your profile, and create a new profile and reinstall the XNA Framework again.

Chapter 2 provides more detailed coverage of the steps required to get a game running on the Xbox 360, but the sample in this chapter also works on the console out-of-the-box. Just start the project, switch to the Xbox 360 output, and press F5. If you have set up everything correctly, you can see the same output on the Xbox 360. Congratulations, you just started your first Xbox 360 game!

Last but not least, if you run into compiler errors from the code in this chapter, here are some final tips:

❑ Make sure you have all required variables defined: graphics, content, backgroundTexture, sprites, and scrollingPosition.

❑ Read the compiler error message and change the code accordingly. Maybe you are trying to use an obsolete method; either replace it with the new method or just comment it out to see how the rest of the code behaves.

❑ If the compiling works, but the program crashes or throws an exception, it is most likely that you have some content file missing (the cityGroundSmall.jpg texture in this project) or that your graphic hardware does not support at least Shader Model 1.1.

Summary

This chapter covered a lot about the background of XNA and how to get XNA Game Studio Express working on your PC, and even how to install XNA on your Xbox 360 if available. You also wrote your first little project — I wouldn't really call it a game, but it has a texture, the Xbox 360 controller input and keyboard input is handled, and you have a response on the screen by scrolling the background texture up and down.

The following chapters focus more on programming cool little games. Here's a recap of what you have learned so far:

❑ Background of the XNA Framework

❑ Installing XNA Game Studio Express

❑ Tips and tricks on how to get XNA running on Visual Studio 2005

❑ Additional tools that might be useful such as TestDriven.NET, SourceSafe, and Ants Profiler

❑ Writing your first XNA project

❑ Concept of the Application Model and the Initialize, Update, and Draw methods

❑ Clearing the background

❑ Drawing a texture with help of a sprite batch

❑ Handling gamepad and keyboard input

❑ Drawing a tiled background based on your input

❑ Changes in XNA 2.0

Creating Your First Game: Pong

This chapter provides information on designing and creating a simple Pong game. Pong was the first video game ever and even before the first Pong versions in the sixties there was a version that could be played on an oscilloscope (Tennis for Two, 1958, by William A. Higinbotham). This shows how easy it is to implement a very basic version of Pong. A TV engineer named Ralph Baer claims that he had the idea of implementing Pong even before that in 1951, but not until 1966 was he able to produce the first prototypes. Atari licensed Pong in the eighties and even fought a court case with another company claiming it was the first to invent Pong. If you think about it today the fight sounds really crazy for such a simple game. You can read the whole Pong story at www.pong-story.com.

Implementing a very simple Pong clone doesn't take much time, but you will also learn about the sprite classes of XNA in this chapter. You start by writing the concept of your game and go through the full design phase of game projects. In future projects, you already know the process of writing a concept first, then create the first unit tests with help of the concept and finally go to the implementation process through each of the unit tests. Then you learn about an effective way to organize and use textures for your games. Additionally you will fine-tune the game, make it more fun, add two-player support, and even test it on the Xbox 360 console.

Although this chapter focuses on the Pong game, it is not the only thing you are going to learn. The Pong game is used to learn more about the Agile Methodology I mention later in this chapter. You will learn why it is important to write unit tests first and design the game up front in a very quick process and then improve it as you go along. In the next chapters, you use unit tests for additional classes, too. For this game, you just have one simple class and a couple of unit tests added at the end of it to test out the graphics and the collision testing, and to position everything correctly.

The types of unit tests used in this chapter are referred to as *static unit tests* as opposed to the *dynamic unit tests* you learn about in the next chapter. The difference is that you have to start static unit tests by hand and check the results yourself by watching the result on the screen. Dynamic unit tests, on the other hand, are executed automatically with the help of a Unit Testing Framework such as NUnit. For more details about the Unit Testing Framework, read Chapter 3.

Game Ideas

Talking about the game concept for a game like Pong seems to be a little ridiculous, but I will try to keep things as general as possible. The important thing is that you think about what the game should look and feel like before you start coding. The bigger the game project is, the more important the design phase is. I'm not saying that you can't write games or applications without any concept at all. In fact, most beginners will just start writing something and then improve it again and again until it looks good. The problem with this approach is that you are highly unlikely to find the best solution on the first try.

The game logic is very simple and it does not require much text or graphics (see Figure 2-1). This makes both the game code and your concept very simple to write. Just think about all the components required for this game (ball, paddles, and the screen borders) and write down your initial ideas.

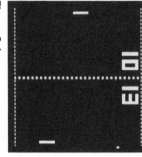

Figure 2-1

Write Down Your Ideas!

Writing a concept does not necessarily mean you have to write down all your ideas, draw UML diagrams like crazy, and start working only when everything is fully planned. I'm completely against that approach because you can't know how everything will work out. Additionally, beginners probably have no idea about the best way to design a full game up front. Instead, you can have a very clear picture of the game in your mind and, after you think you have spent enough time on the design in your mind, you can start working.

If you have other people working on your game project, too, it becomes harder to explain ideas and keep everyone in sync. For this reason alone, you should make it a habit to write down your game idea on just one single page. You can not only show this to other people and get more input, but you will also think about things while writing down some parts of your game idea. Writing down your game ideas will help you gather your thoughts, clarify your ideas, and make sure you did not skip over important issues. For example, for your Pong game you know that you need two paddles and a ball, which moves between the paddles. But maybe only after you write down the initial ideas and think about the sprite textures might you think about the more detailed game play: how many lives does each player have, how do you find out if the ball hits the paddle edges, and how do you handle that? Does the speed of the paddle influence the ball speed and direction? Sure, many of these things can be improved after a while to speed up the game if both players are bored? What about increasing the ball speed after you finish the first version of your game. But it is a lot easier to take all these things into consideration before you write complicated code and then later see that you don't even need that.

As an example, I will write down the design concept for the Pong game you will develop in this chapter. You might want to extend the first step of brainstorming from one page to 5–10 pages for more complex games, but don't write 100 pages of concept text without coding anything. It will take too much time and it will get very hard to manage the concept. You can still come up with a concept containing more than 100 pages, but the concept should evolve as you work on the project. In chapter 16 you can see a highly complex concept of the Dungeon Quest game with over 50 pages, but our team started with just one page of ideas too. For the Agile Methodology you will often update the concept and change details. I usually don't start with UML diagrams until at least 50 percent of the code is done, and the overview diagrams, artworks, and the documentation gets updated later when the project goes final.

Game Idea: Pong

The game is a simple Pong clone for one or two players. In the singleplayer mode the computer will control the other paddle. In the multiplayer mode, two players can either control their paddles with two gamepads, with different keys on the keyboard on the same PC, or on the Xbox 360 console.

The game features a few 2D graphics for the ball and the paddles and a few sound files for the ball hitting one of the paddles or for losing a life. There is a very simple menu allowing you to select the following:

- ❑ Singleplayer
- ❑ Multiplayer
- ❑ Exit

The menu is implemented with a simple texture, the background is just a dark space, and most graphics are bright. You will try to make the game as much fun as possible.

Features and Game Play

The game has two screen modes: Menu and Game. The menu just contains the menu items that were mentioned in the preceding section, and the game consists basically of the ball and the two paddles and a simple scoring system. Take a look at a simple drawing for what you are trying to accomplish (see Figure 2-2).

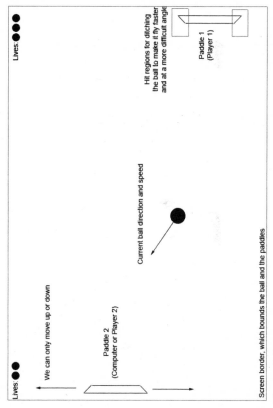

Figure 2-2

Technology

Obviously you are going to use XNA Game Studio Express; there are no additional libraries you are going to use and because you will just render some simple sprites, there are no 3D models or shaders involved here. The game should run on both the Windows platform and the Xbox 360 console.

I never talked about the programming itself in the concept; I just made sure that you know which technology to use. Now it is time to think about the implementation. Don't think about your abilities when writing the game concept; it will just limit you too much. Keep it in the back of your mind.

A more complete example of a game concept is the Rocket Commander concept (see Figure 2-3). You can check it out from the PDF file in the directory for this chapter. It contains four pages and a cover and it features all the ideas for the Rocket Commander game. As you can see from the cover, the game looks very different from the concept, but the general game ideas are there.

Figure 2-3

Agile Methodology

The Agile Methodology is a conceptual framework for software development. The basic idea is to avoid big planning phases, which can often lead to risky and unrealistic project schedules that are hard to keep. For smaller projects you will use short time iterations anyway, but as projects grow bigger, you might see yourself standing in front of problems that require months or even years to finish, and that is very hard to plan.

Instead of planning everything down to the most detailed level, only a very rough concept is done. Each part of the concept is then iterated through the agile process of planning this feature in greater detail, designing the code with help of unit tests, then doing the actual code implementation, and finally testing and documenting this part. This iteration should not take longer than a few weeks and is repeated for all parts of the big project.

Agile methods also include some other ideas about working better together; teaming up developers with the customers, testers, managers and designers; and so on. There are several rules that can be used to bring some structure into this agile framework to avoid having total chaos. Because of the shortened planning phase it looks like there is no detailed plan for the project, similar to a chaotic brute force coding approach. But in reality, the planning process continues throughout the whole project and is much more useful than planning everything just at the beginning and having to live with all the mistakes made in that stage for the whole project.

I will not talk much about the Agile Methodologies in this book, but I will use unit testing and the short concept first, then unit test design, and then code iteration throughout all projects in this book. If you want to read more about unit testing, I recommend reading the website of Martin Fowler at http://martinfowler.com.

Martin has also written several books, and I recommend *Refactoring: Improving the Design of Existing Code*, in particular, which you can also find on the website. You can find many more links and information about the agile software development process on his site, too.

Solving Initial Difficulties

Okay, now you have an idea about your game, but you have not spent much time figuring out where you get the graphics from, what you do about the sound files, and how to implement them. What about the problem with the ball hitting the sides of the paddle? Do you need a simple physics engine for the ball?

All these questions usually arise after the design phase. For more complex projects it can take weeks, if not months, to just figure out some of the basic problems. For example, the first .NET 2.0 game I did was Rocket Commander and I had a nice idea to have thousands of asteroids on the screen, and millions in the level as a whole. I had some cool ideas about letting them collide and bounce off each other. I was not really clear how to implement it in an optimized manner. After some initial tests I found out that I couldn't even render 100 asteroids without a significant performance drop. Instead of rewriting the game concept and making a really boring game without many asteroids at all (which is, after all, the game principle of Rocket Commander — without the many asteroids you don't really have a game at all), I tried to solve this problem by rendering a lot of asteroids sorted by shaders and material settings, doing very early skipping of asteroids if they were not visible, and having the physics apply only to the nearby asteroids.

Even after working and optimizing the asteroids for a week until they rendered at a great performance, the physics were still way too slow. Just updating 5 to 10 thousand asteroids in viewable range every single frame to see if any of them hit any other asteroid was just way too much, even with the best optimizations applied. I still wanted the asteroids to collide and behave correctly after collisions. If I did just check a certain amount of asteroids each frame, the algorithm often missed collisions and only caught up when both asteroids had already penetrated each other, causing even more troubles than removing the physics altogether. I was close to giving up because I had already spent 50 percent of the total project time just solving this single problem, but then I got the idea to separate the space into sectors. Each sector had a certain amount of asteroids and every time an asteroid left a sector it was removed and added to the new sector. For collision checks, asteroids had only to check their own and all neighboring sectors, which still sounds like a lot of collision checks, but the sector logic did improve the physics performance by a factor of 100 and even more after more optimizations.

In most game projects I do nowadays, I spend more than half of the time solving the initial problems and then dividing them up into smaller problems, which again have to be solved. The game itself is then later assembled by just putting these pieces together, and almost like magic the whole game is done in a matter of days. Although this is the best approach to finish a game as quickly as possible, it can be frustrating to see no results for a very long time. In the past, I always iterated the game until I was pleased with the results. This did take a very long time. Thanks to the agile development process, I'm now able to work on the problems and not iterate an almost endless loop of improvements.

What does this mean for your Pong game? Well, the game is very simple and you won't spend a lot of time improving it 100 times. But say you just implement a basic version of Pong with a hard-coded paddle for the computer on the left side moving up and down depending on the ball position and controlling the right paddle. Then later, after improving and testing the single-player game, you might want to add 2-player support, and it gets hard because you hard-coded the computer code. You might comment the computer code out or even remove it and restructure the game play code. Then a little bit later, after testing the 2-player mode, you might want to add the menu and again you have put the code at a different location, re-implement the computer game code, and so on.

Although this is all good practice and forces you to *refactor* (change the layout of your code without changing the functionality to improve maintenance; see Martin Fowler's book, *Refactoring*), it is a lot easier to just focus on one part of the game at a time and have several game versions and tests running side by side. You will do exactly that in the next part of this chapter, and hopefully you can grasp what I mean. Refactoring will occur more naturally, makes your code more usable, and lets you see the result much quicker thanks to unit testing.

One of the problems you will solve in the next part is how to handle the ball physics and how to detect which part of the paddle you hit.

Creating Some Textures

Before you start coding, you need some textures to display stuff on the screen. Even if you use dummy bitmaps here or get some graphics from somewhere else, it is still important to think about the final graphics, which dimensions the ball and paddles should have, and things like that.

Again, for your Pong game it is pretty simple, but more complex games might require an art concept, a lot of sketches, and someone who has a good idea how to manage all this artwork and how to get the artworks to the team members that need them most. Back in the early days of computer games, almost all games were created by one individual, and although this is the easiest way, today no serious game is developed by just one person. Most good artists are not programmers and most programmers are not good artists. If you do a simple game, it does not matter so much, but the bigger your project gets, the more time you will spend finding teammates, skilled artists, and modelers, and putting everything together.

Take a look at the graphics for your game (see Figure 2-4). You will use three textures: SpaceBackground .dds for the background; PongMenu.png, which contains the logo, menu items, and all other texts for your game; and PongGame.png for the paddles and the ball.

Additionally, you will import two sound files (PongBallHit.wav and PongBallLost.wav) into your project and add a simple XACT project to play the sounds. To learn more about sounds and XACT, please read Chapter 9.

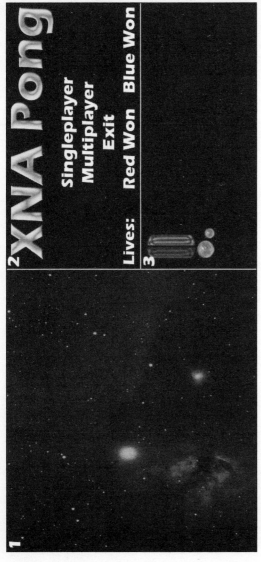

Figure 2-4

Let's Write Pong

You got the concept all figured out and have all the files you need to get started. It's time to do some actual coding. First take a look at the SpriteBatch class and see how you can easily manage all the sprites. The SpriteBatch class is not only useful to render sprites in the same format as the graphics were saved, but it is possible to scale them up or down, recolor them, and even rotate them around.

After putting the menu together, you will add the paddles and move them with help of the input capabilities you already saw in Chapter 1. The ball itself moves with help of some simple variables, and every time you hit one of the paddles you bounce the ball back and play the PongBallHit.wav sound. If the ball goes out of the screen on the left or right side, the PongBallLost.wav sound is played and the player loses one life.

A few unit tests will be used to make sure that the menu and the basic game work. Then you will add additional unit tests to handle the complicated parts such as hitting the ball from the sides of the paddle and fine-tuning the game play. For multiplayer support, you will have a unit test to test out the controls, which are then wired up to the main menu option to support the multiplayer mode.

In the next part of this chapter, you test the whole game on the Xbox 360 and think about more improvements you can make to the game.

Sprites

As you saw in Chapter 1, the SpriteBatch class is used to render your textures directly on the screen. Because you don't have any helper classes yet, you will render everything the same way. For more information about helper classes to make your everyday game programming life easier, check out Chapter 3.

For your Pong game, you use two layers: the Space Background, which is loaded from the SpaceBackground .dds texture, and the menu and game textures showing the menu texts and the game components (paddles and ball).

To load all textures, you use the following lines. First of all, you have to define the textures you are using here:

```
Texture2D backgroundTexture, menuTexture, gameTexture;
```

Then load everything in the Initialize method:

```
// Load all our content
backgroundTexture = content.Load<Texture2D>("SpaceBackground");
menuTexture = content.Load<Texture2D>("PongMenu");
gameTexture = content.Load<Texture2D>("PongGame");
```

And finally you can render the background with the SpriteBatch methods you learned about in Chapter 1:

```
// Draw background texture in a separate pass, else it gets messed up
// with our other sprites, the ordering does not really work great.
spriteBatch.Begin();
spriteBatch.Draw(backgroundTexture,
    new Rectangle(0, 0, width, height),
    Color.LightGray);
spriteBatch.End();
```

LightGray for the color means that you darken down the background a little bit for a better contrast to the foreground items (menu text and game elements). As you can see, it is not just one line to render a sprite on the screen, and it will get a lot more complicated to render just parts of your sprite textures. Take a look at the rectangles you use for the game:

```
static readonly Rectangle
    XnaPongLogoRect = new Rectangle(0, 0, 512, 110),
    MenuSingleplayerRect = new Rectangle(0, 110, 512, 38),
    MenuMultiplayerRect = new Rectangle(0, 148, 512, 38),
    MenuExitRect = new Rectangle(0, 185, 512, 38),
    GameLifesRect = new Rectangle(0, 222, 100, 34),
    GameRedWonRect = new Rectangle(151, 222, 155, 34),
    GameBlueWonRect = new Rectangle(338, 222, 165, 34),
    GameRedPaddleRect = new Rectangle(23, 0, 22, 92),
    GameBluePaddleRect = new Rectangle(0, 0, 22, 92),
    GameBallRect = new Rectangle(1, 94, 33, 33),
    GameSmallBallRect = new Rectangle(37, 108, 19, 19);
```

That is quite a lot of rectangles, but it is still simpler to just use these constant values than to import some XML data, for example. static readonly is used instead of constants here because constants can't be assigned to structures and static readonly behaves the same way as constants. You might ask how to get these values and how to make sure they are correct.

Unit Testing in Games

This is where unit testing comes into play. Unit testing for game programming basically means to split up your problems into small, easily manageable problems. Even for this very simple game, it is still a good idea to write unit tests. Unit testing is perfect to align textures on the screen, test sound effects, and add collision testing. Originally, I planned to write this chapter and the Pong game without using unit testing, but as soon as I programmed the game, I couldn't stop myself and before I knew it I had already written six unit tests. I was convinced that this is the way to go and it would not make sense to delete the very useful tests.

For example, to test out the menu rectangles, you use the following unit test:

```
public static void TestMenuSprites()
{
    StartTest(
        delegate
        {
            testGame.RenderSprite(testGame.menuTexture,
                512-XnaPongLogoRect.Width/2, 150,
                XnaPongLogoRect);
            testGame.RenderSprite(testGame.menuTexture,
                512-MenuSingleplayerRect.Width/2, 300,
                MenuSingleplayerRect);
            testGame.RenderSprite(testGame.menuTexture,
                512-MenuMultiplayerRect.Width/2, 350,
                MenuMultiplayerRect, Color.Orange);
            testGame.RenderSprite(testGame.menuTexture,
                512-MenuExitRect.Width/2, 400,
                MenuExitRect);
        });
} // TestMenuSprites()
```

Please note that this is not the final way you will do unit testing in this book. You just use the very basic idea here to execute unit tests. The delegate holds the code you will execute each frame in the Draw method.

You might ask yourself: What is StartTest? What about testGame or the RenderSprite method? Where do they come from? Well, this is one of the main differences between the old way of game programming and using an agile approach with unit testing. All these methods do not exist yet. Similar to how you planned your game, you also plan your unit tests by just writing down how you want to test something; in this case displaying the game logo and the three menu entries (Singleplayer, Multiplayer, and Exit).

After writing a unit test and all syntax errors are fixed, you can immediately start testing by compiling your code — just press F5 and you will see a couple of errors. These errors have to be fixed step by step and then the unit test can be started. Static unit tests do not use Assert functions very often, but it is possible to add some code to throw exceptions if some values are not as expected. For your unit tests, you will just test them by looking at the result on the screen and then modify the RenderSprite method until everything works the way you want.

The next chapter covers unit testing in greater detail. For the Pong game, you just derive from the PongGame class and add a simple delegate to render custom code in your unit tests:

```
delegate void TestDelegate();
class TestPongGame : PongGame
{
    TestDelegate testLoop;
    public TestPongGame(TestDelegate setTestLoop)
    {
        testLoop = setTestLoop;
    } // TestPongGame(setTestLoop)

    protected override void Draw(GameTime gameTime)
    {
        base.Draw(gameTime);
        testLoop();
    } // Draw(gameTime)
} // class TestPongGame
```

Now you can write the very simple StartTest method to create an instance of TestPongGame and then call Run to execute the Draw method with your custom testLoop code:

```
static TestPongGame testGame;
static void StartTest(TestDelegate testLoop)
{
    using (testGame = new TestPongGame(testLoop))
    {
        testGame.Run();
    } // using
} // StartTest(testLoop)
```

The static instance testGame is used to make writing the unit tests easier, but it can be confusing if you use it somewhere else because it will be valid only after StartTest is called. In the next chapters, you will see a better way to do all this.

Now, two of the errors from the first version of the unit test are fixed; only the RenderSprite method is missing now. It is okay to add an empty method just to make the unit test work:

```
public void RenderSprite(Texture2D texture, int x, int y,
    Rectangle sourceRect, Color color)
{
    //TODO
} // RenderSprite(texture, rect, sourceRect)
public void RenderSprite(Texture2D texture, int x, int y,
    Rectangle sourceRect)
{
    //TODO
} // RenderSprite(texture, rect, sourceRect)
```

After adding these two methods, you can now execute the TestMenuSprites method. How to do that? With TestDriven.NET you can just right-click and select Start Test, but XNA Game Studio Express does

Chapter 2: Creating Your First Game: Pong

not support plugins and you have to write your own way of unit testing by changing the Main method in the Program.cs file:

```
static void Main(string[] args)
{
    //PongGame.StartGame();
    PongGame.TestMenuSprites();
} // Main(args)
```

As you can see, I have also extracted the StartGame method to make the Main method easier to read and to make it easy to change unit tests. StartGame uses just the standard code:

```
public static void StartGame()
{
    using (PongGame game = new PongGame())
    {
        game.Run();
    } // using
} // StartGame()
```

If you press F5 now, the unit test is executed instead of the normal game code. Because RenderSprite does not contain any code yet, you will just see the space background that is drawn in the Draw method of PongGame. Now you add the code to make the menu work. You already know how to render sprites, but it is highly ineffective to start and end a SpriteBatch for every single RenderSprite call. Create a simple list of sprites you want to render each frame and add a new entry every time you call RenderSprite. Then at the end of the frame you will just draw all sprites:

```
class SpriteToRender
{
    public Texture2D texture;
    public Rectangle rect;
    public Rectangle? sourceRect;
    public Color color;
    public SpriteToRender(Texture2D setTexture, Rectangle setRect,
        Rectangle? setSourceRect, Color setColor)
    {
        texture = setTexture;
        rect = setRect;
        sourceRect = setSourceRect;
        color = setColor;
    } // SpriteToRender(setTexture, setRect, setColor)
} // SpriteToRender
List<SpriteToRender> sprites = new List<SpriteToRender>();
```

By the way: You added all this code, including the unit tests, to your PongGame class. Usually you would want to reuse code and extend games later, and it is better to split everything up in multiple classes. To keep things simple and because you won't use much of this code later, everything is just written down in the fastest way possible. Although this is clearly not the cleanest and most elegant way to code, it is usually the fastest and most efficient way to make your unit tests run. At a later point you can refactor your code to make it more elegant and reusable. Thanks to unit testing, you always have a strong tool to make sure everything is still functioning after changing the layout of the code several times.

You might have seen that `Rectangle?` is used instead of just `Rectangle` for the `sourceRect` in the preceding code. `Rectangle?` means that this type is nullable and you can just pass in null for this argument, which makes it possible to create overloads of `RenderSprite` that don't use `sourceRect` to just render the full texture:

```
public void RenderSprite(Texture2D texture, Rectangle rect,
    Rectangle? sourceRect, Color color)
{
    sprites.Add(new SpriteToRender(texture, rect, sourceRect, color));
} // RenderSprite(texture, rect, sourceRect, color)
```

That's pretty straightforward. The `DrawSprites` method, which is called at the end of the `Draw` method, is also not very complicated:

```
public void DrawSprites()
{
    // No need to render if we got no sprites this frame
    if (sprites.Count == 0)
        return;

    // Start rendering sprites
    spriteBatch.Begin(SpriteBlendMode.AlphaBlend,
        SpriteSortMode.BackToFront, SaveStateMode.None);
    // Render all sprites
    foreach (SpriteToRender sprite in sprites)
        spriteBatch.Draw(sprite.texture,
            // Rescale to fit resolution
            new Rectangle(
                sprite.rect.X * width / 1024,
                sprite.rect.Y * height / 768,
                sprite.rect.Width * width / 1024,
                sprite.rect.Height * height / 768),
            sprite.sourceRect, sprite.color);
    // We are done, draw everything on screen with help of the end method.
    spriteBatch.End();

    // Kill list of remembered sprites
    sprites.Clear();
} // DrawSprites()
```

Although it is not very important for this game, at least on the Windows platform where you use 1024768 as the default resolution anyway, you will rescale all sprites from 1024768 to the current resolution. Please note that all textures for this game and all upcoming games in this book are usually stored in the 1024768 resolution. The code in `DrawSprites` makes sure that all sprites are scaled correctly to the currently used resolution. For example, on the Xbox 360, several resolutions are possible and will force the game to run in these resolutions, which you can't know beforehand. For this reason, Xbox 360 games should be resolution independent and allow HDTV-like 1080p (1920×1080) formats if possible.

Basically, `DrawSprites` checks if there are any sprites to render, and if there is nothing to render the function just quits. Then render all sprites with the default alpha blend mode and sorted from back to front without saving the states, which means that if you change any render state of XNA it will not be restored when `End` is called. Usually, you will want to use `SaveStateMode.None` because it is the fastest. Through your unit tests, you make sure everything works out and is not changed in a way that messes up your rendering done after this method.

You might think "All that just to render the main menu graphics?" but if you press F5 now, you can see the screen shown in Figure 2-5. Because you have implemented the basic code for your game, all the sprite rendering code, and everything you need for your unit tests, you have completed almost 50 percent of the work already. You now just need to add the game graphics, the controls, and some simple ball collision code, and you are done.

Figure 2-5

Adding the Ball and Paddles

To add the ball, paddles, and all other game components, you need to do another unit test called `TestGameSprites`:

```
public static void TestGameSprites()
{
    StartTest(
        delegate
        {
            // Show lives
            testGame.ShowLives();
            // Ball in center
            testGame.RenderBall();
            // Render both paddles
            testGame.RenderPaddles();
```

This unit test represents the methodology of the agile development process even better than the last unit test. As you can see, you just took a look at the design concept and implemented everything at a very high level. At the top, you see the number of lives each player has. Then there is the ball in the middle and each player has his paddle. The screen border does not use any special graphics and you already have the background.

Just to make sure you understand the way these unit tests are done, add them, and press F5 after adding this to the Main method and commenting out the old unit test:

```
//PongGame.StartGame();
//PongGame.TestMenuSprites();
PongGame.TestGameSprites();
```

You will get three error messages because none of the three new methods of TestGameSprites is implemented yet. Now after you see these errors you know exactly that these are your next three steps, and if all of them are implemented and tested, this test is complete and you continue with the next part of your game. I cannot mention this often enough: This really makes the overall process much more straightforward. It seems like you planned everything from start to finish, but as you saw earlier, you just wrote down one simple page of your game idea. Everything else is just designed and created as you go from the top-level design down to the implementation at the lowest level. Take a look at the three new methods:

```
public void ShowLives()
{
    // Left players lives
    RenderSprite(menuTexture, 2, 2, GameLivesRect);
    for (int num = 0; num < leftPlayerLives; num++)
        RenderSprite(gameTexture, 2+GameLifesRect.Width+
            GameSmallBallRect.Width*num-2, 9,
            GameSmallBallRect);

    // Right players lives
    int rightX = 1024-GameLifesRect.Width-GameSmallBallRect.Width*3-4;
    RenderSprite(menuTexture, rightX, 2, GameLifesRect);
    for (int num = 0; num < rightPlayerLives; num++)
        RenderSprite(gameTexture, rightX+GameLifesRect.Width+
            GameSmallBallRect.Width*num-2, 9,
            GameSmallBallRect);
} // ShowLives()
```

ShowLives just shows the Lives: text for both players and adds the number of lives as small balls from the game texture. RenderBall is even simpler:

```
public void RenderBall()
{
    RenderSprite(gameTexture,
        (int)((0.05f+0.9f*ballPosition.X)*1024)-
        GameBallRect.Width/2,
        (int)((0.02f+0.96f*ballPosition.Y)*768)-
```

```
    });
} // TestGameSprites()
```

```
    GameBallRect.Height/2,
    GameBallRect);
} // RenderBall()
```

And finally, you have RenderPaddles to show the left and right paddles at the current position:

```
public void RenderPaddles()
{
    RenderSprite(gameTexture,
        (int)(0.05f*1024)-GameRedPaddleRect.Width/2,
        (int)((0.06f+0.88f*leftPaddlePosition)*768)-
        GameRedPaddleRect.Height/2,
        GameRedPaddleRect);
    RenderSprite(gameTexture,
        (int)(0.95f*1024)-GameBluePaddleRect.Width/2,
        (int)((0.06f+0.88f*rightPaddlePosition)*768)-
        GameBluePaddleRect.Height/2,
        GameBluePaddleRect);
} // RenderPaddle(leftPaddle)
```

Before you even wonder about the all the floating-point numbers in RenderBall and RenderPaddles, these are the new variables you need for your game to keep track of the current ball and paddles positions:

```
/// <summary>
/// Current paddle positions, 0 means top, 1 means bottom.
/// </summary>
float leftPaddlePosition = 0.5f,
    rightPaddlePosition = 0.5f;
/// <summary>
/// Current ball position, again from 0 to 1, 0 is left and top,
/// 1 is bottom and right.
/// </summary>
Vector2 ballPosition = new Vector2(0.5f, 0.5f);
/// <summary>
/// Ball speed vector, randomized for every new ball.
/// Will be set to zero if we are in menu or game is over.
/// </summary>
Vector2 ballSpeedVector = new Vector2(0, 0);
```

Now it might be a little bit clearer why you work with floating-point numbers in the render methods. This way you don't have to deal with screen coordinates, multiple resolutions, and checking screen borders. Both the ball and the paddles just stay between 0 and 1. For the x coordinate, 0 means you are at the left border, and 1 means you are at the right border of the screen. Same thing for the y coordinate and the paddles: 0 is the topmost position and 1 is the bottom of the screen. You also use a speed vector to update the ball position each frame, which is discussed shortly.

The paddles are just rendered on the screen; you put the left paddle (red) to the left side and add 5 percent to make it more visible and add a little area behind it where the ball can move to lose a life for this player. The same thing happens for the right paddle (blue) at the right side at 95 percent (which is 0.95f) of the screen width. Take a look at the output you see after pressing F5 now (see Figure 2-6).

That does look like the game is almost done right now. Although unit testing is great and gives you great results in a quick manner, it does not mean you are done yet. The input and the collision testing still have to be done.

Figure 2-6

Handling Player Input

As you saw in Chapter 1, capturing the keyboard and gamepad input is quite easy in XNA. Writing an extra unit test just for that would be overkill; you already know how this works and you just want to test controlling the paddles here. You don't even need a new unit test; you can just use the `TestGameSprites` test and maybe rename it to `TestSinglePlayerGame`. The content of the unit test stays the same; you will now just change input handling and update the paddle positions in the `Update` method of `PongGame`:

```
// Get current gamepad and keyboard states
gamePad = GamePad.GetState(PlayerIndex.One);
gamePad2 = GamePad.GetState(PlayerIndex.Two);
keyboard = Keyboard.GetState();
gamePadUp = gamePad.DPad.Up == ButtonState.Pressed ||
    gamePad.ThumbSticks.Left.Y > 0.5f;
gamePadDown = gamePad.DPad.Down == ButtonState.Pressed ||
    gamePad.ThumbSticks.Left.Y < -0.5f;
gamePad2Up = gamePad2.DPad.Up == ButtonState.Pressed ||
    gamePad2.ThumbSticks.Left.Y > 0.5f;
gamePad2Down = gamePad2.DPad.Down == ButtonState.Pressed ||
    gamePad2.ThumbSticks.Left.Y < -0.5f;

// Move half way across the screen each second
float moveFactorPerSecond = 0.5f *
    (float)gameTime.ElapsedRealTime.TotalMilliseconds / 1000.0f;

// Move up and down if we press the cursor or gamepad keys.
if (gamePadUp ||
```

```
    keyboard.IsKeyDown(Keys.Up))
    rightPaddlePosition -= moveFactorPerSecond;
if (gamePadDown ||
    keyboard.IsKeyDown(Keys.Down))
    rightPaddlePosition += moveFactorPerSecond;
// Second player is either controlled by player 2 or by the computer
if (multiplayer)
{
    // Move up and down if we press the cursor or gamepad keys.
    if (gamePad2Up ||
        keyboard.IsKeyDown(Keys.W))
        leftPaddlePosition -= moveFactorPerSecond;
    if (gamePad2Down ||
        keyboard.IsKeyDown(Keys.S))
        leftPaddlePosition += moveFactorPerSecond;
} // if
else
{
    // Just let the computer follow the ball position
    float computerChange = ComputerPaddleSpeed * moveFactorPerSecond;
    if (leftPaddlePosition > ballPosition.Y + computerChange)
        leftPaddlePosition -= computerChange;
    else if (leftPaddlePosition < ballPosition.Y - computerChange)
        leftPaddlePosition += computerChange;
} // else
// Make sure paddles stay between 0 and 1
if (leftPaddlePosition < 0)
    leftPaddlePosition = 0;
if (leftPaddlePosition > 1)
    leftPaddlePosition = 1;
if (rightPaddlePosition < 0)
    rightPaddlePosition = 0;
if (rightPaddlePosition > 1)
    rightPaddlePosition = 1;
```

You might see a few new variables here (multiplayer, gamePad, gamePad2, keyboard, and ComputerPaddleSpeed), but this section focuses on the code that changes the paddle positions for now. To make sure you always move the ball and the paddles at the same speed no matter how many frames you get, moveFactorPerSecond is calculated. moveFactorPerSecond will be 1 for 1 fps (frame per second), 0.1 for 10 fps, 0.01 for 100 fps, and so on.

Next, you will change the right paddle position if up or down buttons or cursor keys are pressed. The left paddle is either controlled by player 2 using a second gamepad, if available, or the W and S keys. If multiplayer is not true, you are in singleplayer mode and the left paddle is controlled by the computer, which just follows the ball limited by the ComputerPaddleSpeed, which is 0.5f. The ball will initially move much slower, but the speed gets increased at each contact and you can also hit the ball with the edge of the paddles to make it speed up. Then the computer will not catch up and you can win.

To make the new Update method work, add the new variables and constants:

```
/// <summary>
/// Ball speed multiplicator, this is how much screen space the ball
/// will travel each second.
/// </summary>
```

```
const float BallSpeedMultiplicator = 0.5f;
/// <summary>
/// Computer paddle speed. If the ball moves faster up or down than
/// this, the computer paddle can't keep up and finally we will win.
/// </summary>
const float ComputerPaddleSpeed = 0.5f;
/// <summary>
/// Game modes
/// </summary>
enum GameMode
{
    Menu,
    Game,
    GameOver,
} // enum GameMode
GamePadState gamePad, gamePad2;
KeyboardState keyboard;
bool gamePadUp = false,
    gamePadDown = false,
    gamePad2Up = false,
    gamePad2Down = false;
/// <summary>
/// Are we playing a multiplayer game? If this is false, the computer
/// controls the left paddle.
/// </summary>
bool multiplayer = false;
/// <summary>
/// Game mode we are currently in. Very simple game flow.
/// </summary>
GameMode gameMode = GameMode.Menu;
/// <summary>
/// Currently selected menu item.
/// </summary>
int currentMenuItem = 0;
```

For the current test, you just need the variables I mentioned before. However, take a look at all the rest of the variables you need for the game. BallSpeedMultiplicator determines how fast the ball is and therefore how fast the game is. The game mode is used to handle all the three game modes you can be in. Either you just started the game and are in the menu or you are in the game. When you are in the game, but one player lost, the mode is changed to the game over state, showing the winner.

You don't need this code yet, but it is the last part of input you have to handle, so take a look at the input for the menu:

```
// Show screen depending on our current screen mode
if (gameMode == GameMode.Menu)
{
    // Show menu
    RenderSprite(menuTexture,
        512-XnaPongLogoRect.Width/2, 150, XnaPongLogoRect);
    RenderSprite(menuTexture,
        512-MenuSingleplayerRect.Width/2, 300, MenuSingleplayerRect,
        currentMenuItem == 0 ? Color.Orange : Color.White);
    RenderSprite(menuTexture,
        512-MenuMultiplayerRect.Width/2, 350, MenuMultiplayerRect,
        currentMenuItem == 1 ? Color.Orange : Color.White);
    RenderSprite(menuTexture,
```

```
512-MenuExitRect.Width/2, 400, MenuExitRect,
currentMenuItem == 2 ? Color.Orange : Color.White);
if ((keyboard.IsKeyDown(Keys.Down) ||
    gamePadDown) &&
    remDownPressed == false)
{
    currentMenuItem = (currentMenuItem + 1)%3;
} // else if
else if ((keyboard.IsKeyDown(Keys.Up) ||
    gamePadUp) &&
    remUpPressed == false)
{
    currentMenuItem = (currentMenuItem + 2)%3;
} // else if
else if ((keyboard.IsKeyDown(Keys.Space) ||
    keyboard.IsKeyDown(Keys.LeftControl) ||
    keyboard.IsKeyDown(Keys.RightControl) ||
    keyboard.IsKeyDown(Keys.Enter) ||
    gamePad.Buttons.A == ButtonState.Pressed ||
    gamePad.Buttons.Start == ButtonState.Pressed ||
    // Back or Escape exits our game
    keyboard.IsKeyDown(Keys.Escape) ||
    gamePad.Buttons.Back == ButtonState.Pressed) &&
    remSpaceOrStartPressed == false &&
    remEscOrBackPressed == false)
{
    // Quit app.
    if (currentMenuItem == 2 ||
        keyboard.IsKeyDown(Keys.Escape) ||
    gamePad.Buttons.Back == ButtonState.Pressed)
    {
        this.Exit();
    } // if
    else
    {
        // Start game
    .. handle game, etc. ..
```

There are a few new variables such as remDownPressed or gamePadUp, which are used to make handling the input a little easier. Check out the source code for additional details. The next chapter discusses the Input helper class in more detail, and that will simplify the process even more.

That's all you need to know for handling the input in this Pong game. If you execute the unit test again, you can still see the same screen as before, but you can now control the paddles.

Collision Testing

To move the ball away from the middle, the following method startNewBall has to be called in the TestSingleplayerGame unit test. The ball moves to a random location (at least randomly in the four directions you have defined here):

```
/// <summary>
/// Start new ball at the beginning of each game and when a ball is
/// lost.
/// </summary>
```

47

```
public void StartNewBall()
{
    ballPosition = new Vector2(0.5f, 0.5f);
    Random rnd = new Random((int)DateTime.Now.Ticks);
    int direction = rnd.Next(4);
    ballSpeedVector =
        direction == 0 ? new Vector2(1, 0.8f) :
        direction == 1 ? new Vector2(1, -0.8f) :
        direction == 2 ? new Vector2(-1, 0.8f) :
        new Vector2(-1, -0.8f);
} // StartNewBall()
```

In the Update method the ball position gets updated based on the ballSpeedVector:

```
// Update ball position
ballPosition += ballSpeedVector *
    moveFactorPerSecond * BallSpeedMultiplicator;
```

☐ **Collision with Screen Border** at the top and bottom screen borders.

☐ **Collision with a Paddle** to push the ball back to the other player.

☐ **Lose life** if collision with screen border behind paddle happens. Player will lose a life when this happens and the ball is reset with the help of StartNewBall.

If you start the game now, with your unit test the ball will move away from the center and go out of the screen, which is not really cool. This is why you need collision testing. Take a look at the concept again (see Figure 2-7) and add some improvements for the collision code. This is one of the times it makes sense to go back to the concept and make improvements based on your new ideas and knowledge. There are three kinds of collisions that can happen:

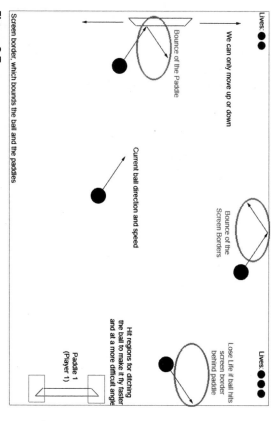

We can only move up or down

Bounce of the Paddle

Current ball direction and speed

Lives: ● ●

Bounce of the Screen Borders

Lives: ● ● ●

Lose Life if ball hits screen border behind paddle

Hit regions for ditching the ball to make it fly faster and at a more difficult angle

Paddle 1 (Player 1)

Screen border, which bounds the ball and the paddles

Figure 2-7

You could continue using TestSingleplayerGame to check out the collisions, but it is far easier to construct a few tests and have every single issue tested. Again, unit testing is great for exactly this kind of problem. You have a clear idea of what you have to do now, but you don't know yet how to do it. Just write a unit test and then work on the implementation:

```
public static void TestBallCollisions()
{
    StartTest(
        delegate
        {
            // Make sure we are in the game and in singleplayer mode
            testGame.gameMode = GameMode.Game;
            testGame.multiplayer = false;
            testGame.Window.Title =
                "Xna Pong - Press 1-5 to start collision tests";
            // Start specific collision scene based on the user input.
            if (testGame.keyboard.IsKeyDown(Keys.D1))
            {
                // First test, just collide with screen border
                testGame.ballPosition = new Vector2(0.6f, 0.9f);
                testGame.ballSpeedVector = new Vector2(1, 1);
            } // if
            else if (testGame.keyboard.IsKeyDown(Keys.D2))
            {
                // Second test, straight on collision with right paddle
                testGame.ballPosition = new Vector2(0.9f, 0.6f);
                testGame.ballSpeedVector = new Vector2(1, 1);
                testGame.rightPaddlePosition = 0.7f;
            } // if
            else if (testGame.keyboard.IsKeyDown(Keys.D3))
            {
                // Thrid test, straight on collision with left paddle
                testGame.ballPosition = new Vector2(0.1f, 0.4f);
                testGame.ballSpeedVector = new Vector2(-1, -0.5f);
                testGame.leftPaddlePosition = 0.35f;
            } // if
            else if (testGame.keyboard.IsKeyDown(Keys.D4))
            {
                // Advanced test to check if we hit the edge of the right paddle
                testGame.ballPosition = new Vector2(0.9f, 0.4f);
                testGame.ballSpeedVector = new Vector2(1, -0.5f);
                testGame.rightPaddlePosition = 0.29f;
            } // if
            else if (testGame.keyboard.IsKeyDown(Keys.D5))
            {
                // Advanced test to check if we hit the edge of the right paddle
                testGame.ballPosition = new Vector2(0.9f, 0.4f);
                testGame.ballSpeedVector = new Vector2(1, -0.5f);
                testGame.rightPaddlePosition = 0.42f;
            } // if
            // Show lifes
            testGame.ShowLives();
            // Ball in center
            testGame.RenderBall();
```

```
        // Render both paddles
        testGame.RenderPaddles();
    });
} // TestBallCollisions()
```

The idea here is to press 1–5 to set up custom collision test scenes. For example, if 1 is pressed, the ball is moved to (0.6, 0.9), which is near the center at the bottom of the screen. The ball speed is set to (1, 1) to make sure it moves to the screen border, where the ball should bounce off as described in the concept of XNA Pong above. If you press 4 or 5, the advanced paddle tests are started to check if you hit the edges of the right paddle, which requires a little bit more fine-tuning than the other quite simple collision tests. Collision testing is done in the Update method of PongGame.

Now you can start testing. Obviously if you just start the test now, it will not work because you have not implemented any collision testing yet.

Testing if you hit the top or bottom screen borders is the easiest test; all of the following code is added to the Update method just before you update the ball position for the next frame:

```
// Check top and bottom screen border
if (ballPosition.Y < 0 ||
    ballPosition.Y > 1)
{
    ballSpeedVector.Y = -ballSpeedVector.Y;
    // Move ball back into screen space
    if (ballPosition.Y < 0)
        ballPosition.Y = 0;
    if (ballPosition.Y > 1)
        ballPosition.Y = 1;
} // if
```

The important part here is to just invert the y part of the ball speed vector. Sometimes it can happen that in the next frame the moveFactorPerSecond is smaller than in this frame. Then the ball position can still be out of the screen border and you would invert the y part of the speed vector every frame. To fix this issue, you make sure the ball position is always inside the screen and does not go outside. The same adjustment is done for the paddles, too.

The paddle collisions are a little bit more complicated. If you just want to test the top and bottom screen collision, just start the unit test with F5 now. To do the paddle collisions, bounding boxes are constructed to perform the intersection tests, which are available in the BoundingBox class of XNA. The BoundingBox struct uses Vector3 struct and works in 3D space. You can just ignore the z value and always use 0, which works just fine in the 2D space of your Pong game:

```
// Check for collisions with the paddles.
// Construct bounding boxes to use the intersection helper method.
Vector2 ballSize = new Vector2(
    GameBallRect.Width / 1024.0f, GameBallRect.Height / 768.0f);
BoundingBox ballBox = new BoundingBox(
    new Vector3(ballPosition.X - ballSize.X / 2,
    ballPosition.Y - ballSize.Y / 2, 0),
    new Vector3(ballPosition.X + ballSize.X / 2,
    ballPosition.Y + ballSize.Y / 2, 0));
```

```
Vector2 paddleSize = new Vector2(
    GameRedPaddleRect.Width / 1024.0f,
    GameRedPaddleRect.Height / 768.0f);
BoundingBox leftPaddleBox = new BoundingBox(
    new Vector3(-paddleSize.X/2,
    leftPaddlePosition-paddleSize.Y/2, 0),
    new Vector3(+paddleSize.X/2,
    leftPaddlePosition+paddleSize.Y/2, 0));
BoundingBox rightPaddleBox = new BoundingBox(
    new Vector3(1-paddleSize.X/2,
    rightPaddlePosition-paddleSize.Y/2, 0),
    new Vector3(1+paddleSize.X/2,
    rightPaddlePosition+paddleSize.Y/2, 0));
// Ball hit left paddle?
if (ballBox.Intersects(leftPaddleBox))
{
    // Bounce of the paddle
    ballSpeedVector.X = -ballSpeedVector.X;
    // Increase speed a little
    ballSpeedVector *= 1.05f;
    // Did we hit the edges of the paddle?
    if (ballBox.Intersects(new BoundingBox(
        new Vector3(leftPaddleBox.Min.X - 0.01f,
        leftPaddleBox.Min.Y - 0.01f, 0),
        new Vector3(leftPaddleBox.Min.X + 0.01f,
        leftPaddleBox.Min.Y + 0.01f, 0))))
        // Bounce of at a more difficult angle for the other player
        ballSpeedVector.Y = -2;
    else if (ballBox.Intersects(new BoundingBox(
        new Vector3(leftPaddleBox.Min.X - 0.01f,
        leftPaddleBox.Max.Y - 0.01f, 0),
        new Vector3(leftPaddleBox.Min.X + 0.01f,
        leftPaddleBox.Max.Y + 0.01f, 0))))
        // Bounce of at a more difficult angle for the other player
        ballSpeedVector.Y = +2;
    // Move away from the paddle
    ballPosition.X += moveFactorPerSecond * BallSpeedMultiplicator;
} // if
```

The bounding boxes are constructed in a similar way as the rendering code is handled in RenderBall and RenderPaddles. The edge detection code makes it a little bit more complicated. It is just a quick and dirty way to speed up the ball if you hit it with the edge of your paddle. But these few lines make the game a lot more fun.

Exactly the same code you use for the left paddle is also used for the right paddle; you just have to replace all left paddle variables with right paddle variables and negate the move away code.

The final thing you have to do for your game to handle all the game play and the final collision test is to check when the ball gets behind the player's paddle and the player loses a life. The code for that is quite simple. You can also directly handle it if one of the players loses all his lives and the game is over then. Displaying the "Red Won" or "Blue Won" messages is done in the Draw method. If the user presses the spacebar or Esc, he will return to the main menu and the game can start again.

51

```
// Ball lost?
if (ballPosition.X < -0.065f)
{
    // Play sound
    soundBank.PlayCue("PongBallLost");
    // Reduce number of lives
    leftPlayerLives--;
    // Start new ball
    StartNewBall();
} // if
else if (ballPosition.X > 1.065f)
{
    // Play sound
    soundBank.PlayCue("PongBallLost");
    // Reduce number of lives
    rightPlayerLives--;
    // Start new ball
    StartNewBall();
} // if
// If either player has no more lives, the other player has won!
if (gameMode == GameMode.Game &&
    (leftPlayerLives == 0 ||
    rightPlayerLives == 0))
{
    gameMode = GameMode.GameOver;
    StopBall();
} // if
```

Well, this was the hardest part for this game; the bounding box collision tests were a little bit complicated, but the rest of the game was very straightforward and could be implemented quite easily. You also learned a bit about unit testing and how to handle sprites in an effective manner. You can now test the game with your unit test by pressing F5 and fine-tune the collisions a bit (see Figure 2-8).

Figure 2-8

Adding Sound

To add sound to your game, you would usually just drop a couple of .wav files into your project and play them back. In XNA, loading .wav files is not supported because Xbox 360 and Windows use different formats for sound and music. To overcome this issue, Microsoft invented the XACT tool, which has been available in the DirectX SDK and the Xbox 360 SDK for quite some time now. XACT is short for "Microsoft Cross-Platform Audio Creation Tool." XNA also makes use of this tool and Microsoft decided to make this the only way to play sound files.

Although XACT is a great tool for adding effects, making a lot of adjustments, and having all sound files managed in one place, it can overcomplicate things a little for a project like this one. There is a full chapter on XACT in this book; check it out in Chapter 9. For your Pong game, you will just use two simple sound files, which can be found in the Sounds directory:

☐ PongBallHit.wav is played every time you collide with something (border or paddle). It is also used for the menu as the sound for changing the selection.

☐ PongBallLost.wav is used when a player loses a life because he didn't catch the ball in time.

To add these files to your game, you have to create a new XACT project. You can find XACT at Start ⇨ All Programs ⇨ Microsoft XNA Game Studio Express ⇨ Tools.

In the new XACT project, add a wave bank by clicking Wave Banks ⇨ Create Wave Bank, and then add a sound bank by clicking Sound Banks ⇨ Create Sound Bank. Now drag the two .wav files into the new XACT wave bank (see Figure 2-9).

Figure 2-9

Next, drag the two new wave bank entries over to the sound bank, and then drag them over to the cues. If you are confused or run into problems, check out Chapter 9 for more details.

These are the main components used in XACT for sounds:

☐ **Wave Bank** stores all your .wav files; you can't add anything but .wav files here. There is no support for .mp3, .wma, or any format. Importing compressed files is also not an option; ACPM for Windows and XMA compression for the Xbox 360 are possible, but you have to follow the rules, which are described in Chapter 9.

☐ **Sound Bank** is used to play back sounds later in the game with help of the cues. You can modify the sound settings here by changing the volume and pitch, adding categories, and attaching sound effects (RPC). You can also define multiple tracks here. Usually you will just set the volume here.

☐ **Sound Cues** are used to play sounds. A sound cue has at least one sound bank entry attached, but you can assign multiple sound files to one cue and set rules, such as whether one of the sounds should be played randomly, and whether you can play only one sound of this kind at a time. You can also set rules for replacing sounds. The important thing here is the cue name, which is used in the game to access the cue and finally play the sound.

Figure 2-10 shows how your XACT project should look like now. You will set the volume of PongBallHit to –8 and the PongBallLost to –4; the default value of –12 is too silent and your hit sound is a little bit too loud, so reducing it sounds nicer in the game. The rest can use the default values and you can just save the project as PongSound.xap. Then add this file to your XNA Studio project and it will use the XNA content pipeline to automatically compile and build all files for both the Windows and Xbox 360 platform for you. Also make sure the two .wav files are in the same directory as the PongSound.xap file; otherwise the content pipeline might not be able to find these files and it won't be able to build your XACT project.

The code to play back the sounds is quite easy. You want to make sure the sounds work fine and the volume is correct. Here is simple unit test for the sounds:

```
public static void TestSounds()
{
    StartTest(
        delegate
        {
            if (testGame.keyboard.IsKeyDown(Keys.Space))
                testGame.soundBank.PlayCue("PongBallHit");
            if (testGame.keyboard.IsKeyDown(Keys.LeftControl))
                testGame.soundBank.PlayCue("PongBallLost");
        });
} // TestSounds()
```

Now all you have to do to implement the sounds to the game is to add a couple of lines at the locations where you want the sound to happen. First of all, add the hit sound to the menu, and add it every time a ball collision occurs with the screen borders or the paddles (see the earlier collision tests).

Then add the lost sound to the code block where you find out if a player lost a life:

```
// Ball lost?
if (ballPosition.X < -0.065f)
```

```
{
    // Play sound
    soundBank.PlayCue("PongBallLost");
    // Reduce life
    leftPlayerLives--;
    // Start new ball
    StartNewBall();
} // if
else if (ballPosition.X > 1.065f)
{
    // Play sound
    soundBank.PlayCue("PongBallLost");
    // Reduce life
    rightPlayerLives--;
    // Start new ball
    StartNewBall();
} // if
```

After adding these lines you can re-enable the `TestSinglePlayerGame` unit test and see if the sounds are played correctly. For more complex games a better system for checking when to play sounds might be required, but most simple games will work fine just with the `PlayCue` method, which just plays the sound and holds the cue as long as it is needed. You can also get a sound cue and manage it yourself; this has the advantage of being able to stop it and resume it, and so on.

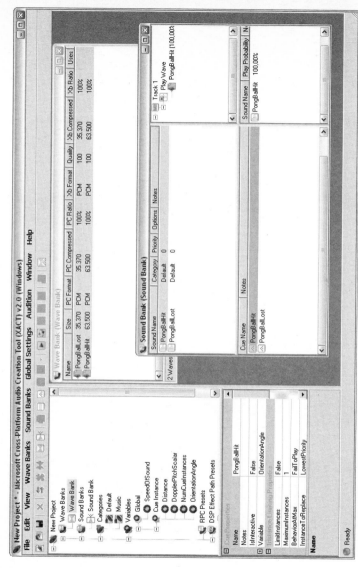

Figure 2-10

How This Looks on the Xbox 360

The game is now finished and you tested it quite a bit on the Windows platform. As I already explained in the first chapter, several steps are required to get the Xbox 360 up and running for the XNA Framework. If the XNA Game Launcher is started on the Xbox 360, you can try to compile your XNA Pong game and deploy it to the console.

There are a few important things to remember for the Xbox 360:

☐ **Do not use any external dlls if not required:** Although it is supported to use XNA Game library dlls, most dlls you will have on the Windows platform will call system dlls that are not available on the Xbox 360, or even worse, call unmanaged dlls with P-Invoke, which is absolutely not supported on the Xbox 360 for security reasons. Also, don't use unsafe code or make any attempts to call external code, access devices, or use unsupported features. It will be a waste of time and you are better off just playing by the rules.

☐ **Don't wait with the testing:** In the middle of the project, test if your code compiles if you change the output settings to the Xbox 360. Often, methods you might get used to might be missing on the Xbox 360. For example, there are no `TryParse` methods in the System.dll on the Xbox 360. Some XNA methods and classes such as the `MouseState` classes are even missing and unsupported.

☐ **Don't load content directly:** On the Windows platform, it is possible to load textures or shaders directly with help of the `Texture2D` or `CompiledEffect` constructors. These methods are completely missing from the Xbox 360; you can only load content from the content pipeline. If you use code that dynamically loads or reloads textures or shaders, it will only work on your Windows platform, so exclude the code with `#if !XBOX360 ... #endif` for the Xbox 360 build.

☐ **Save-Games and loading other content:** For save games you can use the Content namespace and the many available helper classes. To load content, you will always have to make sure you use the correct path with the help of `StorageContainer.TitleLocation`, which works on the Windows platform, too, and just uses your output directory there. Loading from other locations on the Xbox 360 results in Access Denied exceptions for IO operations.

☐ **Test resolutions:** The Xbox 360 supports many different resolutions from the PC and you should test at least 2–3 different resolutions to make sure the game runs fine with them.

☐ **Allow controlling everything with a gamepad:** Most XNA games I've seen to this point made the mistake of allowing only keyboard input or only gamepad input, which means it runs either only on Windows or only if you have an Xbox 360 controller. Always add support to as many input devices as you can think of and that make sense for your game.

☐ **Debug and unit test on the Xbox 360:** Debugging and unit testing is no different on your console; the same rules apply. It might be a little harder to trace errors and log messages, but stepping through code and testing unit tests works great with XNA. Take advantage of that. By the way: "edit and continue" works only on the Windows platform. You can't do that with Xbox 360 games, which can be annoying, but you will probably do the major part of your development on the Windows platform anyway.

XNA Pong was always coded with the Xbox 360 in mind; all methods and features you used are supported on the Xbox 360. Therefore, testing the game on the Xbox 360 is no big deal; you can just deploy it and start it, and it will work fine (see Figure 2-11).

Figure 2-11

Challenge: Improve the Pong Game

It is now your turn to improve the game a little bit; maybe you can exchange the graphics or sounds or you can adjust the game play. Also try to add Rumble support for your Gamepad controller if you have one. You really should have one if you read this book, even if you don't have an Xbox 360; a lot of XNA samples will require an Xbox 360 controller and some of the games are more fun with an Xbox 360 controller than having to play with the keyboard.

Here is the method to add Rumble support for a specific gamepad:

```
GamePad.SetVibration(PlayerIndex.One, leftRumble, rightRumble);
```

Use that code to rumble for a short while if the ball hits your paddle. (Use the same value for left and right rumble, and then the whole controller just shakes). And also rumble if you lost a life, this time longer and stronger.

As always, you can check out the project for this chapter (which can be found on the www.wrox.com site or www.XnaProjects.com as stated before) and see a solution to the challenge. Your solution does not have to be the same, but it might be useful to see another or maybe even an easier way to solve a specific problem.

Have fun with XNA Pong.

Troubleshooting

Let's hope that there is not much that can go wrong in this chapter. This chapter only touched on two major issues: unit testing and sprites. You also might have problems getting the game to run on your Xbox 360, but I already wrote down a bunch of tips and tricks on this issue at the end of Chapter 1; check them out if you still have problems setting up your Xbox 360.

For the few readers who are not experienced with exceptions, especially with the ones from XNA, you need to understand why an exception is thrown and what exactly has to be done to fix it. Always read the exception very closely and try to review the full stack trace. Check out if there are inner exceptions with more detailed information.

Similar to Managed DirectX, sometimes you get exceptions from the underlying DirectX Framework, which can be confusing sometimes. Try to search for help on specific error numbers on the Internet and MSDN. In those cases, the context is usually more important than the error message itself. For example, if compiling a shader fails, you might get strange error codes. Instead of trying to find out what these error codes mean, make sure the shader file exists, that it can be compiled, and that your hardware can handle it. A good tool to check if shader files are valid is FX Composer from Nvidia.

If you run into trouble using unit testing, please also read the troubleshooting section of the next chapter. Basically always remember that the kind of unit tests you used here behave like normal programs; treat them the same way. Debug them and step through them like you would with the final application.

Last but not least, here are some tips about using sprites in XNA:

☐ If you render a lot of sprites on top of each other, there might be many issues in XNA showing random sorting order, or problems when using different textures. Often, the background sprite might kill everything in front of it. As you can see in XNA Pong, you rendered the background in an extra spriteBatch call so that it is separated and cannot interfere with any of the sprites in the game or menu.

☐ Try to render all sprites at once, especially if you can sort them by the blend mode. It is a lot faster if you render all sprites at once in one big call to spriteBatch. Check out the DrawSprites method as an example. If you use different blend modes such as additive for light effects and alpha blending for all other sprites, try to render in two passes, first the alpha blended stuff, then the additive lights on top. Performance can improve 200 to 300 percent if you do that.

☐ Think about resolutions and how to handle different widths and heights; you can get the used resolution in the Initialize method with the following two lines:

```
width = graphics.GraphicsDevice.Viewport.Width;
height = graphics.GraphicsDevice.Viewport.Height;
```

☐ You cannot force a specific resolution; it will not work on the Xbox 360 at all and on Windows it is used as a suggestion only. For example, if you want to test the 720p 16:9 resolution (1280720) on your PC, you must have a monitor that supports this resolution either in windowed mode or in fullscreen mode depending on what you are testing. Add the following lines to the constructor of your main game class (PongGame in this chapter) to suggest the 720p resolution. You can check if that worked in the `Initialize` method by checking the width and height as described earlier:

```
graphics.PreferredBackBufferWidth = 1280;
graphics.PreferredBackBufferHeight = 720;
```

❑ There is no font support in XNA. To show text you can either create textures as in this game with all the text already written down or write your own font support as in Chapter 5. For both solutions, you will use sprites to render text or just a letter at a time on the screen.

❑ Sprites are not the only way to display 2D data in XNA; you can write your own shaders and even do much more advanced effects than is possible with the sprite class. Check out Chapter 5 and see how 2D lines are rendered with the help of shaders.

Summary

I hope you enjoyed this chapter and tried to follow the process of creating a game closely. Pong might not be the most exciting game, but it was a great example to really cover everything from start to finish that would usually happen for any game project. Bigger projects would be impossible to cover in just one chapter. You have now learned about concepts, unit tests, and the basic terminology of agile development. After learning about the helper classes in the next chapter and then diving into the details of the game class and game components, you will be ready to do a rocking 3D engine with lots of cool effects for the final part of this book. In the meantime, you will see a couple of other small fun game projects.

The most important point of this chapter is that agile programming works great for games, and although you are able to dynamically change things and have a very easy top-down approach to solve problems, it is still very important to write a game concept first, even if it is just one-page long. Unit tests also helped a lot, but as you will see in the next chapter, unit tests can also be automated and they are very useful for the helper classes, which are used all over the place in the projects later in this book.

Take a look at what you have learned in this chapter:

❑ It is important to write down your ideas and to develop a small concept.

❑ Just one page of concept can be quite useful.

❑ To solve problems, you use a top-down approach and you use unit testing to stay at just the top level without even thinking of the implementation. This way, you can quickly adopt ideas from the concept and write them down in unit tests, making it easier to see exactly what methods you have to implement.

❑ You created some textures, loaded them into the project, and displayed them as sprites.

❑ Rendering many sprites at once gives better performance.

❑ Using a clever formula helped you to make the game resolution-independent. This way the game works fine on the Xbox 360 and any resolution that is possible.

❑ You added sound using XACT and learned some basics; you can find more details in Chapter 9.

❑ How to handle game input using two gamepads controllers and using the keyboard for multiple players is easily possible in XNA.

Part I: XNA Framework Basics

❑ The BoundingBox structure helped us writing 2D Collision testing code.

❑ Using Vector3 instead of Vector2 works fine if you always set the z component to 0.

❑ Using unit tests for collision testing is very important and greatly reduces the amount of testing you have to do. You can also always switch back to the unit test and test the collisions again, even if you are currently working on a completely different part of the game.

Helper Classes

In the Helper namespace I usually put a lot of helpful little tools and classes, which become quite useful over time. For a single project, it might not be the most important or valuable code, but because it is used again and again, no matter whether other parts of the engine change, helper classes will be the most consistent part of your engines and projects. Most of the helper classes don't have much to do with game programming, and they are useful in other projects or even in websites.

You just saw in the previous chapter that you can write a whole game without any helper classes and without even using any extra files or classes at all. But as the projects become bigger and bigger, you will see that there are a lot of repeating patterns and similar problems occur, which were already solved in the past. Usually most of the reused functionality in XNA is graphic components. In the next chapter and especially in the second part of this book, you learn more about game components and the graphics engine. For now, this chapter keeps the focus on the very basic functionality to log messages, access the game content, and do unit testing effectively, as well as how to generate random numbers, and many other smaller issues.

To make this chapter a little bit more exciting, you also create another little game just for the fun of it. Not all of the helper classes will be used, but building a game engine is not an easy task. For that reason, this and the next chapter start with the helper classes and the game components to make developing your graphic engine in Part II of this book a little easier. Please note that I did not write the helper classes in the way they are presented in this chapter; they evolved over the course of the past couple of years. Just add functionality or your own helper classes whenever you need them. If you solve a problem once and think it might not be useful again, just leave it where it is. But if you find yourself copying that solution over to a new project or maybe just to another class several times, you should seriously consider extracting the logic and putting it into a special class.

Additionally, you learn a little bit more about the content pipeline you already used in the previous chapters to support the Xbox 360. It is possible to directly load textures or shaders without using the content pipeline, but all these methods work only on the Windows platform. If you want to create a cross-platform game you should make sure everything compiles and works on both the Windows and the Xbox 360 platforms. You will continue to do that throughout this book.

At the end of this chapter you will quickly develop a fun Breakout clone game. It will be a lot easier than in the previous chapter because you will write all the helper classes first. For example, sprite rendering is very easy with the help of the SpriteHelper class. You can find more helper classes and game components to improve both the Pong and Breakout games in the next chapter.

Managing the Content Pipeline

As you learned in Chapter 1, the content pipeline is used to import game assets such as textures, models, shaders, and sound files. Instead of just adding them to your project like any other unsupported files for Visual Studio (or XNA Studio), the content files get processed and then are compiled into binary content files, which can be loaded from your game (see Figure 3-1).

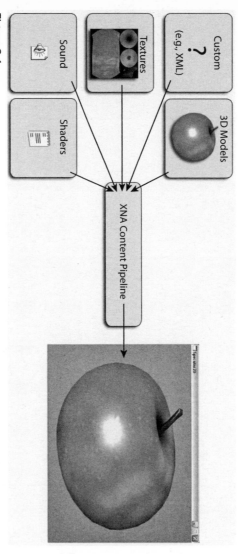

Figure 3-1

In the past, a game programmer had to write his own importer to load game content data or use one of the available formats such as the .x file format in DirectX for model files. But often the available formats are insufficient, too slow, or just too inflexible when trying to add new features to a game. This is the reason why almost every commercial game has its own file formats and custom logic programmed behind it. This has the advantage that only the developers of a game know the layout of their internal format and they can extend it or change it as often as they want. However, it is usually a lot of work to get 3D content in your game this way. Loading textures is usually not that complicated because many libraries exist and even when writing your own file format, it basically just contains pixels, which are stored as 24- or 32-bit color values. It can become a little bit more difficult if you try using compression or if you want to use hardware-compressed textures like with the DXT format, but DirectX has a great repertoire of helpful methods to assist you with that.

On the other hand, loading 3D model data is a lot more complicated, especially in XNA, where you have to have not only the geometry data, but also shaders to render a 3D object and then, of course, material data to tell the shaders which colors, textures, and parameters to use. In DirectX most tutorials and samples just use the .x file format, but the .x file format might not be sufficient for many projects. Especially if you use normal napping and require the geometry data to contain tangents, the .x file format will not be very helpful. You would have to generate tangents in your application and work around problems this might introduce. For example, one of my older games, Rocket Commander, had this exact problem and it required a complex model loading process and tangent regeneration process.

Other game data such as loading sound files (.wav), shaders (.fx), or custom (for example, .xml) data might be straightforward because your game or the framework you are using provides enough helpful classes to load everything quickly, but then you might run into problems running your game with the same content on another platform. You can, for example, use ACPCM sound files on the Windows platform and use compiled Pixel Shader 1.1 files or just load a couple of .jpg files as textures, but there is no ACPCM support on the Xbox 360; sound is either PCM or in the custom XMA format for the Xbox. Shader code has to be in the format the Xbox 360 accepts, and loading textures might work differently, too. This problem would even get more complicated if more platforms are supported in the future.

To simplify loading the game content, XNA allows you now to just drop the raw content files into your XNA Studio project and they will be processed and compiled to the correct output format for the currently selected platform. For example, your sound files can be processed and based on your XACT project settings — you will have different output formats and compressions, but all the raw sound files in the wave bank are the same and have to be updated in only one place. This idea is great, but it would require that *any* raw content file format be supported, which is not practical because there are so many file formats available and you don't know which ones are going to be used. For example, one of your graphic artists might use Photoshop and store .psd files, and other teams might use Gimp or Paint-Shop or just the Paint program of Windows. And there are thousands of other graphic tools and programs around. Additionally, you don't really know which data to extract; many formats can have multiple layers and perhaps the artist wants to have each layer available or just have everything merged down.

Supported File Formats

Instead of just dropping anything, use one of the available processors and supported formats or try to write your own content processors (see Chapter 7) if you think you will need it:

❑ **Texture formats: .dds, .png, .jpg, .bmp, .tga** — Basically everything you can load with the .NET Framework or DirectX. The input format should usually be uncompressed for the best quality. Highly compressed jpg files are bad, especially if you compress them again with DXT for your game. Alternatively, you can use the correct output compression in your input files (dds files with DXT compression) and set the same settings for the content properties again to leave them that way (which is the way I process most of the content in all my projects).

❑ **Sound and Music formats: .xap (XACT Audio Project)** — In XACT you can import only .wav files, but you can set a lot of effects, set parameters, and choose ACPCM compression on the Windows platform or XMA on the Xbox 360 platform. Read more about this in Chapter 9.

❑ **3D Model formats: .fbx and .x model files** — .x files are known from the DirectX SDK and many samples and tutorials. DirectX provides classes to easily load .x files. Most .x files should work fine with XNA, too; the main difference is that DirectX usually doesn't use shaders for .x files and XNA always uses shaders. To export models from 3D Studio Max, use the Panda DirectX Exporter. You can find the Panda Exporter plug-in at www.andytather.co.uk/Panda/directxmax.aspx.

.fbx files are a little bit newer and were originally developed by Alias, the makers of Maya, also a 3D modeling tool. Alias was acquired by Autodesk, the makers of 3D Studio Max and many CAT programs. .fbx stands for "Universal 3D Asset Exchange" and is Autodesk's free format for cross-platform content interchanging. In the new version of 3D Studio Max 9 it is included by default and Maya supports it, too.

There are also many other 3D content creation programs that support importing and exporting the .fbx format. In XNA it is especially useful for animated models, bones, and skinning. It supports more options for that, but it is especially bad for shaders because no material or shader settings can be exported.

Another problem with the .fbx format is the missing format specification. Also, to access the SDK you have to join the Autodesk Developer Network for an annual membership fee, which really sucks. If you take a look at other interchange formats such as Collada, you can see that they are much more open and extensible, and because they are not just developed by one company, many new additions and features are added constantly. In the past Collada did not support shader settings, but the current versions are very good for 3D data; you can export tangents, shader settings, and everything else you need for a game. Sadly, Collada is not supported by XNA and I was not able to convince Microsoft to include it. The XNA Racing Game (see Chapter 12) initially used Collada files for all models, track, and landscape data, but this was changed later to support the content pipeline. You can also import custom file formats — for example xml files or binary files — or even write your own custom processor. This can be useful if you have a bigger project and it is worth the effort or you need a special model format and it is not supported yet by XNA. For example, Quake3/Doom3 uses md3/md5 files and if you would want to use these special file formats for some models an md5 importer would be nice.

In case you have more content files or some custom data for your game you can either decide to write a custom processor and then use the imported and compiled data in your project or just do it the old way by loading the content files yourself. For example, the racer game you will write in the last chapters of this book uses a landscape with landscape height values imported from a bitmap file. Processing the bitmap file and outputting the landscape height data for the game would be possible, but it is too much work — just loading the height data is much simpler and required only once.

Advantages and Disadvantages

Another disadvantage of the content pipeline is that your compiled content cannot be changed anymore. Once you start your game or have your game deployed on client computers or the Xbox 360, all the content files have only the compiled data in them. Say you have just written a particle editor with shader support for all particles. If you want to change the textures, shaders, and other particle settings dynamically while the editor is running, you would have to reload the textures, shaders, and so on. But because you need to have the content compiled first inside of XNA Studio you have to stop your application, add all the files to your XNA Studio project, recompile and wait until all the content is rebuilt, and then start again. Especially in the case of just testing and tweaking effects or particles, this can be very annoying and slows down your work process a lot. It would be more useful to just load textures, shaders, and your particle settings dynamically and not use the content pipeline for programs like that.

Last but not least, here is a trick I use in most projects with many content files: compile them all and make sure you don't change them very often (only every couple of days). Now you can use a dummy project to compile all your game content and copy over all compiled content files to your real project. Especially when using unit testing and the Agile Methodology talked about in the last chapter, you will start the application several hundred times a day and each run should be as fast as possible.

The good thing about the content pipeline is that the compiled data (.xnb files) cannot be read by any programs except from an XNA engine and the loading process is usually also a lot faster because all the data is already in the exact format you need for your game. For example, textures are always stored as DXT files and use mip-maps if you specified that in the content properties. This way the game just has to load the texture data in one quick call and then send it to the graphic card for rendering, again a very fast process. This is even more important for 3D model data. If you take a look at Rocket Commander and profile it a little bit, you can see that loading the 3D models and generating all the extra data and tangents takes most of the initialization time (over 90 percent), whereas XNA games with 10 times as many models load a lot faster. Loading all data as quickly as possible is also a good thing for the Xbox 360 console; console games usually have a short loading time.

Handling Content Directories

Okay, you learned a lot about the advantages and disadvantages of using the content pipeline; here you focus on the game programming a little bit more and the everyday problems. If you take a look at the content directories for the Rocket Commander game and Racing game (see Figure 3-2), you can see that Rocket Commander has a lot of directories, whereas just two simple directories are used in the Racing Game.

Figure 3-2

From the looks of it you would expect that Rocket Commander has a lot more content, but in reality, the Racing Game uses almost ten times as many 3D model files and also has a lot more textures, music, and sound files.

You might ask why Rocket Commander uses so many directories. There is no content pipeline in the game, and to keep everything organized and easy to find, directories are used for each part of the game. For example, the Textures folder holds all the 2D textures for the menu and game interface, the Models subdirectory holds the textures for the 3D models, the Effects subdirectory contains the effect textures, and so on.

In XNA you cannot use this kind of directory structure because most content files, especially the 3D models, can require a lot of other content files to be loaded recursively (see Figure 3-3).

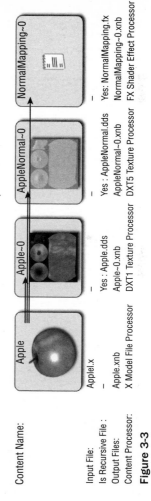

Content Processor Dependencies

Content Name:	Apple	Apple-0	AppleNormal-0	NormalMapping~0
Input File:	Applel.x	–	–	–
Is Recursive File :	–	Yes : Apple.dds	Yes : AppleNormal.dds	Yes: NormalMapping.fx
Output Files:	Apple.xnb	Apple-0.xnb	AppleNormal-0.xnb	NormalMapping~0.xnb
Content Processor:	X Model File Processor	DXT1 Texture Processor	DXT5 Texture Processor	FX Shader Effect Processor

Figure 3-3

As you can see, the Apple model is loaded from the `Apple.x` file, which recursively loads `Apple.dds`, `AppleNormal.dds`, and `NormalMapping.fx`. The content processor expects all these files in the same directory, which forces you to use one directory for all the 3D models and the textures and shaders you use for them. Additionally, most shaders are used for other 3D data as well and it would be very confusing to duplicate the shaders and have them in another directory too. You also sometimes load the textures for custom 3D data, too (for example, the guard rail holder model uses the same texture as the generated guard rail object in the XNA Racing Game).

Anyway, it is important to remember that each piece of content must have a unique name. You can't have an Apple model and an Apple texture. As you can see in the Input File line of Figure 3-3, you add only the `Apple.x` file; all the other files are added automatically through the model processor. Additionally XNA is clever enough to rename all the recursive files because they often use textures with the same names as the model files. Recursive files will end with a tilde (e.g. `Image1~0.xnb`). You also can't set the content properties of these recursive files because you don't add them into your project. For that reason, make sure the input files already use the correct format (DXT1 and DXT5 in the preceding example).

Importing and Accessing Content

You now know enough to import some content and access it from your game. In the previous chapters you already accessed some content files and took a quick look at the content pipeline. Now you will take a closer look at the actual process and how to use content files. In Chapter 7, you learn how to write your own content processors by extending the X Model File Processor with some useful features for your graphics engine.

Back in Chapter 1, you learned how to add textures; just take a texture file (.dds, .jpg, .bmp, or .png) and drop it onto your XNA Studio project. Now you can click the texture and configure the Texture Content Processor settings (see Figure 3-4).

For textures, it is important to set the correct Content Processor mode. For 2D data such as sprites, text, and all user interface (UI) graphics you have in your game, it is usually best to use the 32bpp Sprite format (uncompressed, which means it takes 4MB for a 1024 ×1024 texture with 32bpp).

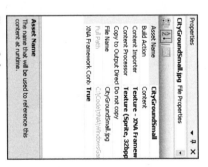

Figure 3-4

Chapter 3: Helper Classes

3D texture data will be used a lot more in a 3D game than 2D UI textures, and textures and levels are getting bigger with every game. For this reason, it is very important to keep the texture sizes small. Instead of just reducing the resolution for your textures and making your games look very bad, use hardware texture compression instead. You can simply select DXT1 for a 1:6 compression ratio for color textures and DXT5 for a 1:4 compression ratio for textures with alpha information (or compressed normal maps). This means that with DXT1 textures, you can have six times as many textures in your game consuming the same amount of video memory as uncompressed textures without losing much of its quality. Another trick is to combine or even generate textures inside your shaders; for example, detail textures can improve landscape details for almost no extra video memory cost.

When importing 3D models, you can currently select only the X Model Importer or the FBX Model Importer (see Figure 3-5). Maybe more formats will be available in the future. If you write custom model processors as you will do in Chapter 7, you can select them the same way you select texture processors. For normal mappings you want to select your custom XNA Tangent Model Processor from Chapter 7. For the next few chapters, just leave the default value.

Figure 3-5

If you followed the way you loaded textures in the last two chapters, you will probably already know how to load content in XNA. Textures are loaded with:

```
backgroundTexture = content.Load<Texture2D>("CityGroundSmall");
```

And 3D models can be loaded the same way — just change the generic type of the Load method:

```
appleModel = content.Load<Model>("apple");
```

Displaying a model is a little bit more complicated. There is no simple draw method so you must go through all model meshes and update all shader effects, and then you can render each part. For more details, see Chapters 5 and 6. Later in this book, in Chapter 7, you will see a new class just for loading and rendering models, which makes it even easier to just show the 3D model in our 3D world with just one single line of code:

```
appleModel.Render(Vector3.Zero);
```

You now know all the basics about the content pipeline. You learn more about the content pipeline in the upcoming chapters when adding 3D models with your custom tangent model processor in your graphics engine, and in Chapter 9, when you learn in detail about XACT.

Logging Error Messages

Debugging game code can be very complicated, especially if you don't get any exceptions, but something in your render loop goes wrong. Just setting a few breakpoints might not be enough, and especially if you experience errors after running the game for a while, debugging is not the right option. You want to know what is going on each frame, but you don't want to step through 500 frames to find it out. For these kinds of problems you can just throw some text to the console, but this will only work inside Visual Studio and you will lose all the console content the next time you start your project.

One of the most important classes in all bigger projects I have done is the Log class, which just writes information, warning, error, or debugging texts to a simple text file. The class itself is very short and simple, but if you use it in the right way it will make your debugging and testing sessions much more enjoyable. More advanced logging classes and frameworks are also available such as Log4Net, which you can find at http://logging.apache.org/log4net/. Logging can be more than just writing a few lines to a text file. You can log data from your application to find out about user errors remotely with a web service. You can fire Windows error events, and you can do a lot more things. This is not covered in this book because it is a very complex topic. For the simple games in this book, using Log class should be sufficient.

Take a look at the Log class (a more complex version can be found in the Breakout game):

```
public class Log
{
    #region Variables
    private static StreamWriter writer = null;
    private const string LogFilename = "Log.txt";
    #endregion
```

The Log class uses the Log.txt file to store all the log messages with the help of the StreamWriter object stored as a static object to have easy access from your static methods. The first time this class is called, it gets instantiated through the static constructor:

```
    #region Static constructor to create log file
    static Log()
    {
        // Open file
        FileStream file = new FileStream(
            LogFilename, FileMode.OpenOrCreate,
            FileAccess.Write, FileShare.ReadWrite);
        writer = new StreamWriter(file);
        // Go to end of file
        writer.BaseStream.Seek(0, SeekOrigin.End);
        // Enable auto flush (always be up to date when reading!)
        writer.AutoFlush = true;
        // Add some info about this session
        writer.WriteLine("");// Session started at: " +
```

```
    StringHelper.WriteIsoDateAndTime(DateTime.Now));
} // Log()
#endregion
```

`FileShare.ReadWrite` makes sure you can always read and write the file from outside while the game is running. Other than that, the writer is set to the end of the file, auto flush is enabled to make sure writing new data is immediately saved to the log file, and finally you add a little text indicating that this session started. For the time stamp, you will use a helper method from the `StringHelper` class you learn about shortly.

And finally, here is the most important method and the only one you will ever call from this class:

```
#region Write log entry
static public void Write(string message)
{
    DateTime ct = DateTime.Now;
    string s = "[" + ct.Hour.ToString("00") + ":" +
        ct.Minute.ToString("00") + ":" +
        ct.Second.ToString("00") + "] " +
        message;
    writer.WriteLine(s);
#if DEBUG
    // In debug mode write that message to the console as well!
    System.Console.WriteLine(s);
#endif
} // Write(message)
#endregion
```

First, a simple time stamp is added in front of the message. Then the message is written to your `Log.txt` file. And finally, you also add the message to the console if the project is in debug mode. Now you can add a new line to the `Log.txt` file every time you complete a level in the Breakout game from Chapter 2 by just adding the following line:

```
Log.Write("Level " + level + " completed.");
```

Unit Testing in XNA

Before going into greater detail about the helper classes for the upcoming projects in this book, this section talks a little bit about unit testing. You already learned about static unit tests in the last chapter. Static unit tests are great for quickly checking visual results, testing physics and the controllers, and building your game in a quick manner. But helper classes and components that do not require user input would require you to think about interfacing with them. That makes no sense because unit testing is all about improving the maintainability of your application and making sure everything runs as errorless as possible. For example, to test if the `Log` class works, you could call the following lines of code:

```
FileHelper.DeleteFile(Log.LogFilename);
Log.Write("New log entry");
```

This code can be executed only inside the `Log` class because `Log.LogFilename` is private.

Now you could go into the application directory and check if the log file exists and has an entry with the "New log entry" text in it. But checking this file yourself over and over again is a bit of a hassle. Instead of logging every error here you should put only the less important warning messages (for example, the user is not connected to the Internet) into the log and throw exceptions when fatal errors occur (for example, "Texture not found", "No shaders available", and so on). This is especially true if the problems become bigger and the tests are much more complex and involve a very lengthy check process. You can avoid checking for errors yourself by letting these tests check themselves, and you can have them executed automatically instead of calling them yourself from the Program class as static unit tests.

NUnit and TestDriven.Net

To do this, you can use the popular NUnit Framework, which you can download at www.nunit.org/. Just when I started to work on the second edition of this book, the new xUnit Framework came out, which is the successor of NUnit and MbUnit, another popular .NET unit testing framework. It works more closely together with .NET 2.0 and .NET 3.5, using more generic methods, a more clean framework with many removed attributes, and a simplified interface. If you are using the code for this book from www.XnaProjects.net (Chapters 1 through 14), stick with NUnit. It will work fine for you. In case you are writing new code or start your own project, I suggest xUnit. The last chapters of this book (Chapters 15 through 17) and the Dungeon Quest game will use xUnit instead of NUnit. Again, it is very similar. Just some attributes have been removed and some methods have been simplified and refactored a little. You can get xUnit from www.codeplex.com/xunit.

Alternatively, you can also use TestDriven.NET from www.testdriven.net/ if you are using Visual Studio 2005 Standard or better. It supports many cool features and you can start tests directly with hotkeys or the pop-up menu, which is really cool and simple. Internally, it just uses NUnit or one of the other unit testing frameworks. It also works with MbUnit or xUnit, for example. TestDriven.Net does not work in VC# Express or XNA Studio Express (it did work a year ago, but the developer had to remove the plug-in support for Express because Microsoft wants developers to use the Professional Edition for serious programmers). See Chapter 1 on how to get XNA 1.0 working in Visual Studio 2005; if you are using XNA 2.0, it will work out-of-the-box with Visual Studio 2005 and you can directly use TestDriven.Net. Visual Studio 2008 is also supported by TestDriven.Net, but for XNA projects you might need to convert the project files, either with my VSProjectChanger tool (see Chapter 1) or by just upgrading to a VS2008 project when opening the project file with VS2008. While you can also do most work with VS2008 or later versions, it does not support the content pipeline at the moment, so to get it to work with XNA 1.0, you have to use Visual C# Express. With XNA 2.0 you can use Visual C# Express or one of the Visual Studio 2005 editions.

It does not matter which one you install. Just add the NUnit.Framework.dll from the installation folder to your project. Right-click your project references and add a new reference; use Browse if you can't find it in the Global Assembly Cache (GAC), which is represented in the first tab. Now you can add the following using directive:

```
#if DEBUG
using NUnit.Framework;
#endif
```

I usually add this at the very top of the using directives region. This is used only in debug mode because you will only use the unit tests in your debug build. For the final game, you don't want the extra NUnit .Framework.dll and all the testing code because it is not required for your game. This style is used throughout the book except for the very last chapters where xUnit is used (just include xUnit.dll and add a using Xunit; directive). Because of the small size of xUnit we are still using it in Release mode, even when the if debug condition blocks out any unit tests in the Release mode. Please also note that some of the unit test code looks different in the last chapters because of xUnit. TestFixtures are no longer required and the Assert methods are named differently, but the overall idea is the same. Stay with NUnit if you don't want to be on the bleeding edge; it will work just fine and is a good way to learn more about test-driven development if you are doing it for the first time.

As an example, take a look at the first unit test in the StringHelper class, which checks if the IsInList helper method works as expected:

```
[TestFixture]
public class StringHelperTests
{
    /// <summary>
    /// Test IsInList
    /// </summary>
    [Test]
    public void TestIsInList()
    {
        Assert.IsTrue(IsInList("whats",
            new string[] { "hi", "whats", "up?" }, false));
        Assert.IsFalse(IsInList("no way",
            new string[]
            { "omg", "no no", "there is no way!" }, false));
    } // TestIsInList()
    ...
```

Assert is a helper class inside the NUnit Framework, and it contains methods to check if the return values are as expected. If the value is not as expected an exception is thrown and you can immediately see which line of your test failed. For example, Assert.IsTrue checks if the return value of IsInList is true. If the return value is false, an exception is thrown. Luckily the string list contains "whats" and the test should pass. The next test checks for "no way" and that string is not in the second string list. Therefore, the second test line should return false as it does. Note that the statement "there is no way!" contains "no way," but you were not checking the Contains method, which also exists in the StringHelper class. IsInList returns true only if the exact string was found in the list.

Starting Unit Tests

You can run the test in TestDriven.Net by right-clicking and selecting "Run Test" (see Figure 3-6) or you can use the NUnit GUI program if you don't have or cannot use TestDriven.Net. You can also test static unit tests the same way with TestDriven.Net, but the NUnit GUI does not support static unit tests. For this reason, I added the unit tests in Program.cs (or the UnitTesting.cs class in later projects) to support all users and XNA Studio Express. TestDriven.Net can be used to start both dynamic and static unit tests, but since version 2.0 you will have to remove the [Test] attribute from static unit tests in order for it to work properly (you don't use the [Test] attributes for static unit tests in this book anyway).

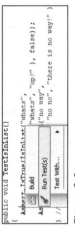

Figure 3-6

The test will execute without any error, but if you were to change the test by changing "whats" to "whats up" the first Assert test would fail and you would see the following results from TestDriven.Net:

```
TestCase 'M:XnaBreakout.Helpers.StringHelperTests.TestIsInList' failed:
at NUnit.Framework.AssertionException
at NUnit.Framework.Assert.DoAssert(IAsserter asserter)
at NUnit.Framework.Assert.IsTrue(Boolean condition, String message, Object[] args)
at NUnit.Framework.Assert.IsTrue(Boolean condition)
C:\code\Xna\RacingGame\Helpers\StringHelper.cs(1387,0): at
    XnaBreakout.Helpers.StringHelper.StringHelperTests.TestIsInList()

0 passed, 1 failed, 0 skipped, took 0.48 seconds.
```

This tells you exactly where to look (you can even double-click the error and jump to the line 1387) and what you should change. The error becomes even more visible if using the NUnit GUI (see Figure 3-7).

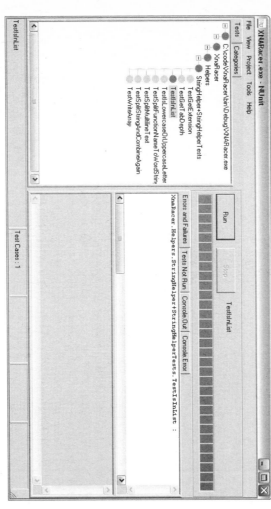

Figure 3-7

The NUnit GUI is a good tool to run many unit tests at once and quickly see which ones did not work properly and then investigate further in the source code. You can use File ⇨ Load to select your program or just drag and drop any .NET .exe or .dll file onto the NUnit GUI program. Then you see all the tests in that assembly and can test them by clicking Run. The program is nice, but I usually don't go outside of my programming environment when coding and testing, and therefore I like TestDriven.Net a lot more and use it all the time. To fix the error, you just change the "whats up" line back to "whats" and all your tests will pass and you get a green light.

Golden Rules

I did not go much into writing unit tests here because Chapter 2 already discussed the basic rules, which of course also apply for dynamic unit tests. Keep these guidelines in mind when you start writing your first unit tests:

❑ Think about your problems and divide them into small manageable parts.

❑ Write the tests first and do not think about the implementation. Just write them down as you think the final code should look or as you want to have your game code.

❑ Try to make sure you test as much as possible. For example, the TestIsInList method tests both a successful call to IsInList and a failure from the IsInList call. Spend time with your unit tests, but never more than 50 percent of your time — you should not have to write 30 checks for a method that has only two lines of code.

❑ Start the test constantly from this point on, even when you think it does not make sense. It will force you to see what has to be done and how far you are in the implementation process. At first, the test will not even compile because you haven't implemented anything. Then, after implementing empty methods, the test should fail because you are not doing anything yet. Later when everything works, you will feel much better.

❑ Although you will not test your static unit tests very often, dynamic unit tests can be tested every single time you compile your code (if they all run quick enough). Always try to run all unit tests once a day or once a week to make sure your latest code changes did not add new bugs or errors.

RandomHelper Class

Take a look at one of the helper classes. RandomHelper will not be used often in a single project, but almost any game uses some random number generation to make the game content appear less periodic and to add more variation to the game.

In the Breakout game you will write in a little bit, the blocks are generated randomly. For level 1, you use a probability of 10 percent, level 2 uses a probability of 20 percent, and so on. This way, the level gets more filled and the game gets harder. You could just use the Random class and call the Next method to get a new random number, but in case you want to generate a random normalized vector you would have to write the following lines of code:

```
Random randomGenerator = new Random((int)DateTime.Now.Ticks);
Vector3 randomNormalVector = new Vector3(
    (float)randomGenerator.NextDouble() * 2.0f - 1.0f,
    (float)randomGenerator.NextDouble() * 2.0f - 1.0f,
    (float)randomGenerator.NextDouble() * 2.0f - 1.0f);
randomNormalVector.Normalize();
```

Instead of repeating this code over and over again, a helper class such as RandomHelper might be very useful. Figure 3-8 shows the basic layout of the RandomHelper class.

As you can see, the methods are very simple and it would take only a couple of minutes to write the whole class. However, the class is still useful and thanks to the internal globalRandomGenerator instance of the Random class, the RandomHelper class is much quicker at generating random values than creating a new Random class every time you need a random number.

Figure 3-8

Generate Random Vectors

Here you can see a method from the RandomHelper class:

```
/// <summary>
/// Get random Vector2
/// </summary>
/// <param name="min">Minimum for each component</param>
/// <param name="max">Maximum for each component</param>
/// <returns>Vector2</returns>
public static Vector2 GetRandomVector2(float min, float max)
{
    return new Vector2(
        GetRandomFloat(min, max),
        GetRandomFloat(min, max));
} // GetRandomVector2(min, max)
```

It does not make sense to unit test any method in the RandomHelper class because all return values are random and you don't really have to check if GetRandomVector2 returns a Vector2; it just does that. There is not much that can go wrong.

StringHelper Class

The StringHelper class is one of the biggest helper classes and it was the very first helper class I ever wrote because working with strings involves so many things, it is very easy to think about many ways to improve performance, handle lists of strings easier, output string data easily, and so on.

If you take a look at the StringHelper class (see Figure 3-9) you will immediately notice the many methods and all the method overloads supporting many different parameter types. It also contains quite a lot of unit tests; you just saw a unit test from the StringHelper class.

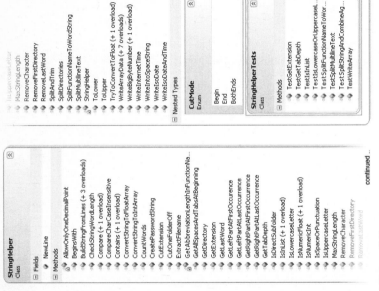

StringHelper
Class

Fields
- NewLine

Methods
- AllowOnlyOneDecimalPoint
- BeginsWith
- BuildStringFromLines (+ 3 overloads)
- CheckStringWordLength
- Compare (+ 1 overload)
- CompareCharCaseInsensitive
- Contains (+ 1 overload)
- ConvertStringToFloatArray
- ConvertStringToIntArray
- CountWords
- CreatePasswordString
- CutExtension
- CutOneFolderOff
- ExtractFilename
- GetAbbreviationLengthInFunctionNa...
- GetAllSpacesAndTabsAtBeginning
- GetDirectory
- GetExtension
- GetLastWord
- GetLeftPartAtFirstOccurrence
- GetLeftPartAtLastOccurrence
- GetRightPartAtFirstOccurrence
- GetRightPartAtLastOccurrence
- GetTabDepth
- IsDirectSubfolder
- IsInList (+ 1 overload)
- IsLowercaseLetter
- IsNumericFloat (+ 1 overload)
- IsNumericInt
- IsSpaceOrPunctuation
- IsUppercaseLetter
- MaxStringLength
- RemoveCharacter
- RemoveFirstDirectory
- RemoveLastWord

continued ...

- IsUppercaseLetter
- MaxStringLength
- RemoveCharacter
- RemoveFirstDirectory
- RemoveLastWord
- SplitAndTrim
- SplitDirectories
- SplitFunctionNameToWordString
- SplitMultilineText
- StringHelper
- ToLower
- ToUpper
- TryToConvertToFloat (+ 1 overload)
- WriteArrayData (+ 7 overloads)
- WriteBigByteNumber (+ 1 overload)
- WriteInternetTime
- WriteIntoSpaceString
- WriteIsoDate
- WriteIsoDateAndTime

Nested Types

CutMode
Enum
- Begin
- End
- BothEnds

StringHelperTests
Class

Methods
- TestGetExtension
- TestGetTabDepth
- TestIsInList
- TestIsLowercaseOrUppercaseL...
- TestSplitFunctionNameToWor...
- TestSplitMultilineText
- TestSplitStringAndCombineAg...
- TestWriteArray

Figure 3-9

You might ask yourself why there are only a couple of unit tests, but so very many methods in this class. The reason for this is that I started coding this class many years ago, a long time before I started using unit testing. Some methods don't make much sense in .NET 2.0 because the framework implements them now, but I got used to my own methods. I just hope you can find some useful methods in this class. It might take a while to get used to the many methods, but when you need a complicated string operation you will thank me (or yourself if you have your own helper class) for a useful method.

Extracting Filenames

Many methods such as GetDirectory and CutExtension are available in the Path class from the System.IO namespace, too, but one of the most useful methods in StringHelper for filenames is the ExtractFilename method, which cuts off both the path and the extension to just get the name of a file, nothing else. Path.GetFileNameWithoutExtension does a similar thing, but I like my own method better for some reason. It might also be interesting if you want to implement your own methods and need some working code you can start with. Again: You don't have to write your own Path methods, but sometimes you don't know what the framework provides or you just want to investigate yourself. It's been a long time since I tested the performance of these methods, but I would still guess that most of the StringHelper methods are faster than some of the Path methods.

```
/// <summary>
/// Extracts filename from full path+filename, cuts of extension
/// if cutExtension is true. Can be also used to cut of directories
/// from a path (only last one will remain).
/// </summary>
static public string ExtractFilename(string pathFile, bool cutExtension)
{
    if (pathFile == null)
        return "";

    // Support windows and unix slashes
    string[] fileName = pathFile.Split(new char[] { '\\', '/' });
    if (fileName.Length == 0)
    {
        if (cutExtension)
            return CutExtension(pathFile);
        return pathFile;
    } // if (fileName.Length)
    if (cutExtension)
        return CutExtension(fileName[fileName.Length - 1]);
    return fileName[fileName.Length - 1];
} // ExtractFilename(pathFile, cutExtension)
```

Writing a unit test for a method like this is also very simple. Just check if the expected result is returned:

```
Assert.AreEqual("SomeFile",
    StringHelper.ExtractFilename("SomeDir\\SomeFile.bmp"));
```

Writing Lists

A little bit more unique is the `WriteArrayData` method in the `StringHelper` class, which writes any type of lists, arrays, or `IEnumerable` data to a text string, which then can be used for logging. The implementation is again quite simple:

```
/// <summary>
/// Returns a string with the array data, ArrayList version.
/// </summary>
static public string WriteArrayData(ArrayList array)
{
    StringBuilder ret = new StringBuilder();
    if (array != null)
        foreach (object obj in array)
            ret.Append((ret.Length == 0 ? "" : ", ") +
                obj.ToString());
    return ret.ToString();
} // WriteArrayData(array)
```

`Lists`, even generic ones, are derived from the `ArrayList` class and therefore you can call this method with any dynamic list. For arrays, a special overload exists, as it does for special collections and byte or integer arrays, which would work with `IEnumerable`, too, but it is faster to use overloads that don't use the object class.

To test the WriteArrayData method you could write a method like the following:

```
/// <summary>
/// Test WriteArrayData
/// </summary>
[Test]
public void TestWriteArrayData()
{
    Assert.AreEqual("3, 5, 10",
        WriteArrayData(new int[] { 3, 5, 10 }));
    Assert.AreEqual("one, after, another",
        WriteArrayData(new string[] { "one", "after", "another" }));
    List<string> genericList = new List<string>();
    genericList.Add("whats");
    genericList.AddRange(new string[] { "going", "on" });
    Assert.AreEqual("whats, going, on",
        WriteArrayData(genericList));
} // TestWriteArray()
```

Other Helpers

The Helpers namespace contains a few more helper classes; most of them are simple like the RandomHelper class. It is not very exciting to go through all of them, so please review the ones that are not mentioned in this chapter yourself and test them out with the included unit tests if you want to know more about them.

Before you go into the Breakout game at the end of this chapter, take a quick look at some of the remaining helper classes, which will be used more frequently in the next chapters: SpriteHelper, EnumHelper, and ColorHelper.

SpriteHelper Class

You used a lot of sprite rendering in the previous chapter and because of the unit tests, you forced yourself to write an easy way to handle sprites in XNA. This approach and the fact that you should put useful code that is used more than once into reusable classes leads us to the SpriteHelper class (see Figure 3-10). Basically it provides a constructor to create new SpriteHelpers storing the texture and graphics rectangle data and a few Render methods to easily draw the sprites to the screen as you did in the last chapter with a list of SpriteToRender classes.

Most methods here don't do much; the constructor just sets the values, Render just adds a new SpriteToRender instance to the sprites list, RenderCentered renders the sprite centered at the specified location, and DrawSprites finally draws all the sprites on the screen. Take a look at the DrawSprites method, which will look similar to the DrawSprites method from the previous chapter, but with some improvements:

```
public static void DrawSprites(int width, int height)
{
    // No need to render if we got no sprites this frame
```

```
        if (sprites.Count == 0)
            return;
        // Create sprite batch if we have not done it yet.
        // Use device from texture to create the sprite batch.
        if (spriteBatch == null)
            spriteBatch = new SpriteBatch(sprites[0].texture.GraphicsDevice);
        // Start rendering sprites
        spriteBatch.Begin(SpriteBlendMode.AlphaBlend,
            SpriteSortMode.BackToFront, SaveStateMode.None);
        // Render all sprites
        foreach (SpriteToRender sprite in sprites)
            spriteBatch.Draw(sprite.texture,
                // Rescale to fit resolution
                new Rectangle(
                sprite.rect.X * width / 1024,
                sprite.rect.Y * height / 768,
                sprite.rect.Width * width / 1024,
                sprite.rect.Height * height / 768),
                sprite.sourceRect, sprite.color);
        // We are done, draw everything on screen.
        spriteBatch.End();
        // Kill list of remembered sprites
        sprites.Clear();
    } // DrawSprites(width, height)
```

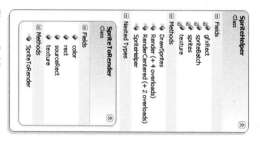

Figure 3-10

This method is called with the current width and height of the render window resolution to scale all sprites up and down depending on the resolution, which is important to support all Xbox 360 screen resolutions. In the DrawSprites method, you first check if there is something to render. Then you make sure the static sprite batch was created, which will be used for all sprites you draw here. After beginning the sprite batch, you go through all sprites for this frame and rescale their rectangles to fit correctly on the screen. Finally, you let everything draw on the screen by calling End. The sprites list is also killed to start fresh the next frame. For an example of how this class works, see the Breakout game at the end of the chapter.

EnumHelper Class

The EnumHelper class (see Figure 3-11) is useful when you want to enumerate through any enum or quickly find out the number of enum values contained in an enum. For the Pong and Breakout games, you are not using any enums, but in the next chapter, the Enum class becomes useful when going through the types of blocks for the game there. Please also note that the EnumHelper class uses some methods of the Enum class, which are not implemented in the .NET Compact Framework. To avoid any compilation errors, the whole class is usually left out of the Xbox 360 project, but you can still use it on the Windows platform if you like.

Figure 3-11

The unit test for TestGetAllEnumNames looks like this and also illustrates how GetAllEnumNames works. It goes through each enum value with the help of the EnumEnumerator helper class inside of EnumHelper:

```
[Test]
public void TestGetAllEnumNames()
{
    Assert.AreEqual(
        "Missions, Highscore, Credits, Help, Options, Exit, Back",
        EnumHelper.GetAllEnumNames(typeof(MenuButton)));
} // TestGetAllEnumNames()
```

And the `GetAllEnumNames` just uses the `WriteArrayData` helper method of the `StringHelper` class just covered:

```
public static string GetAllEnumNames(Type type)
{
    return StringHelper.WriteArrayData(GetEnumerator(type));
} // GetAllEnumNames(type)
```

ColorHelper Class

Initially, the `ColorHelper` class (see Figure 3-12) was a lot longer and had many methods, but because the new `Color` class in XNA is much more powerful than the `Color` class from `System.Drawings` that is used in Managed DirectX, many of the methods are not required anymore. It still contains some useful methods you use for color manipulation.

Figure 3-12

For example, the `Color.Empty` field is used to initialize shader effect parameters to unused values — 0, 0, 0, 0 is usually not a valid color; it is completely transparent. Even black has 255 for the alpha value.

```
/// <summary>
/// Empty color, used to mark unused color values.
/// </summary>
public static readonly Color Empty = new Color(0, 0, 0);
```

The Breakout Game

Alright, in this chapter, I talked a lot about helper classes, and it is finally time to put them to some use. I will skip the concept phase here and basically just say that Breakout is an abbreviation of Pong for just one player to play against a wall of blocks. Breakout was initially created by Nolan Bushnell and Steve Wozniak and released by Atari in 1976. In this early version it was just a black and white game like Pong, but to make it more "exciting," transparent stripes were placed over the monitor to color the blocks (see Figure 3-13).

You will actually go a similar road by reusing some of the Pong components and using the helper classes you learned about in this chapter. Breakout is a more complex game than Pong; it can have many levels and can be improved quite a lot. For example, Arkanoid is a clone of Breakout and there were many games in the 1980s and 1990s that still used this basic game idea and added weapons, better graphics effects, and many levels with different block placements.

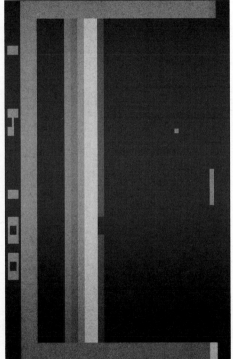

Figure 3-13

As you can see in Figure 3-14, the BreakoutGame class is structured in a similar way to the Pong class from the last chapter. The sprite handling is missing because it is done now with help of the SpriteHelper class. Some other internal methods and calls are also replaced by some of the helper classes. For example, StartLevel generates a random new level based on the level value, and to generate the random values you will use the RandomHelper class.

Please also note that many test methods are visible in the class. This will be improved similar to the helper classes in the next chapter, which introduces the BaseGame and TestGame classes that make handling the game class, and especially unit testing, a lot easier and more organized.

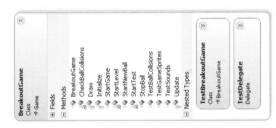

Figure 3-14

Take a look at Figure 3-15 for a quick overview of the Breakout game you are going to develop in the next few pages. It is quite a lot of fun and certainly has a greater replay value than Pong, which is only fun with two human players anyway. The Breakout game uses the same background texture and the two sound files from the Pong project, but you also add a new texture (BreakoutGame.png) for the paddle, ball, and blocks, and you have new sounds for winning a level (BreakoutVictory.wav) and for destroying blocks (BreakoutBlockKill.wav).

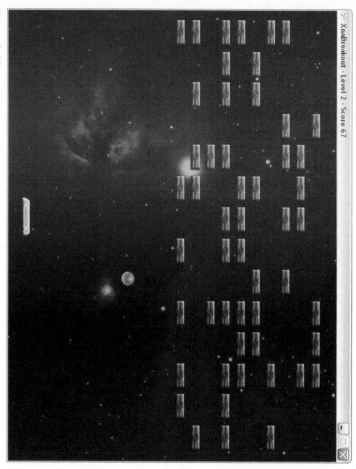

XnaBreakout - Level 2 - Score 67

Figure 3-15

Unit Testing in Breakout

Before you start copying and pasting code over from the last project, using your new helper classes, and drawing the new game elements, you should think about the game and the problems you might run into. Sure you can just go ahead and implement the game, but it will be much harder to test the collisions, for example, which are the hardest part of this game. The unit tests help you out and provide you with an easy way to at least check all the basic parts of your game, and they also help you to organize your code and force you to program only what is really required. As always, start with the most obvious part of the game and unit test it, then add more unit tests until you are done, and finally put everything together and test the final game.

Here is a quick overview of the unit tests for the Breakout game; check the full source code for this chapter for more details. You don't have the TestGame class yet, so you still use the same kind of unit testing you used in the last chapter. Check out the next chapter on a better way to do static unit tests. You have only three unit tests, but they were used and changed a lot as I implemented the game.

- **TestSounds** — Just a quick test to check out all the new sounds for your project. Press the spacebar, Alt, Control, or Shift to play the sounds. I also added a little pause after playing the next sound to make it a little easier to hear the sounds. This test was used to check out the new XACT project I created for this game.

- **TestGameSprites** — This test was initially used to test the `SpriteHelper` class, but then all the code was moved to the `Draw` method of the game. The test was also used to initialize all the blocks in the game; the code was moved to the constructor, which is shown at the end of this chapter. This test shows you just having four lines of code can be enough to test huge parts of your game engine. Copy and paste useful parts of unit tests to your code as often as you need. Static unit tests also don't have to be intact as do dynamic unit tests for the helper classes because you use them only to build and test your game. When the game works, you don't need the static unit tests anymore except for testing parts of the game at a later point in time.

- **TestBallCollisions** — As in the previous chapter, testing the ball collisions is the most useful unit test. Here you check if the collisions happen with the screen borders and paddle as expected. Only minor changes were required to get this to work. Then you can go to the more complicated block collision code, which is explained in more detail a bit later. You might even be able to think of more ways to test the collision and improve the game if you like. For example, it would make sense to trap the ball behind the wall of blocks and see if it destroys all the blocks correctly.

Breakout Levels

Because you are using many of the existing Pong ideas, you can skip the code that is similar or identical. You should focus on the new variables for now:

```
/// <summary>
/// How many block columns and rows are displayed?
/// </summary>
const int NumOfColumns = 14,
    NumOfRows = 12;
/// <summary>
/// Current paddle positions, 0 means left, 1 means right.
/// </summary>
float paddlePosition = 0.5f;
/// <summary>
/// Level we are in and the current score.
/// </summary>
int level = 0,  score = -1;
/// <summary>
/// All blocks of the current play field. If they are
/// all cleared, we advance to the next level.
/// </summary>
bool[,] blocks = new bool[NumOfColumns, NumOfRows];
/// <summary>
/// Block positions for each block we have, initialized in Initialize().
/// </summary>
Vector2[,] blockPositions = new Vector2[NumOfColumns, NumOfRows];
/// <summary>
```

```
/// Bounding boxes for each of the blocks, also precalculated and
/// checked each frame if the ball collides with one of the blocks.
/// </summary>
BoundingBox[,] blockBoxes = new BoundingBox[NumOfColumns, NumOfRows];
```

First you define the maximum number of columns and blocks you can have. In the first levels, you will not fill all the lines and will use only 10 percent of the blocks. The paddle position is also a little bit easier than in Pong because you have just one player. Then you store the current level and the score, which is new. In Pong, each player just had three balls and the game was over if all balls were lost. In Breakout, the player starts at level 1 and works his way up until he finally loses a ball. You don't have a high score here or any game font, so the level and score data is just updated in the title of the window.

Then all the blocks are defined; the most important array is *blocks*, which just tells you which block is currently used. The blocks are initialized before each level starts, whereas the blockPositions and blockBoxes are initialized only once in the constructor of the game; blockPositions is used to determine the centered position of the block for rendering and blockBoxes defines the bounding box of the block for collision testing. It is important to note that none of these lists or position values use screen coordinates. All position data is stored in the 0–1 format: 0 is left or top, and 1 is right or bottom. This way, the game stays resolution-independent and makes both rendering and collision checking easier.

The levels are generated in the StartLevel method, which is called at the beginning of the game and every time you advance one level:

```
void StartLevel()
{
    // Randomize levels, but make it more harder each level
    for (int y = 0; y < NumOfRows; y++)
        for (int x = 0; x < NumOfColumns; x++)
            blocks[x, y] =
                RandomHelper.GetRandomInt(10) < level+1;

    // Use the lower blocks only for later levels
    if (level < 6)
        for (int x = 0; x < NumOfColumns; x++)
            blocks[x, NumOfRows - 1] = false;
    if (level < 4)
        for (int x = 0; x < NumOfColumns; x++)
            blocks[x, NumOfRows - 2] = false;
    if (level < 2)
        for (int x = 0; x < NumOfColumns; x++)
            blocks[x, NumOfRows - 3] = false;

    // Halt game
    ballSpeedVector = Vector2.Zero;
    // Wait until user presses space or A to start a level.
    pressSpaceToStart = true;
    // Update title
    Window.Title =
        "XnaBreakout - Level " + (level+1) +
        " - Score " + Math.Max(0, score);
} // StartLevel
```

In the first for loop, you just fill the whole block array with new values depending on the level. In level 1, the level value is 0 and you will fill only 10 percent of the blocks. RandomHelper.GetRandomInt(10) returns 0–9, which is smaller than 1 in only 10 percent of the cases. In level 2, this goes up to 20 percent until you reach level 10 or higher, where 100 percent of the level is filled. The game actually has no limit; you can play as long as you want.

Then you clear the lower three lines for the first levels to make the first levels easier. At level 3, only two lines are removed and at level 5, just one line is removed until you reach level 7 where all the lines are used.

Unlike Pong, the ball speed vector is not immediately started for a new game. The ball stays on the paddle until the user presses the spacebar or A. Then the ball bounces off the paddle to a random location and the ball goes between the wall blocks, the screen borders, and the player paddle until either all blocks are removed to win a level or the player loses by not catching the ball.

Finally, the window's title is updated to show the current level number and the score the player has reached so far. In this very simple game, the player gets only one point for every block he destroys; reaching a score of 100 is really good, but as I said before, there is no limit. Try to go higher and have fun with the game.

The Game Loop

The game loop in Pong was quite easy and contained mostly input and collision code. Breakout is a little bit more complicated because you have to handle two states of the ball. It is either still on the paddle and awaits the user to press the spacebar or you are in the game and have to check for any collisions with the screen borders, the paddle, or any of the blocks in the game.

Most of the Update method looks the same way as in the previous chapter; the second player was removed and a little bit of new code was added at the bottom:

```
// Game not started yet? Then put ball on paddle.
if (pressSpaceToStart)
{
    ballPosition = new Vector2(paddlePosition, 0.95f - 0.035f);
    // Handle space
    if (keyboard.IsKeyDown(Keys.Space) ||
        gamePad.Buttons.A == ButtonState.Pressed)
    {
        StartNewBall();
    } // if
} // if
else
{
    // Check collisions
    CheckBallCollisions(moveFactorPerSecond);
    // Update ball position and bounce off the borders
    ballPosition += ballSpeedVector *
        moveFactorPerSecond * BallSpeedMultiplicator;

    // Ball lost?
    if (ballPosition.Y > 0.985f)
    {
        // Play sound
        soundBank.PlayCue("PongBallLost");
```

```
            // Game over, reset to level 0
            level = 0;
            StartLevel();
            // Show lost message
            lostGame = true;
        } // if
        // Check if all blocks are killed and if we won this level
        bool allBlocksKilled = true;
        for (int y = 0; y < NumOfRows; y++)
            for (int x = 0; x < NumOfColumns; x++)
                if (blocks[x, y])
                {
                    allBlocksKilled = false;
                    break;
                } // for for if
        // We won, start next level
        if (allBlocksKilled == true)
        {
            // Play sound
            soundBank.PlayCue("BreakoutVictory");
            lostGame = false;
            level++;
            StartLevel();
        } // if
    } // else
```

First you check if the ball was not started yet. If not, update the ball position and put it on the center of the player's paddle. Then check if the spacebar or A was pressed and start the ball then. (This just randomizes the ballSpeedVector for you and bounces the ball off to the wall of blocks.)

The most important method is checkBallCollisions, which you will check out in a second. Then the ball is updated as in the Pong game and you check if the ball is lost. If the player did not catch the ball, the game is over and the player can start over at level 1.

Finally, you check if all blocks were removed and the level is complete. If all blocks are killed, you can play the new victory sound and start the next level. The player sees a "You Won!" message on the screen (see Draw method) and can press the spacebar to start the next level.

Drawing Breakout

Thanks to the SpriteHelper class, the Draw method of the Breakout game is short and easy:

```
protected override void Draw(GameTime gameTime)
{
    // Render background
    background.Render();
    SpriteHelper.DrawSprites(width, height);
    // Render all game graphics
    paddle.RenderCentered(paddlePosition, 0.95f);
    ball.RenderCentered(ballPosition);
    // Render all blocks
    for (int y = 0; y < NumOfRows; y++)
```

```
        for (int x = 0; x < NumOfColumns; x++)
            if (blocks[x, y])
                block.RenderCentered(blockPositions[x, y]);

        if (pressSpaceToStart &&
            score >= 0)
        {
            if (lostGame)
                youLost.RenderCentered(0.5f, 0.65f, 2);
            else
                youWon.RenderCentered(0.5f, 0.65f, 2);
        } // if
        // Draw all sprites on the screen
        SpriteHelper.DrawSprites(width, height);
        base.Draw(gameTime);
    } // Draw(gameTime)
```

You start by rendering the background; you don't have to clear the background because the background texture fills the complete background. To make sure everything is rendered on top of the background, you draw it immediately before rendering the rest of the game sprites.

Next, you draw the paddle and the ball, which is very easy to do because of the RenderCentered helper method in the SpriteHelper class, which works like this (the three overloads are just for a more convenient use of this method):

```
public void RenderCentered(float x, float y, float scale)
{
    Render(new Rectangle(
        (int)(x * 1024 - scale * gfxRect.Width/2),
        (int)(y * 768 - scale * gfxRect.Height/2),
        (int)(scale * gfxRect.Width),
        (int)(scale * gfxRect.Height)));
} // RenderCentered(x, y)
public void RenderCentered(float x, float y)
{
    RenderCentered(x, y, 1);
} // RenderCentered(x, y)
public void RenderCentered(Vector2 pos)
{
    RenderCentered(pos.X, pos.Y);
} // RenderCentered(pos)
```

RenderCentered takes a Vector2 or x and y float values and rescales the positions from 0 to 1 (the format you use in your game) to 1024 × 768. The Draw method of SpriteHelper then rescales everything to the current screen resolution from 1024 × 768. It may sound complicated, but it is really easy to use.

Then all the blocks of the current level are rendered and again that is very easy thanks to the position you have calculated in the constructor of your game. Take a look at the code on how to initialize all block positions at the upper part of the screen:

```
// Init all blocks, set positions and bounding boxes
for (int y = 0; y < NumOfRows; y++)
    for (int x = 0; x < NumOfColumns; x++)
```

```
{
  blockPositions[x, y] = new Vector2(
    0.05f + 0.9f * x / (float)(NumOfColumns - 1),
    0.066f + 0.5f * y / (float)(NumOfRows - 1));
  Vector3 pos = new Vector3(blockPositions[x, y], 0);
  Vector3 blockSize = new Vector3(
    GameBlockRect.X/1024.0f, GameBlockRect.Y/768, 0);
  blockBoxes[x, y] = new BoundingBox(
    pos - blockSize/2, pos + blockSize/2);
} // for for
```

The blockBoxes bounding boxes are used for the collision testing discussed in a second. The calculation of the position is also no big deal; the x coordinate goes from 0.05 to 0.95 in as many steps as you have columns (14 if I remember correctly). You can try to change the NumOfColumns constant to 20 and the field will have many more blocks.

Finally, a small message is rendered on the screen with a scaling factor of two in case the player has won a level or lost the game. Then you just call the Draw method of SpriteHelper to render all game elements on the screen. Check out the unit tests in the game for how the rendering of the blocks, paddle, and game messages was developed. I started with the unit tests again and then wrote the implementation.

Collision Testing

The collision testing for the Breakout game is a little bit more complicated than just checking the paddles and the screen border in Pong. The most complicated part is to correctly bounce off the blocks the ball hits. For the complete code, check the source code for this chapter.

As in the last game, you have a ball with a bounding box, screen borders, and the paddle. The blocks are new and to check for any collisions you have check all of them each frame. See Figure 3-16 for an example collision happening with a block in the game.

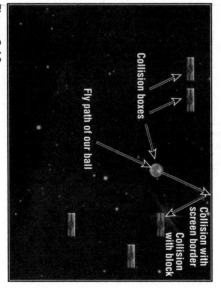

Figure 3-16

Take a closer look at the basic collision code with the blocks. The collision with the screen border and paddle is pretty much the same as in the Pong game and is checked with the help of the `TestBallCollisions` unit test. To check for collisions with the blocks, you iterate through all of them and check if the bounding box of the ball hits the bounding box of the blocks. The actual game code is more complex because we also have to check which side of the bounding box was hit and in which direction the ball has to bounce off, but the rest of the code and the general idea are still the same.

```
// Ball hits any block?
for (int y = 0; y < NumOfRows; y++)
  for (int x = 0; x < NumOfColumns; x++)
    if (blocks[x, y])
    {
      // Collision check
      if (ballBox.Intersects(blockBoxes[x, y]))
      {
        // Kill block
        blocks[x, y] = false;
        // Add score
        score++;
        // Update title
        Window.Title =
          "XnaBreakout - Level " + (level + 1) + " - Score " + score;
        // Play sound
        soundBank.PlayCue("BreakoutBlockKill");
        // Bounce ball back
        ballSpeedVector = -ballSpeedVector;
        // Go outta here, only handle 1 block at a time
        break;
      } // if
    } // for for if
```

Challenge: Improve the Breakout Game

Try to improve the game by giving the player more than one life, and maybe also add a menu as in the previous chapter. You can also use the Breakout game as a test platform to check out the helper classes you implemented so far. For example, you could write a log message every time the player completes a level or destroys a block and then check out the log file.

The next chapter introduces the `Input` class to make it easier to catch all controller inputs. A nice improvement to the game would be to implement rumble support for gamepads as in the last chapter and also shake the screen or add simple explosion graphics when blocks get destroyed. The sky is the limit; if you really like arcade games, there are many ways you can improve this game and make it much more fun.

Maybe you are more interested in the helper classes and have several of your own helper classes you would like to add and test using your new knowledge. Now is the time to do that. The next chapter focuses more on reusability; the chapters after that talk only about creating a 3D engine and you might forget about all the useful helper classes until you miss some feature. The good thing about helper classes is that it is easy to improve them all the time. They may become a little bit big as the StringHelper class, but you can always refactor them.

Anyway, have fun with XNA Breakout and relax for a while. Try to get to level 5 without cheating — it is not easy.

Summary

You covered a lot of classes in this chapter, which will be useful in your later projects. Unit testing is also important, and I hope I convinced you that writing unit tests first is the way to go. The Breakout game got a little attention at the end of the chapter. The chapter is long enough as it is and luckily you could skip a few points of the Breakout game because many parts of the game could be reused from the Pong game of the last chapter.

The next chapter focuses a little bit more on game programming and how to build a game with several components. In this chapter, you saw the usefulness of the helper classes and now you are ready to extend this idea to your game code, which is important for creating more complex games.

Here's a recap of what you have learned in this chapter:

☐ Use helper classes wherever possible; put code to methods or helper classes especially if you have used it more than twice.

☐ Always write unit tests first and then work on the implementation.

☐ Keep the unit tests simple. You don't have to waste time writing overly complex unit tests for helper classes or make static unit tests more complex than the game itself. Unit tests are not important for the final game (in fact they are not even included thanks to the #if DEBUG directives) and they are used only to make your life easier and help you to test and reuse new and existing code.

☐ When changing code, always run the tests to make sure everything still works correctly:

☐ Use TestDriven.Net to run single tests or run every test of a class or namespace in the Solution Explorer.

☐ Alternatively, use the NUnit GUI to test all unit tests of your assembly. For static unit tests, use the Program class and start the tests manually.

☐ Test the most complicated parts of your game as much as possible, such as the collision testing in Breakout.

Game Components

This chapter covers the Game class and the game components you can add to it. To get your graphics engine up and running in the next chapter, you still need some new helper classes before starting with 3D concepts. The BaseGame class is used to implement more features and to include all the other classes you have written so far. It is derived from the Game class to take advantage of all the existing XNA features. In the same way our main test class TestGame is derived from BaseGame to help you execute static unit tests in your game. Then you will add the TextureFont class to your Helpers namespace to allow you to draw text on the screen, which is not possible out-of-the-box in XNA. Finally, you also add some of the existing functionality from the previous chapters such as input, controller handling, and sound output into special classes to make it much easier to write a new game. Instead of speaking in the abstract, this chapter provides a concrete example game.

In contrast to the previous chapter you are not going to write any helper classes first, but instead you are going to write the unit tests and the game class first and then add all the game components you need to your project. In the last few projects, the problems were fairly simple and once you resolved them there was no need to go through them again. For the game you are going to develop in this chapter many improvements can be made and you will see this becomes even more true the bigger the game projects become. Refactoring is still the most important thing you have to remember when working over existing code and improving your game. Sometimes you will even see the code used in the unit tests ending up somewhere else in the final game code.

For an example, I'll use a simple Tetris clone. It will feature a big play field with colored blocks falling down, support for keyboard and gamepad input, a next block field showing you what comes next, and a little scoreboard containing the current level, score, highscore, and lines you destroyed. If you are a Tetris fan like me and like to play it every once in a while, this game is great fun. Tetris is one of the most popular puzzle arcade games ever. It was invented by a Russian, Alexey Pazhitnov, in 1985, and became very popular after Nintendo released it on the Game Boy system in 1989.

The **Game Class**

You already used the Game class in the previous chapters, but other than starting the game by calling the Run method from the Program class and your unit tests, and using the Initialize, Update, and Draw methods, those chapters did not talk about the underlying design. Well, you don't really need to know anything else if you are just creating a few simple games, but as games become bigger and have more features you might want to think about the class overview and class design of your game.

The Game class itself is used to hold the graphics device in the GraphicsDeviceManager instance and the content manager in the content field. From the Program class you just have to create an instance of your game class and call the Run method to get everything started. Unlike in the old days with Managed DirectX or OpenGL, you don't have to manage your own window, create your game loop, handle Windows messages, and so on. XNA does all that for you, and because it is handled in such a way, it is even possible to run your game on the Xbox 360 platform where no window classes or Windows events are available.

It is still possible to access the window of the game through the Window property of the game class. It can be used to set the window's title, specify if the user is allowed to resize the window, get the underlying Windows handle for interop calls, and so on. All these methods do nothing on the Xbox 360 platform. There is no window, there is no window title, and it can certainly not be resized. As you already saw in the previous game, you used the Window.Title property to set some simple text to the title for showing the current level and score to the user. You did that because there is no font support in XNA; to render text on the screen you have to create your own bitmap font and then render every letter yourself. In the next games, and even for the Tetris game you will need that feature, and therefore the TextureFont class is introduced shortly.

Additionally, it is worth mentioning that it is possible to set the preferred resolution in the game class constructor by setting the graphics properties, as in the following example, which tries to use the 1024768 resolution in fullscreen mode:

```
graphics.PreferredBackBufferWidth = 1024;
graphics.PreferredBackBufferHeight = 768;
graphics.IsFullScreen = true;
```

There is no guarantee that the game will actually run in that mode; for example, setting 16001200 on a system that just supports up to 1024768 will use only the maximum available resolution.

You already know that Update and Draw are called every frame, but how do you incorporate new game components without overloading the game class itself? It's time to look at the game classes and components overview of the Tetris clone game (see Figure 4-1).

The first thing you will notice is that you have now three game classes instead of just one, as in the previous game examples. The reason for that is to make the main game class shorter and simpler. The BaseGame class holds the graphics manager with the graphics device and the content manager, and it stores the current width and height values of the current resolution you use in the game. The Update and Draw methods also handle the new Input, Sound, and TextureFont classes to avoid having to update them in the main game class. Then the TetrisGame class is used to load all the graphics from the content pipeline and initialize all sprites and game components, which you learn about shortly.

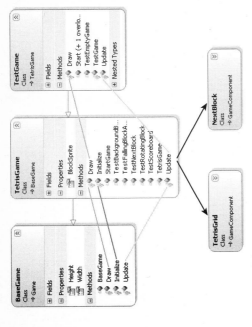

Figure 4-1

Finally, the TestGame class derives itself from the TetrisGame class to have access to all the textures, sprites, and game components. It is only used in debug mode to start unit tests. The functionality of the TestGame class is very similar to the previous chapters, but this time it is organized in a nice way and separate from your main game class. The TetrisGame class uses several unit tests to make sure each part of the game works as you have planned.

Game Components

The TetrisGame class also holds all game components in the Components property derived from the game class. You can add any class that is derived from the GameComponent class to this list and it will automatically be called when your game is started and when it is updated. It will not be called when you draw your game because the GameComponent does not have a Draw method. You can, however, implement your own drawing methods or just use the DrawableGameComponent class, which does have a Draw method. XNA does not have a direct Draw support for the game components; you have to call it yourself to make sure all components are called in the correct order. Because of this and for several other reasons, you will not use many game components later in this book. Forcing you to use this model has not many advantages, it makes unit testing harder, and writing your own game classes might be more effective or specific anyway. It is generally a nice idea, but you can live without it because you have to create game components yourself anyway and you have to call Draw for them yourself, too. Just for the Update method, it did not make much sense to use the GameComponent class in XNA 1.0.

Please note that this has changed in XNA 2.0 quite a lot, with a much better support for game components. Not only does it make more sense to use them because of a better integrated update and draw system, which now lets you just add a game component without worrying about the implementation details, but you can also nest game components inside one another and thus build more complex components. For more details about using the new kind of game components in XNA 2.0, check out Chapters 14 and 15, where game components are used for the Dungeon Quest game and networking components of the game. Please excuse my dislike of the early game components from the XNA 1.0 beta days when the first edition of this book was written. The game components have become better since then and they are in fact used more in later parts of this book.

As I mentioned in Chapter 1, the basic idea is to have users collaborate and share their game components to allow others to use parts of their game engine. For example, a frame counter component or even a full-blown 3D landscape rendering engine could be implemented as a game component, but just because someone does not use a game component does not mean it is harder to copy over. For example, if you have a complicated game component such as a landscape rendering module, it will probably involve some other classes, too, and use its own rendering engine, which might not work out-of-the-box in your engine if you just copy one file over. Either way, plugging in external code often requires quite a bit of refactoring until it is usable in your own game engine. In beta 1 of the XNA Framework, a graphical designer was available in XNA Game Studio Express for the game components and you could easily drag and drop components into your Game class or even into other game components to add features to your game without writing a single line of code. Because this feature was very complicated and buggy, and did not work on the Xbox 360, it was abandoned in the beta 2 release of the XNA Framework.

It is not a sure thing that game components will not be used, and maybe it does not matter to most programmers that the designer is missing and you have to call the Draw methods yourself. Then a lot of game components might be available and it would be useful to know all the basics about them. In the case of the Tetris game, a few components come to mind:

☐   The grid itself with all the colored blocks and the current falling block

☐   The scoreboard with the current level, score, high-score, and number of lines you destroyed

☐   The next block type box for the game

☐   More simple things such as a frame counter, handling the input, and so on

I decided to implement the Tetris grid and the next block feature as game components; some of the other code is just way too simple for implementing several new game components for them too. If you will reuse the scoreboard, for example, you could always put it in a game component, but I cannot think of any other game I would like to write that uses that scoreboard.

Take a closer look at the Game class and the components that were added to it (see Figure 4-2).

The gray arrows indicate that these methods are called automatically because TetrisGame and NextBlock were added to the Components list of the Game class. In TetrisGame.Draw the Draw method of TetrisGrid is called, which again calls the NextBlock.Draw method. TetrisGame itself holds just an instance of TetrisGrid. The NextBlock instance is only used inside of the TetrisGrid class.

You can see that using the game components for these three classes forced you to think about the calling order and it made your game more organized just by the fact that you did not put everything into one big class. This is a good thing and, although you can do all this by yourself if you are an experienced programmer, it might be a good idea for beginners to anticipate the idea of the game components in XNA.

In XNA 2.0, you can also use nested game components. The main advantage of this technique is that you can create much more complex game components, and that it provides you with a solid framework to build more complex games without having to invent your own game application model. If you are just writing a frame counter game component or a screenshot capturer as in this chapter, it won't matter to you if you can nest game components or not. Other use cases would be putting some of your most often used game components in a parent game component class to manage them all at once. The more game components you have and the more actual game logic is hidden inside of them, the more sense it will make to nest them and hide game logic inside of them. Most games in this book will not go that far, but you can see a few examples of nested game components in the Dungeon Quest game at the end of this book. Dungeon Quest gives you some practical ideas where nested game components would make sense. As you will see from the code in the game, nested components perform their best work for game logic code, which will get updated automatically for you via the Update method.

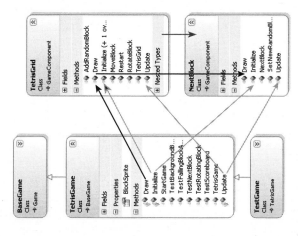

Figure 4-2

More Helper Classes

Didn't talk enough about helper classes in the last chapter? Yes we did. The two new classes you are going to use for the Tetris game are not discussed here in great detail and they are just stripped-down versions of the real classes you use later in this book. But they are still useful and help you to make the programming process of your game easier.

TextureFont Class

You already learned about the missing font support in XNA and you know that using bitmap fonts is the only option to display text in XNA (apart from using some custom 3D font rendering maybe). In the first games of this book, you just used some sprites to display fixed text in the game or menu. This approach was very easy, but for your scoreboard you certainly need a dynamic font allowing you to write down any text and numbers the way you need it in the game.

Let's go a little bit ahead and take a look at the `TestScoreboard` unit test in the `TetrisGame` class, which renders the background box for the scoreboard and then writes down all the text lines to display the current level, score, highscore, and number of lines you destroyed in the current game:

```
int level = 3, score = 350, highscore = 1542, lines = 13;
TestGame.Start("TestScoreboard",
delegate
{
    // Draw background box
    TestGame.game.backgroundSmallBox.Render(new Rectangle(
        (512 + 240) - 15, 40 - 10, 290 - 30, 190));

    // Show current level, score, etc.
    TextureFont.WriteText(512 + 240, 50, "Level: ");
    TextureFont.WriteText(512 + 420, 50, (level + 1).ToString());
    TextureFont.WriteText(512 + 240, 90, "Score: ");
    TextureFont.WriteText(512 + 420, 90, score.ToString());
    TextureFont.WriteText(512 + 240, 130, "Lines: ");
    TextureFont.WriteText(512 + 420, 130, lines.ToString());
    TextureFont.WriteText(512 + 240, 170, "Highscore: ");
    TextureFont.WriteText(512 + 420, 170, highscore.ToString());
});
```

You might notice that you are now using the `TestGame` class to start your unit test. For this test, you use a couple of variables (level, score, and so on), which are replaced by the real values in the game code. In the render loop, you first draw the background box and display it immediately to avoid display errors with sprites you draw later. Then you write down four lines of text with the help of the `WriteText` method in the new `TextureFont` class at the specified screen positions. You actually call `WriteText` eight times to properly align all the numbers at the right side of your background box, which looks much nicer than just writing down everything in four lines.

After writing this unit test, you will get a compiler error telling you that the `TextureFont` class does not exist yet. After creating a dummy class with a dummy `WriteText` method, you will be able to compile and start the test. It will just show the background box, which is drawn in the upper-right part of the screen with the help of the `SpriteHelper` class you learned about in the last chapter.

Before you even think about implementing the `TextureFont` class, you will need the actual bitmap texture with the font in it to render text on the screen. Without a texture, you are just doing theoretical work, and unit testing is about practical testing of game functionality. You will need a texture like the one in Figure 4-3 to display all the letters, numbers, and signs. You can even use more Unicode letters in bigger textures or use multiple textures to achieve that, but that would go too far for this chapter. Please check out the websites I provided at the top of the `TextureFont` class comment in the source code to learn more about this advanced topic.

Take a look at the implementation of the `TextureFont` class (see Figure 4-4). Calling the `TextureFont` class is very easy; you just have to call the `WriteText` method as in the unit test shown earlier. But the internal code is not very easy. The class stores rectangles for each letter of the `GameFont.png` texture, which is then used in `WriteAll` to render text by drawing each letter one by one to the screen. The class also contains the font texture, which is `GameFont.png`, a sprite batch to help render the font sprites on the screen, and several helper variables to determine the height of the font. For checking how much width a text will consume on the screen, you can use the `GetTextWidth` method.

Figure 4-3

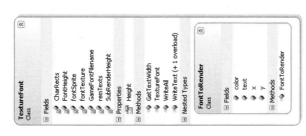

Figure 4-4

The internal FontToRender class holds all the text you want to render each frame, which is very similar to the process the SpriteHelper class uses to render all sprites on the screen at the end of each frame. In the same way SpriteHelper.DrawAll is called by BaseGame, TextureFont.WriteAll is also called and flushes everything on the screen and clears all lists. To learn more about the TextureFont class, check out the source code and run the unit tests, or try stepping through the WriteAll method.

Input Class

Another new class that is used in the Tetris game is the Input class, which encapsulates all the input handling, checking, and updating yourself in the previous chapters. Chapter 10 talks about the Input class in greater detail and some nice classes that really need all the features from the Input class (see Figure 4-5).

As you can see, the Input class has quite a lot of properties and a few helper methods to access the keyboard, the gamepad, and the mouse data. It will be updated every frame with the help of the static Update method, which is called directly from the BaseGame class. For this game you are mainly going to use the key press and gamepad press methods such as GamePadAJustPressed or KeyboardSpaceJustPressed. The RandomHelper class is also not hard to figure out, and you already implemented much of the functionally in the previous chapter. For more details and uses, you can check out Chapter 10.

Figure 4-5

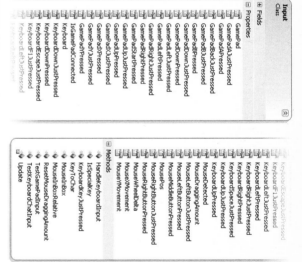

Sound Class

Well, you already had sound in the first game in Chapter 2 and you also used it in Chapter 3 for the Breakout game. To keep things simple and to allow you to add more sound functionality later without having to change any of the game classes, the sound management is now moved to the Sound class. Take a quick look at the class (see Figure 4-6). It looks very simple in this version, but in Chapter 9, which also talks about XACT in greater detail, you will extend the Sound class quite a bit and make it ready for your great racing game at the end of this book.

As you can see, all the sound variables are now in this class and the Game class no longer contains any sound variables. The Sound constructor is static and will be called automatically when you play a sound for the first time with the Play method. The Update method is called automatically from the BaseGame class.

The Sounds enum values and the TestPlayClickSound unit test depend on the actual content in your current game. These values will change for every game you are going to write from here on, but it is very easy to change the Sounds enum values. You might ask why you don't just play the sounds with help of the cue names stored in XACT. Well, many errors could occur by just mistyping a sound cue and it is hard to track all changes in case you remove, rename, or change a sound cue. The Sounds enum also makes it very easy to quickly add a sound effect and see which ones are available through IntelliSense.

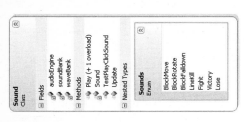

Figure 4-6

The Tetris game uses the following sounds:

- ❑ **BlockMove** for moving the block left, right, or down. It is a very quiet sound effect.

- ❑ **BlockRotate** is used when you rotate the current block and it sounds very "whooshy."

- ❑ **BlockFalldown** is used when the current block reaches the ground and finally lands.

- ❑ **LineKill** is played every time you manage to kill a line in the game.

- ❑ **Fight** is played at the start of each game to motivate the player.

- ❑ **Victory** is used when the player reaches the next level and contains an applause sound.

- ❑ **Lose** is an old-school dying sound and is played when the player loses the game.

Tetris, Tetris, Tetris!

Enough with all the helper classes and game components discussions. It is time to write another cool game. Thanks to the many classes available in the little game engine it is now easy to write text on the screen, draw sprites, handle input, and play sounds.

Before going into the details of the Tetris game logic, it would be useful to think about the placement of all game elements as you did in the previous games. Instead of drawing all game components on the screen, you just show the background boxes to see what is going to be displayed. For the background you use the space background once again (I promise, this will be the last time). The background box is a new texture and exists in two modes (see Figure 4-7). It is used to separate the game components and make everything fit much nicer on the screen. You could also just reuse the same box for both parts of the game, but because the aspect ratio is so different for them it would either look bad for the background box or for the extra game components, which are smaller, but also need the background box graphic, just a smaller version of it.

Rendering the Background

To render these boxes on the screen, you use the `SpriteHelper` class again and test everything with the help of the following unit test:

```
public static void TestBackgroundBoxes()
{
    TestGame.Start("TestBackgroundBoxes",
        delegate
    {
        // Render background
        TestGame.game.background.Render();
        // Draw background boxes for all the components
        TestGame.game.backgroundBigBox.Render(new Rectangle(
            (512 - 200) - 15, 40 - 12, 400 + 23, (768 - 40) + 16));
        TestGame.game.backgroundSmallBox.Render(new Rectangle(
            (512 - 480) - 15, 40 - 10, 290 - 30, 300));
        TestGame.game.backgroundSmallBox.Render(new Rectangle(
            (512 + 240) - 15, 40 - 10, 290 - 30, 190));
    });
} // TestBackgroundBoxes()
```

This unit test will produce the output shown in Figure 4-8.

You might ask why the right box is a little bit smaller and where I got all these values from. Well, I just started with some arbitrary values and then improved the values until everything in the final game fit. First, the background is drawn in the unit test because you will not call the Draw method of `TetrisGame` if you are in the unit test (otherwise the unit tests won't work anymore later when the game is fully implemented).

Figure 4-7

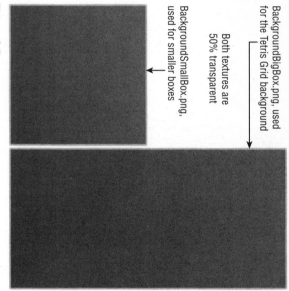

BackgroundBigBox.png, used for the Tetris Grid background

Both textures are 50% transparent

BackgroundSmallBox.png, used for smaller boxes

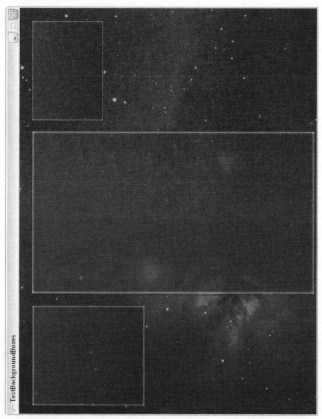

Figure 4-8

Then three boxes are drawn. The upper-left box is used to show the next block. The center box shows the current Tetris grid. And finally, the upper-right box is used to display the scoreboard. You already saw the unit test for that earlier.

Handling the Grid

It is time to fill the content of these boxes. Start with the main component: the TetrisGrid. This class is responsible for displaying the whole Tetris grid. It handles the input and moves the falling block and it shows all the existing data as well. You already saw which methods are used in the TetrisGrid class in the discussion about the game components. Before rendering the grid you should check out the first constants defined in the TetrisGrid class:

```
#region Constants
   public const int GridWidth = 12;
   public const int GridHeight = 20;
   .
```

There are a couple more interesting constants, but for now you only need the grid dimensions. So you have 12 columns and 20 lines for your Tetris field. With help of the Block.png texture, which is just a simple quadratic block, you can now easily draw the full grid in the Draw method:

```
// Calc sizes for block, etc.
   int blockWidth = gridRect.Width / GridWidth;
   int blockHeight = gridRect.Height / GridHeight;
   for ( int x=0; x<GridWidth; x++ )
```

```
for ( int y=0; y<GridHeight; y++ )
{
    game.BlockSprite.Render(new Rectangle(
        gridRect.X + x * blockWidth,
        gridRect.Y + y * blockHeight,
        blockWidth-1, blockHeight-1),
        new Color(60, 60, 60, 128)); // Empty color
} // for for
```

The gridRect variable is passed as a parameter to the Draw method from the main class to specify the area where you want the grid to be drawn to. It is the same rectangle as you used for the background box, just a little bit smaller to fit in. The first thing you are doing here is calculating the block width and height for each block you are going to draw. Then you go through the whole array and draw each block with the help of the SpriteHelper.Render method using a half transparent dark color to show an empty background grid. See Figure 4-9 to see how this looks. The unit test just draws the background box and then calls the TetrisGrid.Draw method to show the results (see the TestEmptyGrid unit test).

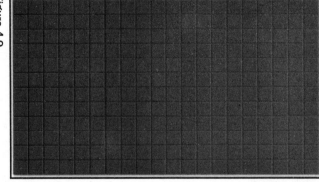

Figure 4-9

Block Types

Before you can render anything useful on your new grid, you should think about the block types you can have in your game. The standard Tetris game has seven block types; all of them consist of four small blocks connected to each other (see Figure 4-10). The favorite block type is of course the line type because you can kill up to four lines giving you the most points.

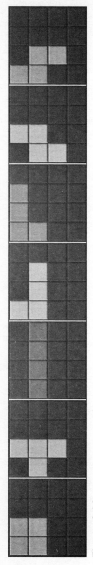

Figure 4-10

These block types have to be defined in the TetrisGrid class. One way of doing that is to use an enum holding all the possible block types. This enum can also hold an empty block type allowing you to use this data structure for the whole grid, too, because each grid block can contain either any part of the predefined block types or it is empty. Take a look at the rest of the constants in the TetrisGrid class:

```
/// <summary>
/// Block types we can have for each new block that falls down.
/// </summary>
public enum BlockTypes
{
    Empty,
    Block,
    Triangle,
    Line,
    RightT,
    LeftT,
    RightShape,
    LeftShape,
} // enum BlockTypes
/// <summary>
/// Number of block types we can use for each grid block.
/// </summary>
public static readonly int NumOfBlockTypes =
    EnumHelper.GetSize(typeof(BlockTypes));
/// <summary>
/// Block colors for each block type.
/// </summary>
public static readonly Color[] BlockColor = new Color[]
{
    new Color( 60, 60, 60, 128 ),  // Empty, color unused
    new Color( 50, 50, 255, 255 ), // Line, blue
    new Color( 160, 160, 255 ),    // Block, gray
    new Color( 255, 50, 50, 255 ), // RightT, red
    new Color( 255, 255, 50, 255 ), // LeftT, yellow
    new Color( 50, 255, 255, 255 ), // RightShape, teal
    new Color( 255, 50, 255, 255 ), // LeftShape, purple
    new Color( 50, 255, 50, 255 ),  // Triangle, green
}; // Color[] BlockColor
/// <summary>
/// Unrotated shapes
/// </summary>
public static readonly int[][,] BlockTypeShapesNormal = new int[][,]
{
```

```
// Empty
new int[,] { { 0 } },
// Line
new int[,] { { 0, 1, 0 }, { 0, 1, 0 }, { 0, 1, 0 }, { 0, 1, 0 } },
// Block
new int[,] { { 1, 1 }, { 1, 1 } },
// RightT
new int[,] { { 1, 1 }, { 1, 1, 1 } },
// LeftT
new int[,] { { 1, 1 }, { 0, 1, 0 }, { 1, 1 } },
// RightShape
new int[,] { { 0, 1 }, { 0, 1 }, { 0, 1 } },
// LeftShape
new int[,] { { 0, 1, 1 }, { 1, 1, 0 } },
// Triangle
new int[,] { { 0, 1, 0 }, { 1, 1, 1 }, { 0, 0, 0 } },
}; // BlockTypeShapesNormal
```

`BlockTypes` is the enum we talked about; it contains all the possible block types and also is used to randomly generate new blocks in the `NextBlock` game component. Initially all of the grid fields are filled with the empty block type. The grid is defined as:

```
/// <summary>
/// The actual grid, contains all blocks,
/// including the currently falling block.
/// </summary>
BlockTypes[,] grid = new BlockTypes[GridWidth, GridHeight];
```

By the way, `NumOfBlockTypes` shows you the usefulness of the enum class. You can easily determine how many entries are in the `BlockTypes` enum.

Next, the colors for each block type are defined. These colors are used for the `NextBlock` preview, but also for rendering the whole grid. Each grid has a block type and you can easily use the `BlockColors` by converting the enum to an int number, which is used in the `Draw` method:

```
BlockColor[(int) grid[x,y]]
```

And finally, the block shapes are defined, which looks a little bit more complicated, especially if you take into consideration that you have to allow these block parts to be rotated. This is done with help of the `BlockTypeShapes`, which is a big array of all possible blocks and rotations calculated in the constructor of `TetrisGrid`.

To add a new block to the Tetris grid, you can just add each of the block parts to your grid, which is done in the `AddRandomBlock` method. You keep a separate list called `floatingGrid` to remember which parts of the grid have to be moved down (see the following section, "Gravity"; you can't just let everything fall down) each time `Update` is called:

```
// Randomize block type and rotation
currentBlockType = (int) nextBlock.SetNewRandomBlock();
currentBlockRot = RandomHelper.GetRandomInt(4);
// Get precalculated shape
int[,] shape = BlockTypeShapes[currentBlockType, currentBlockRot];
int xPos = GridWidth/2-shape.GetLength(0)/2;
```

```
// Center block at top most position of our grid
currentBlockPos = new Point(xPos, 0);
// Add new block
for ( int x=0; x<shape.GetLength(0); x++ )
    for ( int y=0; y<shape.GetLength(1); y++ )
        if ( shape[x,y] > 0 )
        {
            // Check if there is already something
            if (grid[x + xPos, y] != BlockTypes.Empty)
            {
                // Then game is over dude!
                gameOver = true;
                Sound.Play(Sound.Sounds.Lose);
            } // if
            else
            {
                grid[x + xPos, y] = (BlockTypes)currentBlockType;
                floatingGrid[x + xPos, y] = true;
            } // else
        } // for for if
```

First you determine which block type you are going to add here. To help you do that, you have a helper method in the NextBlock class, which randomizes the next block type and returns the last block type that was displayed in the NextBlock window. The rotation is also randomized; say "Hi" to the RandomHelper class.

With that data you can now get the precalculated shape and put it centered on the top of your grid. The two for loops iterate through the whole shape. It adds each valid part of the shape until you hit any existing data in the grid. If that happens, the game is over and you hear the lose sound. This will happen if the pile of blocks reaches the top of the grid and you cannot add any new blocks.

You now have the new block on your grid, but it is boring to just see it on the top there; it should fall down sometimes.

Gravity

To test the gravity of the current block, the TestFallingBlockAndLineKill unit test is used. The active block is updated each time you call the Update method of TetrisGrid, which is not very often. In the first level, the Update method is called only every 1000ms (every second). There you check if the current block can be moved down:

```
// Try to move floating stuff down
if (MoveBlock(MoveTypes.Down) == false ||
    movingDownWasBlocked)
{
    // Failed? Then fix floating stuff, not longer moveable!
    for ( int x=0; x<GridWidth; x++ )
        for ( int y=0; y<GridHeight; y++ )
            floatingGrid[x,y] = false;
    Sound.Play(Sound.Sounds.BlockFalldown);
} // if
movingDownWasBlocked = false;
```

105

Most of the Tetris logic is done in the `MoveBlock` helper method, which checks if moving in a specific direction is possible at all. If the block can't be moved anymore, it gets fixed and you clear the `floatingGrid` array and play the sound for landing a block on the ground.

After clearing the `floatingGrid` array, there is no active block you can move down, and the following code is used to check whether a line was destroyed:

```
// Check if we got any moveable stuff,
// if not add new random block at top!
bool canMove = false;
for ( int x=0; x<GridWidth; x++ )
    for ( int y=0; y<GridHeight; y++ )
        if ( floatingGrid[x,y] )
            canMove = true;
if (canMove == false)
{
    int linesKilled = 0;
    // Check if we got a full line
    for ( int y=0; y<GridHeight; y++ )
    {
        bool fullLine = true;
        for ( int x=0; x<GridWidth; x++ )
            if ( grid[x,y] == BlockTypes.Empty )
            {
                fullLine = false;
                break;
            } // for if
        // We got a full line?
        if (fullLine)
        {
            // Move everything down
            for ( int yDown=y-1; yDown>0; yDown-- )
                for ( int x=0; x<GridWidth; x++ )
                    grid[x,yDown+1] = grid[x,yDown];
            // Clear top line
            for ( int x=0; x<GridWidth; x++ )
                grid[0,x] = BlockTypes.Empty;
            // Add 10 points and count line
            score += 10;
            lines++;
            linesKilled++;
            Sound.Play(Sound.Sounds.LineKill);
        } // if
    } // for

    // If we killed 2 or more lines, add extra score
    if (linesKilled >= 2)
        score += 5;
    if (linesKilled >= 3)
        score += 10;
    if (linesKilled >= 4)
        score += 25;

    // Add new block at top
    AddRandomBlock();
} // if
```

The first thing that is done here is to check if there is an active moving block. If not, you go into the "if block," checking if a full line is filled and can be destroyed. To determine if a line is filled, you assume it is filled and then check if any block of the line is empty. Then you know that this line is not fully filled and continue checking the next line. If the line is filled, however, you remove it by copying all the lines above it down. This is the place where a nice explosion could occur. Anyway, the player gets 10 points for this line kill, and you hear the line kill sound.

If the player was able to kill more than one line, he gets awarded more points. And finally, the AddRandomBlock method you saw before is used to create a new block at the top.

Handling Input

Handling the user input itself is no longer a big task thanks to the Input helper class. You can easily check if a cursor or gamepad key was just pressed or is being held down. Escape and Back are handled in the BaseGame class and allow you to quit the game. Other than that, you need only four keys in your Tetris game. To move to the left and right, the cursor keys are used. The up cursor key is used to rotate the current block and the down cursor key, or alternatively the space or A keys, can be used to let the block fall down faster.

Similar to the gravity check to see if you can move the block down, the same check is done to see if you can move the current block left or right. Only if that is true do you actually move the block; this code is done in the TetrisGame Update method because you want to check for the player input every frame and not just when updating the TetrisGrid, which can happen only every 1000ms as you learned before. The code was in the TetrisGrid Update method before, but to improve the user experience it was moved and improved quite a lot, also allowing you to move the block quickly left and right by hitting the cursor buttons multiple times.

Well, you have learned a lot about all the supporting code and you are almost ready to run the Tetris game for the first time. But you should take a look at the MoveBlock helper method because it is the most integral and important part of your Tetris game. Another important method is the RotateBlock method, which works in a similar way, testing if a block can be rotated. You can check it out yourself in the source code for the Tetris game. Please use the unit tests in the TetrisGame class to see how all these methods work:

```
#region Move block
public enum MoveTypes
{
    Left,
    Right,
    Down,
} // enum MoveTypes
/// <summary>
/// Remember if moving down was blocked, this increases
/// the game speed because we can force the next block!
/// </summary>
public bool movingDownWasBlocked = false;
/// <summary>
/// Move current floating block to left, right or down.
/// If anything is blocking, moving is not possible and
/// nothing gets changed!
/// </summary>
/// <returns>Returns true if moving was successful, otherwise false</returns>
```

```
public bool MoveBlock(MoveTypes moveType)
{
    // Clear old pos
    for ( int x=0; x<GridWidth; x++ )
        for ( int y=0; y<GridHeight; y++ )
            if ( floatingGrid[x,y] )
                grid[x,y] = BlockTypes.Empty;

    // Move stuff to new position
    bool anythingBlocking = false;
    Point[] newPos = new Point[4];
    int newPosNum = 0;
    if ( moveType == MoveTypes.Left )
    {
        for ( int x=0; x<GridWidth; x++ )
            for ( int y=0; y<GridHeight; y++ )
                if ( floatingGrid[x,y] )
                {
                    if ( x-1 < 0 ||
                        grid[x-1,y] != BlockTypes.Empty )
                        anythingBlocking = true;
                    else if ( newPosNum < 4 )
                    {
                        newPos[newPosNum] = new Point( x-1, y );
                        newPosNum++;
                    } // else if
                } // for for if
    } // if
    else if ( moveType == MoveTypes.Right )
    {
        for ( int x=0; x<GridWidth; x++ )
            for ( int y=0; y<GridHeight; y++ )
                if ( floatingGrid[x,y] )
                {
                    if ( x+1 >= GridWidth ||
                        grid[x+1,y] != BlockTypes.Empty )
                        anythingBlocking = true;
                    else if ( newPosNum < 4 )
                    {
                        newPos[newPosNum] = new Point( x+1, y );
                        newPosNum++;
                    } // else if
                } // for for if
    } // if (right)
    else if ( moveType == MoveTypes.Down )
    {
        for ( int x=0; x<GridWidth; x++ )
            for ( int y=0; y<GridHeight; y++ )
                if ( floatingGrid[x,y] )
                {
                    if ( y+1 >= GridHeight ||
                        grid[x,y+1] != BlockTypes.Empty )
                        anythingBlocking = true;
                    else if ( newPosNum < 4 )
                    {
                        newPos[newPosNum] = new Point( x, y+1 );
```

```
                newPosNum++;
            } // else if
        } // for for if
        if ( anythingBlocking == true )
            movingDownWasBlocked = true;
    } // if (down)
    // If anything is blocking restore old state
    if ( anythingBlocking ||
        // Or we didn't get all 4 new positions?
        newPosNum != 4 )
    {
        for ( int x=0; x<GridWidth; x++ )
            for ( int y=0; y<GridHeight; y++ )
                if ( floatingGrid[x,y] )
                    grid[x,y] = (BlockTypes)currentBlockType;
        return false;
    } // if
    else
    {
        if ( moveType == MoveTypes.Left )
            currentBlockPos =
                new Point( currentBlockPos.X-1, currentBlockPos.Y );
        else if ( moveType == MoveTypes.Right )
            currentBlockPos =
                new Point( currentBlockPos.X+1, currentBlockPos.Y );
        else if ( moveType == MoveTypes.Down )
            currentBlockPos =
                new Point( currentBlockPos.X, currentBlockPos.Y+1 );
        // Else we can move to the new position, let's do it!
        for ( int x=0; x<GridWidth; x++ )
            for ( int y=0; y<GridHeight; y++ )
                floatingGrid[x,y] = false;
        for ( int i=0; i<4; i++ )
        {
            grid[newPos[i].X,newPos[i].Y] = (BlockTypes)currentBlockType;
            floatingGrid[newPos[i].X,newPos[i].Y] = true;
        } // for
        Sound.Play(Sound.Sounds.BlockMove);
        return true;
    } // else
} // MoveBlock(moveType)
#endregion
```

There are three kinds of moves you can do: Left, Right, and Down. Each of these moves is handled in a separate code block to see if the left, right, or down data is available and if it is possible to move there. Before going into the details of this method there are two things that should be mentioned. First of all, a helper variable called movingDownWasBlocked is defined above the method. You have this variable to speed up the process of checking if the current block reached the ground. It is stored at the class level to let the Update method pick it up later (which can be several frames later) and make the gravity code you saw earlier update much faster than it does when the user doesn't want to drop the block down right here. This is a very important part of the game because if each block were immediately fixed when reaching the ground the game would become very difficult, and all the fun is lost when it gets faster and the grid gets more filled.

Then you use another trick to simplify the checking process by temporarily removing the current block from the grid. This way, you can easily check if a new position is possible because your current position does not block you anymore. The code also uses several helper variables to store the new position and that code is simplified a bit to account for only four block parts. If you change the block types and the number of block parts, you should also change this method.

After setting everything up, you check if the new virtual block position is possible in the three code blocks. Usually it is possible and you end up with four new values in the `newPosNum` array. If fewer than three values are available, you know that something was blocking you and the `anythingBlocking` variable is set to true anyway. In that case, the old block position is restored and both the `grid` and the `floatingGrid` arrays stay the same way.

But in case the move attempt was successful, the block position is updated and you clear the `floatingGrid` and finally add the block again to the new position by adding it both to the `grid` and the `floatingGrid`. The user also hears a very silent block move sound and you are done with this method.

Testing

With all that new code in the `TetrisGrid` class, you can now test the unit tests in the `TetrisGame` class. In addition to the tests you saw before, the two most important unit tests for the game logic are:

- ☐ `TestRotatingBlock`, which tests the `RotateBlock` method of the `TetrisGrid` class.

- ☐ `TestFallingBlockAndKillLine`, which is used to test the gravity and user input you just learned about.

It should be obvious that you often go back to older unit tests to update them according to the newest changes you require for your game. For example, the `TestBackgroundBoxes` unit test you saw earlier is very simple, but the layout and position of the background boxes changed quite a lot while implementing and testing the game components and it had to be updated accordingly to reflect the changes. One example for that would be the scoreboard, which is surrounded by the background box, but before you can know how big the scoreboard is going to be you have to know what the contents are and how much space they are going to consume. After writing the `TestScoreboard` method, it became very obvious that the scoreboard has to be much smaller than the `NextBlock` background box, for example.

Another part of testing the game is constantly checking for bugs and improving the game code. The previous games were pretty simple and you had to make only minor improvements after the first initial runs, but the Tetris game is much more complex and you can spend many hours fixing and improving it.

One last thing you could test is running the game on the Xbox 360 — just select the Xbox 360 console platform in the project and try to run it on the Xbox 360. All the steps to do that were explained in Chapter 1, which also has a useful troubleshooting section in case something does not work on the Xbox 360. If you write new code, you should make sure from time to time that it compiles on the Xbox 360, too. You are not allowed to write any interop code calling unmanaged assemblies, and some of the .NET 2.0 Framework classes and methods are missing on the Xbox 360.

Challenge: Create the NextBlock Game Component

This chapter did not really talk about the NextBlock game component and there is a reason for that. I want you to create it yourself. In the source code for this book, the NextBlock class is empty and you have the task of filling it with life. The NextBlock game component is already added to the TetrisGrid class and you already saw all the available methods. If you are unsure about your solution, you can check the complete source code with all the improvements and the full NextBlock class I made in the XNA Tetris full project source code, but I recommend you try coding the game component and maybe some other improvements to the game yourself to get more familiar with all the new classes.

The NextBlock component should show the next block type. Just use the BlockTypes enum from the TetrisGrid class and display the next block in a 55 grid and add a little text on top (see Figure 4-11).

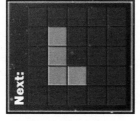

Figure 4-11

A little tip: Don't waste too much time playing Tetris. It can be an addictive game, but you have more to come in this book.

Summary

Your little game engine now has three new namespaces and you have many helper classes you can use for future projects. The new TextureFont class especially can be very useful for the next chapters. It is not only useful to display game data such as the scoreboard, but it will also be used for unit tests. It is very useful to display help texts in unit tests to tell the user about all the available hotkeys and it is especially useful for displaying test data or debugging data in case you run into problems. For example, a camera class unit test can output the camera position and rotation values to see what is going on while the test is running.

I hope these last four chapters were fun to read and you enjoyed the sample games you developed here. Arcade games can be fun, but just writing simple 2D games is not state of the art and you will certainly not get much attention if you program another Pong clone. For learning purposes, to introduce all the helper classes and for learning more about the Agile Methodology and unit testing, it was very useful to have these real projects instead of just talking about some theoretical uses and some boring helper classes.

However, in the next part of this book you dive into the world of 3D graphics and learn how to write your own 3D graphic engine in XNA. You don't really have to be a math professor to understand how to render a model on the screen. Thanks to XNA and the content pipeline, it is possible to render 3D data on the screen without knowing much about the underlying math and 3D geometry involved. If you are serious about 3D graphics programming, you should certainly know about vectors, matrices, and how to manipulate them in the right order. There are many tricks and knowing about all issues in the 3D game programming world not only requires a clever person, but you will also have to read constantly about new developments in this sector.

If you are a game programmer, you might not care so much about the underlying graphic engine code and want to focus on the game itself. While most people just want to create cool games, it usually means that they also have to create the graphic engine because there is no perfect 3D engine available and every effect in the game might require another way to render the 3D data. The last part of this book talks more about game programming after your game engine is complete enough to handle more complex games.

Here's a final look at what you have learned in the previous chapters:

☐ It is important to write down your ideas and to develop a small concept, preferably limited to one page.

☐ To solve problems, you use a top-down approach and you use unit testing.

☐ You learned about handling user input, playing sounds, and drawing sprites. All this can be done quite easily in XNA, but to avoid repeating the same code over and over again you put it in helper classes.

☐ I introduced a lot of helper classes to help you with rendering texture fonts, handling strings, going through enums, manipulating colors, writing log files, and much more.

☐ In every game you wrote, some kind of collision testing was required. In the first two games, you used the BoundingBox structure to check for collisions in 2D, and in this chapter you handled all the collisions in the Tetris grid yourself in the MoveBlock method.

☐ Unit testing rules: I can't repeat that often enough. Especially the static unit tests helped you out a lot and made creating the games in this chapter a lot more fun and productive than without using unit testing.

☐ Use static unit tests to check out if your game code provides the visual result you expect and use automatic dynamic unit tests to make sure helper classes and the internal game logic always work the way they should.

Part II: Basic Graphics Engine

Chapter 5: Writing Your Own XNA Graphics Engine

Chapter 6: Shader Management

Chapter 7: Realism Through Normal Mapping

Chapter 8: Post-Screen Shaders and the Rocket Commander Game

Writing Your Own XNA Graphics Engine

In the first section of this book you learned all about the XNA Framework and rendering 2D graphics with the help of the SpriteBatch class. You also made some fun games. Now it is time to explore the much more exciting world of 3D graphic programming. Creating 3D games is a lot more work than just putting together a 2D game, but many games would not be possible without the great advances in 3D graphics technology. Some games such as strategy games are also possible in 2D, and the most successful strategy games of all time (StarCraft, WarCraft, Command & Conquer, Age of Empires) show that 2D games are still very popular. But if you take a look at shooter games, they would just not be possible without 3D graphics, and the better and more realistic the graphics get, the more fun the games often are. Other game genres such as beat-'em-ups, adventures, sport games, and so on have also benefited from the advancements in recent years. Sure, Pong and the early tennis games were a lot of fun 10 or 20 years ago, but they don't compare in any way with today's sport games.

XNA is a great framework for quickly creating 2D games. Even without a team of people behind you, you will probably be able to quickly throw together a game idea, make some graphics, or find someone to make some graphics for your game, and then program the whole game in a matter of weeks or months.

However, most game programmers are much more excited about creating 3D games, and a common mistake almost everyone makes is to compare their own game ideas with the most successful AAA titles that took big game studios many years to create. As an individual, you will probably not be able to compete with the next EA game, which will have had an experienced game studio with more than 100 people working on it, even if you think that their game is not as good as it could be in your opinion.

But this does not matter; most of us got into the game development scene because we like creating games and often because we think we can make it much better than all the other guys.

The good thing is that although it is hard to create a full-blown 3D game that can compete with AAA titles, you have to start somewhere, and getting into the world of 3D programming is getting easier and easier. Many great websites, tutorials, frameworks, and books are available to quickly guide even very inexperienced programmers through the first steps of creating 3D graphics for games.

Because there are already so many resources available I will not focus on the math basics, how to work with matrices, or other 3D graphics basics. It would just be boring for many programmers who already know about it and it would take away many pages for more interesting projects in this book. The same way I told you in the first chapter that you should start by reading a C# book first if you are inexperienced with C#, I suggest that if you really want to know all the basics about 3D graphics, pick up a book for that. If you have worked with Direct3D or OpenGL before, you are good to go and should know all the basics already (let's hope that covers most of the readers here).

This chapter takes the classic approach of first writing down the requirements and creating the unit test for that and then goes into detail for every required new class you need. Your goal is to create your own graphics engine and the basic framework for all the projects and games for the rest of this book. The Tetris game from the last chapter already had many useful helper classes and some new graphics classes that will be refactored in this chapter. You will also add some new classes. Refactoring means that the classes will be rewritten to fit your new requirements.

What Should Your Engine Be Able to Do?

Usually you would just write down the game idea here and then determine which classes you need to get the game and all components running. We still want to create a game at the end of this part, in Chapter 8, but for now we focus on creating a reusable graphics engine to make the creation process of future games easier. This and the next two chapters just focus on the graphics engine programming and how to get textures, models, fonts, shaders, effects, and so on working for your engine. Chapter 7 introduces advanced shaders, and in Chapter 8, you learn more about post screen shaders and how to write a game with the graphics engine developed in this part.

Thanks to the XNA Framework, which already gives you many helper classes and an easy way to manage the game window, game components, and content files (models, textures, shaders, and sound files), you don't have to worry that much about custom file formats, writing your own window management class, or how to get 3D models into your engine and then on the screen. If you have worked with DirectX or OpenGL before, you probably know that the samples and tutorials were not that hard, but as soon as you wanted to get your own textures, 3D models, or sound files into the engine, you often ran into problems like unsupported file formats, no support for the 3D models, or no ability to play your sound files. Then you would either continue your search or write your own classes to support those features. Texture and model classes do exist, but that does not mean they are perfect. Sometimes you want to add more functionality or have an easier way to load and access textures and models. For this reason, you are going to write new classes for texture and model management, which internally still use the XNA classes, but will make it easier for you to work with textures, models, and later, materials and shaders, too.

Okay, first of all you want a cool 3D model displayed on your screen. It should not only have a texture, but also use an exciting shader effect on it. Just watching a static 3D model in the center of the screen is not very exciting and can also be accomplished by just showing a screenshot, so you have to create a camera class to move around a little in your 3D world.

To help you in your future unit tests and for the UI (user interface) you also need the ability to render 2D lines as well as 3D lines to help you find out if 3D positions are correct for unit tests and debugging. You might now say "Hey, rendering lines is nothing special. Can't XNA do that already like the OpenGL graphics framework with a method like glLine, which easily draws a line on the screen?" Well, it would be nice, but the creators of XNA removed all the fixed function capabilities of DirectX, and although you can still render some lines with the help of vertex buffers and then render line primitives, it is just way too complicated. Remember that you are always going to write your unit test first and think about what should happen instead of implementing it first; you just want to draw a line from (0, 50) to (150, 150), or in 3D from (−100, 0, 0) to (+100, 0, 0). Besides that, the performance of your application will be really bad if you render each line by itself and create a new vertex buffer or vertex array for it and then get rid of it again, especially in the unit tests you will do at the end of this book with several thousand lines rendered every frame.

Then you also want the capabilities you had in the previous games to render text on the screen with the help of the TextureFont class. Your engine should also be able to render sprites, but you should stop thinking of sprites and just use textures. For example, if I load the background texture, I don't want to think about the sprite class; I just put the background texture on the whole background or put a UI texture at the location I want it to be. This means you will hide the SpriteHelper class from the user and let the Texture class manage all this in the background for you — very similar to the TextureFont class, which also handles the entire sprite rendering in the background for you.

The Engine Unit Test

Before you go deeper into the implementation details and problems of the 3D graphics engine, write your unit test for the end of this chapter first and therefore specify what the engine should be capable of by then. Please note that the initial version of this unit test looked a little different; it is absolutely okay to change it a bit if you forgot something or if you have some dependencies that were not used in the unit test, but make sense in the engine and should be used. Generally, you should try to make the unit test work without changing them. In the unit test, I initially just wrote testModel.Render(); to render the test model, but it makes more sense to specify a matrix or vector to tell the model where it has to be rendered in the 3D world.

Enough talk; take a look at the code:

```
/// <summary>
/// Test render our new graphics engine
/// </summary>
public static void TestRenderOurNewGraphicEngine()
{
    Texture backgroundTexture = null;
    Model rocketModel = null;
    TestGame.Start("TestRenderOurNewGraphicEngine",
        delegate
        {
            // Load background and rocket
            backgroundTexture = new Texture("SpaceBackground");
            rocketModel = new Model("Rocket");
        },
        delegate
        {
```

```
        // Show background
        backgroundTexture.RenderOnScreen(
            BaseGame.ResolutionRect);
        SpriteHelper.DrawSprites(width, height);
        // Render model in center
        BaseGame.Device.RenderState.DepthBufferEnable = true;
        rocketModel.Render(Matrix.CreateScale(10));
        // Draw 3d line
        BaseGame.DrawLine(
            new Vector3(-100, 0, 0), new Vector3(+100, 0, 0), Color.Red);
        // Draw safe region box for the Xbox 360, support for old monitors
        Point upperLeft = new Point(width / 15, height / 15);
        Point upperRight = new Point(width * 14 / 15, height / 15);
        Point lowerRight = new Point(width * 14 / 15, height * 14 / 15);
        Point lowerLeft = new Point(width / 15, height * 14 / 15);
        BaseGame.DrawLine(upperLeft, upperRight);
        BaseGame.DrawLine(upperRight, lowerRight);
        BaseGame.DrawLine(lowerRight, lowerLeft);
        BaseGame.DrawLine(lowerLeft, upperLeft);
        // And finally some text
        TextureFont.WriteText(upperLeft.X + 15, upperLeft.Y + 15,
            "TestRenderOurNewGraphicEngine");
    });
} // TestRenderOurNewGraphicEngine()
```

The test starts by initializing a background texture and a rocket model in the first delegate, and then another delegate is used to render everything on the screen each frame. In the previous chapters, you used only very simple unit tests with just one render delegate; now you also allow data to be created in a special init delegate, which is required because you need the graphics engine to be started before you can load any content from the content manager in XNA.

You might wonder why I call a RenderOnScreen method of the Texture class or the Render method of the Model class, when these methods don't exist. The unit test also uses many properties and methods of the BaseGame that do not exist yet, but that does not mean you can't write it this way and want this to work out later. For example, you might say that the following line is too long and too complicated to write:

```
BaseGame.Device.RenderState.DepthBufferEnable = true;
```

Then just write it in a simpler way by using a new imaginary method BaseGame.EnableDepthBuffer and worry about the implementation later. The reason why I use a Texture and Model class and have methods like Render in this unit test is quite simple: That's the way I think about this problem. Sure, I know XNA does not have these methods for me, but nothing stops me from writing my own Texture and Model classes to do just that. If you'd like to simplify the unit test even more or have other additions you would like to make, feel free to edit the unit test and then implement the features as you read through this chapter.

As a little note before you get started, I should mention that there are several additions to the BaseGame class and some new game components such as the camera class, which are also used in this unit test, but are not visible in the form of code because they are executed automatically. You learn more about these additions, new classes, and improvements as you go through this chapter.

3D Models

Before you can start rendering 3D models, you need to have an idea first of what the 3D model should look like or, even better, have some working 3D models to use. If you are not really a professional in 3D Studio Max, Maya, or Softimage, or don't have an artist who can throw some models at you quickly, don't start with that yourself. Instead, use files that are freely available from samples and tutorials or files from previous projects. This chapter uses the Rocket model from the Rocket Commander game I wrote last year (see Figure 5-1).

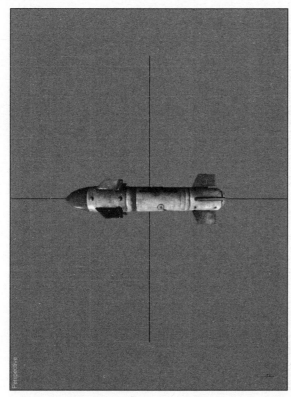

Figure 5-1

The Rocket model consists of the 3D geometry data (vectors, normals, tangents, and texture coordinates), the `ParallaxMapping.fx` shader, and the textures for this shader:

❏ `Rocket.dds` for the rocket texture (red head, gray, all logos in the middle, and so on).

❏ `RocketNormal.dds` for the normal mapping effect discussed in Chapter 7.

❏ `RocketHeight.dds` for the parallax mapping effect used in the Rocket Commander game.

All this is created by the 3D model artist, who also specifies how the rocket should look by setting additional shader and material settings for the ambient, diffuse, and specular color and any other parameters defined in the shader or material that can be set in 3D Studio. This model file is saved as a .max file, which is a custom format just for 3D Studio Max (or in whatever modeling programs you or your artist uses). To get this into your game you would need a .max importer, which does not exist for DirectX or XNA. The .max files can get very big and it would not make sense to have a 100MB file with all kinds of high polygon objects for your game if you just need the low polygon rocket model, which might fit into 100KB. You need an exporter to just get the model data you need for your game. Many formats are available, so why do I even talk about this for so long? Well, none of the standard export formats in 3D Studio Max support the shader settings you need for your game. And XNA is also able to import only .x and .fbx files. That really sucks.

You probably could just import a .x file or use the .fbx format and live with the fact that there will be no imported shader settings, tangent data, and whatever else you need to perform normal mapping, parallax mapping, or whatever custom shader you want to use in your game. But then you would have a lot of work in your game engine to fix this for every single model. Or alternatively, you can write your own custom importer for 3D Studio Max, which many big game studios do, but they have a lot more time and money than you can ever have as an individual. Another way might be to have some custom XML files that store all the shader settings for each model. The shader data is then exported into an XML file and merged in your game engine, which again can lead to a lot of work, not only in implementing the exporting and merging, but also in keeping the XML settings file up-to-date. I have seen all these approaches used and you are free to do whatever you like, but I strongly suggest choosing a painless process if possible.

In this case the Rocket model can be imported to a custom .x file with the help of the community-created Panda-Exporter for 3D Studio Max (see Figure 5-2), which then can be exported to the XNA Framework. It does not support all the features (tangent data is missing) and having more complex objects with bone and skinning data can be a pain, but you won't need that for your games yet. A good alternative is the new Collada format, which exports data from many 3D modeling programs in a very clear and easy-to-use XML data file, which can then be exported into your game more easily than writing your own custom importer and exporter for model data. For skinned models I would suggest the .fbx format (.x format also works in XNA) or just search for a .md3, .md5, or similar model format exporter, which is the famous format used in the Quake and Doom series of games. Skinned models are 3D models that also use a bone skeleton and each vertex has several skinning factors to apply any bone movement to them, often used in shooter games and whenever your game has any character models running around.

Figure 5-2

The imported rocket.x file can now be used in your XNA engine the same way you use textures or other content files. Just drop the content file into your project and it will automatically pick up all used shaders and textures and warn you if they are missing. You don't have to add the used textures and shaders yourself; the XNA .x Model processor will do that automatically for you. You just have to make sure the dependent files can be found in the same directory; in this case it would be the files Rocket.dds,

`RocketNormal.dds`, `RocketHeight.dds`, and `ParallaxMapping.fx`. The implementation of the Model class and how to render the Rocket model on the screen is handled in the next part of this chapter.

Rendering of Textures

Until now you used the `Texture` class of the XNA Framework to load textures and then used the `SpriteHelper` class you wrote in Chapter 3 to render sprites on the screen with the help of the `SpriteBatch` class. This worked nice for your first couple of games, but it is not really useful for using textures in a 3D environment and it is still too complicated to use with all these sprite helper classes. As you just saw in the unit test for this chapter, there should be a new method called `RenderOnScreen` to render the whole texture or just parts of it directly on the screen. In the background, you still use the `SpriteHelper` class and all the code you wrote to render sprites, but this makes using textures much easier and you don't have to create instances of the `SpriteHelper` class anymore. Additionally, you could later improve the way sprites are rendered and maybe even implement your own shaders to accomplish that without having to change any UI code or any unit tests.

Figure 5-3 shows the layout of the new `Texture` class; the code is pretty straightforward and the previous chapters already covered most of the functionality. The only important thing to remember is that you now have two texture classes, the one from the XNA Framework and the one from your own engine. Sure, you could rename your own class to something crazy, but who wants to write `MyOwnTextureClass` all the time, when you can just write `Texture`? Instead you will just rename the use of the XNA `Texture` class, which is not required anymore except in your new `Texture` class, which internally still uses the XNA texture. To do that, you write the following code in the using region:

```
using Texture = XnaGraphicEngine.Graphics.Texture;
```

Or this code when you need to access the XNA texture class:

```
using XnaTexture = Microsoft.Xna.Framework.Graphics.Texture;
```

Some of the properties and methods are not important yet and I just included them here to have the complete `Texture` class working right now so you can use it later in this book without having to re-implement any missing features (for example, rendering rotated texture sprites).

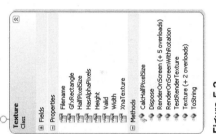

Texture
Class

⊞ Fields

⊟ Properties
  Filename
  GfxRectangle
  HalfPixelSize
  HasAlphaPixels
  Height
  Valid
  Width
  XnaTexture

⊟ Methods
  CalcHalfPixelSize
  Dispose
  RenderOnScreen (+ 5 overloads)
  RenderOnScreenWithRotation
  TestRenderTexture
  Texture (+ 2 overloads)
  ToString

Figure 5-3

Before you analyze the code in this class, you should first look at the unit test, which always gives a quick overview on how to use the class. Please note that I split up the static unit tests into different classes now instead of having them all in the main game class. It is more useful this way because there will be a lot of classes in your engine and it makes it easier to check out functionality and quickly test the capabilities of each class. The unit test just loads the texture with the help of the texture constructor, which takes the content name, and then you can render it with the `RenderOnScreen` method:

```
/// <summary>
/// Test render textures
/// </summary>
public static void TestRenderTexture()
{
    Texture testTexture = null;
    TestGame.Start("TestTextures",
        delegate
        {
            testTexture = new Texture("SpaceBackground");
        },
        delegate
        {
            testTexture.RenderOnScreen(
                new Rectangle(100, 100, 256, 256),
                testTexture.GfxRectangle);
        });
} // TestTextures()
```

The most important method for you right now is the `RenderOnScreen` method. The `Valid` property indicates if the loading of the texture succeeded and if you can use the internal `XnaTexture` property. `Width` and `Height` and `GfxRectangle` give you the dimensions of the texture, and the other properties are not important to you right now. They will be used later when you render materials with shaders.

```
/// <summary>
/// Render on screen
/// </summary>
/// <param name="renderRect">Render rectangle</param>
public void RenderOnScreen(Rectangle renderRect)
{
    SpriteHelper.AddSpriteToRender(this,
        renderRect, GfxRectangle);
} // RenderOnScreen(renderRect)
```

Looks quite simple, doesn't it? There are several overloads that all add sprites to the `SpriteHelper` class, which uses code you already wrote in Chapter 3. Only the `AddSpriteToRender` method was changed to be static now and accept `GfxRectangles` instead of creating new instances of the `SpriteHelper` class:

```
/// <summary>
/// Add sprite to render
/// </summary>
/// <param name="texture">Texture</param>
/// <param name="rect">Rectangle</param>
/// <param name="gfxRect">Gfx rectangle</param>
public static void AddSpriteToRender(
    Texture texture, Rectangle rect, Rectangle gfxRect)
```

```
    {
        sprites.Add(new SpriteToRender(texture, rect, gfxRect, Color.White));
    } // AddSpriteToRender(texture, rect, gfxRect)
```

Finally, you also use the TextureFont class. It was moved to the graphics namespace, it uses the new Texture class now instead of the XNA Texture class, and it has a new unit test for text rendering. Other than that, the class remains unchanged; you use it directly to write text on the screen with the help of the static WriteText methods (a few more overloads were added):

```
    /// <summary>
    /// Write text on the screen
    /// </summary>
    /// <param name="pos">Position</param>
    /// <param name="text">Text</param>
    public static void WriteText(Point pos, string text)
    {
        remTexts.Add(new FontToRender(pos.X, pos.Y, text, Color.White));
    } // WriteText(pos, text)
```

Line Rendering

To render lines in XNA, you can't just use a built-in method; you have to do it your own way. As I said before, there are several ways and the most efficient one is to create a big vertex list and render all lines at once after you've collected them throughout the frame (see Figure 5-4).

cam pos={X:-1,093441 Y:-11,36231 Z:2,097521}

Figure 5-4

Additionally, you use a very simple shader to draw the lines. You could also use the `BasicEffect` class of XNA, but it is much faster to use your own custom shader, which just spits out the vertex color for each line. Because rendering 2D and 3D lines is basically the same, just the vertex shader looks a tiny bit differ-ent; this section only talks about rendering 2D lines. The `LineManager3D` class works in almost the same manner (see Figure 5-5).

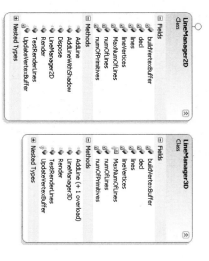

Figure 5-5

To learn how to use these classes, just take a look at the `TestRenderLines` unit test:

```
/// <summary>
/// Test render
/// </summary>
public static void TestRenderLines()
{
    TestGame.Start(delegate
    {
        BaseGame.DrawLine(new Point(-100, 0), new Point(50, 100),
            Color.White);
        BaseGame.DrawLine(new Point(0, 100), new Point(100, 0),
            Color.Gray);
        BaseGame.DrawLine(new Point(400, 0), new Point(100, 0),
            Color.Red);
        BaseGame.DrawLine(new Point(10, 50), new Point(100, +150),
            new Color(255, 0, 0, 64));
    });
} // TestRenderLines()
```

So all you have to do is to call the `BaseGame.DrawLine` method, which accepts both 2D points and 3D vectors to support 2D and 3D lines. Both `LineManager` classes work as shown in Figure 5-6. Just call the `DrawLine` method of the `BaseGame` class a couple of times and let the `LineManager` class handle the rest.

LineManager Process

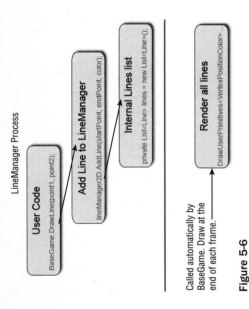

User Code
BaseGame.DrawLine(point1, point2);

Add Line to LineManager
lineManager2D.AddLine(startPoint, endPoint, color);

Internal Lines list
private List<Line> lines = new List<Line>();

Render all lines
DrawUserPrimitives<VertexPositionColor> ...

Called automatically by
BaseGame. Draw at the
end of each frame.

Figure 5-6

The interesting code is in the Render method, which renders all the lines you have collected this frame. The collecting of the lines and adding them to your lines list is really not complicated; check it out yourself if you want to take a close look. The Render method uses the VertexPositionColor structure for all the vertex elements and the vertex array is created in the UpdateVertexBuffer method. This is the main part of the method:

```
// Set all lines
for (int lineNum = 0; lineNum < numOfLines; lineNum++)
{
  Line line = (Line)lines[lineNum];
  lineVertices[lineNum * 2 + 0] = new VertexPositionColor(
    new Vector3(
    -1.0f + 2.0f * line.startPoint.X / BaseGame.Width,
    -(-1.0f + 2.0f * line.startPoint.Y / BaseGame.Height), 0),
    line.color);
  lineVertices[lineNum * 2 + 1] = new VertexPositionColor(
    new Vector3(
    -1.0f + 2.0f * line.endPoint.X / BaseGame.Width,
    -(-1.0f + 2.0f * line.endPoint.Y / BaseGame.Height), 0),
    line.color);
} // for (lineNum)
```

First you might wonder why each start point and end point of a line is divided through the width and height of your game and then multiplied by two and then subtracted by one. This formula is used to convert all 2D points from screen coordinates into your view space, which goes from –1 to +1 for both x and y. In the LineManager3D class, this is not really required because you already have the correct 3D points. For each line, you store two points (start and end) and each vertex gets the position and the color, hence the VertexPositionColor structure from the XNA Framework.

125

In the `Render` method, you now just go through all primitives you have added (which are the lines; you got half as much as you have points) and render them with the help of the `LineRendering.fx` shader:

```
// Render lines if we got any lines to render
if (numOfPrimitives > 0)
{
BaseGame.AlphaBlending = true;
BaseGame.WorldMatrix = Matrix.Identity;
BaseGame.Device.VertexDeclaration = decl;
ShaderEffect.lineRendering.Render(
"LineRendering2D",
delegate
{
BaseGame.Device.DrawUserPrimitives<VertexPositionColor>(
PrimitiveType.LineList, lineVertices, 0, numOfPrimitives);
});
} // if
```

The `AlphaBlending` property of `BaseGame` makes sure you can render lines with alpha blending to allow blending them in and out. The `WorldMatrix` is discussed later; for now, just make sure here that the world matrix is reset to use the original position values of the `lineVertices` list. This is especially important for the `LineManager3D`.

Then the vertex declaration is set, which just makes sure that you can render `VertexPositionColor` vertices now. (This is just the way DirectX does this and XNA works very similar to that, but you still have the advantage of using generics and other cool .NET functionality.)

```
decl = new VertexDeclaration(
BaseGame.Device, VertexPositionColor.VertexElements);
```

That looks simple, doesn't it? Well, why even bother with the declaration; couldn't XNA do that for you automatically? Yes, it could, but remember you can also create your own custom vertex declaration if you need a custom format, which makes sense if you write your own custom shaders. See Chapter 7 on how to do that, in the discussion of the `TangentVertexFormat`.

The final thing you have to figure out to understand the rendering of the lines is to render data with shaders. Yeah, I know — it's a lot of work just to render a few lines, but you will need all the shader functionality for anything you do in 3D anyway. You cannot render anything in XNA without shaders — period! You might now say "What about the `SpriteBatch` class? You used it to render 2D graphics and you never talked about shaders yet?" That is correct; you don't have to know anything about shaders if you just want to create a simple 2D game. But that does not mean the `SpriteBatch` class does not use shaders internally. Another class that hides the shader capability is the `BasicEffect` class, which allows you to render 3D data without writing your custom shader effects first. It uses a basic shader internally to mimic the fixed function pipeline functionality. It is similar to the fixed function pipeline, but it is not as fast as writing your own custom shaders, and it does not support anything special.

The model class that is discussed in a little bit also uses shaders, but XNA allows you to hide all the shader management. You can just set the shader parameters for the matrices and then use the `Draw` method to let XNA render all mesh parts of the 3D model.

Shaders are discussed in great detail in Chapter 6. Before you take a look at the `LineRendering.fx` shader that brings the lines on the screen, you should first look at the `ShaderEffect` class that allows rendering of 3D data for the shader, with help of a `RenderDelegate`:

```
/// <summary>
/// Render
/// </summary>
/// <param name="techniqueName">Technique name</param>
/// <param name="renderDelegate">Render delegate</param>
public void Render(string techniqueName,
    BaseGame.RenderDelegate renderDelegate)
{
    SetParameters();
    // Start shader
    effect.CurrentTechnique = effect.Techniques[techniqueName];
    effect.Begin(SaveStateMode.None);
    // Render all passes (usually just one)
    //foreach (EffectPass pass in effect.CurrentTechnique.Passes)
    for (int num = 0; num < effect.CurrentTechnique.Passes.Count; num++)
    {
        EffectPass pass = effect.CurrentTechnique.Passes[num];
        pass.Begin();
        renderDelegate();
        pass.End();
    } // foreach (pass)
    // End shader
    effect.End();
} // Render(passName, renderDelegate)
```

The `ShaderEffect` class uses the effect instance to load the shader from the content pipeline. You then can use the effect to render 3D data with it. This is done by first selecting the technique either by name or index; then the shader is started and you have to call `Begin` and `End` for each pass the shader has. Most shaders in this book and most shaders you will ever encounter will have only one pass, and that means you have to call `Begin` and `End` only once for the first pass. Usually only post screen shaders are more complex, but you can write shaders with many passes, which might be useful for fur shaders or things of this nature with multiple layers. In between `Begin` and `End`, the 3D data is rendered with the help of the `RenderDelegate` you used earlier to call `DrawUserPrimitives` with the `lineVertices` array.

3D Programming

So how do you get the 3D data imported from a model file such as `rocket.x` on your screen? Your screen can display 2D data only; this means you need a way to convert 3D data to your 2D screen. This is called projection, and there are many ways this can be done. In the early days of 3D games, techniques such as ray-casting were used and done all on the CPU. For each pixel column of the screen, the upper and lower bounds were calculated by a simple formula and this led to the first 3D games, including Ultima Underground, Wolfenstein 3D, and later Doom, which was quite popular.

Not long after that, more realistic games such as Descent, Terminal Velocity, Quake, and so on were developed, which used a better way to convert 3D data to 2D. In the mid-nineties, 3D hardware was becoming more popular and more and more gaming PCs suddenly had the ability to help render many polygons in a very efficient matter.

Luckily, you don't have to worry about all the early problems of 3D games anymore. 3D graphics today are all created on the GPU (graphic processing unit on the graphic card). The GPU not only renders polygons on the screen and fills pixels, but it also performs all the transformations to project 3D data to 2D (see Figure 5-7). Vertex shaders are used to transform all 3D points to screen coordinates, and pixel shaders are then used to fill all visible polygons on the screen with pixels. Pixel shaders are usually the most interesting and important part of shaders because they can greatly manipulate the way the output looks (changing colors, mixing textures, having lighting and shadows influence the final output, and so on). Older hardware that does not support vertex and pixel shaders is not even supported in XNA, so you don't have to worry about falling back to the fixed function pipeline or even doing software rendering. For XNA you need at least Shader Model 1.1, which means you need at least a GeForce 3 or ATI 8000 graphic card.

The code and images I discuss in the next pages include only the basics of 3D programming and how to work with matrices in XNA. If you want to know more, I strongly recommend reading the XNA documentation and, even better, the original DirectX documentation, which has very good topics about getting started with 3D programming, matrices, and how everything is handled in the framework (which is very similar to XNA).

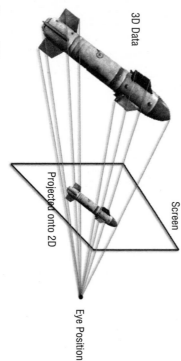

3D Data

Screen

Projected onto 2D

Eye Position

Figure 5-7

I won't have time to go into great detail about all these calculations and thanks to the many helper classes and methods in the XNA Framework, you can get along without knowing much about matrix transformations. Projecting 3D data usually consists of the following steps:

☐ Bring the 3D data to the correct 3D position with help of the `WorldMatrix`. This means for the rocket, which was created in 3D Studio Max, to rotate it in the direction you want, scale it accordingly to fit correctly into your 3D scene, and then position it to wherever you want it to be. You can use the `Matrix` methods to help you do that; use `CreateRotation`, `CreateScale`, and `CreateTranslation` methods and combine them by multiplying the resulting matrixes:

```
BaseGame.WorldMatrix =
    Matrix.CreateRotationX(MathHelper.Pi / 2) *
    Matrix.CreateScale(2.5f) *
    Matrix.CreateTranslation(rocketPosition);
```

❑ Every single point of your 3D model is then transformed with this `WorldMatrix` to bring it to the correct position in your 3D world. In DirectX and the fixed function pipeline, you didn't have to do that yourself, but as soon as you write shaders in XNA you have to transform all vertices yourself. And as you know, everything in XNA is rendered with shaders; there is no support for the fixed function pipeline.

❑ What is visible on the screen depends on the location and orientation of your camera or eye (see Figure 5-7 earlier). Everything is projected to this camera location, but you can also rotate the world, tilt it, or do more crazy things with your camera matrix. You will probably just want to use the `Matrix.CreateLookAt` method in the beginning to create your camera matrix, which is then used in the vertex shader to transform the 3D world data to the camera space:

```
BaseGame.ViewMatrix =
    Matrix.CreateLookAt(cameraPosition, lookTarget, upVector);
```

❑ Bring the projected camera space data to your screen. This operation is not already done in the `ViewMatrix`, in order to allow the view matrix to be calculated and changed more easily. The visible camera space goes from –1 to +1 for both x and y, and z contains the depth value for each point in relation to the camera position. The `ProjectionMatrix` converts these values to your screen resolution (for example, 1024×768) and it also specifies how deep you can look into the scene (near and far plane values). The depth is important in helping you find out which object is in front of which other object when you finally render the polygons in the pixel shaders (which are all 2D, because you can only render 2D data on your screen). The projection matrix is constructed this way:

```
/// <summary>
/// Field of view and near and far plane distances for the
/// ProjectionMatrix creation.
/// </summary>
private const float FieldOfView = (float)Math.PI / 2,
    NearPlane = 1.0f,
    FarPlane = 500.0f;
...
aspectRatio = (float)width / (float)height;
BaseGame.ProjectionMatrix = Matrix.CreatePerspectiveFieldOfView(
    FieldOfView, aspectRatio, NearPlane, FarPlane);
```

There is an important change in XNA that should be mentioned: In DirectX, all the `Matrix` methods, tutorials, and samples used left-handed matrices, but in XNA everything is right-handed; there are no methods to create any left-handed matrices. If you create a new game or if you are new to 3D programming this will probably not matter much to you, but if you have old code or old models, you might run into problems because of the way the 3D data is used. Using left-handed data in a right-handed environment means that everything looks turned inside out if you don't modify your matrices. Culling is also the other way around in XNA; it works counter-clockwise, which is the mathematically correct way. DirectX used clockwise culling by default. If your models are inside out and you switch from clockwise to counter-clockwise, they will look correct again; they are just mirrored now (the 3D data is still left-handed).

This is especially true if you import .x files, which use, by default, a left-handed system (see Figure 5-8). You can either convert all matrices or points yourself or just live with the fact that everything is mirrored. In this book, you will use a lot of .x files and it does not matter if they are left-handed (such as the Rocket model from Rocket Commander) or right-handed (as all new 3D content created here) because you do not care if left-handed data is mirrored. If you have to make sure all data in your game is correctly aligned, please make sure you have all the 3D data in an exportable format so you can later re-export any wrong data instead of having to fix it in your code yourself.

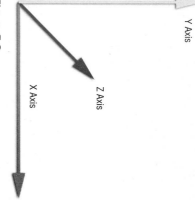

Figure 5-8

You probably remember from school that the left-handed coordinate system is named after the left hand, which can be used to show you the x (thumb), y (forefinger), and z (middle finger) axes. Just hold up your left hand and align these three fingers in 90 degrees to each other and you have your left-handed coordinate system. In school, both math and physics used only the right-handed coordinate system and if you were writing with your right hand and held up your left hand to show you the axes, you got it all wrong.

Anyway, the right-handed coordinate system is much cooler because almost all 3D modeling programs work with right-handed data, and most programs except games work with right-handed data, too. Right-handed coordinate systems can be shown by using your right hand for the x (thumb), y (forefinger), and z (middle finger) axes (see Figure 5-9).

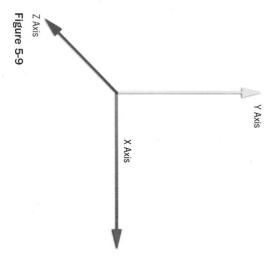

Figure 5-9

Looks almost the same, but having the z axis coming toward you is kind of unnatural if you have worked with left-handed systems before. It might also be useful to rotate this system to have it behave the same way as in 3D modeling programs where z points up. I also like x and y lying on the ground for positioning 3D data and building 3D landscapes (see Figure 5-10).

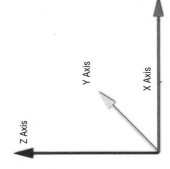

Z Axis

Y Axis

X Axis

Figure 5-10

Enough talk about converting 3D to 2D and coordinate systems. You should now know enough about basic 3D calculations to render 3D models. If you are still unsure and want to learn more about 3D math and programming, please pick up a good book about that or read more on the Internet. Many great websites and tutorials are available there; just search for 3D programming.

Model Unit Test

You should now have the Rocket.x model file discussed earlier imported into your project (use the content directory to keep code and content data separated). Rendering the model data is not very complicated, but there is no Render method in the XNA Model class and you want to have such a method for your unit test. To accomplish this and to make it easier to later extend the model rendering, optimizing it and adding more cool features, you write your own Model class (similar to the Texture class you just wrote). It will just use the XNA model class internally, provide you with a Render method, and handle all the scaling issues and set all required matrices automatically for you.

It is a good practice to write another unit test just for the class you are currently developing, even if another unit test already covers the basic functionality. In this class unit test, you can make more special considerations and check more details. It is also useful to quickly check if new data is valid by just exchanging the content loaded in the unit test. Here is the very simple, but still very useful, unit test for the Model class:

```
public static void TestRenderModel()
{
    Model testModel = null;
    TestGame.Start("TestRenderModel",
        delegate
        {
            testModel = new Model("Rocket");
        },
```

```
delegate
{
    testModel.Render(Matrix.CreateScale(10));
});
} // TestRenderModel()
```

So you just load a test model named Rocket in the content system and then you render it every frame with a scaling of 10 directly in the 3D scene. All the other stuff is handled somewhere else and you don't have to worry about it. This includes setting shaders, updating matrices, making sure the render states are correct for rendering 3D data, and so on.

The only interesting method in the Model class (see Figure 5-11) is the Render method.

Figure 5-11

The constructor just loads the model from the content and sets the internal variables to make sure you got the correct object scaling and matrix to make it easier to fit it into your world:

```
/// <summary>
/// Create model
/// </summary>
/// <param name="setModelName">Set Model Filename</param>
public Model(string setModelName)
{
    name = setModelName;
    xnaModel = BaseGame.Content.Load<XnaModel>(
        @"Content\" + name);

    // Get matrices for each mesh part
    transforms = new Matrix[xnaModel.Bones.Count];
    xnaModel.CopyAbsoluteBoneTransformsTo(transforms);

    // Calculate scaling for this object, used for rendering.
    scaling = xnaModel.Meshes[0].BoundingSphere.Radius *
        transforms[0].Right.Length();
    if (scaling == 0)
        scaling = 0.0001f;

    // Apply scaling to objectMatrix to rescale object to size of 1.0
    objectMatrix *= Matrix.CreateScale(1.0f / scaling);
} // Model(setModelName)
```

After the `xnaModel` instance is loaded from the content directory, the transformations are pre-calculated because you don't support any animated data here (XNA does not really support it yet anyway). The transforms matrix list holds the render matrix for each model mesh part you have to render (the rocket consists just of one mesh part using only one effect). This transformation is set by the 3D Modeler in the 3D creation program and aligns your model the way the modeler wants it to be. Then you determine the scaling and make sure it is not zero because dividing by zero is not really fun. Finally, you calculate the object matrix, which will be used together with the transform matrices and the render matrix for rendering.

The `Render` method now just goes through all meshes of your model (for good performance always make sure you have as few meshes as possible) and calculates the world matrix for every mesh. Then each used effect is updated with the current world, view, and project matrix values as well any other dynamic data such as the light direction, and then you are good to go. The `MeshPart.Draw` method calls the internal shader of the model the same way you did earlier for the line rendering. The next two chapters talk in more detail about this process and you re-implement it in your own way to be much more efficient when rendering many 3D models each frame.

```
/// <summary>
/// Render
/// </summary>
/// <param name="renderMatrix">Render matrix</param>
public void Render(Matrix renderMatrix)
{
    // Apply objectMatrix
    renderMatrix = objectMatrix * renderMatrix;
    // Go through all meshes in the model
    foreach (ModelMesh mesh in xnaModel.Meshes)
    {
        // Assign world matrix for each used effect
        BaseGame.WorldMatrix =
            transforms[mesh.ParentBone.Index] *
            renderMatrix;
        // And for each effect this mesh uses (usually just 1,multimaterials
        // are nice in 3ds max, but not efficiently for rendering stuff).
        foreach (Effect effect in mesh.Effects)
        {
            // Set technique (not done automatically by XNA framework).
            effect.CurrentTechnique = effect.Techniques["Specular20"];
            // Set matrices, we use world, viewProj and viewInverse in
            // the ParallaxMapping.fx shader
            effect.Parameters["world"].SetValue(
                BaseGame.WorldMatrix);
            // Note: these values should only be set once every frame!
            // to improve performance again, also we should access them
            // with EffectParameter and not via name (which is slower)!
            // For more information see Chapter 6 and 7.
            effect.Parameters["viewProj"].SetValue(
                BaseGame.ViewProjectionMatrix);
            effect.Parameters["viewInverse"].SetValue(
                BaseGame.InverseViewMatrix);
            // Also set light direction (not really used here, but later)
            effect.Parameters["lightDir"].SetValue(
```

```
    BaseGame.LightDirection);
  } // foreach (effect)
  // Render with help of the XNA ModelMesh Draw method, which goes
  // through all mesh parts and renders them (with vertex and index
  // buffers).
  mesh.Draw();
  } // foreach (mesh)
} // Render(renderMatrix)
```

As you can see, there are quite a lot of comments in this code and you will see this in all methods written by me that are a little longer. I think it is very important to understand the code quickly later when you want to change something, refactor code to new requirements, or just for optimizing your code. For most programmers this is a hard step. We are all lazy, and it takes a long time to understand how useful these comments can be, not only if other people read your code, but also if you come back to a part of code at a later point in time. Please also try to write your comments in English and use a language that simplifies the reading process and does not use code in the comments.

The render matrix you passed from the unit test (which was just a scaling matrix with the factor of 10) is now multiplied with the object matrix, which again scales the render matrix by the factor required to bring the object to the size 1, so in total your rocket now has a size of 10 units in your 3D world. Then you go through each model mesh (your rocket just has one mesh) and calculate the world matrix for this mesh by using the pre-calculated transforms matrix list and the render matrix. By using the world matrix in the vertex shader, you can now be sure that every single 3D point of your rocket is transformed the way you want it to be. Before calling this method the view and projection matrices must obviously be set, too, because the vertex shader expects all these values to be able to convert the 3D data for the pixel shader to render it onto the screen.

XNA models store all the used effects for each model mesh and you can have multiple effects for one single mesh, but most models have usually just one effect assigned to them. You will later see that the most efficient way to render a lot of 3D data is to render them in a bunch using the same shader for a long time and then flush everything to the screen at once. This allows you to render thousands of objects every frame with a very high frame rate. Please read Chapters 6 and 7 for more information about shaders and how to work with them in an efficient way.

But before you can render your mesh here, you have to set the used technique first, which is not done automatically by XNA, even though it is set by the model artist. You will see in Chapter 7 how to get around this issue. Then you set the world, view, and project matrices the way the shader expects these values. For example, the view matrix is never directly required; you just use the view inverse matrix to figure out the camera position and use it for specular light calculations. All these shader parameters are set with the Parameters property of the effect class by using the names of these parameters. This is not a very efficient way to set effect parameters because using strings to access data is a huge performance penalty. You will later find better ways to do this, but for now it works and you should be able to see your little rocket from the unit test after mesh.Draw is called (see Figure 5-12).

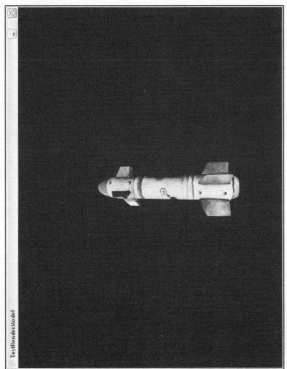

Figure 5-12

Testing Other Models

If you have other .x files on your disk, or if you just want to test other .x files from the Rocket Commander game or one of its many game mods, you can quickly test that by dragging in the .x file to the content directory and changing the unit test to load the new model.

Let's do that with the Apple.x model from the Fruit Commander mod:

```
public static void TestRenderModel()
{
    Model testModel = null;
    TestGame.Start("TestRenderModel",
        delegate
        {
            testModel = new Model("Apple");
        },
        delegate
        {
            testModel.Render(Matrix.CreateScale(10));
        });
} // TestRenderModel()
```

This results in the screen shown in Figure 5-13. Please note that the specular color calculations are based on the normal mapping effect in the shader, which does not work correctly here because the tangent data of the apple is not correct. (It was not even imported because XNA models don't support tangent data, and you have to implement it in your own way in Chapter 7.)

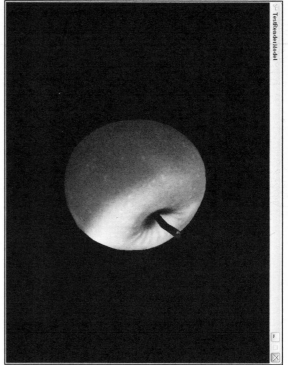

Figure 5-13

Plugging in More Game Components

Before you even noticed it, your graphics engine has grown to a respectable size and you have a lot of useful classes right now, which help you to render both 2D and 3D data quite easily, as you can see in the many unit tests available in most of the classes (see Figure 5-14).

You haven't used many game components until now and in my opinion it does not make much sense to write the base graphics engine with components. You did not use any Update or Draw methods the way game components are used. Okay, the Model class uses a Render method and the Input class has an Update method, but other than that you did not have any functionality that is compatible with game components. The Render methods in the model and texture classes work quite differently because they expect the user to call them with different values and very often each frame. I guess the Input class could be changed to a game component, but I'm not quite excited about that idea.

Instead let's think of components, which fit perfectly into the game components model. It makes sense if you have a class that needs to be updated and drawn each frame. Examples of these kinds of classes include frame per second counters, or a camera class, which is still missing from your engine.

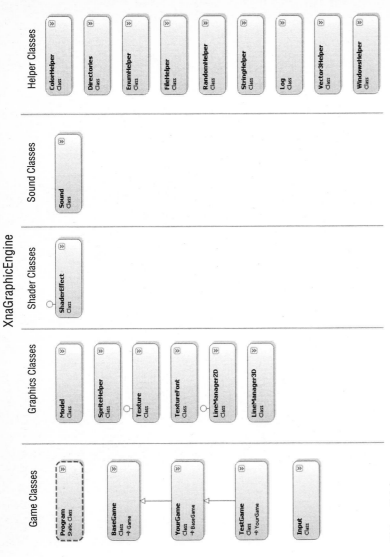

Figure 5-14

Simple Camera Class

You don't need a complex camera for your unit tests, but it would be nice to move around a little and to have a simple 3D look at the objects you render in your engine unit tests. With the help of the view matrix and the Matrix.CreateLookAt method, you can easily create such functionality and set it wherever you need it. Even better would be the use of a game component class to do all this automatically. Simply create an instance of the camera class in the constructor of the YourGame class, which is derived from the BaseGame class, and suddenly all unit tests and other 3D code will use the new camera class without any extra code because Update is called automatically for each game component you have in the YourGame class.

```
public YourGame()
{
    // Init simple camera
    this.Components.Add(new SimpleCamera(this));
} // YourGame()
```

The SimpleCamera class has a constructor and an Initialize and Update method, which are both called automatically (see Figure 5-15). The class also has three fields for the x, y, and z position of the camera, which is initialized to (0, 0, 15). Update then changes x and y based on the mouse movement, or if you have a gamepad, based on the right thumb stick movement. Additionally you can zoom in and out with the left thumb stick.

Figure 5-15

The class is quite simple and it is easy to read through the code of the whole class:

```
/// <summary>
/// Simple camera class just to move around a little.
/// Always focuses on the center and uses the same height.
/// </summary>
class SimpleCamera : GameComponent
{
    #region Variables
    float x = 0, y = 0;
    float zHeight = 15.0f;
    #endregion

    #region Constructor
    public SimpleCamera(BaseGame game)
        : base(game)
    {
    } // SimpleCamera(game)
    #endregion

    #region Initialize
    public override void Initialize()
    {
        base.Initialize();
    } // Initialize()
    #endregion

    #region Update
    public override void Update(GameTime gameTime)
    {
        base.Update(gameTime);
        // Update camera position (allow mouse and gamepad)
        x += Input.MouseXMovement / 10;
        y += Input.MouseYMovement / 10;
        x += Input.GamePad.ThumbSticks.Right.X;
```

```
        y += Input.GamePad.ThumbSticks.Right.Y;
        zHeight += Input.GamePad.ThumbSticks.Left.Y;
        BaseGame.ViewMatrix = Matrix.CreateLookAt(
            new Vector3(x, y, zHeight), Vector3.Zero, Vector3.Up);
    } // Update(gameTime)
    #endregion
} // class SimpleCamera
```

The important thing here is the ViewMatrix from the BaseGame class, which is set at the end of the Update method. When rendering a shader in the model class or in any other class like the line managers, you will use this view matrix and make sure that all your 3D data is converted to your view space with this exact matrix until you change it again in the next frame.

You now have everything together for the TestRenderOurNewGraphicEngine test you wrote at the beginning of this chapter, and if you take a look at all the classes in the project you imported and wrote, it is quite a nice engine that is both easy to use and extensible, which you will explore in the next chapters.

ScreenshotCapturer Class

There is also another helper class in the engine called ScreenshotCapturer, which allows you to take screenshots with the Print-Screen key. It is implemented as a game component, too, and it is initialized in the BaseGame constructor. The Update method is called automatically and just calls MakeScreenshot if the user just pressed the Print-Screen key:

```
public override void Update(GameTime gameTime)
{
    if (Input.KeyboardKeyJustPressed(Keys.PrintScreen))
        MakeScreenshot();

    base.Update(gameTime);
} // Update(gameTime)
```

The MakeScreenshot method creates a temporary texture and stores the back buffer with the help of the ResolveBackBuffer method of the device. The result is then saved to disk with the help of some other helper methods in the class:

```
using (Texture2D dstTexture = new Texture2D(
    BaseGame.Device, BaseGame.Width, BaseGame.Height, 1,
    ResourceUsage.ResolveTarget,
    SurfaceFormat.Color,
    ResourceManagementMode.Manual))
{
    // Get data with help of the resolve method
    BaseGame.Device.ResolveBackBuffer(dstTexture);
    dstTexture.Save(
        ScreenshotNameBuilder(screenshotNum),
        ImageFileFormat.Jpg);
} // using (dstTexture)
```

Making Sure Games Run on the Xbox 360

The first two chapters already talked about the Xbox 360 and how to deploy some simple 2D games to it. This is the section in which I want to make sure that you have the XNA Game Launcher ready to work on your Xbox 360 console. You can test the graphics engine and games in each chapter as you go along. In the creation of my first XNA game, I was not able to test it on the Xbox 360 early on. I finally tested it on the Xbox 360 when it was almost done and I encountered many problems. 2D games ran fine and the only thing that I did wrong was to not respect the safe region on the Xbox 360 to support older TV sets. For 3D games and shaders, especially post screen shaders, so many things can go wrong; I just want to make sure that none of you have to go through the same troubles.

If you don't have an Xbox 360 or if you are not interested in Xbox 360 console development, you can probably skip this section. XNA is still a great platform for Windows and superior to Managed DirectX because it supports .NET 2.0 and simplifies many processes, but having the ability to create console games is really great.

Before you get started, take a quick look at the completed TestRenderOurNewGraphicEngine unit test, which shows some of the features of your new graphics engine (see Figure 5-16). It looks much cooler in real time, especially if you move around with the mouse or gamepad.

As you can see on the image, I have drawn a white rectangle at the border of the visible render area. This rectangle is not described in the XNA Framework and you will not find much information about that on the Internet because this safe region is not really documented well. It means that if you have a TV set, the signal that is sent to it is usually overdrawn, even if it is a new HDTV set; that's just the way TVs work and accept signals. The older the TV set is, the more pixels in the outer regions can be skipped. For this reason you should make sure that all the important game content is in the inner "safe region." On the PC, you can put anything you want in the top-left corner or in the lower right and the user will still see it in the fullscreen mode because all pixels are rendered 1:1 onto the screen, but consoles and TV sets don't work this way. It is usually best to design your game in a way that the outer regions are not so important and have only some less important UI or 3D data on them — so it looks okay on the PC, which uses the full resolution, and one mode for the Xbox 360, which cuts off 5–10 percent of the borders to make the game fit on all TV sets. Note: If you connect your Xbox 360 to a VGA monitor with a VGA cable, none of this will matter because then the Xbox 360 will render the full screen the same way the PC does; this applies only to TV sets.

Downloading the XNA Game Launcher

To get the XNA Framework on your Xbox 360, you have to download the XNA Game Launcher first. On the PC you can just install the XNA Framework Redistributables or you can install XNA Game Studio Express, which also installs the XNA Framework. Either way, you will need .NET 2.0 to start any XNA application on the PC and in the same way you will need .NET 2.0 on the Xbox 360, which is obviously not installed by default (because none of the Xbox 360 components use .NET or any Managed code at all).

You can't just put a CD or DVD into your Xbox 360 and install XNA or .NET. The Xbox 360 does not allow any unauthorized data and it protects itself very well against any hacking attempts. Although this is good for the Xbox 360 game developers because games can't be copied that easily and the Xbox 360 can't be used for anything other than the expected use by the manufacturers, it is not a good thing if you want to bring your custom content and game ideas to your Xbox 360.

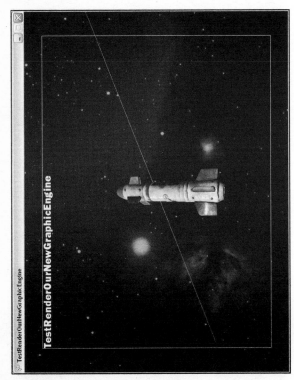

Figure 5-16

For that reason, and because Microsoft and especially the Xbox 360 team are very afraid of misuse and security risks, you have to join the so-called "XNA Creator's Club" first before you are allowed to download and install XNA on your console. Other than XNA it is not free to join the XNA Creator's Club; it will cost you a couple of bucks ($99 per year or just $49 for four months). To join, you can log in with any Xbox Live account (create one first if you don't have one yet; make sure your console is connected to the Internet) and then go to All Games ➪ Memberships. There you can select the XNA Creator's Club memberships and subscribe to them.

After you have done that, you can download the XNA Game Launcher, which will be installed to your Games ➪ All Demos/Games section of your Xbox 360 Dashboard.

Xbox 360 Setup and Deploying Games

You can now start the XNA Game Launcher, which is the program you use to start all your XNA games, no matter if written by you or if you have downloaded them. The XNA Game Launcher can be found on your Games ➪ All Demos/Games page if you are logged into an Xbox Live account that has the XNA Creator's Club membership. If you don't see it, go back to the Memberships page and make sure you are subscribed. After you start the XNA Game Launcher, you can see the screen shown in Figure 5-17. Please make sure you are connected to the Internet at all times when the XNA Game Launcher is started, or you will lose the connection to Xbox Live and the XNA Game Launcher will end itself.

As already discussed in Chapter 1, you have to go into Settings first if this is your first time using the launcher and you want to deploy your games from your PC to the console. In Settings, you can then generate a key, which you have to enter in XNA Game Studio Express under Tools ➪ Options ➪ XNA Game Studio ➪ Add Console (see Chapter 1). You may have to repeat that step in case the connection to the PC does not work anymore or if you have reinstalled XNA Game Studio Express on your PC.

After the key is set, you can connect the Xbox 360 to your computer and start deploying games from your PC. To deploy games, the PC and the Xbox 360 must be in the same network and because both have to be on the Internet, it makes sense to use a router or modem to connect all the devices together. You can deploy games by just opening an Xbox 360 project in XNA Game Studio Express and pressing F5 to start it. Alternatively you can just deploy the game without starting it in the Build menu. In any case the deployed games (if there were no build errors) are automatically stored on your Xbox 360 and can be accessed later with the "My XNA Games" menu entry of the XNA Game Launcher (see Figure 5-17). This is quite useful if you just want to play a game or show it to a friend without having to connect to the PC first.

Figure 5-17

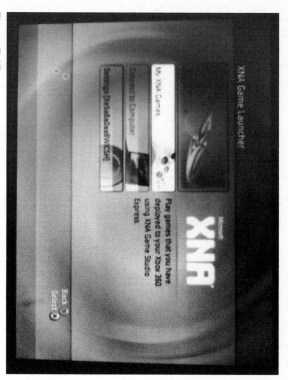

Console Debugging and Tools

When you press F5 in XNA Game Studio a project will be debugged, no matter whether you start it on the PC or the Xbox 360. The cool thing is that debugging works great on the console, too. This can be especially useful if you just have one PC monitor and then your Xbox 360 connected to a TV set. Then you can use your PC to do all the work and step through the code in the debugging mode while you can see the result on the Xbox 360 screen.

Additionally there are some tools to help you out with the Xbox 360 development. For example, XACT allows you to create and test sound projects for Windows and the Xbox 360. You learn all about that in Chapter 9. Professional Xbox 360 developers also have access to the XDK (Xbox Development Kit), which is not available to home users and it costs quite a lot of money to get such a kit, if your company is even accepted to be a certified Xbox 360 developer. There are many useful tools in the XDK, especially to find out about the performance of the console, get and log errors, and so on. All of this is not available to XNA developers. For this reason, Microsoft created a special tool just for XNA to help you analyze the performance of your game project on the Xbox 360. The program is called "XNA Framework Remote Performance Monitor for Xbox 360" and you can find it at Start ➪ All Programs ➪ XNA Game Studio ➪ Tools. Check it out if you are serious about XNA console development.

Challenge: Write a Game Component

It is now your turn to write some code and test it on both the Windows and Xbox 360 platforms. To make it easy you just have to write a simple "frames per second" display in the upper-left corner of the screen. Remember the safe region on the Xbox 360; it would make sense to have different code for the Xbox 360 and the PC for the location of the frame per second number. Take a look at the following code to see how this can be done:

```
#if XBOX360
    Point fpsPos = new Point(2 + width / 15, 2 + height / 15);
#else
    Point fpsPos = new Point(2, 2);
#endif
```

You should plug the game component in the same way as the `SimpleCamera` class, and you should put it in the game namespace, too. For drawing the frames per second counter, use the last line of the `BaseGame` `.Draw` method before `base.Draw` is called. Then test a couple of unit tests (see the program class) and see if the frames per seconds counter is displayed correctly on Windows and the Xbox 360 if you have one.

To calculate the frames per second while a frame is rendered you could use a frame counter variable and then find out how long the application runs and divide these two values to get the number of frames you have each second on average. A better way would be just to count the frames every second and then start over at 0 every time a second has passed. See the Time and Fps Properties of the `Game` class and the `FpsCounter` class for more detail about this technique.

If you are unsure about your implementation, skip a few chapters ahead and see the code that is used in the games there (they all have fps counters and the code for it in them). For example, the Rocket Commander game always uses an fps display in debug mode and for all unit tests to quickly help you to see any performance drops if you do anything wrong. For just the component code take a look at the `FpsCounter` class from the source code for this chapter.

Summary

In this chapter, you learned a lot about the creation of a full-blown graphics engine, and you have gone through quite a lot of new graphics classes. Most of them were quite simple, but they are all still very important for the upcoming projects in this book.

In addition to the many unit tests you explored, you also learned about the process of converting 3D data to the 2D screen space and how to use right-handed matrices properly in XNA. To use these matrices in shaders, which are required to render anything in XNA, you took a quick look at vertex and pixel shaders, but you will dive much deeper into shaders in the next chapters.

If you take a look at the new classes (refer to Figure 5-15) and the project overview (refer to Figure 5-13) you can see that there are a lot more namespaces than in the previous projects. You also moved some classes around and refactored them to your new needs. This was important because the switch from 2D to 3D is not an easy one and you can always improve the way the classes work and make the unit tests simpler. When your engine becomes more and more complex, it is even more important to have solid framework with many unit tests you can fall back on in case something does not work the way you want it to. Otherwise it would just not be possible to write a unit test at the end of the book that renders a complex car with many shaders and over 20,000 polygons into a scene with shadow mapping, post screen effects, and cool glass shaders in just a few lines of code.

BaseGame is now your main entry point for the application and all internal classes are somehow connected to this class. BaseGame not only stores the device or content manager, but it also allows you to get the width and height of the render area, and all the matrices you need to render shaders. It stores many more useful capabilities in the properties that allow you, for example, to quickly enable or disable alpha blending.

Finally you learned a little bit more about using the Xbox 360 to test your graphics engine and all the pitfalls that can happen if you don't test your game on the console early enough. In the next chapter, you learn all about shaders and in Chapter 7, you will do some cool normal mapping, and you finally fix all these problems with the XNA models, tangent data, and so on. Then in Chapter 8, you learn about the powerful post screen shaders, which quickly give your whole game another look. As an example game, you can play Rocket Commander on the Xbox 360 with the help of XNA.

Shader Management

With the basic graphics engine now up and running you can focus on shader development for a while. As mentioned in the last chapter, everything that is rendered in XNA is done with the help of shaders, even if you don't interact with shaders directly when using the SpriteBatch class or the SimpleEffect class to simulate fixed function behavior. This chapter goes through the whole process of writing a shader from the ground up, and then you learn all about vertex buffers, the vertex shader process, and how pixel shaders finally bring the pixels on the screen. If you are already a shader expert, you probably want to skip this chapter or just quickly fly over it. But because the next chapters all rely on a fundamental knowledge of shaders, I want to make sure everyone is on the same level.

Because shaders are so very important in XNA, you should really try to follow all steps in this chapter if you don't have a strong foundation in shaders yet. The chapter is designed to let you follow every single step, and by the end of the chapter you will have written your first shader and you will not only understand all the steps in the process of shader creation, but also how to use them easily. Then you will be ready for the next chapters and you will be able to write your own shaders easily.

Before starting with cool normal mapping effects or post screen shaders in the next chapters, you have to learn the basics first. Shaders are not just used for high-quality effects; they also replace very simple rendering processes that were used in the days of the fixed function pipeline. After learning a little bit about the history of shaders and graphic card developments, you will go through the process of creating a simple shader just to render an example 3D model with per-pixel specular lighting and then import the shader into your graphics engine. To create shaders and test them out before you even start putting more code in your engine, you'll use FX Composer from NVIDIA, which is a great tool to get started and play around with your own shader ideas.

Shader Overview

Fixed function means that the GPU developers have programmed a fixed way to transform vertices and output pixels in a pre-programmed way directly on the GPU hardware. Early graphics hardware had no support for processing and transforming vertices, but after T&L (Transform & Lightning) able cards were introduced, it was much faster to calculate many vertices at once. But it was not possible to change the T&L behavior; you can only enable and disable certain features. For early games, this was quite nice because the GPU hardware did a lot of work and kept the CPU free for other tasks, and the GPU was a lot faster rendering 3D data than the CPU because the GPU is heavily optimized just for rendering polygons. If you hear of Direct3D 7.0-capable graphics cards, this is exactly what they could do; earlier cards had a similar behavior, but in Direct3D 5.0 and before, it was really hard to program directly on the hardware level of the GPU with execute buffers and things like that. Direct3D 7.0 simplified the rendering process when the NVIDIA GeForce series of graphic cards were available around 1999. It was now possible to render polygons with multiple textures at once, use texture compression to fit more textures in video memory, and use vertex buffers directly in video memory for improved performance.

History

Even after these great advancements in Direct3D 7.0, the games did not look much different — they just ran faster, maybe had more polygons, and made use of texture compression and multi-texture effects to show more textures and mix them together a little. The real revolution came with DirectX 8 and DirectX 9. DirectX 8 did finally remove the DirectDraw component and introduced vertex shaders, pixel shaders, and many effects — bump mapping, custom texture mapping, and so on — but it supports only Shader Model 1.0, and it was not very user-friendly in the beginning. Because of the many API changes, writing assembly shaders is no piece of cake.

DirectX 9 added support for HLSL (High Level Shader Language, which you learn about in this chapter) and new features with upcoming graphics cards such as HDR (high dynamic range) rendering and multiple render targets, which allow techniques such as deferred shading. DirectX 9 was very popular and many developers switched from OpenGL to DirectX just because OpenGL did not support shaders properly in the beginning and the OpenGL 2.0 Standard took way too long until it was approved. The extension model is also inferior for shaders than the Direct3D shader classes and it took a long time until better mechanisms were available in OpenGL. Direct3D 10 is also again much ahead of OpenGL, supporting Shader Model 4.0 and geometry shaders for more than a year now, and OpenGL has a lot of catching up to do. Geometry shaders are used to modify the geometry by adding, removing or otherwise modifying vertices before they even reach the vertex shader. While many cool techniques are possible this way, such as generating displacement mapped vertices from a height texture on-the-fly, or generating new 3D data on-the-fly, or modifying existing data, it is certainly hard to do and beyond the scope of this book anyway. Direct3D 10 works currently only on Windows Vista, but you can still do some shader model 4.0 development with OpenGL extensions in XP. But most Windows game developers will switch to Vista just for Direct3D 10 in a few years. Contrary to the belief of some people, there is no support for Shader Model 4.0 in DirectX 9; the so-called "DirectX 9.0L" is just a way to support DirectX 9.0 games and applications in Vista.

In my opinion, it is not a good thing to have so many different versions of DirectX around. Supporting DirectX 9, DirectX 10 and maybe even falling back to older hardware, which can only do DirectX 7 or 8, can increase the amount of work to get a good game engine up and running by several factors. Especially since implementing Direct3D 10 for the newest effects only works in Windows Vista and you probably always need to make a DirectX 9.0 version for anyone running Windows XP. That does not sound like a joy ride. Luckily for you, XNA does not have these problems; only one version is available and it will just support Shader Models 1–3 (DirectX 8 and 9) — you don't have to worry about anything else. It will run fine on Windows XP, Vista, and even on the Xbox 360.

For more information about the history of DirectX and the relationship to the Windows versions and the available hardware technology, see Figure 6-1. It shows that DirectX versions were usually bound in some way to the newest operating system from Microsoft and you can expect this to be true in the future, too. DirectX 1 and 2 were not really used. DirectX 3 did still have support for the retained (high level) mode, but that mode was not used much by game developers and it was depreciated in the next versions. DirectX 5 came out together with Windows 98 and was more widely used (the DirectX 4 Version number was skipped). DirectX advanced almost every year by a version until DirectX 7, which was more widely used, and the graphic hardware was becoming faster and faster every year. Together with Windows XP, DirectX 8 was released and introduced shaders for the first time. Half a year later DirectX 9 was already available and there were many versions. In the first years (2002, 2003, 2004) Microsoft named each new version with a new letter (DirectX 9.0a, DirectX 9.0b, and so on) and each version allowed the use of a new shader model for the newest graphic hardware; after 9.0c they stopped renaming the version, but many DirectX 9.0c versions (11 by now) were released, often only a very few months apart. Direct3D 10 has been in beta since late 2005 and will finally be released with Windows Vista in early 2007. Graphics hardware for Shader Model 4.0 was already available by the end of 2006 (NVIDIA GeForce 8800).

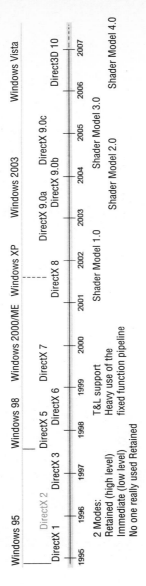

Figure 6-1

Shaders Everywhere in XNA

You already saw in the previous chapter that shaders are essential to render anything in XNA; you could not even put a line on the screen without having a shader to output the pixels on the screen. Sure, you can use the sprite classes for 2D interface graphics and maybe you will also use the SimpleEffect class to display some 3D data, but I don't like the SimpleEffect class and I will not use it in this book at all. I think it is too complicated to use and it really has no benefits when you are able to write your own shaders, which can be much simpler, faster, and more flexible. If you use simple effects, you have to use the pre-defined features. If you need anything more, you have to start over and write your own shader anyway. For the upcoming games in this book, you will mainly use normal mapping shaders to display 3D data and then some cool post screen shader effects to manipulate the final screen data. Both of these shader types cannot be emulated with the SimpleEffect class from the XNA framework, you will need custom shader code to make them work.

When you have worked with OpenGL or DirectX before and just used the fixed function pipeline, you might wonder why you put so much effort into shaders and why you can't just render some 3D data on the screen and be done with it. Well, writing is a little bit harder than that and although you could just render

.x models in DirectX without even knowing much about matrices or how the GPU works internally, you could not really modify much if you never learned about the details. It may be harder to learn all about shaders, but at least you get a much closer look at the graphics hardware and you will be able to understand much better how polygons are rendered on the screen, why certain bugs can occur, and how to quickly fix them.

One final thing I want to mention is the increased amount of work connected with the use of shaders. Not only will you, as a programmer, have to learn all about shaders — and you will probably write most of them unless you have a "shader guy" in your team — but your graphics artists (hopefully not you again) have to know about shaders, too. For example, it makes sense to use normal mapping shaders to achieve great looking effects, as in the following games (for example, Doom 3), but only if your 3D data not only consists of the basic geometry, but also provides you with the normal maps to achieve those effects.

Although it is discussed in greater detail in the following chapter, for now it will help you to know that you usually need a high-poly version (with up to several million polygons) of a 3D object and a low-poly version (just a couple of hundred or maybe few thousand polygons) for rendering. As you can see in Figure 6-2, the low-poly object can look quite bad without normal mapping applied, but once it is activated (see right side), the sphere looks much better.

As an alternative to creating high-detail models, which are usually a lot more work, you can also use a paint program to "paint" your own normal map by first drawing a height map and then converting it into a normal map. Usually such maps look much worse and you will never achieve the graphic quality of top games with this approach, but from time to time you can see games implementing normal maps this way to save money. In any case, your 3D graphic artist should be aware of all the new techniques and you should think about the way content is created before you start writing your engine or game code.

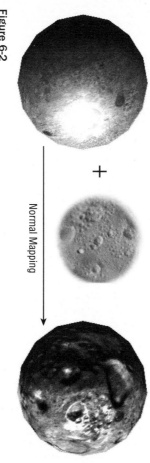

Normal Mapping

Figure 6-2

Example Games

If you want to see shaders in action just play any recent game — they almost all support shaders and even if you don't see heavy use of normal mapping and post screen effects, shaders might still be used for rendering the 3D models efficiently or executing shadow mapping techniques.

3D shooter games such as Doom 3, Half-Life 2, and Far Cry, and more recent games such as Fear, Ghost Recon, and Gears of War show really top-notch graphics and make great use of shader effects. Shooters benefit greatly from most new graphic technologies because you see your surrounding world in many different scaling and levels of details. First you see yourself or at least your weapons, and then you might be indoors and see walls and surrounding objects close up, but there are also big rooms and even the outside world where you can see to great distances. This means levels are usually big and you are still able to look closely everywhere you want to because you can move wherever you want to. Obviously graphics cards, especially earlier ones, are not able to store that much detail in video memory. Just mapping one big texture over the whole 3D level or just using the same wall texture all over the place is not really a good option. Instead, the game developers have to think of many cool techniques to improve the visual quality by using detail maps, using normal mapping to make the player think geometry is much more detailed, and mixing in post screen effects to make the overall game appear more realistic.

Other games such as strategy games or role playing games also benefit from shaders, but it took longer before strategy or role playing games even implemented shaders. These games focus more on the game play, how to render many units at once, and problems with zooming in and out.

Anyway, you want cool shader effects in your game, too, and if you look at a screenshot of Rocket Commander (see Figure 6-3), you can see some normal mapping and post screen shaders at work. Without shaders enabled (left screen), the game looks really boring and asteroids don't really look very real because the lighting is just not right. Please note that the non-shader version was just provided as an option to support older graphics hardware; the game was designed with shaders in mind. It would be possible to create a better screenshot for the fixed function version, but in real time the game would look even more unrealistic if the lighting did not change and if you didn't have any post screen effects.

For better examples of using shaders and the fixed function pipeline in games, take a look at water effects in 3D games. Water surfaces have evolved so much in the past few years that it is hard to keep up.

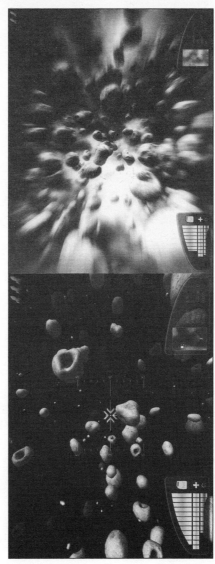

Figure 6-3

If you want to see more examples in games or have additional instruction, I recommend that you watch my Rocket Commander Video Tutorials at www.RocketCommander.com. Or check out one of the many existing XNA games that use shaders nowadays; some of my XNA games can be found at www.XnaProjects.net. There are also more links to useful XNA game development and shader resource sites.

Step-by-Step Shader Tutorial

This section goes through the whole process of creating your own shader. It will not be the most useful shader in the world, but it shows how to get shaders done and which tools can be used, and it prepares you for future shaders, which might be more exciting.

To see where you are heading, take a look at Figure 6-4, which shows the apple model from the last chapter, but this time your new shader SimpleShader.fx is applied onto it and another texture is used with some text on it.

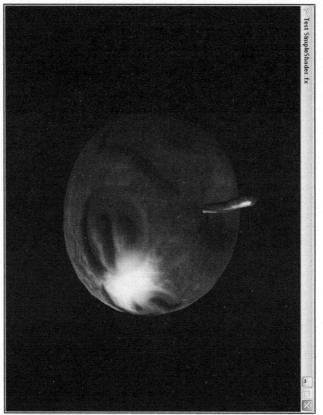

Figure 6-4

The SimpleShader.fx uses a normal vertex shader, which just transforms the 3D data, and a simple specular per-pixel technique for the pixel shader, which processes every pixel and calculates the ambient, diffuse, and specular components for it. This kind of calculation is not possible with a fixed function shader because you cannot program any special formulas for the pixel shader and the only way to show specular light effects is to do them in the vertex shader. You might ask why it is that bad to calculate the specular color component in the vertex shader. Well, if you have a low-polygon object like the apple here, or the sphere from the normal mapping example earlier, just calculating color components in the vertex shader will look very bad because you can only calculate the resulting colors for every vertex. If you take a look at the wireframe for the apple (see Figure 6-5), you can see that there are only a bunch of vertices, but you have many more pixels to fill in between. If you calculate only the vertices (the points that connect the wires), all data in between is not calculated the right way and can only be interpolated. But if a highlight like the one in Figure 6-4 is between two vertices, it will not be visible at all. By the way, if you want to render in wireframe mode, just add the following line before you render any 3D data:

```
BaseGame.Device.RenderState.FillMode = FillMode.WireFrame;
```

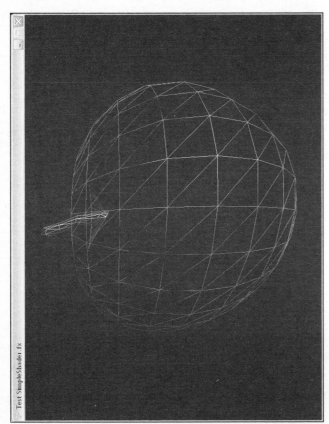

Test SimpleShader.fx

Figure 6-5

FX Composer

To get started with the little simpleShader.fx shader, you are going to use the freely available FX Composer tool, which you can download at the NVIDIA home page (www.Nvidia.com) in the developers section (or just Google for it).

After you have installed and started FX Composer, you will see the screen shown in Figure 6-6. It shows you several panels and can even be used by artists to test out textures and shader techniques, and to modify shader parameters such as color values, effect strengths, and more. For you as the developer, the most important panel is in the center, which shows the source code of the currently selected .fx file (similar to Visual Studio). As you can see, the .fx file looks very similar to C# or CPP and it has syntax highlighting and many keywords, which look similar to C#. For example, string is just a text string, float is just a floating-point number, and so on, just like in C#. But there are also other types such as float3 or float4x4. These numbers behind the float name just indicate the dimensions; float3 is the same structure as a Vector3 in XNA, which contains three floats, too (x, y, and z). Float4x4 describes a matrix and contains 16 float values (4 × 4); it is also in the same format as the XNA Matrix structure. The last variable types you have to know are for textures. Textures are defined with the texture type and you also have to specify a sampler to tell the shader how to use this texture (which filtering to use, which dimensions the texture has, and so on).

Last but not least, you see the optional semantics values (WorldViewProjection, Diffuse, Direction, and so on) behind variables indicated by a column. They tell FX Composer how to fill in this value and how to use it. For your XNA program these values do not matter, but it is very common to always specify these semantics. It allows you to use the shader in other programs such as FX Composer and 3D Studio

151

Max, and it is also helpful when you read through the shader later. The semantics tell you exactly which variable was intended for what use. In XNA, you are not limited to the use; you can set the `world` matrix to the `viewInverse`, for example, but that would be very confusing after a while, wouldn't it?

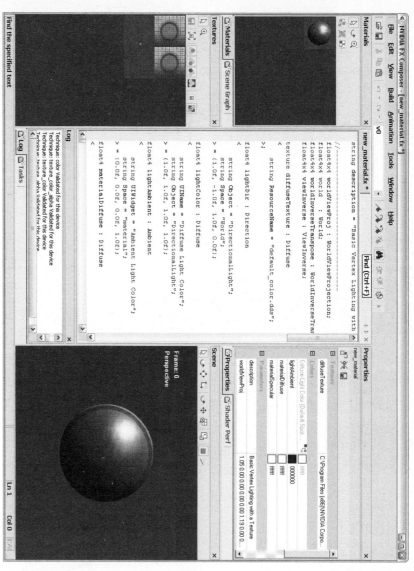

Figure 6-6

The other panels are not so important to you right now, but here's an explanation of what each of them does:

☐ Use the toolbar on the top to quickly load a shader and save your current file. The last button in the toolbar builds your shader and shows you any compiler errors in the log panel below (very similar to Visual Studio). Every time you build a shader, it gets saved automatically and you should use this button (or the Ctrl+F7 hotkey) as often as possible to make sure your shader always compiles and is saved.

☐ The Materials panel on the left side shows you a list of all shaders you have currently loaded into FX Composer with a little preview sphere, which changes as soon as you change any shader. The most important button here is the Assign to Selection button, which you use to set this material to the currently selected Scene panel object.

□ Textures panel on the lower-left side shows the textures used in the current shader. If you load external shaders, texture files are often not found because they reside in another directory or were not shipped with the .fx shader file. Textures that could not be loaded are shown as all blue bit-maps. You should make sure to load a texture first; otherwise the shader output is usually black and useless.

□ The Properties panel on the right side shows all the parameters in the shader you can set (or not, because they are already filled in by FX Composer, such as world, viewInverse, and so on). To make the shader work the same way in your XNA engine, you have to set all these values in your game engine, too, especially the matrices, which are dependent on the current camera position, viewport, and object in the 3D world. If you don't set a parameter, the default value is used, which can be set directly in the source code of the .fx file. To make sure all parameters always have valid values, even if the user or engine does not set any of the color parameters, for example, you should always make sure the parameters have useful default settings, such as setting the diffuse color to white:

```
float4 diffuseColor : Diffuse = {1.0f, 1.0f, 1.0f, 1.0f};
```

□ The Scene panel shows a simple example object such as the standard sphere to test your shader. You can also change it to a cube, cylinder, or something else. Alternatively, you can even import model files and play around with them, but most files do not work very well and the camera in FX Composer always gets messed up when you import scenes. I would just stick with the stan-dard sphere object and do all advanced tests in your XNA engine. FX Composer 2.0 will be much better for loading and handling custom 3D data and model files. You can use Collada files and even manage all the shaders that are used by every mesh in your model. Use FX Composer 2.0 if it is available by the time you read this.

FX File Layout

If you have worked with OpenGL before and had to write your vertex and fragment shaders (which just means vertex and pixel shaders in DirectX) yourself, you will be happy to hear that .fx files have all the shader code in one place and you can have many different pixel shader blocks in your .fx files to support multiple target configurations, such as pixel shader 1.1 for the GeForce 3 and pixel shader 2.0 support for the Nvidia GeForce FX or the ATI Radeon 9x series. Another useful side effect of supporting multiple ver-tex and pixel shaders in one single .fx file is to put similar shaders together and have them all use some common methods and the same shader parameters, which makes shader development much easier. In the past, especially for OpenGL you would define pixel and vertex shaders in separate files and they could not reuse any of your existing functionality again, which made shader programming much harder. For example, if you have a normal mapping shader for shiny metal surfaces, which looks really good on metal, you maybe want another more diffuse looking shader for stones, and you can put another shader technique in the same shader file and then select the used technique in your engine based on the material you want to display.

Figure 6-7 shows the SimpleShader.fx file layout as an example of a typical .fx file. More complex shaders will have more vertex and pixel shaders and more techniques. You don't have to create new ver-tex shaders or pixel shaders for each technique; you can combine them in any way you want to. Some shaders might also use multiple passes, which means they render everything with the first pass, and then the second pass is rendered with the exact same data again to add more effects or layers to a material. Using multiple passes is usually too slow for real-time applications because rendering with ten passes means your rendering time will be ten times higher than just rendering one pass with the same shader. In some cases it can be useful to use multiple passes to achieve effects that would otherwise not fit into the shader instruction limit or for post screen shaders where you can use the results from the first pass and modify them in the second pass to achieve much better effects. For example, blurring takes a lot of instructions because to get a good blurred result you have to mix many pixels to calculate every blurred point.

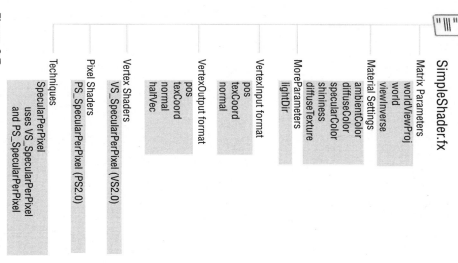

Figure 6-7

SimpleShader.fx

Matrix Parameters
worldViewProj
world
viewInverse

Material Settings
ambientColor
diffuseColor
specularColor
shininess
diffuseTexture

MoreParameters
lightDir

VertexInput format
pos
texCoord
normal

VertexOutput format
pos
texCoord
normal
halfVec

Vertex Shaders
VS_SpecularPerPixel (VS2.0)

Pixel Shaders
PS_SpecularPerPixel (PS2.0)

Techniques
SpecularPerPixel
uses VS_SpecularPerPixel
and PS_SpecularPerPixel

As an example, blurring with the range of 10 × 10 pixels would take 100-pixel read instructions, and that does not sound good if you have one or two million pixels you want to blur the whole screen. It is much better in this case just to blur in the x direction (10 pixel read instructions) and then take the result and blur it in the y direction in the second pass with another set of 10 pixel read instructions. Now your shader runs five times faster and looks pretty much the same. You can even achieve much better performance by first sampling down the background image from 1600 × 1200 to 400 × 300 and then perform the blurring, which gives you another performance improvement by the factor of 16 (now that is amazing).

Chapter 8 covers post screen shaders; but first, write the SimpleShader.fx file. As you see in Figure 6-7, the shader file uses quite a lot of shader parameters. Some of them are not so important because you could also hard-code the material settings directly into the shader, but this way you have the ability to change the color and appearance of the material in your engine and you can use the shader for many different materials. Other parameters such as the matrices and the texture are very important, and you cannot use the shader if these parameters are not set by the engine. Material data such as the color values and the texture should be loaded at the time you create the shader in your engine. The world matrices, light direction, and so on should be set each frame because this data can change every frame.

Parameters

If you want to follow the creation steps of this shader closely you might want to open up FX Composer now and start with an empty .fx file. Select File ⇨ New to create a new empty .fx file and delete all content. You will start with a completely empty file.

The first thing you might want to do to quickly remember what this file is about when you open it up later is to add a description or comment at the top of the file:

```
// Chapter 6: Writing a simple shader for XNA
```

As you saw in the SimpleShader.fx overview, you need several matrices first to be able to transform the 3D data in the vertex shader. This would be the worldViewProj matrix, the world matrix, and the viewInverse matrix. The worldViewProj matrix combines the world matrix, which puts the object you want to render at the correct position in the world; the view matrix, which transforms the 3D data to your camera view space (see Figure 5-7 from the previous chapter); and finally, the projection matrix, which puts the view space point to the correct screen position. This matrix allows you to quickly transform the input position with just one matrix multiply operation to get the final output position. The world matrix is then used to perform operations in the 3D world such as calculating the world normal, lighting calculations, and more. These calculations are important because the model data in the input vertices are not transformed yet, they are stored in the way the 3D modeler has created them, but in a game we usually want to rotate them, move them around or even scale them. The viewInverse is usually just used to get more information about the camera position, which can be extracted from this matrix by getting the fourth row:

```
float4x4 worldViewProj : WorldViewProjection;
float4x4 world : World;
float4x4 viewInverse : ViewInverse;
```

Each of these matrix values is a float 4 × 4 type (which is the same data type as Matrix in XNA) and you use the shader semantics to describe these values better and to have support in applications such as FX Composer or 3D Studio Max, which is important when the modeler wants to see how his 3D model looks with your shader. The cool thing is that it will look absolutely the same no matter whether it is displayed in FX Composer, 3D Studio, or in your engine. This fact can save you a lot of game development time; it especially shortens the testing process to get the appearance of all 3D objects right.

Time to save your file now. Just press the Build button or Ctrl+F7 and you are prompted to enter a name for the new shader. Just name it SimpleShader.fx and put it into your XnaGraphicEngine content directory so you can quickly use it in XNA later. After saving, FX Composer will tell you that "There were no techniques" and "Compilation failed" in the Tasks panel below the source code. That's okay — you will implement the techniques soon, but first implement the rest of the parameters. Because your shader uses a light to lighten up your apple (see Figure 6-4), you need a light, which can be either a point light or a directional light. Using point lights is a little bit more complicated because you have to calculate the light direction for every single vertex (or even for every single pixel if you like). The calculation becomes even more complex if you use a spot light. Another problem with point lights is that they usually become weaker over the distance and you will need a lot of lights if your 3D world is big. Directional lights are much easier and are very useful to quickly simulate the sun in an outside environment, like for the game you will create in the next chapters.

```
float3 lightDir : Direction
<
    string Object = "DirectionalLight";
    string Space = "World";
> = { 1, 0, 0 };
```

In addition to ambient lighting, which just adds a general brightness to all materials, the following light types are commonly used in games:

❑ **Directional Lights** — Simplest light type, very easy to implement. You can directly use the light direction for the internal lighting calculations in shaders. In the real world, no directional lighting exists; even the sun is just a big distant point light, but it is much easier to implement it for outdoor lighting scenes.

❑ **Point Lights** — Calculating a single point light is not much harder, but you have to calculate the falloff to make the light weaker over distance. If you need the light direction, it needs to be calculated in the shader, too, which slows things down. But the main problem for point lights is that you need more than one light for any scene bigger than just a room. 3D shooters usually use tricks to limit the amount of point lights that can be seen at the same time, but for outdoor games such as strategy games, it is much easier to use a directional light and just add a few light effects and simple point lights for special effects.

❑ **Spot Lights** — These are the same thing as point lights, but they point in just one direction and lighten only a small spot with help of a light cone calculation. Spot lights are a little bit more difficult to calculate, but if you are able to skip the hard part of the lighting calculation (for example, when using a complex normal mapping shader with multiple spot lights), it can even be a lot faster than using point lights. Currently, you can only do conditional statements such as "if" in Shader Model 3.0; previous Shader versions support these statements, too, but all "if" statements and "for" loops will just be unrolled and expanded — you will not gain a great performance benefit as you do on Shader Model 3.0.

Now the preceding code does look a little bit more complicated; the first line is pretty much the same as for the matrices. float3 specifies that you use a Vector3 and Direction tells you that lightDir is used as a directional light. Then inside the brackets an Object and a Space variable are defined. These variables are called *annotations* and they specify the use of the parameter for FX Composer or other external programs such as 3D Studio Max. These programs now know how to use this value and they will automatically assign it to the light object that may already exist in the scene. This way, you can just load the shader file in a 3D program, and it will work immediately without having to link up all light, material settings, or textures by hand.

Next you are going to define the material settings; you are going to use the same material settings that a standard DirectX material uses. This way, you can use similar shaders or older DirectX materials in programs such as 3D Studio Max, and all color values are automatically used correctly. In the engine, you usually will just set the ambient and diffuse colors and sometimes you also specify another shininess value for the specular color calculation. You might notice that you did not use any annotations — you can specify them here, too, but material settings work fine in both FX Composer and 3D Studio Max even if you don't define annotations. The engine can also just use the default values in case you don't want to over-write the default values for your unit test later.

```
float4 ambientColor : Ambient  = { 0.2f, 0.2f, 0.2f, 1.0f };
float4 diffuseColor : Diffuse  = { 0.5f, 0.5f, 0.5f, 1.0f };
float4 specularColor : Specular = { 1.0, 1.0f, 1.0f };
float shininess : SpecularPower = 24.0f;
```

Last but not least, your shader needs a texture to look a little bit more interesting than just showing a boring gray sphere or apple. Instead of using the apple texture from the original apple, as in the last chapter, you are going to use a new test texture, which will become more interesting in the next chapter when you add normal mapping. The texture is called marble.dds (see Figure 6-8):

```
texture diffuseTexture : Diffuse
<
    string ResourceName = "marble.dds";
>;
sampler DiffuseTextureSampler = sampler_state
{
    Texture = <diffuseTexture>;
    MinFilter=linear;
    MagFilter=linear;
    MipFilter=linear;
};
```

The ResourceName annotation is used in FX Composer only, and it automatically loads the marble.dds file from the same directory the shader is in (make sure the marble.dds file is in the XnaGraphicEngine content directory, too). The sampler just specifies that you want to use linear filtering for the texture.

Figure 6-8

Vertex Input Format

Before you can finally write your vertex and pixel shader, you have to specify the way vertex data is passed between your game and the vertex shader, which is done with the VertexInput structure. It uses the same data as the XNA structure VertexPositionNormalTexture, which is used for the apple model. The position is transformed with the worldViewProj matrix defined earlier in the vertex shader later. The position is just used to get the texture coordinate for every pixel you are going to render in the pixel shader later, and the normal value is required for the lighting computation.

You should always make sure that your game code and your shaders are using the exact same vertex input format. If you don't do that, the wrong data might be used for the texture coordinates or vertex data might be missing and mess up the rendering. The best practice is to define your own vertex structure in the application (see the TangentVertex structure in the next chapter) and then define that same vertex structure layout, in your game code before calling the shader. Also set the used vertex declaration, which describes the vertex structure in the shader. You can find more details about that in the next chapter.

```
struct VertexInput
{
    float3 pos      : POSITION;
    float2 texCoord : TEXCOORD0;
    float3 normal   : NORMAL;
};
```

Similarly, you must define the data that is passed from the vertex shader to the pixel shader. This may sound unfamiliar at first and I promise you this is the last thing you have to do to finally get to the shader code. If you take a look at Figure 6-9, you can see the way 3D geometry is traveling from your application content data to the shader, which uses the graphics hardware to finally end up on the screen in the way you want it to be. Although this whole process is more complicated than just using a fixed function pipeline as in the old DirectX days, it allows you to optimize code at every point, and you can modify data in every single step. Either at the application level, or dynamically when the vertices are processed in the vertex shader or you can modify the color of the final pixel when it is rendered on the screen.

The VertexOutput structure of your shader passes the transformed vertex position, the texture coordinate for the used texture, and a normal and halfVec vector to perform the specular color calculation directly in the pixel shader. Both vectors have to be passed as texture coordinates because the data passed from the vertex to the pixel shader can only be position, color, or texture coordinate data. But that does not matter; you can still use the data the same way as in the VertexInput structure. It is very important to use the correct semantics (Position, TexCoord0, and Normal) in the VertexInput structure to tell FX Composer, your application, or any other program that uses the shader.

Because you define the VertexOutput structure yourself and it is only used inside the shader, you can put anything you want in here, but you should keep it as short as possible. You are also limited by the number of texture coordinates you can pass over to the pixel shader (four in pixel shader 1.1, eight in pixel shader 2.0).

```
struct VertexOutput
{
    float4 pos      : POSITION;
    float2 texCoord : TEXCOORD0;
    float3 normal   : TEXCOORD1;
    float3 halfVec  : TEXCOORD2;
};
```

The Journey of the 3D Geometric Data

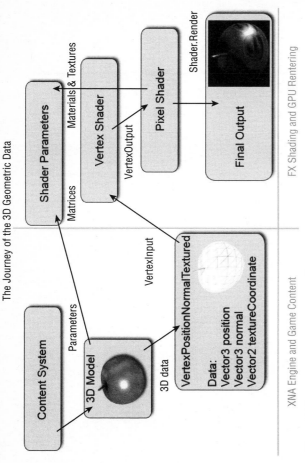

Content System	Shader Parameters
Parameters	
Matrices	Materials & Textures

3D Model

3D data

VertexPositionNormalTextured

Data:
Vector3 position
Vector3 normal
Vector2 textureCoordinate

VertexInput

Vertex Shader

VertexOutput

Pixel Shader

Shader.Render

Final Output

XNA Engine and Game Content   FX Shading and GPU Rentering

Figure 6-9

Vertex Shader

The vertex shader now takes the VertexInput data and transforms it to the screen position for the pixel shader, which finally renders the output pixel for every visible polygon point. The first lines of the vertex shader usually look very much the same as for every other vertex shader, but you often pre-calculate values at the end of the vertex shader for use in the pixel shader. If you are using pixel shader 1.1, you cannot do certain things such as normalizing vectors or executing complex mathematical functions such as power. But even if you use pixel shader 2.0 (as you are for this shader), you might want to pre-calculate certain values to speed up the pixel shader, which is executed for every single visible pixel. Usually you will have far fewer vertices than pixels, and every complex calculation you make in the vertex shader can speed up the performance of the pixel shader several times. The following code shows a typical vertex shader, where all the important variables are calculated and whatever is needed in the pixel shader is passed through the VertexOutput structure.

```
// Vertex shader
VertexOutput VS_SpecularPerPixel(VertexInput In)
{
    VertexOutput Out = (VertexOutput)0;
    float4 pos = float4(In.pos, 1);
    Out.pos = mul(pos, worldViewProj);
    Out.texCoord = In.texCoord;
    Out.normal = mul(In.normal, world);
    // Eye pos
    float3 eyePos = viewInverse[3];
    // World pos
    float3 worldPos = mul(pos, world);
    // Eye vector
```

```
float3 eyeVector = normalize(eyePos-worldPos);
// Half vector
Out.halfVec = normalize(eyeVector+lightDir);

return Out;
} // VS_SpecularPerPixel(In)
```

The vertex shader takes the VertexInput structure as a parameter, which is automatically filled in and passed from the 3D application data by the shader technique you will define at the end of the .fx file. The important part here is the VertexOutput structure, which is returned from the vertex shader and then passed to the pixel shader. The data is not just passed 1:1 to the pixel shader, but all values are interpolated between every single polygon point (see Figure 6-10).

An example polygon with 3 vertices

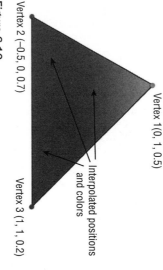

Vertex 1 (0, 1, 0.5)

Vertex 2 (−0.5, 0, 0.7)

Vertex 3 (1, 1, 0.2)

Interpolated positions and colors

Figure 6-10

This is of course a good thing for any position and color values because the output looks much better when values are interpolated correctly. But if you use normalized vectors, they can get messed up in the process of the interpolation that the GPU does automatically. To fix this, you have to re-normalize vectors in the pixel shader (see Figure 6-11). Sometimes this can be ignored because the artifacts are not visible, but for your specular per pixel calculation, it will be visible on every object with a low polygon count. If you are using pixel shader 1.1, you can't use the normalize method in the pixel shader. Instead you can use a helper cube map, which contains pre-calculated normalized values for every possible input value. For more details, please take a look at the NormalMapping and ParallaxMapping shader effects of the next chapters.

If you take a quick look at the source code again (or if you are typing it in yourself to write your first shader), you can see that you start by calculating the screen output position. Because all matrix operations expect a Vector4, you have to convert your input Vector3 value to Vector4 and set the w component to 1 to get the default behavior of the translation part of the worldViewProj matrix (translation means movement for matrices).

Next, the texture coordinate is just passed over to the pixel shader; you are not interested in manipulating it. You can, for example, multiply the texture coordinates here or add an offset. Sometimes it can even be useful to duplicate the texture coordinate and then use it several times in the pixel shader with different multiplication factors and offsets for detail mapping or water shaders.

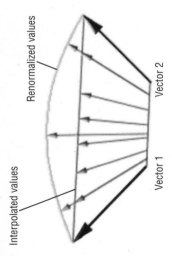

Renormalized values

Interpolated values

Vector 1

Vector 2

Figure 6-11

Each normal vector from the apple model is then transformed to the world space, which is important when you rotate the apple model around. All normals are rotated then as well; otherwise, the lighting will not look correct because the `lightDir` value does not know how each model is rotated, and the `lightDir` values are just stored in the world space. Before applying the world matrix, your vertex data is still in the so-called object space, which can be used for several effects, too, if you like to do that (for example, wobble the object around or scale it in one of the object directions).

The last thing you do in the vertex shader is to calculate the half vector between the light direction and the eye vector, which helps you with calculating the specular color in the pixel shader. As I said before, it is much more effective to calculate this here in the vertex shader instead of re-calculating this value for every single point over and over again. The half vector is used for phong shading and it generates specular highlights when looking at objects from a direction close to the light direction (see Figure 6-12).

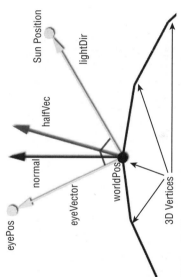

Sun Position

lightDir

halfVec

normal

eyeVector

worldPos

eyePos

3D Vertices

Figure 6-12

Pixel Shader

The pixel shader is responsible for finally outputting some pixels on the screen. To test this, you can just output any color you like; for example, the following code outputs just a red color for every pixel that is rendered on the screen:

```
// Pixel shader
float4 PS_SpecularPerPixel(VertexOutput In) : COLOR
{
    return float4(1, 0, 0, 1);
} // PS_SpecularPerPixel(In)
```

If you press Build now the shader still does not compile because you have not defined a technique yet. Just define the following technique to get the shader to work. The syntax of techniques is always similar; usually you just need one pass (called P0 here) and then you define the used vertex and pixel shaders by specifying the used vertex and pixel shader versions:

```
technique SpecularPerPixel
{
    pass P0
    {
        VertexShader = compile vs_2_0 VS_SpecularPerPixel();
        PixelShader = compile ps_2_0 PS_SpecularPerPixel();
    } // pass P0
} // SpecularPerPixel
```

Now you are finally able to compile the shader in FX Composer and you should see the output shown in Figure 6-13. Make sure you have the shader assigned to the selection in the Scene panel in FX Composer (click the sphere, and then click the SimpleShader.fx material in the Materials panel and click the Apply Material button).

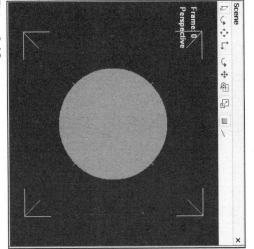

Figure 6-13

The next step you should take is to put the marble.dds texture onto the sphere. This is done with the help of the tex2D method in the pixel shader, which expects a texture sampler as the first parameter and the texture coordinates as the second parameter. Replace the return float4 line from the previous code with the following code to texture your 3D object:

```
float4 textureColor = tex2D(DiffuseTextureSampler, In.texCoord);
return textureColor;
```

After compiling the shader you should now see the result shown in Figure 6-14. If you just see a black sphere or no sphere at all you probably don't have the marble.dds texture loaded. See the Textures panel and make sure the texture is loaded as described previously; you can click the diffuseTexture in the Properties panel and load it yourself.

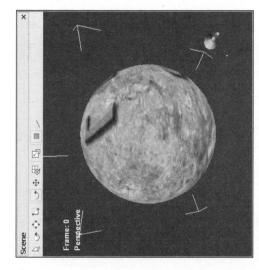

Figure 6-14

The last thing you have to do is calculate the diffuse and specular color components based on the lightDir and halfVec values. As mentioned, you also want to make sure the normals are re-normalized in the pixel shader to get rid of any artifacts.

```
// Pixel shader
float4 PS_SpecularPerPixel(VertexOutput In)   : COLOR
{
    float4 textureColor = tex2D(DiffuseTextureSampler, In.texCoord);
    float3 normal = normalize(In.normal);
    float brightness = dot(normal, lightDir);
    float specular = pow(dot(normal, In.halfVec), shininess);
    return textureColor *
        (ambientColor +
        brightness * diffuseColor) +
        specular * specularColor;
} // PS_SpecularPerPixel(In)
```

163

The diffuse color is calculated by taking the dot product of the re-normalized normal (in world space, see the vertex shader discussion earlier in this chapter) and the lightDir, which is also in world space. It is always important that you are in the same space if you do any matrix, dot, or cross product calculations. Otherwise, the results will be wrong. The dot product behaves just the way you need for the diffuse color calculation. If the lightDir and the normal point in the same direction it means that the normal is point-ing right at the sun and the diffuse color should be at the maximum value (1.0); if the normal is at a 90 degree angle, the dot product will return 0 and the diffuse component is zero. To even see the sphere from the dark side, the ambient color is added, which lights up the sphere even when no diffuse or specular light is visible.

Then the specular color is calculated with the Phong formula to take the dot product of the normal and the half vector you calculated in the vertex shader. Then you take the power of the result by the shininess fac-tor to make the area affected by the specular highlight much smaller. The higher the shininess value, the smaller the highlight gets (play around with the shininess value if you want to see it). At the end of the pixel shader you can finally add all color values together. You multiply the result by the texture color and return everything to be painted on the screen (see Figure 6-15).

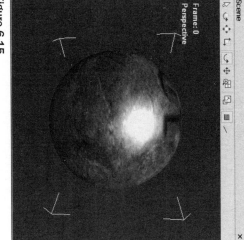

Figure 6-15

You are now finished with working on the shader. The saved shader file can now even be used in other programs such as 3D Studio Max to help artists to see how the 3D models will look in the game engine. Next you are going to implement the shader into your XNA engine.

Importing the Shader into Your Engine

To get the shader you just wrote into your graphics engine, you basically do the same thing FX Composer does to display the shader. Thanks to DirectX or XNA, it is easy to load a shader effect file and set all required parameters (you already did that in the last chapter for the line rendering shader). In the next chapter, you are going to use a more general class that accepts many different shaders and uses a more optimized way to set all required shader parameters, but for this chapter you just want to get the SimpleShader.fx file to work in your engine.

As usual, you start by defining the unit test. Create a new file called `SimpleShader.cs` in the `Shaders` namespace and write the following code:

```
#region Unit Testing
public static void TestSimpleShader()
{
    SimpleShader shader = null;
    Model testModel = null;
    Texture testTexture = null;
    TestGame.Start("Test SimpleShader.fx",
        delegate
        {
            shader = new SimpleShader();
            testModel = new Model("Apple");
            testTexture = new Texture("Marble");
        },
        delegate
        {
            // Render model
            shader.RenderModel(testModel.XnaModel, testTexture);
        });
} // TestSimpleShader
#endregion
```

The unit test should compile except for the `RenderModel` method of the new `SimpleShader` class, which has not been defined. Let's quickly define that method:

```
public void RenderModel(XnaModel someModel, Texture texture)
{
} // RenderModel(someModel, texture)
```

The unit test compiles now and you can start it just to see a blank screen.

Compiling Shaders

To get anything useful on the screen for your little unit test, you have to load and compile the shader first. To do that, you use the content pipeline of XNA as you did for models and textures before. Just drop the .fx file into your project (put it into the content directory together with the rest of the textures and models) and it will get compiled automatically when the project is built. You will even get a shader compilation error in case the shader does not compile. This way, you don't have to start your game and then have to track down an exception thrown by the shader compiler at runtime; you can already make sure the shader is correct before the game is run. While you are at it, make sure the `marble.dds` texture is also in the content directory and gets compiled by XNA; you use this texture in your unit test.

Loading the compiled effect is as simple as loading a texture. Just define an effect variable and then load it in the `SimpleShader` constructor:

```
#region Variables
Effect effect = null;
#endregion
#region Constructor
public SimpleShader()
```

```
{
    effect = BaseGame.Content.Load<Effect>(
        Path.Combine(Directories.ContentDirectory, "SimpleShader"));
} // SimpleShader()
#endregion
```

If you are on the Windows platform, you can also dynamically load shaders (not precompiled already by the XNA Framework), which can be useful to test and change shaders while your game is running. I usually use un-compiled shader files for most of the shader development time and then I put them into the content pipeline when the game is done or I don't want to change the shaders anymore. The following code is used to compile and load shaders yourself.

Please note that these classes and methods are available only on the Windows platform. Use #if !XBOX360 #endif around these lines if you want the code to get compiled on the Xbox 360 (where dynamically reloading shaders is not supported and does not make so much sense anyway):

```
CompiledEffect compiledEffect = Effect.CompileEffectFromFile(
    Path.Combine("Shaders", shaderContentName + ".fx"),
    null, null, CompilerOptions.None,
    TargetPlatform.Windows);
effect = new Effect(BaseGame.Device,
    compiledEffect.GetEffectCode(), CompilerOptions.None, null);
```

Using Parameters

As you learned in the process of creating your shader, the world, view, and projection matrices are really important to transform your 3D data and get everything correctly on the screen. To set all these shader parameters, you just use the RenderModel method, which is called by your unit test:

```
BaseGame.WorldMatrix =
    Matrix.CreateScale(0.25f, 0.25f, 0.25f);
effect.Parameters["worldViewProj"].SetValue(
    BaseGame.WorldMatrix *
    BaseGame.ViewMatrix *
    BaseGame.ProjectionMatrix);
effect.Parameters["world"].SetValue(
    BaseGame.WorldMatrix);
effect.Parameters["viewInverse"].SetValue(
    BaseGame.InverseViewMatrix);
effect.Parameters["lightDir"].SetValue(
    BaseGame.LightDirection);
effect.Parameters["diffuseTexture"].SetValue(
    texture.XnaTexture);
```

The first thing that happens in this code is that the world matrix is set. This is very important because if the world matrix is not set and perhaps has some crazy values from any previous operation, the 3D model is rendered at some random location you don't want it to be. Because your apple model is pretty big, you scale it down a little to fit on the screen with your default SimpleCamera class from the last chapter.

Then the worldViewProj matrix is calculated and you also set all the other matrices, the lightDir value, and even the diffuseTexture, which is important because by just loading the shader effect, none of the textures are loaded automatically as in FX Composer; you still have to set these values yourself. If you load

Models from the XNA content pipeline, XNA does help you out a little and will automatically load all used textures from the Model data. In your case, you just set the texture you have loaded in the unit test to display the marble.dds texture, as in FX Composer.

Vertex Formats

Before you can render the data used in your 3D apple model, you have to make sure that your application and the shader know which vertex format to use. In DirectX it was possible to just set one of the predefined fixed function vertex formats, but these formats do not exist anymore and you can't just set them. Instead, you have to define the full vertex declaration in a similar way as you did in the shader for the VertexInput structure. Because you are just using the built-in VertexPositionNormalTexture structure, you don't have to define everything yourself, but in the next chapter you will learn how to do that with your custom TangentVertex format.

```
// Use the VertexPositionNormalTexture vertex format in SimpleShader.fx
BaseGame.Device.VertexDeclaration =
    new VertexDeclaration(BaseGame.Device,
    VertexPositionNormalTexture.VertexElements);
```

You don't really have to create a new vertex declaration every time you call RenderModel, but just to keep things simple you build a new vertex declaration every call. It takes the graphics device as the first parameter and the vertex elements array from the XNA VertexPositionNormalTexture structure as the second parameter. For more information, refer to Chapter 7.

Rendering with Shaders

To render the apple with your shader now, you first specify the technique you want to use (which is by default set to the first technique anyway, but it is good to know how to set techniques). For rendering a shader, you will always use the CurrentTechnique property of the effect class. Then you go through the technique the same way FX Composer does — you draw all 3D data for every pass you have in the technique (as I said before, usually you just have one pass). Rendering the apple itself is not that easy because the only method XNA gives you to render it is to call mesh.Draw for every mesh that is in the model after setting the required shader parameters first — as you saw in the last chapter when you wrote the Model class.

Also missing from the XNA Framework are the mesh helper methods to create boxes, spheres, or teapots. You will also notice that most of the Direct3DX namespace functionality is just non-existent in XNA. You can only access some of these methods when writing your own content processor, but that does not help you when writing your engine or wanting to test models, meshes, or shaders. You also can't access any of the vertices or the index data of the loaded models because all the vertex and index buffers are write-only, which is good for fast hardware access, but bad if you just want to modify anything. In the following code block, you are just mimicking the behavior of the mesh.Draw method, just without the effect code that is used because you have your own effect class here.

```
effect.CurrentTechnique = effect.Techniques["SpecularPerPixel"];
effect.Begin();
foreach (EffectPass pass in effect.CurrentTechnique.Passes)
{
    pass.Begin();
```

```
// Render all meshes
foreach (ModelMesh mesh in someModel.Meshes)
{
    // Render all mesh parts
    foreach (ModelMeshPart part in mesh.MeshParts)
    {
        // Render data our own way
        BaseGame.Device.Vertices[0].SetSource(
            mesh.VertexBuffer, part.StreamOffset, part.VertexStride);
        BaseGame.Device.Indices = mesh.IndexBuffer;
        // And render
        BaseGame.Device.DrawIndexedPrimitives(
            PrimitiveType.TriangleList,
            part.BaseVertex, 0, part.NumVertices,
            part.StartIndex, part.PrimitiveCount);
    } // foreach
    pass.End();
} // foreach
} // for
effect.End();
```

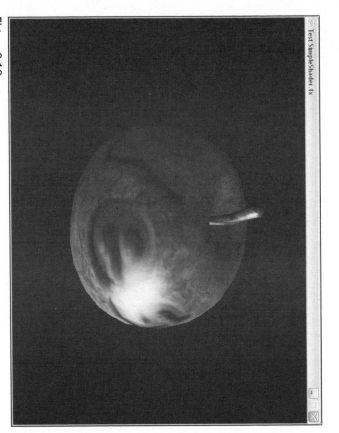

Figure 6-16

This means you go through every pass (again, you just have one) and draw all meshes (also just one for your apple) and then you draw all mesh parts (guess what, again only one) by setting the vertex and index buffers with help of the XNA properties of the Device class. Finally you call DrawIndexedPrimitives to render all the vertices inside the shader. Then the pass and the shader are closed and you can finally see your apple with the marble.dds texture on the screen (see Figure 6-16).

Testing the Shader

Just because everything works now, it does not mean you can't play around a little bit with your shader and test other material settings, textures, or render modes.

To achieve the wireframe effect that you saw in Figure 6-5 previously, you can just change the `FillMode` before starting the shader:

```
BaseGame.Device.RenderState.FillMode = FillMode.WireFrame;
```

Or you can manipulate the shader material a little bit; if you want you can load another texture or even another model. The shader class is written in a way that allows you to load any XNA model and texture and test it out. One simple way to modify the output of the shader would be to change the ambient, diffuse, and specular values to make an evil alien apple (see Figure 6-17).

```
effect.Parameters["ambientColor"].SetValue(
    Color.Blue.ToVector4());
effect.Parameters["diffuseColor"].SetValue(
    Color.Orange.ToVector4());
effect.Parameters["specularColor"].SetValue(
    Color.Orchid.ToVector4());
```

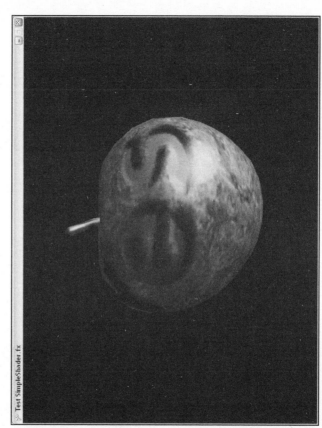

Figure 6-17

Please note that you have to convert the colors to `Vector4` because `SetValue` does not have an overload for color values (seems like there was someone really lazy). When you set any effect parameters between a shader `Begin` and `End` call, you should also call the `Effect CommitChanges` method to make sure that all your changes are sent to the GPU. If you call Begin after setting the parameters like in the SimpleShader class you don't have to worry about that.

In the next chapter, you are going to use effect parameters much more effectively because setting them by name is not really fast and is also error prone. If you mistype one of the parameters, an exception will occur and that's never good.

Challenge

As a little challenge to get more familiar with shaders, you should now write a simple DiffusePerPixel shader, which works the same way as the SpecularPerPixel shader except for the specular color component, which is cut out. DiffusePerPixel will be more useful for non-shiny materials. To switch between SpecularPerPixel and DiffusePerPixel you should have two techniques in the SimpleShader .fx file.

With the following code you can then dynamically choose between the two techniques based on whether or not the user currently pressed space:

```
if (Input.Keyboard.IsKeyDown(Keys.Space))
    effect.CurrentTechnique = effect.Techniques["DiffusePerPixel"];
else
    effect.CurrentTechnique = effect.Techniques["SpecularPerPixel"];
```

If you are still very excited about the whole shader idea, you also might want to check out the shaders included with FX Composer in the HLSL directory of the program. Maybe you can play around with them a little or even try to implement them into SimpleShader.fx.

Have fun!

Summary

This chapter reinforced how shaders work, why you have to do certain things such as declaring vertex formats, and how vertex data is processed through the shaders. Most of the time when I talk to other developers who have not worked with shaders before, they are afraid of shaders and do not have a clear concept of what they are all about. If you have worked with shaders before, this chapter might not have been the most exciting, but maybe you learned some details you didn't know.

The following steps describe how 3D data is processed in XNA:

❑ Get the 3D geometry data from the Model class (or define it yourself with vertex buffers).

❑ Make sure your shader and your XNA code use the same vertex formats.

❑ Call the shader technique and execute each pass by rendering your 3D data.

❑   The vertex shader processes the input data and passes it to the pixel shader with the `VertexOutput` structure. The positions get transformed from world coordinates to the screen position.

❑   The pixel shader finally brings each pixel of every rendered visible polygon on the screen. Always try to make the pixel shader as short and fast as possible.

In the next chapter, you use this information and create great looking `NormalMapping` shader effects. Then you will be ready to create your next game in Chapter 8, where you also add cool post screen shader effects.

7

Realism Through Normal Mapping

The really cool advantage of using shaders is that every step of the rendering pipeline can be customized. For Pixel Shader version 1.1 (GeForce 3), you have just eight instructions available. As such, the programmable pipeline is not so great because all it does is emulate the Pixel Shader instructions with preprogrammed hardware. Pixel Shader 2.0 is much more flexible by allowing many more functions (as you saw in the previous chapter the `normalize` and `pow` methods are only available for Pixel Shader 2.0 and up) and enabling you to write more instructions (the limit is 96 here, but some methods require more than one instruction).

Pixel Shader version 3.0 is even better by enabling better flow control, which means you can exit the shader code based on programmed conditions to optimize the performance. Complex shaders in Pixel Shader 3.0 can have up to 512 instructions, and even with very fast graphics hardware, this is a lot. When rendering many millions of pixels it takes a lot of time to execute that many instructions for every single pixel, even when you have 16, 24, or 32 pixel shader units working in parallel. The new NVidia 8800 GTX graphic card has even more shader units working in parallel — it has 128. Sometimes you might want to skip complex calculations if a pixel is not affected by several lights or doesn't lie in the shadow. This way you can still achieve great looking and expensive Pixel shader effects, but you limit them to where they are required. Sounds great, but in reality most new games just use Pixel Shader 2.0 because it is supported by many graphics cards. Most games do not support the more expensive graphics hardware.

While the Shader Model 4.0 was introduced with Direct3D 10 in early 2006, the first graphics hardware (GeForce 8800) to support it wasn't available until the end of 2006. Meanwhile, Direct3D 10 only works on Vista, and the hardware is quite expensive. It will take a while until game developers can fully utilize shader model 4.0. XNA currently only supports shader models 1.1 up to 3.0. Shader Model 4.0 allows even more instructions and introduces geometry shaders that manipulate and add geometry data before your vertex and pixel shaders are executed. All shader units are also unified in Shader Model 4.0, which means you can use them for whatever you want. There are no longer just 8 vertex and 16 pixel units; you have 128 shader units and they all can be used for geometry, vertex, and pixels shaders. This is great for amazing effects such as displacement mapping and level-of-detail effects. In 2007, you may see some cool demos, but games will probably not use geometry shaders until 2008 or later.

Adding Detail to Objects

For your next couple of games in this book, you want to use Normal Mapping shaders. These greatly improve the realism of many 3D objects, especially if they have a lot of structure on the surface and many little details, riffs, tubes, cables, and so on, that would normally cost many million of polygons to display all those details correctly (see Figure 7-1). You will often see Normal Mapping examples on Internet sites that compare totally ridiculous looking objects and bad textures with a super high resolution Normal Mapped object. I tried to use a real object from a real game here (it is used in the racer game later in this book). You can see that the version without Normal Mapping looks okay, too. The diffuse texture, however, is already shaded a little bit. You can render without using the Normal Map and the object still looks okay. With Normal Mapping enabled, the object looks even better and even though it has only 1000 polygons, it looks very smooth (see right side of Figure 7-1).

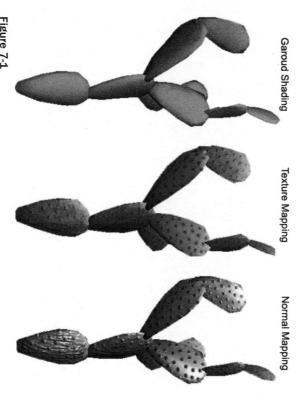

Garoud Shading   Texture Mapping   Normal Mapping

Figure 7-1

Even better effects can be achieved through Parallax Mapping (faking the height) Offset Mapping (multiple layers to fake the height even better), or Displacement Mapping (really moving vertices around, possible with Shader Model 4, but very expensive and slow computation). These techniques are a bit more complex and they also require a height map in addition to the diffuse and Normal Map textures. But just using Normal Mapping looks fine, too.

Chapter 7: Realism Through Normal Mapping

The good thing about Normal Mapping is that it is not that hard to implement if you have a shader-enabled graphics card. It even works with the very old GeForce 3 (Pixel Shader version 1.1), and can also be improved for Pixel Shader 2.0 support to enable better specular lighting effects on today's hardware. In the previous chapter you already learned about creating pixel shaders, how vertices are transformed and how each pixel finally gets rendered on the screen.

Normal Mapping uses an additional texture. The diffuse texture is used to display the basic material structure, color, and so on. The Normal Map then adds additional 3D detail by supplying an additional normal vector for every single pixel you are going to render in the Pixel Shader (see Figure 7-2).

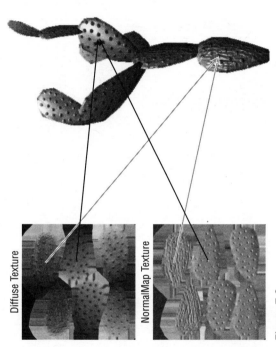

Diffuse Texture

NormalMap Texture

Figure 7-2

Please note that if you open up the KaktusSeg.dds and KaktusSegNormal.dds textures of the cactus 3D model, the Normal Map bitmap will look different. The Normal Map texture represents a normal vector for the surface of the polygon. This data is stored in tangent space, which is discussed in Figure 7-4 in a bit. To get a normal vector from the color data in the texture, the formula (each r, g and b value-0.5)/0.5 is used (see Figure 7-3). The RGB data in the Normal Map viewed as floats lets you use this formula. To convert from RGB to floats, just divide by the floating value 255. This is done automatically in your pixel shader. It is always easier to work with these floating-point values instead of the byte data stored in the bitmap file. and red channels reversed. This trick is used to compress the normal texture by a factor of 1:4 without losing much detail, and the result still looks great. More details about this technique in a second — just remember that internally the Normal Map texture resembles the texture in Figure 7-2; the compressed version just stores the data differently.

To compute the light for every pixel in the Pixel Shader of your Normal Mapping shader, the Normal Map texture data is used. Every pixel in the Normal Map texture represents a normal vector for the surface of the polygon. This data is stored in tangent space, which is discussed in Figure 7-4 in a bit. To get a normal vector from the color data in the texture, the formula (each r, g and b value-0.5)/0.5 is used (see Figure 7-3). The RGB data in the Normal Map viewed as floats lets you use this formula. To convert from RGB to floats, just divide by the floating value 255. This is done automatically in your pixel shader. It is always easier to work with these floating-point values instead of the byte data stored in the bitmap file.

Most pixels in the Normal Map are light blue (RGB 128, 128, 255) and this means that most resulting vectors just point up like Vector3 (0, 0, 1). If the complete texture is light blue, it means every vector is (0, 0, 1). Thus, the Normal Map will have no effect because this is the behavior you have with normal diffuse lighting calculations.

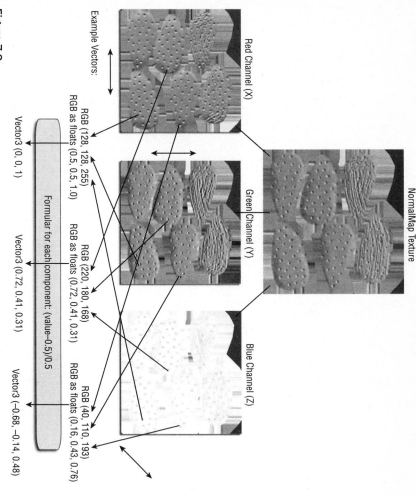

Example Vectors:

Red Channel (X)

NormalMap Texture

Green Channel (Y)

Blue Channel (Z)

RGB (128, 128, 255)
RGB as floats (0.5, 0.5, 1.0)

RGB (220, 180, 168)
RGB as floats (0.72, 0.41, 0.31)

RGB (40, 110, 193)
RGB as floats (0.16, 0.43, 0.76)

Formular for each component: (value−0.5)/0.5

Vector3 (0, 0, 1)

Vector3 (0.72, 0.41, 0.31)

Vector3 (−0.68, −0.14, 0.48)

Figure 7-3

These Normal Mapping pixels are usually stored in the tangent space, which means that each normal is stored relative to the polygon surface. It is called tangent space because you can construct the tangent matrix with the help of the tangent and binormal vectors of each vertex point. If you don't have a binormal, it can easily be created with the help of the cross product of the normal and tangent vectors (see Figure 7-4). In the previous chapter, you only had the position, normal, and texture coordinate for each point. This data is not sufficient for Normal Mapping. You need at least the tangent vector for each vertex to build this very important tangent matrix. Without it, Normal Mapping will not look correct. You should not even bother to implement it if you don't have these tangents.

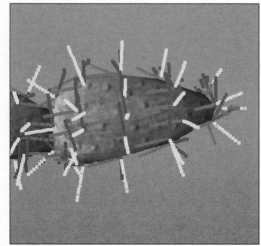

Figure 7-4

You can think of the tangent and binormal vectors as being the vectors that point to the next vertex in the x and y direction, but they are still octagonal (in a 90-degree angle) to the normal vector. This means even if your 3D geometry does not have any tangent data, you can construct it yourself by going through all vertices (not easy, but possible).

Problems

The problem with vertex shaders is that often vertices are used for more than one polygon and sometimes the texture coordinates do not merge well. For diffuse mapping, this does not matter because you use the normal vectors only for lighting calculations, but if you rely on the tangent space to transform your normals for each pixel, the data must fit. This means it is much better to have the tangent data generated in the 3D program, which was used to create the 3D geometry. It knows which tangents are used and the exported normals are much better for the Normal Mapping shader. Inside the vertex shader you only have access to the current vertex you are processing; you can't get the next vertex or build a new vector pointing to the next vertex. This means it is very important to pass valid tangent data to the vertex shader. If you define the vertex input structure to support tangents in the shader, it does not mean the application is able to pass valid tangent data. By default, if you have a .x or .fbx file in your content pipeline, it does not have any tangent data (see Figure 7-5).

This means that you only have the valid normals, but the missing tangents will not allow you to construct the tangent space for the Normal Mapping. For simple objects, such as this apple, it does not matter so much, but the more curves and texture coordinates you have in a model that do not fit together, the worse this problem gets. Figure 7-6 shows the tangent errors of the apple model; you can check it out by starting the demo application from the previous chapter.

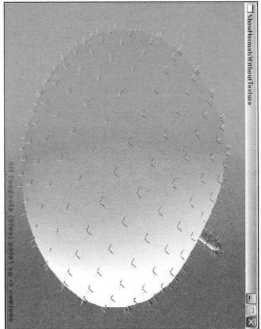

Figure 7-5

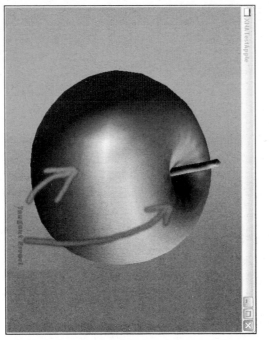

Figure 7-6

After understanding all these issues, you can get to the 3D models and shaders now.

Asteroids! Wrong Game or What?

It is hard to create good looking 3D objects such as the ones you saw in Figure 7-1; your modeler usually will spend most of the time creating the high-poly version, which can have several million polygons. You will probably spend a lot of time fine-tuning shaders and optimizing them to allow your engine to display many objects at the same time with high frame rates. To keeps things simple, you will use some

Chapter 7: Realism Through Normal Mapping

cool-looking asteroid objects, which have several million polygons in the high-poly versions (although they were not that hard to create) and the low-poly version has around 1000 polygons. These models will be used in the next chapter for the Rocket Commander XNA game.

To optimize the performance even further, more versions with 500, 200, and even 50 polygons were created of the same asteroids. This was not very hard to do because the same high-poly object can be used, and even the Normal Maps from the higher polygon objects look okay with the low-poly versions. In performance tests, the 200 polygon version was the most efficient. It renders almost as fast as the 50 polygon version, but it looks much nicer. The 500 polygon version did not look much better, but took longer to render, especially on low-end computers. Thus, the final game ended up with the 1000 polygon and 200 polygon versions of all asteroids (see Figure 7-7).

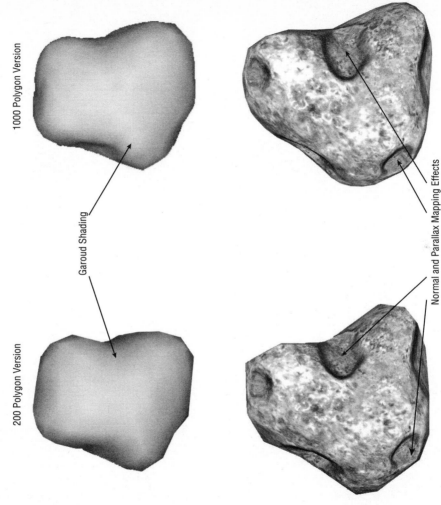

Figure 7-7

Figure 7-8 shows the three textures used for this asteroid. Because all asteroid models of Rocket Commander use a parallax mapping shader, you need a diffuse, normal, and height map for each object. As mentioned before, the Normal Maps are compressed. As a result, they will look reddish instead of the default bluish of Normal Maps. The compressed Normal Map is red because the red color channel is completely white and the alpha channel, which stores the original red channel, is not visible. For more details check out the `ParallaxMapping.fx` shader in the next chapter and open up the Normal Mapping textures.

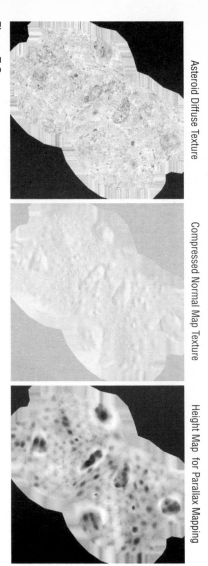

Asteroid Diffuse Texture

Compressed Normal Map Texture

Height Map for Parallax Mapping

Figure 7-8

I wrote a little tool in 2005 named NormalMapCompressor (see Figure 7-9), which is available from my blog at `http://abi.exdream.com`. It can be used to convert Normal Maps to compressed Normal Maps. You will save 75 percent of the disk and texture space that these textures use without losing much quality. That is really cool because you can get into a lot of video memory problems just by using Normal Mapping or parallax mapping. In the past, you had only a diffuse texture and small resolutions, such as 128 × 128, 256 × 256, and sometimes 512 × 512 were common.

The 128 × 128 textures stored as uncompressed bitmaps with 32 bits per channel (RGBA) take 128 × 128 × 4 bytes = 64KB. Compressed as a DXT1 dds file, it is only 8KB in size. As a JPG file it is only around 5–10KB. For 256 × 256, these sizes are four times as big (256KB uncompressed, 32KB for DXT1, around 20KB for JPEG), and for 512 × 512 it is again four times bigger. Even here, you only have 1MB if you use no compression at all.

But today texture sizes of 1024 × 1024, 2048 × 2048, and even 4096 × 4096 are more common. Even if you just take 1024 × 1024 textures, you already have 4MB of texture space for the diffuse map if you don't use compression. Because you also need the Normal Map and the height map now for cool shader effects, you have suddenly up to 12MB just for one single texture. If your game uses a few hundred different textures, this is completely impractical. You just have to use compression and think about loading only the data you really need. This is why console games often reload level data and generally don't use very high texture resolution; it just costs too much memory, especially on the Xbox 360 and older consoles.

Diffuse textures can be compressed quite easily with DXT1, which uses eight times less space than RGBA or six times less for RGB. If you still need alpha data for transparent objects, you can use DXT5, which still is four times smaller than uncompressed RGBA data. You might say "Why not use .jpg or .png files?" Well, you could save disk space by using .jpg files, but in video memory you would still need to uncompress the files and store them in video memory. The great thing about dds files is that the DXT format is compatible with today's graphics hardware and saves video memory too.

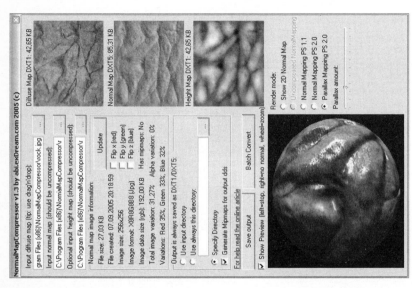

Figure 7-9

For Normal Maps, the major problem here is that the DXT compression algorithms were designed for color data; the green channel eats up most of the compression because green colors are more visible. The blue channel is not that important in Normal Maps because it is usually very bright anyway (see Figure 7-3), but the red channel will look like crap after the DXT1 compression. Especially in Pixel Shader 1.1, you can't normalize the normals again, and the vector length will be completely wrong in many cases. In addition, the Normal Map lighting will look very wrong and weak (see Figure 7-10).

It is really hard to explain without switching the compression on and off. On the screen, the visual difference is clearly visible. The NormalMapCompressor solves this problem by using the DXT5 compression format and storing the red channel in the alpha channel, which gets compressed separately in DXT5. This gives the green and blue a little better compression ratio because the red channel is all white now. In the shader, you just have to switch the red and alpha channel and you are good to go. If you look closely at the NormalMapCompressor (refer to Figure 7-9) you can see that the red channel has the highest variation (information panel on the left side), which means that the red channel has the most different color values and variations. The blue channel is usually very low. Try out several Normal Maps to see the different variance values.

For the diffuse and height map you can use DXT1. If you just use Normal Mapping, you don't need a height map and you can save even more video memory. Now a 1024 × 1024 texture only takes 512KB for the diffuse map, 1MB for the Normal Map (DXT5 takes twice as much space), and another 512KB for the optional height map, if needed. If you use mip-mapping you can add another 25 percent to that. Mip-mapping is a texturing technique in which the best fitting mip-map inside a texture is automatically choosen. A texture with mip-maps contains the original texture and then smaller versions with half the size until they reach 1 pixel (256x256, 128x128, 64x64, 32x32, etc.).

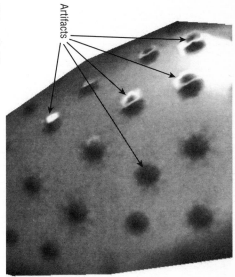

Artifacts

Figure 7-10

With 2–2.5MB, it looks almost as good as the uncompressed 12MB of textures for 1024 × 1024. I should also mention that although the cool looking Normal Mapping or parallax mapping effects textures often look a lot sharper, you can get away with 512 × 512 textures instead of using 1024 × 1024 textures as I did in Rocket Commander. The amazing thing is that the complete Rocket Commander game is under 10MB, including two sound tracks, many sound effects, five asteroid types, five item models, the rocket model and many more models, textures and effects, and four cool-looking levels. On the Xbox 360, it takes a little bit more because playing MP3s is not possible, but it is amazing to display a 3D game with less than 15MB to a screen with a resolution of 1920 × 1080 pixels (HDTV), which looks sharper than most commercial games for the Xbox 360.

The later chapters of this book also discuss how to use Normal Mapping for your own custom 3D data such as the track and other vertex buffer generated 3D data, which looks great with Normal Maps and does not take much texture space, thanks to the compression technique discussed here.

So How Do Shaders Work?

Enough pictures, let's do some coding. For the shader, you are going to write in FX Composer (see Chapter 6 for an introduction). You'll use the asteroid textures you saw in Figure 7-8.

If you like, you can try to follow the steps described here and program your own Normal Map shader like the simple shader in the last chapter, but you don't have to. You can just follow the shader code and play around with the complete vertex and Pixel Shader once you get through everything here. Normal Mapping

Chapter 7: Realism Through Normal Mapping

is quite a cool effect, but fine-tuning can take a lot of time and it can be a lot of fun to tweak. Leave some tweaking options to the model artist and write some different shaders for Normal Mapping so the artist can choose which effect to use for which material. For example, metal should look different from stone or wood materials.

Start FX Composer and open the NormalMapping.fx shader file. The layout for the shader file is similar to the SimpleShader.fx file, but you use more annotations and you will see that future shaders in this book all use a similar file structure. This way it is easier to work with shaders from the C# code.

The basic file layout is:

- ❑ Header comment and description of the shader
- ❑ Matrices (world, worldViewProj, viewInverse, and whatever else is required)
- ❑ Other global variables such as time, factors, or testing values
- ❑ Material data, first the material colors, then all used textures and samplers
- ❑ Vertex structures, most importantly the VertexInput structure, which is always the same and uses the TangentVertex format you have also defined in your engine.

For each technique in the shader you have a code block usually separated by a comment line starting with the usual //.

- ❑ Vertex Shader
- ❑ Pixel Shader
- ❑ Technique that puts these shaders together, often using the same vertex shaders for different shader models over and over again

To keep things simple, I am just going to explain the vertex and Pixel Shader for the default Normal Mapping effect used for all the upcoming games in this book called Specular. There is also a technique called Specular20, which works the same way on shader model 1.1, but has some features turned off or reduced because of the eight instruction limit in Pixel Shader 1.1. Older GPUs did only support Pixel Shader 1.1, which allowed just eight instructions for pixel shaders and the instruction set was also more limited than for Pixel Shader 2.0.

Please go through the shader file header and parameters after you open the file; they are basically in the same form as for SimpleShader.fx from the last chapter. What has changed since last chapter is the VertexInput format, which looks similar, but it expects a tangent input now. You already learned about the problems with .x and .fbx content files before. We will be solve this later in this chapter. Assume for now that you have valid tangent data, which can be used in the shader. Lucky for you, FX Composer always gives you valid tangent data for the standard test objects (sphere, teapot, cube, and so on).

```
// Vertex input structure (used for ALL techniques here!)
struct VertexInput
{
    float3 pos     : POSITION;
    float2 texCoord : TEXCOORD0;
    float3 normal  : NORMAL;
    float3 tangent : TANGENT;
};
```

In `SimpleShader.fx`, you simply started coding and once it worked you did not refactor the shader code anymore. This is totally fine, but the more shaders you write, the more you will think about reusing components. One way to do that is to define the most commonly used methods directly in the shader file:

```
// Common functions
float4 TransformPosition(float3 pos)//float4 pos)
{
    return mul(mul(float4(pos.xyz, 1), world), viewProj);
} // TransformPosition(.)
float3 GetWorldPos(float3 pos)
{
    return mul(float4(pos, 1), world).xyz;
} // GetWorldPos(.)
float3 GetCameraPos()
{
    return viewInverse[3].xyz;
} // GetCameraPos()
float3 CalcNormalVector(float3 nor)
{
    return normalize(mul(nor, (float3x3)world));
} // CalcNormalVector(.)
// Get light direction
float3 GetLightDir()
{
    return lightDir;
} // GetLightDir()

float3x3 ComputeTangentMatrix(float3 tangent, float3 normal)
{
    // Compute the 3x3 tranform from tangent space to object space
    float3x3 worldToTangentSpace;
    worldToTangentSpace[0] =
        mul(cross(normal, tangent), world);
    worldToTangentSpace[1] = mul(tangent, world);
    worldToTangentSpace[2] = mul(normal, world);
    return worldToTangentSpace;
} // ComputeTangentMatrix(..)
```

The first common function is `TransformPosition`, which just converts the 3D vertex position in the vertex shader to the screen space. It works exactly the same way as in the last chapter except that you don't have a combined `worldViewProj` matrix anymore. Instead, you have a `world` matrix, which you had in `SimpleShader.fx`, too, but the `viewProj` matrix is new. After multiplying `world` with `viewProj` you would have `worldViewProj` again. This is not done in the code, but in the shader instead, which costs you one additional vertex shader instruction.

Another way would be to store methods or even parameters and constants in separate .fxh files, similar to C++ header files. I don't prefer that approach because FX Composer can only show one source file at a time and you will most likely still change a lot of code at this stage.

By separating the world matrix from the `worldViewProj` matrix, you only have to worry about one single matrix that changes for every object, mesh, or custom 3D data you are going to render. The more data you have to pass from the program to the shader, the longer it takes. It can significantly slow down your rendering code if you set parameters over and over again and even start shaders too often per frame. It is much better to just set up the shader once and then render thousands of objects in a bunch by just changing the world matrix for each of them. You can take this idea even further by using an array of world matrices to store 20 or more matrices at once and then go through all of them. This technique is called *instancing* and is sometimes used by shooter games to optimize the performance even more if many objects of the same kind with the same shader are used. In earlier versions of Rocket Commander, I had instancing implemented also, but it was too much work to get it to work in all shader models (1.1, 2.0, and 3.0) and also have it support the fixed function pipeline. It did not matter anyway because the performance was quite good after all the other shader optimizations.

The other helper methods are pretty simple and you should understand them quickly just by looking at them, except for the last one, which is used to build the tangent space matrix. Check out Figures 7-4 and 7-5 again to see which vector is which. CalculateTangentMatrix is used in the vertex shader (as with all the other helper methods) and it expects the tangent and the normal vector for each vertex point. Good thing you got these from the VertexInput structure. The binormal vector is generated by calculating the cross product between the normal and tangent vectors. You can reconstruct this matrix with your right hand (remember Chapter 5?) — the middle finger is the normal vector, the forefinger is the tangent, and the thumb represents the binormal, which is the cross product of the middle and forefinger and is in a 90 degree relationship with them because of that.

This tangent space matrix is very useful to quickly transform normals and the light direction from the world space to the tangent space, which is required for the Pixel Shader Normal Mapping calculation. The reason you need this tangent space matrix is to make sure all vectors are in the same space. This space lies directly on top of the polygon and points up (z) as the normal vectors do, whereas x and y describe the tangent and binormal. Using this tangent space is easiest and fastest in the Pixel Shader and in order to get to the correct order of the binormal and tangent that are used to construct this tangent space matrix. The order and even the cross product for the binormal might have to be reversed for a left-handed engine. Use unit testing to figure out which way is the correct one; you can also take a look at the shaders from the original Rocket Commander game (left-handed) to see the differences that were made in the XNA port (right-handed).

Vertex Shaders and Matrices

With all these helper methods it should be easy to write the vertex shader now. Before you do that you should define the VertexOutput structure first. I'm only discussing the Pixel Shader 2.0 version here because the Pixel Shader 1.1 version is really complicated and uses a lot of assembly shader code, which is outside the scope of this book. Please pick up a good shader book to learn more about shader details and the shader assembly language if you really want to support Pixel Shader 1.1. I recommend the Programming Vertex and Pixel Shader, GPU Gems, or Shader X series books. Wolfgang Engel, a hardcore shader expert, is involved with most of them and you can learn a lot of shader tricks that were developed in the last few years by many professionals. This topic is so big that a new programmer job is born: Shader Programmer.

If you are in a small team or even have to do all the programming yourself, this can be a hassle because you have to learn so much and you have very little time because the technology is advancing so fast. Try to keep it simple and use the easiest shader model for you. It may be bad for some gamers that XNA does not support the fixed function pipeline and it also does not support Direct3D 10 shader model 4.0, but this way you can concentrate on just creating Pixel Shader 2.0 shaders (or maybe use Pixel Shader 3.0 too) and getting a game done.

185

Your vertex structure needs the screen space position, as always, and you have to pass the texture coordinates over to the Pixel Shader, too, so the diffuse and Normal Maps can be used correctly. Please note that you have to duplicate the texture coordinates in Pixel Shader 1.1 because each texture vertex input in the Pixel Shader can only be used once. This is one of the many problems with Pixel Shader 1.1; you also can't do normalize there or even use the pow function. It is also harder to uncompress the compressed Normal Map back to a useful format.

```
// vertex shader output structure
struct VertexOutput_Specular20
{
    float4 pos       : POSITION;
    float2 texCoord  : TEXCOORD0;
    float3 lightVec  : TEXCOORD1;
    float3 viewVec   : TEXCOORD2;
};
```

The lightVec and viewVec variables are just helpers to make the Pixel Shader computation a little bit easier. The lighting calculation is basically the same as in the previous chapter, but this time you have to calculate all vectors in the tangent space because it is easier to work in the tangent space than to convert all tangent space vectors to the world space. That makes sense because you have a lot more pixels than vertices. Converting every pixel with a complex matrix operation in the Pixel Shader would be too slow and converting only the light direction and the view vector in the vertex shader does not cost much time.

Take a look at the whole vertex shader code. The important part here is the use of the worldToTangentSpace matrix, which is calculated by the ComputeTangentMatrix method you saw before.

```
// Vertex shader function
VertexOutput_Specular20 VS_Specular20(VertexInput In)
{
    VertexOutput_Specular20 Out = (VertexOutput_Specular20) 0;
    Out.pos = TransformPosition(In.pos);
    // We can duplicate texture coordinates for diffuse and Normal Map
    // in the Pixel Shader 2.0.
    Out.texCoord = In.texCoord;
    // Compute the 3x3 tranform from tangent space to object space
    float3x3 worldToTangentSpace =
        ComputeTangentMatrix(In.tangent, In.normal);
    float3 worldEyePos = GetCameraPos();
    float3 worldVertPos = GetWorldPos(In.pos);
    // Transform light vector and pass it as a color (clamped from 0 to 1)
    // For ps_2_0 we don't need to clamp from 0 to 1
    Out.lightVec = normalize(mul(worldToTangentSpace, GetLightDir()));
    Out.viewVec = mul(worldToTangentSpace, worldEyePos - worldVertPos);
    // And pass everything to the pixel shader
    return Out;
} // VS_Specular20(.)
```

Pixel Shader and Optimizations

The Pixel Shader now takes the vertex output and computes the light influence for each pixel. The first thing you have to do is to get the diffuse and Normal Map colors. The diffuse map just has the RGB values and maybe an alpha value if you use alpha blending (not really right now, but it is supported by this shader). The more complicated call is getting the normal vector from the compressed Normal Map. If you remember the way the compressed Normal Maps were built earlier with the NormalMapCompressor tool you can probably guess that you have to exchange the red and alpha channels again to make the RGB data valid and usable as an XYZ vector again. The first step to do this is to use a so-called swizzle, which takes the RGBA or XYZW data from a texture or a shader register and changes the order. For example, ABGR reverses the order of RGBA. In your case you just need the alpha channel (x) and the green (y) and blue (z) channels, so you use the .agb swizzle.

Then you use the formula described earlier to get the floating-point color values to vector values by subtracting 0.5 and dividing by 0.5, which is the same as multiplying by 2 and subtracting 1 (because 0.5×2 is 1). To fix any remaining compression errors you normalize the vector again, which takes one extra Pixel Shader instruction, but it is definitely worth it.

```
// Pixel Shader function
float4 PS_Specular20(VertexOutput_Specular20 In) : COLOR
{
    // Grab texture data
    float4 diffuseTexture = tex2D(diffuseTextureSampler, In.texCoord);
    float3 normalVector = (2.0 * tex2D(normalTextureSampler,
        In.texCoord).agb) - 1.0;
    // Normalize normal to fix blocky errors
    normalVector = normalize(normalVector);
    // Additionally normalize the vectors
    float3 lightVector = In.lightVec;//not needed: normalize(In.lightVec);
    float3 viewVector = normalize(In.viewVec);
    // For ps_2_0 we don't need to unpack the vectors to -1 - 1
    // Compute the angle to the light
    float bump = saturate(dot(normalVector, lightVector));
    // Specular factor
    float3 reflect = normalize(2 * bump * normalVector - lightVector);
    float spec = pow(saturate(dot(reflect, viewVector), shininess));
    //return spec;
    float4 ambDiffColor = ambientColor + bump * diffuseColor;
    return diffuseTexture * ambDiffColor +
        bump * spec * specularColor * diffuseTexture.a;
} // PS_Specular20(.)
```

With this normalVector (still in tangent space) you can now do all the lighting calculations. The light vector and view vector are extracted from the VertexOutput_Specular20 structure. The light vector is the same for every vertex and pixel because you just use a directional light source, but the view vector can be very different if you are close to the object you are rendering. Figure 7-11 again shows why it is important to re-normalize this view vector as discussed in the previous chapter. For Normal Mapping, it is even more important because you calculate the light for every single pixel and the vectors can vary a lot from pixel to pixel through the variation in the Normal Map.

The bump value is calculated the same way you calculated the diffuse color in the previous chapter. For every normal pointing toward the light you use a bright color, and if it points away, it gets darker. Both the normal vector and the light vector are in tangent space and this way the basic formula stays the same. You can test out simple lighting effects in the SimpleShader.fx file and then re-implement them here together with Normal Mapping, which is cool because even though this shader is a lot more complex, the basic lighting calculation is still simple and exchangeable. If you take a look at the Normal Mapping and parallax mapping shaders of the next chapters, you will see that this is the only place you make modifications; the rest of the Normal Mapping shader stays the same.

The last thing you have to calculate is the specular color component before putting the final color together. You don't have a half vector yet, but you have the view vector in tangent space and you know in which way the normal points. The code uses a little bit simplified formula by just subtracting the light vector from two times the normal vector to generate a pseudo normalized half vector. Doing the same computation as in the SimpleShader.fx vertex shader would be very expensive in a Pixel Shader. The Normal Mapping shader looks fine with this computation as well. It does not really matter how exact the half vector is. The important thing is the pow method that makes the shiny effect small. You should fine-tune the shininess and specularColor values for each material because they greatly influence the appearance of the final output (see Figure 7-12).

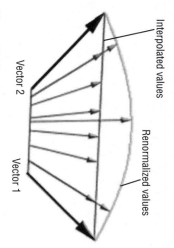

Figure 7-11

Interpolated values

Renormalized values

Vector 2   Vector 1

Putting together the final color may seem a little strange to you. The first two lines are pretty easy to understand. First, you mix together the ambient color with the result of the bump value with the diffuse color. This operation is actually just one instruction in the shader and that's why it is written this way. (It is easier to read the assembly output and use the same code for Pixel Shader 1.1 this way.)

Then the specular color is multiplied by the spec value, which shows the highlights. It is then multiplied again by the bump value and finally by the diffuseColor alpha value. The bump value makes sure that the specular value gets darker when you point away from the light and the diffuseColor alpha value helps you to fade out the specular highlights in case the texture is transparent here (alpha blending feature, not used in Rocket Commander).

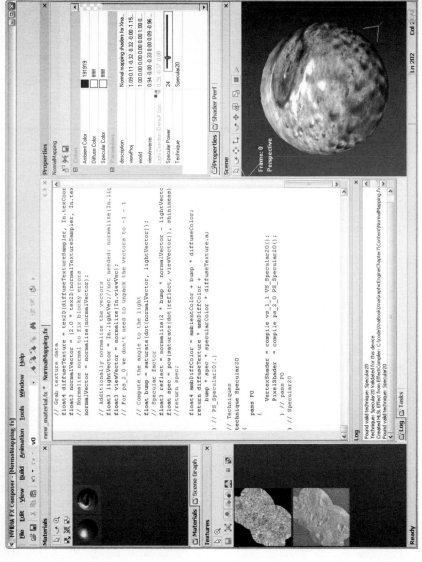

Figure 7-12

That's everything you have to know for now to get the Normal Mapping shader to work in FX Composer. Feel free to play around with it a little bit — change color values and use different textures and parameters. Now you have to worry about getting the correct tangent data in the application, as well as ensuring the ability to easily import model files a model artist might have created for you.

ShaderEffect Class

To render the shader you will use the ShaderEffect class introduced in Chapter 5. All the basics were covered in Chapter 6; the only thing you are going to add here is more shader parameters. The rest of the functionality stays the same (see Figure 7-13). You also use the Render method to render 3D data with the shader like in the line manager class in Chapter 5.

To render 3D data, you do not only need the 3D geometry or the 3D render code, but also the material parameters, which include the material color values and textures, as in FX Composer. To manage this data, a new helper class, Material.cs, has been introduced to store all this material data in one place (see Figure 7-14).

The ShaderEffect SetParameters method accepts the Material class as a parameter, which can also be passed in the Render method. This way you can easily assign materials without having to set all the effect parameters yourself.

Figure 7-13

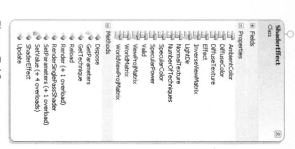

Figure 7-14

With the new classes you can now easily write a new unit test to change the apple model from the previous chapter to support your new NormalMapping.fx shader. Additionally you change the material to the asteroid material by loading the asteroid diffuse and Normal Map to test out your new Material class.

TangentVertex Format

Before you can write the unit test to test out the Normal Mapping shader, you need the same VertexInput structure from the .fx file in your code too. Unlike the VertexPositionNormalTexture structure from Chapter 6, there is no predefined structure that contains tangent data. You have to define it yourself. The following TangentVertex class (see Figure 7-15) is used to define the VertexInput structure used by NormalMapping.fx and all the shaders that you will write in this book from this point on.

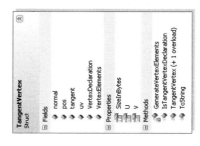

Figure 7-15

Defining the fields of this structure is nothing special. You simply define the four types you need — pos, normal, tangent, and UV texture coordinates, as follows:

```
/// <summary>
/// Position
/// </summary>
public Vector3 pos;
/// <summary>
/// Texture coordinates
/// </summary>
public Vector2 uv;
/// <summary>
/// Normal
/// </summary>
public Vector3 normal;
/// <summary>
/// Tangent
/// </summary>
public Vector3 tangent;
```

Some methods for vertex buffers require that you specify the size of this structure. In MDX you could use a Direct3DX method or you could use unsafe code to use the sizeof method. In XNA, it is not that easy. You must define the size yourself.

```
/// <summary>
/// Stride size, in XNA called SizeInBytes.
/// </summary>
public static int SizeInBytes
{
    get
    {
        // 4 bytes per float:
        // 3 floats pos, 2 floats uv, 3 floats normal and 3 float tangent.
        return 4 * (3 + 2 + 3 + 3);
    } // get
} // StrideSize
```

The rest of the structure is pretty straightforward. The only other field that you need externally is the Vertex Declaration, which has to be generated by custom code, as follows:

```
#region Generate vertex declaration
/// <summary>
/// Vertex elements for Mesh.Clone
/// </summary>
public static readonly VertexElement[] VertexElements =
    GenerateVertexElements();

/// <summary>
/// Vertex declaration for vertex buffers.
/// </summary>
public static VertexDeclaration VertexDeclaration =
    new VertexDeclaration(BaseGame.Device, VertexElements);

/// <summary>
/// Generate vertex declaration
/// </summary>
private static VertexElement[] GenerateVertexElements()
{
    // Construct new vertex declaration with tangent info
    // First the normals (we should already have that)
    VertexElement[] decl = new VertexElement[]
    {
        // Construct new vertex declaration with tangent info
        // First the normals (we should already have that)
        new VertexElement(0, 0, VertexElementFormat.Vector3,
            VertexElementMethod.Default,
            VertexElementUsage.Position, 0),
        new VertexElement(0, 12, VertexElementFormat.Vector2,
            VertexElementMethod.Default,
            VertexElementUsage.TextureCoordinate, 0),
        new VertexElement(0, 20, VertexElementFormat.Vector3,
            VertexElementMethod.Default,
            VertexElementUsage.Normal, 0),
        // And now the tangent
        new VertexElement(0, 32, VertexElementFormat.Vector3,
            VertexElementMethod.Default,
            VertexElementUsage.Tangent, 0),
```

```
    };
    return decl;
} // GenerateVertexElements()
#endregion
```

`VertexElement` takes the following parameters to define in which order the 3D data is declared:

❑ **Stream (first parameter):** Usually just 0, use it only if you have multiple vertex buffer streams, which is complicated stuff.

❑ **Offset (second parameter):** Offset from the start of the stream in bytes. Just calculate how far you are in the structure in bytes. Most data types, like floats, integers and dwords take 4 bytes.

❑ **Vertex element format (third parameter):** Defines which type of data is used. This is the same name as defined in the `VertexInput` format in the shader. Usually you will use `Vector2`, `Vector3`, and `Vector4` here. Integer numbers or other floating-point values are usually only used for skinning and skeletal animation.

❑ **Vertex element method:** Simply use default. Allows also UV and Lookup, but that's not really required often.

❑ **Vertex element usage:** How should this data type be used? This is similar to the semantics value you defined in the shader. You should always set this to the data type that is used because, even if the order is not the same as in the shader, the data will be reordered based on this usage type. If you don't specify tangent here, the `VertexInput` data might be completely messed up and XNA usually complains if the format does not fit.

❑ **Usage index:** You can also specify the usage index, but again you probably will never need this value. Simply leave it at 0. The usage index can be useful for complex shaders and multiple vertex buffers to specify where which parts of the vertex data is coming from.

Normal Mapping Unit Test

Normally you would write the unit test first, but you already have a unit test for shaders from the previous chapter. Thus, you need to define how your new shader works first to figure out which classes are required. Now it is much easier to write shader unit tests. Please note that you should not write any unit tests in the `ShaderEffect` class because once `ShaderEffect` gets called all shaders get initialized, which should not happen before the device is initialized!

Take a look at the following Normal Mapping shader unit test:

```
public static void TestNormalMappingShader()
{
    Model testModel = null;
    Material testMaterial = null;
    TestGame.Start("TestNormalMappingShader",
    delegate
    {
        testModel = new Model("apple");
        testMaterial = new Material(
            Material.DefaultAmbientColor,
            Material.DefaultDiffuseColor,
```

```
            Material.DefaultSpecularColor,
            "asteroid4~0", "asteroid4Normal~0", "", "");
    },
    delegate
    {
        // Render model
        BaseGame.WorldMatrix = Matrix.CreateScale(0.25f, 0.25f, 0.25f);
        BaseGame.Device.VertexDeclaration =
            TangentVertex.VertexDeclaration;
        ShaderEffect.normalMapping.Render(testMaterial, "Specular20",
        delegate
        {
            // Render all meshes
            foreach (ModelMesh mesh in testModel.XnaModel.Meshes)
            {
                // Render all mesh parts
                foreach (ModelMeshPart part in mesh.MeshParts)
                {
                    // Render data our own way
                    BaseGame.Device.Vertices[0].SetSource(
                        mesh.VertexBuffer, part.StreamOffset, part.VertexStride);
                    BaseGame.Device.Indices = mesh.IndexBuffer;
                    // And render
                    BaseGame.Device.DrawIndexedPrimitives(
                        PrimitiveType.TriangleList,
                        part.BaseVertex, 0, part.NumVertices,
                        part.StartIndex, part.PrimitiveCount);
                } // foreach
            } // foreach
        });
    });
} // TestNormalMappingShader()
```

The model is loaded as in the unit test from the previous chapter, but instead of loading a texture you now load a complete material with several color values and the diffuse and Normal Maps of your asteroid4 model. In the render loop, you simply ensure that the world matrix is set as before and then you set your new TangentVertex structure. The render code itself is the same as in SimpleShader RenderModel and just goes through all the meshes and renders everything with the new asteroid material. Figure 7-16 shows the result of this unit test.

The apple is still there, but it is very dark. The Normal Map also does not appear as it should yet, and it certainly does not appear the way it looked in FX Composer. Why? Well, it is the tangent issue again. You are telling XNA how to use the input data, but the tangent data is still missing and has to be generated before the model lands in your content pipeline.

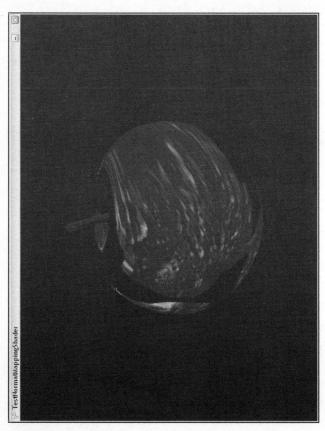

TestNormalMappingShader

Figure 7-16

Adding Tangent Data with a Custom Processor

It is not easy to get this tangent problem right, and writing a custom processor is also not an easy task. The basic steps are described here. If you want to know more about writing custom processors or how to write a whole new content importer class, you should refer to the XNA documentation and additional samples on the Web.

First, you have to create a new DLL project. You simply add it to the existing solution and choose XNA DLL or C# DLL as the type. Second, make sure that the XNA Framework and XNA pipeline DLLs are added in the references section of this new project (see Figure 7-17).

- XnaGraphicEngineContentProcessors
  - Properties
  - References
    - Microsoft.Xna.Framework
    - Microsoft.Xna.Framework.Content.Pipeline
    - mscorlib
    - System
  - StringHelper.cs
  - XnaGraphicEngineModelProcessor.cs

Figure 7-17

Third, write the following code into the main class of the DLL. You are deriving from the ModelProcessor class and extending the default behavior of XNA models. The code just calls CalculateTangentFrames for each mesh in the model. The code in the project for this chapter is much more complex and also fixes several other things and prepares the model for complex highly optimized rendering.

```
/// <summary>
/// XnaGraphicEngine model processor for x files. Loads models the same
/// way as the ModelProcessor class, but generates tangents and some
/// additional data too.
/// </summary>
[ContentProcessor(DisplayName = "XnaGraphicEngine Model (Tangent support)")]
public class XnaGraphicEngineModelProcessor : ModelProcessor
{
    #region Process
    /// <summary>
    /// Process the model
    /// </summary>
    /// <param name="input">Input data</param>
    /// <param name="context">Context for logging</param>
    /// <returns>Model content</returns>
    public override ModelContent Process(
        NodeContent input, ContentProcessorContext context)
    {
        // First generate tangent data because x files don't store them
        GenerateTangents(input, context);
        // And let the rest be processed by the default model processor
        return base.Process(input, context);
    } // Process
    #endregion

    #region Generate tangents
    /// <summary>
    /// Generate tangents helper method, x files do not have tangents
    /// exported, we have to generate them ourselfs.
    /// </summary>
    /// <param name="input">Input data</param>
    /// <param name="context">Context for logging</param>
    private void GenerateTangents(
        NodeContent input, ContentProcessorContext context)
    {
        MeshContent mesh = input as MeshContent;
        if (mesh != null)
        {
            // Generate trangents for the mesh. We don't want binormals,
            // so null is passed in for the last parameter.
            MeshHelper.CalculateTangentFrames(mesh,
                VertexChannelNames.TextureCoordinate(0),
                VertexChannelNames.Tangent(0), null);
        } // if
        // Go through all childs
        foreach (NodeContent child in input.Children)
        {
```

```
        GenerateTangents(child, context);
    } // foreach
    } // GenerateTangents(input, context)
    #endregion
} // class
```

The `MeshHelper` class is only available in the content pipeline here. There are several methods that assist you if you want to modify the incoming data. The method `GenerateTangents` generates the tangent frames from the first set of texture coordinates and it ignores the creation of binormal values. While it is nice to finally have some generated tangents, they will often look wrong, especially if the model was created a while ago. Newer versions of 3D Studio Max (8 and 9) use the so-called Rocket Mode (named after the Rocket model in Rocket Commander) for Normal Map creation, but older versions and other tools might generate rounded Normal Maps, which will be messed up by the auto-tangent creation of XNA (or MDX for that matter). In the original XNA game, I implemented my own tangent processor and generator, but in XNA this is not that easy. You don't have direct access to the vertex data of the model, but there are some helper methods. It still would be a lot of work to extract all data and put it back together.

It is easier to write a completely new content importer than to mess with an existing format if you really need a lot of changes and additional features for your 3D model data. For example, many 3D models exist in many different formats, such as the popular md3 or md5 in the Quake/Doom world. Often, people write their own importers to get some cool looking models from other games to be shown in their own graphics engine. Please refer to the XNA documentation for how to write your own custom content importer. Additionally, there will be a lot of user-written custom content importers on the Web in the future. The easiest format to import in my opinion is the Collada format if you don't want to mess with .x or .fbx files. It requires some custom code, but once you have done that it is quite easy to extend your importer, add new features, and change the behavior completely in whatever way you like. More information can be found in the following blog post about the Collada format and some sample code that I wrote to help you understand using the format, and how to do skinning and render Collada models on the screen:
http://exdream.no-ip.info/blog/2007/02/25/
SkeletalBoneAnimationAndSkinningWithColladaModelsInXNA.aspx.

Most likely, you are happy with your custom model processor for now. It generates tangent data and that is all you need for your Normal Mapping shaders. To get a custom processor working in your XNA project you have to select it yourself by opening each content file properties. Before you can even select your own custom model processor you have to ensure the content pipeline knows it exists. For now, you simply create a DLL file somewhere on the disk. To include your processor, open up your project properties (right-click in the Solution Explorer on the XnaGraphicEngine .csproj file on the top, right below the XnaGraphicEngine solution, and select `Properties` here). The last option in the project properties is called `Content Pipeline` and this is where you can select additional content importers and processors (see Figure 7-18). If you click Add, you can select the `XnaGraphicEngineContentProcessors.dll` file by browsing two levels up and then selecting its bin\Debug\ directory. For release mode, you want to select bin\Release\.

After the new content pipeline assembly is loaded, you should now be able to select "XnaGraphicEngine Model (Tangent support)" for each .x file model you have in your project. You can also select multiple .x files in the Solution Explorer and then change the model content processor for all of them (see Figure 7-19).

With all that heavy lifting behind you, you can now start your last unit test again and check out what has changed. Please note that you did not change a single line of code in your project for the new content processor support; it is all done in the processor DLL. If you made any mistake in the content processor or one of the content files does not contain valid data, you will get a warning or error before the project is started because the content pipeline builds all the content before you start the project. Once the content is built with your new processor it does not change anymore and it does not have to be rebuilt again. XNA skips that automatically for you.

As you can see in Figure 7-20, your apple with the asteroid material now looks much better and you can even assign different materials on it (just for fun). Please note that the internal structure of the apple is different from your own TangentVertex format. If you set the apple material directly on it, make sure the correct vertex declaration from the mesh is used and not your own, or else the texture coordinates will not match (but that does not matter for your testing; none of the textures fit).

Figure 7-18

Figure 7-19

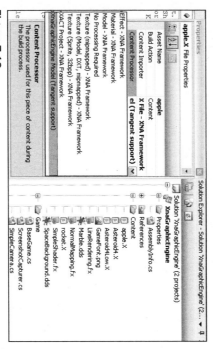

Apple with Asteroid4 Material   Apple with Rocket Material   Apple with Marble Test Material

Figure 7-20

You might notice that both the rocket and the marble test textures seem to be mirrored. This is normal because the apple model was generated for DirectX and uses a left-handed matrix. You could export all models again with a right-handed mode (which the Panda DirectX Exporter in 3D Studio Max luckily supports) or you could just ignore this issue because it does not matter very much in Rocket Commander. If you have text on textures in your game, or you want the textures to fit and not to be mirrored, make sure that everything is aligned the correct way from day one. It is always important to use the same format in the modeling program your artists use and in your graphics engine. If it does not fit, either adjust your engine or convert the content the way you need it to be.

Final Asteroid Unit Test

You do not need to have all this knowledge to display a simple asteroid model because the following unit test shows it is possible to load the model and use the shader that was selected in 3D Studio automatically. The problem with this approach becomes apparent when you try to render 1000 asteroids per frame. It is simply too slow and impractical to start a new shader for every single asteroid, set all the parameters all over again, and then use the un-optimized mesh draw method.

Instead, you are going to start your own shader class in the future and then initialize the material and shader settings only once and render a lot of models as fast as possible. In this way, you can achieve great performance in the Rocket Commander game.

```
public static void TestAsteroidModel()
{
    Model testModel = null;
    TestGame.Start("TestNormalMappingShader",
    delegate
    {
        testModel = new Model("asteroid4");
    },
    delegate
    {
        // Render model
```

```
    });
} // TestAsteroidModel1()
```

```
testModel1.Render(Matrix.CreateScale(10.25f, 10.25f, 10.25f));
```

If the asteroid4 model (by the way, you can also use asteroid4Low for testing here) uses the correct model processor with tangent support, you should be able to see it correctly in 3D (see Figure 7-21) with the parallax mapping effect on it (which is the same as Normal Mapping, it just uses an additional height texture to move the output texture around a little bit for a fake displacement effect). One problem with the asteroid model is that there are visible raw edges on it. It appears as if the texture mapping does not match, but if you disable the Normal Mapping effect, it looks okay. So the problem comes from the tangent data. The Normal Map is correct as you can see in the DirectX version of Rocket Commander (fits perfectly thanks to the custom way tangent data is re-generated, which is sadly not possible in XNA for .x files). Other models such as the rocket and future models created for XNA games look fine, but this is still an un-fixable problem with older models and a limitation of XNA. So, you have to live with it.

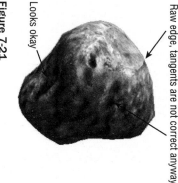

Raw edge, tangents are not correct anyway

Looks okay

Figure 7-21

It probably would be possible to somehow fix all asteroids, re-export them, make sure all data is correct, and maybe even re-generate the Normal Map to fit correctly. But that is a lot of work and the asteroid looks good enough now. The original Rocket Commander game still exists and shows how it is done; for the XNA port you can live with some minor glitches.

For a native XNA game this should not happen. In the following games for this book, you will ensure that all models are exported and displayed correctly. Please note that it can be arduous to work with 3D models, exporting them correctly, importing them again into your engine, writing all the shaders required to make them look the way the artist intended them to look, and so on. Sometimes you will be better off using an existing engine (such as the one you develop in this book) for a while until you see your custom needs and start writing your own 3D code anyway. But don't spend all your time just developing a 3D engine without writing a game. XNA is about game development. A common mistake in the DirectX world was that everyone wrote his own engine, but only very few people made games out of their engines. Be smarter than that.

More Shaders

Normal Maps are great, but there are many more ways to improve the visual quality of 3D objects. For the Rocket Commander game, we are satisfied with a little parallax mapping and some cool post screen shaders. If you are more ambitious, you probably want to implement glass shaders, reflection effects, cool water shaders, and more. This section gives a small overview about possible shaders you could write for your XNA graphics engine. There are many more examples available online or in the many shader books out there. Good examples are the NVidia home page, www.shadertech.com, the GPU Gems (by NVidia), or Game Programming Gems books (by Charles River Media), or Shader X book series (by Charles River Media, edited by Wolfgang Engel). You can learn a lot from these books, but in the end you will probably end up writing your own shader code unless you find someone that does it for you.

Offset Mapping

Parallax mapping is sometimes also called offset mapping because the points are remapped, but usually offset mapping means that the original parallax mapping effect is taken to another level by going through several height layers in the pixel shader. Another popular name for offset mapping is steep parallax mapping, which was originally demonstrated in a paper by Morgan McGuire and Max McGuire in April, 2005. The game F.E.A.R. is a prominent example of this technique. It uses parallax mapping with approximately two or three height layers. The results are fine-tuned and look pretty good.

The steep parallax mapping approach is a little more complex and usually takes 20 or more height steps until it looks really good. The advantage of this approach is that you can also calculate self-shadowing (see Figure 7-22), which looks really amazing if you consider that all of this happens in the pixel shader, there is no actual 3D geometry, and it is all faked.

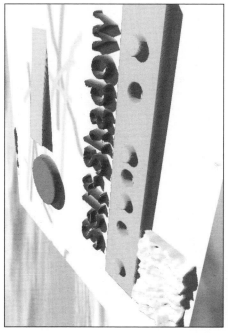

Figure 7-22

Part II: Basic Graphics Engine

The major problem with this technique, however, is the high cost associated with it. Not only will you spend a lot of time implementing this technique and trying to get it right, but, more important, it will cost an insane amount of Pixel Shader power to execute. The shader is about 20 times slower than a normal parallax mapping shader, and while it is possible to create cool looking scenes in demos with very few polygons, in a real game you will need a lot more than one cool effect. In the future, it may be an option to improve existing games or to enable really high-end graphics hardware to make the game look even better.

Glass Shader

Simulating glass is not that easy, at least if you try to get it right. The main problem with glass is that it does two things: it reflects the side of the world you are on and it refracts the world behind the glass. Reflection means that light from the viewer side of the glass is reflected as if on a mirror, and so will not be seen by the viewer, including his own image if he stands in front of the glass and the lighting conditions are correct. Refraction means that the world behind the glass (for example, if you are looking outside through a window) is distorted a bit depending on the glass thickness, the structure, and even the color of the glass. This is especially true if you have a glass surface with a structure on it (such as glass in the bathroom window).

To make things even more complicated glass does not always behave the same way. Viewing it from the top gives you other values for reflection than viewing the glass from the side, this usually gives you a better reflection similar to a mirror. If the lighting conditions are poor or the glass is dirty, it might not be so reflective at all, and so on. There are many more options that can be considered.

Because you don't have a lifetime to get it right and you just want it to work, you usually leave out everything that is not really important. But you are still left with some cool looking effects (see Figure 7-23). You can find more information about the cars and the shaders in the last part of this book.

Figure 7-23

Reflection and Water

For glass, you can get away with implementing a simple reflection shader, which reflects the sky cube box (see Chapter 8 for more information about the sky) on the glass. For more shiny metal surfaces or mirrors, just reflecting the sky might not be sufficient. You may have to think about reflecting the world around certain objects for more realistic effects. This is neither easy nor fast because for a complete reflection around a simple 3D object you would have to render a reflection cube map to show the world in every direction from that reflective material. In Direct3D 10 it is possible to render this in one step, but you still need a fast graphics card for this kind of dynamic update for materials in your engine. In DirectX 9 or XNA it will probably be too slow because you have to render the scene six times for every cube direction just for one materials reflective cube map.

Reflection can be a little bit simpler when you just reflect the world on a planar surface such as a mirror. Now you only have to render the world mirrored on this surface once and you are good to go for your reflection effects. This technique is also used for many water shaders and it can look really cool, especially if you don't just reflect the sky, but also the objects and effects of the world. Additionally, water has many effects (reflection, refraction, water color, water animation, waves, and so on), which can take a lot of time to fine-tune, but it can also be a lot of fun playing around with water shaders (see Figure 7-24).

Figure 7-24

Challenge: Add Parallax Mapping

Phew, that was a lot of reading. I hope you still have some energy left for your little task here. This chapter talked a lot about Normal Mapping and parallax mapping, but you only saw how Normal Maps were implemented. It is now your turn to implement parallax mapping. Don't worry — it is not very hard once you get the basic idea.

First of all you have to understand that each pixel produced by the Pixel Shader shows the interpolated texture coordinates you passed in through the vertices. But if you are able to interpolate and scale the texture coordinates, you should also be able to move them around depending on your location. This is already the basic idea of parallax mapping, as shown in Figure 7-25.

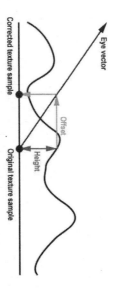

Figure 7-25

To get this effect in your shader, you have to define a height-texture first (the black curvy line in the figure represents the height for each pixel). Simply add it after the Normal Map and use the default sampler values (linear interpolation). Now you can access the height map data in the Pixel Shader with the following code:

```
float height = tex2D(heightTextureSampler, In.texCoord);
```

Only a float value is used because you only need the height value, not the real color in the height map (which is gray anyway). Now you have to calculate the offset that this height value produces. Then use very small values here, or else parallax mapping will look very bad if the effect is too strong. This is the basic code for that:

```
// Calculate parallax offset, parallaxAmount should be 0.05 or less.
float2 offsetTexCoord = In.texCoord +
(height*parallaxAmount - parallaxAmount*0.6f) * normalize(In.viewVec);
```

The last thing you have to do now is to use this offsetTexCoord for the diffuse and Normal Map instead of In.texCoord and your parallax mapping effect should work. Fine-tune it a little and use a variable in FX Composer for the parallaxAmount for easier testing. Good luck. If you don't get it to work right away or run into trouble, please take a look at the ParallaxMapping.fx shader in the content directory for additional assistance.

Summary

You learned a lot about advanced shader effects in this chapter and you should be ready now to create your own shaders and play around with some ideas you might have. Because shaders are completely programmable today, it is impossible to explain all the possibilities and ways shaders can be used. In the future, many more new techniques might appear and make games look even better. But shaders are not only used for games; certain applications try to use the GPU power for other uses too and there are several experiments that show how to use the GPU for math calculations or physics. It may sound crazy, but for some of these tasks the GPU is a far better processing unit than the CPU because it works so well for just processing pixels and it works in parallel with 24-pixel processing units or even more.

Here's the list of shaders and problems you encountered in this chapter:

❏ You saw that Normal Mapping can greatly improve 3D models. Objects with a few hundred polygons can look almost as good as 3D objects with millions of polygons. To get them to work correctly, however, you need valid tangent data in the 3D geometry.

❏ By compressing Normal Maps you can save a lot of video memory while still having great visual quality. Use the NormalMapCompressor tool to quickly generate compressed Normal Maps.

❏ FX Composer is still the program to do all the heavy lifting for your shader code. Visual Studio is nice for code, but FX Composer is clearly the better IDE for shaders. The preview scene is especially useful.

❏ To work painlessly with shaders in the future, several new classes were introduced into the graphics engine that enable you to load and render shaders (ShaderEffect class), assign and set materials (Materials class), and to use 3D geometry data with tangent support (TangentVertex structure).

❏ Finally, you saw several other shaders including offset mapping/steep parallax mapping, glass shaders, reflection and water shaders, and the parallax mapping shader in the Challenge (I hope you got it right).

❏ Playing around with shaders can be fun.

With all this new code you are now ready for a new game in the next chapter, where you also learn about post screen shaders to greatly improve the visual quality and overall look of your upcoming games.

Post-Screen Shaders and the Rocket Commander Game

Well, it was fun to write the graphics engine the last couple of chapters, but where is the next game? Don't worry; in this chapter a really cool game will be examined: Rocket Commander. The original version was released in March 2006, when the German www.Coding4Fun.de site went online and Visual Studio 2005 came out in Germany. One month and many thousands of played games later, the English Rocket Commander Tutorial Videos were created and two additional mods were released with it. Half a year later, 100,000 games were played online — even more if you consider the number of people who were playing offline. Many other mods were also created and the engine proved to be reliable enough, even for two commercial games that were released with the Rocket Commander engine: Pizza Commander and Rocket Racer.

The Rocket Commander game and the complete source code are free to download, and you are encouraged to play around with it or even use it to create your own games. I received many nice stories via e-mail of people learning C# for the first time, and they were able to create their own engines and games in a short time thanks to the Rocket Commander and the video tutorials on the German and English Coding4Fun sites.

Let's just say the Rocket Commander game was a success. I didn't get rich or anything, just famous. In December 2006, the final version of the XNA Framework and XNA Game Studio Express were finally released and I was working hard on the release of Rocket Commander XNA, a complete port of the Rocket Commander engine to XNA to make it possible to play the Rocket Commander game on the Xbox 360. The performance of the XNA port is great; it runs even better than the old version and the game has no problems with thousands of asteroids rendered at the highest detail level with anti-aliasing in the highest HDTV resolution (1920 × 1080, which is a pretty big screen resolution) on the Xbox 360. One major improvement of the new version is the support for multiple cores, which is important for both the Xbox 360 and today's PCs. The game now calculates all the physics, collision testing, and other game data in an extra thread that is executed on another CPU core (if available, as on the Xbox 360) than the rendering thread, which is always busy pushing data to the GPU.

Before you get into the Rocket Commander game, you are going to learn all about post-screen shaders first, which are also a major part of Rocket Commander in addition to the powerful rendering engine and the physics. For more information about physics, please read Chapter 13. Most information about the shaders for the 3D objects were already discussed in the previous chapters and if you are interested in the game logic, take a look at the source code or watch the Rocket Commander Video Tutorials.

For the rest of the book you will, of course, still use the XnaGraphicsEngine, but any improvements such as the heavily optimized render system in Rocket Commander XNA or the physics system can still be used for future projects. Most importantly for the look of all upcoming games, including Rocket Commander, will be the many pre- and post-screen shaders that are introduced in this chapter. Pre-screen shaders are executed before the 3D scene is rendered and allow you to render textures, sky cubes, and other effects in the background. Writing such a shader is quite easy.

Post-screen shaders, on the other hand, are much more complex and they are executed at the very end of the frame rendering process. They take the fully rendered scene as a texture on a render target and modify it in several steps to output the post-screen shader result on the screen, which the user then finally sees. Getting this render target right is not a piece of cake, but once you've got the system up you can easily plug in more post-screen shaders and play around with effects. Don't overuse bloom and motion blur effects; it is cool to use those kinds of shader effects, but overusing them will not make your game better. Try also to make sure that the post-screen shaders run as fast as possible because they can heavily reduce perform-ance on high resolutions, especially if you have five or more passes and modify every single pixel on the screen.

Handling Post-Screen Shaders

The first thing you have to get for any post-screen shader is the rendered scene and put it into a render target (see Figure 8-1). The image illustrates some example post-screen shaders in FX Composer, which can be used to test out the post-screen effects before you include them into your graphics engine.

Before getting into the more complex post-screen shaders and how you can get the scene render target with help of the new RenderToTexture helper class, you will first test out the Pre-Screen Sky Cube Mapping shader and get it to work in your engine the same way it works in FX Composer.

Pre-Screen Sky Cube Mapping

First of all, you need a sky cube map, which consists of six faces like a cube. Each of these faces should be in high resolution because in the game you only look in one direction. It's okay to use 512×512 for each face if you use a lot of post-screen shaders; 1024×1024 is even better because the sky on high-resolution screens will look much better this way.

It is not easy to create such a sky cube texture. You can either use the DirectX DxTexture tool and put together the cube map with six separate faces yourself (or do the same thing in your code, but it is much easier to load one single cube map file that contains all six faces instead of loading six separate textures and putting them together yourself). Alternatively a program like Photoshop can be used to store a big $6*512 \times 512$ texture and save it as a cube-map dds (a texture with 6 bitmaps in it, one for each cube side) with help of the Nvidia DDS Exporter plug-in for Photoshop (see Figure 8-2).

Chapter 8: Post-Screen Shaders and the Rocket Commander Game

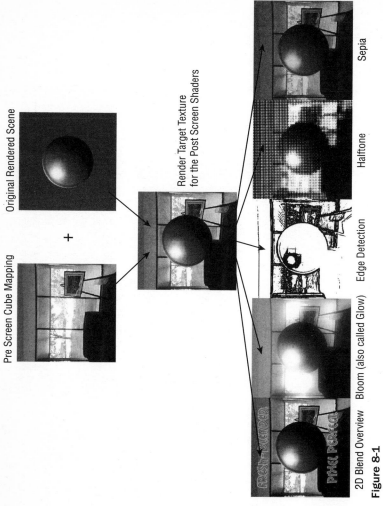

Original Rendered Scene

Pre Screen Cube Mapping

+

Render Target Texture
for the Post Screen Shaders

2D Blend Overview   Bloom (also called Glow)   Edge Detection   Halftone   Sepia

Figure 8-1

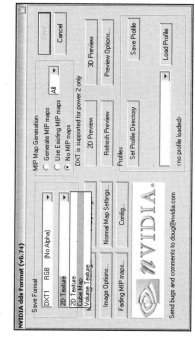

Figure 8-2

If you don't have a good looking cube map, search the Web for one; some example textures are available. Most of them have bad resolutions, but for testing they are fine. Or just use the cube map from this book if you like it. For the Rocket Commander game, you use a space cube map that looks a little different on each of the six sides to help you with navigating through the 3D space levels of the game (see Figure 8-3).

209

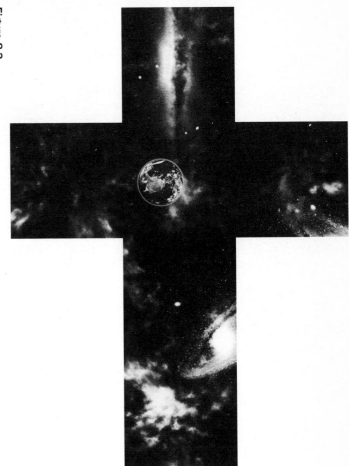

Figure 8-3

Take a look at the shader to put this cube texture on the screen. You call this shader even before rendering the scene. The sky should always be visible.

The following code is from the `PreScreenSkyCubeMapping.fx` shader:

```
struct VertexInput
{
    // We only need 2d screen position, that's all.
    float2 pos      : POSITION;
};
struct VB_OutputPos3DTexCoord
{
    float4 pos      : POSITION;
    float3 texCoord : TEXCOORD0;
};
VB_OutputPos3DTexCoord VS_SkyCubeMap(VertexInput In)
{
    VB_OutputPos3DTexCoord Out;
    Out.pos = float4(In.pos.xy, 0, 1);
    // Also negate xy because the cube map is for MDX (left handed)
    // and is upside down
    Out.texCoord = mul(float4(-In.pos, scale, 0), viewInverse).xyz;

    // And fix rotation too (we use better x, y ground plane system)
    Out.texCoord = float3(
```

```
    -Out.texCoord.x*1.0f,
    -Out.texCoord.z*0.815f,
    -Out.texCoord.y*1.0f);
    return Out;
} // VS_SkyCubeMap(..)
float4 PS_SkyCubeMap(VB_OutputPos3DTexCoord In)  : COLOR
{
    float4 texCol = ambientColor *
        texCUBE(diffuseTextureSampler, In.texCoord);
    return texCol;
} // PS_SkyCubeMap(.)
technique SkyCubeMap < string Script = "Pass=P0;"; >
{
    pass P0 < string Script = "Draw=Buffer;"; >
    {
        ZEnable = false;
        VertexShader = compile vs_1_1 VS_SkyCubeMap();
        PixelShader  = compile ps_1_1 PS_SkyCubeMap();
    } // pass P0
} // technique SkyCubeMap
```

For rendering the shader, you need only a Vector2 screen position, which can be converted to the sky cube position by multiplying it with the inverse view matrix. The scale variable can be used to tweak the zooming a little bit, but usually this value should be 1.0. After getting the texture coordinate for the sky cube map, you need to convert it from the standard left-handed system cube that maps are usually stored in. To do that, you have to swap the y and z coordinates and you also invert the direction the cube map texture coordinate is pointing to. And finally, you multiply the y value by a custom value of 0.815 to make the sky rendered in a 1:1 aspect ratio mode look correct on a 4:3 aspect ratio of the screen. All these tweaking variables were tested with the unit test presented next until the background sky just looked correct.

If you want to build your own sky cube map, you can use the DirectX Texture Tool from the DirectX SDK to load normal 2D images on each of the six cube map faces of a cube texture. Additionally, many tools are available to directly render 3D scenes into cube maps such as Bryce, 3D Studio Max, and many other 3D content creation applications.

Then you rotate the sky cube map for XNA compatibility because it was created for MDX and uses a left-handed system. Rendering the sky cube map is pretty easy — just grab the cube texture color value and multiply it by the optional ambient color value, which is usually white. The shader is not using any advanced Shader Model 2.0 functionality, and it is absolutely no problem to compile it to Shader Model 1.1.

To get it to work in your XNA graphics engine, use the following unit test:

```
public static void TestSkyCubeMapping()
{
    PreScreenSkyCubeMapping skyCube = null;
    TestGame.Start("TestSkyCubeMapping",
        delegate
        {
            skyCube = new PreScreenSkyCubeMapping();
        },
        delegate
        {
```

```
      skyCube.RenderSky();
  }); 
} // TestSkyCubeMapping()
```

The class is derived from the ShaderEffect class from the previous chapters and it just loads the
PreScreenSkyCubeMapping.fx shader in the constructor; all other shader effect parameters are already
defined in the ShaderEffect class. The important new method in this class is RenderSky, which executes
the following code:

```
AmbientColor = setSkyColor;
InverseViewMatrix = BaseGame.InverseViewMatrix;
// Start shader
// Remember old state because we will use clamp texturing here
effect.Begin(SaveStateMode.SaveState);
for (int num = 0; num < effect.CurrentTechnique.Passes.Count; num++)
{
    EffectPass pass = effect.CurrentTechnique.Passes[num];
    // Render each pass
    pass.Begin();
    VBScreenHelper.Render();
    pass.End();
} // foreach (pass)
// End shader
effect.End();
```

VBScreenHelper generates a very simple screen quad for you and handles all the vertex buffer initialization
and rendering. The following code initializes the vertex buffer with just VertexPositionTexture vertices.
You have only one static instance of the helper class and it is used only in pre- and post-screen shaders.

As in any other shader you wrote before, you set the effect parameters first. You can leave most parameters
to their default values, but you should always set the ambient color and the inverse view matrix to see
something on the screen. This shader actually does not use anything else yet. Then the shader is started
and you render all passes (well, you have only one pass) with the help of the VBScreenHelper Render
method, which is also used for all post-screen shaders.

```
public VBScreen()
{
    VertexPositionTexture[] vertices = new VertexPositionTexture[]
    {
        new VertexPositionTexture(
            new Vector3(-1.0f, -1.0f, 0.5f),
            new Vector2(0, 1)),
        new VertexPositionTexture(
            new Vector3(-1.0f, 1.0f, 0.5f),
            new Vector2(0, 0)),
        new VertexPositionTexture(
            new Vector3(1.0f, -1.0f, 0.5f),
            new Vector2(1, 1)),
        new VertexPositionTexture(
            new Vector3(1.0f, 1.0f, 0.5f),
            new Vector2(1, 0)),
    };
    vbScreen = new VertexBuffer(
```

```
      BaseGame.Device,
      typeof(VertexPositionTexture),
      vertices.Length,
      ResourceUsage.WriteOnly,
      ResourceManagementMode.Automatic);
    vbScreen.SetData(vertices);
    decl = new VertexDeclaration(BaseGame.Device,
      VertexPositionTexture.VertexElements);
  } // VBScreen()
```

As discussed in Chapter 5 and Chapter 6, the view space uses –1 to +1 as the minimum and maximum values for the screen borders. Everything above these values will not be on the screen. The projection matrix then puts the pixels at the real screen positions. You use simple VertexPositionTexture vertices here. For the sky cube mapping shader you don't even need the texture coordinates, but they will be used for the post-screen shaders later. Please note that the position in screen coordinates of +1, +1 is the lower-left corner of the screen and –1, –1 is the upper-right corner. If you want the top-left corner of a screen texture to be displayed on the top left, the texture coordinates of 0, 0 should be in the –1, +1 corner.

You should always specify WriteOnly and Automatic when creating VertexBuffers; this way, the hardware can access them much faster without having to worry about read access from the CPU, and Automatic makes it easier to get rid of the vertex buffer and let XNA handle re-creation issues when the vertex buffer gets lost and has to be re-created (which can happen when the user presses Alt+Tab in a full-screen application and then returns).

With all these new classes up and ready, you should now be able to execute your TestSkyCubeMapping unit test and see the result shown in Figure 8-4.

Figure 8-4

Writing a Simple Post-Screen Shader

Writing post-screen shaders is no picnic. It involves a lot of testing and the ability to handle render targets correctly, and it is not always easy to get the shader to work in both FX Composer and your engine, and behave the same way. To make it a little simpler for the first post-screen shader, you are just going to add a very simple effect to your scene. Instead of really modifying the rendered scene, you are just going to darken down the screen borders to give the game a TV-like look. To change something that would not be possible without a post-screen shader, you also turn the whole screen to black and white.

Start with the `PostScreenDarkenBorder.fx` shader file in FX Composer. After the header comment and the description of the shader, you define a script, which is only used for FX Composer to indicate that this shader is a post-screen shader and should be rendered a certain way. All variables starting with an upper-case letter are considered to be constant for your purposes.

Neither your engine nor FX Composer are case sensitive, but by using uppercase letters for constants you can easily spot which variables should be constant and not be changed in the app and which ones have to be set from the application. `ClearColor` and `ClearDepth` are both used only in the FX Composer. In your application, you don't have to worry about that because you handle your own clearing. For testing, you can set other colors as black for `ClearColor` or `1.0` for depth if you like, but most of the time, these values will always be the same and they default to the same values for all upcoming post-screen shaders.

```
// This script is only used for FX Composer, most values here
// are treated as constants by the application anyway.
// Values starting with an upper letter are constants.
float Script : STANDARDSGLOBAL
<
    string ScriptClass = "scene";
    string ScriptOrder = "postprocess";
    string ScriptOutput = "color";
    // We just call a script in the main technique.
    string Script = "Technique=ScreenDarkenBorder;";
> = 0.5;
const float4 ClearColor : DIFFUSE = { 0.0f, 0.0f, 0.0f, 1.0f };
const float ClearDepth = 1.0f;
```

Post-screen shaders need to know about the screen resolution and you need access to the scene map render target. The following code is used to allow you to assign the window size and the scene map. The window size is the resolution you render into and the scene map render target contains the fully rendered scene as a texture. Please note the semantics such as `VIEWPORTPIXELSIZE` used here to help FX Composer to assign the correct values for the preview rendering automatically. If you don't use them, FX Composer will not be able to use the correct window size and you would have to set it yourself in the properties panel.

```
// Render-to-Texture stuff
float2 windowSize : VIEWPORTPIXELSIZE;
texture sceneMap : RENDERCOLORTARGET
<
    float2 ViewportRatio = { 1.0, 1.0 };
    int MIPLEVELS = 1;
>;
sampler sceneMapSampler = sampler_state
```

```
{
    texture = <sceneMap>;
    AddressU = CLAMP;
    AddressV = CLAMP;
    AddressW = CLAMP;
    MIPFILTER = NONE;
    MINFILTER = LINEAR;
    MAGFILTER = LINEAR;
};
```

For darkening down the screen border, you also use a little helper texture with the name
screenBorderFadeout.dds (see Figure 8-5):

```
// For the last pass we add this screen border fadeout map to darken the borders
texture screenBorderFadeoutMap : Diffuse
<
    string UIName = "Screen border texture";
    string ResourceName = "ScreenBorderFadeout.dds";
>;
sampler screenBorderFadeoutMapSampler = sampler_state
{
    texture = <screenBorderFadeoutMap>;
    AddressU  = CLAMP;
    AddressV  = CLAMP;
    AddressW  = CLAMP;
    MIPFILTER = NONE;
    MINFILTER = LINEAR;
    MAGFILTER = LINEAR;
};
```

Figure 8-5

**This texture has to be added to your content directory along with the .fx shader file.
XNA will not automatically add any textures when you just add a shader, unlike when
adding 3D models where the contained materials and textures are also imported and
added for you.**

To achieve the darkening effect, every pixel from the scene map is simply multiplied by the color value in
the screen border fadeout texture. This way, most pixels stay the same (white middle); pixels at the screen
border will get darker and darker, but not completely black (or else the border would be black), so you
just want to make it a little darker.

Take a look at the very simple vertex shader, which just passes the texture coordinates to the Pixel Shader. To make the shader compatible to Pixel Shader 1.1, you have to duplicate the texture coordinates because you need to access them twice, once for the scene map and once for the screen border fadeout texture. Please also note that you are adding half a pixel to the texture coordinates to fix a very common problem of rendering textures on the screen. In DirectX (and XNA) all the pixels have an offset of 0.5 pixels; you just fix this by moving the pixel to the correct location.

You can read more about this issue online. You don't have to worry about it normally because all the helper classes (for example, SpriteBatch) take care of this issue for you, but if you render your own post-screen shader, you might want to fix this. For this shader it does not matter so much, but if you have a very precise shader that shadows certain pixels you want to make sure to completely hit the pixel position and not draw somewhere else. The following vertex shader shows how to use the correct texel positions:

```
struct VB_OutputPos2TexCoords
{
    float4 pos       : POSITION;
    float2 texCoord[2] : TEXCOORD0;
};

VB_OutputPos2TexCoords VS_ScreenQuad(
    float4 pos       : POSITION,
    float2 texCoord : TEXCOORD0)
{
    VB_OutputPos2TexCoords Out;
    float2 texelSize = 1.0 / windowSize;
    Out.pos = pos;
    // Don't use bilinear filtering
    Out.texCoord[0] = texCoord + texelSize*0.5;
    Out.texCoord[1] = texCoord + texelSize*0.5;
    return Out;
} // VS_ScreenQuad(..)
```

The position is already in the correct space and will just be passed over. The Pixel Shader now accesses the scene map, and for testing if everything is set up correctly you can just return the scene map colors here:

```
float4 PS_ComposeFinalImage(VB_OutputPos2TexCoords In) : COLOR
{
    float4 orig = tex2D(sceneMapSampler, In.texCoord[0]);
    return orig;
} // PS_ComposeFinalImage(...)
```

After adding the ScreenDarkenBorder technique, you should see the normal scene as always in FX Composer (see Figure 8-6). Please note that all the annotations here are required for FX Composer only! For rendering, you use the pre-screen sky cube mapping shader described earlier and the standard sphere.

```
// ScreenDarkenBorder technique for ps_1_1
technique ScreenDarkenBorder
<
    // Script stuff is just for FX Composer
```

```
string Script = "RenderColorTarget=sceneMap;"
"ClearSetColor=ClearColor; Clear=Color;"
"ClearSetDepth=ClearDepth; Clear=Depth;"
"ScriptSignature=color; ScriptExternal=;"
"Pass=DarkenBorder;";
>
{
    pass DarkenBorder
    <
        string Script = "RenderColorTarget0=; Draw=Buffer;";
    >
    {
        VertexShader = compile vs_1_1 VS_ScreenQuad();
        PixelShader  = compile ps_1_1 PS_ComposeFinalImage(sceneMapSampler);
    } // pass DarkenBorder
} // technique ScreenDarkenBorder
```

Figure 8-6

Improvements

Just to test if the shader is activated (which can be done in FX Composer by clicking the shader in the materials panel and selecting "Apply to Scene"), you can now easily modify the output. Just change the last line in the Pixel Shader:

```
return 1.0f - orig;
```

This will subtract the color value from 1.0 for each component (shaders will automatically convert from float to float3 or float4 if required; you don't have to specify float4 (1, 1, 1)). You can probably guess that this formula will invert the whole image (see Figure 8-7), which looks funny, but is not really useful.

217

Okay, back to your initial mission: Apply the screen border texture. To darken down the edges, you first load the screen border texture and then multiply the original scene map color value with it — that's it. You just have to return the result, and you are almost done (see Figure 8-8):

```
float4 orig = tex2D(sceneSampler, In.texCoord[0]);
float4 screenBorderFadeout =
    tex2D(screenBorderFadeoutMapSampler, In.texCoord[1]);
float4 ret = orig;
ret.rgb *= screenBorderFadeout;
return ret;
```

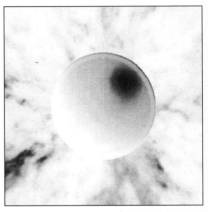

Figure 8-7

Figure 8-8

You could now also convert the image to black and white by applying the Luminance formula, which just tells you which component to weight how much (green is always the most visible color):

```
// Returns luminance value of col to convert color to grayscale
float Luminance(float3 col)
```

```
{
    return dot(col, float3(0.3, 0.59, 0.11));
} // Luminance(.)
```

This method can be applied to the original scene map by just modifying one line in your Pixel Shader to finally achieve the expected post-screen shader effect: Darken down the screen borders and apply a black-and-white effect (see Figure 8-9):

```
float4 ret = Luminance(orig);
```

Frame: 0
Perspective

Figure 8-9

Writing post-screen shaders can be a lot of fun once you have your basic setup, but you should try to implement the shader first into your engine before moving on to even more cool post-screen shaders and possibilities.

Implementing Post-Screen Shaders

We have already covered the helper class VBScreenHelper and the PreScreenSkyCubeMapping shader class, but for post-screen shaders, you really need render targets, which can be accessed and handled through the RenderTarget class in XNA. The problem with that class is that you still have to call a lot of methods and handle a lot of things yourself. This is especially true if you also want to use the depth buffer for render targets and restore them after they have been modified, which is useful for shadow mapping shaders.

Please note that XNA 2.0 has improved the RenderTarget class and made its behavior more similar on the Xbox 360 and Windows. Now the rendered data stays persistent even if you change the render target and render something else. Render targets were a major problem of the XNA Racing Game after Shadow Mapping was added because, it used two separate render targets, rendered one after another. The rendering worked fine on Windows, but was in the wrong order for the Xbox 360 causing the second render target to kill the first one. It was not easy to figure out and it can be annoying if you have not developed on the Xbox 360 before. XNA 2.0 helps you out in such cases, keeping the code more consistent over the two supported platforms. Another nice improvement of XNA 2.0 is the ability to use multiple render targets (MRT) to render data into several render targets at once, which is cool for some advanced shader techniques, but beyond the scope of this book.

RenderToTexture Class

For that reason a new helper class is introduced here: RenderToTexture, which provides important methods to make post-screen shaders easy to handle (see Figure 8-10). The most important methods for you are the constructor, which takes SizeType as a parameter, Resolve, and SetRenderTarget. Getting XnaTexture and RenderTarget via the properties is also very useful. Please note that this class also inherits all the features from the Texture class.

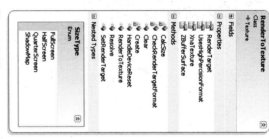

Figure 8-10

The constructor does the following:

```
sceneMapTexture = new RenderToTexture(
    RenderToTexture.SizeType.FullScreen);
```

For example, if you want to create a full-screen scene map for the PostScreenDarkenBorder.fx shader, you would use the following line:

```
/// <summary>
/// Creates an offscreen texture with the specified size which
/// can be used for render to texture.
/// </summary>
public RenderToTexture(SizeType setSizeType)
{
```

```
        sizeType = setSizeType;
        CalcSize();
        texFilename = "RenderToTexture instance " +
            RenderToTextureGlobalInstanceId++;
        [...]
        SurfaceFormat format = SurfaceFormat.Color;
        // Create render target of specified size.
        renderTarget = new RenderTarget2D(
            BaseGame.Device,
            texWidth, texHeight, 1,
            format);
    } // RenderToTexture(setSizeType)
```

To use this render target and let everything be rendered into it, you just have to call SetRenderTarget now, which uses some new helper methods in the BaseGame class to take care of multiple stacked render targets (required for more complex post-screen shaders):

```
sceneMapTexture.SetRenderTarget();
```

After all the rendering is done, you can call Resolve to copy the render target results to the internal texture (which can be accessed through the XnaTexture property). This step is new in XNA; it was not required in DirectX and the reason this method was added is to support the Xbox 360 hardware, which works quite differently than PC graphics cards. On the PC, you can directly access the render target and use it for post-screen shaders, but on the Xbox 360, the render target results reside in a write-only hardware location and cannot be accessed. Instead you have to copy the render target over to the internal texture. This call takes some time but it is still very fast, so don't worry about it.

After resolving the render target, you have to reset the render target back to the default background buffer, or else you are still rendering into the render target and will see nothing on the screen. To do that, just call the BaseGame ResetRenderTarget method and pass in true to get rid of any started render targets. The method will also work if you don't have any render targets started. In that case, ResetRenderTarget just returns and does nothing.

```
// Get the sceneMap texture content
sceneMapTexture.Resolve();
// Do a full reset back to the back buffer
BaseGame.ResetRenderTarget(true);
```

That is almost everything you have to know to work with the RenderToTexture class. Additional functionality will not be required for a while (until the last chapters of this book). Check out the unit tests of the RenderToTexture class to learn more about it.

PostScreenDarkenBorder Class

Before even thinking about writing the PostScreenDarkenBorder class, you should define a unit test and specify the entire feature set you want to have in your post-screen class. Please note that you derive this class from ShaderEffect, the same way as you do for the pre-screen shader, and have easier access to the effect class and the effect parameters. But you still have to specify the new effect parameters used in PostScreenDarkenBorder.fx.

221

Take a look at the unit test for this post-screen shader:

```
public static void TestPostScreenDarkenBorder()
{
    PreScreenSkyCubeMapping skyCube = null;
    Model testModel = null;
    PostScreenDarkenBorder postScreenShader = null;
    TestGame.Start("TestPostScreenDarkenBorder",
    delegate
    {
        skyCube = new PreScreenSkyCubeMapping();
        testModel = new Model("Asteroid4");
        postScreenShader = new PostScreenDarkenBorder();
    },
    delegate
    {
        // Start post screen shader to render to our sceneMap
        postScreenShader.Start();
        // Draw background sky cube
        skyCube.RenderSky();
        // And our testModel (the asteroid)
        testModel.Render(Matrix.CreateScale(10));
        // And finally show post screen shader
        postScreenShader.Show();
    });
} // TestPostScreenDarkenBorder()
```

By the way, always try to name your shader and source code files the same way; it will make it much easier when looking for bugs. Another nice thing you can sometimes do if shaders use similar features is to derive from one post-screen shader class when writing a new one. This trick is used for most of the following games to save you from having to code the same effect parameters and render target code over and over again.

You use three variables in the unit test:

□ skyCube initializes and renders the sky cube mapping shader as in FX Composer.

□ testModel loads the asteroid4 model and displays it with a scaling factor of 10 after rendering the sky cube map background.

□ postScreenShader holds an instance of the PostScreenDarkenBorder class. Because this shader needs a valid scene map, you have to call it twice, first with the Start method to set up the scene map render target and then at the end of the frame rendering, Show is then called to bring every-thing to the screen.

If you take a look at the final unit test in the PostScreenDarkenBorder.cs file, you may notice some additional code to toggle the post-screen shader and show some help on the screen. This was added later and only improves the usability of the shader; the basic layout is the same.

The layout of post-screen shader classes is very similar to the one you already saw in PreScreenSkyCube-Mapping. You just need a new Start and Show method and some internal variables to hold the new effect parameters and check whether or not the post-screen shader was started (see Figure 8-11).

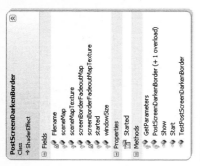

Figure 8-11

The `Start` method just calls `setRenderTarget` for the scene map texture; the important code is in the `Show` method:

```
/// <summary>
/// Execute shaders and show result on screen, Start(..) must have been
/// called before and the scene should be rendered to sceneMapTexture.
/// </summary>
public virtual void Show()
{
    // Only apply post screen glow if texture and effect are valid
    if (sceneMapTexture == null || Valid == false || started == false)
        return;
    started = false;
    // Resolve sceneMapTexture render target for Xbox360 support
    sceneMapTexture.Resolve();
    // Don't use or write to the z buffer
    BaseGame.Device.RenderState.DepthBufferEnable = false;
    BaseGame.Device.RenderState.DepthBufferWriteEnable = false;
    // Also don't use any kind of blending.
    BaseGame.Device.RenderState.AlphaBlendEnable = false;
    if (windowSize != null)
        windowSize.SetValue(new float[]
            { sceneMapTexture.Width, sceneMapTexture.Height });
    if (sceneMap != null)
        sceneMap.SetValue(sceneMapTexture.XnaTexture);
    effect.CurrentTechnique = effect.Techniques["ScreenDarkenBorder"];
    // We must have exactly 1 pass!
    if (effect.CurrentTechnique.Passes.Count != 1)
        throw new Exception("This shader should have exactly 1 pass!");
    effect.Begin();
    for (int pass= 0; pass < effect.CurrentTechnique.Passes.Count; pass++)
    {
        if (pass == 0)
            // Do a full reset back to the back buffer
```

```
    BaseGame.ResetRenderTarget(true);
    EffectPass effectPass = effect.CurrentTechnique.Passes[pass];
    effectPass.Begin();
    VBScreenHelper.Render();
    effectPass.End();
} // for (pass, <, ++)
effect.End();
// Restore z buffer state
BaseGame.Device.RenderState.DepthBufferEnable = true;
BaseGame.Device.RenderState.DepthBufferWriteEnable = true;
} // Show()
```

First you are checking if Start was called properly and if you still have the shader started; otherwise, the content in the scene map render target will not contain any useful data. Then you resolve the render target for full Xbox 360 support, and you can start setting up all required effect parameters and the technique. You might ask why the technique is added by name here and you are right — it would be faster to do this by a reference to the technique, which could be initialized in the constructor. But it does not matter so much; you call this shader only once per frame and this performance difference will never show up in any profiler tool (because one line for a frame that goes through many thousands lines of code is not affecting performance that much). If you will call a shader more often, you should definitely cache this technique reference and maybe not even set it again and again every frame (it is still set from the last frame). See the ShaderEffect class for more information about this kind of optimization.

Now the shader is started and you render the screen quad with the VBScreenHelper class as usual, but you have to make sure that the correct render target is set for each pass. In your case, you just have one pass and all you have to do is to reset it to the back buffer (you will always have to do that for the last pass in post-screen shaders, or else you will not see anything on the screen). For a more complex example you can check out the PostScreenGlow class.

Unit Test Result

After you are done with rendering the device, render states are restored (maybe you still want to render some 3D data after showing the shader). If you look at the code in the project, you can also see some additional try and catch blocks to make sure that the render engine stays stable even if a shader crashes. The shader will just set to an invalid state and not be used anymore. An error is logged and the user will no longer see the post-screen shader, but the rest of the game still runs.

You should always provide alternatives if some code does not work or crashes. Most of the time, the code is providing only visual elements to your game like this post-screen shader. The game is still the same even if you don't use this shader; it will just not look as pretty. In practice, a shader will never crash and you don't have to worry about this for your final game, but during development, you can easily mess up an effect parameter or try new things in the Pixel Shader, and you don't want your whole game or unit test to crash.

You should now see the result shown in Figure 8-12 when running the TestPostScreenDarkenBorder unit test. Feel free to play around with the shader and change code in your application. For example, you could try to render into a smaller render target — for example, using only one quarter of the screen — and see how this affects the final output (big blocky pixels).

You should also test out all post-screen shaders as early as possible on your Xbox 360 if you have one. This is very important because shaders can sometimes behave differently and you have to make sure that all render targets fit in the Xbox 360 memory and still perform well. The PostScreenDarkenBorder and the RenderToTexture classes are fully compatible with the Xbox 360; and they work great on Xbox 360, too.

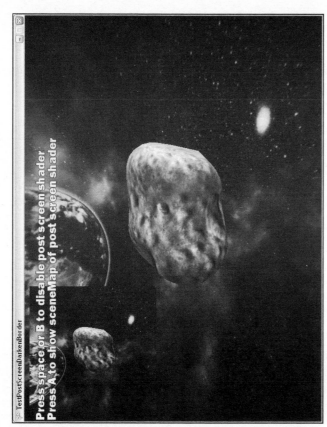

Figure 8-12

More Post-Screen Shaders

Changing the screen border, adding the sky in the background, and inverting or grayscaling your scene map is nice, but there are many more possibilities and way more powerful post-screen shaders possible. The Rocket Commander game uses a pretty complex glow shader by faking HDR lighting in the alpha channel and performing several passes, adding radial motion blur by mixing the result with the scene map result from the last frame and doing a lot of glow effects.

The shader is called PostScreenGlow and it can be found in the Rocket Commander game (both the DirectX and the XNA version). Figure 8-13 shows the basic functionality; the shader is even more complex than that because it supports multiple Shader Models (1.1 and 2.0) and there are some optimizations built in to improve the performance for slow computers. In the Rocket Commander game, the Shader Model can be chosen or you can disable the post-screen shader for very slow computers, but the game is only half the fun without the cool effects.

Well, that does look a little bit complicated and it is quite a lot of work to get it right, but there are many good shader books available and you can often achieve something quickly by taking a shader from someone else and playing around with it.

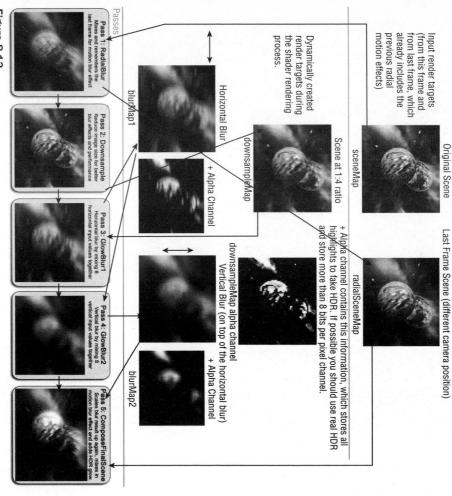

Input render targets (from this frame and from last frame, which already includes the previous radial motion effects)

Original Scene

Last Frame Scene (different camera position)

sceneMap

radialSceneMap

Dynamically created render targets during the shader rendering process.

Scene at 1:4 ratio

+ Alpha channel contains this information, which stores all highlights to fake HDR. If possible you should use real HDR and store more than 8 bits per pixel channel.

Horizontal Blur

downsampleMap

+ Alpha Channel

blurMap1

downsampleMap alpha channel
Vertical Blur (on top of the horizontal blur) + Alpha Channel

blurMap2

Passes

Pass 1: RadialBlur
Mixes and remembers the last frame for motion blur effect

Pass 2: Downsample
Reduce image size for better blur effects and performance

Pass 3: GlowBlur1
Horizontal blur by mixing 8 horizontal input values together

Pass 4: GlowBlur2
Vertical blur by mixing 8 vertical input values together

Pass 5: ComposeFinalScene
Scales blur result up again, mixes in motion blur effect and adds HDR glow.

Figure 8-13

The effect of this shader becomes most apparent if you hold two images right beside each other with and without the post-screen glow shader (see Figure 8-14).

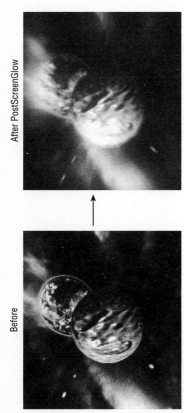

Before   After PostScreenGlow

Figure 8-14

Motion Blur

You already saw a simple way to do motion blur with post-screen shaders in the `PostScreenGlow` example. It may not seem simple to you, but the motion blur effect is the easiest part of the glow and it can be extended quite a bit by using the so-called "Per Pixel Motion Blur" effect. To do per-pixel motion blur, you have to save the velocity for every pixel in the scene with the help of a special shader. You don't have to render the full geometry with all the shaders; just render the objects that are moving and leave the rest of this special texture black (unused).

Then, in the motion blur post-screen shader, you take each pixel and determine how far it should be blurred based on the current direction the player is looking and overall velocity, as well as the per pixel velocity and direction. Several newer racing games implemented this technique and also some upcoming game engines are able to do such effects, but it is not easy to implement and it also costs a lot of performance to render the special texture and then a lot of shader instructions to get it to work in the post-screen shader.

The way motion blur was implemented earlier in this chapter works only with such big motion blur values because you always reuse the last screen. This means you have to add only 10 percent new motion blur and reuse 90 percent of the motion blur from the last screen. Per-pixel motion blur could do that, too, but it will be a lot harder to track if everything is moving (you, many objects in the scene, and so on) and therefore it is probably best to calculate the whole motion blur with many pixels trailing after each object in the per-pixel motion blur shader.

One relatively simple trick is to divide the screen quad you are going to render for the post-screen shader into 10×10 grid pieces and then render them like the big quad, but allow the vertex shader to use different weights depending on how strong the motion blur should be for each vertex. See Figure 8-15 for a comparison between rendering motion blur with just a screen quad and using a 5×5 grid as an example. Using a 10×10 grid looks even a little bit better.

Color Correction

I often use color correction in my post-screen shaders because they are easy to use and can greatly influence the way the final output looks. It also helps you to make all textures look more equal and more realistic because the color correction affects all pixels, like real lighting situations in the outside world. For example, if you staying in a cave or dark room it will be dark inside and only a little light comes from the outside world. But if you have some bright stone material it might look a lot brighter than the rest of materials in the cave. Using color correction shaders on the rendered scene will not fix this problem (because you should really put better objects in your cave that fit together in a better way), but it makes the scene a little bit better by changing all the color values a bit. For example, if you give the whole scene a dark look (brightness down), and add a little blue color to each pixel, then all materials will fit together better because the color values are more similar (see Figure 8-16). The scene in the figure is from a prototype game I coded one year ago. It was developed without any color correction shader and one day I thought, Hey, why not do it like in the movies, where everyone uses a lot of color correction and contrast adjustment shaders. The result was pretty good and all new games I do will always have a color correction shader.

Figure 8-15

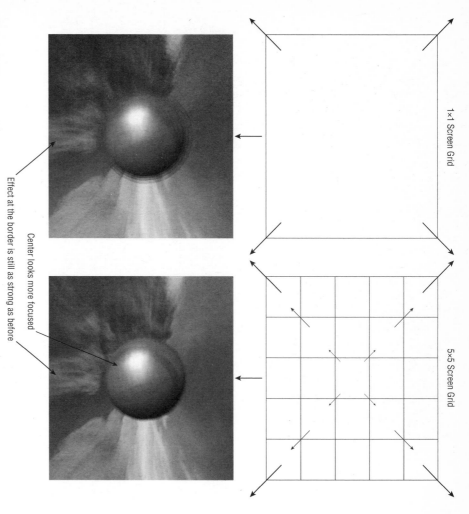

1x1 Screen Grid

5x5 Screen Grid

Effect at the border is still as strong as before

Center looks more focused

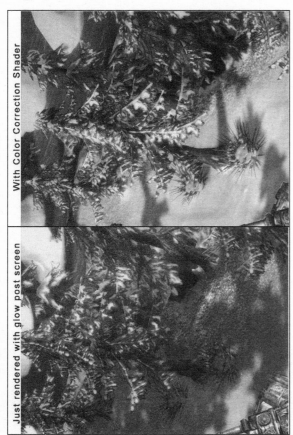

With Color Correction Shader

Just rendered with glow post screen

Figure 8-16

The basic code to do brightness effects just multiplies the color with a constant (or variable if you want to change it dynamically). For example, 0.5 makes the whole image half dark, 2.0 makes it two times brighter, 0.0 makes it completely black, and so on. The following line costs only one shader instruction and you can even combine it with the color correction shader, which is shown later in this chapter. It will still cost only one shader instruction. Figure 8-17 shows the brightness effect in action.

```
return brightness * originalColorValue;
```

Normal Image with brightness 1.0 **Dark Image with brightness 0.66** **Bright Image with brightness 2.0**

Figure 8-17

Changing the contrast is a little bit trickier. A value of 1.0 should let everything stay the same way, 0.0 should make the image completely gray (no more contrast left), and higher values should make the image a lot sharper. To achieve this effect, you have to subtract 0.5 from each color channel first, then multiply the result with the contrast value, and finally add 0.5 to each color channel again.

This way values below 1.0 make the image lose a lot of color, and 0.0 makes it completely gray (because only the 0.5 you add at the end is used; the rest is canceled out). Higher values give the image more contrast by darkening dark values down and bright light color values up (see Figure 8-18).

```
return (originalColorValue-float3(0.5, 0.5, 0.5)) * contrast +
float3(0.5, 0.5, 0.5);
```

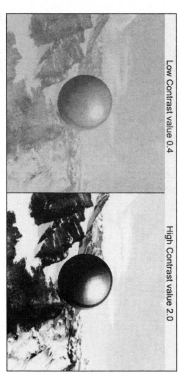

| Low Contrast value 0.4 | High Contrast value 2.0 |

Figure 8-18

To achieve the effect in Figure 8-18, use only very dense values close to 1 for the brightness and contrast. I used values like 0.96 for brightness and 1.2 for contrast. Additionally, you can change the color by adding a little color to each resulting pixel.

```
inputColor = float3
inputColor.r-0.04f,
inputColor.g,
inputColor.b+0.05f);
```

Be aware that the green color is more visible than blue or red and as soon as you add or subtract more than 0.1 to any color channel, the final output will look way too colorful; use very small values between 0.01 and 0.05. The following code makes the output image more bluish and removes a little bit of the red color. It was used for an arctic world. In the desert you probably want orange tones, for a Vulcan world you might use more red colors, and so on.

This is only a very easy way to change the colors; if you want to do more complex operations or even optimize the color correction part of your shader, you can use a matrix for each operation and then precalculate the result of all these matrices combined. Then you would have to modify each pixel only once. Here are some example matrices:

```
brightnessMatrix = float4x4(
brightness, 0, 0, 0,
0, brightness, 0, 0,
0, 0, brightness, 0,
0, 0, 0, 1);
contrastMatrix = float4x4(
1, 0, 0,
0, 1, 0,
0, 0, 1, 0,
```

```
      -0.5, -0.5, -0.5, 1);
contrastMatrix *= float4x4(
      contrast, 0, 0,
      0, contrast, 0, 0,
      0, 0, contrast, 0,
      0, 0, 0, 1);
contrastMatrix *= float4x4(
      1, 0, 0, 0,
      0, 1, 0, 0,
      0, 0, 1, 0,
      +0.5, +0.5, +0.5, 1);
addColorMatrix = float4x4(
      1, 0, 0, 0,
      0, 1, 0, 0,
      0, 0, 1, 0,
      -0.04, 0.0, +0.05, 1);
```

You can obviously do a lot more things with matrices such as rotations or scaling only one row, and so on. Rotations can be useful to change the colors completely and switch color channels; scaling rows differently can be used to do a luminance effect you saw earlier. Feel free to play around.

Menu Effects

In the last game of this book you will also use a menu post-screen effect, which is pretty similar to the PostScreenGlow shader you saw earlier. It does not glow as strong, but the glow effect is still visible. More important, it adds a film-like effect as in old movies, which looks funny when you see it animated. It might not fit into every game, but it was quite cool for the racing game and it fits to the menu music.

The basic idea here is to take a noise texture and go through it very slowly and power up the values so much that only the brightest points get used. Then the whole effect is stretched from the top to the bottom and several other effects are added on top of it (see Figure 8-19).

Figure 8-19

231

There are many more possibilities with post-screen shaders and sometimes you don't even want to do anything in the post-screen space, but it is just easier to remember and mark some pixel data in the rendering process and then later use it in a post-screen shader to show some effects with it. Not only can this be a lot faster than doing complicated calculations for each pixel, but in the post-screen space it is easier to do things like mixing neighboring pixels together, moving around a few pixels, and changing colors. For example, for shadow mapping shaders, you first render the scene into a special shadow map rendered from the lights perspective (a virtual camera at the light position) and then you render the scene again and use the shadow map for comparisons. It works great, but if you have a lot of different shaders you need to modify all of them. Often, the shaders, especially for Pixel Shader 1.1, are at the instruction limit and you can't just add more instructions. Then you have to add another pass and render the geometry again.

Another approach is to render the shadowed scene again, but this time just for a scene shadow map, which is later used in a post-screen shader to mix in the normally rendered scene without any special shadow shaders with the shadows. Thanks to the screen space, you can then also easily blur the shadow or change the intensity of the shadow without much trouble.

For more information about shaders, post-screen shaders, shadow mapping, and rendering techniques for today's hardware I recommend that you read one of the many good advanced books about shaders (yes, you are an advanced shader coder now if you read through all this) such as *Shader X*, *GPU Gems*, *Game Programming Gems*, and many vertex and Pixel Shader books you can easily find on sites like Amazon.com. I also recommend downloading the Nvidia SDK and checking out the many sample shaders.

Rocket Commander Game

This chapter has already covered so much about post-screen shaders, there is barely space left to talk about the Rocket Commander game. Well, that doesn't matter so much because the Rocket Commander game has already been out for a year now and many tutorials are available, including the very popular video tutorials series on Coding4Fun (which you can find on www.msdn.com or in any search engine).

It would not make sense to repeat all that again here. The Rocket Commander game is also written in Managed DirectX for .NET 1.1; the game itself runs in .NET 2. Managed DirectX is quite different from XNA — a lot of things could be ported easily, but all the font rendering, sprite handling, and so on is completely different code in DirectX and several features such as animated models are not supported yet in XNA (or at least they are not easy to import).

For that reason, Rocket Commander XNA shows only the basic engine, but it is still a great game and a lot of fun, even on the Xbox 360 with the Xbox 360 controller, for which the game was never intended. This section covers only the transition problems from MDX to XNA. If you want to know more about Rocket Commander, please visit its website at www.RocketCommander.com and check out the video tutorials. Read the source code and documentation and play one of the many game modifications that exist today.

Performance in XNA

No one believes how well XNA performs. The main reason for that is that most of the XNA games that exist today are just simple 2D games, which do not care much about archiving high performance and using 3D hardware effects and shaders. The other reason is that many people think it is bad for performance to wrap DirectX to Managed DirectX or XNA, because XNA just redirects the calls to the DirectX base framework. The important part here is how much code you can save and how much easier it is to write

Chapter 8: Post-Screen Shaders and the Rocket Commander Game

games in XNA, especially if you want to do a cross-platform game for both the Windows and Xbox 360 platforms. It would be a lot more work to get all these features by just using C++. You would probably need at least twice as many programmers to get everything to work as fast as an experienced XNA team could create a game. More likely, you will also run into more problems with memory issues, pointer management, and overall manageability in an unmanaged environment.

I have proven in the past that most programmers are just plain wrong in assuming Managed DirectX is a lot slower than DirectX; it does not really matter. If your code uses 100 percent of the GPU and 100 percent CPU you probably don't have a game, but just a benchmark to stress test or play around. Even in these situations Managed DirectX reaches almost the same performance (98–99 percent), but for a real game it does not matter anyway because you will not have time to optimize every single line of your code. Instead, you will focus on the important parts and try to get 10–20 percent of the code, which is called the most often, to work as fast as possible. Adding performance improvements to the other 80–90 percent takes five times longer and the improvements would only bring you a slightly better frame rate.

Instead, you should focus on the game itself. The gamer does not care if the game runs at 59 or 58 frames; he wants a fun game and if you allow different settings he can even minimize the resolution and disable effects to get to a higher frame rate. Too many games today focus on the graphics only (as I do in this book). At least this book trys to show many cool game ideas, and hopefully you can use the base code and make your own games without writing graphics engines for a long time without writing any new game.

Anyway, the Rocket Commander code was heavily optimized and I did a lot of performance tests back when I developed the first version. The whole game was also coded in just four weeks and it is not always easy to get the most out of the shaders if you have so little time. I still managed to get over 100 frames per second on a medium PC with a Shader Model 2.0 card and a high screen resolution while showing up to 5000 asteroids (in some cases over 30 million polygons were rendered each second) at the same time in each frame, and I had time to do collision testing and to create some other effects. Lower-end PCs, even ones completely without shader support, were still able to run the game. It did not look as pretty, but it ran very nicely.

Today, computers are even faster and CPUs have multiple cores, which can be used to execute several tasks at the same time. The Xbox 360 has three cores, too, and it uses six threads, which execute all the game code you need. I don't know of any game today that really needs this immense CPU power on the Xbox 360; the GPU is pretty fast, too, but especially on high resolutions it is still the GPU that will prevent you from getting better frame rates.

The Rocket Commander game is actually a nice example of how to split the work into two cores. The physics calculations and the pre-testing if asteroids and sectors are even visible take up half of the CPU time (sometimes even more). The rendering plus additional effects take the other half of the CPU time each frame. The physics can be done in parallel to the rendering because the physics calculation checks only whether two asteroids intersect with each other. In that case, it bounces both asteroids back (see Figure 8-20) and makes sure they don't intersect anymore.

In the next frame the newly updated physics positions, movement vectors, and so on can be used, which is only a slight disadvantage because the physics are now calculated for the next frame and not for the current frame. (It would be too late to try to render the new physics positions because most of the asteroids will already be rendered when the physics update is complete.) As you can see in the image, you don't have to check every asteroid, only the ones near to each other, and this can even be optimized further by putting them into sectors, which helped to improve the physics performance by a factor of 10 in the original Rocket Commander.

The important thing here is that Rocket Commander XNA performs even better than the original. It is possible to play the game in HDTV 1080p resolution on the Xbox (or the PC) and still use all the graphics effects, use full anti-aliasing, and show several thousand asteroids at the same time at very high frame rates.

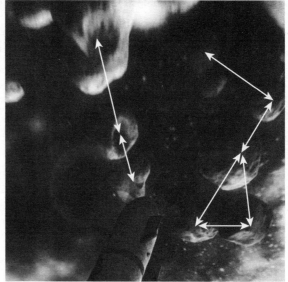

Figure 8-20

Moving from MDX to XNA

The base engine of Rocket Commander is similar to the XnaGraphicsEngine. There are more features in the Rocket Commander engine such as animated models or better handling and rendering of many asteroids. For example asteroids all use the same shaders and materials and allow the game to render them in a very efficient way. But some other features are implemented in an easier and better way in XnaGraphicsEngine than in Rocket Commander — such as the font and sprite management in XNA. You also can take advantage of the new shader classes you wrote and you can even plug in new shaders if you want to play around with the visual appearance of Rocket Commander XNA a bit.

Please also note that some features such as the animated model support or the occlusion testing for the lens flare effects in the original Rocket Commander were not possible in XNA 1.0 at the time XNA Rocket Commander was written. Thanks to XNA 2.0, occlusion querying is now possible again and several frameworks and engines are available today that allow you to use animated 3D models. Check out the code at the end of this book for examples on how to use these new features. The occlusion testing is something that was just missing from the XNA 1.0 Framework. I would guess it was too hard to get it to work on both the PC and the Xbox 360 the same way, but it is still bad for the lens flare effect because it will no longer disappear and blend in and out when an asteroid moves in front of the sun. The animated model can still be done by doing custom model processing or even introducing a new format for all the models, but you want to keep the port as simple as possible and you certainly don't want to re-export every single model and re-test it all over again.

The network code of the game was also ripped out in the Xbox 360 version because there isn't any access to the System.Net namespace on the Xbox 360. On the Windows platform, the game still sends and receives high scores to and from the Internet server via Web services. All other game data and the levels are 100 percent compatible and even porting the mods to XNA would be possible, but I have other things to do. Feel free to write more Rocket Commander Mods, especially on the XNA Framework. I'm always happy to receive e-mails from people all over the world who are using the code and writing mods, and who have success stories to tell about learning from the tutorials and the source code.

At the end of 2006, I wrote a long blog post on my website comparing MDX with XNA and talking all about the advantages and disadvantages of using XNA. If you worked with MDX before and are still wondering if XNA is worth the effort, read this article. In Rocket Commander XNA some new features were added, especially more unit tests and the multithreading that I will talk about in a second, but the overall number of source code lines decreased by more than 10 percent, which shows you that even porting a project makes it simpler. This effect is obviously even greater if you start fresh with an XNA project.

Using Threads to Improve Performance

The overall performance of Rocket Commander XNA is great on both Windows and the Xbox 360, especially when just doing some benchmarks, and performance is absolutely perfect. The GPU is pushed to its limits and there is no reason why you should be afraid of Managed code. Windows performance is especially great; all my programs and games are completely GPU bound even in low resolutions and even when they have only one thread.

On the Xbox 360, the performance is a little bit worse and you have to take many things into consideration, which is hard because there is again not much documentation around. For example, the worst thing you can do on the Xbox 360 is to generate new data each frame, and even if you just create an enumerator by executing a foreach loop, it will affect your performance. The good thing is that you have three cores (and six hardware threads) at your fingertips, which allow you to optimize performance. It was possible for the Rocket Commander game to optimize the game loop a lot because the physics and update threads eat up almost 50 percent of the CPU time. On the PC it does not matter much because my GPU is slowing everything down (see Figure 8-21), but on the Xbox 360, I was able to almost double the frame rate using multiple threads. Nice.

Result and Screenshots

Rocket Commander XNA is a great game and it runs even better than the original. It now has support for the Xbox 360 and the XNA Framework on the PC. Thanks to the new multithreading ability of the game and the fact that you can split up the physics and the rendering engine so easily, the physics are now more precise, and the rendering engine has more time to render more asteroids if you like or add other cool effects.

Both games look so similar that it is hard to tell the difference between the original game and the XNA port. You will probably detect it only through the missing features (such as animated models and occlusion checking for lens flares) or by just looking at the new game font. I added the XNA logo in the main menu to tell the difference between running the original game and the XNA version (see Figure 8-22).

I hope you have fun with the game. It is freely available, as was the original Rocket Commander game, and you can use it for your own game ideas or just to play around with it a little. Check out Figure 8-23 for a screenshot of Rocket Commander XNA in action.

Rocket Commander, Single-threaded (simplified):

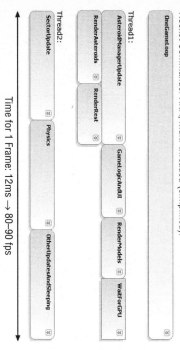

OneGameLoop

AsteroidManagerUpdate

SectorUpdate · Physics · RenderAsteroids · RenderRest · …

GameLogicAndUI

RenderModels

WaitForGPU

Time for 1 Frame: 20ms → 50 fps

Rocket Commander XNA, Multi-threaded (simplified):

OneGameLoop

Thread1:

AsteroidManagerUpdate

RenderAsteroids · RenderRest

GameLogicAndUI

RenderModels

WaitForGPU

Thread2:

SectorUpdate

Physics

OtherUpdatesAndSleeping

Time for 1 Frame: 12ms → 80–90 fps

Figure 8-21

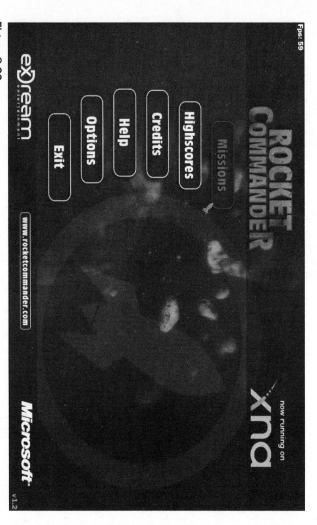

Figure 8-22

Figure 8-23

Challenge: Write an Edge Detection Shader

This chapter offered detailed discussion of post-screen shaders and covered almost every basic post-screen shader that exists. You learned about the basic components to write similar shaders. For example, the color correction shader can be used to achieve sepia effects, as shown previously in Figure 8-1. One shader I left out intentionally is the Edge Detection shader. It may not be useful for every single game, but there are a lot of other shaders that use the basic functionality of an edge detection shader. Here are some examples:

❑ Edge detection shaders for an evil alien-like look or for a high-tech special ops view mode that allows you to see much sharper in the night.

❑ Comic and toon shaders, which just take the input color and reduce it to very few colors — for example, from a color table or simple image that maps each color value to certain predefined colors. Then the thick border lines are drawn for every 3D surface, which can be done via an edge detection shader. You could also improve it a bit by drawing the lines in 3D and then adding the solid geometry on top of it, leaving you with the outlines for each 3D object, which the edge detection shader can pick up more easily. Note: You can also check out the non-realistic rendering sample on the XNA Creators Club to learn more about this technique at http://Creators.xna.com.

❑ Edge detection shaders can be used to add contrast to the scene or to find lines or contours. Edge detection is often the opposite of a blur effect, which mixes everything together, making the final

237

result too washed out sometimes. An edge detection shader can help if you want a sharper image to start with before doing additional glow and blur effects.

☐ Edge detection shaders can also be used to create very artistic images that look like they were painted and not rendered. You just use a very high edge detection amount and add other filters such as strain effects or the half-tone shader from Figure 8-1.

To complete this exercise you have to create a simple edge detection filter. The basic idea here is to take several pixels from the original scene map and compare them with the neighboring pixels. In Shader Model 1.1, you can take only four texture inputs, and in Shader Model 2.0 only eight; therefore, you are limited in how many pixels you can use in the Pixel Shader. Doing comparisons is also not that easy and not a good thing for Pixel Shader 1.1. Instead, just take a center point, multiply it by 2, and then subtract two surrounding points (top and bottom, and left and right). Then take the grayscale value with the help of the Luminance function of the result, and you have your edges.

The following is the basic Pixel Shader code; if you are in Shader Model 2.0, you can do even more texture fetches. If you are unsure how to extend the shader, please check out the edge detection shader of Nvidia's FX Composer. You should try to develop the whole shader in FX Composer anyway, and then you can work on a C# class if you want to import it into your engine. The variables $col1$, $col2$, $col3$, and $col4$ are four colors from the scene map through four texture coordinates you passed to the Pixel Shader.

```
return Luminance(
    // Horizontal
    (col1*2.0f-col2-col3)+
    // Vertical
    (col2*2.0f-col1-col4));
```

If you managed to get your shader to work, you should see something similar to Figure 8-24.

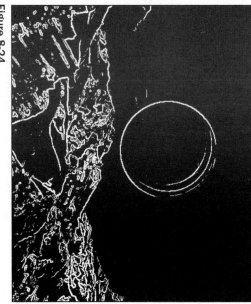

Figure 8-24

Summary

In this chapter you learned all about post-screen shaders. This concludes your graphics engine for now. Graphics effects are nice and can be a lot of fun to play around with, but this book is about game development, and doing graphics work is only a part of it. In the next part of this book you will focus a little bit more on the other aspects such as sound, input, and a general game engine. Some of that code was already used in the previous games. In particular, the Rocket Commander game uses sounds and advanced input classes, and also has a lot of game logic.

Here is a recap of some of the things that post-screen shaders can be used for:

❑ Sky cube mapping (okay, it is a pre-screen shader, but it works similarly).

❑ Rendering textures on top of the scene (blend overlay).

❑ Inverting the scene map (that's easy, just use 1-color).

❑ Turning the scene map into black and white with help of the Luminance function.

❑ Adding screen border effects, in this case to darken the screen borders for a TV-like effect.

❑ Glowing techniques and how to get them to perform very fast through downsampling.

❑ HDR faking by using an extra alpha channel in the glow shader. Alternatively, you can try using better render targets supporting more than 8 bits per channel and allowing you to save HDR colors in the scene map, which then can later be used for real HDR effects.

❑ Edge detection (well, that was your part).

❑ Menu effects, noise textures in shaders, half-tone effects, and so on.

❑ Color correction including brightness changing, contrast adjustments, and adding colors to influence the overall look of the scene. The sepia effect is also possible with a color-correction post-screen shader.

❑ Motion blur, either per-pixel or just for the whole screen. The chapter also covered additional tricks to improve the screen, including rendering a 10 × 10 screen grid instead of just one screen quad.

❑ And many more shaders.

I hope you found these last chapters useful and that you were able to create your XNA graphics engine in a short time thanks to the many samples I provided with each chapter. In this chapter, you can test out many post-screen shaders with the source code of XnaGraphicsEngine, which is now quite a big and powerful engine that enables you to work with shaders, 3D geometry, sprites, post-screen shaders, and many more things without your having to worry about any implementation details because it is all handled for you.

Using a multithreaded solution also provided you with great performance results for the Rocket Commander XNA game, but it is harder to program multithreaded.

It is easy now to rely on the graphics engine and stop writing unit tests, but don't do that. It will hurt you later when you try to figure out why menu x does not work the way it should or unity does this instead of that. With a menu unit test, you can quickly find out what's wrong. A unit test for the in-game units is probably also a lot faster to test and debug than going through the whole game, setting everything up, and then waiting for the error to happen again.

More graphics effects, physics, and the racing game are discussed in the last part of this book, but now check out Part III, which also gives you another great game (say hello to my little shoot-'em-up) and you dive a little bit deeper into the details for sound, input, and game logic classes.

Part III: Improving Your Game Engine

Chapter 9: Adding Sound with XACT

Chapter 10: Player Input and the User Interface

Chapter 11: Creating XNA Shooter

Adding Sound with XACT

This chapter takes a closer look at XACT. XACT is the name for Microsoft's Cross-Platform Audio Creation Tool, which allows you to create audio projects for the Windows and Xbox 360 platforms. It is actually the only way to play sounds in XNA on the Xbox 360. It doesn't matter so much for the Windows platform because you can plug in any other sound engine you want (DirectSound of DirectX, OpenAL, FMod, and so on) and play sound or music this way. It is not that easy on the Xbox 360 because you can use only the XNA Framework here and it is absolutely not possible to use any other framework for playing sound but XACT because you cannot use any unmanaged code in XNA. To play sound or use any low-level hardware on the Xbox 360, you would need unmanaged code to access it. For the same reason you cannot use any other graphics or input engine than the one XNA provides for you.

XACT was implemented into XNA to make sure it is possible to use the same sound content and sound playback code for both the Windows and the Xbox 360 platforms. For example, the Xbox 360 supports only XMA compression; the PC uses other compression formats for sound and music such as MP3, OGG, ADPCM, and many other custom compression formats, but only ADPCM and uncompressed sound files are supported in XACT. Voice-over-IP applications often use their own proprietary sound compression format because the human voice can be compressed better than music, for example. Luckily, XNA does allow you to use Voice via Xbox Live and Games for Windows Live services in the new XNA 2.0 networking API (for more details see Chapter 14). Sound effects are very short and small anyway, but as a game developer, you want the highest quality possible for sound effects. Therefore, sound effects are often uncompressed or use lossless compressions. Music, on the other hand, takes up a lot of space. If your game is on a DVD or you have plenty of hard disk space you can waste, you could just store the music as uncompressed .wav files or directly on the CD or DVD. For XNA games this is not an option because you can't access the DVD on the Xbox 360, and wasting a few hundred MB for just the music is not a good idea for your game.

In the past, with DirectX or Managed DirectX applications, you would most likely use DirectSound for the sound playback or use other frameworks such as OpenAL or commercial sound engines like FMod (but FMod is free for personal use or open source projects). Even with these frameworks you will still have to do a lot of custom code; you have to decide which sound format is the best for you and you will have to worry about sound compression yourself. Additionally, you must implement a way to play music yourself, too. For example, DirectSound is really not usable for music — it just supports .wav files — but if you want to play MP3 or OGG music files, you have to use other frameworks such as DirectShow, Windows MCI, ActiveX sound playback codecs, or other free and commercial frameworks and sound engines. Yes, you are right, this sounds like a lot of work. The actual code to play back sounds or music is very simple for most games. It gets a little bit more complicated if you want to use complex 3D sound calculations and if you want to support surround sound, but it is still way easier to program these things than to develop your 3D engine.

More information about the improvements of XACT in XNA 2.0 will be provided later in this chapter. For the games in this book, it does not matter if you are using XACT from XNA 1.0 or the version from XNA Game Studio 2.0. The source code of the games for this book will be updated when XNA 2.0 final comes out, but the general way to play back sounds will stay the same as described in this chapter.

No DirectSound

I'm assuming that most of you have worked with DirectSound before and when you write your first game in XNA you will notice that the sound namespace is very different from DirectSound of DirectX. Take a quick look at how DirectSound was used in Managed DirectX. First, you had to initialize the DirectSound device:

```
soundDevice = new DirectSound.Device();
soundDevice.SetCooperativeLevel(form, CooperativeLevel.Priority);
```

Now you can load all the sounds, but it can be a little bit more complicated to make sure you have multiple sound buffers and to catch instances in which the file does not exist, which would cause DirectSound just to throw an InvalidOperationException with no additional error message. In the Managed DirectX Rocket Commander code, the following was used to make sure all sound files exist and to make sure you can play back sounds multiple times:

```
if (File.Exists(Directories.SoundsDirectory + "\\" + filename) ==
    false)
{
    Log.Write("Sample " + filename + " was not found!");
    loaded = false;
    return;
} // if (File.Exists)
BufferDescription bufferDesc = new BufferDescription();
bufferDesc.StaticBuffer = true;
bufferDesc.ControlPan = true;
bufferDesc.ControlVolume = true;
bufferDesc.ControlFrequency = true;
buffer = new SecondaryBuffer[setNumberOfSimultaneousSounds];
channelVolume = new float[setNumberOfSimultaneousSounds];
channelPanning = new float[setNumberOfSimultaneousSounds];
buffer[0] = new SecondaryBuffer(
    Directories.SoundsDirectory + "\\" + filename,
    bufferDesc,
    Sound.Device);
defaultFrequency = buffer[0].Frequency;
for (int i = 1; i < buffer.Length; i++)
    buffer[i] = buffer[0];
```

```
try
{
  for (int i = 1; i < buffer.Length; i++)
    buffer[i] = buffer[0].Clone(Sound.Device);
} // try
catch { } // catch
```

And finally, the following is the code required to play the sound effect. Additionally, you can set the volume and panning of each sound buffer channel thanks to the code in the constructor of the Sample class (ControlPan, ControlVolume, ControlFrequency, and so on). The extra code to manage all the sound buffers and the properties for each sound (volume, panning, frequency) are not shown here because there is a lot of code in the Sample class of Rocket Commander. Take a look at the freely available Rocket Commander source code if you are interested further.

```
// Make sure to start at position 0
buffer[currentBufferNum].SetCurrentPosition(0);
// And play the sound
buffer[currentBufferNum].Play(0, BufferPlayFlags.Default);
```

In XNA, you no longer need a Sample class. You can extend the Sound class to support everything you need, including the MusicManager of Rocket Commander. You replace the Sample class, and everything else in the Sound namespace of Rocket Commander.

Because of the structure of XACT, which is discussed shortly, you have to load the XACT project and the used wave and sound banks yourself. But don't worry; the code for that is very simple. You already used XACT in the first chapters for all the arcade games.

```
audioEngine = new AudioEngine("YourSoundProject.xgs");
waveBank = new WaveBank(audioEngine, "Wave Bank.xwb");
soundBank = new SoundBank(audioEngine, "Sound Bank.xsb");
```

And that's it; all you have to do to play a sound now is to call the following:

```
soundBank.PlayCue(soundName);
```

Looks much easier, doesn't it? You might ask about all the extra functionality you had to implement for DirectSound. No, it is not missing, but you have to think differently about sound in XNA. Sound files are no longer managed completely by the custom code of your game. Instead the XACT sound project contains all the predefined sound parameters for you. Instead of modifying each sound volume yourself or changing the pitching to reuse existing sounds yourself, you could set all this inside of the XACT tool. This is especially useful to make sure all sound effects are at the same volume level and to make sure the music is not too loud. You can even specify that certain sounds are only allowed to be played once (such as the background music) or if you want your engine to allow playing multiple instances of the same sound for firing sounds or explosions. You learn more about this later in this chapter.

Handling .wav Files

For both DirectSound and XACT all your sound files must be in the .wav file format, especially for all sound effects. If you have different sound files in other formats, you have to convert them first. For example, MP3 files are not supported and you cannot play them in DirectSound or just drop them into your XACT project. You have to convert them to .wav files first. Please also note that certain .wav files are not supported in XACT and you will get a warning message that the format is not supported when you add the sound files into a wave bank in XACT.

It is not easy to make sure a music file is in the correct format and that it can be compressed the best way possible in XACT for both the Xbox 360 and the Windows platform (see Figure 9-1).

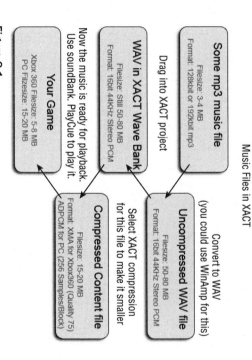

Music Files in XACT

Some mp3 music file
Filesize: 3-4 MB
Format: 128kbit or 192kbit mp3

Drag into XACT project

Convert to WAV
(you could use WinAmp for this)

Uncompressed WAV file
Filesize: 50-80 MB
Format: 16bit 44KHz Stereo PCM

WAV in XACT Wave Bank
Filesize: Still 50-80 MB
Format: 16bit 44KHz Stereo PCM

Select XACT compression
for this file to make it smaller

Compressed Content file
Filesize: 15-20 MB
Format: XMA for Xbox360 (Quality 75)
ADPCM for PC (256 Samples/Block)

Now the music is ready for playback.
Use soundBank. PlayCue to play it.

Your Game
Xbox 360 Filesize: 5-8 MB
PC Filesize: 15-20 MB

Figure 9-1

Just convert all your sounds to 16-bit 44 KHz Stereo PCM .wav files to make sure you can compress them. Even if your music is only mono, you still have to save it in stereo and if you have 8-bit PCM files, don't try to use them. Convert to 16-bit and stereo or XACT will not allow you to compress the sound files correctly. For 8-bit files, you will get the error message shown in Figure 9-2, and mono files compress badly. You will also lose quality for your 16-bit stereo files, but choosing the right XMA and ADPCM compression level for you might tweak the sound quality a little bit.

Figure 9-2

Please note that music files are not really supported by XACT and it is a much better tool for sound effect files than for music files. For the PC platform, using ADPCM files for your music might not make much sense if you have MP3 files and already have some code to play them back. On the Xbox 360 platform, you currently have no choice but to use XMA compression and XACT for your music files.

You can use compression for your sound effects, too, but I recommend that you try to use high compression ratios. For a PC game, it is also very uncommon to use heavily compressed sound files; instead, you will just use files of lower quality (22 KHz mono) because loading them is much faster, and using MP3 files for sounds is impractical because the CPU would have to decompress them every time you play them or you would have to decompress all files at the start of your game, which could take a while. In most cases, adding a few extra megabytes to your game will not affect much, but if you are an optimization freak like I am and you want to make sure the game is as small as possible without losing any feature or noticing any quality drop, you will still try to compress all the files with various options until everything is small and still sounds right.

I also compressed all texture files of all games in this book several times and used different formats to find out which one was the optimal format for each texture. For example, menu and interface graphics are compressed very well with the PNG format because it stores the bitmap in a lossless manner, but PNG files are just too big for model textures or landscape textures. In these cases, DDS files are used, which also have the advantage of saving video memory, which is another important point for the Xbox 360. Don't waste your main memory, disk space, or video memory — all of them are very rare on a console.

For example, the Rocket Commander game from the previous chapter uses about 15 sound files (see Figure 9-3) and with compression enabled, the game is nearly 1MB smaller on the Xbox 360. Not much, but every bit counts.

Enough talk about the basics and file formats; next you create your first sound project in XACT.

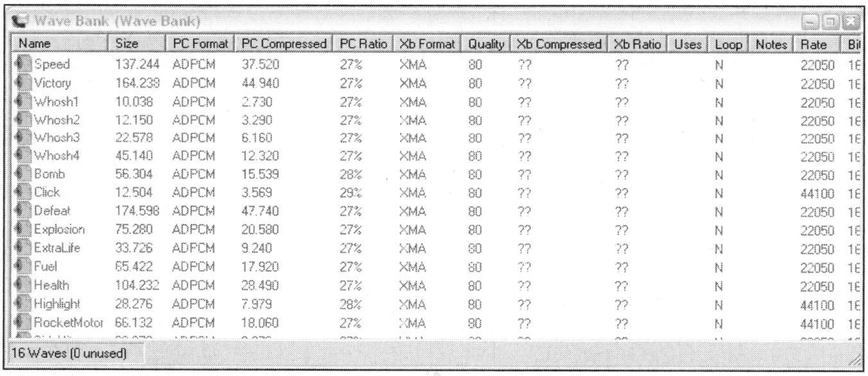

Figure 9-3

Name	Size	PC Format	PC Compressed	PC Ratio	Xb Format	Quality	Xb Compressed	Xb Ratio	Uses	Loop	Notes	Rate	Bit
Speed	137.244	ADPCM	37.520	27%	XMA	80	??	??		N		22050	16
Victory	164.238	ADPCM	44.940	27%	XMA	80	??	??		N		22050	16
Whosh1	10.038	ADPCM	2.730	27%	XMA	80	??	??		N		22050	16
Whosh2	12.150	ADPCM	3.290	27%	XMA	80	??	??		N		22050	16
Whosh3	22.578	ADPCM	6.160	27%	XMA	80	??	??		N		22050	16
Whosh4	45.140	ADPCM	12.320	27%	XMA	80	??	??		N		22050	16
Bomb	56.304	ADPCM	15.539	28%	XMA	80	??	??		N		22050	16
Click	12.504	ADPCM	3.569	29%	XMA	80	??	??		N		44100	16
Defeat	174.598	ADPCM	47.740	27%	XMA	80	??	??		N		22050	16
Explosion	75.280	ADPCM	20.580	27%	XMA	80	??	??		N		22050	16
ExtraLife	33.726	ADPCM	9.240	27%	XMA	80	??	??		N		22050	16
Fuel	65.422	ADPCM	17.920	27%	XMA	80	??	??		N		22050	16
Health	104.232	ADPCM	28.493	27%	XMA	80	??	??		N		22050	16
Highlight	28.276	ADPCM	7.979	28%	XMA	80	??	??		N		44100	16
RocketMotor	66.132	ADPCM	18.060	27%	XMA	80	??	??		N		44100	16

16 Waves (0 unused)

Using XACT

XACT used to be a tool just for Xbox 360 developers and you could not get it easily. You would have to be a certified Xbox 360 developer and have access to the XDK (Xbox Development Kit). Not an easy thing even if you are a professional game developer and have worked many years in the industry, if you ask me.

But all that has changed. Microsoft decided to include XACT in the DirectX SDK a year ago and although not many have used it for PC-only games, XACT becomes important now for XNA game development. It is the only way to get any sound files for XNA on the Xbox 360. You don't have to install the DirectX SDK to get access to the XACT tool; it is also included in the XNA Game Studio Express Installation. You can find it under Start ⇨ All Programs ⇨ Microsoft XNA Game Studio Express ⇨ Tools ⇨ XACT Auditioning Utility. If you use another version of XACT, please make sure that it is supported by XNA; for example, the August 2006 DirectX SDK has XACT 2.0, too, but it saves content files in version 40. The October 2006 DirectX SDK and the XNA Framework use version 41 content files, which are not compatible with previous versions. If you load older XACT sound projects, you might get very strange errors (for example, files are missing) or just get an InvalidOperationException. Future versions might also behave differently. To make sure your XACT project is supported, check the content version in the .xap file (which is just a simple text file; you can open it with any text editor you want).

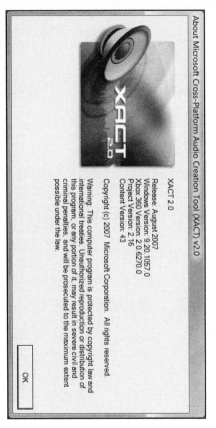

About Microsoft Cross-Platform Audio Creation Tool (XACT) v2.0

XACT 2.0

Release: August 2007
Windows Version: 9.20.1057.0
Xbox 360 Version: 2.0.6270.0
Project Version: 2.16
Content Version: 43

Copyright (c) 2007 Microsoft Corporation. All rights reserved.

Warning: This computer program is protected by copyright law and international treaties. Unauthorized reproduction or distribution of this program, or any portion of it, may result in severe civil and criminal penalties, and will be prosecuted to the maximum extent possible under the law.

OK

Figure 9-4

The .xap file is structured in a simple way and looks similar to XML files. The version numbers are a little bit confusing, but you just have to check for version 13 (which is content version 41 of the XACT tool and can be checked in its About dialog box; see Figure 9-4). Older versions such as 11 or 12 (of older DirectX SDKs) are not supported. This issue can also happen to you if you open up an early XNA project from the XNA beta times (August through October 2006), which still used the old XACT tool. XACT for XNA 2.0 uses version 16 and has the content version 43, but you can still load all older XACT files without problems.

```
Signature = XACT2;
Version = 13;
Options
{
```

```
}
Global Settings
{
[...]
}
```

If you just want to make a simple change to some sound volume of a sound file inside your XACT project inside Visual Studio, you can just open the .xap file in the text editor of Visual Studio and edit the value yourself instead of minimizing Visual Studio, searching for the .xap file, opening it, searching for the correct location where the volume is stored, and then changing the value with the XACT tool.

The best thing that can happen to you as a game developer for sounds is having someone that does the sound effects and music for you. Explain the XACT tool to this person and you won't have to worry much about sound, volumes, and formats anymore. That's business for the sound guy. Unfortunately, most small teams don't have a dedicated person for sound and if you program on your own, make your own graphics and other game content files, you will also have to make your own sound effects. Try to use existing sound effects or freely available sounds at first and exchange them later. For music, it often makes sense to choose similar music, maybe even music from your MP3 library, just for testing and presenting your game. For the final version you will need your own music, of course; you can't just use someone else's music and put it in your game. Some music files are free to use in your game projects, but most music you hear every day is not free to use. Getting sound effect files is a little bit easier. For some simple sound effects, you can use the sound effect files of the example games from this book. I also suggest that you search for free sound effect sites on the Internet if you don't have any of your own sound effect files or know anyone that can help you out.

To make things a little bit more interesting, you are going to create the sound project for the game at the end of Part III in this book: XNA Shooter, which is a simple shoot-'em-up style game with cool 3D graphics, sound effects, and keyboard, mouse, and Xbox 360 controller support (which is discussed in detail in the next chapter).

Creating Projects

After you open the XACT tool you will see a new empty project (see Figure 9-5). It does not contain any sound files, wave or sound banks yet, but certain variables and settings are already created for you in each new project:

☐ The project tree, which always contains the same root elements. You cannot change it.

☐ Two default categories: Default and Music, which you can use to mark your sound files as sound effects or music files to make your sound files behave differently.

☐ One global variable, SpeedOfSound, which is always 343.5 and 4 cue instance variables for the Distance, Doppler Shift, Number of Cue Instances, and Orientation Angle. All these variables are important only for 3D sounds, which are sadly not possible in XNA yet. More about this issue will be discussed when you write the code to play back sound effects.

☐ A global effect path preset with nothing in it.

☐ All the other root elements are empty. You have to create the child elements for each of them yourself by either clicking on the toolbar or just right-clicking on the element and selecting New. For example, "New Wave Bank" creates a new wave bank.

249

To get any .wav files into your new XACT project, you have to create a wave bank first, which stores all the .wav files into a wave bank, and is then loaded and used by your game. This is more work than just loading .wav files yourself, but the idea behind XACT is to give the sound artist more flexibility in setting all kinds of sound parameters himself instead of nagging the programmer every time he wants to tweak some sound effect. This will not help you much when you have to do the XACT work and the programming yourself anyway, but XACT gives your project at least a little bit of organization for your sound files and you always know where you can change any sound parameters without having to go into your game code. The disadvantage of using XACT is that you can no longer dynamically load sound files; all content files (such as compiled models) have to be created and loaded when you start your game, and nothing can be added while the game is running. This inflexibility was very annoying to me at first because I always add stuff dynamically while writing and debugging my unit tests, but once I got used to it, it was fine. I now create all sound files and the XACT project early in the project and use only existing sounds in the unit tests.

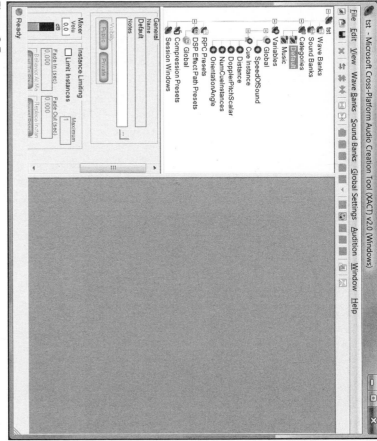

Figure 9-5

Creating Your Wave Bank

To create a wave bank for your project, you can either right-click Wave Banks and select New Wave Bank, use the menu, or you can use the toolbar icon for creating a wave bank (eighth entry, the orange-white rectangle with the wave effect; see Figure 9-5). The wave bank is just the storage for all the sound files you want to use. You can even have different wave banks; for example, if you have multiple levels in your game and you only want to load the wave files for the current level, you could separate the wave files and optimize your game this way. All projects of this book and all other projects I ever made contain only one wave bank, and other than separating the music files and sound files to support streaming the music files, I really don't think it is important to have multiple wave banks, and you will probably never need them either.

After you have created your wave bank, you can drag and drop .wav files into it or alternatively use the Insert Wave Files entry from the context menu. Figure 9-6 shows all the sound files you are going to use for the XNA Shooter game imported into your newly created XACT project.

As you can see, all sound files are still unused, which is indicated by the italic red font. As soon as you add these imported .wav files to a sound bank, they become green. But before you do that, you should make sure all of the files have the correct settings. By default, no compression is chosen and most of the sound files are pretty small; except for the music file, all sound effects are below 1MB data. The music file, which takes a whopping 36MB of disk space, is 3½ minutes long and in the format discussed previously (16-bit 44 KHz Stereo PCM).

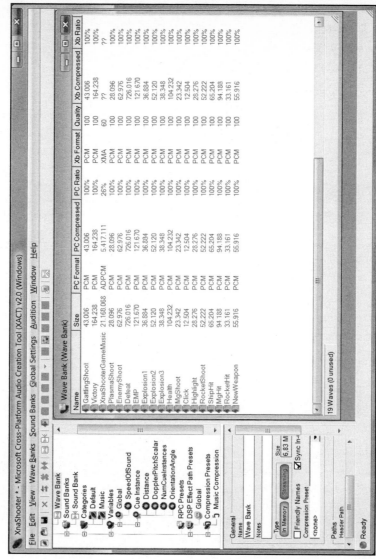

Figure 9-6

If you want to compress the music sound file, click it and select your desired compression preset in the wave properties panel. It currently shows <none>, but if you click the drop-down list, it has no other options for you. You have to create a compression preset first and then you can use it for any wave file you want (or just assign it to the whole wave bank). XACT works similarly with other presets, too. For example, if you want to create a custom variable for a sound effect, you have to create it first in the variables section and then you can select and use it in the sound bank.

Compressing Music Data

To create a new compression preset click Compression Presets and select New Compression Preset (see Figure 9-7). Now enter a name for your compression; in this case, you just want to create a music compression schema. The notes field is just for you and is never used anywhere outside the XACT tool. Lots of other panels also have note fields and optional parameters you will not need. You will probably find XACT very confusing when using it for the first time. I didn't like it at first either, but after a while you get used to it and you have to remember that this is the only way to get any sound files onto the Xbox 360 with XNA. If you create a Windows-only game, you can still use DirectSound or other sound engines, which might be simpler to use or have other advantages. Finally, set Windows compression (only ADPCM is available) with 128 samples per block (the default). Higher values will make the file smaller, but you can lose a little quality. Thirty-two samples per block is the highest ADPCM quality, but the file is about 30 percent bigger.

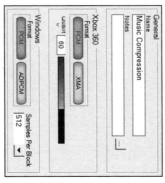

Figure 9-7

For the Xbox 360 you can select only XMA, but the compression is much better here. You might wonder why there are so many options when you can choose only one compression anyway. Well, that's XACT and we all can just hope that we get more compression formats in the future. XMA is fine for the Xbox 360; sometimes it produces file sizes that are a little too big, but it sounds good and works great. But ADPCM for the Windows platform is just unusable. It sounds worse than MP3 files and it is 4–5 times bigger. WMA or MP3 support would be great here.

Unfortunately, XACT does not show the resulting file size for XMA right away. You have to compile the project first, and then it shows you how compressed each wave is in the XMA format for the Xbox 360. To compile the project, you can click the last toolbar button or just press F7. By default, the project will compile to the Windows platform and you will still not see the XMA compression results. To finally get there you have to switch to the Xbox 360 output in the View menu, then compile the XACT project, and your wave bank will show the file sizes for the Xbox 360, too. (The PC Compression rates are always shown and they are always in the same ratio: 27 percent for the default ADPCM setting.)

The following table shows the compression ratios for the XnaShooterGameMusic.wav file (36MB uncompressed).

Compression	File Size	Compression Rate
Uncompressed	36MB	100%
MP3 with 192kbit	4.8MB	13%
MP3 with 128kbit	3.1MB	8.5%
AccPlus with 48kbit, similar to MP3 192kbit	1.2MB	3%
AccPlus with 24kbit, similar to MP3 96kbit	0.6MB	1.6%
OGG with 160kbit	3.8MB	11%
XACT ADPCM 32 samples per block	12.5MB	34%
XACT ADPCM 128 samples per block (default)	9.9MB	27%
XACT ADPCM 512 samples per block	9.3 MB	26%
XACT XMA 100% Quality	14.3 MB	40%
XACT XMA 90% Quality	8.9 MB	25%
XACT XMA 75% Quality	5.5 MB	15%
XACT XMA 60% Quality (default)	4.7 MB	13%
XACT XMA 30% Quality	3.5 MB	10%
XACT XMA 10% Quality	2.9 MB	8%

The lower-quality XMA files look very similar to the MP3 in size, but the quality is much worse. I would not recommend using any XMA file with very low compression settings. Use 50 percent or higher; the file size is still very similar with 60 percent (the default setting), and 75 percent is one of my favorite settings because for very good quality settings the file stays very small (below 15 percent, similar to MP3 with 192kbit) and also sounds similar. If you just have a game without music or with just one track, this will not matter to you, but if you have 10+ music tracks in your game, you want to think twice about the compression settings and explore all possibilities.

After setting the new compression for the music file you should now get file sizes of around 5–6MB for the Xbox directory and 10MB for the Win directory (see Figure 9-8). For the Rocket Commander XNA project, these file sizes are almost twice as much because you use two music files there. In later games of this book, more music is used and the file sizes go up even more.

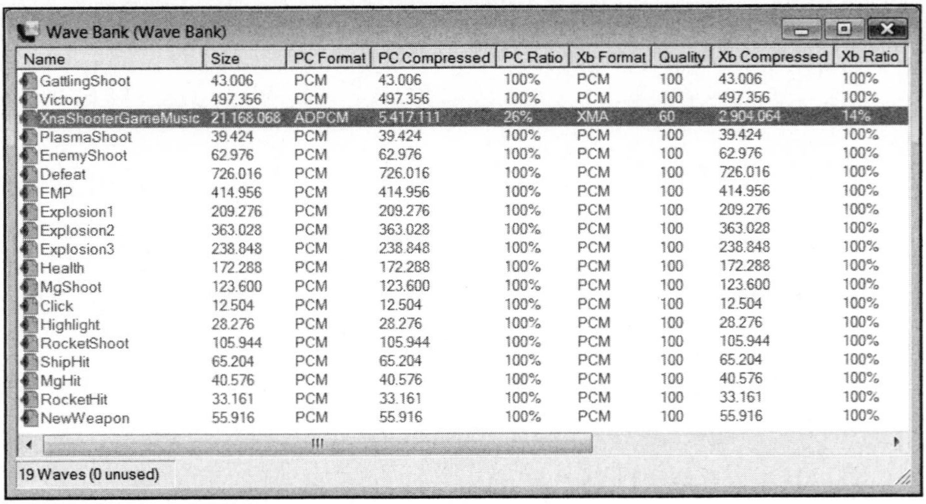

Sound Banks

Although you can compile the project and even load it in your XNA game, you can't use any sound yet because the XACT project just contains wave files right now. But for playback, you need sound cues, which have to be created in a sound bank first. Again you have the opportunity to create multiple sound banks here, but you probably will never need to do that.

The simplest way to get all the wav files working is to drag them over to your sound bank. But wait, where is the sound bank? You don't have one yet. As with the wave bank, you have to create it first. You can do this by clicking the Sound Banks entry or clicking the second orange icon in the toolbar (the one with the orange wave going over the orange-white box on the right side). The new sound bank is just named "Sound Bank"; if you just have one wave bank and one sound bank, just leave the default names. If you have multiple wave or sound banks, you should name them properly so you can find them more easily.

To drag all wave files from the wave bank over to your sound bank, you should position the windows in a way that allows you to see both of them completely. The sound bank window consists of two parts: the sound names on the top and the cue names on the bottom. Select all files from the wave bank and drag them over to the sound names section of the sound bank now (see Figure 9-9). Each sound here can get additional settings, such as changing the volume or frequency (pitch), or applying other variations or effects. You can add the same wave file multiple times and give it different sound names. For more complex games, you can even mix several wave files in multiple tracks and blend them on top of each other; then for playback this "mix" is used instead of a wave file. To add more than one track to a sound name, just drag another file on top of it and XACT will automatically create a second track for it. However, you will not use this feature in this chapter.

While you are editing the sounds in the sound bank you should make sure that the music (XnaShooterGameMusic) uses the category Music instead of Default (you can edit that in the sound properties panel on the left side). I usually also tell the music category to play sounds softer than the default sounds because I want the music to be more in the background. In your game, you can use the music category to control the volume of the music if you like. Additionally, you probably want to make sure only

Figure 9-8

Name	Size	PC Format	PC Compressed	PC Ratio	Xb Format	Quality	Xb Compressed	Xb Ratio
GattlingShoot	43.006	PCM	43.006	100%	PCM	100	43.006	100%
Victory	497.356	PCM	497.356	100%	PCM	100	497.356	100%
XnaShooterGameMusic	21.168.068	ADPCM	5.417.111	26%	XMA	60	2.904.064	14%
PlasmaShoot	39.424	PCM	39.424	100%	PCM	100	39.424	100%
EnemyShoot	62.976	PCM	62.976	100%	PCM	100	62.976	100%
Defeat	726.016	PCM	726.016	100%	PCM	100	726.016	100%
EMP	414.956	PCM	414.956	100%	PCM	100	414.956	100%
Explosion1	209.276	PCM	209.276	100%	PCM	100	209.276	100%
Explosion2	363.028	PCM	363.028	100%	PCM	100	363.028	100%
Explosion3	238.848	PCM	238.848	100%	PCM	100	238.848	100%
Health	172.288	PCM	172.288	100%	PCM	100	172.288	100%
MgShoot	123.600	PCM	123.600	100%	PCM	100	123.600	100%
Click	12.504	PCM	12.504	100%	PCM	100	12.504	100%
Highlight	28.276	PCM	28.276	100%	PCM	100	28.276	100%
RocketShoot	105.944	PCM	105.944	100%	PCM	100	105.944	100%
ShipHit	66.204	PCM	66.204	100%	PCM	100	66.204	100%
MgHit	40.576	PCM	40.576	100%	PCM	100	40.576	100%
RocketHit	33.161	PCM	33.161	100%	PCM	100	33.161	100%
NewWeapon	55.916	PCM	55.916	100%	PCM	100	55.916	100%

19 Waves (0 unused)

Chapter 9: Adding Sound with XACT

one music file is played at a time (maybe you call a StartMusic method several times or you just have multiple music files and you don't want to stop and restart them yourself).

For optimal music playback you should put all music files you want to play at a certain part of your game randomly into one sound bank entry (for example, MenuMusic and GameMusic; see Rocket Commander XNA as an example). Then click Play Wave on the right side of the sound bank window when the music sound entry is selected. Here you can force to loop this sound; some sounds are already looped, but for music it is always best to force it to make sure all music files work fine.

Finally, you have to make sure only one music file is played at a time, and if another music file is selected a nice fade-over effect would also be nice. Luckily, XACT provides all that for you. You could now set instance limiting and fade in/out durations for each single music file or you could be cleverer and just set it once for the Music category (see Figure 9-10). By default, LimitInstances is set to false; once you set it to true the properties below it become active. If you try to play another music item now after one music item is already started, an exception is thrown because BehaviorAtMax is set to FailToPlay. Change it to Replace for the correct behavior for music playback. For the rest of the settings, see Figure 9-10.

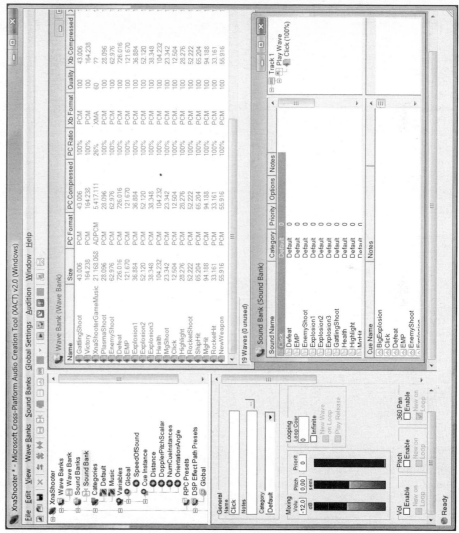

Figure 9-9

255

Cue Variables

If you want, to you can compile the project again now, but in your XNA code you still have no access to any sound effects. XNA allows you to access only sound cues, which have to be created first. This step is quite easy — just select all sound names and drag them down to the cue section of the sound bank window. The names are automatically taken from the filenames, but you can rename any entry if you like. I usually rename the music files to make access in XNA a little easier.

Another cool feature you can use for your XNA Shooter game is to assign multiple sound effects to one single sound cue. You'll use this feature for the explosion sound effect. You have three explosion wave files, but for simplicity you just want to tell XACT to play an explosion and it should randomly choose between one of the explosions for you. To do that, remove the Explosion2 and Explosion3 sound cues from the cue list again by selecting them and pressing the Del key. Now rename the Explosion1 cue to just Explosion. Finally, drag both the Explosion2 sound name and the Explosion3 sound name onto the Explosion sound cue. You should now see what's shown in Figure 9-11.

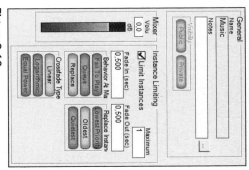

Figure 9-10

> **To make editing a little easier, make the sound bank window bigger or maximize it. XACT sometimes messes with you and when scrollbars appear and disappear all the time you might drop entries to the wrong location or duplicate items unwillingly (happens to me all the time).**

You might also notice that I renamed the game music sound cue to just GameMusic to make it easier to enter the name in your XNA code. Also make sure all the other sound cue names are easy to remember.

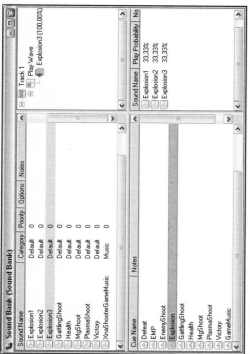

Figure 9-11

After compiling the project again, you can use the XACT project in XNA now and access all the sound cues. Please note that you don't have to compile the XACT project yourself all the time in XACT; XNA will automatically do that for you if you add the .xap project file to your XNA Game Studio project. Alternatively, you can also just add the compiled files and load them yourself in XNA. It does not matter how you do it, but the .xap file in your XNA project is certainly the most comfortable solution. When using XACT, however, I recommend pressing F7 to compile the project a lot in a similar way you would test a newly written unit test all the time until it works fine.

Other Effects

XACT allows you to set other effects and sound parameters, which is especially useful for 3D sound effects, where you can set all kinds of parameters for your sound effects. Combined with a little custom programming you can do very powerful things such as changing sound effects depending on the location they are played at, and automatically detecting halls from 3D geometry or open space. Your engine might also distort effects if they are played under water or after the player has been hit by a grenade. The possibilities are endless.

For this little game, you won't need any special effects, but as an example I will show you how to create a custom variable that allows you to change the frequency (pitch) of a sound effect during runtime. Changing it directly in XACT is easy, but you don't have direct access to these settings in XNA. You have to expose a public cue variable first, and you must make sure the sound uses this custom variable.

This is not just for fun. For both the Rocket Commander XNA and the game in the last part of this book, you need this effect to distort the motor sound of the rocket or the car you are currently driving with, depending on the current speed.

To create your new cue instance variable, click Cue Instance and select New Cue Instance Variable from the pop-up menu. You can type in anything you want here and use whatever values you like; they are not bound to anything yet. In this case you call the new variable `Pitch` and allow a range of −100 to +100; the rest of the properties can stay as they are (see Figure 9-12).

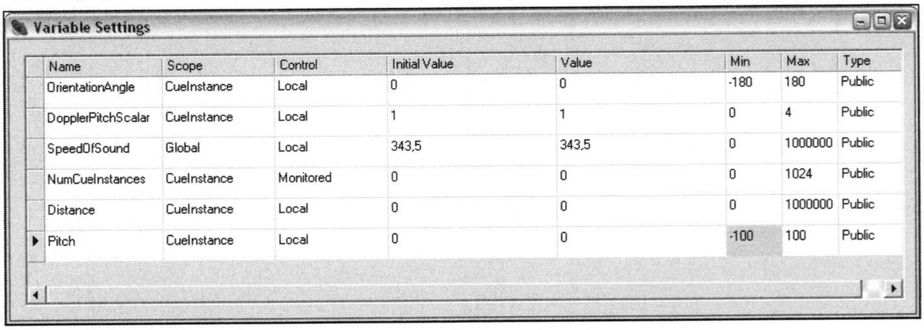

Name	Scope	Control	Initial Value	Value	Min	Max	Type
OrientationAngle	CueInstance	Local	0	0	-180	180	Public
DopplerPitchScalar	CueInstance	Local	1	1	0	4	Public
SpeedOfSound	Global	Local	343.5	343.5	0	1000000	Public
NumCueInstances	CueInstances	Monitored	0	0	0	1024	Public
Distance	CueInstance	Local	0	0	0	100000	Public
Pitch	CueInstance	Local	0	0	-100	100	Public

Figure 9-12

Next, you have to make sure XACT does something useful with this variable. You can set it now and assign it to any sound effect, but it will do nothing but store the value yet. In this case, you can use the existing parameters of the RPC Presets (Runtime Parameter Control), but the selections are very limited right now (you can change only the Volume, Pitch, and Reverb Send Level, whatever that is). Maybe more options will come in the future. For example, it is not possible to set the panning for Rocket Commander XNA, which was used in the Managed DirectX version to fake 3D sound effects. If XACT would support 3D sounds, this would not matter because you could easily do real 3D sound calculations, but sadly the 3D listener was dropped after the first XNA beta. It is possible to set 3D sound parameters in XACT and you could use them in native XACT projects, but XNA does not support it yet (not funny if you had implemented it before, as I did, and then everything stops working).

Anyway, for changing the pitch of a sound effect, you can easily use a new RPC Preset. Just click RPC Presets and add a new RPC Preset; call it RPC Pitch or just leave the default name. Select Sound::Pitch as the parameter and use the newly created `Pitch` variable. Now you can drag the left and right points in the graph below to let −12 equal −100 of your `Pitch` variable and +12 equal +100 (see Figure 9-13).

The final thing you have to do before this preset can be used is to assign all sounds to the preset that should be able to use this new variable. To do that, just drag a sound file from the sound bank (don't use a wave or cue; they won't work) onto the PRC Preset.

The following code can be used to start a sound cue and change the pitch cue variable dynamically. If you just want to set a static pitch value, don't go through this trouble; just create a new cue in XACT and set different pitch values. But for motor sounds you have to change the pitch dynamically and therefore you have to go through all this trouble.

```
rocketCue = soundBank.GetCue("RocketMotor");
rocketCue.Play();
// Set the global volume for this category
motorsCategory.SetVolume(MathHelper.Clamp(volume, 0, 1));
// Set pitch from -55 to +55 (little more than half the max values)
rocketCue.SetVariable("Pitch", 55 * MathHelper.Clamp(pitch, -1, 1));
```

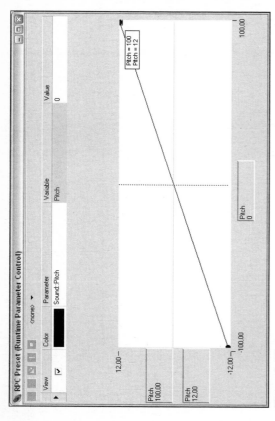

Figure 9-13

As you will see in a second, the rest of the Sound class is even easier and you will probably spend most of the time in XACT and then code your Sound class in a matter of minutes.

In the preceding example you can also see a way to change the volume for a category. Changing the volume of a cue directly is not supported by default, but you could create a volume cue variable the same way you just created the pitch variable to set custom volume values to your sound cues.

Changes in XNA 2.0

XACT will be improved in XNA 2.0, but at the time of this writing not much information is publicly available. The Gamefest conference had a session about XAudio 2, an improved low-level framework for Audio programming that works on both Xbox 360 and Windows, but support for XNA is not yet implemented. It will probably not be implemented for XNA 2.0 directly, but in a later version. Similar to XACT, which is build on top of low-level XAudio, it will probably be implemented in a similar way allowing you to access the functionality in the high-level XACT framework. XAudio is harder to use and only available directly with C++, while XACT is possible via XNA on a higher level.

The first thing you will notice when you open up XACT from XNA Game Studio 2.0 is the new properties panel in the lower left. As you can see in Figure 9-5, the new XACT version has now a lot of improved controls to modify volumes and other sound values. There are also many new visualizations that help you to understand what value means and how it affects your sound effects. But the overall functionality of XACT is pretty much the same as before, there are some new features here and there, but mostly XACT for XNA 2.0 is just a nicer looking version of the old XACT application.

XAudio was created to replace DirectSound from the DirectX SDK, which was once the most popular sound framework for Windows, but is more and more replaced with other APIs as described above in the Introduction to XACT. The XACT tool was originally available only on the Xbox platform, but now it is included in the DirectX SDK download and can be used with both DirectX and XNA. XAudio is not widely used on the PC yet most programmers still use DirectSound. In XNA, you will only use XACT and the Audio classes provided in the XNA Framework directly. XAudio 2 hopes to change this and tries to finally replace DirectSound, add new functionality and support for 3D Sounds and Dolby Surround formats.

You can read more about the comparison between DirectSound, XAudio, XACT, and the supported platforms on this wiki site: http://en.wikipedia.org/wiki/DirectSound.

The code in this chapter is based on XACT from XNA 1.0, but an updated version of the source code will be provided when XNA 2.0 is released. It will also state what has changed and how you can take advantage of the new Audio features of XNA 2.0 for new projects. If you are interested in XAudio 2 specifically, Microsoft provides a beta that lets you play around with the new API. While it is not yet implemented in XNA, in the future there will be support in the Audio classes of XNA and you can use the same methods from inside XNA then, too.

The XAudio 2 FAQ states the following:

Is XAudio 2 available for XNA? [added 7.31.07]
Just to clarify, I presume you're referring to XNA Game Studio? The term 'XNA' in general applies to all Microsoft game technologies, including the DirectX SDK, Xbox 360 XDK, etc. Regardless, specific to XNA Game Studio, we are currently evaluating XAudio 2 for future deployment on the platform. Note that as XNA Game Studio is a managed code space, the API would likely be somewhat simplified, just as XACT and graphics APIs have been. Certainly no changes would be made while XAudio2 is in beta. XACT remains the best avenue for implementing game audio on XNA Game Studio at present.

Sound Class

Creating the sound class is really simple. You already saw several sound classes in the first chapters and sound cue playback is easy. To make your life even easier, you can define an enum with all the sound cue names in it. This way, you make sure that every sound cue really exists and you don't mistype any sound. Another great advantage of this approach is IntelliSense, which will now show you all the available sound cues that are hidden in the XACT project if you don't have an enum like this. Spending two minutes to write this enum is the most valuable thing you can do for sound playback in XNA. Playing a sound cue is easy now with the help of the Play method in the Sound class.

```
/// <summary>
/// Play
/// </summary>
/// <param name="soundName">Sound name</param>
public static void Play(string soundName)
{
    try
    {
        if (soundBank == null)
            return;

        soundBank.PlayCue(soundName);
```

```
        } // try
        catch (Exception ex)
        {
            Log.Write("Playing sound " + soundName + " failed: " +
                ex.ToString());
        } // catch
    } // Play(soundName)
    /// <summary>
    /// Play
    /// </summary>
    /// <param name="sound">Sound</param>
    public static void Play(Sounds sound)
    {
        Play(sound.ToString());
    } // Play(sound)
```

You can also make the string version private to allow only the Sounds enum version. In case the sound bank could not be initialized in the constructor (for example, if the file is missing), this method will immediately return and you will not be able to play any sounds. A log file error will have already been reported in the constructor if that happened. Then you just call PlayCue to play and forget about the sound cue. In case this fails, you log an error message, but you don't throw the exception down to the caller because you always want to have the sound played and not to interrupt your program logic just because some sound file is missing or some effect did not work out.

As you saw before, you can also use the GetCue method to remember a sound cue and then do multiple things with it. This is also useful if you want to stop the cue yourself instead of waiting until it is finished playing. This is used to stop music playback in the following example:

```
someSoundCue = soundBank.GetCue("SomeSound");
someSoundCue.Play();
...
someSoundCue.Stop(AudioStopOptions.Immediate);
```

Although most of the Sound class is the same for most of the projects in this book, take a look at the differences and the special functionality because the basic playback code was already discussed (see Figure 9-14).

The first thing you will notice is the different sound cue names in the Sounds enum. Both Rocket Commander XNA and the Racing Game use the custom pitch cue variable just discussed. The XNA Shooter game does not use anything special; you just start the music at the beginning of the game, and then play all sound effects as you need them and that's it.

To make typing in the code to play sounds more comfortable, several helper methods were created. For example, PlayExplosionSound just replaces the following code, making it faster and easier to write the code required to play this sound effect:

```
Sound.Play(Sound.Sounds.Explosion);
```

For music playback, two additional methods are added, which also keep track of the music cue in case you want to stop or restart the music: StartMusic and StopMusic.

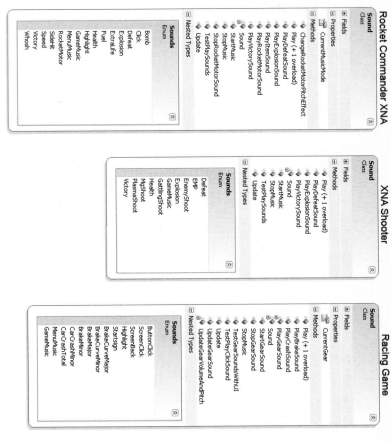

Figure 9-14

There is also a unit test in each sound class to check if the sound playback works the way you want it to. It is also used to check if all sounds have the proper volume settings. This is the unit test from the Rocket Commander XNA Sound class:

```
/// <summary>
/// Test play sounds
/// </summary>
public static void TestPlaySounds()
{
    TestGame.Start(
        delegate
        {
            if (Input.MouseLeftButtonJustPressed ||
                Input.GamePadAJustPressed)
                Sound.Play(Sounds.Bomb);
            else if (Input.MouseRightButtonJustPressed ||
                Input.GamePadBJustPressed)
                Sound.Play(Sounds.Click);
            else if (Input.KeyboardKeyJustPressed(Keys.D1))
                Sound.Play(Sounds.GameMusic);
            else if (Input.KeyboardKeyJustPressed(Keys.D2))
```

```
            Sound.Play(Sounds.MenuMusic);
        else if (Input.KeyboardKeyJustPressed(Keys.D3))
            Sound.Play(Sounds.Explosion);
        else if (Input.KeyboardKeyJustPressed(Keys.D4))
            Sound.Play(Sounds.Fuel);
        else if (Input.KeyboardKeyJustPressed(Keys.D5))
            Sound.Play(Sounds.Victory);
        else if (Input.KeyboardKeyJustPressed(Keys.D6))
            Sound.Play(Sounds.Defeat);
        else if (Input.KeyboardKeyJustPressed(Keys.D7))
        {
            Sound.PlayRocketMotorSound(0.75f);
            Sound.ChangeRocketMotorPitchEffect(0.5f);
        } // else if
        else if (Input.KeyboardKeyJustPressed(Keys.D8))
            Sound.StopRocketMotorSound();
        TextureFont.WriteText(2, 30,
            "Press 1-8 or A/B or left/right "+
            "mouse buttons to play back sounds!");

    });
} // TestPlaySounds()
```

Finally, the Update method is called automatically by the Update method of your BaseGame class inside the graphics engine. The Update method just makes sure that all parameters, looping, and timing values are updated inside XACT for you.

Rocket Motor Sound

Take a quick look at the Rocket Motor sound from Rocket Commander XNA. You already saw all the code required for this to work, but it might be nice to see it all thrown together and compatible with the Rocket Commander engine, which was written for DirectSound initially, but works fine with XACT now, too:

```
/// <summary>
/// Play rocket motor sound
/// </summary>
public static void PlayRocketMotorSound()
{
    // Get new cue every time this is called, else we get
    // Xact throwing this error: The method or function
    // called cannot be used in the manner requested.
    rocketMotorSound = soundBank.GetCue(Sounds.RocketMotor.ToString());
    // Plays the sound looped, set in XACT
    rocketMotorSound.Play();
    // Make motor category a little silent
    motorCategory.SetVolume(0.86f);
} // PlayRocketMotorSound(volume)

/// <summary>
/// Change rocket motor pitch effect
/// </summary>
/// <param name="pitchFactor">Pitch factor</param>
public static void ChangeRocketMotorPitchEffect(float pitchFactor)
{
```

```
rocketMotorSound.SetVariable("Pitch",
  55 * MathHelper.Clamp(pitchFactor - 1, -1, 1));
} // ChangeRocketMotorPitchEffect(pitchFactor)

/// <summary>
/// Stop rocket motor sound
/// </summary>
public static void StopRocketMotorSound()
{
  rocketMotorSound.Stop(AudioStopOptions.Immediate);
} // StopRocketMotorSound()
```

To start the rocket sound, you just call the PlayRocketMotorSound method after a mission starts; then you modify it during the flight with the help of the ChangeRocketMotorPitchEffect method:

```
// Adjust rocket playback frequency to flying speed
Sound.ChangeRocketMotorPitchEffect(0.66f + speed * 0.9f);
```

And finally, StopRocketMotorSound can be called to stop the rocket sound when you die or the mission is over.

The gear sound logic in the racing game works in a similar way, but it is a little bit more complicated because you have 13 different gear motor sounds and not just one rocket motor sound, as in Rocket Commander XNA. Check out the Sound class of the racing game for more details.

Whoosh, What Was That?

The original Rocket Commander game used its own 3D sound calculation formula and used the volume and panning properties of a DirectSound sample to achieve the correct effect for the player. In XNA, it's sadly not possible to change the panning. All sounds are played the way they are created and set in XACT. For 3D sounds you should use real 3D sound code anyway. In the XNA beta 1, I wrote some code to play 3D sounds and have a 3D listener object moving around the 3D world.

This 3D listener object is now missing from XNA; you can't use 3D sound effects currently. Let's hope this will change in the future, and I will certainly update the code for the games in this book when 3D sounds are possible again, but for now, you can play back sounds in mono only. There's no stereo or surround sound support.

In case you can use X3DAudio and X3DAudioListener (the classes might have different names; it is just important that you can somehow set and play 3D audio and that you can position yourself with the help of the 3D listener class), the following code could be used to play 3D sounds after you set all important cue variables:

```
// Setup 3D listener for 3D sound
Sound.Listener = new X3DAudioListener(
  zAxis, yAxis, cameraPosition, movementVector);
```

Now set the emitter for each sound you want to play in your 3D world and play the 3D audio instances. Currently, there is no C# code available to do this and if you are still puzzling about this when XNA finally supports it some time in the future, you can check out the following link to see how the X3DAudio classes are used in C++. The ideas will be the same in C#, but much easier to write.

```
http://msdn.microsoft.com/library/default.asp?url=/library/en-us/directx9_c/audio_x
act_overview_x3daudio.asp
```

Menu Sounds

Here are some quick tips for menu sounds:

❑ Use helper methods such as `PlayMenuHighlight` or `PlayMenuClick` to play menu sound effects instead of using the `Sounds` enum.

❑ If you want to play certain menu sounds at different volumes, for example a loud highlight sound for major buttons and a more silent highlight sound for smaller controls, then create two sound cues in XACT instead of writing your own custom volume code, which is more work and not necessary at all.

❑ Try to write helper methods to find out if the mouse was moved over a control this frame, and reuse this code or method for all controls to unify the highlight or mouse-click code. This way, you don't have to play click or highlight sounds yourself for every custom button method you use in your game.

❑ Make sure you also support the Xbox 360 controller and the keyboard. Writing a mouse-only game makes no sense on the Xbox 360 because you have absolutely zero mouse support in XNA for your Xbox 360.

❑ Play highlight sounds when navigating through menu entries and play click sounds when the user clicks the gamepad or presses the spacebar or the Enter key on the keyboard to go into the current menu selection.

Challenge: Create Your XACT Project

The challenge for this chapter is simple; just create your own XACT project like the one that was shown in this chapter. It is important that you feel comfortable in XACT; otherwise you will spend a lot of time rewriting code that is not necessary or you have to search for functionality in XACT that is hidden somewhere you have never looked before.

Additionally, write your own `Sound` class for the XACT project you created and start with the unit test first. Then implement the constructor and load the XACT project and the wave and sound banks. Finally, implement the `Play` methods to make your unit test work. As an example of how it's done, you can check out the `XnaShooterSoundProject` for this chapter and the `TestSounds` unit test in there.

That's it; you are now an experienced XACT user. For more details about XACT, you can also visit the official XACT forum at `http://forums.xna.com/28/ShowForum.aspx`. You'll find many tips, and you can ask all the XACT experts for help if you run into trouble with your game code and XACT.

If available at the time you are reading this book, try to use X3DAudio and check if there is a newer version of Rocket Commander XNA available to show how it's done.

In XNA 2.0, you no longer have to keep a reference to each cue that is playing in order to prevent the garbage collector from destroying the cue as it is being played. In XNA 2.0, you simply call Cue.Play — and you don't have to worry about it.

Summary

In this chapter you learned all about sound effects in XNA. XACT is the tool you have to use, no matter if you think it is great or you are annoyed by it. XACT allows you to play sound effects and even music on the Xbox 360 and Windows with the help of the XNA Framework.

Here are all the important points about XACT you learned in this chapter:

❑ XACT is the only way to play sounds on the Xbox 360 with XNA, it is build on top of the XAudio Framework, which works natively on the Xbox 360 and Vista and via DirectSound on Windows XP. In the future, XNA will be updated to the XAudio 2 Framework and support even more cool features.

❑ The XACT tool might be annoying at first, but once you get used to it, you'll enjoy the new cool features. For example, using the fade in and fade out settings for music items is much cooler than having to write your own fade in and out code. XNA 2.0 also has a much improved XACT tool.

❑ MP3, OGG, or ACC compression or other custom compression formats are not supported by XACT. The only two formats supported are ADPCM for the Windows platform and XMA for the Xbox 360 platform.

❑ XMA is a good and useful compression format for the Xbox 360, but ADPCM is not really useful. If you have the time and you want smaller sound files on Windows, implement DirectAudioVideoPlayback from the DirectX SDK into your engine or use other external sound engines for the Windows part of your game.

❑ I recommend using the 75 percent quality setting for the XMA format in XACT and 128 or 256 samples per block setting for the ADPCM format. Whatever you choose, you have to live with the fact that the Windows version of your game will probably be twice as big as the Xbox 360 version in XNA just because of the sound files and the bad ADPCM compression.

❑ Make sure your Sound class is easy to use and accessible from everywhere.

❑ Use the Sounds enum to quickly access and play all available sound cues.

❑ Write helper methods for code you call often.

❑ Custom cue variables are first configured in XACT and then programmed into your XNA code. SetVariable is the method for all the dirty cue instance variable modifying.

The next chapter discusses the Input class for handling the keyboard, the mouse, and the Xbox 360 gamepad controller devices, which is already in the graphics engine you wrote, but all the methods have not been discussed in detail. Additionally, you will learn about the menu system and other UI (user interface) code that directly interacts with the Input class. For example, sounds are played by the UI code automatically every time you hover over a control or if you click a control. For custom controls you have to do all the checking and handling yourself. You will also learn more about the XNA Shooter game, which will then be completed in Chapter 11.

Player Input and the User Interface

This chapter takes a closer look at the Input class that has been used so many times now. Then it discusses the ways to implement a good graphical user interface (GUI) for XNA Shooter. Handling the user input is very simple in XNA because, thanks to the Input namespace, you can easily get the mouse, keyboard, and gamepad states with just three lines of code:

```
mouseState = Mouse.GetState();
keyboardState = Keyboard.GetState();
gamePadState = GamePad.GetState(PlayerIndex.One);
```

If you don't have the XNA Input namespace added to the file you are currently working on, go with the text cursor over Mouse, Keyboard, or GamePad and press Ctrl+., which automatically adds the following line to your using directives:

```
using Microsoft.Xna.Framework.Input;
```

Now you can use these states and check if the gamepad is connected at all, if the spacebar is pressed on your keyboard, or where the mouse position is currently. This is exactly what you did in the first and second chapter when you wrote your first XNA game.

The more complex your games become, the more often you will have to repeat the same code over and over again. As with the classes in the graphics engine, you often do not add more functionality, but instead you make the existing functionality easier to use. For example, the Texture class was used to store the XNA texture, the texture size, and whether or not it has alpha; it also contains many useful methods to render the texture directly on the screen with the help of the SpriteHelper class.

All this is possible with the standard XNA Framework, too, but you will have to write more code. If you just want to put one single texture on the screen, it would not make sense to write all these helper classes, but if you write many projects and use hundreds of textures you will probably thank yourself for all the helper classes you wrote earlier. Only by simplifying the texture, shaders, and materials is it possible to write complex graphics in a few lines of code, as you can see in the unit tests of the graphics classes.

The same logic applies to the Input class, too. The advantages are not that obvious, but you will notice after a while that writing new UI (user interface) code for your custom buttons or menu controls gets much easier thanks to the many helper classes, including the Input class.

Just writing a helper class is kind of boring, and you already know how to use this Input class because you already used it so many times. To get something useful done for your next game, XNA Shooter, you will also program all the UI classes and see the menu logic for the more advanced games shown in this book. The idea here is to reuse the existing Rocket Commander XNA game screen classes for newer projects. Some classes have to be removed and you might need a new class here and there, but the overall program logic is pretty much the same.

The game itself shows the user interface (ammunition, health, points, and so on) in the Mission class just like Rocket Commander did. For more complex games, like the racing game in the next part of this book, the game logic and the UI rendering code is separated into more classes. As with unit testing, you should always make sure that writing your game code is as simple as possible, but not simpler. It does not make sense to write 30 helper classes if all you want to do is to output "Hello World" on the screen.

Game UI and especially menu UI is a big topic for games. There was a time a few years back when almost every game had very complex menu animations or even 3D graphics, but they were very hard to use. You should try to keep things simple, not only for you as the programmer, but also for the user. You learn about a good menu design at the end of this chapter.

Input Class

The Input class has many properties to easily access all the most-used keyboard, mouse, and gamepad key states (see Figure 10-1). The class also provides some helper methods to manage keyboard input and typing in text, but you will probably not need most of the code in the Input class for your first game projects. It becomes more useful the bigger your game grows and the more UI code you have in it. The most important method is the Update method, which has to be called every frame (done automatically from the BaseGame class at the beginning of each frame in the Update method there).

Please note that all the mouse functionality is missing if you run XNA on your Xbox 360, and you can't even get the mouse states when you compile for the Xbox 360 (the class is just missing). So you have to comment out all your mouse code just to make the game run on the Xbox 360. That can cause quite a few problems when compiling on the Xbox 360 for the first time, especially if you have hundreds of mouse calls all over the place in your project. A much better solution is to completely hide the mouse state (make it private) and only access the mouse parameters through properties in the Input class. As you can see in Figure 10-1, you have access to the Gamepad and Keyboard states directly in case you want to check another key or button yourself, but for the mouse, you can access only the properties the Input class gives you. Now all these properties return just what you would expect on the PC, but on the Xbox 360 they all return false or just the virtual mouse position. You can set and get the mouse position the same way as on the PC, but the user does not control it directly.

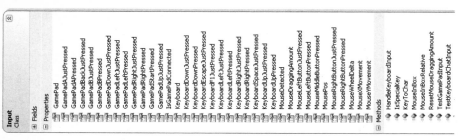

Input
Class

⊞ Fields

⊟ Properties

- GamePad
- GamePadAJustPressed
- GamePadAPressed
- GamePadBackJustPressed
- GamePadBJustPressed
- GamePadBPressed
- GamePadDownJustPressed
- GamePadLeftJustPressed
- GamePadLeftPressed
- GamePadRightJustPressed
- GamePadRightPressed
- GamePadStartPressed
- GamePadUpJustPressed
- IsGamePadConnected
- Keyboard
- KeyboardDownJustPressed
- KeyboardDownPressed
- KeyboardEscapeJustPressed
- KeyboardF1JustPressed
- KeyboardLeftJustPressed
- KeyboardLeftPressed
- KeyboardRightJustPressed
- KeyboardRightPressed
- KeyboardSpaceJustPressed
- KeyboardUpJustPressed
- KeyboardUpPressed
- MouseDetected
- MouseDraggingAmount
- MouseLeftButtonJustPressed
- MouseLeftButtonPressed
- MouseMiddleButtonPressed
- MousePos
- MouseRightButtonJustPressed
- MouseRightButtonPressed
- MouseWheelDelta
- MouseXMovement
- MouseYMovement

⊟ Methods

- HandleKeyboardInput
- IsSpecialKey
- KeyToChar
- MouseInBox
- MouseInBoxRelative
- ResetMouseDraggingAmount
- TestGamePadInput
- TestKeyboardChatInput

Figure 10-1

XNA 1.0 basically just supports the mouse, keyboard and the Xbox 360 controller. You can also use other XInput-compatible devices and access them the same way you control the Xbox 360 controller as I have done for the XNA Racing Game. In XNA 2.0, the support for other XInput-compatible devices has been improved, especially devices specifically designed for the Xbox 360 and some of the casual games on that console.

XNA 2.0 adds support for the following devices, mostly new devices, which were released in 2007 or later:

❑ **Chatpad device:** To help you enter text messages on the Xbox 360. This may also improve how text can be entered in XNA 2.0, which is still a lot of work to get right (see later in this chapter).

❑ **Big-Button-Pad:** For simpler games or old school games. It is basically a huge red button on the top of the controller and the standard A, B, X, and Y buttons below it, but much smaller.

269

❑ **Guitars:** For games such as the very popular and famous Guitar Hero 2 game on the Xbox 360. Not sure how you get the input values from a guitar, but it is nice to see XNA 2.0 supporting all these innovative devices.

❑ **Drum Sticks:** For other music games. There are probably many more special devices like this, that are both simple and simple to program against.

And, of course, there are other devices such as old school joysticks, flight sticks, and devices like that, which are especially good for flight simulators.

Take a look at the Input classes of the XNA 2.0 Framework to learn more about the capabilities. In most cases it is best to just test it out with a special controller and see how it feels. Most devices such as wheels or joysticks will work just right out-of-the-box if you already have added support for the standard Xbox 360 controller. The XNA Racing Game did not require any special code for supporting racing wheel controllers on the Xbox 360 — just a little bit of fine-tuning and testing had to be done.

Now the same code for mouse, keyboard, and gamepad input can be used on both platforms. XNA had the goal to have 98 percent of the code behave the same way; go to 100 percent for your engine.

For example, the A button of the Xbox 360 gamepad or the cursor keys for the keyboard are used very often. It is far easier to write code like the following to allow navigating through the menu entries with the up/down keyboard keys. Additionally supporting the gamepad up/down cursor or even controlling the menu with the gamepad left thumb stick is easier to do with these helper properties. If you had to write all the state checking yourself every time you needed to check if a key or button was currently pressed and had not been pressed before, you would probably go crazy after a while.

```
// Handle GamePad input, and also allow keyboard input
if (Input.GamePadUpJustPressed ||
    Input.KeyboardUpJustPressed)
{
    Sound.Play(Sound.Sounds.Highlight);
    selectedButton =
        (selectedButton + NumberOfButtons - 1) % NumberOfButtons;
} // if (BaseGame.GamePadLeftNowPressed)
else if (Input.GamePadDownJustPressed ||
    Input.KeyboardDownJustPressed)
{
    Sound.Play(Sound.Sounds.Highlight);
    selectedButton = (selectedButton + 1) % NumberOfButtons;
} // else if
```

For example, the GamePadUpJustPressed method does the following:

```
/// <summary>
/// Game pad up just pressed
/// </summary>
/// <returns>Bool</returns>
public static bool GamePadUpJustPressed
{
    get
    {
        return (gamePadState.DPad.Up == ButtonState.Pressed &&
```

```
        gamePadStateLastFrame.DPad.Up == ButtonState.Released) ||
        (gamePadState.ThumbSticks.Left.Y > 0.75f &&
        gamePadStateLastFrame.ThumbSticks.Left.Y < 0.75f);
    } // get
} // GamePadUpJustPressed
```

The code uses the current gamepad state, which is assigned at the beginning of each frame, and the gamepad state from the last frame to check if any button state has changed. As you can see, if you had to write this code again and again every time you wanted to check if the gamepad up cursor was pressed, you would go crazy. Copy and paste works fine for the first one or two times, but if you use the same code over and over again, write a helper method or property to let it do the work for you. In the future, when you write more UI code, it will become much easier to check all input states and work with many different input devices.

The Update Method in the Input Class

The Update method does nothing really complicated, but it is the most important part of the Input class because all the last frame states are copied over from the previous states and then you get each new state for the keyboard, mouse, and gamepad input. To help out with relative mouse movement there is some extra code to handle it. Relative mouse movement is something that is not supported in XNA unlike the DirectInput classes from DirectX, which allow you to get relative mouse data instead of the absolute mouse positions such as (−3.5, +7.0) instead of position (350, 802).

```
/// <summary>
/// Update, called from BaseGame.Update().
/// Will catch all new states for keyboard, mouse and the gamepad.
/// </summary>
internal static void Update()
{
#if XBOX360
    // No mouse support on the XBox360 yet :(
    mouseDetected = false;
#else
    // Handle mouse input variables
    mouseStateLastFrame = mouseState;
    mouseState = Microsoft.Xna.Framework.Input.Mouse.GetState();
    // Update mouseXMovement and mouseYMovement
    lastMouseXMovement += mouseState.X - mouseStateLastFrame.X;
    lastMouseYMovement += mouseState.Y - mouseStateLastFrame.Y;
    mouseXMovement = lastMouseXMovement / 2.0f;
    mouseYMovement = lastMouseYMovement / 2.0f;
    lastMouseXMovement -= lastMouseXMovement / 2.0f;
    lastMouseYMovement -= lastMouseYMovement / 2.0f;
    if (MouseLeftButtonPressed == false)
        startDraggingPos = MousePos;
    mouseWheelDelta = mouseState.ScrollWheelValue - mouseWheelValue;
    mouseWheelValue = mouseState.ScrollWheelValue;
    // Check if mouse was moved this frame if it is not detected yet.
    // This allows us to ignore the mouse even when it is captured
    // on a windows machine if just the gamepad or keyboard is used.
    if (mouseDetected == false)
        mouseDetected = mouseState.X != mouseStateLastFrame.X ||
```

```
#endif
      // Handle keyboard input
      keysPressedLastFrame = new List<Keys>(keyboardState.GetPressedKeys());
      keyboardState = Microsoft.Xna.Framework.Input.Keyboard.GetState();
      // And finally catch the XBox Controller input (only use 1 player)
      gamePadStateLastFrame = gamePadState;
      gamePadState = Microsoft.Xna.Framework.Input.GamePad.GetState(
          PlayerIndex.One);

      // Handle rumbling
      if (leftRumble > 0 || rightRumble > 0)
      {
          if (leftRumble > 0)
              leftRumble -= 1.5f * BaseGame.MoveFactorPerSecond;
          if (rightRumble > 0)
              rightRumble -= 1.5f * BaseGame.MoveFactorPerSecond;
          Microsoft.Xna.Framework.Input.GamePad.SetVibration(
              PlayerIndex.One, leftRumble, rightRumble);
      } // if (leftRumble)
  } // Update()
```

You might also notice the code for the gamepad rumbling at the end of the Update method, which allows you to use the following method to let the gamepad rumble for a while without having to worry about it anymore. The Update method will automatically reduce the rumbled effect if GamePadRumble is not called again in the next frame. You can also use a weaker rumble effect for smaller events. Playing XNA Shooter is a lot more fun with rumbling enabled.

```
      /// <summary>
      /// Game pad rumble
      /// </summary>
      /// <param name="setLeftRumble">Set left rumble</param>
      /// <param name="setRightRumble">Set right rumble</param>
      public static void GamePadRumble(
          float setLeftRumble, float setRightRumble)
      {
          leftRumble = setLeftRumble;
          rightRumble = setRightRumble;
      } // GamePadRumble(setLeftRumble, setRightRumble)
```

Mouse Rectangles

The Input class also has some methods to help you detect if the mouse is over a UI element such as a menu button. Use the following method to check if the mouse is hovering over a UI element. The method will also automatically play the highlight sound for you if you just entered this rectangle.

```
      /// <summary>
      /// Mouse in box
      /// </summary>
      /// <param name="rect">Rectangle</param>
      /// <returns>Bool</returns>
      public static bool MouseInBox(Rectangle rect)
      {
```

```
#if XBOX360
  return false;
#else
  bool ret = mouseState.X >= rect.X &&
    mouseState.Y >= rect.Y &&
    mouseState.X < rect.Right &&
    mouseState.Y < rect.Bottom;
  bool lastRet = mouseStateLastFrame.X >= rect.X &&
    mouseStateLastFrame.Y >= rect.Y &&
    mouseStateLastFrame.X < rect.Right &&
    mouseStateLastFrame.Y < rect.Bottom;
  // Highlight happened?
  if (ret &&
    lastRet == false)
    Sound.Play(Sound.Sounds.Highlight);
  return ret;
#endif
} // MouseInBox(rect)
```

You can use the preceding code to allow users to select the main menu elements, as in Figure 10-2. As I said before, try to keep it simple. A menu should just show all important parts of the game. The background texture should also be a nice picture from your game — some artwork or a custom-made texture (e.g. with a paint program) from your skilled graphics artist (if you have one).

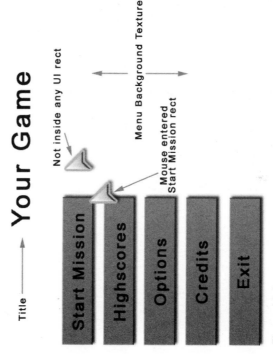

Title ⟶ **Your Game**

Not inside any UI rect

Menu Background Texture

Mouse entered
Start Mission rect

Start Mission

Highscores

Options

Credits

Exit

Figure 10-2

To get this to work, you would use some code similar to the following code snippet:

```
// Render background
game.RenderMenuBackground();
// Show all buttons
```

```
int buttonNum = 0;
MenuButton[] menuButtons = new MenuButton[]
{
    MenuButton.Missions,
    MenuButton.Highscore,
    MenuButton.Credits,
    MenuButton.Exit,
    MenuButton.Back,
};
foreach (MenuButton button in menuButtons)
{
    // Don't render the back button
    if (button != MenuButton.Back)
    {
        if (game.RenderMenuButton(button, buttonLocations[buttonNum]))
        {
            if (button == MenuButton.Missions)
                game.AddGameScreen(new Mission());
            else if (button == MenuButton.Highscore)
                game.AddGameScreen(new Highscores());
            else if (button == MenuButton.Credits)
                game.AddGameScreen(new Credits());
            else if (button == MenuButton.Exit)
                quit = true;
        } // if
        buttonNum++;
        if (buttonNum >= buttonLocations.Length)
            break;
    } // if
} // if

// Hotkeys, M=Mission, H=Highscores, C=Credits, Esc=Quit
if (Input.KeyboardKeyJustPressed(Keys.M))
    game.AddGameScreen(new Mission());
else if (Input.KeyboardKeyJustPressed(Keys.H))
    game.AddGameScreen(new Highscores());
else if (Input.KeyboardKeyJustPressed(Keys.C))
    game.AddGameScreen(new Credits());
else if (Input.KeyboardEscapeJustPressed)
    quit = true;

// If pressing XBox controller up/down change selection
if (Input.GamePadDownJustPressed)
{
    xInputMenuSelection =
        (xInputMenuSelection + 1) % buttonLocations.Length;
    SelectMenuItemForXInput();
} // if (Input.GamePad)
else if (Input.GamePadUpJustPressed)
{
    if (xInputMenuSelection <= 0)
        xInputMenuSelection = buttonLocations.Length;
    xInputMenuSelection --;
    SelectMenuItemForXInput();
} // if (Input.GamePad)
```

If you have more controls — such as in your options screen to enable or disable checkboxes, handle slide bars, or edit boxes — the code will get a little bit more complicated. Before you have to copy and paste the same code over and over again, you should introduce a UI class to handle all the UI code for you. If you just have to use an edit box once, you could also write the code directly into the Options class as I did for Rocket Commander XNA. But the code should be refactored if you use it multiple times. Handling text boxes is also a little bit more complicated in XNA because you have to implement your own keyboard input methods for text.

Entering Text in XNA

You might also have noticed that there is no keyboardStateLastFrame variable in the Input class, because unlike the MouseState and GamePadState, you cannot use the KeyboardState struct again the next frame; the data is no longer valid. This happens because the KeyboardState struct uses an internal list for all the keys, which is used in the next frame again and overwritten to all the new keyboard key states when you call Keyboard.GetState. To fix this issue you just keep your own list of keys, which is cloned every time you assign it from the last frame keys. Using the constructor of the generic List class will automatically clone all elements for you.

Using this list works almost the same way as using the keyboard state directly. For an example, take a look at the KeyboardSpaceJustPressed property of the Input class:

```
/// <summary>
/// Keyboard space just pressed?
/// </summary>
/// <returns>Bool</returns>
public static bool KeyboardSpaceJustPressed
{
    get
    {
        return keyboardState.IsKeyDown(Keys.Space) &&
            keysPressedLastFrame.Contains(Keys.Space) == false;
    } // get
} // KeyboardSpaceJustPressed
```

The rest of the Input class is very similar to all the code you already saw except for the keyboard input text methods I mentioned a minute ago. To get the keyboard input for text boxes the same as you would with a normal Windows text box, the following unit test can be used to test if this works as expected:

```
/// <summary>
/// Test keyboard chat input
/// </summary>
public static void TestKeyboardChatInput()
{
    // Better version with help of Input.HandleKeyboardInput!
    string chatText = "";
    TestGame.Start("TestKeyboardChatInput",
        null,
        delegate
        {
            TextureFont.WriteText(100, 100,
                "Your chat text: " + chatText +
                // Add blinking |
                ((int)(BaseGame.TotalTime / 0.35f) % 2 == 0 ? "|" : ""));
            Input.HandleKeyboardInput(ref chatText);
```

```
    },
    null);
} // TestKeyboardChatInput()
```

The unit test just displays the `chatText` string and a blinking | sign behind it. Then the `HandleKeyboardInput` method is used to allow the user to type in new chat text. Take a look at the `HandleKeyboardInput` method:

```
/// <summary>
/// Handle keyboard input helper method to catch keyboard input
/// for an input text. Only used to enter the player name in the
/// game.
/// </summary>
/// <param name="inputText">Input text</param>
public static void HandleKeyboardInput(ref string inputText)
{
    // Is a shift key pressed (we have to check both, left and right)
    bool isShiftPressed =
        keyboardState.IsKeyDown(Keys.LeftShift) ||
        keyboardState.IsKeyDown(Keys.RightShift);

    // Go through all pressed keys
    foreach (Keys pressedKey in keyboardState.GetPressedKeys())
        // Only process if it was not pressed last frame
        if (keysPressedLastFrame.Contains(pressedKey) == false)
        {
            // No special key?
            if (IsSpecialKey(pressedKey) == false &&
                // Max. allow 32 chars
                inputText.Length < 32)
            {
                // Then add the letter to our inputText.
                // Check also the shift state!
                inputText += KeyToChar(pressedKey, isShiftPressed);
            } // if (IsSpecialKey)
            else if (pressedKey == Keys.Back &&
                inputText.Length > 0)
            {
                // Remove 1 character at end
                inputText = inputText.Substring(0, inputText.Length - 1);
            } // else if
        } // foreach if (WasKeyPressedLastFrame)
} // HandleKeyboardInput(inputText)
```

The method uses two other helper methods in the `Input` class. First, `IsSpecialKey` is used to see if the key can be used for the chat text or if it was just F1, cursor, Delete, Enter, and so on, which will not be added directly to the chat text. Then you handle the special case for the Backspace key. You could also extend the code to handle the Enter or Delete keys in your text boxes if you need that in your game.

The next problem is that you can't just add keys to your input text. First, the A key would add A to the input text string regardless of whether the user pressed the Shift key or not. Then there are special keys such as +, -, {, and so on, which would show up as `Plus`, `Minus`, and `OemOpenBrackets` in your input text. To help you out with that, it would be nice if XNA would provide you with the real key meaning, but it does not; you have to do it yourself with the help of the `KeyToChar` helper method in the `Input` class:

```
/// <summary>
/// Keys to char helper conversion method.
/// Note: If the keys are mapped other than on a default QWERTY
/// keyboard, this method will not work properly. Most keyboards
/// will return the same for A-Z and 0-9, but the special keys
/// might be different. Sorry, no easy way to fix this with XNA ...
/// For a game with chat (windows) you should implement the
/// Windows events for catching keyboard input, which are much better!
/// </summary>
/// <param name="key">Keys</param>
/// <returns>Char</returns>
public static char KeyToChar(Keys key, bool shiftPressed)
{
    // If key will not be found, just return space
    char ret = ' ';
    int keyNum = (int)key;
    if (keyNum >= (int)Keys.A && keyNum <= (int)Keys.Z)
    {
        if (shiftPressed)
            ret = key.ToString()[0];
        else
            ret = key.ToString().ToLower()[0];
    } // if (keyNum)
    else if (keyNum >= (int)Keys.D0 && keyNum <= (int)Keys.D9 &&
        shiftPressed == false)
    {
        ret = (char)((int)'0' + (keyNum - Keys.D0));
    } // else if
    else if (key == Keys.D1 && shiftPressed)
        ret = '!';
    else if (key == Keys.D2 && shiftPressed)
        ret = '@';
    [etc. about 20 more special key checks]
    // Return result
    return ret;
} // KeyToChar(key)
```

With that method, the `HandleKeyboardInput` method works the way you expect it to and your unit test can be started and tested. There are even more unit tests in the `Input` class; check them out to learn more about the available properties and methods.

Game Screens

In Figure 10-2, you already saw an example for a simple main menu, but your games contain more than just the game screen itself and a menu. You typically need a credits screen to make you famous, an options screen to let the user comfortably set all settings and change the screen resolution, and a help screen explaining the basic game principle (see Figure 10-3).

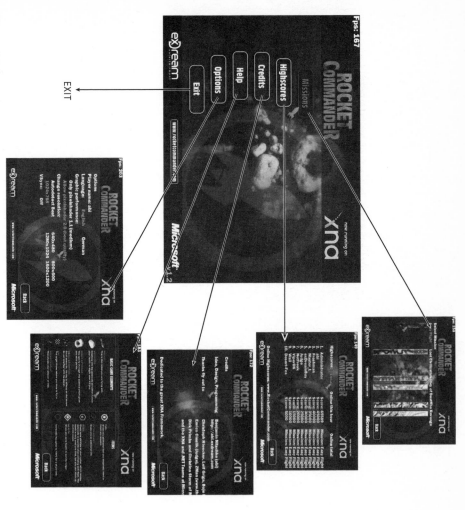

Figure 10-3

Most game screens use a special background texture to show most of the information on the screen. In the Mission selection screen, you can select one of the four missions and then start the game. The other screens just show some information and only the options screen allows the user to change anything. All game screens return to the main menu after you press Back.

To handle all game screens automatically, you use a stack of game screens in your main game class (see Figure 10-4). This allows you to use even more complex menu systems with several levels where you can always return to the previous screen. In case you want to return to the main menu, just remove all entries on the stack except for the last one. Another trick I often use for demos is to add another game screen

Chapter 10: Player Input and the User Interface

before the main menu is added just to show a demo "buy this game now" screen when the user exits the game. The class itself is only a couple of lines and you need to add only one extra line to your main class. Most game screen classes are very simple, too.

GameScreen Stack in Rocket Commander XNA

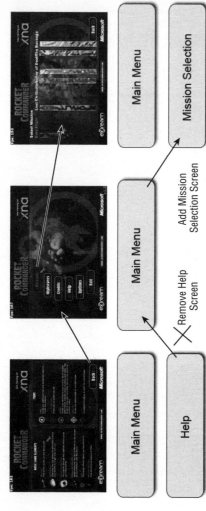

Figure 10-4

Why is this game screen stack so great? Well, all you have to do is to derive all your game screen classes from IGameScreen (see Figure 10-5) and then you can use the following code to render and handle them automatically. The Render method of each game screen class returns true if you are finished with it, and you will return to the previous screen. After all game screens have been removed, you can exit the game.

```
// No more game screens?
if (gameScreens.Count == 0)
{
    // Then quit
    Exit();
    return;
} // if (gameScreens.Count)

// Handle current screen
if (gameScreens.Peek().Render())
{
    // Play sound for screen back
    Sound.Play(Sound.Sounds.ScreenBack);
    gameScreens.Pop();
} // if (gameScreens.Peek)
```

Figure 10-5

Help Screen

Here is the complete code of the `Help` class in the `GameScreens` namespace. Other game screen classes are not much more complex except for the `Mission` class, which handles the whole game.

```
/// <summary>
/// Help
/// </summary>
class Help : IGameScreen
{
    #region Properties
    /// <summary>
    /// Name of this game screen
    /// </summary>
    /// <returns>String</returns>
    public string Name
    {
        get
        {
            return "Help";
        } // get
    } // Name
    #endregion

    #region Run
    /// <summary>
    /// Run game screen. Called each frame.
    /// </summary>
    /// <param name="game">Form for access to asteroid manager</param>
    public bool Run(RocketCommanderGame game)
    {
```

```
// Render background
game.RenderMenuBackground();
// Show helper screen texture
game.helpScreenTexture.RenderOnScreen(
    new Rectangle(0,
        174 * BaseGame.Height / 768,
        BaseGame.Width,
        510 * BaseGame.Height / 768),
    new Rectangle(0, 0, 1024, 510));
if (game.RenderMenuButton(MenuButton.Back,
        new Point(1024 - 210, 768 - 140)) ||
        Input.KeyboardEscapeJustPressed)
    return true;

return true;
} // Run(game)
} // class Help
```

That's it. Looks pretty simple, doesn't it? Please take a look at the game screen classes yourself if you want to learn more about them. Some of them also have unit tests to show the behavior and use cases of each game screen.

In-Game User Interface

In this section I want you to follow all the steps I took to make the In-Game UI for the XNA Shooter game. The UI is not very complex, but you will encounter several issues anyway. The following elements are displayed in the shoot-'em-up game:

❑ **Mission time:** Minutes and seconds showing you how long you played.

❑ **Current score:** You get points for shooting, killing, and collecting items and weapons.

❑ **Highscore:** The score you have to beat to become number one.

❑ **Your current health:** If you lose all of it, you die.

❑ **Current weapon:** The current weapon you are firing with and number of EMP bombs you can throw.

Figure 10-6 shows all of these elements together on the screen with help of the following textures:

❑ HudTop.png for the top bar on the screen, showing time, score, and highscore

❑ HudButton.png for the bottom counterpart, showing health and the current weapons

❑ GameFont.png, the game font you already used in several games in this book

❑ NumbersFont.png for the numbers on the top part; looks cooler than the default font

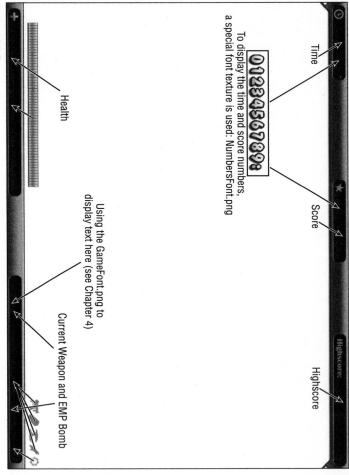

To display the time and score numbers,
a special font texture is used: NumbersFont.png

Time   Score   Highscore

Using the GameFont.png to
display text here (see Chapter 4)

Health

Current Weapon and EMP Bomb

Figure 10-6

After the new class to display the numbers from the NumbersFont was implemented, and thanks to the Texture class and the RenderOnScreen methods, adding the In-Game UI isn't too difficult anymore.

The NumbersFont.png texture is handled in the NumbersFont class and it is very similar to the TextureFont class from Chapter 4, but much simpler because you have only eleven rectangles here, ten for the numbers 0 to 9 and one for the column for displaying times.

```
private void RenderHud()
{
    // Render top hud part
    hudTopTexture.RenderOnScreenRelative4To3(0, 0,
        hudTopTexture.GfxRectangle);

    // Time
    BaseGame.NumbersFont.WriteTime(
        BaseGame.XToRes(73), BaseGame.YToRes(8),
        hudTopTexture.GfxRectangle);
    // Score
    BaseGame.NumbersFont.WriteNumberCentered(
        BaseGame.XToRes(485), BaseGame.YToRes(8), (int)Player.gameTimeMs);
    BaseGame.NumbersFont.WriteNumberCentered(
        BaseGame.XToRes(485), BaseGame.YToRes(8), Player.score);
```

```
// Highscore
BaseGame.NumbersFont.WriteNumberCentered(
    BaseGame.XToRes(920), BaseGame.YToRes(8), Highscores.TopHighscore);
// Render bottom hud part
Rectangle bottomHudGfxRect = new Rectangle(0, 24, 1024, 40);
hudBottomTexture.RenderOnScreenRelative4To3(0, 768 - 40,
    bottomHudGfxRect);
// Health
Rectangle healthGfxRect = new Rectangle(50, 0, 361, 24);
hudBottomTexture.RenderOnScreenRelative4To3(50, 768 - 31,
    new Rectangle(healthGfxRect.X, healthGfxRect.Y,
    (int)(healthGfxRect.Width * Player.health), healthGfxRect.Height));
// Weapon and Emps!
Rectangle weaponMgGfxRect = new Rectangle(876, 0, 31, 24);
Rectangle weaponGattlingGfxRect = new Rectangle(909, 0, 27, 24);
Rectangle weaponPlasmaGfxRect = new Rectangle(939, 0, 33, 24);
Rectangle weaponRocketsGfxRect = new Rectangle(975, 0, 24, 24);
Rectangle weaponEmpGfxRect = new Rectangle(1001, 0, 23, 24);
TextureFont.WriteText(BaseGame.XToRes(606),
    BaseGame.YToRes(768 - 20) - TextureFont.Height / 3, "Weapon: ");
// Show weapon icon!
Rectangle weaponRect =
    Player.currentWeapon == Player.WeaponTypes.MG ? weaponMgGfxRect :
    Player.currentWeapon == Player.WeaponTypes.Gattling ?
    weaponGattlingGfxRect :
    Player.currentWeapon == Player.WeaponTypes.Plasma ?
    weaponPlasmaGfxRect : weaponRocketsGfxRect;
hudBottomTexture.RenderOnScreenRelative4To3(
    715, 768 - 31, weaponRect);
// And weapon name
TextureFont.WriteText(BaseGame.XToRes(717+weaponRect.Width),
    BaseGame.YToRes(768 - 20) - TextureFont.Height / 3,
    Player.currentWeapon.ToString());
TextureFont.WriteText(BaseGame.XToRes(864),
    BaseGame.YToRes(768 - 20) - TextureFont.Height / 3, "EMPs: ");
// Show emp icons if we have any
for (int num = 0; num < Player.empBombs; num++)
    hudBottomTexture.RenderOnScreenRelative4To3(
    938 + num * 23, 768 - 31, weaponEmpGfxRect);
} // RenderHud()
```

This solution works fine on the PC, but as soon as you start the game (or the TestHud unit test I wrote before even writing the RenderHud method) on the Xbox 360 connected to a TV screen you will see that the HUD is not completely visible, or worse, almost not visible at all.

If you have never developed a game on a console connected to a TV before, this may be a new issue for you because on a PC monitor you can always use 100 because of the visible area because there is no safe region. Well, on most TV screens you do not see 100 percent of the screen — more like 90 percent — which means about 10 percent of the width and height are not visible at the screen borders (see Figure 10-7).

You might ask why XNA does not put everything inside this safe region automatically. Well, it is not that easy. The TV set receives the full signal, and depending on the input cables and the model of the TV set, you see different results. These are some examples I have encountered:

□   PC connected to a monitor with a VGA or DVI cable lets you see 100 percent.

□   Xbox 360 connected through a VGA cable to a PC monitor lets you see 100 percent, too (or close to 100 percent if the resolution is not the native one).

□   Xbox 360 connected to an old-style monitor with SCART: around 92 percent visible.

□   Xbox 360 connected through Component cables to a big 24″ monitor (yeah HDTV): around 93–95 percent visible (depends on the resolution).

□   Some old TV sets (according to the XNA docs and tips on the Web) have a save region of 80–90 percent, but I never saw the 80 percent case; that is probably the worst-case scenario.

As you can see, it is not just 90 percent on the Xbox 360 and you don't have to worry about it. The results on the screen can be very different in many different situations, which can be checked by neither your game nor the XNA Framework. The only thing for sure is that on the PC you can be sure that 100 percent of all screen pixels are visible, which is the reason why many PC games use the borders of the screen to display UI elements and other information. If you take a look at Xbox 360 (or any console games for that matter) you will notice that they often have a simpler interface and they never show any information at the very screen borders.

Figure 10-7

You can't just put the HUD bars in the 90 percent safe region because if the user sees more it will look very wrong because you have no graphics behind the 90 percent region, and if the user sees even less you still have the same problem as before. Instead of continuing to work around this issue, you should stop here and rethink the problem. It is just not a good idea to have UI elements, as shown in Figure 10-6, for an Xbox 360 game. The best solution is to change the UI graphics and put them in the safe region if you are running the game in a situation where the user cannot see 100 percent of the screen such as starting it on the Xbox 360. Figure 10-8 shows how to change the HUD graphics to have them work on both the PC, where you put them at the screen borders, and on the Xbox 360, where they are put in the inner 92 percent. Your UI or HUD might still be visible with a safe region of 90 percent, but it gets harder to see elements or text if only 85 percent or less are visible. I never saw this worst-case scenario; most TV sets allow seeing around 90–95 percent of the rendered screen.

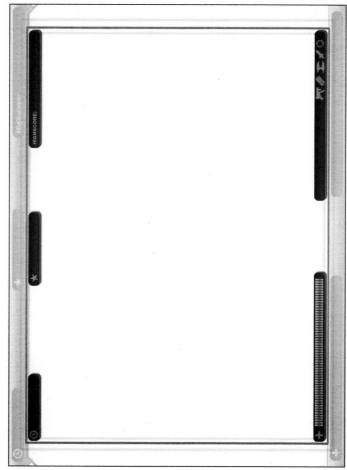

Figure 10-8

Figure 10-9 shows the final screen layout of XNA Shooter after going through all the steps of this chapter. Please check out the RenderHud method in the Mission class for more details. It was mainly developed for widescreen resolutions and to look good on the Xbox 360, but even with smaller resolutions on the PC it looks okay, as in the screenshot on Figure 10-9. To test the menu and game screens from this chapter, run the sample game project for this chapter, which is still based on the XnaGraphicEngine project you started in Chapter 5, but you have some new and updated game classes now.

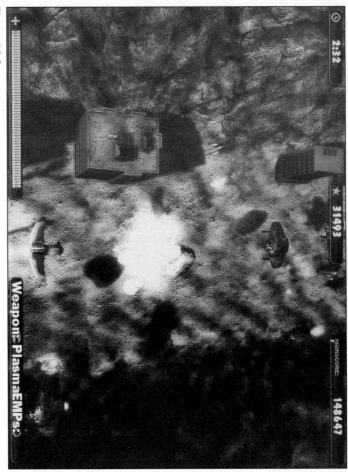

Figure 10-9

Tips

From my experience there are a couple of things you have to remember when developing XNA games on the Xbox 360. All of these issues are not a big deal on the PC, but they can cost some extra time until you get them right. One of the main problems is that if you develop your game on the PC only and then test it on the Xbox 360 only at the end, a lot of things may go wrong (bad performance on the PC only and then test Framework; UI elements at the border of the screen, which are just not visible on some TVs; bad Xbox 360 controller support, which is the main input device for Xbox 360s; and so on). Please read more about these issues on my blog if you are interested. Keep the following tips in mind when working with user interfaces in XNA:

☐ **Test, test, and test.** This is the most important tip. Write unit tests and constantly test them on your PC *and* your Xbox 360. I keep two projects open at the same time. (Both of them use the same files, but I develop only the PC solution and use the Xbox 360 solution for deploying and testing only.) Almost all of my classes have unit tests and I constantly test them until they are completed. **Don't use foreach loops, especially not in tight render loops.** This may sound a little crazy because it does not matter on a PC game and today's CPUs are fast enough to handle the creation and deletion of many thousands of objects each frame, which most games don't even need. But on the compact framework you will spam the memory even with things like foreach loops because a new enumerator instance is created every time you start a foreach loop. After a while, there will be a lot of dead objects, which have to be collected. This can take some time and slow down your game immensely. The PC version might run at over 200 frames, but your Xbox 360 version is stuck at something like 30–40 frames. Avoiding creation of new data each frame and avoiding foreach loops (just replace them with normal for loops; it is mostly just one line of extra code) can improve your performance by a factor of 100 percent or more.

☐ **Don't create lots of data in the game loop.** In Arena Wars (the first .NET game I developed, which was also the first commercial .NET game ever), I never created any data during the game. All objects were created at the beginning of each mission and they were reused (which was no big deal since the game principle did not allow an infinite number of units; it always stayed around the same because you get your money back from dead units to build new units). This approach was taken to reduce the Garbage Collector performance impact that could happen on slow computers in .NET 1.1. In later projects, I did not care so much about creating new objects and I coded just the easy way because unit tests drive you into a direction to quickly develop solutions, which work and are tested, but may not be the best in other situations, such as for the Xbox 360 .NET Compact Framework. That is okay because you can now use the unit tests to check if other solutions work just the way you expect them to work. For XNA Shooter and XNA Racer (and a couple of other new game projects) I now make sure that most of the game data is created at the beginning of each level and not dynamically during the game. This makes writing the code far easier and enables you to refactor it much more freely allowing you to improve both the overall code design and the execution speed. I advise you to always take the "clean code" approach first and think about optimizations in the beginning, but do not evolve important code around ugly optimized code that is hard to manage early in the project. Thanks to many improvements that have been made in .NET 2.0, the performance of the Garbage Collector — reusing existing objects and Exception Handling — is now much better and faster. Also keep in mind we have much faster computers today making these problems less important.

☐ **Safe-Regions on TVs can be problematic.** Just Google for Xbox 360 screenshots and you will notice that the GUI (graphical user interface) looks a lot different from most PC games. PC games often use user interfaces at the screen border showing you tips, little buttons, and other not-so-important things. If you do that in your Xbox 360 game, all of these UI elements may be cut off on a regular TV. For the XNA Shooter, I had to rework all the UI elements because they just did not fit on a TV screen and it was not practical to put them in a bar (such as the Windows task bar) because it looks so different on the PC and certain TV monitors. Instead, I put all UI elements in floating bars, which will be adjusted depending on the screen the user is looking at.

The important thing is to keep often used UI elements in this inner 90 percent (or 93 percent if you want to be close to the edges) rectangle. This means that instead of using a full 1920 × 1080 pixel resolution, you use only 90 percent of it (1728 × 945). Or just start rendering UI elements at about 5 percent of the screen (x coordinate: 96, y coordinate: 54). These pixel locations obviously depend on the screen resolution; just calculate them in your main class and use them whenever you render UI.

For more information about the .NET Compact Framework and how it is best used for the XNA Framework on the Xbox 360, please read the great article by the .NET compact framework team, which you'll find at http://blogs.msdn.com/netcfteam/archive/2006/12/22/managed-code-performance-on-xbox-360-for-the-xna-framework-1-0.aspx.

Cameras

Handling the input and managing the game screens is important and you will look at a more professional game and a more complete looking game after you have implemented all the game screens, even if your background textures are still placeholders.

For the game itself, especially if it is in 3D and if you can move around freely in the game world, you need a camera class. Chapter 5 introduced the SimpleCamera class to move around and zoom in a simple 3D environment. More interesting and useful are the camera classes in the Rocket Commander game (SpaceCamera class) and the one in the racing game (ChaseCamera class). The camera required for XNA Shooter can be pretty simple; you can just reuse the SimpleCamera class and move the "look at target" position through the level.

Figure 10-10 shows a comparison of all camera classes used in this book. The SpaceCamera class is discussed here, and in a few chapters you are going to check out the ChaseCamera class, too. Thanks to the GameComponent class the SimpleCamera is derived from, you should be able to add new camera classes yourself with ease.

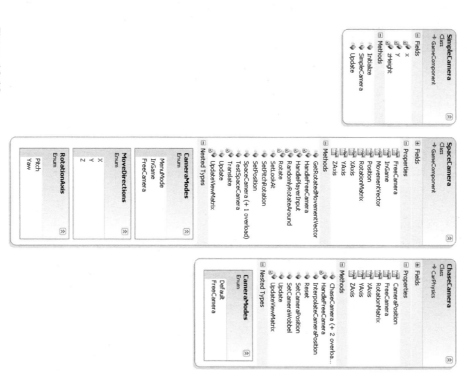

Figure 10-10

Space Camera

The SpaceCamera class is a lot more complex than the SimpleCamera class, and even the ChaseCamera class for the racing game looks simpler. The main reason for the complex code of the SpaceCamera class is that it was the first space camera class I ever wrote and getting the Quaternion math is not that easy. The camera class also supports several modes for the menu camera, one for the in-game camera, and a free camera mode for unit tests. The SpaceCamera of Rocket Commander XNA is a little bit simpler because the Quaternion math was removed and the controlling of the rocket is a little bit simplified by just allowing pitch and yaw rotations. The roll rotation around the z axis of the rocket is now handled by the engine automatically, which makes it easier to fly around and not get disoriented. The main reason for this change is to allow the player to control the rocket nicely with the Xbox 360 controller, which is harder than in the original Rocket Commander game that also supports the Xbox 360 controller.

Take a quick look at the most important method in SpaceCamera, which handles all the player input and updates the camera position of each frame:

```
/// <summary>
/// Handle player input for the game.
/// This is where all the input happens in the game.
/// </summary>
private void HandlePlayerInput()
{
    if (Player.lifeTimeMs < Player.lifeTimeZoomAndAccelerateMs)
    {
        float speedPercentage =
            Player.lifeTimeMs / (float)Player.lifeTimeZoomAndAccelerateMs;
        // Use quadradric product for better speed up effect
        Player.SetStartingSpeed(speedPercentage * speedPercentage);
        // Always move forward
        Translate(Player.Speed * BaseGame.MoveFactorPerSecond *
            Player.MovementSpeedPerSecond, MoveDirections.Z);
        if (Player.gameTimeMs < 100)
        {
            yawRotation = 0;
            pitchRotation = 0;
            pos = Vector3.Zero;
        } // if
    } // if
```

The preceding code increases the speed of the rocket in Rocket Commander and it also resets the rotation and position values if the game just started. Next you do some checking if the game is over and handle the special case to allow moving. Then the mouse and keyboard input is handled. This is pretty much the original code from the very first version I implemented for the SpaceCamera class; all the other code was added later to add more input devices:

```
#region Mouse/keyboard support
if (Input.MouseXMovement != 0.0f ||
    Input.MouseYMovement != 0.0f)
{
```

289

```
  float xMovement = Input.MouseXMovement;
  float yMovement = Input.MouseYMovement;
  Rotate(RotationAxis.Yaw, -xMovement * rotationFactor);
  Rotate(RotationAxis.Pitch, -yMovement * rotationFactor);
} // if (Mouse.left.Pressed)

// Use asdw (qwerty keyboard), aoew (dvorak keyboard) or
// cursor keys (all keyboards?) to move around.
// Note: If you want to change any keys, use Settings!
if (Input.Keyboard.IsKeyDown(moveForwardKey) ||
  Input.Keyboard.IsKeyDown(Keys.Up) ||
  Input.Keyboard.IsKeyDown(Keys.NumPad8))
{
  float oldPlayerSpeed = Player.Speed;
  Player.Speed += 0.75f * BaseGame.MoveFactorPerSecond;
} // if
if (Input.Keyboard.IsKeyDown(moveBackwardKey) ||
  Input.Keyboard.IsKeyDown(Keys.Down) ||
  Input.Keyboard.IsKeyDown(Keys.NumPad2))
{
  float oldPlayerSpeed = Player.Speed;
  Player.Speed -= 0.75f * BaseGame.MoveFactorPerSecond;
} // if
if (Player.speedItemTimeout > 0)
{
  Player.speedItemTimeout -= BaseGame.ElapsedTimeThisFrameInMs;
  if (Player.speedItemTimeout < 0)
  {
    Player.speedItemTimeout = 0;
    // Reduce to max. possible speed
    if (Player.Speed > Player.MaxSpeedWithoutItem)
      Player.Speed = Player.MaxSpeedWithoutItem;
  } // if
} // if

// Adjust current speed by the current player speed.
float moveFactor = Player.Speed * maxMoveFactor;
float slideFactor = maxSlideFactor;

// Always move forward
Translate(+moveFactor, MoveDirections.Z);
// Slide
if (Input.Keyboard.IsKeyDown(moveLeftKey) ||
  Input.Keyboard.IsKeyDown(Keys.Left) ||
  Input.Keyboard.IsKeyDown(Keys.NumPad4))
{
  consumedAdditionalFuel = true;
  Translate(-slideFactor, MoveDirections.X);
} // if
if (Input.Keyboard.IsKeyDown(moveRightKey) ||
  Input.Keyboard.IsKeyDown(Keys.Right) ||
  Input.Keyboard.IsKeyDown(Keys.NumPad6))
{
  consumedAdditionalFuel = true;
  Translate(+slideFactor, MoveDirections.X);
} // if
```

```
// Up/down
if (Input.Keyboard.IsKeyDown(Keys.F))
{
    Translate(+slideFactor, MoveDirections.Y);
} // if
if (Input.Keyboard.IsKeyDown(Keys.V))
{
    Translate(-slideFactor, MoveDirections.Y);
} // if
#endregion
```

To support the Xbox 360 controller, I added the following code in the beginning of 2006 just one day before the game was released. Implementing XInput was very easy and I'm glad XNA uses XInput for all the input classes. The general idea to have all input devices in one namespace is very good in XNA; the only problematic part is the missing mouse class for the Xbox 360 runtimes. Even if the class is not supported, Microsoft should implement a dummy class to have the code at least compile without having to change all input code that optionally uses a mouse. Well, you fixed that with your own Input class anyway.

Here's the Xbox 360 controller code in Rocket Commander XNA:

```
#region Input support for the XBox360 controller
// 2006-03-09: Added Input support
rotationFactor = 3.0f * BaseGame.MoveFactorPerSecond;
// Change camera rotation when right thumb is used.
if (Input.GamePad.ThumbSticks.Right.X != 0.0f ||
    Input.GamePad.ThumbSticks.Right.Y != 0.0f)
{
    float xMovement = Input.GamePad.ThumbSticks.Right.X;
    float yMovement = Input.GamePad.ThumbSticks.Right.Y;
    Rotate(RotationAxis.Yaw, -xMovement * rotationFactor);
    Rotate(RotationAxis.Pitch, yMovement * rotationFactor);
} // if (Mouse.left.Pressed)
// Use left thumb for moving around
if (Input.GamePad.ThumbSticks.Left.Y != 0)
{
    float oldPlayerSpeed = Player.Speed;
    Player.Speed += 0.75f * Input.GamePad.ThumbSticks.Left.Y *
        BaseGame.MoveFactorPerSecond;
    // Only decrease fuel if change happened
    if (oldPlayerSpeed != Player.Speed)
        consumedAdditionalFuel = true;
} // if
// slide
if (Input.GamePad.ThumbSticks.Left.X != 0)
{
    consumedAdditionalFuel = true;
    Translate(slideFactor * Input.GamePad.ThumbSticks.Left.X * 2,
        MoveDirections.X);
} // if
#endregion
} // HandlePlayerInput()
```

You can see all the code that used a lot of helper methods such as Rotate and Translate, and made heavy use of the Input class properties and some helper values from the BaseGame class such as MoveFactorPerSecond.

Translate moves the current camera along the x, y, or z axis. The x axis is used for sliding to the left and right, which can be done with the A and D keys or the cursor keys in Rocket Commander. The y axis allows you to move up and down, and the z axis allows you to move forward and backward. In Rocket Commander, the z axis is the most important and you fly with very high speed moving on this axis.

```
/// <summary>
/// Translate into x, y or z axis with a specfic amount.
/// </summary>
/// <param name="amount">Amount</param>
/// <param name="direction">Direction</param>
private void Translate(float amount, MoveDirections direction)
{
    Vector3 dir =
        direction == MoveDirections.X ? XAxis :
        direction == MoveDirections.Y ? YAxis : ZAxis;
    pos += dir * amount;
} // Translate(amount, direction)
```

Finally, the Rotate method is used to rotate the camera around. Yaw rotates you left and right, and Pitch allows you to rotate up and down. The original Rocket Commander used a Quaternion here and it allowed you to roll around the rocket, too. In Rocket Commander XNA the rocket is automatically aligned for you to make it easier on the Xbox 360.

```
/// <summary>
/// Rotate around pitch, roll or yaw axis.
/// </summary>
/// <param name="axis">Axis</param>
/// <param name="angle">Angle</param>
private void Rotate(RotationAxis axis, float angle)
{
    if (axis == RotationAxis.Yaw)
        yawRotation -= angle;
    else
        pitchRotation -= angle;
    Rotate(axis, angle)
} // Rotate(axis, angle)
```

All camera classes have unit tests to test them out. Make sure you test them if you try to create your own camera class or run into trouble.

Challenge: Write a Free Camera Class

You already learned everything there is to know to handle input devices. Optional input devices such as an Xbox 360 Wheel Controller are supported automatically as a gamepad in the Input class. You could, for example, play Rocket Commander XNA with an Xbox Wheel Controller if you like. It will be unnatural, but it works and it looks funny. With XNA 2.0 you can also try more strange input devices such as the Big-Button-Pad.

You also have a lot of game screen classes, and you will try to reuse them for the next games. The XNA Shooter game, for example, uses almost the same menu structure as Rocket Commander XNA, just more simplified. In the next chapter, you learn more about the XNA Shooter game.

Your task for this chapter is to write your own free camera class. You could implement a free camera in 3D space, enabling you to move in any direction you want. Just exchange the SimpleCamera class in BaseGame and replace it with your camera class; then you can check out all the unit tests that show 3D data to see if your camera is working as expected. If you are unsure about how to start, check out the existing code in the SpaceCamera class, which provides most functionality for this kind of camera handling.

Alternatively, you could implement a shooter camera, which also allows you to freely rotate and move around, but you stay on the ground. You could even improve this camera and do simple collision tests with the ground allowing you to go up or down when the underground allows it. If you want to do this I recommend that you write a unit test that shows some objects and a ground plane first to test out your camera class.

Summary

You learned a lot about input devices and how to handle them in XNA. The Xbox 360 controller code is the easiest, but most PC users will not have an Xbox 360 controller and many games are not optimal for this kind of controller. For example, strategy or 3D shooter games work much better with a mouse and keyboard setup instead of using a gamepad. The sad thing about XNA is that the mouse device is not supported on the Xbox 360, so all mouse code you implement on the PC version of your game will not work on the Xbox 360. Keyboard devices are supported on both platforms, but Xbox 360 users will usually just have the Xbox 360 controller. This means you have to implement all three input devices for all your games if you want them to run on both platforms correctly. Thanks to your new Input class, this is not a difficult job.

Then you learned about the game screen classes. With the help of the game screen stack, it is easy to execute all game screen classes derived from the IGameScreen interface. For example, the Rocket Commander game uses the following game screen classes (most other games in this book behave similarly):

❑ MainMenu

❑ MissionSelection

❑ Mission (the game itself)

❑ Highscores

❑ Credits

❑ Help

❑ Options

Finally, the chapter covered many camera classes and it was your job to implement another one. You really have a powerful graphics engine now. Writing a complete game with it is still not a piece of cake, but you can get the job done much faster now and it will be more fun to write a game like XNA Shooter, as you can see in the next chapter.

Creating XNA Shooter

In this chapter, I want to guide you through the creation of XNA Shooter, a little shoot-'em-up game, which is actually quite fun to play. It looks and feels better than the usual boring arcade games thanks to many cool effects, nice-looking 3D models and a 3D landscape in the background with houses and plants, real-time shadow mapping, a cool sound track, and nice sound effects. I did not really expect to get such a great game when I started programming XNA Shooter (as you can probably guess from the name, which is not that great). But after I added shadow mapping, which is also used in the racing game in the last part of this book, the background and the 3D buildings looked very nice. The nice UI from the previous chapter and some cool post-screen shaders (see Chapter 8) also help.

This chapter allows you to follow every step in the process of creating XNA Shooter. The basic game was coded in two to three days and only some of the more advanced classes such as the EffectManager and the shadow mapping needed some additional tweaking. Shadow mapping is one of those things that is not only hard to implement at first, but you can spend days or even weeks tweaking it over and over again to make it look a little better and fix some issues (and there are always issues). XNA Shooter is completely based on the XnaGraphicEngine from Chapter 5 and on Rocket Commander XNA from Chapter 8. Only in this way is it even possible to create such a good looking game in that short timeframe.

It didn't require a great deal of work to create the 3D models because I already had most of them from older projects. Thanks to the simple camera, which is fixed and always looks down on the ground, some 3D classes such as rendering sky cube maps or lens flares could be ignored. The camera also simplifies the way you can do the shadow mapping because you always see about the same 3D area in size.

The game logic itself is handled in the following four classes:

☐ The Player class, which you already know from the Rocket Commander game, is even easier to use here because you only need to keep track of the current time, score, health, and the selected weapons.

☐ The Unit class handles all enemy units. It updates their positions and AI and renders them on the screen.

☐ The Projectiles class is used to keep track of all the weapon projectiles you or any enemy unit shoot out. This includes plasma balls, your rockets, fireballs, or enemy rockets. Instant weapons such as the MG or Gatling-gun do not have projectiles; they hit the target immediately and you see the effects directly on the screen.

☐ The Item class is used to drop items after killing transporter or rocket frigate ships and allowing the player to pick them up by flying over them. Items can be health, EMP bombs, or simply one of the four weapon types.

The game logic is a little bit more complex than the logic for the Rocket Commander game. After you go through all these classes, you can see that the code in the Mission class is really easy. Then, after you put everything together, the game is almost complete. Just a little bit of play testing and fixing bugs and the game is ready.

Putting It All Together

You saw some bits and pieces of XNA Shooter in the previous two chapters. Before you can start, you need all files in the XNA Shooter project, which has to be created first. The project needs all the sound effects together with the XACT project, and all the usual files such as shaders, standard textures for fonts, testing, the menu, and so on. Finally, after adding the .x files for the 3D models and their textures, you can go ahead and test them out with help of the unit tests you have in the Texture, Shader, and Model classes.

Figure 11-1 shows the new project, which is just called XnaShooter, after performing the following actions:

☐ Create a new Windows XNA Game project in XNA Game Studio Express with the name "XnaShooter."

☐ Drag in all source code files from the Rocket Commander XNA project, which was based on the XnaGraphicEngine. The following files, sorted by namespaces, were removed because you won't need them in XnaShooter:

   ☐ Game namespace: Asteroid.cs, BaseAsteroidManager.cs, GameAsteroidManager.cs, Level.cs, PhysicsAsteroidManager.cs, SmallAsteroid.cs, and SpaceCamera.cs

   ☐ GameScreens namespace: Help.cs, MissionSelection.cs, and Options.cs

   ☐ Graphics namespace: AnimatedModel.cs and LensFlare.cs

   ☐ Shaders namespace: ParallaxShader.cs and PreScreenSkyCubeMapping.cs

☐ Game1.cs was also removed and the RocketCommanderGame class was renamed to XnaShooterGame.

- The `RocketCommanderXna` namespace that is used in all files is replaced with the `XnaShooter` namespace.

- Most code from the `Mission.cs`, `Player.cs`, `MainMenu.cs`, and `XnaShooterGame.cs` had to be commented out in order to allow compiling the project.

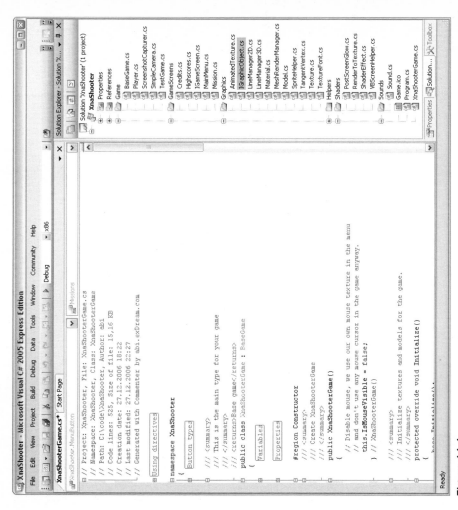

Figure 11-1

Sounds

The source code files are important, but without any textures, sounds, and 3D models you would not have a real game. Because the XnaShooter XACT project was already discussed in Chapter 9, it is the first thing you are going to add to your new project. The only file that has to be in your project is the `XnaShooter.xap` file, but it uses many `.wav` files. I tend to add all these `.wav` files to the project because I like to see which files are used directly in the project.

After the XACT project is added to the `Sounds` namespace, you can change the `Sound` class and test all the sounds with help of the `TestPlaySounds` unit test. The unit test does not cover all sounds, but the most important sound effects are tested here. Some sounds such as GameMusic and Explosion are using more than one sound file. This means if you play the Explosion sound, one of three explosion sound files is randomly selected and played. There is no special code required for this to work; everything is set up in XACT.

```
public static void TestPlaySounds()
{
  TestGame.Start(
    delegate
    {
      if (Input.MouseLeftButtonJustPressed ||
        Input.GamePadAJustPressed)
        Sound.Play(Sounds.Defeat);
      else if (Input.MouseRightButtonJustPressed ||
        Input.GamePadBJustPressed)
        Sound.Play(Sounds.Victory);
      else if (Input.KeyboardKeyJustPressed(Keys.D1))
        Sound.Play(Sounds.GameMusic);
      else if (Input.KeyboardKeyJustPressed(Keys.D2))
        Sound.Play(Sounds.EnemyShoot);
      else if (Input.KeyboardKeyJustPressed(Keys.D3))
        Sound.Play(Sounds.Explosion);
      else if (Input.KeyboardKeyJustPressed(Keys.D4))
        Sound.Play(Sounds.Health);
      else if (Input.KeyboardKeyJustPressed(Keys.D5))
        Sound.Play(Sounds.PlasmaShoot);
      else if (Input.KeyboardKeyJustPressed(Keys.D6))
        Sound.Play(Sounds.MgShoot);
      else if (Input.KeyboardKeyJustPressed(Keys.D7))
        Sound.Play(Sounds.GattlingShoot);
      else if (Input.KeyboardKeyJustPressed(Keys.D8))
        Sound.Play(Sounds.EMP);
      TextureFont.WriteText(2, 30,
        "Press 1-8 or A/B or left/right mouse buttons to play back "+
        "sounds!");
    });
} // TestPlaySounds()
```

User Interface

The UI and menu textures should be added now. The previous chapter talked quite a bit about handling the input, the UI, and the game screen's logic, so add the required files (MainMenu.png, MouseCursor.dds, and GameFont.png) and take a look at the game screen logic (see Figure 11-2). Implementing the main menu and the other game screens should not take long. It is very similar to the Rocket Commander game, but several complicated screens such as the Options and Mission Selection screens were removed because they were not really necessary for XnaShooter.

You already learned about the in-game UI for XnaShooter, and the game logic for the whole game is discussed at the end of this chapter. For the menu, you only have three screens and all of them are easy to implement. The Main Menu just shows four menu buttons, which add a new game screen on the stack to allow you to return to the main menu after quitting the newly added game screen. The Highscore list is a stripped-down version of the Rocket Commander Highscore screen, showing a local highscore because

Chapter 11: Creating XNA Shooter

there is no network support for an online highscore in XNA. Last but not least, the Credits screen just shows a bunch of text plus the Back button.

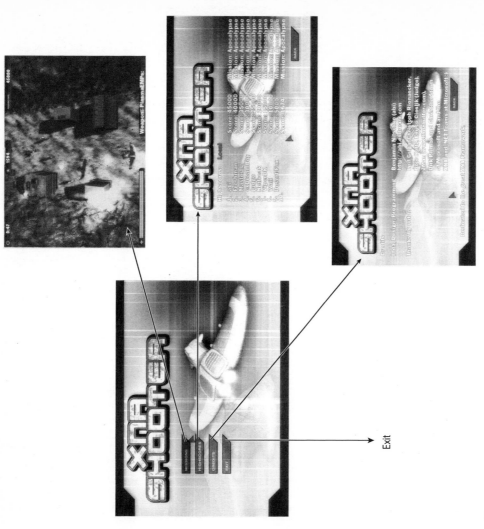

Exit

Figure 11-2

Take a quick look at the MainMenu Run method, which handles the main menu and the four buttons to the other game screens:

```
// Render background
game.RenderMenuBackground();
// Show all buttons
int buttonNum = 0;
foreach (MenuButton button in menuButtons)
  // Don't render the back button
  if (button != MenuButton.Back)
```

```
            {
                if (game.RenderMenuButton(button, buttonLocations[buttonNum]))
                {
                    if (button == MenuButton.Missions)
                        game.AddGameScreen(new Mission());
                    else if (button == MenuButton.Highscore)
                        game.AddGameScreen(new Highscores());
                    else if (button == MenuButton.Credits)
                        game.AddGameScreen(new Credits());
                    else if (button == MenuButton.Exit)
                        quit = true;
                } // if
                buttonNum++;
                if (buttonNum >= buttonLocations.Length)
                    break;
            } // foreach if

            // Hotkeys, M=Mission, H=Highscores, C=Credits, Esc=Quit
            if (Input.KeyboardKeyJustPressed(Keys.M))
                game.AddGameScreen(new Mission());
            else if (Input.KeyboardKeyJustPressed(Keys.H))
                game.AddGameScreen(new Highscores());
            else if (Input.KeyboardKeyJustPressed(Keys.C))
                game.AddGameScreen(new Credits());
            else if (Input.KeyboardEscapeJustPressed)
                quit = true;
```

Textures

In addition to the menu, mouse, and game font textures, you need a bunch more textures for the game. First of all, there are the HUD textures you already saw in the previous chapter and the new NumbersFont.png texture for some colorful numbers you are going to display on the top HUD bar. Then there are also many effect textures you need for the effect system discussed later in this chapter. It is hard to explain which texture is used for which part of the game. Please take a look at Figure 11-3 for a quick explanation on how each texture is used in XNA Shooter.

All these texture files have to be added to the project, but the content importer settings are not all the same. Some files like the mouse cursor, the main menu, and the game font should not be compressed with the DXT compression format (used in dds files). They should stay uncompressed in 32bpp (bits per pixel), but other textures like the explosion effects need compression to become smaller. For example, the BigExplosion effect consists of about 30 textures with the size 128 × 128. Without compression this would be about 2MB of texture data just for one explosion effect.

With DXT5 compression you can get it down to half a megabyte, enabling you to implement several explosion effects and still save disk and video memory space. To support the alpha channel of the explosion textures the DXT5 compression format has to be used instead of DXT1, which would compress even better.

The game has about 3MB of textures, where 1MB is just for the two explosion effects, and another megabyte goes to the menu graphics. The rest of the textures are used for the visual effects, the HUD, and fonts. Effect systems can be much more complex with many little particles acting together to form cool, big explosions. Sometimes effects are even combined with a physics engine and enable you to let the particles, smoke, and explosion pieces interact with the 3D environment and even with each other.

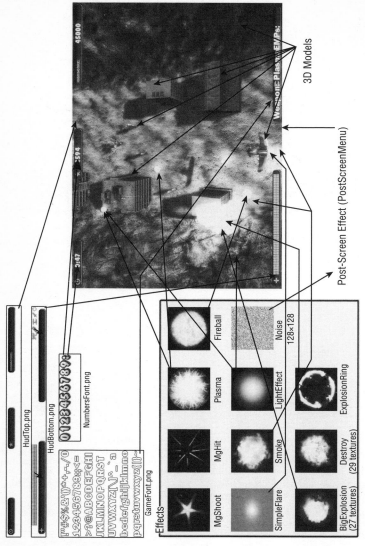

Figure 11-3

For the XnaShooter game, the simple effect system is sufficient; all effects are hard coded, but it is very easy to change them or to add new effects using the existing textures. Simply add another Add method and test it with help of the TestEffects unit test in the EffectManager class.

3D Models

The game uses a lot of 3D models (see Figure 11-4).

I just started with a ship and some effects, but after a while I noticed that the game is not fun without at least 3 to 4 different enemy units that behave differently. The units in XNA Shooter are very different, as follows:

☐ OwnShip is the model for your own ship. It enables you to shoot with an MG, Plasma, Gatling-Gun, or the Rocket Launcher. Additionally, you can fire EMP bombs to kill everything on the screen. Your ship is the fastest one in the game, but when the screen gets filled with enemy units, that won't help you. You have to kill everything before the enemies can overwhelm you.

☐ Corvette is the basic enemy unit; it shoots two small MGs mounted on the left and right side of the ship. It does not have many hitpoints and the weapon is very weak. This unit's main advantage is that the weapon hits you instantly if you are in the shooting direction of the Corvette. If the screen fills up with many Corvettes, you will constantly lose energy if you don't kill them fast enough.

XNA Shooter 3D Models

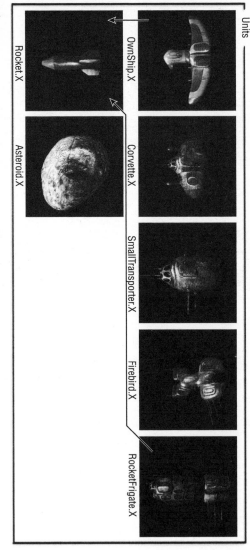

Units

OwnShip.X Corvette.X SmallTransporter.X Firebird.X RocketFrigate.X

Rocket.X Asteroid.X

Items

ItemHealth.X ItemMg.X ItemPlasma.X ItemGattling.X ItemRockets.X ItemEMP.X

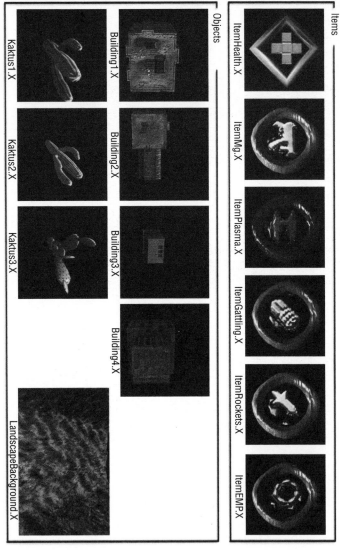

Objects

Building1.X Building2.X Building3.X Building4.X

Kaktus1.X Kaktus2.X Kaktus3.X LandscapeBackground.X

Figure 11-4

❑ Small-Transporter is a little ship that carries supplies. There's a 25 percent to 50 percent chance these ships have something useful for you, especially health items, which are useful if you are low on health. EMP bombs can be collected after you kill these transporters. They carry all the other items too, enabling you to switch your weapon after collecting new weapon items.

- Transporters do not shoot, but you should not collide with them. They are small and have even fewer hitpoints than the Corvette ship.

- The Firebird is a very powerful unit because it shoots fireballs directly at you. It even calculates the position you are currently flying to forcing you to constantly evade the incoming fireballs. It has more hitpoints than the other smaller ships and it is a little bigger. Do not collide with Firebirds; they can immensely reduce your energy. Often only an EMP can help you if too many Firebirds are on the screen.

- The Rocket-Frigate is the biggest ship in the game. Originally, I also wanted to create a Boss-Enemy at the end of the level, but it was too much work creating the 3D model and implementing the additional game logic. It should not be hard to add a Boss-Enemy and more levels to the game if you are really interested in developing a shoot-'em-up game. The Rocket-Frigate fires rockets, similar to the rockets your own ship can fire, but they are a lot smaller and do not inflict as much damage. In addition to the heavy armor and high amount of hitpoints this unit has, the main advantage of the rockets that are fired by the Rocket-Frigate is the homing ability of the rockets, which will always follow your ship until they run out of fuel. Handling just one Rocket-Frigate is not a big problem. If you are skilled enough to evade the incoming rockets and are able to still hit the Rocket-Frigate, it will be demolished after a short while. It becomes a lot harder if you have to deal with multiple Rocket-Frigates at the end of the mission. Make sure you have a heavy weapon and EMP bombs on your ship to prepare for these situations.

Asteroids are not really a unit; they just fly around and block your way. They cannot shoot, but if you collide with them you lose a high amount of hitpoints. They are almost indestructible with normal weapons, but with help of EMP bombs you are able to take them out. You have probably noticed that I borrowed this model from the Rocket Commander game.

The units are very important for your game, but without the items (new weapons, extra health, etc.) it would be no fun and without the background objects it would look boring. The items give you back health or EMP bombs or allow you to change the weapon to the four available weapons: MG, Plasma Gun, Gatling-Gun, and the Rocket Launcher.

The background objects do not interact with the game at all; they just sit in the background and receive shadows. The LandscapeBackground.X model is rendered and repeated for the mission. Later in this chapter you learn more details about the creation process and the level generation. After rendering the landscape, all buildings and plants are rendered on top of it. Because the center of the landscape model forms a valley that has the same height at all locations, you can easily add the buildings and plants here. All the objects are randomly added and generated as you fly through the level. You can also add more objects if you want to. It is very easy to change the landscape models list; just add another model and it will automatically be generated on the ground.

Animated Textures

You used animated textures before in the Rocket Commander game, but you never learned how to implement them. Basically, you just have a bunch of textures, which are changed every $1/30$ of a second. In XNA Shooter, two animated textures are implemented for the two explosion effects used when units explode. You could just load the 30 textures for each explosion effect and handle them yourself, but because you need that code more than once it should be abstracted to a new class: AnimatedTexture (see Figure 11-5).

The constructor of `AnimatedTexture` is very similar to the `Texture` constructor, but you also check for additional textures with the help of the filename. The big explosion has sequential texture names such as `BigExplosion0001.dds`, `BigExplosion0002.dds`, `BigExplosion0003.dds`, and so on. The following code in the constructor is used to load all these filenames into the internal `xnaTextures` array. Please note that in the original Rocket Commander code (Managed DirectX) dds files were loaded, but in XNA you should load the already compiled .xnb files, which is the only way to load textures on the Xbox 360 (the Windows platform, however, also supports loading directly from dds files).

Figure 11-5

```
// Ok, now load all other animated textures
List<XnaTexture> animatedTextures =
    new List<XnaTexture>();
animatedTextures.Add(internalXnaTexture);
int texNumber = 2;
while (File.Exists(filenameFirstPart +
    texNumber.ToString("0000")+".xnb"))
{
    animatedTextures.Add(BaseGame.Content.Load<Texture2D>(
        filenameFirstPart + texNumber.ToString("0000")));
    texNumber++;
} // while (File.Exists)
xnaTextures = animatedTextures.ToArray();
```

With the help of the `Select` method, you can now select any of the loaded textures, and the rest of the class behaves exactly the same as the original texture class. This means you can select and render textures on the screen or pass the texture to shaders because the internal `xnaTexture` field is assigned to the correct selected texture. You can also just call `GetAnimatedTexture` to access any animated texture number.

```
/// <summary>
/// Select this animated texture as the current texture
/// </summary>
/// <param name="animationNumber">Number</param>
public void Select(int animationNumber)
{
    // Select new animation number
    internalXnaTexture =
        xnaTextures[animationNumber % xnaTextures.Length];
    if (xnaTextures != null &&
        xnaTextures.Length > 0)
    {
        // Select this animated texture as the current texture
        xnaTextures.Length > 0)
    } // if
} // Select(num)
```

Billboards

You now have all the content in place for your XNA Shooter game. You still need to think about a way to display all this new content. You do not have any rendering code for the landscape and all the objects on it yet. You also don't have code to display the new effects in your 3D environment. In Rocket Commander you displayed the explosion, which was the only effect you had, directly on the screen. In your new game, it would not look very convincing to put all effects directly on top of the screen. Having the effects directly in your 3D scene as 3D polygons has the following advantages:

□ You don't need to calculate the 2D position and size for every 3D effect. When using 3D polygons, they will be transformed to the screen like everything else.

□ Thanks to the depth buffer it is possible to render effects in front of and behind other 3D objects. This way flare and smoke effects behind the ship engines look correct, even if parts of the ship or other 3D objects are in front.

□ If you sort the effects back to front, you can render them on top of each other with alpha blending turned. This way many effects are combined to give greater looking 3D effects.

To be able to render 3D effects directly on the screen, billboards are usually used. Billboards are just 3D quads (two triangles) showing the texture. Sometimes special graphic card features such as point sprites can be used. In any case, the billboards should be visible when you view them. But as with any 3D polygon, if it faces in the wrong direction you can't see it or it gets distorted and smaller (see Figure 11-6).

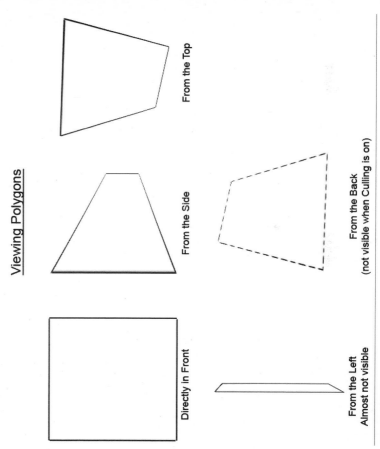

Viewing Polygons

Directly in Front

From the Side

From the Top

From the Left
Almost not visible

From the Back
(not visible when Culling is on)

Figure 11-6

For some effects this behavior is good. For example, a 3D explosion ring would look correct from the front and the sides, although it may not work from a 90 degree angle, when it nearly disappears. Most other effects, however, are not designed to look good from the side. Explosions, light effects, fire and plasma balls, and so on are all effects that are captured from the front, but they look nearly the same from all other sides too. Take the fireball effect as an example. A fireball should look like a ball from all directions. It should not be distorted, become small, or disappear if you look from the other side. To achieve a successful effect, you have to look the effect in the eye, so to speak. This is accomplished by always rotating the effect polygons in a way that faces directly to the viewer. The Billboard class helps you achieve this task (see Figure 11-7).

The most important methods of the Billboard class are the Render methods that put the billboards into the billboards list, which is finally rendered when you call RenderBillboards at the end of each frame. There are six overloads of the Render method, but you can also call the RenderOnGround methods to render billboards on the xy plane. One of the Render methods even allows you to specify the right and up vectors, which span the billboard vectors. This way you can randomly align explosion rings for the ship explosion in addition to the other explosion effects.

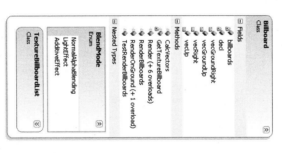

Figure 11-7

Before you take a look at the Render methods, check out the unit test of the Billboard class, which shows you how to use this class:

```
Billboard.Render(plasma,
    new Vector3(-40.0f, 0.0f, 0.0f), 5.0f,
    BaseGame.TotalTimeMs * (float)Math.PI / 1000.0f,
    Color.White);
Billboard.Render(fireball,
    new Vector3(-40.0f, +50.0f, 0.0f), 5.0f,
    Color.White);
Billboard.RenderOnGround(ring,
```

```
new Vector3(-25.0f, 0.0f, -100.0f), 5.0f, 0, Color.White,
    vecGroundRight, vecGroundUp);
// etc.
// Render all billboards for this frame
Billboard.RenderBillboards();
```

In the Render methods the vecRight and vecUp vectors are used to construct the billboard polygons. These vectors can be directly extracted from the view matrix you currently use. Thanks to the BaseGame class it is easy to extract these vectors, which is automatically done every time you call RenderBillboards through the CalcVectors helper method.

```
/// <summary>
/// Calc vectors for billboards, will create helper vectors for
/// billboard rendering, should just be called every frame.
/// </summary>
public static void CalcVectors()
{
    // Only use the inverse view matrix, world matrix is assumed to be
    // Identity, simply grab the values out of the inverse view matrix.
    Matrix invViewMatrix = BaseGame.InverseViewMatrix;
    vecRight = new Vector3(
        invViewMatrix.M11, invViewMatrix.M12, invViewMatrix.M13);
    vecUp = new Vector3(
        invViewMatrix.M21, invViewMatrix.M22, invViewMatrix.M23);
} // CalcVectors()
```

Take a quick look at one of the Render methods of the Billboard class:

```
/// <summary>
/// Render 3D Billboard into scene. Used for 3D effects.
/// This method does not support rotation (it is a bit faster).
/// </summary>
/// <param name="tex">Texture used for rendering</param>
/// <param name="lightBlendMode">Blend mode for this effect</param>
/// <param name="pos">Position in world space</param>
/// <param name="size">Size in world coordinates</param>
/// <param name="col">Color, usually white</param>
public static void Render(XnaTexture tex, BlendMode lightBlendMode,
    Vector3 pos, float size, Color col)
{
    // Invisible?
    if (col.A == 0)
        return;
    TextureBillboardList texBillboard =
        GetTextureBillboard(tex, lightBlendMode);
    Vector3 vec;
    int index = texBillboard.vertices.Count;
    vec = pos + ((-vecRight + vecUp) * size);
    texBillboard.vertices.Add(
        new VertexPositionColorTexture(
            vec, col, new Vector2(0.0f, 0.0f)));
    vec = pos + ((-vecRight - vecUp) * size);
    texBillboard.vertices.Add(
```

```
new VertexPositionColorTexture(
    vec, col, new Vector2(0.0f, 1.0f)));
vec = pos + ((vecRight - vecUp) * size);
texBillboard.vertices.Add(
    new VertexPositionColorTexture(
    vec, col, new Vector2(1.0f, 1.0f)));
vec = pos + ((vecRight + vecUp) * size);
texBillboard.vertices.Add(
    new VertexPositionColorTexture(
    vec, col, new Vector2(1.0f, 0.0f)));
texBillboard.indices.AddRange(new short[]
    {
        (short)(index+0), (short)(index+1), (short)(index+2),
        (short)(index+0), (short)(index+2), (short)(index+3),
    });
} // Render(tex, pos, size)
```

As you can see, four vertices are constructed and added to the vertices list for this billboard type. Each texture and light blend mode combination gets its own `TextureBillboardList`. Then indices for the two polygons that form a screen quad are added to the indices list. Both the vertex and index buffers from the `TextureBillboardList` are then rendered together with the texture and the effect shader in the `RenderBillboards` method.

Landscape Rendering

The landscape in XNA Shooter is a simple 3D model with one 1024 × 1024 texture. However, landscape rendering is not an easy topic. You will spend a whole chapter in the next part of this book rendering the landscape and the tracks for the upcoming racing game.

But I did not want to spend so much time for this simple shoot-'em-up game, especially given that it's just for the landscape rendering in the background, something that you don't even interact with in the game. So instead of implementing a landscape engine to render many thousands of polygons, you can use tile-able textures on these polygons and maybe even implement alpha blending between the different ground texture types. I just took the easy road and used a finished 3D model for the whole landscape. It is just enough to fit on one screen and it does not enable you to scroll to the left or right, but that is not required for this game; you just move up. The mission is approximately 60 of these landscape parts long and you simply put them on top of each other, always showing the current one and the next. It does not fit together perfectly because the lighting on the borders is hard to fix (texture has to fit, normal map has to fit, 3D model normals have to fit), but it is good enough for our purpose.

In this section I want to show you the necessary steps to create such a background model because I'm not the only one who uses this easy technique to get something on the screen quickly (for example, one game modification of Rocket Commander called Canyon Commander uses a similar technique to show 3D canyons).

Base Texture and Normal Map

Before you start with any 3D data or height-map for the background landscape, you should have an idea of what is displayed in the background. My idea was to have desert sand in the middle and rocks at the sides, which form a little canyon. I quickly grabbed two textures that would fit and threw them together into the BackgroundRock.dds texture (see Figure 11-8). To be honest, I did not initially think of the sand part. I thought the rock texture was sufficient, although it looked boring and was too repetitive.

The normal map is mixed together in a similar way, but for these two textures I did not have a normal map at first. I used the Nvidia Photoshop plugins to generate normal maps from the two base textures. You have to play around a little bit with the values until it looks good and sometimes you have to repaint the base texture to fix wrong places. The diffuse textures that are used here have no information about the height or normals in it, so the only thing this normal map generator plugin can do is to convert the image to a grayscale format and generate normals from this fake height map.

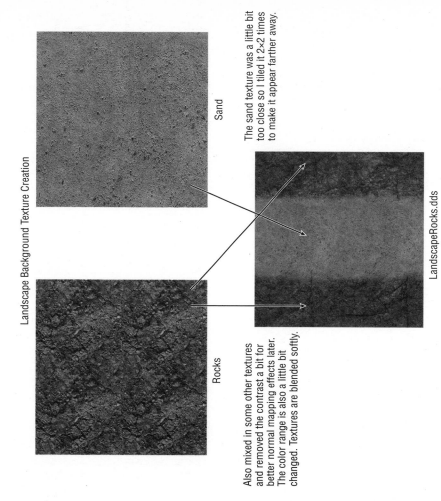

Landscape Background Texture Creation

Sand

The sand texture was a little bit too close so I tiled it 2×2 times to make it appear farther away.

Rocks

Also mixed in some other textures and removed the contrast a bit for better normal mapping effects later. The color range is also a little bit changed. Textures are blended softly.

LandscapeRocks.dds

Figure 11-8

Sometimes the normal maps look okay. Other times it is just plain wrong to generate normals this way. It would be much better if these textures were created by an artist who also provides normal maps or at least height maps with them, but you will not always have this luxury. On occasion, only the diffuse texture exists. If you take a photo with your camera height and normal map, data is not recorded either. Again, try to keep things simple here. You create more complex landscape textures and normal maps in the next chapter for the more complex racing game. Figure 11-9 shows the normal maps mixed together. You will notice that the normals for the rocks use a stronger normal map than for the sand, and that is good because you want to have the rocks appear curvier than the sand on the ground. But even the sand has some variations in it (added on top of the relatively plain sand texture) to get a little bit better lighting from the normal mapping shader used in the game.

Height Map

With the diffuse and normal texture in place you could now display the landscape background on a simple polygon, but it would not look very convincing or even appear to be 3D this way. You need some real height for the cliffs and the canyon in the middle. To create this canyon I used 3D Studio Max (but you can use whatever 3D content creation tool you feel comfortable with or ask someone who knows how to use these tools if you don't want to create 3D models yourself) and I created a simple plane object on the xy ground (z pointing up) with 64 × 64 intersection points forming 63*63*2 = 7938 polygons. I used 63 because each polygon needs a start and end position. I multiplied by 2 because each landscape quad is formed from two triangles (see Figure 11-10).

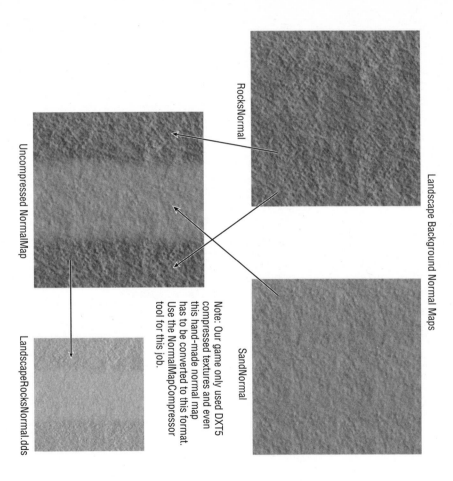

RocksNormal

Landscape Background Normal Maps

SandNormal

Uncompressed NormalMap

Note: Our game only used DXT5 compressed textures and even this hand-made normal map has to be converted to this format. Use the NormalMapCompressor tool for this job.

LandscapeRocksNormal.dds

Figure 11-9

To give each height point another z value than the default 0.0 you could drag them up or down in your 3D modeling program, but I'm not skilled or patient enough to create a landscape this way. A much easier approach is to use a height texture and then displace all height points of your plane according to this height map. Height maps are also often used for geological landscape maps, so it is not very hard to find some cool looking height maps on the Internet, even from other planets.

Luckily for us, 3D Studio Max has a simple modifier called Displace, which does just what you need (not easy to find, but once you know where it is, it becomes very useful). From here you can add your newly created height map (I painted it myself; not spectacular, but it works) to the 3D model (see Figure 11-11).

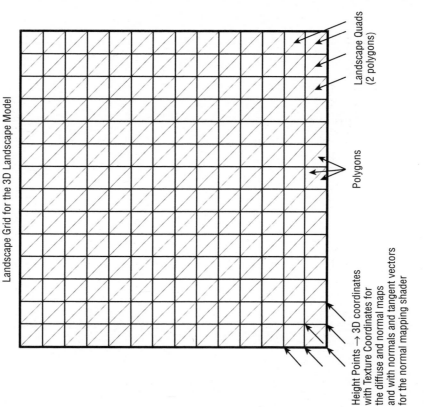

Landscape Grid for the 3D Landscape Model

Landscape Quads
(2 polygons)

Polygons

Height Points → 3D coordinates
with Texture Coordinates for
the diffuse and normal maps
and with normals and tangent vectors
for the normal mapping shader

Figure 11-10

Nothing happens now; you might ask why that is. Well, Max has many settings and it is not always easy to find out which one is responsible for what. Just play around with the settings until something changes. In this case you need to adjust the Strength setting at the top. Set it to something between 30 and 40 to see a result like the one shown in Figure 11-12.

The final action you have to do in 3D Studio Max is to assign the diffuse and normal textures to a new normal mapping shader material. Then you can assign this material to your 3D model (see Figure 11-13) and export it. It is now ready to be used in your game.

This landscape is now rendered from the top in the game and you will only see the valley and the inner borders of the cliffs. The landscape rendering was tested with support of 16:9 widescreen resolutions, which means on 4:3 resolutions some parts of it might not always be visible. All the action happens in the middle anyway. After you add the 3D buildings and plans in the game everything is up and ready for some shoot-'em-up action.

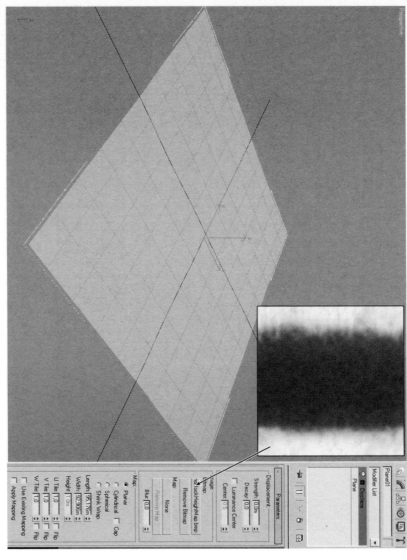

Figure 11-11

Adding Objects

The landscape looks nice (at least better than a simple xy plane), but it is still kind of empty. To make it a little bit more exciting, the buildings and plants you saw earlier are added to it. Check out the

Check out the unit test in the `Mission` class to see how this landscape model is rendered in the game. For just taking a look at the 3D model you can also use the unit test in the `Model` class, which shows all used models in the game.

Chapter 11: Creating XNA Shooter

`TestRenderLandscapeBackground` unit test at the end of the `Mission` class, which just calls `RenderLandscapeBackground` of the `Mission` class. This method takes the current level position as a parameter and always shows only the current and the next landscape part to ensure you always have 3D models in front of you even when you move up. The player will not notice this because the current landscape part is replaced with the next if you move up enough and a new landscape part is generated at the top until you are done with the level.

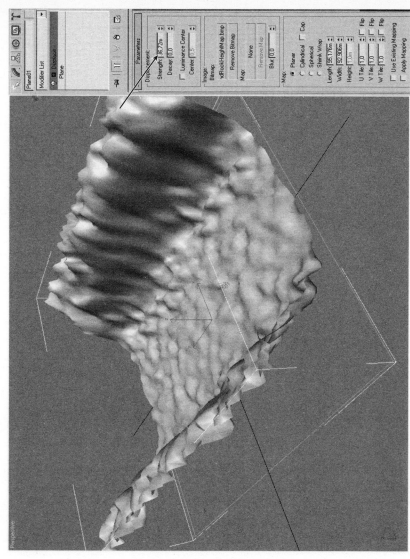

Figure 11-12

The more interesting code is the object generation, which takes the array of loaded models and randomly adds new objects to the visible landscape object list. Plants are randomly placed and rotated, but buildings only appear on the left and right side and they are only rotated in 90 degree steps to fit better together.

```
// From the GenerateLandscapeSegment method:
List<MatrixAndNumber> ret = new List<MatrixAndNumber>();
int numOfNewObjects = RandomHelper.GetRandomInt(
    MaxNumberOfObjectsGeneratedEachSegment);
if (numOfNewObjects < 8)
    numOfNewObjects = 8;
```

```
for (int num = 0; num < numOfNewObjects; num++)
{
    int type = 1+RandomHelper.GetRandomInt(NumOfLandscapeModels-1);
    // Create buildings only left and right
    if (type <= 5)
    {
        int rotSimple = RandomHelper.GetRandomInt(4);
        float rot = rotSimple == 0 ? 0 :
            rotSimple == 1 ? MathHelper.PiOver2 :
            rotSimple == 1 ? MathHelper.Pi : MathHelper.PiOver2 * 3;
        bool side = RandomHelper.GetRandomInt(2) == 0;
        float yPos = segmentNumber * SegmentLength + 0.94f *
            RandomHelper.GetRandomFloat(-SegmentLength / 2, SegmentLength / 2);
        Vector3 pos = new Vector3(side ? -18 : +18, yPos, -16);
        // Add very little height to each object to avoid same height
        // if buildings collide into each other.
        pos += new Vector3(0, 0, 0.001f * num);
        ret.Add(new MatrixAndNumber(
            Matrix.CreateScale(LandscapeModelSize[type]) *
            Matrix.CreateRotationZ(rot) *
            Matrix.CreateTranslation(pos),
            type));
    } // if
    else
    {
        ret.Add(new MatrixAndNumber(
            Matrix.CreateScale(LandscapeModelSize[type]) *
            Matrix.CreateRotationZ(
            RandomHelper.GetRandomFloat(0, MathHelper.Pi * 2)) *
            Matrix.CreateTranslation(new Vector3(
            RandomHelper.GetRandomFloat(-20, +20),
            segmentNumber * SegmentLength +
            RandomHelper.GetRandomFloat(
            -SegmentLength / 2, SegmentLength / 2),
            -15)),
            type));
    } // else
} // for
```

The `ret` list is then returned to the caller, which saves it to the requested landscape part. The full `GenerateLandscapeSegment` code also adds all enemy units, checks for colliding landscape objects, and prevents objects from being too close to each other.

If you execute the `TestRenderLandscapeBackground` unit test you should see the landscape and the ground objects as shown in Figure 11-14. Note that the shadow map generation is not discussed in this chapter. Please read the last part of this book for more information about shadow mapping techniques. You can also check out the `ShadowMappingShader` class if you are interested now.

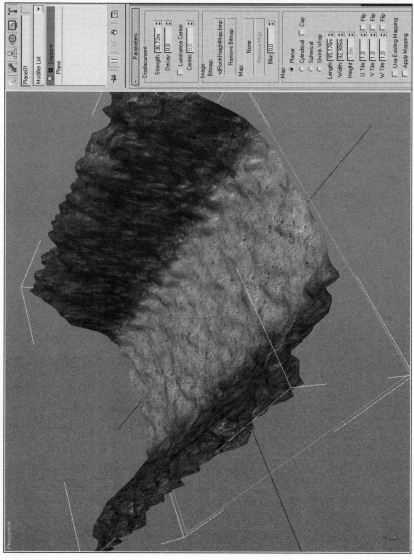

Figure 11-13

XNA Shooter Game

It is time for some action now. You have all the 3D models, all effect files and textures, and your sound effects ready to be used, and you don't have to worry about the landscape background anymore because it already works fine. The landscape itself is below the surface (z is below 0). Thus, you can easily add all your game objects at the z height 0.0, which makes adding effects, collision checking, and testing a little bit easier for the game.

You can now add your own ship in the landscape rendering method of the `Mission` class and control it in the `Player` class. Rendering just requires the following lines of code:

```
Player.shipPos =
    new Vector3(Player.position, AllShipsZHeight) + levelVector;
AddModelToRender(
    shipModels[(int)ShipModelTypes.OwnShip],
    Matrix.CreateScale(ShipModelSize[(int)ShipModelTypes.OwnShip]) *
```

```
Matrix.CreateRotationZ(MathHelper.Pi) *
Matrix.CreateRotationX(Player.shipRotation.Y) *
Matrix.CreateRotationY(Player.shipRotation.X) *
Matrix.CreateTranslation(Player.shipPos));
// Add smoke effects for our ship
EffectManager.AddRocketOrShipFlareAndSmoke(
    Player.shipPos + new Vector3(-0.3f, -2.65f, +0.35f), 1.35f,
    5 * Player.MovementSpeedPerSecond);
EffectManager.AddRocketOrShipFlareAndSmoke(
    Player.shipPos + new Vector3(0.3f, -2.65f, +0.35f), 1.35f,
    5 * Player.MovementSpeedPerSecond);
```

Figure 11-14

All the scaling and rotation is just done to get the ship to the correct size and to rotate it correctly. The z rotation lets it point upwards and the x and y rotations let the ship wiggle when moving to the sides or up and down. Then two flare and smoke effects are added where your ship engine is. The EffectManager is discussed shortly.

Game Logic

The code to control your ships is located in the Player class, where most of the other game logic is handled for you including firing your weapons, moving the ship, getting points for killing ships, and handling items:

```
// From Player.HandleGameLogic:
// [Show victory/defeat messages if game is over]
// Increase game time
gameTimeMs += BaseGame.ElapsedTimeThisFrameInMs;
// Control our ship position with the keyboard or gamepad.
// Use keyboard cursor keys and the left thumb stick. The
// right hand is used for fireing (ctrl, space, a, b).
Vector2 lastPosition = position;
Vector2 lastRotation = shipRotation;
float moveFactor = mouseSensibility *
  MovementSpeedPerSecond * BaseGame.MoveFactorPerSecond;
// Left/Right
if (Input.Keyboard.IsKeyDown(moveLeftKey) ||
  Input.Keyboard.IsKeyDown(Keys.Left) ||
  Input.Keyboard.IsKeyDown(Keys.NumPad4) ||
  Input.GamePad.DPad.Left == ButtonState.Pressed)
{
  position.X -= moveFactor;
} // if
if (Input.Keyboard.IsKeyDown(moveRightKey) ||
  Input.Keyboard.IsKeyDown(Keys.Right) ||
  Input.Keyboard.IsKeyDown(Keys.NumPad6) ||
  Input.GamePad.DPad.Right == ButtonState.Pressed)
{
  position.X += moveFactor;
} // if
if (Input.GamePad.ThumbSticks.Left.X != 0.0f)
{
  position.X += Input.GamePad.ThumbSticks.Left.X;// *0.75f;
} // if
// Keep position in bounds
if (position.X < -MaxXPosition)
  position.X = -MaxXPosition;
if (position.X > MaxXPosition)
  position.X = MaxXPosition;
// [Same for Down/Up changes position.Y, see Player.cs]
// Calculate ship rotation based on the current movement
if (lastPosition.X > position.X)
  shipRotation.X = -0.5f;
else if (lastPosition.X < position.X)
  shipRotation.X = +0.5f;
else
  shipRotation.X = 0;
// [Same for shipRotation.Y, see above]
// Interpolate ship rotation to be more smooth
shipRotation = lastRotation * 0.95f + shipRotation * 0.05f;
```

HandleGameLogic first checks if the game is over and displays a message on the screen telling you if you have won or lost. Then the current game time is increased. After that, your ship control is handled, and then the weapon firing and items are handled at the end of the method together with some code that gives you scores for killing enemy units.

You allow input from the keyboard and gamepad input devices. The mouse is not supported, because tweaking it is hard for a shoot-'em-up game and I personally don't like controlling a shoot-'em-up game with the mouse; it feels wrong. With the help of the MaxXPosition and MaxYPosition constants you make sure that your ship does not move outside the visible screen area and the shipRotation is calculated based on the movement you made. If no movement was made it will slowly get back to zero.

The following lines show how the firing is handled. Additional details can be found in the Player class.

```
// Fire?
if (Input.GamePadAPressed ||
    Input.GamePad.Triggers.Right > 0.5f ||
    Input.Keyboard.IsKeyDown(Keys.LeftControl) ||
    Input.Keyboard.IsKeyDown(Keys.RightControl))
{
    switch (currentWeapon)
    {
        case WeaponTypes.MG:
            // Shooting cooldown passed?
            if (gameTimeMs - lastShootTimeMs >= 150)
            {
                // [Shooting code goes here ...]
                shootNum++;
                lastShootTimeMs = gameTimeMs;
                Input.GamePadRumble(0.015f, 0.125f);
                Player.score += 1;
            } // if
            break;
        case WeaponTypes.Plasma:
            // [etc. all other weapons are handled here]
            break;
    } // switch
} // if
```

As soon as you press the A button, the right trigger on the gamepad, or the Ctrl keys on the keyboard, you enter the firing code, but the weapon will not fire until you reach the next cool-down phase (each weapon has different cool-down times). Then the weapon firing and weapon collision detection is handled and lastShootTimeMs is reset to the current game time waiting for the next cool-down phase.

After handling the weapons the only thing left is to create the winning and losing conditions. You achieve victory if you successfully reach the end of the level and you lose if you run out of hitpoints before that happens.

```
if (Player.health <= 0)
{
    victory = false;
    EffectManager.AddExplosion(shipPos, 20);
    for (int num = 0; num<8; num++)
        EffectManager.AddFlameExplosion(shipPos+
            RandomHelper.GetRandomVector3(-12, +12));
    Player.SetGameOverAndUploadHighscore();
} // if
```

The rest of the game logic is part of the enemy units, the items, and the weapon projectiles, which are all handled in their own separate classes that are described at the end of this chapter.

3D Effects

Back to the 3D effects. You already learned a lot about them and thanks to the Billboard class it is not hard to render textures in 3D now. The effects are now handled at a higher level; you worry about the effect length, animation steps, and fading them in and out. All the 3D polygon generation and rendering is handled by the Billboard and Texture classes. All effects are managed through the EffectManager class (see Figure 11-15), which allows you to add new effects from anywhere in the code thanks to the many static Add methods.

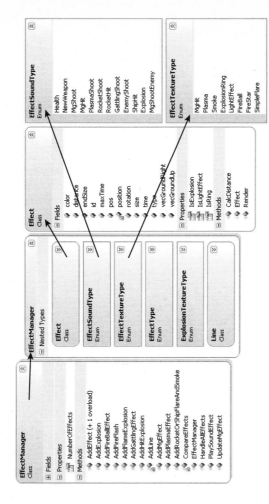

Figure 11-15

You can see the many fields inside the Effect classes, which are used to allow you to create many different kinds of 3D effects. Explosions are optimized differently than light effects. For example, regular effects are just blended out with an alpha value, but for light effects this does not work because if the alpha value was modified the effect would get darker and look very strange. Instead of darkening down light effects we just make them get smaller at the end of their lifetime. The other enumeration values help you to quickly identify effect types and to add them easily through the AddEffect method.

The best way to learn about the EffectManager class is to look at the TestEffects unit test at the end of the class. Then add new effects here and implement them after changing the unit test or just write new unit tests for more effects.

```
public static void TestEffects()
{
    TestGame.Start("TestEffects",
        delegate
        {
```

```
        // No initialization code necessary here
    },
    delegate
    {
        // Press 1-0 for creating effects in center of the 3D scene
        if (Input.Keyboard.IsKeyDown(Keys.D1) &&
            BaseGame.EveryMs(200))
            AddMgEffect(new Vector3(-10.0f, 0, -10),
                new Vector3((BaseGame.TotalTimeMs % 3592) / 100.0f, 25, +100),
                0, 1, true, true);
        if (Input.Keyboard.IsKeyDown(Keys.D2))
        {
            AddPlasmaEffect(new Vector3(-50.0f, 0.0f, 0.0f), 0.5f, 5);
            AddPlasmaEffect(new Vector3(0.0f, 0.0f, 0.0f), 1.5f, 5);
            AddPlasmaEffect(new Vector3(50.0f, 0.0f, 0.0f), 0.0f, 5);
        } // if (Input.Keyboard.IsKeyDown(Keys.D2))
        if (Input.Keyboard.IsKeyDown(Keys.D3))
        {
            AddFireBallEffect(new Vector3(-50.0f, +10.0f, 0.0f), 0.0f, 10);
            AddFireBallEffect(new Vector3(0.0f, +10.0f, 0.0f),
                (float)Math.PI / 8, 10);
            AddFireBallEffect(new Vector3(50.0f, +10.0f, 0.0f),
                (float)Math.PI * 3 / 8, 10);
        } // if (Input.Keyboard.IsKeyDown(Keys.D3)
        if (Input.Keyboard.IsKeyDown(Keys.D4))
            AddRocketOrShipFlareAndSmoke(
                new Vector3((BaseGame.TotalTimeMs % 4000) / 40.0f, 0, 0),
                5.0f, 150.0f);
        if (Input.Keyboard.IsKeyDown(Keys.D5) &&
            BaseGame.EveryMs(1000))
            AddExplosion(Vector3.Zero, 9.0f);
        // etc.
        // Play a couple of sound effects
        if (Input.Keyboard.IsKeyDown(Keys.P) &&
            BaseGame.EveryMs(500))
            PlaySoundEffect(EffectSoundType.PlasmaShoot);
        // etc.
        // We have to render the effects ourselfs because
        // it is usually done in RocketCommanderForm (not in TestGame)!
        // Finally render all effects before applying post screen shaders
        BaseGame.effectManager.HandleAllEffects();
    });
} // TestEffects()
```

Unit Class

Maybe this class should be called EnemyUnit because it is only used for the enemy ships; your own ship is already handled in the Player class. Originally, I wanted to unify all units (your own ship and the enemy ships) in this class, but they behave very differently and it only made the code more confusing and complicated. In more complex games you should create a base class for units and then derive it once for enemy units and once for your own and friendly player ships (for example, for multiplayer code, where you want to make sure that all the other players get the same ship movement you do locally on their machines). Anyway, take a look at the class in Figure 11-16.

Figure 11-16

The class uses many fields internally to keep track of each unit's hitpoints, shoot times, position values, and so on, but from the outside the class looks very simple. It just has one method you have to call every frame: Render. The constructor creates the unit and assigns the unit type, position, and all the default hitpoints and damage values to it (from constant arrays inside the class — more complex games should load these values from XML files or other external data sources that can be changed easily).

As always you should check out the unit test to learn more about this class:

```
public static void TestUnitAI()
{
    Unit testUnit = null;
    Mission dummyMission = null;
    TestGame.Start("TestUnitAI",
        delegate
        {
            dummyMission = new Mission();
            testUnit = new Unit(UnitTypes.Corvette, Vector2.Zero,
                MovementPattern.StraightDown);

            // Call dummyMission.RenderLandscape once to
            // initialize everything
            dummyMission.RenderLevelBackground(0);
            // Remove the all enemy units (the start enemies) and
            // all neutral objects
            dummyMission.numOfModelsToRender = 2;
```

```
},
delegate
{
    // [Helper texts are displayed here, press 1-0 or
    // the C, S, F, R, A etc. keys]
    ResetUnitDelegate ResetUnit =
    delegate(MovementPattern setPattern)
    {
        testUnit.movementPattern = setPattern;
        testUnit.position = new Vector2(
            RandomHelper.GetRandomFloat(-20, +20),
            Mission.SegmentLength/2);
        testUnit.hitpoints = testUnit.maxHitpoints;
        testUnit.speed = 0;
        testUnit.lifeTimeMs = 0;
    };

    if (Input.KeyboardKeyJustPressed(Keys.D1))
        ResetUnit(MovementPattern.StraightDown);
    if (Input.KeyboardKeyJustPressed(Keys.D2))
        ResetUnit(MovementPattern.GetFasterAndMoveDown);
    // [etc.]
    if (Input.KeyboardKeyJustPressed(Keys.Space))
        ResetUnit(testUnit.movementPattern);
    if (Input.KeyboardKeyJustPressed(Keys.C))
        testUnit.unitType = UnitTypes.Corvette;
    if (Input.KeyboardKeyJustPressed(Keys.S))
        testUnit.unitType = UnitTypes.SmallTransporter;
    if (Input.KeyboardKeyJustPressed(Keys.F))
        testUnit.unitType = UnitTypes.Firebird;
    if (Input.KeyboardKeyJustPressed(Keys.R))
        testUnit.unitType = UnitTypes.RocketFrigate;
    if (Input.KeyboardKeyJustPressed(Keys.A))
        testUnit.unitType = UnitTypes.Asteroid;

    // Update and render unit
    if (testUnit.Render(dummyMission))
        // Restart unit if it was removed because it was
        // too far down
        ResetUnit(testUnit.movementPattern);

    // Render all models the normal way
    for (int num = 0;
        num < dummyMission.numOfModelsToRender; num++)
        dummyMission.modelsToRender[num].model.Render(
            dummyMission.modelsToRender[num].matrix);
    BaseGame.MeshRenderManager.Render();

    // Restore number of units as before.
    dummyMission.numOfModelsToRender = 2;

    // Show all effects (unit smoke, etc.)
    BaseGame.effectManager.HandleAllEffects();
}); 
} // TestUnitAI()
```

The unit test allows you to press C, S, F, R, or A to change the unit type to the five available units: Corvette, Small Transporter, Firebird, Rocket-Frigate, and Asteroid. By pressing 1-0 you are able to change the AI behavior of this unit. Discussing AI here is a little bit crazy because all the AI does for the unit is to handle the movement differently. The unit just follows certain movement patterns and is in no way intelligent. For example, the GetFasterAndMoveDown movement code looks like the following:

```
case MovementPattern.GetFasterAndMoveDown:
  // Out of visible area? Then keep speed slow and wait.
  if (position.Y - Mission.LookAtPosition.Y > 30)
    lifeTimeMs = 300;
  if (lifeTimeMs < 3000)
    speed = lifeTimeMs / 3000;
  position += new Vector2(0, -1) * speed * 1.5f * maxSpeed * moveSpeed;
  break;
```

Other movement patterns are even simpler. The name of each movement pattern should tell you enough about the behavior. In the game you randomly assign a movement pattern to each new unit. You could also create a level with predefined positions and unit values including the movement AI for a shoot-'em-up game, but I wanted to keep things simple. The rest of the unit test just renders the unit and the background landscape. It was used to create the whole Unit class and it should cover everything except the shooting and dying of units, which is tested easier directly in the game.

Projectile Class

The code required to let the Corvette shoot is not so complicated because it immediately starts shooting and will hit targets like your ship if they are directly below it. It checks its and your x and y position and acts accordingly. Otherwise the Corvettes just shoot into the emptiness, which happens most of the time.

All other units do not fire instant weapons. Instead, they fire projectiles such as rockets, fireballs, or plasma balls. These projectiles stay active for a short while and fly toward their target position. The Projectile class (see Figure 11-17) helps you manage these objects and simplifies the weapon logic because you can now shoot a projectile and forget about it. The projectile will handle collisions with any enemy ships, and after it runs out of fuel, or goes out of the visible area, it is removed, too.

There are three different projectiles in XNA Shooter and they all behave a little differently, as follows:

☐ Plasma projectiles are only fired from your own ship and you fire them only if you currently have the Plasma weapon. Plasma projectiles are fast and inflict more damage than the MG can, but the Gatling-Gun and the Rocket Launcher are more powerful, although they have their disadvantages, too.

☐ Fireballs are fired from enemy Firebird ships and they fly slowly toward you. They do not change direction, but the enemy Firebird's AI shoots them a little bit ahead of you, so you always have to evade them.

☐ Rockets are used by both you and the enemy Rocket Frigate ship. Your rockets are bigger and inflict more damage, but they just fly straight ahead. Enemy rockets are more intelligent and will adjust their target to your ship position, constantly making it much harder to evade them.

Compared to the Unit class Render method, the Projectile class Render method is not very complex. The most interesting part is the collision handling after updating the position and rendering the projectile in the Render method.

Figure 11-17

```
public bool Render(Mission mission)
{
    // [Update movement . . .]
    // [Render projectile, either the 3D model for the rocket
    // or just the effect for the Fireball or Plasma weapons]

    // Own projectile?
    if (ownProjectile)
    {
        // Hit enemy units, check all of them
        for (int num = 0; num < Mission.units.Count; num++)
        {
            Unit enemyUnit = Mission.units[num];
            // Near enough to enemy ship?
            Vector2 distVec =
                new Vector2(enemyUnit.position.X,
                    enemyUnit.position.Y) -
                new Vector2(position.X, position.Y);
            if (distVec.Length() < 7 &&
                (enemyUnit.position.Y - Player.shipPos.Y) < 60)
            {
                // Explode and do damage!
                EffectManager.AddFlameExplosion(position);
                Player.score += (int)enemyUnit.hitpoints / 10;
                enemyUnit.hitpoints -= damage;
                return true;
            } // if
        } // for
    } // if
    // Else this is an enemy projectile?
    else
    {
        // Near enough to our ship?
```

```
Vector2 distVec =
    new Vector2(Player.shipPos.X, Player.shipPos.Y) -
    new Vector2(position.X, position.Y);
if (distVec.Length() < 3)
{
    // Explode and do damage!
    EffectManager.AddFlameExplosion(position);
    Player.health -= damage / 1000.0f;
    return true;
} // if
} // else

// Don't remove projectile yet
return false;
} // Render()
```

If this is your own projectile (plasma or rocket), you must determine if it collides with any enemy ship that is currently active. If this happens, you inflict the projectile damage, and then the explosion effect is added. You also get some points for this kill (10 percent of the unit's remaining health). Then `true` is returned to tell the caller of this method that you are done with this projectile and it can be removed from the currently active projectiles list. This also happens if the projectile goes outside of the visible landscape area.

If the projectile was shot by an enemy unit, the collision checking code is much simpler. You only have to check if it collides with the player ship and then the damage is inflicted the same way. Both your unit and the enemy unit's death are handled by their own `Render` method. Earlier, you saw the defeat condition that is triggered when you run out of health. The enemy unit's death condition looks very similar. Once again, you would return true to allow removing this unit from the current unit list.

Item Class

Last but not least, the `Item` class is used to handle all the items in the game. It is very simple as you can see in Figure 11-18, but without it the game would not be half the fun. As you can see from the `ItemTypes` enum inside the class, there are six available items. Four of them are the weapons for your ship and the other two are: the health item, which completely refreshes your ship's health, and the EMP bomb, which allows you to kill all units on the screen by pressing the space key. You can stack up to three bombs at the same time.

The `Render` method is similar to the one from the `Projectiles` class; you just don't kill anyone that collides with this projectile. Instead, the player can collect these items and their effect is immediately handled. This means you either get a new weapon or you can get back 100 percent of your health or you get another EMP bomb.

```
/// <summary>
/// Render item, returns false if we are done with it.
/// </summary>
/// <returns>True if done, false otherwise</returns>
public bool Render(Mission mission)
{
    // Remove unit if it is out of visible range!
    float distance = Mission.LookAtPosition.Y - position.Y;
```

```
const float MaxUnitDistance = 60;
if (distance > MaxUnitDistance)
    return true;

// Render
float itemSize = Mission.ItemModelSize;
float itemRotation = 0;
Vector3 itemPos = new Vector3(position, Mission.AllShipsZHeight);
mission.AddModelToRender(mission.itemModels[(int)itemType],
    Matrix.CreateScale(itemSize) *
    Matrix.CreateRotationZ(itemRotation) *
    Matrix.CreateTranslation(itemPos));

// Add glow effect around the item
EffectManager.AddEffect(itemPos + new Vector3(0, 0, 1.01f),
    EffectManager.EffectType.LightInstant,
    7.5f, 0, 0);
EffectManager.AddEffect(itemPos + new Vector3(0, 0, 1.02f),
    EffectManager.EffectType.LightInstant,
    5.0f, 0, 0);

// Collect item and give to player if colliding!
Vector2 distVec =
    new Vector2(Player.shipPos.X, Player.shipPos.Y) -
    new Vector2(position.X, position.Y);
if (distVec.Length() < 5.0f)
{
    if (itemType == ItemTypes.Health)
    {
        // Refresh health
        Sound.Play(Sound.Sounds.Health);
        Player.health = 1.0f;
    } // if
    else
    {
        Sound.Play(Sound.Sounds.NewWeapon);
        if (itemType == ItemTypes.Mg)
            Player.currentWeapon = Player.WeaponTypes.MG;
        else if (itemType == ItemTypes.Plasma)
            Player.currentWeapon = Player.WeaponTypes.Plasma;
        else if (itemType == ItemTypes.Gattling)
            Player.currentWeapon = Player.WeaponTypes.Gattling;
        else if (itemType == ItemTypes.Rockets)
            Player.currentWeapon = Player.WeaponTypes.Rockets;
        else if (itemType == ItemTypes.Emp &&
            Player.empBombs < 3)
            Player.empBombs++;
    } // else
    Player.score += 500;
    return true;
} // else
// Don't remove item yet
return false;
} // Render()
```

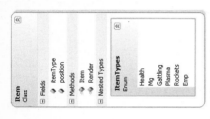

Figure 11-18

The render code puts the item at the given screen location, rotated and scaled correctly. It also adds two light effects to make the item glow a little. If you don't look at the items, you might not notice the glow effect, but when it is missing it is a lot harder to detect the items currently flying around.

If you are closer than five units to any item, you automatically collect it. Your ship has a radius of about five units too, which means you can touch the item with any part of your ship. The item is then handled either giving you health or the new weapon. After that, you even get a little bit of extra points for your heroic act of collecting this item. The item can now be removed. If you did not collide with the item, it stays active until you do or it is no longer visible.

Final Screenshot

Yeah, you finally made it. You now have everything you need for your XNA Shooter game. See Figure 11-19 for the result. I hope this chapter was informative.

I hope that you enjoy XNA Shooter, and you find it useful if you want to create your own shoot-'em-up game. Remember that it was created in only a couple of days and you can probably make it much better, add more levels, enemy ships, or a better AI. Have fun with it.

Challenge: Write a Game with Your Engine

A lot of games were already discussed in this book and before you get to your final blockbuster game, I want you to think about creating your own little game with your existing engine. You saw all the important steps in this chapter, from creating the project based on the Rocket Commander XNA engine to the XNA Shooter engine, which is even a more powerful engine now thanks to the additions we made (like the effect system and ship AI). You probably have some great game idea in your head and you should not wait any longer to start working on it, if you haven't done so already.

It took me more than half the time to implement all the additional helper classes for XNA Shooter. It required even more time if I put the shadow mapping in, which had to be adjusted quite a lot to look good in the game. Coding the game itself was a lot more fun and having to play it over and over again was also a lot of fun, especially at the end when all the effects and units were correctly implemented.

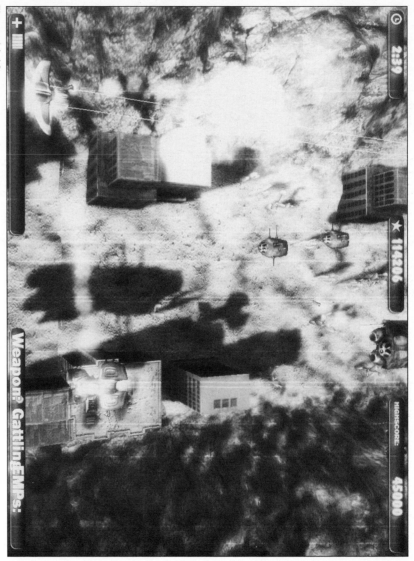

Figure 11-19

If you have a really big game idea, and not a simple arcade game idea, you should try to build a prototype first because doing a MMORPG (which stands for Massive Multiplayer Online Role Playing Game), such as World of WarCraft is impossible. You might spend years before you realize that you can never get as big as those monster games. When I give advice to beginners and game programmers this is my number one tip: Start with a small game and work your way up. This does not mean you have to create Tetris or a Jump'n'Run game first. If all you want to do is to create an RPG (role playing game), try to implement only one small part of your game idea (maybe running around with your hero and slaying or shooting at some simple monsters) and go from there.

It's not easy to write games today. It has gotten a lot easier thanks to XNA and many useful tutorials you can find on the Internet. But don't underestimate what it takes to get everything together and to get it working. Try to get your first game working (including UI, input, the menu, and some simple game logic) and then think about your next monster project, instead of the other way around. This is the number one reason why more than half of all game projects on the Internet are canceled before they are halfway done.

Anyway, good luck with your game project. Feel free to contact me and tell me about it, especially if it is based on one of my game engines.

Summary

In this chapter you learned all about the XNA Shooter game. It not only introduced 3D effects, billboards, simple landscape rendering, and handling the game logic with all the new game classes, but it also prepared you for the more advanced racing game project you are going to encounter next.

Your graphics engine is now capable of rendering textures, 3D models, 3D effects, shaders, handling sound effects with XACT. It also handles the user input and all game classes easily for you. You are also very familiar with some of the game classes by now. The Player class for handling most of your own game logic has been proven worthy in the Rocket Commander XNA and in the XNA Shooter games. Other aspects of the game programming world such as landscape rendering and shadow mapping were also introduced for the first time in this chapter. You learn about these advanced topics in the next chapters in greater detail.

Part IV of this book is devoted completely to a cool looking racing game. You are going to create a beautiful 3D landscape for the game and generate tracks from spline data. Additionally, you are going to take a tour through the world of physics for games, which was discussed a little bit in the Rocket Commander game. The racing game, however, needs a much more complex model. Finally, you are going to learn about the game logic in the racing game and how to fine-tune such a big project.

Part V of this book covers network programming with the help of the XNA 2.0 framework, or Windows Sockets if you just want to use the Windows platform. If you are interested in adding multiplayer support to the XNA Shooter game, make sure you read Chapters 15 first. You can also use the multiplayer classes presented there and import them into earlier games of this book, which would help you to add networking capabilities to the XNA games you have written so far.

Part IV: Writing a Racing Game

Chapter 12: Generating Landscapes and Tracks

Chapter 13: Physics

Chapter 14: Fine-Tuning and "Modding" the Racing Game

12

Generating Landscapes and Tracks

To create the last big game for this book, the XNA Racing Game, we are going to explore some of the more advanced topics of game programming in the next chapters, like 3D landscape generation, physics, more complex controls and shadow mapping algorithms.

This chapter covers the whole landscape generation and render techniques as well as the track data for the roads in all levels. The next chapter takes a closer look at the physics engine required for the racing game. In the final chapter you learn all about the game screens, game logic, and fine-tuning of the racing game, and you get some final tips about game development. The game that is covered in this book is a complete racing game, but it shows you only one track and a simplified game principle. The complete XNA Racing Game is available as a starter kit for the XNA Framework by Microsoft at http://Creators.xna.com. The complete game covers more missions, more cool features, several cars, more cool-looking 3D objects, which you can download and watch to learn more. We are going to cover all the basics to allow you to create a cool game like the Racing Game, but I want to cover more than just one game with the game engine we have written so far. It is not only possible to create game modifications of the Racing Game, but as we saw in the previous chapters it is helpful to have developed a full game with the game engine before starting with the next game.

Before you go ahead and design your little racing game, you should think a little bit about what exactly the game should be capable of. Thanks to the many available racing games, especially on the console platforms, it is not very hard to figure out what these games need. Most racing games have great looking cars and show nice scenery around the road itself. The games themselves are often very simple, but the game designers take great care in fine-tuning the controller input and adding small features to make the racing games more fun.

After you are sure in which direction your game is heading, you can think about the required 3D models, textures, effects, and other data such as the landscape and track data, which will become very important for your game. I spent more than half the development time just getting the landscape rendering and track generation right. You will see later in this chapter why there was so much work involved and why several new shaders for the landscape and road rendering were required.

When I say "so much work," I mean relatively speaking. Keep in mind that the racing game was developed in a few weeks and is similar to Rocket Commander in that it's a nice looking game, but you cannot compare it to an AAA game title that took years and many people to develop. Console games especially are developed by big game companies with 100 people or more.

The time is over when one man could code, design, and test his game in a few days or weeks as in the seventies or eighties (see Figure 12-1). But wait, there is XNA now and it is possible again to create your own games in short time frames. And if you think about it, the past was not really friendly to game developers. You had to implement your own routines to even get a pixel on the screen. I'm better off not mentioning that this most likely involved a lot of assembly machine code just to get it to work on one single hardware configuration. If you take a look at the Dream-Build-Play XNA Game Studio Contest of Microsoft at www.dreambuildplay.com, you can see many impressive games that were created in relatively short timeframes with XNA — both by hobbyists and professionals. The contest winners were announced at the Gamefest in August 2007 and while most games were in 2D, they all look very colorful, have refreshing game ideas and really unique styles. Let's hope that XNA 2.0 will bring even more skillful developers to the table and allow even more complex and bigger games in the future.

Figure 12-1

Game Comparisons

I would say most racing games can be split up into three main categories. Sometimes games fall into multiple categories. You could, of course, think of many more categories and if you add various similar games such as kart games, motor truck games, motor bicycle games, futuristic games, and so on, you could create many more categories, but I want to keep things simple here and talk only about classic racing games:

- ❑ **Realistic racers:** Racing simulations and typical racing games such as Gran Turismo, Colin McRae Rally, Test Drive, and Formula One would be examples of realistic racing games. These games are all about realism and giving the player the impression that they are really driving a racing car. At fairs, these games are often shown with wheel controllers, sometimes in stage cars with monitors, in special racing chairs, or with multiple monitors or other devices attached to enhance the realism aspect. The basic game principle for these games is to beat the fastest lap time, but it gets more complicated with many available cars and sometimes added game modes.

❑ **Street racers:** Underground racers such as Need for Speed, Midnight Club, Street Racing, or Juiced have become popular in the past years. The basic game principle is still the same, but the realism is not so important anymore. It is more like watching a movie; everything has to be cool, gangster-style, and you need tuned cars and cool music for this kind of game. They are very popular, especially on the console platforms.

❑ **Fun racers:** Arcade racers such as Trackmania, Wipeout, and Carmageddon that are no longer focusing on being real would fall into this category. They are all about having fun and having crazy tracks or modified cars that can shoot or do other crazy things. You can even count all crazy racing games such as Crazy Taxi or Grand Theft Auto in this category, although they're not all racing games. In some games, you just drive around with cars to get somewhere else. The mission is not to drive around, but rather to accomplish certain goals. You would also not call an adventure game a 3D shooter just because it is in 3D, but there are adventure elements in some shooter games as well, so what the heck.

Some games such as Project Gotham Racing would fall into more than one category. They are more real-istic than street racers, but they are not really as much of a simulation like Grand Tourismo or Formula One because you can also tune your cars and you drive through streets. Need for Speed, on the other hand, is no longer realistic; you can't crash your car, no matter how fast you drive into a wall, and you can drive over other cars, escape the police, damage public property, and so on. The game falls much more into the underground and street racer category.

The next sections take a quick look at some racing games that fall into these categories and which ones could be implemented with the XNA Racing Game engine.

Gran Tourismo

Most of the realistic racing games were originally developed for the PlayStation games. Games like Gran Tourismo, Formula One, Enthusia Professional Racing, Colin McRae Rally, and others fall into this cate-gory. Most games are also available on the PC platform, and sometimes also on the Xbox platform, but not often. You will find a lot more street racers and fun racers on the Xbox than on the PlayStation.

Anyway, I do not know much about these games and I usually fall asleep before completing the first lap. Better ask my brother about details here. I can just leave you with a nice picture of Gran Tourismo (see Figure 12-2).

For the Xbox 360, the most popular game in this category is probably Project Gotham Racing, which is a little fun to play thanks to the additional street racer angle of the game, but even here I do not get very far; after a couple of missions it is always the same over and over again. But I must say that the game is done very well and I would expect other classic racing games to evolve into street racer style games because it's a very popular game type right now. And it is obviously more fun to have some additional game modes instead of just driving around in circles, but hey, that's what racing games are all about.

Need for Speed

Need for Speed is an extremely popular game by EA Sports and many versions of the game exist. The latest two games are Need for Speed Underground (2005, see Figure 12-3) and Need for Speed Carbon (2006). Usually all Need for Speed games come out for all the latest console platforms and even for the PC, which makes them less of a system seller, but nevertheless an incredibly well selling game over all platforms combined.

Games like these have great graphics and also a lot of details in the background. Additionally you get some extra game modes and bonus points for drifting around or achieving special tricks. You are also able to tune your car, paint directly onto it, or apply stickers, which is highly anticipated by the car tuning scene.

Figure 12-2

Trackmania

And finally there are the fun racers. Most recently Trackmania has got a lot of attention. I will leave the crazy racing games out because they are often not pure racing games, but more like shooters like Carmagedon, which is basically a first person shooter with cars.

In Trackmania (see Figure 12-4), you have to reach the finish line, but there are several checkpoints where you can see your current time and whether or not you improved since the last time you passed this checkpoint. It is not always easy to reach the goal and sometimes tracks are only as long as a few seconds, but the game is designed in a way that you constantly want to beat your own times or your opponents' times if you play together with some friends in a multiplayer game. You often reach the bronze medal, but you also want the silver or gold medal for the current track by driving just a bit faster. This makes the game highly addictive and you might wonder why you just played the same track 30 times in a row just to be half a second faster.

Other than the basic game principle, the tracks are really defining Trackmania. You don't see many games with that many loopings and opportunities to fly around in the level with your car or driving up walls just to fall into the right spot somewhere else. The levels are also very different and you could play Trackmania just for a few minutes to test out a track or even for hours trying to solve all singleplayer tracks. While we are not going to develop a level editor and certainly will not have as many tracks, the Racing Game is similar to Trackmania in the way it is played.

Figure 12-3

XNA Racing Game

Let's talk about the Racing Game and in which category it would fit best. Before the street racers became popular, it was either realistic games or fun games and I always liked the fun games much more. Just driving a car, as in Test Drive, was always boring to me. But many people like the realistic racing games.

Anyway, the racing game I want to develop is more like a fun racer because creating realistic graphics is really hard. It is okay to mix in a little bit of the street racer and underground racer genres, but only to make the game look and sound cooler. The game I liked the most recently is Trackmania, which just lets you drive through crazy tracks with loopings, ramps, holes in the road, and so on. The game principle is still to get to the finish line as fast as possible, but I like the fact that getting there becomes a lot harder. Just driving slowly forward will not get you through any loopings or above certain ramps. And if you fall out of the track, you have to start over. It is much more like an arcade game than an old-fashioned racing game where you drive in circles.

The recent release of Trackmania (Sunrise and Nations) also has great graphics. They may not be as good looking or realistic as the other racers mentioned here, but it's still a fun racer. Some of the techniques used are very nice, especially given that producing a game like Trackmania has many challenges: such as handling so many road pieces and seeing far into the level. In games such as Need for Speed or Project Gotham Racing you hardly ever see more than the current road piece plus the next curve.

You are going to face the same problems, and therefore I want to make sure that both the landscape rendering and the track rendering is as fast as possible and that you can optimize landscape objects to skip away if a certain frame limit is reached.

Figure 12-4

Landscape Rendering

You already saw a simplified way to generate a 3D landscape with the help of the .x model in the previous chapter. There you created the diffuse texture first and then created a normal map from that, and finally you added a simple height map to generate the canyon for the XNA Shooter game.

For this game you are still going to use a very simplified approach to render the landscape because the development time was so short and developing a highly sophisticated landscape rendering engine alone can take months. The landscape engine in Arena Wars, for example, supports very big landscapes, but it was never used in the game. It was a lot of work to get it optimized on the many available hardware configurations, especially because 24 different ground texture types are supported there.

To keep things simple in the racing game, only one very big ground texture is used, but you also have a normal map for it and an additional detail texture to add a little detail in case you look very closely at the ground, which can happen in the game if you stay still and are close to the landscape ground. Originally I created a 4096 × 4096 texture, but it was very hard to constantly update a texture this big and have to manage a normal map for it, too. Uncompressed, this texture is about 64MB just for the diffuse texture, and another 64MB for the normal map. Now imagine you have ten or more layers of each of these textures when creating them and a computer with only about 1GB of RAM. The story does not end nicely. Even compressed as a DXT5 texture, the 4096 × 4096 normal map was still about 12MB and the loading process alone was too annoying when I was developing the landscape class with the help of the unit test in there. What finally stopped me from using 4096 × 4096 textures ever again in XNA was the content pipeline because it can forever to convert textures this big into the .xnb content files.

I went down to 2048 × 2048 textures, which look almost as good as the 4096 × 4096 ones, but take up only a quarter of the space and loading time. The normal map was even reduced to 1024 × 1024 a little later because it did not make much of a visual difference. Another reason you might choose not to use that big of a texture size is that the Xbox 360 has a limited amount of video memory (64MB). If you load too much stuff or your textures are too big, the performance will go down. Instead of creating a super-sized texture, I added the detail texture to make the landscape look better when zooming in. The rendering texture to accomplish this is discussed in the next pages.

Textures

First you need a height map and an idea of how big your landscape will be. I initially wanted each landscape texel (1 pixel of a texture) to be 1 meter (3.3 feet) and by having a 4096 × 4096 texture, the whole landscape would be 4 × 4 km big (about 2.5 × 2.5 miles). Even after the texture was reduced to 2048 × 2048, the landscape size stayed the same; now each texel is 2 × 2 meters.

So where do you get this many height values for your landscape? Just painting them yourself will probably not look very good. You don't have a good program for that and certainly not enough time to write a custom landscape height-map editor. A good idea is to search for height maps on the Internet and try to use existing height-map data from one of the many sources that provide it (geological organizations, NASA, which even has height-map data for other planets, and so on).

For the racing game I tried to get some mountains and I mixed them in together. It was good enough for testing, but later I needed mountains around the landscape and I had to modify the landscape height map a bit to create a big mountain in the middle and mountains around the border of the landscape. The final height map result can be seen in Figure 12-5. Please note that the LandscapeGridHeights.png height map that is used for the game in the Landscapes directory has a size of only 257 × 257 pixels because the grid that is generated in the Landscape class generates only 257 × 257 vertices (which are 66,049 vertices) for the 256*256*2 polygons (which are around 130,000 polygons). Having more polygons would slow down rendering too much, but handling 130,000 polygons is not a big problem for today's graphics cards. The Xbox 360 handles it fine, too (at several hundred frames per second).

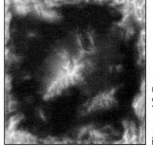

Figure 12-5

You may notice flat areas on the height map, which are used for city areas where it is simpler to have all the buildings and objects generated at the same height along with the palms at the side of the road. The white area in the middle is the big mountain and you can see the gray to white areas around the border of the map, which serve as the mountains at the border and hide the fact that you have nothing behind them.

This height map is now used together with a little bumpy grain texture to generate the normal map. Additionally you can also mix in the diffuse map as you did in the last chapter, but I changed the diffuse map so often for this landscape that the normal map is not really affected anymore by the diffuse texture. Figure 12-6 shows the used diffuse and normal maps for the landscape in the game.

Please note that I changed these textures a lot until I got them this way and I'm not completely pleased with them, but you have to stop at some point, especially if you don't have more time to improve the landscape. The normal map, for example, looks really great from a distance, but if you look more closely, it doesn't have many variations and it could perhaps be improved to fit better to the diffuse texture. Anyway, it looks fine in the game and I have not had any complaints yet.

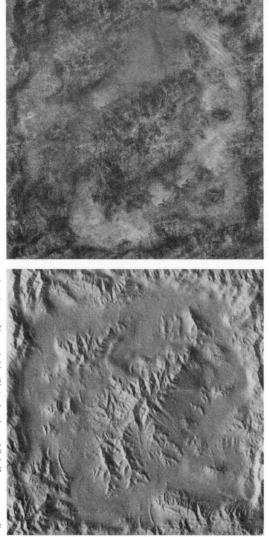

Figure 12-6

Landscape.dds

LandscapeNormal.dds (Note: Looks reddish if compressed)

Landscape Textures in the Racing Game

Finally, a detail map is also added for when you look closely at the landscape. You will not notice the detail map after a while, but Figure 12-7 shows the difference quite convincingly between using a detail map and not using it. You will never go without a detail texture ever again if you have a big landscape and allow zooming in, as you do for the racing game.

Rendering

If you open up the Racing Game project, you can see a lot of the classes from the previous chapters, but also two new namespaces, which are discussed in this chapter: Landscapes and Tracks. There is just one class in the Landscapes namespace called Landscape (see Figure 12-8), which is responsible for rendering the landscape, all objects on it, all the tracks and track objects, and basically everything in the game except your own car. In the Mission class, you are just calling the Render method of this class to perform all the rendering. For shadow mapping, several helper methods are available. More details about the shadow mapping are discussed in Chapter 14.

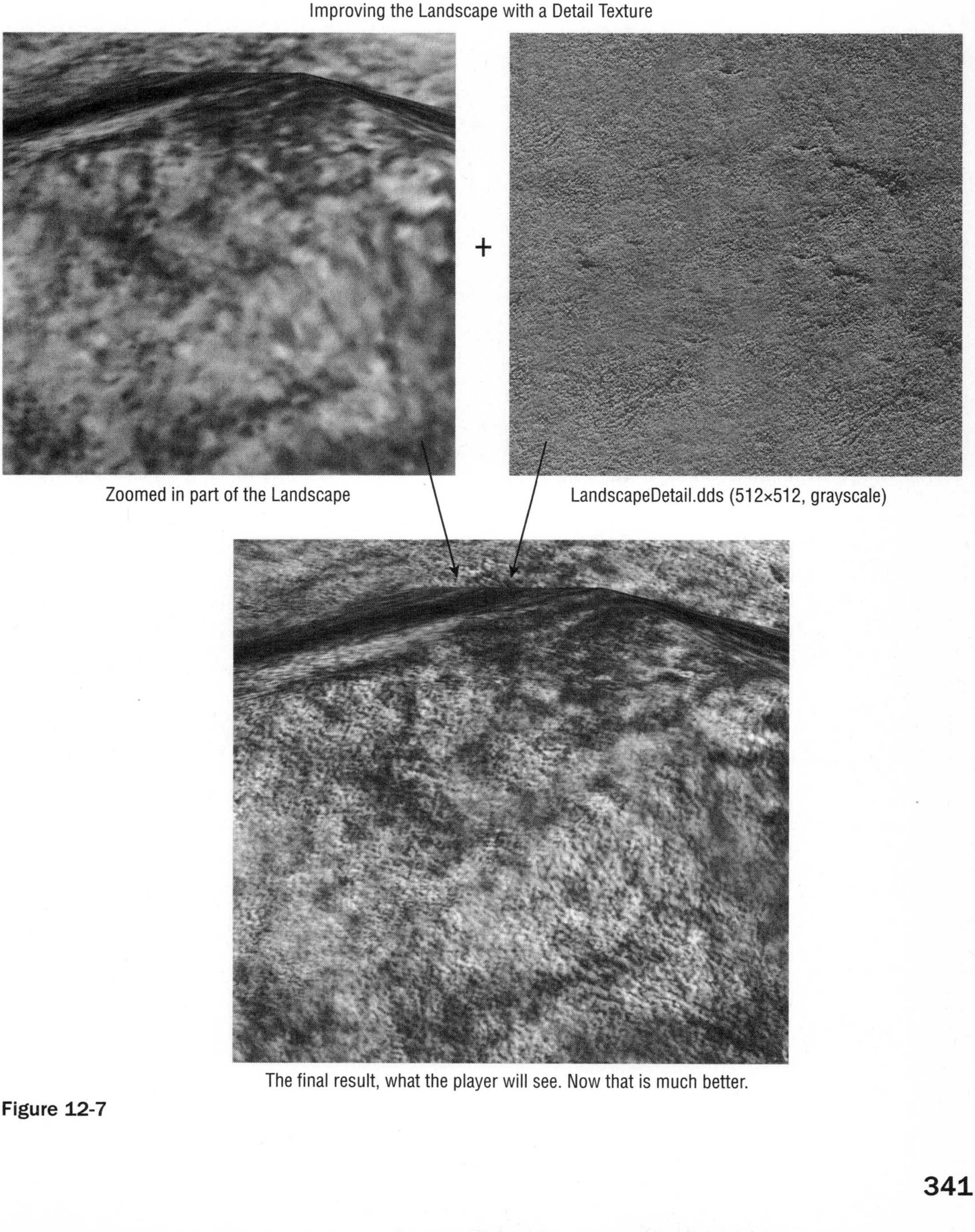

Improving the Landscape with a Detail Texture

LandscapeDetail.dds (512×512, grayscale)

+

Zoomed in part of the Landscape

The final result, what the player will see. Now that is much better.

Figure 12-7

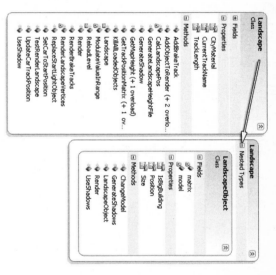

Figure 12-8

All landscape objects are generated at the creation time of the Landscape class, especially in the constructors of the Track classes, which are used inside the Landscape class. You will take a quick look at some of the 3D models in a second.

The first thing you have to do to be able to render your landscape is to generate it first in the constructor. Before you take a look at that, you should check out the TestRenderLandscape unit test of the Landscape class in the same way the unit test was written before the class was implemented. You may also notice the other unit test, GenerateLandscapeHeightFile, which generates a level file for the landscape height map just as you had to generate a special content file for Rocket Commander XNA levels because loading bitmap data is not possible on the Xbox 360.

```
/// <summary>
/// Test render landscape
/// </summary>
public static void TestRenderLandscape()
{
    TestGame.Start("TestRenderLandscape",
        delegate
        {
            RacingGame.LoadLevel(RacingGame.Level.Beginner);
            RacingGame.Landscape.SetCarToStartPosition();
        },
        delegate
        {
            if (BaseGame.AllowShadowMapping)
            {
                // Generate shadows
                ShaderEffect.shadowMapping.GenerateShadows(
                    delegate
```

```
{
    RacingGame.Landscape.GenerateShadow();
    RacingGame.CarModel.GenerateShadow(
        RacingGame.Player.CarRenderMatrix);
});
// Render shadows
ShaderEffect.shadowMapping.RenderShadows(
delegate
{
    RacingGame.Landscape.UseShadow();
    RacingGame.CarModel.UseShadow(
        RacingGame.Player.CarRenderMatrix);
});
} // if (BaseGame.AllowShadowMapping)
BaseGame.UI.PostScreenGlowShader.Start();
BaseGame.UI.RenderGameBackground();
RacingGame.Landscape.Render();
RacingGame.CarModel.RenderCar(0, Color.Goldenrod,
    RacingGame.Player.CarRenderMatrix);
// And flush render manager to draw all objects
BaseGame.MeshRenderManager.Render();
if (BaseGame.AllowShadowMapping)
    ShaderEffect.shadowMapping.ShowShadows();
BaseGame.UI.PostScreenGlowShader.Show();
TestGame.UI.WriteText(2, 50, "Number of objects: "+
    RacingGame.Landscape.landscapeObjects.Count);
});
} // TestRenderLandscape()
```

The unit test does a lot of things; it even shows the car and all landscape objects. Even the track and all the shadow mapping and post-screen shaders are tested here to make sure they work fine together with the landscape. If you just want to test the landscape itself, call Render of the Landscape class; that's already enough to test the landscape rendering.

The LoadLevel method of the RacingGame class, which is actually the main class for this game, loads one of the levels. All levels currently use the same landscape, which means you don't have to reload it. But you should check out the code for generating the landscape vertices anyway. The landscape constructor does the following things:

❑ Loads the map height data from the level file and builds tangent vertices with it

❑ Generates and smoothes normals for the whole landscape, and also regenerates the tangents with the new normals

❑ Sets the vertex buffer with these vertices

❑ Calculates the index buffer (very similar to the landscape triangles you saw in the last chapter)

❑ Sets the index buffer for the landscape rendering

❑ Loads and generates all track data for the current level, including all landscape objects

❑ Adds additional objects such as the city ground planes to give the city objects a better looking ground texture.

The most important part of the constructor is the tangent vertex generation from the height-map data, which goes through all 257 × 257 points of the height map and generates vertices for you:

```
// Build our tangent vertices
for (int x = 0; x < GridWidth; x++)
  for (int y = 0; y < GridHeight; y++)
  {
    // Step 1: Calculate position
    int index = x + y * GridWidth;
    Vector3 pos = CalcLandscapePos(x, y, heights);
    mapHeights[x, y] = pos.Z;
    vertices[index].pos = pos;

    // Step 2: Calculate all edge vectors (for normals and
    // tangents). This involves quite complicated
    // optimizations and mathematics, hard to explain ...
    Vector3 edge1 = pos -
      CalcLandscapePos(x, y + 1, heights);
    Vector3 edge2 = pos -
      CalcLandscapePos(x + 1, y, heights);
    Vector3 edge3 = pos -
      CalcLandscapePos(x - 1, y + 1, heights);
    Vector3 edge4 = pos -
      CalcLandscapePos(x + 1, y + 1, heights);
    Vector3 edge5 = pos -
      CalcLandscapePos(x - 1, y - 1, heights);

    // Step 3: Calculate normal based on the edges
    // (interpolate from 3 cross products we build from our
    // edges).
    vertices[index].normal = Vector3.Normalize(
      Vector3.Cross(edge2, edge1) +
      Vector3.Cross(edge4, edge3) +
      Vector3.Cross(edge3, edge5));

    // Step 4: Set tangent data, just use edge1
    vertices[index].tangent = Vector3.Normalize(edge1);

    // Step 5: Set texture coordinates, use the full 0.0f
    // to 1.0f range!
    vertices[index].uv = new Vector2(
      y / (float)(GridHeight - 1),
      x / (float)(GridWidth - 1));
  } // for for (int)
```

You can see that this code generates the vertices in five steps. First, the position vector is calculated. Then all edge vectors are calculated for constructing the normal from three cross products and assigning the tangent. Finally, the texture coordinates are assigned, but you flip x and y to make xy rendering easier later. The vertices list is already generated when it is defined because you support only 257 × 257 height-map grids. The CalcLandscapePos helper method that is used here is quite simple and just extracts a height vector from the height-map data:

```
private Vector3 CalcLandscapePos(int x, int y,
  byte[] heights)
```

```
{
    // Make sure we stay on the valid map data
    int mapX = x < 0 ? 0 :
        x >= GridWidth ? GridWidth - 1 : x;
    int mapY = y < 0 ? 0 :
        y >= GridHeight ? GridHeight - 1 : y;
    float heightPercent =
        heights[mapX+mapY*GridWidth] / 255.0f;
    return new Vector3(
        x * MapWidthFactor,
        y * MapHeightFactor,
        heightPercent * MapZScale);
} // CalcLandscapePos(x, y, texData)
```

With all the vertices and indices generated now, you can finally render the landscape with the help of the LandscapeNormalMapping.fx shader. You will not believe how easy that is now. The following lines of code will render 130,000 polygons with the LandscapeNormalMapping shader using the landscape diffuse map, the normal map, and the additional detail map:

```
// Render landscape (pretty easy with all the data we got here)
ShaderEffect.landscapeNormalMapping.Render(
    mat, "DiffuseWithDetail20",
    delegate
    {
        BaseGame.Device.VertexDeclaration =
            TangentVertex.VertexDeclaration;
        BaseGame.Device.Vertices[0].SetSource(vertexBuffer, 0,
            TangentVertex.SizeInBytes);
        BaseGame.Device.Indices = indexBuffer;
        BaseGame.Device.DrawIndexedPrimitives(
            PrimitiveType.TriangleList,
            0, 0, GridWidth * GridHeight,
            0, (GridWidth - 1) * (GridHeight - 1) * 2);
    });
```

The ShaderEffect class from Chapter 7 allows you to render the landscape material with the specified technique using the RenderDelegate code for rendering.

The Render method of the Landscape class also renders the track and all landscape objects. The track rendering is discussed throughout the rest of this chapter. We will not talk about all the landscape models used in the game because there are so many. Check out the TestRenderModels unit test of the Model class to view them all; a quick overview is shown in Figure 12-9.

Optimizing Tips

Handling landscape engines is not easy. Even if you have developed a great-looking landscape engine that supports many different shaders and texture sets, you might find yourself worrying about performance. On the other hand, if you already have a great performing landscape engine like the one from the racing game or the shoot-'em-up game from the last chapter, you might want to improve the visual quality of it without affecting the performance too much. It is a challenge to get a landscape engine just right for your game. As I mentioned, in the past I tried to create a more complex landscape and graphics engine than actually required for a game like Arena Wars. It was possible to create huge landscapes 100 times as big as the ones that were finally used, but it did not make sense after a while to optimize these cases when the game never utilizes these features.

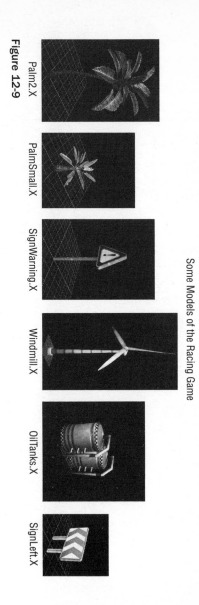

Some Models of the Racing Game

Figure 12-9

Palm2.X   PalmSmall.X   SignWarning.X   Windmill.X   OilTanks.X   SignLeft.X

Instead, you should focus on what the game is doing. Take the racing game as an example. It is much easier to have one fixed landscape, which is always the same. Testing is easier and you can reuse existing parts of the landscape for other levels without having to redesign everything. The landscape is also big enough (4096 × 4096 meters) for many different tracks because the first level shows you only a small part of it (maybe 20–30 percent).

There are three disadvantages to a more-or-less fixed landscape rendering technique like used here and in the last chapter:

☐ You can't just change the size of the landscape that easily. It will involve a lot of work just to make it smaller or bigger. If you are already using 4096 × 4096 textures, you probably cannot use even bigger textures to improve the texture quality because this is the hardware limit for many GPUs today, and if your game is very close to the ground, it may still look very blurry even with extra detail textures.

☐ Changing the diffuse texture map is really hard. You not only have to mix all different texture types together yourself, but it is also hard to see the result and it involves a lot of testing. To make things worse, the bigger the mega-texture gets, the slower the development time.

☐ The landscape engine is just not powerful enough to handle advanced effects such as adding craters or extra textures (tracks, roads, leaves, riffs, and so on) to the ground, and you can't even change the visual appearance dynamically. This means the landscape will always look the same. If you wanted to build a level editor you would need a more dynamic solution that would allow you to change the texture types and offer a way to mix them together automatically.

The best way to get around these issues is to use a landscape rendering technique called *splatting*, which basically takes a bunch of textures and renders them based on a texture map that uses the same resolution as the height map onto the landscape. Because it would not look very good to have different ground textures sitting side by side, you need a smooth interpolation between them. You could either fade from tile to tile, but that would still look too harsh, or you could save percentage values for each texture type.

The landscape is rendered separately for all ground texture types and you should make the lowest one completely opaque to make sure you can never look through the landscape. Then the other ground types are alpha blended on top of the previous ones until you are done with all of them (see Figure 12-10).

You can also use an alpha texture for blending or just blend softly with color values (see the example in Figure 12-10). Because you will use shaders in XNA you might also want to combine four (pixel shader 1.1) or even eight (pixel shader 2.0) textures together into one shader pass to optimize performance. If your landscape engine needs to handle more textures, however, you will need multiple passes until everything is rendered. Sometimes it can even be faster not to render all textures on top of each other, but just the ones that are visible. It becomes harder when you have to generate the vertex and index buffers, but if you really have a lot of textures, such as 20 or 30 different ground types, the performance will greatly increase because each ground texture type is used only 10 percent or less and it does not make sense to render it all the time.

Landscape Texture Splatting Techniques

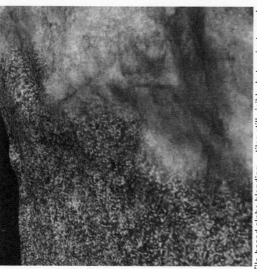

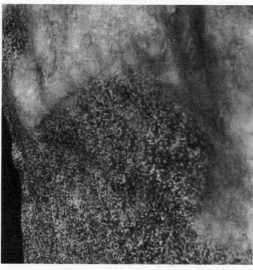

Tile-based alpha blending—tiles still visible, but easier to render

Customized application of an alpha mask for each blending— can look the best

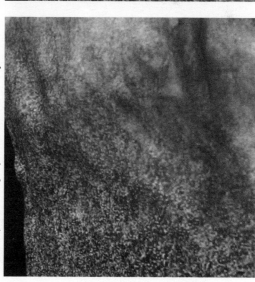

No alpha blending—just the textures side-by-side

Softly blending through interpolated alpha values— does not always fit

Figure 12-10

Whichever technique you choose, I strongly suggest you start with something simple like just rendering a big landscape with one texture type tiled over it. You can then improve it later when your game is more than just a landscape engine. You might also want to make sure your landscape can always be rendered at several hundred frames to make sure the game still runs fast enough after you add all the landscape models, 3D units, and effects, plus the game logic, into it.

There are many more tips and tricks about creating good landscapes. You could implement pre-calculated lighting and huge landscape shadows; there are also many opportunities for great looking shaders, especially if you have water involved. Grass could be done with fur shaders. The 3D appearance of rocks and cliffs could be enhanced with parallax or even offset mapping. If you are interested in these topics, please pick up a good shader book such as the *Game Programming Gems* or *ShaderX* books by Charles River Media, or search the Internet for many tips and tricks as well as tutorials.

Figure 12-11 shows the final appearance of the landscape in the racing game after also applying the post-screen shaders, the in-game HUD, and the sky cube mapping (see Chapters 5 and 6 for more information about these kinds of shaders if you need a refresher).

Figure 12-11

Tracks

Except for the HUD, the game does not really look like a racing game right now — more like a fantasy RPG thanks to the glow and color-correction post-screen shaders. The road track and the car itself are not implemented at this point, which will make the game look more like a racing game. Just putting the car somewhere in your landscape might look funny, but you don't want to drive around on the ground, especially since the landscape does not look so great from this zooming level (1 landscape texel for 2 × 2 meter, so the whole car stays on 2 texels).

The idea for this game was to create some tracks like the ones from Trackmania, but after investigating Trackmania and the editor in the game you can see how complex the rendering process is in the game. Instead of just rendering the track as one piece and adding landscape objects as I wanted to do, Trackmania levels are constructed with many different road building blocks, which fit together perfectly. This way you can put three loopings after each other without having to paint or construct them yourself. The disadvantage of this technique is that you are limited by the available building blocks, and from the developer's point of view you really will have a lot of work creating hundreds of these building blocks, not to mention all the levels you need to test them out.

So this idea was thrown out of the window in seconds. I returned to my original approach of creating just a simple 2D track and adding a little height to it through the landscape height map. I wanted to use a bitmap with the track painted on it as a white line and then import into the game, extracting all bitmap positions and building 3D vertices from it. But after playing around with this idea it was very clear that the track heavily depends on the landscape ground, and doing things like loopings, ramps, and crazy curves was just not possible or at least very hard to implement with just a bitmap track.

So again another idea flew out the window. To get a better understanding of how a track might look, I used 3D Studio Max and played around with the spline functions there to create a simple circle track with just four points (see Figure 12-12). Rotated by 90 degrees to the left, this looked almost like looping and much more appealing as a fun racer than the bitmap approach.

I had to get this spline data out of 3D Studio Max and somehow into my engine. This way I could make the creation process of the tracks very easy by just drawing a 3D spline in Max and exporting it into the racing game engine. The hard part would be to generate a useful track out of this data because each spline point is just a point, and not a road piece with orientation, a road width, and so on.

Before spending more time trying to figure out the best way to generate tracks and before you can start importing this spline data into your game, you should make sure that this idea even works.

Unit Testing to the Rescue

This is a great time again to do some heavy unit testing. Start with the first simple unit test of the new TrackLine class, called TestRenderingTrack, which only creates a simple spline like the one from 3D Studio Max and displays it on the screen:

```
public static void TestRenderingTrack()
{
    TrackLine testTrack = new TrackLine(
        new Vector3[]
        {
```

```
            new Vector3(20, -20, 0),
            new Vector3(20, 20, 0),
            new Vector3(-20, 20, 0),
            new Vector3(-20, -20, 0),
};
TestGame.Start(
    delegate
    {
        ShowGroundGrid();
        ShowTrackLines(testTrack);
        ShowUpVectors(testTrack);
    });
} // TestRenderingTrack()
```

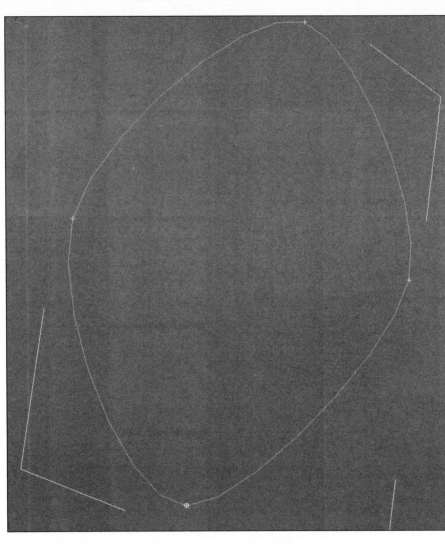

Figure 12-12

ShowGroundGrid simply displays some grid lines on the xy ground plane to help you see where the ground is. I wrote this method a while back for the models class; it is just reused here. ShowTrackLines is the important method here because it shows all the lines and interpolated points that have been generated for you through the constructor of the `TrackLine` class. Finally, the `ShowUpVectors` method shows you in which direction the up vector points for every position on the track. Without the up vector, you will not be able to generate the right and left side of the road correctly. For example, in curves the road should tilt and for loopings you need the up vectors pointing to the center of the loop and not just upward.

The `ShowTrackLines` helper method shows each point of the track connected through white lines. When you execute the `TestRenderingTrack` unit test you can see a screen like the one in Figure 12-13.

```
public static void ShowTrackLines(TrackLine track)
{
    // Draw the line for each line part
    for (int num = 0; num < track.points.Count; num++)
        BaseGame.DrawLine(
            track.points[num].pos,
            track.points[(num + 1)%track.points.Count].pos,
            Color.White);
} // ShowTrackLines(track)
```

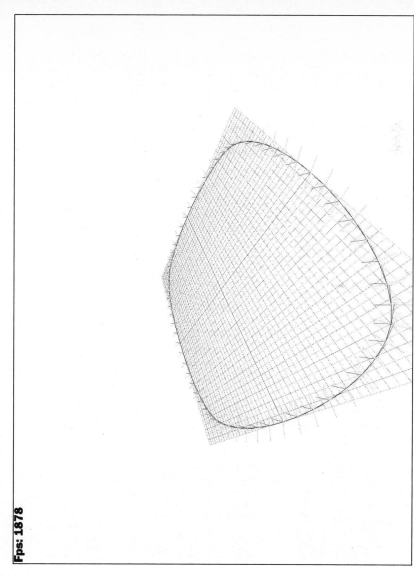

Fps: 1878

Figure 12-13

The track almost looks like a road thanks to the red up vectors and the green tangent vectors. All you have to do now is to tweak the track generation code and maybe test out a couple more splines. In the `TrackLine` class, you can see several of the test tracks I created all by adding a couple of 3D points by hand, and more tracks are available through the Collada files used later to import track data from 3D Studio Max into your engine.

Before you take a look at the spline interpolation code in the constructor, you can also test out a simple looping by just switching the x and z values of the track points (see Figure 12-14). To make the spline look more round I've also added four new points. The new `TestRenderingTrack` unit test now looks like the following:

```
public static void TestRenderingTrack()
{
    TrackLine testTrack = new TrackLine(
        new Vector3[]
        {
            new Vector3(0,  0,  0),
            new Vector3(0,  7,  3),
            new Vector3(0, 10, 10),
            new Vector3(0,  7, 17),
            new Vector3(0,  0, 20),
            new Vector3(0, -7, 17),
            new Vector3(0, -10, 10),
            new Vector3(0, -7,  3),
        });
    // [Rest stays the same]
} // TestRenderingTrack()
```

Interpolating Splines

You might ask how you even get all these points from just passing in four or eight input points and how these points are interpolated so nicely. It all happens in the `TrackLine` constructor, or to be more precise, in the protected `Load` method, which allows you to reload the track data any time you need it to be regenerated. The `Load` method will not look very easy when you see it for the first time. It is the main method for all the track loading, track data validation, interpolation, and up and tangent vector generation. Even the tunnels and neutral landscape objects are generated here from the helpers you can pass to this method.

The `Load` method does the following things:

☐ It allows reloading, which is important for loading levels and starting over. Any previous data is killed automatically if you call `Load` again.

☐ All data is validated to make sure you can generate the track and use all the helpers.

☐ Each track point is checked to see if it is above the landscape. If not, the point is corrected and the surrounding points are also lifted up a bit for a smoother road. This way, you can easily generate a 3D track in Max without having to worry about the actual landscape height that is used later when the track is put on top of the landscape.

☐ Loopings are simplified by just putting two spline points on top of each other. The loading code automatically detects this and replaces these two points with a full looping of nine points, which are interpolated to even more points to generate a very smooth and correct looking looping.

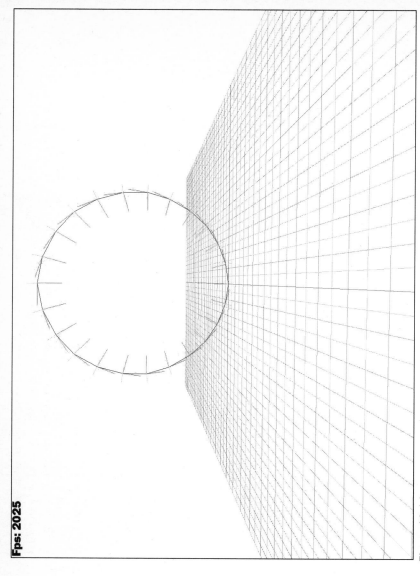

Fps: 2025

Figure 12-14

- [ ] Then all track points are interpolated through a Catmull-Rom spline interpolation method. You take a closer look at that shortly.

- [ ] Up and tangent vectors are generated and interpolated several times to make the road as smooth as possible. The tangent vectors especially should not suddenly change direction or flip to the other side, which would make driving on this road very hard. This code took the longest time to get it right.

- [ ] Then all helpers are analyzed and the road width for each track position is saved and will be used later when the actual rendering happens in the TrackLine class, which is based on the TrackLine class.

- [ ] Texture coordinates for the road texture are also generated here because you store the track points as a TrackVertex array to make the rendering easier later. Only the u texture coordinate is stored here; the v texture coordinate is then later just set to 0 or 1 depending on whether you are on the left or right side of the road.

- [ ] Then all the tunnel helpers are analyzed and the tunnel data is generated for you. Basically the code here just constructs a few new points for later use. They are used to draw the tunnel box with the tunnel material in the Track class.

☐ All landscape models are added. They are also saved together with the track data to form a complete level with everything you need. Additional landscape objects are also automatically generated in the `Track` class — for example, palms and lanterns at the side of the road.

When I started developing the `TrackLine` class, the constructor only generated the new interpolated points from the input points through the Catmull-Rom spline helper method. The code looked like this and can still be found in the `Load` method:

```
// Generate all points with help of catmull rom splines
for (int num = 0; num < inputPoints.Length; num++)
{
    // Get the 4 required points for the catmull rom spline
    Vector3 p1 = inputPoints[num-1 < 0 ? inputPoints.Length-1 : num-1];
    Vector3 p2 = inputPoints[num];
    Vector3 p3 = inputPoints[(num + 1) % inputPoints.Length];
    Vector3 p4 = inputPoints[(num + 2) % inputPoints.Length];
    // Calculate number of iterations we use here based
    // on the distance of the 2 points we generate new points from.
    float distance = Vector3.Distance(p2, p3);
    int numberOfIterations =
        (int)(NumberOfIterationsPer100Meters * (distance / 100.0f));
    if (numberOfIterations <= 0)
        numberOfIterations = 1;
    Vector3 lastPos = p1;
    for (int iter = 0; iter < numberOfIterations; iter++)
    {
        TrackVertex newVertex = new TrackVertex(
            Vector3.CatmullRom(p1, p2, p3, p4,
            iter / (float)numberOfIterations));
        points.Add(newVertex);
    } // for (iter)
} // for (num)
```

More Complex Tracks

The unit tests are nice to get everything up and running, but the more complex the tracks get, the more difficult it is to even generate them by typing in the 3D position for each spline point. It would be much easier to use the data from exported splines of 3D Studio Max, which allows you to construct and modify the spline positions easier.

Take a look at the expert track for the XNA Racing Game in Figure 12-15. The track alone contains about 85 points, which are interpolated to about 2,000 track points resulting in about 24,000 polygons for the road alone. Additional data for the guard rails and additional road 3D models are also generated later in the game. Constructing a track like this one and tweaking it is just not possible without a nice editor. You can be glad that you can use Max for that.

Exporting this data was not as easy as I initially thought. X files do not support splines and .fbx files also do not help. Even if they would export the splines you would still have to do a lot of work extracting the track data before you could use it in the game because it is not possible to get any vertex data from imported models in XNA. I decided to go with the currently very popular Collada format, which was built to allow exporting and importing 3D content and 3D scenes from one application to the next.

The main advantage of Collada over other formats is the fact that everything is stored as XML data and you can quickly see which data is used for what purpose just by looking at the exported file. You don't even need to look at any documentation; just search for the data you need and extract it. (In this case, you are looking for the spline and helper data; the rest is not important for you.)

Collada is not really a good export format for a game because it usually stores way too much information and the file sizes are a lot bigger than binary file formats because XML data is just a bunch of text. For that reason and because I was not allowed to use any external data formats for the XNA Starter Kit, all the Collada data is converted to the internal level data format in the `TrackImporter` class. Using your own data format speeds up the loading process and ensures that no one can figure out how to construct his own levels. Hey, wait a second; don't you want people to create their own tracks? I really want this to be easier and it is not good that you even need 3D Studio Max to construct or change the levels. I really have to implement some other way to import or build tracks in the game later.

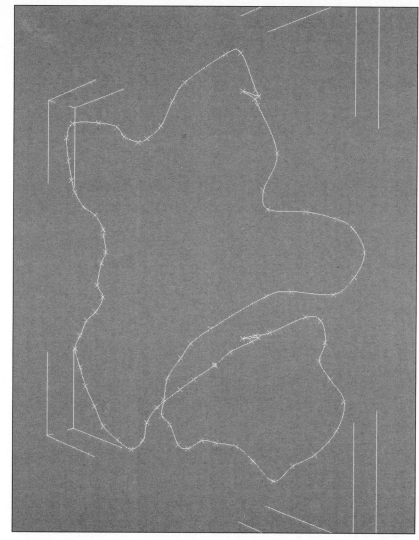

Figure 12-15

Importing the Track Data

To make the loading of Collada files a little bit easier, several helper classes are used. First of all, the XmlHelper class (see Figure 12-16) really helps you out with loading and managing XML files.

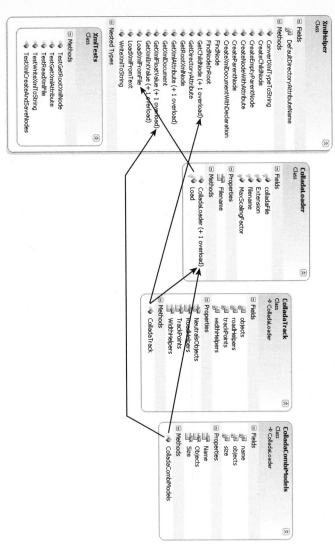

Figure 12-16

The ColladaLoader class is just a very short class that loads the Collada file (which is just an XML file) for you and lets the derived classes use the XmlHelper methods more easily.

❑ ColladaTrack is used to load the track itself (trackPoints), but also all helper objects such as the widthHelpers to make the road bigger and smaller and the roadHelpers for tunnels, palms, lanterns, and other objects on the side of the road. Finally, all additional landscape objects are loaded to be displayed as you drive close enough to them (because there can be a lot of landscape objects in the scene).

❑ ColladaCombiModels is a little helper class to load and display multiple models at once by just setting one combo model that contains up to ten models with relative positions and rotation values in them. For example, if you want to set a city block of nine buildings, just use the Buildings.CombiModel file, or if you need a bunch of palms plus a few stone models use the Palms.CombiModel file.

To learn more about the loading process, you can use the unit tests in the TrackLine and Track classes. More important, check out the ColladaTrack constructor itself:

```
public ColladaTrack(string setFilename)
    : base(setFilename)
{
    // Get spline first (only use one line)
    XmlNode geometry =
        XmlHelper.GetChildNode(colladaFile, "geometry");
    XmlNode visualScene =
        XmlHelper.GetChildNode(colladaFile, "visual_scene");
    string splineId = XmlHelper.GetXmlAttribute(geometry, "id");
    // Make sure this is a spline, everything else is not supported.
    if (splineId.EndsWith("-spline") == false)
        throw new Exception("The ColladaTrack file " + Filename +
            " does not have a spline geometry in it. Unable to load " +
            "track!");

    // Get spline points
    XmlNode pointsArray =
        XmlHelper.GetChildNode(geometry, "float_array");
    // Convert the points to a float array
    float[] pointsValues =
        StringHelper.ConvertStringToFloatArray(
        pointsArray.FirstChild.Value);
    // Skip first and third of each input point (MAX tangent data)
    trackPoints.Clear();
    int pointNum = 0;
    while (pointNum < pointsValues.Length)
    {
        // Skip first point (first 3 floating point values)
        pointNum += 3;
        // Take second vector
        trackPoints.Add(MaxScalingFactor * new Vector3(
            pointsValues[pointNum++],
            pointsValues[pointNum++],
            pointsValues[pointNum++]));
        // And skip thrid
        pointNum += 3;
    } // while (pointNum)
    // Check if we can find translation or scaling values for our
    // spline
    XmlNode splineInstance = XmlHelper.GetChildNode(
        visualScene, "url", "#" + splineId);
    XmlNode splineMatrixNode = XmlHelper.GetChildNode(
        splineInstance.ParentNode, "matrix");
    if (splineMatrixNode != null)
        throw new Exception(
            "The ColladaTrack file " + Filename +
            " should not use baked matrices. Please export " +
            "without baking matrices. Unable to load track!");
    XmlNode splineTranslateNode = XmlHelper.GetChildNode(
        splineInstance.ParentNode, "translate");
    XmlNode splineScaleNode = XmlHelper.GetChildNode(
        splineInstance.ParentNode, "scale");
    Vector3 splineTranslate = Vector3.Zero;
    if (splineTranslateNode != null)
    {
```

```
    float[] translateValues =
        StringHelper.ConvertStringToFloatArray(
        splineTranslateNode.FirstChild.Value);
    splineTranslate = MaxScalingFactor * new Vector3(
        translateValues[0], translateValues[1], translateValues[2]);
} // if (splineTranslateNode)
Vector3 splineScale = new Vector3(1, 1, 1);
if (splineScaleNode != null)
{
    float[] scaleValues = StringHelper.ConvertStringToFloatArray(
        splineScaleNode.FirstChild.Value);
    splineScale = new Vector3(
        scaleValues[0], scaleValues[1], scaleValues[2]);
} // if (splineTranslateNode)

// Convert all points with our translation and scaling
for (int num = 0; num < trackPoints.Count; num++)
{
    trackPoints[num] = Vector3.Transform(trackPoints[num],
        Matrix.CreateScale(splineScale) *
        Matrix.CreateTranslation(splineTranslate));
} // for (num)
[Now Helpers are loaded, the loading code is similar]
} // ColladaTrack(setFilename)
```

Getting the spline data itself is not very hard, but getting all the translation, scaling, and rotation values is a little bit of work (and even more complicated for the helpers), but after you have written and tested this code (there are several unit tests and test files that were used to implement this constructor) it is very easy to create new tracks and get them into your game.

Generating Vertices *from the* Track Data

Just getting the track points and helpers imported is only half the story. You already saw how complex the TrackLine constructor loading is and it really helps you out to generate the interpolated track points, and to build up vectors and the tangents. Even the texture coordinates and all the helpers and landscape models are handled here. But you still have only a bunch of points and no real road your car can drive on. To render a real road with the road textures (see Figure 12-17) you need to construct render-able vertices first for all the 3D data that forms your final road, including all the other dynamically created objects such as the guard rails. The most important texture is the road texture itself, but without the normal map it looks boring in the game. The normal map adds a sparkly structure to the road and makes it shiny when looking toward the sun. The other road textures for the road sides and background (RoadBack.dds) and for the tunnels (RoadTunnel.dds) are also important, but you won't see them that often.

The class that handles all these textures as road materials, as well as all the other road data such as the road cement columns, the guard rails, and the checkpoint positions, is the Track class, which is based on the TrackLine class. The Landscape class is used to render the track and all the landscape objects together with the landscape, which is finally everything you need to put the car on the road and start driving straight ahead. You still need a physics engine to stay on the road and to collide with the guard rails, but that is covered in the next chapter.

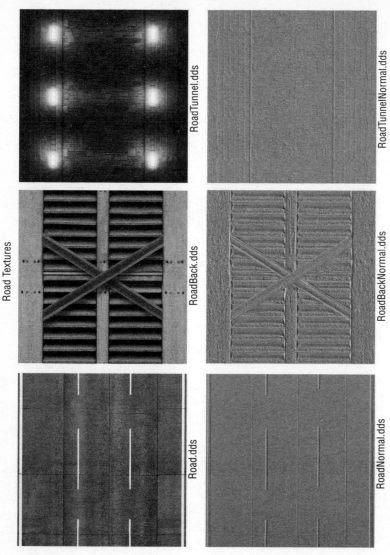

Road Textures

Road.dds

RoadBack.dds

RoadTunnel.dds

RoadNormal.dds

RoadBackNormal.dds

RoadTunnelNormal.dds

Figure 12-17

So the Track class is responsible for all the road materials, generating all vertices as well as the vertex and index buffers, and finally for rendering all the track vertices with the help of the shaders you use in the game. Most materials use the Specular20 technique of the NormalMapping shader for a nice shiny road, but the Diffuse20 technique is also quite popular for the tunnels and other non-shiny road materials.

The unit test to render the track is quite simple; all you want to do is to render the track. There is not much else you have to verify here:

```
public static void TestRenderTrack()
{
    Track track = null;
    TestGame.Start(
        delegate
        {
            track = new Track("TrackBeginner", null);
        },
        delegate
        {
            ShowUpVectors(track);
```

As you can see, you can still use the protected ShowUpVectors helper method from the TrackLine class because you derived the Track class from it. The Render method is also similar to the first render code you had in the previous chapter for the landscape rendering in the Mission class.

```
    track.Render();
  });
} // TestRenderingTrack()

public void Render()
{
  // We use tangent vertices for everything here
  BaseGame.Device.VertexDeclaration = TangentVertex.VertexDeclaration;
  // Restore the world matrix
  BaseGame.WorldMatrix = Matrix.Identity;
  // Render the road itself
  ShaderEffect.normalMapping.Render(
    roadMaterial, "Specular20",
    delegate
    {
      BaseGame.Device.Vertices[0].SetSource(roadVb, 0,
        TangentVertex.SizeInBytes);
      BaseGame.Device.Indices = roadIb;
      BaseGame.Device.DrawIndexedPrimitives(
        PrimitiveType.TriangleList,
        0, 0, points.Count * 5,
        0, (points.Count - 1) * 8);
    });
  // [etc. Render rest of road materials]
} // Render()
```

Well, that does not look very complicated. Take a look at the code that generates the road vertex and index buffers. The private GenerateVerticesAndObjects helper method is where all the magic happens:

```
private void GenerateVerticesAndObjects(Landscape landscape)
{
  #region Generate the road vertices
  // Each road segment gets 5 points:
  // left, left middle, middle, right middle, right.
  // The reason for this is that we would have bad triangle errors if the
  // road gets wider and wider. This happens because we need to render
  // quads, but we can only render triangles, which often have different
  // orientations, which makes the road very bumpy. This still happens
  // with 8 polygons instead of 2, but it is much better this way.
  // Another trick is to not do so many iterations in TrackLine, which
  // causes this problem. Better to have a not so round track, but at
  // least the road up/down itself is smooth.
  // The last point is duplicated (see TrackLine) because we have 2 sets
  // of texture coordinates for it (begin block, end block).
  // So for the index buffer we only use points.Count-1 blocks.
  roadVertices = new TangentVertex[points.Count * 5];
  // Current texture coordinate for the roadway (in direction of
  // movement)
```

```
for (int num = 0; num < points.Count; num++)
{
  // Get vertices with the help of the properties in the TrackVertex
  // class. For the road itself we only need vertices for the left
  // and right side, which are vertex number 0 and 1.
  roadVertices[num * 5 + 0] = points[num].RightTangentVertex;
  roadVertices[num * 5 + 1] = points[num].MiddleRightTangentVertex;
  roadVertices[num * 5 + 2] = points[num].MiddleTangentVertex;
  roadVertices[num * 5 + 3] = points[num].MiddleLeftTangentVertex;
  roadVertices[num * 5 + 4] = points[num].LeftTangentVertex;
} // for (num)
roadVb = new VertexBuffer(
  BaseGame.Device,
  typeof(TangentVertex),
  roadVertices.Length,
  ResourceUsage.WriteOnly,
  ResourceManagementMode.Automatic);
roadVb.SetData(roadVertices);

// Also calculate all indices, we have 8 polygons for each segment
// with 3 vertices each. We have 1 segment less than points because
// the last point is duplicated (different tex coords).
int[] indices = new int[(points.Count - 1) * 8 * 3];
int vertexIndex = 0;
for (int num = 0; num < points.Count - 1; num++)
{
  // We only use 3 vertices (and the next 3 vertices),
  // but we have to construct all 24 indices for our 4 polygons.
  for (int sideNum = 0; sideNum < 4; sideNum++)
  {
    // Each side needs 2 polygons.
    // 1. Polygon
    indices[num * 24 + 6 * sideNum + 0] = vertexIndex + sideNum;
    indices[num * 24 + 6 * sideNum + 1] =
      vertexIndex + 5 + 1 + sideNum;
    indices[num * 24 + 6 * sideNum + 2] = vertexIndex + 5 + sideNum;
    // 2. Polygon
    indices[num * 24 + 6 * sideNum + 3] =
      vertexIndex + 5 + 1 + sideNum;
    indices[num * 24 + 6 * sideNum + 4] = vertexIndex + sideNum;
    indices[num * 24 + 6 * sideNum + 5] = vertexIndex + 1 + sideNum;
  } // for (sideNum)
  // Go to the next 5 vertices
  vertexIndex += 5;
} // for (num)
// Set road back index buffer
roadIb = new IndexBuffer(
  BaseGame.Device,
  typeof(int),
  indices.Length,
  ResourceUsage.WriteOnly,
  ResourceManagementMode.Automatic);
roadIb.SetData(indices);
#endregion

// [Then the rest of the road back, tunnel, etc. vertices are
```

```
// generated here and all the landscape objects, checkpoints, palms,
// etc. are generated at the end of this method]
} // GenerateVerticesAndObjects(landscape)
```

Good thing I wrote so many comments when I wrote this code. The first part generates a big tangent vertex array with five times as many points as the track vertices you get from the TrackLine base class. This data is directly passed into the vertex buffer for the road and then used to construct the polygons in the index buffer. Each road piece gets eight polygons (four parts with two polygons each) and therefore the index buffer needs 24 times as many indices as you have track points. To make sure you are still able to properly access all these indices, you have to use int values here instead of short values that I would usually use for index buffers. Using shorts reduces the memory size by half. But in this case, for the roads you can have many more than just 32,000 indices. (2000 road pieces from the expert track example times 24 is already 48,000 indices.) You need many iteration points for your road because it is not hand-crafted, but automatically generated, which can lead to overlapping errors if you don't have enough iterations and don't generate the road smoothly enough (see Figure 12-18).

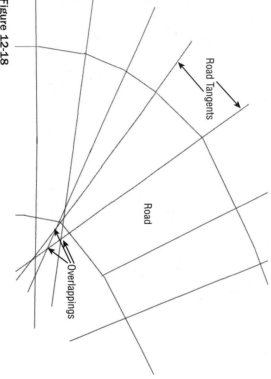

Figure 12-18

You might ask why four parts are generated for each road segment. It's not that I enjoy throwing more polygons at the poor GPU. This technique is used to improve the visual quality of the road, especially in curves.

Figure 12-19 explains this problem much better than I can with words. As you can see two polygons that form an uneven quad are not always the same size, but they still use the same number of texels. On the right, you can see an extreme situation where the bottom-right part of the road is heavily distorted and does not look good anymore.

This problem can be fixed by dividing the road into multiple parts. You use four parts for each segment in the racing game to make the road look much better.

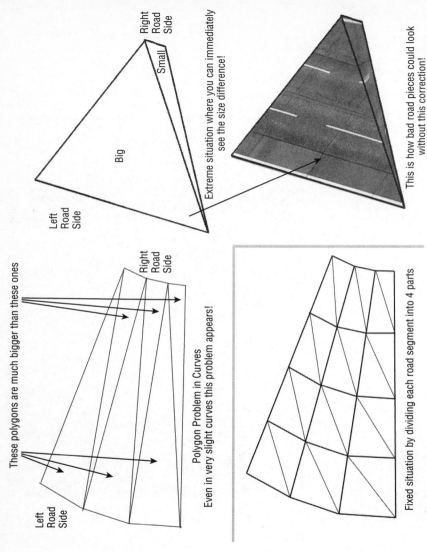

Figure 12-19

Final Result

That was really a lot of work to get the landscape and road rendering right, but now you have a really good portion of the game ready; at least the graphical parts are good to go. There are, of course, many smaller tricks and tips you can find in the classes of the `Tracks` namespace. Please check out the unit tests to learn more about rendering the road back sides, the loopings, and tunnels.

Figure 12-20 shows the final result of the `TestRenderTrack` unit test of the `Track` class.

Together with the landscape rendering from the first part of this chapter, you have a pretty nice rendering engine. Together with the pre-screen sky cube mapping shader for the background, the landscape and the road rendering looks quite good (see Figure 12-21). The post-screen glow shader of the game also makes everything fit together even better, especially if you have many landscape objects in the scene, too.

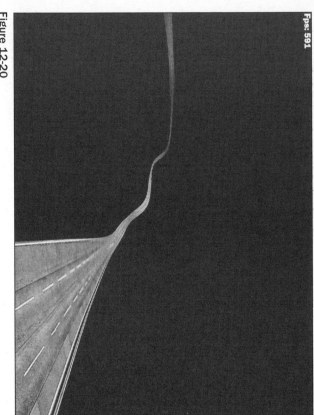

Figure 12-20

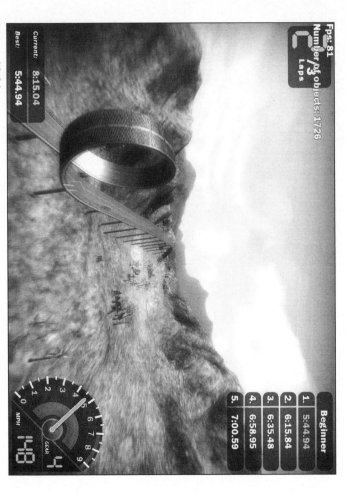

Figure 12-21

Challenge: Create a New Unit Test Track

Go into the TrackLine class and add a new unit test for a simple track. You just have to add a bunch of vectors and test them until you think the track looks good enough.

Figure 12-22 shows an example of such a custom track. Please note that I inverted the screenshot to be better visible in this book. You could also use an invert post-screen shader as described in Chapter 8.

If you have some energy left, try to import a track from 3D Studio Max through the TrackImporter class and then test it in the Track or Landscape class. Anyway, enjoy the landscape and track rendering code. I hope it is also useful for other game projects.

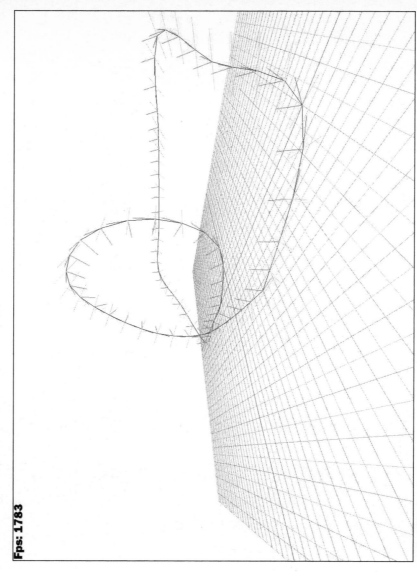

Fps: 1783

Figure 12-22

Summary

In this chapter you learned a lot about rendering complex 3D objects such as the landscape, the track, and the many 3D models used to create the levels in the racing game you are creating here. It will, I hope, be useful for other games, too, but there are a couple of things you might want to remember when creating landscapes for games:

- [ ] Always figure out first how the player looks at the landscape in the game later. It does not make sense to have a great looking landscape, which looks good only at a close distance and covers only 50×50 meters if, in reality, you need huge terrains for strategy, role playing, or racing games. You need something bigger for these kinds of games and this means you either have to repeat textures or have clever rendering techniques combining detail textures with big textures, or use splatting to "paint" the landscape ground this way.

- [ ] Splatting is a great technique for huge terrains. Most games go with texture splatting and use many different ground textures and additional special textures, tracks, and so on for great looking terrains. If you don't have much development time or if you don't really need huge terrains you might find simpler solutions like the one from the last chapter, which was okay for a shoot-'em-up kind of game.

- [ ] Additional layers, shaders, and effects, especially water shaders and shadow mapping, can be a very time-consuming task. I intentionally left out water from the game because in my last couple of projects it always took several weeks to get great looking water.

- [ ] There are many tips and tricks you can learn from other people; you can find many tutorials on the Internet and seek out books such as the *Game Programming Gems* or *ShaderX* series by Charles River Media.

For the track generation you have similar rules, and the rule to create unit tests first is always important. Always test your performance, especially if you get into high polygon areas as you did this chapter, with more than 130,000 polygons just for the landscape and up to 24,000 polygons for the road plus maybe 50,000 polygons for additional road data such as guard rails, tunnels, and the cement columns the road stands on. This means that even without any additional landscape objects, you already have more than 200,000 polygons each frame, which means that to even achieve a frame rate of 100 frames per second you need to push more than 20 million polygons per second to the GPU just for the landscape and the track. The car has about 25,000 polygons and the landscape objects all have several thousand polygons, too, which means that you can end up with several million polygons per frame if you have 1000 landscape objects or more in the scene. This may sound like a lot, but if you take a look at the screenshots from the TestRenderLandscape unit test, you can see that you have almost 2000 objects in all of them.

You can probably guess that the GPU will not be able to push 2–3 million polygons each frame to the screen and still run at over 60 frames per second on the Xbox 360. On the PC it is even worse because 75 Hz is the most-used screen refresh rate and the GPU of most players is much slower, not at all able to handle that much 3D geometry each frame. To make sure the game still runs great even on mid to low spec PCs, the following tricks are used:

- [ ] Never render anything that is not visible. Well, the landscape and the track are always visible, so you can't just skip them. But many of the landscape models might be behind you or just not in your field of view and can be easily skipped. Another trick is to skip any models that are just too far away to be noticed anymore. Especially smaller 3D models can be skipped after 100 meters. This is the biggest performance gain in the whole game. Check out the Model class and the Render method to learn more about this trick.

❏ Render the GPU-heavy data at the beginning of each frame. This way you can prepare the landscape models and other rendering data while the GPU is still working with the many landscape and track polygons.

❏ Always sort rendering by shaders. You already saw in the previous games how the MeshRenderManager is used and how it can greatly improve the performance. In the many performance tests I did with the racing game (see the Model class for some of them) I constantly improved the performance of the MeshRenderManager class. Especially for many objects of the same type using the same shader the performance can be really astonishing in the engine. Check out the TestRenderManyModels unit test, which pushes more than 100 million polygons to the GPU on the Xbox 360 (and your PC if your GPU is fast enough).

❏ Use short shaders! In the original Rocket Commander game everything used the ParallaxShader, which just has a few extra instructions compared to the NormalMapping shader, but it will still take more time to render a parallax mapped 3D object than just a normal mapped 3D object. For that reason you use only normal mapping in the racing game and it does not make any visual difference. Only the landscape uses a more complex shader to add the detail map effect (see Figure 12-7; it is really worth the effort).

Okay, before your brain explodes with all this new knowledge, relax for a while. Chapter 13 is about physics and involves a lot of math. By the time you read Chapter 14, you will finally be able to put everything together for the racing game — and you can drive a few test rounds!

13

Physics

The use of physics in games has become quite popular in recent years. It is not as if older games do not use physics engines, but recently many shooter games have complex physics systems that are only possible because of the immense increase in computing power and multi-core systems. Even hardware PPUs (physics processing units) are available today, similar to GPUs that just handle graphics. These processors are just for calculating physics.

The games that use physics the most are first-person shooters, especially if the games permit a lot of freedom and enable the player to walk around freely and interact with the scenery. One of the most popular games, Half-Life 2 (launched in 2004), used a lot of innovative physics techniques and also involved physics in the game play and mission design.

Half-Life 2 uses the commercial physics engine Havok internally, but there are several other physics frameworks, which are discussed in a short while. Sadly none of these frameworks work on the Xbox 360 with the XNA Framework because they all use unmanaged code, which is not allowed on the Xbox 360 when you develop games with XNA. On the PC you can use whatever you like, and this chapter discusses which framework might be the best to use right now. The Racing Game that you are currently developing will not make use of any advanced physics framework for that reason. It is also a lot of work to implement and test such a powerful framework, and most of the physics engines are expensive to license. In Half-Life 2, the engineers spent several years tweaking and fine-tuning the physics until they were pleased with the result.

Physics always comes along with some heavy mathematics. It is certainly possible to use a physics framework or apply a simple formula such as the famous $F = m * a$ without knowing much about physics or math. However, as soon as you want to develop your own physics system for your game, you will need at least a basic understanding of Newton's laws of motion. Having a physics formula book nearby, or at least having Google at your fingertips, for help is also a good idea. Figure 13-1 shows a typical example of a physics problem involving several objects, transmitting forces, gravity, and so on.

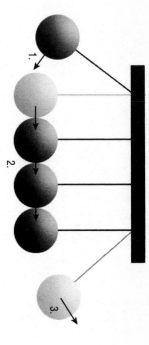

1. Gravity pulls first ball down and pushes it towards the other balls through the attached string.
2. The force gets transmitted through the balls until it reaches the last ball, where the force can be used to lift up the last ball.
3. The last ball flies up, all the other balls stay still. After a while gravity reverses the direction of the ball and the game begins again.

Figure 13-1

When you talk about physics you just have to mention Isaac Newton, the apple, and the tree. You know the story. Physics has evolved quite a bit since then. There are many theories about the extremely small world of atoms, quarks, electrons, and so on. Of course, many other theories exist about the macro cosmos, the solar system, stars, planets, and so on. But for most games, you use just a bunch of simple physics formulas to help you accelerate and decelerate objects. It is just not practical to work on a smaller scope due to limited processing power. In addition, it just has to look good, so you don't need every virtual atom to behave as it would in the real world.

While formulas such as Newton's laws of motion are heavily used, you are going to spend most of the time with collision issues, such as those in the Rocket Commander game (Chapter 8). At least physics are fun. Unit testing enables you to quickly try things out. Be aware, however, that you can spend a lot of time with physics without seeing the results of your work if the world of your game does not allow too much interaction. It is nice to have real physics for a puzzle game, but if all you can do is click on objects to be removed, you really don't need a complex physics engine. Just fake it!

Newton's Laws of Motion

Let's take a quick look at the important laws of motion by our friend Isaac Newton. Check out Figure 13-2 to see these physics laws in action:

☐ **First Law:** Objects stay in motion unless some external force interacts with them. This is really easy because all objects that can move usually have a movement vector or some velocity value. Just don't change that value unless you apply some force to slow it down, accelerate it, or change the direction. That's it.

☐ **Second Law:** When you do apply an external force, it means you can accelerate or decelerate an object. If you have more than one dimension (well, you have three for 3D games), you can also change the direction the object is moving. In that case, you work with vectors instead of scalar values. As a result, all vector components (x, y, and z) will be changed instead of one simple value. Because masses for your objects will always be constant (at least in most games I know), you can use the simplified $F = m * a$ formula, where "a" is the acceleration defined by the change of velocity divided by the change of time: $a = dv/dt$.

☐ **Third Law:** Each action has an equal and opposite reaction. Thus, if you have a force such as the gravity of the earth acting on an object, there is a force that reacts, applying pressure in the opposite direction. Because the earth has a much greater mass than a small object, such as a stone or apple, it may not matter if the earth is acting on it. But if you take a much bigger object, such as the sun, the gravity of the earth is comparatively smaller to that of the sun. Good thing our earth is always in motion rotating around the sun, keeping it in orbit, the same way the moon is orbiting around the earth.

Newton's Laws on Steroids, er, I mean, Asteroids!

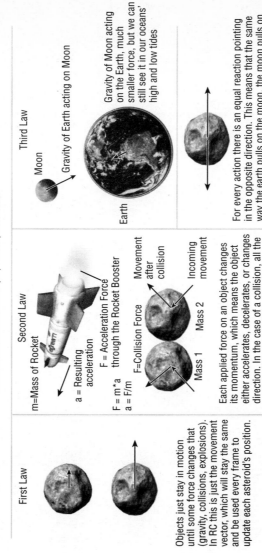

First Law

Objects just stay in motion until some force changes that (gravity, collisions, explosions). In RC this is just the movement vector, which will stay the same and be used every frame to update each asteroid's position.

Second Law

m=Mass of Rocket

a = Resulting acceleration

F = Acceleration Force through the Rocket Booster

$F = m*a$
$a = F/m$

F=Collision Force

Mass 1   Mass 2

Movement after collision

Incoming movement

Each applied force on an object changes its momentum, which means the object either accelerates, decelerates, or changes direction. In the case of a collision, all the momentum of both objects builds the collision Force, which is then used to either break the objects or give the force back to them and let them bounce off in opposite directions.

Third Law

Moon

Gravity of Earth acting on Moon

Earth

Gravity of Moon acting on the Earth, much smaller force, but we can still see it in our oceans' high and low tides

For every action there is an equal reaction pointing in the opposite direction. This means that the same way the earth pulls on the moon, the moon pulls on the earth. Since the masses are very different, the effect is much greater on the moon. But even a simple moving asteroid from the first example has an opposite force of the movement, or else it would get faster and faster and then would not comply with the first law.

Figure 13-2

In "Principia Mathematica," Newton discussed the laws of motion for the first time, along with his law of universal gravitation, which explains planetary movements — that is, why the moon orbits the earth, and the earth orbits the sun. Pretty exciting stuff back then, but today every school kid can understand this, at least if they pay attention in physics class. Computers are more powerful than just giving them one planet moving around another one, which you could probably calculate on paper. In Rocket Commander, you saw thousands of asteroids interacting with one another. The asteroids aren't affected by gravity and just collide and bounce off one another, but adding more reality to the unit tests by adding gravity would not be a big challenge.

Keep It Simple

Because physics is a big topic and implementing physics into your game requires your full attention, you should try to keep things simple. Often you don't even have to know which formula is the correct one — just find something that works. For example, you don't have to code anything to follow the first law of motion. The third law can be ignored, as well, because you are only interested in forces that change motion for your objects.

Before you dive deeper into the world of physics, and take a quick look at the available physics engines, you should make sure you know exactly what you need for your Racing Game. There is no need to implement a highly complex physics engine allowing you to stack boxes and throw them over, if all you need is to be able to just drive around with your car and stay on the road. I wish I would have had more time for implementing physics into the Racing Game, but the game had to be completed quickly. For that reason, the Racing Game uses only a simple approach to physics and the collisions are handled in a very simplified way. But it works, and even though it still requires a lot of fine-tuning and special care, as you can see in the next chapter, you can get your car on the road and drive around.

Figure 13-3 shows the basic physics requirement for the Racing Game. Because you do not interact with any other object in the world and no landscape object has physics, you can fully turn your attention to the car. Don't worry about anything else.

These rules are implemented in the following few lines of code, but it gets harder to tweak all the values to enable the car to interact correctly with the road:

```
// [From CarPhysics.cs]
// Handle car engine force
float newAccelerationForce = 0.0f;
if (Input.KeyboardUpPressed ||
    Input.Keyboard.IsKeyDown(Keys.W) ||
    Input.MouseLeftButtonPressed ||
    Input.GamePadAPressed)
    newAccelerationForce +=
        MaxAccelerationPerSec;

// [etc.]


// Add acceleration force to total car force, but use the
// current car direction!
carForce +=
    carDir * newAccelerationForce * (moveFactor * 85);

// Change speed with standard formula, use acceleration as
// ourforce, gravity is handled below in the ApplyGravity
// method.
float oldSpeed = speed;
Vector3 speedChangeVector = carForce / CarMass;

// Only use the amount important for our current direction
// (slower rotation)
if (speedChangeVector.Length() > 0)
{
    float speedApplyFactor =
        Vector3.Dot(Vector3.Normalize(speedChangeVector), carDir);
    if (speedApplyFactor > 1)
        speedApplyFactor = 1;
```

```
    speed += speedChangeVector.Length() * speedApplyFactor;
} // if (speedChangeVector.Length)
```

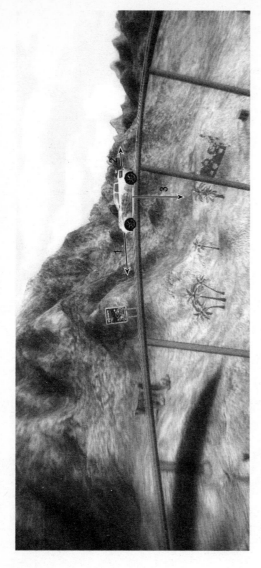

Figure 13-3

1. Our car engine pushes the car forward as we step on the gas.
2. Wind, road friction, etc., pull the car back and slow it down. We can also brake the car ourselves.
3. Gravity pulls the car down and keeps the car on the road. If we drive fast enough, we might stay in the air for a few seconds through the momentum of the car until gravity pushes us down again.

The code is maybe a little bit more complicated than it was when I implemented the solution the first time with the help of the unit test of the `CarPhysics` class. However, it still basically increases the speed of the car when you accelerate through the keyboard up keys or the equivalent input keys and buttons. To enable the car to drift in a different direction than you are actually heading, I split up the car direction and the movement vector. Speed was used to update the length of the movement vector, but I ran into many problems. To simplify the problem, I use a scalar value for the speed now. This way it is also very easy to just drive backwards a little bit with the help of negative speed vectors while the car is still pointing forward.

Because your track is not just going straight ahead, you need to rotate your car with the help of the left and right keyboard cursors or the gamepad, or even by using the mouse. Figure 13-4 shows the basic rules for the rotation of your car, which are very simple and implemented in a few lines of code. To make rotations smoother, the last rotation value is still used, but reduced a bit.

```
// First handle rotations (reduce last value)
rotationChange *= 0.825f;// 75f;
// Left/right changes rotation
if (Input.KeyboardLeftPressed ||
    Input.Keyboard.IsKeyboard(Keys.A))
    rotationChange += MaxRotationPerSec * moveFactor / 2.5f;
else if (Input.KeyboardRightPressed ||
    Input.Keyboard.IsKeyDown(Keys.D) ||
    Input.Keyboard.IsKeyDown(Keys.E))
    rotationChange -= MaxRotationPerSec * moveFactor / 2.5f;
else
```

```
rotationChange = 0;
if (Input.MouseMovement != 0)
    rotationChange -=
        (Input.MouseXMovement / 15.0f) *
        MaxRotationPerSec * moveFactor;
// Rotate dir around up vector
// Interpolate rotation amount.
virtualRotationAmount += rotationChange;
// Smooth over 200ms
float interpolatedRotationChange =
    (rotationChange + virtualRotationAmount) *
    moveFactor / 0.225f;// / 0.200f;
virtualRotationAmount -= interpolatedRotationChange;
// We can't rotate our car ourself if it is currently not on the ground
if (isCarOnGround)
    carDir = Vector3.TransformNormal(carDir,
    Matrix.CreateFromAxisAngle(carUp, interpolatedRotationChange));
```

Figure 13-4

1. Forward movement through the car engine.
2. We can turn the car left and right or just crash into the guard rail when a curve comes. Anyway we will stay on the road because gravity pulls us down. Only if we manage to fly above the guard rails, we die. We can also fall out of the track in loopings.
3. Friction through wind and the road, or if the player brakes himself.

A more complex way to handle the car physics makes sense if you have more than a few weeks to develop your game. If you really want more realistic calculations, you could use more constants and forces to make the car behavior more realistic than I did. But my solution works too, and it did not take much time to implement it.

If you want to check it out please use the TestCarPhysicsOnPlaneWithGuardRails unit test in the CarPhysics class. The unit test started simply with the car and a plane on the ground, rendered with the help of the new PlaneRenderer class. Later the guard rails and collision checking and response were added, which are discussed later in this chapter. This is an earlier version of the unit test before it was renamed to TestCarPhysicsOnPlaneWithGuardRails. It shows you my test environment for handling the basic car physics. Figure 13-5 shows the result. Testing is done with the normal keys and input devices the game uses for controlling the car (up, down, left, right, and so on).

Figure 13-5

```
static public void TestCarPhysicsOnPlane()
{
    PlaneRenderer plane = null;

    TestGame.Start("TestCarPhysicsOnPlane",
    delegate
    {
        plane = new PlaneRenderer(Vector3.Zero,
            new Plane(new Vector3(0, 0, 1), 0),
            new Material("CityGround", "CityGroundNormal"), 500.0f);
        // Put car on the ground and use standard direction and up vectors
        RacingGame.Player.SetCarPosition(
            new Vector3(0, 0, 0),
            new Vector3(0, 1, 0),
            new Vector3(0, 0, 1));
    },
    delegate
    {
        // Test slow computers by slowing down the framerate with Ctrl
        if (Input.Keyboard.IsKeyDown(Keys.LeftControl))
            Thread.Sleep(75);

        Matrix carMatrix = RacingGame.Player.UpdateCarMatrixAndCamera();

        // Generate shadows, just the car does shadows
        ShaderEffect.shadowMapping.GenerateShadows(
        delegate
        {
            RacingGame.CarModel.GenerateShadow(carMatrix);
        });

        // Render shadows (on both the plane and the car)
        ShaderEffect.shadowMapping.RenderShadows(
        delegate
        {
            RacingGame.CarModel.UseShadow(carMatrix);
            plane.UseShadow();
        });

        BaseGame.UI.RenderGameBackground();
        // Show car and ground plane
        RacingGame.CarModel.RenderCar(0, Color.White, carMatrix);
        plane.Render();
        // Just add brake tracks (we don't render the landscape here)
        RacingGame.Landscape.RenderBrakeTracks();
        // Render all 3d objects
        BaseGame.MeshRenderManager.Render();
        // Add shadows
        ShaderEffect.shadowMapping.ShowShadows();
        RacingGame.Player.DisplayPhysicsValuesAndHelp();
    });
} // TestCarPhysicsOnPlane()
```

Gravitation

Driving around on a plane surface is easy to do, but not much fun, especially because the Racing Game enables you to drive crazy tracks with loopings, tunnels, hard curves, and so on. The collision detection and response techniques are discussed later in this chapter, but you can add gravity relatively quickly to your current TestCarPhysicsOnPlane unit test and fine-tune it a little bit later.

You are just going to make a very simple change to the TestCarPhysicsOnPlane unit test by putting the car 10 meters above the ground in the initialization code. It should fall down now, but because you have not implemented any real physics yet (only the car controlling, accelerating, and steering was done until now) it just stays in the air (see Figure 13-6).

Fps: 184
Cursor: Move and Rotate Car; Space: Brake; Mouse: View
Car position: {X:0 Y:0 Z:10}
Camera pos: {X:-4.102058 Y:16.54896 Z:19.09231}
Speed: 0
Force: {X:0 Y:0 Z:0}
Car dir: {X:0 Y:1 Z:0}
Car up: {X:0 Y:0 Z:1}
rotateCarAfterCollision: 0
isCarOnGround: False
groundPlanePos: {X:0 Y:0 Z:0}
guardrailLeft: {X:-10 Y:0 Z:0}
guardrailRight: {X:10 Y:0 Z:0}
viewDistance: 1

Figure 13-6

```
// Put car 10m above the ground to test gravity and ground plane!
RacingGame.Player.SetCarPosition(
    new Vector3(0, 0, 10),
    new Vector3(0, 1, 0),
    new Vector3(0, 0, 1));
```

The Player class is derived from the ChaseCamera class, which is again derived from the CarPhysics class. This way all the car controlling, physics, player logic, and so on, can be handled and accessed from one single place: the `Player` class. The `ChaseCamera` has the following two modes, similar to the modes of the `SpaceCamera` class from Rocket Commander:

☐ The Free Camera Mode is used for all unit tests. Sometimes, you have to change it for unit tests like the one you are currently working on to allow the same controller features as in the game.

☐ Default Chase Car Game Camera is used for the game. It can be used for the menu or replays to chase the camera behind the car. Of course, it can be used in the game to show and control the car.

Use the following lines in the initialization code to make sure the game camera is used and you don't use any zoom-in time like in the game, so you can see the car falling down at the beginning:

```
// Make sure we are not in free camera mode and can control the car
RacingGame.Player.FreeCamera = false;
RacingGame.Player.ZoomInTime = 0;
RacingGame.Player.SetCameraPosition(new Vector3(0, -5, 8));
```

The rest of the unit test can stay the same. The actual gravity computation happens in the `Update` method of the `CarPhysics` class, which calls the `ApplyGravity` method, as follows:

```
/// <summary>
/// Apply gravity
/// </summary>
private void ApplyGravity()
{
    // Fix car on ground
    float distFromGround = Vector3Helper.SignedDistanceToPlane(
        carPos, groundPlanePos, groundPlaneNormal);
    isCarOnGround = distFromGround > -0.1f;
    // Use very hard and instant gravity to fix if car is below ground!
    float moveFactor = BaseGame.MoveFactorPerSecond;
    float maxGravity = Gravity * moveFactor;
    // Use more smooth gravity for jumping
    float minGravity = -Gravity * moveFactor;
    if (distFromGround > maxGravity)
    {
        distFromGround = maxGravity;
        gravitySpeed = 0;
    } // if (distFromGround)
    if (distFromGround < minGravity)
    {
        distFromGround = minGravity;
        gravitySpeed -= distFromGround;
    } // if (distFromGround)
    carPos.Z += distFromGround;
} // ApplyGravity()
```

This code basically reduces the z position value of the car position until you reach the ground. Because the car might be lower than the road when you drive uphill or because of some precision error, the z position value is also corrected to reset the car back to the road level.

For tweaking, the many constants are used, which are all defined at the very beginning of the `CarPhysics` class. The following code block shows the first three constants. Changing the `CarMass`, for example, gives you control if the car is very heavy and almost glued to the ground, or if it is as light as a feather and can fly a long time until gravity kicks in again:

```
#region Constants
/// <summary>
/// Car is 1000 kg
/// </summary>
const float CarMass = 1000;//1000.0f;
/// <summary>
/// Gravity on earth is 9.81 m/s^2
/// </summary>
const float Gravity = 9.81f;
/// <summary>
/// Max speed of our car is 275 mph. While we use mph for
/// the display, we calculate internally with meters per
/// sec since meter is the unit we use for everthing in the
/// game. And it is a much nicer unit than miles or feet.
/// </summary>
public const float MaxSpeed =
    275.0f * MphToMeterPerSec;
/// <summary>
/// Convert our meter per sec to mph for display.
/// 1 mile = 1.609344 kilometers
/// Each hour has 3600 seconds (60 min * 60 sec).
/// 1 kilometer = 1000 meter.
/// </summary>
public const float MeterPerSecToMph =
    1.609344f * ((60.0f*60.0f)/1000.0f),
    MphToMeterPerSec = 1.0f / MeterPerSecToMph;
// [etc.]
```

You probably saw a couple of times now that I use meters instead of feet, inches, yards, or miles. Sorry to those in the U.S. — the rest of the world uses meters, and it is an easier unit system for measuring and setting constants. I don't even know constants such as gravity in other unit systems and you can see that whenever I have other formats like mph (miles per hour) I use helper constants to convert from one format to the next. You can also use Google to convert from one format to another. Just type in "1500 meters as miles" and you will get the value in miles.

The new TestCarPhysicsOnPlane unit test allows you to control the car and it handles gravity correctly (see Figure 13-7). It also handles displaying the brake tracks on the ground after you suddenly try to stop the car.

Physics Engines

With all this new knowledge about the basics of physics you can now compare existing physics engines. After these basics are handled, and after making sure you have the correct constants defined and feel comfortable in your unit system, you should think a little bit about the requirements for your game (which object should have physics, where we can ignore it, etc.). Physics engines can often do a lot of different things and while many physics demos and tutorials look pretty cool, they cannot be used for most games. Having a bunch of boxes on top of one another and kicking them over is fun the first time, but not many games even allow direct control of boxes. After a while, it really gets boring seeing boxes fall over. It is like being in kindergarten again.

But not all demos are just a bunch of boxes. There are many good examples showing you specific features of physics engines. My point, however, is that most games only need certain features. First-person shooter games can use most of the features from physics engines. You can see that by looking at the released games in the past couple of years. Almost all first-person shooters have some kind of physics implemented, whereas other games such as role playing games, strategy games, and so on, have either no physics or rudimentary physics, which are only used to improve the visual effects, but not the game logic itself.

Fps: 219
Cursor: Move and Rotate Car; Space: Brake; Mouse: View
Car position: {X:0.5209404 Y:134.7605 Z:-5.890568E-06}
Camera pos: {X:0.0497843 Y:128.7445 Z:2.599998}
Speed: 82.07549
Force: {X:-0.006459513 Y:-16.70989 Z:7.304126E-07}
Car dir: {X:0.0003865682 Y:1 Z:-4.371139E-08}
Car up: {X:-3.82137E-15 Y:4.371139E-08 Z:1}
rotateCarAfterCollision: 0
isCarOnGround: True
groundPlanePos: {X:0 Y:0 Z:0}
guardrailLeft: {X:-10 Y:0 Z:0}
guardrailRight: {X:10 Y:0 Z:0}
viewDistance: 1

Figure 13-7

I personally don't like physics in strategy games because they are not implemented very well and do not improve the game. They often add better visuals but cause such side effect as killing your units if a big building collapses or falls over. It is like playing chess while an earthquake is going on. You would not be able to make clever moves because everything would be shaking and falling over. Maybe it will take time until the developers figure out how to use physics in the game play to make the game predictable and not luck-based.

I really like physics for explosions, effects, and for improving the visual quality. There are several games that have really nice simulations for water, explosion, and smoke effects that interact with the surrounding environment, and so on.

As I said before, you will not be able to use any of the physics engines on the Xbox 360 when using XNA because they are based on unmanaged code, which is just not supported in XNA. There are some XNA-compatible physics engines written in pure .NET code in the works at the time of this writing. They do not really compare to the professional physics engines yet, but they keep improving. On the Windows platform you can use whatever you prefer, but even on Windows most engines do not have a proper .NET interface that enables you to easily use and handle physics directly in your game. The possibilities for .NET are discussed later with the engine types. For now, take a quick look at some of the features of physics engines available today:

❑ Forces such as gravity, friction, kinetic and contact friction, buoyancy, and so on.

❑ Basic physics objects support for defining and handling boxes, spheres, cylinders, plates, and so on. Often these engines also support connected objects and more complex predefined models such as cars, planes, hovercrafts, ships, and so on to enable you to quickly play around with them.

❑ Checking for collisions between many objects, especially if they are not just spheres. This is usually the main place for optimizations because collision calculations are used very often and require checking a lot of objects, bounding spheres, and even polygon-based checks.

❑ Collision response, which is executed when a collision is detected. Either you let the objects bounce off one another (as in Rocket Commander), or you can even damage or break them (collision force is transformed to kinetic energy and breaks up your models). Games usually use predefined 3D models for explosions, wrecks, and broken parts because it is hard to generate this data in real time. The results, however, are still great looking if the 3D artist does a good job.

❑ Projectile physics can help you with bullets, rockets, and other projectiles that are fired. You saw how to use projectiles in the last chapter. If you have a physics engine that handles projectiles too, you can add the projectile to it. This enables you to use physics parameters and to add special behavior depending on the 3D surroundings (for example, bullets are slower under water).

❑ Complete particle systems can be done with physics. As I stated earlier, I really like effect systems that can make good use of a physics engine, but effect systems require a lot of work.

There are many more features a physics engine can have such as supporting rigid body simulators. A rag-doll physics engine can make characters fall down, or you can create deformable objects such as clothes, flags, fluids, and other complex bodies.

Ageia PhysX

PhysX is the name for the physics engine and SDK by AGEIA, which was formerly known as NovodeX SDK. PhysX is also the name of the PPU (physics processing unit), developed by AGEIA. The PhysX PPU is the world's first card devoted to calculating physics on the PC. It can be used in any game that uses the PhysX SDK. Currently, there are not many games that support the PhysX engine. However, many engines and upcoming games have already licensed the PhysX SDK. Most recently, Sony licensed PhysX for its Playstation 3 console game development.

Even without having the PPU, the engine is really powerful and the developers have been doing physics engines for a long time now. Physics engines are very widely used, coming in second place for usage behind the Havok engine, which is more widely used, not only in games, but also in 3D content creation programs such as 3D Studio Max. While the idea is nice to offload the heavy lifting for physics calculations to a special card, the PPU is just too expensive ($250–$300). In addition, not many people will have this card. Most people who buy a physics card will probably be developers or artists that can benefit from the card in the content creation process. You can't expect your gamers, however, to have this card in order for your game to work. But PhysX also performs well on the CPU, and thanks to multi-core systems it runs well on today's hardware, too.

Only a handful of games use the PhysX engine right now, such as Ghost Recon, Gothic 3, Joint Task Force, and most recently Gears of War (Xbox 360). But games in the future will use the engine such as the Unreal Tournament 2007 game, the Unreal 3 engine, Splinter Cell, Monster Madness, and so on.

PhysX focuses a lot on games, game engines, and handling effects, the game logic that uses physics, and having a lot of cool looking examples and tutorials. The main advantage of PhysX is that they have the PPU hardware to run faster than all the other physics engines. PhysX also uses a more unified architecture to handle all physics calculations the same way.

Ageia made its PhysX API free to use in the summer of 2007. This is really great for many projects, especially if you are writing an open source project or do not have the budget for a big expensive physics engine. While there are already C# Wrappers around to use PhysX in XNA, it is still limited to Windows because you can't run any native code with XNA on the Xbox 360. If you can live with that limitation, PhysX is currently the best choice for getting a very solid and feature rich physics engine into your game. At the time I wrote the XNA Racing Game, I did not know much about this great physics engine except for some nice samples and the games that were using it. After using it a bit, you learn quickly that it can boost productivity quite a lot and keep your head clear for game logic programming (you won't have to figure out your own physics programming problems).

You can find more information about PhysX on the official website at www.ageia.com.

Havok

Havok is the name of the very popular and widely known Havok Game Dynamics SDK (currently at version 4, released in 2006). It is also the name of the company that develops this SDK. T the first SDK (v 1.0) was released in 2000. More than 100 games use the Havok physics engine today, the most famous of which is Half-Life 2. The Source engine by Valve also uses Havok and is based on Half-Life. Havok is mainly used by first-person shooter games, but some other game genres also use the Havok engine.

Havok is available on many platforms including the PC (Windows and Linux) and almost every console that came out since it was released (Xbox, Xbox 360, PS 2, PS 3, WII, Game Cube). It is written in C/C++ and is very portable to any system that allows compiling C code. For you, as a .NET developer, there is not much support. While there may be wrappers out there, I have not heard of any .NET game or engine that uses Havok.

This physics engine is not only used in games, but it is also available in 3D Studio Max, which uses the middleware internally and is quite popular in the 3D artist community for simulating physics effects. In previous versions, it was implemented as a plug-in named reactor. In recent versions, it is implemented into the basic version of 3D Studio Max. Havok was even used in the movie production of the *Matrix* trilogy.

Havok supports two major physics operations. Effect physics are used for anything that does not affect the game play and they can even be offloaded to a GPU that supports Shader Model 3.0 such as the

GeForce 7x and 8x series, especially if the GPU is fast. Then there are game physics, which are calculated on the CPU. Havok is the main competitor of PhysX. It proves that you can do really great things without having an extra PPU. Even the Half-Life 2 game from 2004, proved that it was possible to improve game play with pretty good physics without an extra PPU.

You can find more information about Havok on the official website at www.havok.com/.

ODE

ODE stands for Open Dynamics Engine, and unlike PhysX and Havok it's not a commercial engine, which may be more interesting to most beginner developers or teams that just don't have the money to use a big commercial physics engine.

ODE is an open source physics engine, which uses the BSD license (or LGPL if you like that). It was started in 2001, and many games have been developed with it. It is not, however, as feature-complete as PhysX or Havok and certainly not that successful.

ODE basically supports rigid body dynamics and collision detection. You will still have a lot of work to do for more advanced physics. ODE, however, gives you a nice basic framework, which gives you all the basic geometries (such as boxes, spheres, cylinders, and so on) and physics calculations you need to do some basic physics demos. There are also frameworks that have been built on top of ODE or use ODE.

Now comes the cool part: ODE has a nice .NET wrapper called ODE.NET, which can be found on the following website. There are several samples available. It is always nice to see some .NET code between all these physics engines, which are all using C++ code and only give you C++ samples. The samples show basic physics problems such as stacking boxes and pushing them over, as well as rag-doll physics and controlling basic objects such as cars or toys are also presented on ODE.NET at www.thejamesrainenetwork.co.uk/ode/ode.html.

You can also take a look at the official website of ODE. If it is down, check out the Wikipedia entry about the Open Dynamics Engine at www.ode.org/.

Other

There are many other physics engines available and I certainly do not know about all of them. Maybe there are even other useful engines that can be used in .NET, but I have not found any other wrappers that were as useful as ODE.NET.

Here are a couple of other physics engines I have encountered:

❑ Farseer Physics Engine is a 2D Physics engine with some nice effects. It is not really useful, however, if you need a 3D physics engine like we do for the XNA Racing Game. It can be a useful and fun way to try out some easier ideas in 2D first. Check out the samples to learn more. You can check this project out at www.codeplex.com/FarseerPhysics.

❑ XPA is a physics API designed specifically for XNA. It is based on OPAL (Open Physics Abstraction Layer) and uses ODE (see above) right now. It is planned to support the XNA Bullet Engine (also called BulletX, see below) at a later point in time to run on both the Xbox 360 and Windows. While XPA sounds promising, even at the time of writing the second edition of this book, it is far from complete and useable yet. You should check it out from time to time at www.codeplex.com/xnadevru.

❑ Newton Game Dynamics is a free physics engine with really nice samples and good documentation. It is used both recreationally and commercially. It also supports the Windows, Mac, and Linux platforms. Nearly a year ago, there was a .NET wrapper for this engine, but the source code for the base engine was not available. This makes it very hard to implement it into .NET or to change it if you want to improve the engine. ODE, on the other hand, is highly customizable to meet your every need. Check it out at www.newtondynamics.com/.

❑ Tokamak Game Physics is another nice physics engine that is completely free to use for both noncommercial and commercial projects. It also has quite a few samples and tutorials. Once again, there is no source code available for the core engine itself, just for the samples. Sadly this engine has not been updated for almost two years now. Furthermore, the forum is completely overrun by spam. The last news entry was March 2005. I implemented a simple .NET wrapper a few years back and played around with the engine a little bit, but I never found the time to get any further. Today, I would probably use one of the other available engines, especially ODE.NET because it already works with .NET. Visit www.tokamakphysics.com/.

❑ Physics and Math Library (also called Game Physics Engine) is a German-based engine that was originally developed for a book. It focuses on implementing many of the available features of the commercial engines such as Havok and PhysX. While it is free to use, I could not find many screenshots or forum discussions. It is hard to tell if this engine type is really worth the effort you would probably put into it (making it run in your project and maybe even porting it to .NET). The project, however, looks pretty promising. The website is http://game-physics-engine.info/.

❑ nV Physics Engine (also called The Physics Engine) has a nice website and some screenshots on it (which is always good for a website presenting a product). It looks promising but all samples are C++ again and you probably don't even have access to the source code. The website is www.thephysicsengine.com/.

❑ Bullet Physics Library is yet another free physics engine. This engine is hosted by sourceforge.net. It includes the full source code. The author of the Bullet Physics Library worked at Havok before. The Bullets Physics engine is already used by several engines, especially open source engines and the 3D modeler tool Blender 3D. It also supports the latest file formats and has several advanced features already. The website is www.continuousphysics.com/Bullet/. ∎

Many more physics engines are available, especially smaller ones, but it is not easy to use them in .NET. Try searching for something specific when you encounter a certain problem and don't really need a full-blown physics engine. The lack of .NET physics engines doesn't have much to do with XNA. It is just annoying that you can't use them on the Xbox 360 because they are developed in C++ and use unmanaged code.

But even if you don't use a physics engine in the end, checking them out and playing around with the many available samples and tutorials may provide you with a clearer picture of what is possible with a physics engine. Then you can determine which parts will probably be hard to re-implement if you do it yourself. You don't really need a complex physics engine in the Racing Game. While it would be nice to have a good solid foundation, you are back to doing it yourself because implementing a physics engine is so difficult in .NET and because you want the game to run on the Xbox 360, too.

Implementing Physics

Time to dive a little bit deeper into the implementation of the physics required for your Racing Game. You saw some of the features of the many powerful physics engines available today, but because it is not easy to implement them and because they are not written in .NET you are going to continue implementing physics in your own way.

You handled some of the car controlling and simple gravity at the beginning of the chapter. The element you are currently missing is an accurate collision detection system for your car. The car should be stopped when you crash into one of the guard rails. You are also going to check some of the more complex situations such as driving through loopings. Loopings are actually not hard to implement. Thanks to the track generation code from the last chapter, they can be added to your tracks quite easily by putting two of the spline points on top of each other. When driving along the road, the loopings are almost handled automatically, if your physics system for the car is handling all the car forces correctly.

Handling Loopings

Before you continue with the hard stuff (collision detection and response, which is actually most of the code in the CarPhysics class), please take a look at Figure 13-8, which simply shows how the forces act on your car when you drive through a looping.

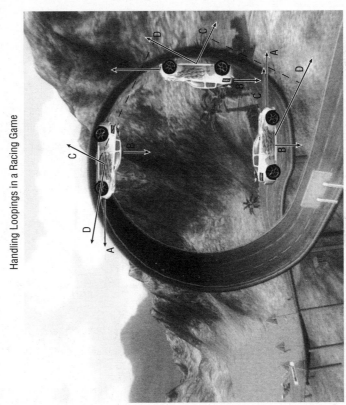

Handling Loopings in a Racing Game

A Car Engine Force
B Gravity always pulls us down
C Momentum from the previous movement
D Current resulting force for the car

Figure 13-8

If you put the car on the top part of the looping without applying any forces, gravity (red) will pull it down and you will not be able to move or drive the car because you will lose contact with the road immediately. So to get to the top part of the looping, the car must be always pushed toward the road, which is upwards at the top of the looping. This force must be stronger than the gravity or your car will lose contact with the road and begin to fall down again (see Figure 13-9). It is important that you have enough momentum to keep the car on the road. Momentum is the force the car had from the car's previous movement in the current time frame you are looking at.

Situations Where the Car Is Too Slow for Loopings

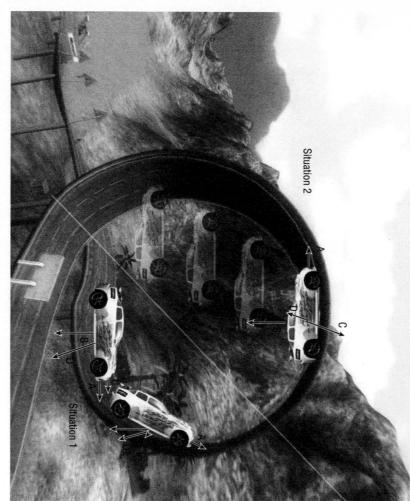

Figure 13-9

Situation 1: Car is too slow to even get up to the first part of the looping. Gravity is stronger than the decreasing momentum and the car engine together. Finally the car stops and falls down again (basically rolls/slides back).

If you drive straight up a wall (with a ramp in front of it to get some momentum first), the gravity pulls you down, and after a while you are going to lose all of the momentum and finally fall down. Because looping is always changing the direction of the car, you are able to keep the car on the road relatively easily. Beating gravity is no big deal if you have a centrifugal force that is stronger than the gravity. Figure 13-10 shows you an example of circling around a ball attached to a string. Even with a slow swinging force, you will be able to let the ball fly in circles. The faster you go, the less you will notice the gravity the ball usually has. It will just get harder to keep the string in your hand because the ball is strongly pulling on it, thanks to the centrifugal force.

You can see the centrifugal force pushes the ball away from the hand and the gravity is relatively slow in comparison to that force when you move the ball fast enough. The momentum keeps the ball in the circulating motion, even if you stop moving your hand.

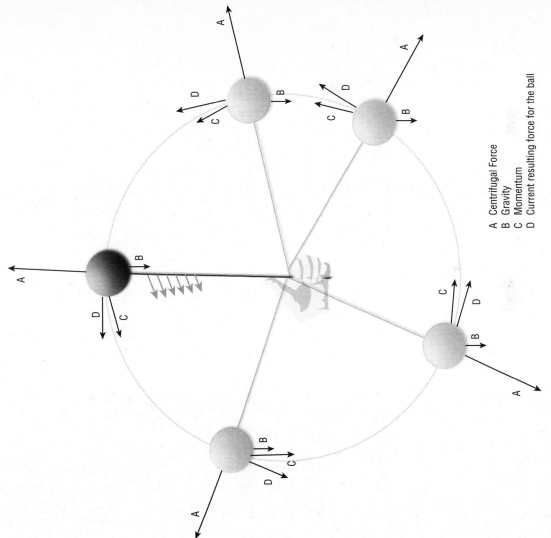

Centrifugal Force on a Rotating Ball Attached to a String

A Centrifugal Force
B Gravity
C Momentum
D Current resulting force for the ball

Figure 13-10

Spring Physics

Most formulas for your game are simplified and the car movement is not as complex as it could be. You do not care much about the car engine, about any of the car internals, or use. It is possible to implement many more parameters to use the power, rpm, starting and stalling forces, better braking and friction formulas, and so on. For a more detailed description about car physics please check out the following link at www.racer.nl/reference/carphys.htm.

Because of your simplified car logic, many of these resulting effects are not implemented, such as pitching the car backwards when you accelerate and forward when you brake. But you still can implement this in a simplified way yourself.

All car wheels are connected to springs on the car allowing the car to stay more stable on the road even if you drive over smaller bumps on the road. When you accelerate, the wheels push the car forward but it takes a while until enough energy is created to move the huge mass of the car itself. The effect becomes even more apparent when you suddenly stop the car. The wheels stop, but the car itself is still in motion. Then the still moving car mass pulls the entire car forward and tilts the car a little bit (see Figure 13-11).

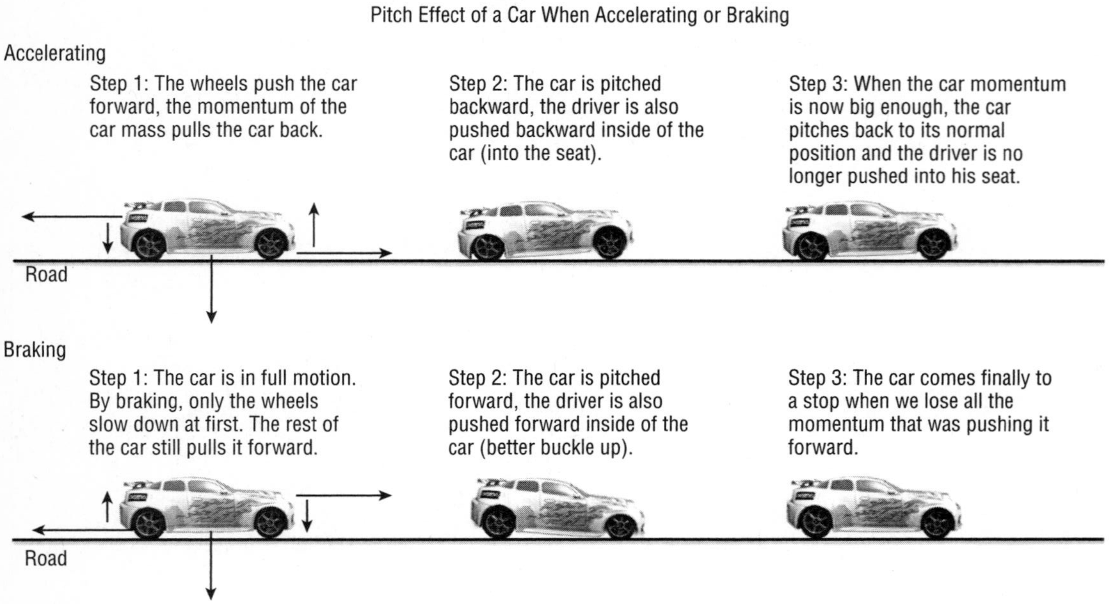

Pitch Effect of a Car When Accelerating or Braking

Accelerating

Road

Step 1: The wheels push the car forward, the momentum of the car mass pulls the car back.

Step 2: The car is pitched backward, the driver is also pushed backward inside of the car (into the seat).

Step 3: When the car momentum is now big enough, the car pitches back to its normal position and the driver is no longer pushed into his seat.

Braking

Road

Step 1: The car is in full motion. By braking, only the wheels slow down at first. The rest of the car still pulls it forward.

Step 2: The car is pitched forward, the driver is also pushed forward inside of the car (better buckle up).

Step 3: The car comes finally to a stop when we lose all the momentum that was pushing it forward.

Figure 13-11

Gravity always pushes you down, but different parts of the car, especially the wheels and the rest of the car, behave differently. The wheels are attached to springs on the car enabling the car to pitch forward and backwards, which happens when you accelerate or decelerate, even if you stay on a road that is not straight (if you drive uphill, the car will be pulled backwards).

You do not really have a representation of the springs. You also don't render the wheels the way they are shown in Figure 13-11. The car wheels go into the ground if the car is pitched, but because you don't see the car from the side you will not notice it in the game. The chase camera is always behind the car. Thus, you are going to see most of the pitch effect just from the top of and behind the car.

Because the effect is relatively simply described, you can pitch the car whenever the speed changes for it, as follows:

- ❑ When accelerating, pitch the car backwards — the faster you are accelerating, the bigger the pitch angle is going to be.

- ❑ When braking, pitch the car forward — this pitch effect is usually stronger than the accelerating pitch effect because you brake much faster than you accelerate the car.

You already saw this behavior in the last game, XNA Shooter, where your own ship was rotated horizontally and vertically when you moved in either direction. The same formula can be used for the car, too. To fix the problem that the wheels and the rest of the car would disappear into the road, you are going to limit the effect, as follows:

```
// Calculate pitch depending on the force
float speedChange = speed - oldSpeed;
// Limit speed change, never apply more than 8 mph change per sec.
if (speedChange < -8 * moveFactor)
    speedChange = -8 * moveFactor;
if (speedChange > 8 * moveFactor)
    speedChange = 8 * moveFactor;
carPitch = speedChange;
```

When the car is not changing its speed, the car pitch value will stay 0 and behave correctly. If you are accelerating or decelerating the car, it also behaves the correct way. But even after applying a better smoothing formula, the effect does not look very convincing. In the real world, the car would pitch forward and then backwards, swinging out until the springs of the cars lose all force to friction.

All you need now is to let the car swing forward and backwards with a simple spring formula. The `SpringPhysicsObject` class (see Figure 13-12) of the Racing Game helps you with that. It calculates the position of a single object with a certain mass attached to a spring with a specific spring constant. This position swings up and down, but it slows down through the friction constant also used in this class. You are going to use a big mass and a strong friction. As a result, the car achieves a slow pitch effect, which becomes weaker very quickly. You don't want the car to bounce around.

This helper class is directly used in the `CarPhysics` class. It is initialized with the `CarMass` constant — 1.5 for the friction and 120 for the spring constant (both relatively high values). The initial position for the virtual spring object is 0 (car in its normal state):

```
/// <summary>
/// Car pitch physics helper for a simple spring effect for
/// accelerating, decelerating and crashing.
/// </summary>
SpringPhysicsObject carPitchPhysics = new SpringPhysicsObject(
    CarMass, 1.5f, 120, 0);
```

To update the current virtual spring object position when the car changes speed, you can use the `ChangePos` helper method, as follows:

```
carPitchPhysics.ChangePos(speedChange);
```

Finally, you simply call Simulate with the current time factor for this frame to simulate the pitch behavior. Then, when rendering, you are going to use the pos value of this class to get the current pitch value, as follows:

```
// Handle pitch spring
carPitchPhysics.Simulate(moveFactor);
```

Figure 13-12

The interesting part of the SpringPhysicsObject class is obviously the Simulate method. All the other methods only set values. To understand what the spring formula does, you have to know about the restoring force for the spring by applying Hooke's law to the well known $F = m * a$ formula.

Hooke's law describes how stress is directly proportional to strain, using a constant pressure value. In this way elasticity, spring, stress, and strain physics can be described.

If you want to read more about Hooke's law, please read a good formulary book or check out the Internet. Wikipedia and Wolfram Research (http://scienceworld.wolfram.com) have great articles about many physics problems.

You are just going to use the simple spring formula $F = -k * x$ where F is the restoring force that pulls the object attached to your spring back or forward and k is the spring constant. Figure 13-13 describes this formula and the effect it has over time on the spring object you are going to use for the car pitch effect.

When no force is acting on the object and it is in the initial position (0), the object will stay that way (no position change). But if you pull it down the spring expands and forces the object back to its initial position. When it reaches the position 0 again, the spring restoring force is also back to zero. The speed of the attached object, however, is still fast and its momentum still pushes it up. The spring restoring force becomes negative now and prevents the object from moving up when it reaches its highest position of 1. Now the restoring force is −1 and that pulls the object down again. When it is at the bottom position, the game starts from the beginning again.

The only thing that slows you down is friction, which should be very strong hereto ensure the car does not bounce around too much. Please also note that you are ignoring gravity here. It is not really important for your car pitch effect because the car handles gravity itself. For the spring effect, you can safely ignore gravity because it pulls everything down to the same direction and does not affect any calculations.

The code to make this all work is in the Simulate method. You should be able to quickly understand it with the help of the knowledge you just acquired:

```
/// <summary>
/// Simulate spring formular using the timeChange.
/// The velocity is increased by the timeChange * force / mass,
/// the position is then timeChange * velocity.
/// </summary>
public void Simulate(float timeChange)
{
    // Calculate force again
    force += -pos * springConstant;
    // Calculate velocity
    velocity = force / mass;
    // And apply it to the current position
    pos += timeChange * velocity;
    // Apply friction
    force *= 1.0f - (timeChange * friction);
} // Simulate(timeChange)
```

The SpringPhysicsObject class can be found in the Game Physics namespace (see Figure 13-13). If you want to add more physics classes and try to implement more physics behaviors, you should do it in this namespace. It gets easier when you try to reuse some of the physics in future projects; simply copy over and use the physics namespace.

Collision Detection

The final task for this chapter is to do the collision detection for the car and the guard rails. The car cannot collide with any other cars because you are the only car on the road. I also made sure that there are no other objects on the road to collide with. Collision detection, and especially the response, would be a lot more complex if you allowed other objects on the road, such as lanterns, signs, trash cans, and so on. If these objects are found on the road, you would have to kick them away with your car if you hit them. Then again, these objects need to collide with one another and also with the surrounding world.

If you have a good physics engine, this is possible. However, it is still a lot of work to tweak these objects and the general physics constants. Plus, you must constantly test all the different kinds of collisions that can occur. It would probably be fun to implement such techniques and play around with them. Because XNA doesn't have a full-blown physics engine, getting the basics up and running would take longer than the whole project took.

The principles for collision detection and collision response are still the same. You can, however, simplify them to your needs and only involve the car and the guard rails. Because the guard rails are indestructible, the only object that is affected by any collision is your car.

The biggest part of the physics in the Rocket Commander game was the asteroid-to-asteroid collision detection and optimization. The collision response is not very complex. Thanks to the many unit tests, even the basic collision detection could be done in a very simple way.

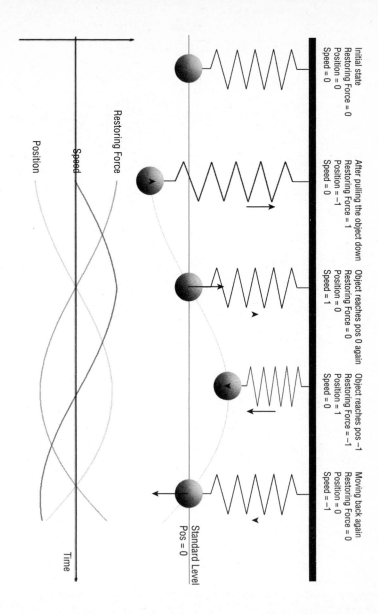

Figure 13-13

PhysicsAsteroidManager

The `TestAsteroidPhysicsSmallScene` unit test of the `PhysicsAsteroidManager` class in Rocket Commander shows a good way to test collision detection. The unit test enables you to press 1–7 to test out various scenarios and shows the result of an asteroid collision event.

Figure 13-14 shows this unit test in action by using two asteroids of the same size flying toward each other and bouncing off in opposite directions after the collision happens. The method `SetupScene` is used to set the asteroids to their initial positions while the unit test itself handles all the collision testing.

```
case 2:
    // Collide with crazy movement vectors
    AddAsteroid(new Vector3(-35, +19, 8) * (-2),
        12.5f, asteroidModel.ObjectSize,
        new Vector3(-35, +19, 8));
    AddAsteroid(new Vector3(+15, 40, 14) * (-2),
```

```
    12.5f, asteroidModel.ObjectSize,
    new Vector3(+15, 40, 14));
    break;
```

The `TestAsteroidPhysicsSmallScene` unit test then calls the `HandleSectorPhysics` method. This method checks all asteroids in a certain sector and performs a simple bounding spheres test if they are too close to one another and if you should handle such a collision.

The method not only checks the asteroids from your own sector, but also all asteroids from all surrounding sectors, which could collide with one of your own asteroids. Even with very good sector optimization, there are still several thousand collision detection checks being performed in each frame of Rocket Commander. Thus, it gets slower the more asteroids you have. For this reason, it is a good thing that Rocket Commander XNA now uses two different threads to handle the physics and the rendering code.

Figure 13-14

The collision detection adds up the radii of both asteroids to determine if they are smaller together than is physically possible. If so, a collision has occurred and you have to handle it. The following code shows the collision test for one single sector. The code for testing all surrounding sectors is similar, but a lot longer.

```
// Only check this sector! Crosscheck with any other asteroid in
// this sector.
foreach (Asteroid otherAsteroid in thisSectorAsteroids)
    if (asteroid != otherAsteroid)
    {
```

```
        float maxAllowedDistance =
            otherAsteroid.collisionRadius +
            asteroid.collisionRadius;
        // Distance smaller than max. allowed distance?
        if ((otherAsteroid.position -
            asteroid.position).LengthSq() <
            maxAllowedDistance * maxAllowedDistance)
        {
            HandleAsteroidCollision(asteroid, otherAsteroid);
        } // if (otherAsteroid.position)
    } // foreach if (asteroid)
```

The `HandleAsteroidCollision` method now handles a collision and it moves the asteroids away from one another so they don't intersect:

```
// Put both circles outside of the collision
// Add 1% to add a little distance between collided objects!
otherAsteroid.position = middle +
    otherPositionRel * otherAsteroid.collisionRadius * 1.015f;
asteroid.position = middle +
    positionRel * asteroid.collisionRadius * 1.015f;
```

Then the method reflects both movement vectors of the two asteroids away from the collision plane (the purple line in Figure 13-14) by using the total collision force and applying it to the masses of the asteroids. This way, a smaller asteroid gets pushed away by a bigger asteroid with a far greater force than the other way around. Check out the unit tests to see this behavior in action.

The method is actually quite long. It performs extra checking. It also calculates masses and directions, and even adds rotation speed to the asteroids. The code for handling the collision resembles the following:

```
// Normalize movement
Vector3 asteroidDirection = asteroid.movement;
asteroidDirection.Normalize();
Vector3 otherAsteroidDirection = otherAsteroid.movement;
otherAsteroidDirection.Normalize();
// Get collision strength (1 if pointing in same direction,
// 0 if 90 degrees) for both asteroids.
float asteroidCollisionStrength = Math.Abs(Vector3.Dot(
    asteroidDirection, asteroidNormal));
float otherAsteroidCollisionStrength = Math.Abs(Vector3.Dot(
    otherAsteroidDirection, otherAsteroidNormal));
// Calculate reflection vectors from the asteroid direction and the
// normal towards the reflection plane.
Vector3 asteroidReflection =
    Reflect Vector(asteroidDirection, asteroidNormal);
Vector3 otherAsteroidReflection =
    ReflectVector(otherAsteroidDirection, otherAsteroidNormal);
// Make sure the strength is calculated correctly
// We have also to correct the reflection vector if the length was 0,
// use the normal vector instead.
if (asteroidReflection.Length() <= 0.01f)
{
    asteroidCollisionStrength = otherAsteroidCollisionStrength;
    asteroidReflection = asteroidNormal;
```

```
    } // if (asteroidDirection.Length)
if (otherAsteroidDirection.Length() <= 0.01f)
{
    otherAsteroidCollisionStrength = asteroidCollisionStrength;
    otherAsteroidReflection = otherAsteroidNormal;
} // if (otherAsteroidDirection.Length)
// Ok, now the complicated part, everything above was really easy!
asteroid.movement = asteroidReflection *
    // So, first we have to reflect our current movement speed.
    // This will be scaled to 1-strength to only account the reflection
    // amount (imagine a collision with a static wall). In most cases
    // Strength is close to 1 and this reflection will be very small.
    ((1 - asteroidCollisionStrength) * asteroidSpeed +
    // And finally we have to add the impuls, which is calculated
    // by the formula ((m1-m2)*v1 + 2*m2*v2)/(m1+m2), see
    // http://de.wikipedia.org/wiki/Sto%C3%9F_%28Physik%29 for more help.
    (asteroidCollisionStrength *
    (Math.Abs(asteroidMass - otherAsteroidMass) * asteroidSpeed +
    (2 * otherAsteroidMass * otherAsteroidSpeed)) / bothMasses));
    // Same for other asteroid, just with asteroid and otherAsteroid
    // inverted.
    otherAsteroid.movement = otherAsteroidReflection *
    // Same as above.
    ((1 - otherAsteroidCollisionStrength) * otherAsteroidSpeed +
    (otherAsteroidCollisionStrength *
    (Math.Abs(otherAsteroidMass - asteroidMass) * otherAsteroidSpeed +
    (2 * asteroidMass * asteroidSpeed)) / bothMasses));
```

Car Collision

Thanks to the preceding code, I knew how to determine whether or not the car would collide with one of the guard rails. I simply built two collision planes, one for each guard rail, and then I would check to see if any of the four wheels collide with these collision planes. Because the car is not a sphere, and can't be handled as easily as the asteroids, all four sides have to be checked. You can, however, just check the four wheel positions (or at least the most outer parts of the car) to do the basic collision detection (see Figure 13-15).

The code for these collision checks can be found in the `ApplyGravityAndCheckForCollisions` method of the `CarPhysics` class. The code basically goes through all four car corners to check if any are not between the collision planes (see the two lines on either side of the road in Figure 13-15). The four car corners are defined by calculating the car corners based on actual car length and width values:

```
// Check all 4 corner points of our car.
Vector3 carRight = Vector3.Cross(carDir, carUp);
Vector3 carLeft = -carRight;
// Car dimensions are 2.6m (width) x 5.6m (length) x 1.8m (height)
// Note: This could be improved by using more points or using
// the actual car geometry.
// Note: We ignore the height, this way the collision is simpler.
// We then check the height above the road to see if we are flying
// above the guard rails out into the landscape.
Vector3[] carCorners = new Vector3[]
{
```

```
    // Top left
    pos + carDir * 5.6f/2.0f - carRight * 2.6f/2.0f,
    // Top right
    pos + carDir * 5.6f/2.0f + carRight * 2.6f/2.0f,
    // Bottom right
    pos - carDir * 5.6f/2.0f + carRight * 2.6f/2.0f,
    // Bottom left
    pos - carDir * 5.6f/2.0f - carRight * 2.6f/2.0f,
};
```

Car with Guard Rail Collisions

Car is crashing into the left
guard rail.

Collision happens at the front
left side of the car. Collision
response is to rotate the car
to the right and slow it down
due to the crash.

Car is crashing into the right
guard rail.

Collision happens at the front
right side of the car. Collision
response is to rotate the car
to the left and slow it down
due to the crash.

If we collide with an angle of
45 degrees or more, the car
does a full stop and we hear
the total crash sound.

Figure 13-15

The collision test is now relatively easy, thanks to all the helper values that have been calculated before
in this method:

```
// Check for each corner if we collide with the guard rail
for (int num = 0; num < carCorners.Length; num++)
```

```
{
    // Hit any guardrail?
    float leftDist = Vector3Helper.DistanceToLine(
        carCorners[num], guardrailLeft, nextGuardrailLeft);
    float rightDist = Vector3Helper.DistanceToLine(
        carCorners[num], guardrailRight, nextGuardrailRight);
    // If we are closer than 0.1f, thats a collision!
    if (leftDist < 0.1f ||
        // Also include the case where we are farther away from rightDist
        // than the road is wide.
        rightDist > roadWidth)
    {
        // Handle collision with left guard rail here
    } // if (leftDist < 0.1f)
    if (rightDist < 0.1f ||
        // Also include the case where we are farther away from leftDist
        // than the road is wide.
        leftDist > roadWidth)
    {
        // Handle collision with right guard rail here
    } // if (rightDist < 0.1f)
} // for (num)
```

The final part of the collision handling is now to respond to this collision event. But before you do that, you should set some field in your unit test to show you that your collision detection code works. Or just set a breakpoint inside the "if" statement blocks to see if you ever reach the conditions.

Now all you have to do is to play the crash sound and rotate the car around depending on which of the four car corners had the collision. The car will also be slowed down. Allow the camera to wobble a bit to notify the player that he just crashed. If the collision was straight ahead (0–45 degrees to the wall), you immediately stop the car and play the total crash sound:

```
// Force car back on the road, for that calculate impulse and
// collision direction (same stuff as in Rocket Commander).
Vector3 collisionDir =
    Vector3.Reflect(carDir, guardrailRightNormal);
float collisionAngle =
    Vector3Helper.GetAngleBetweenVectors(
        carLeft, guardrailRightNormal);
// Flip at 180 degrees (if driving in wrong direction)
if (collisionAngle > MathHelper.Pi / 2)
    collisionAngle -= MathHelper.Pi;
// Just correct rotation if collison happened at 0-45 degrees (slowly)
if (Math.Abs(collisionAngle) < MathHelper.Pi / 4.0f)
{
    // Play crash sound
    Sound.PlayCrashSound(false);
    // For front wheels to full collision rotation, for back half!
    if (num < 2)
    {
        rotateCarAfterCollision = +collisionAngle / 1.5f;
        speed *= 0.935f;//0.85f;
        if (viewDistance > 0.75f)
```

```
        viewDistance -= 0.1f;//0.15f;
    } // if (num)
    else
    {
        rotateCarAfterCollision = +collisionAngle / 2.5f;
        //slowdownCarAfterCollision = 0.8f;
        speed *= 0.96f;//0.9f;
        if (viewDistance > 0.75f)
            viewDistance -= 0.05f;//0.1f;
    } // else
    // Shake camera
    ChaseCamera.SetCameraWobbel(0.00075f * speed);
} // if (collisionAngle)
// If 90-45 degrees (in either direction), make frontal crash
else if (Math.Abs(collisionAngle) < MathHelper.Pi * 3.0f / 4.0f)
{
    // Also rotate car if less than 60 degrees
    if (Math.Abs(collisionAngle) < MathHelper.Pi / 3.0f)
        rotateCarAfterCollision = +collisionAngle / 3.0f;
    // Play crash sound
    Sound.PlayCrashSound(true);
    // Shake camera
    ChaseCamera.SetCameraWobbel(0.005f * speed);
    // Just stop car!
    speed = 0;
} // if (collisionAngle)
// For all collisions, kill the current car force
carForce = Vector3.Zero;
// Always make sure we are OUTSIDE of the collision range for
// the next frame. But first find out how much we have to move.
float speedDistanceToGuardrails =
    speed * Math.Abs(Vector3.Dot(carDir, guardrailLeftNormal));
if (rightDist > 0)
{
    float correctCarPosValue = (rightDist + 0.01f +//0.11f +
        0.1f * speedDistanceToGuardrails * moveFactor);
    carPos += correctCarPosValue * guardrailRightNormal;
} // if (rightDist)
```

With this code, you are now able to test the `TestCarPhysicsOnPlaneWithGuardRails` unit test and fine-tune the crash into the guard rails. The code for the game is a little bit more complex, but the same rules apply and all the collision code and physics calculations are exactly the same as you use for the unit test.

Challenge: Figure Out the Road Collision

In the previous chapter, I let you off easily, so this time it will be a little harder. Your job is to check out the `CarPhysics` class and to figure out how the same physics code and collision detection is actually used in the Racing Game. You need to determine how the code keeps the car on the road and how it handles the collision with the guard rails, which are not straight lines as in the unit test.

The best thing for this job would be to write a unit test that renders the road and enables you to control the car the same way you controlled it in the TestCarPhysicsOnPlaneWithGuardRails unit test, and the same way it is actually handled in the game itself. But you can also use the game to test the physics by setting a breakpoint in the Update method of the CarPhysics class and then stepping through the code to see how the variables change. Figure 13-16 shows such a unit test in action.

You can of course also try to improve the physics or maybe even try to implement a physics engine if you are really eager to extend the game and add more features. At least on the Windows platform this can be an opportunity to change the game play, add effects, and to handle more complex collision scenarios.

If you don't know where to look or how the road can use the same simple collision logic as the simple plane unit test does, please look at the UpdateCarMatrixAndCamera method of CarPhysics and the GetTrackPositionMatrix of the Track class. The track matrix transforms the current road piece into a space that can be used in the exact same way you used the car matrix in the simple plane collision unit test.

Figure 13-16

Summary

Physics engines are an important part of games today. However, it is not easy to get an existing physics engine implemented into an XNA game. But you can still implement physics your own way to ensure that the game runs on the Xbox 360, where unmanaged code is not allowed.

There are many topics related to physics, and it is certainly not easy to implement all physics elements yourself. Even with a good physics engine, you still have to do a lot of fine-tuning and testing. However, if another game has great physics and uses the laws of physics in a way that does not destroy the game play or the fun of the game, the other game will appear superior to one that only has very basic rules. But you should also be aware of the work associated with physics. You can probably guess by this chapter's length and position in this book that physics is not the easiest topic, especially for beginners. Although this chapter did not cover all possibilities, you did take a nice tour through available physics engines. If you are interested in reading more about physics, there is a lot of information available both on the Web and in many good books and series of books such as the *Game Programming Gems*.

The Racing Game and the game logic and how everything else is handled in the game is discussed in the next chapter. Other games of this book also used a little bit of physics, but you can get away with ignoring many other issues. For example, the XNA Shooter only handles ship, unit, and projectile movements and handles simple collisions by checking distances. But the game works and that is what counts in the end. In the same manner you only implemented what was necessary for the Racing Game — nothing more, and nothing less.

In this chapter you learned about the following topics, which are all used in the Racing Game:

□ Newton's Laws of Motion may be old, but they are still useful and allow you to quickly implement simple physics into your game. You also saw that the famous $F = m * a$ formula was used several times. It is the most important formula you need for most physics calculations.

□ Always keep the problems as simple as possible; split them up into smaller problems and write unit tests to figure out what to do next. You also won't end up implementing any unnecessary code that will not be used later anyway.

□ You learned all about the physics engines that are available today: PhysX and Havok are the major players here. They are, however, both commercial engines and you can't just plug them into XNA and expect them to work on your Xbox 360 because they use unmanaged code, which is not supported or even allowed on the Xbox 360 with XNA. Because they are expensive you will probably be better off using one of the free alternatives, which have great samples and tutorials, but suffer from the same lack of .NET support. ODE.NET is a nice solution. A lot of work has already been done with it, and although it just supports some basic features, it is still a very powerful physics engine that can save you months of work.

□ Then you went step by step through the problems you encounter in a Racing Game such as driving through loopings, handling spring physics, and handling the collision detection. A more complex collision detection system was used in Rocket Commander, but the collisions themselves were pretty simple because you only checked if the bounding spheres collide.

□ After detecting a collision, it must be handled, and when the collision detection is accurate you will spend most of the time tweaking this code to ensure that the collision feels real. In the Racing Game, I did not have much time to fine-tune a lot, but the basic rules are implemented. So, it should be possible for anyone that is interested to improve the game and maybe add more physics collisions and calculations.

In Chapter 14, you learn all about the Racing Game and how to create modifications, which will be pretty exciting.

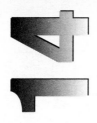

14

Fine-Tuning and "Modding" the Racing Game

You are finally going to learn about all the details of the Racing Game here. In this chapter, you learn all about the game screens used in the racing game and the game logic, the scoring system, and everything else you need for the game itself. Most of the rendering techniques for the landscape and the track were already discussed in Chapter 12, but this chapter shines a little more light on the whole shadow mapping thing. Thanks to the previous chapter, which covered everything about the game physics and car controlling, you should now be able to plug in this code and start actually testing out the game itself.

The whole purpose of this chapter is to get you familiar with the racing game and the underlying code. At the end of this chapter you should know everything you need to create your own game modifications (better known as *mods*) of the racing game. A game modification can be as simple as just changing a couple of graphics and 3D models or it can change the whole game logic in a way that it is no longer a racing game. The Rocket Commander game, for example, was also mod-able, but the game logic and the rendering code itself were pretty much fixed. You could more or less just change the models and add a little bit of game logic. Although most Rocket Commander mods looked quite different (see Figure 14-1), the game logic was always similar. The game principle in Rocket Commander is always to fly around and avoid colliding with certain objects (such as asteroids) while also collecting items such as health, fruits, pizza pieces, and so on. Some mods had an even faster game speed; other mods were much slower and focused on solving puzzles like collecting the correct ingredients or fruits (Pizza Commander and Fruit Commander). The good thing about creating mods in Rocket Commander was that it was relatively easy to change the original game. If there are just a couple of different 3D models it is simple to change them. It was also not hard to change the game logic because you would only have to worry about the Mission and the Player classes; the rest of the classes were just used for the menu and graphics rendering engine.

The latest mod (at the time of this writing) is Canyon Commander, and it shows that the graphics and game play can be changed quite a lot without much effort. The mod was created by a .NET beginner in Canada and this was his first game project. Quite impressive I would say.

Rocket Commander Mods

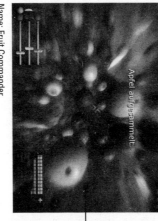

Name: Rocket Commander
Development time: 4 weeks (whole game)
Game: Avoid asteroids, collect items, fly fast.
First .NET 2.0 game ever.
Game was made to help beginners programming games in .NET, but the game is also fun.
Over 120,000 online played games in 2006.

Name: Flower Commander
Development time: 4 hours
Game: Collect flowers instead of avoiding asteroids.
The rest of the game stayed the same.
Code changes were pretty easy.
First Mod ever.

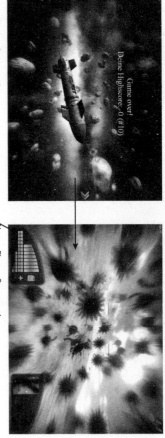

Name: Fruit Commander
Development time: Less than a week
Game: Keep your vitamin levels (A, B, and C) up.
Collecting fruits gives you more vitamins and health.
Collecting bad fruits will reduce health.
Quite a lot of UI, 3D model, and code changes.

Name: Canyon Commander
Development time: Maybe 2 weeks
Game: Fly through the canyons and collect items.
Game principle is still similar, but the game looks very different. The landscape rendering technique is also quite impressive and put together cleverly.
Not many changes in the UI or game logic, but a lot of new code for the landscape rendering through 3D models.

Figure 14-1

The racing game of this chapter, on the other hand, is a little bit more complex and allows even greater game changes. There is no reason why it should not be possible to take the code and 3D models and make a completely different game out of it. Landscape engines can be found in strategy or role-playing games, but even outdoor shooters or adventures could greatly benefit from an existing landscape rendering engine. It would, however, be a little bit more work to make a total mod and to change the whole game logic and even removing the code responsible for generating the roads when you don't need it for your mod.

It is obviously a lot easier to stay in the same genre and just change a couple of 3D models and maybe tweak some of the game parameters. This is what you are going to do at the end of this chapter with the

Speedy Racer mod, but you are free to implement your own game ideas yourself by then. The Speedy Racer mod exchanges the car model and also makes the road much wider and simpler to drive on, but it greatly increases the car speed. This mod is discussed in detail at the end of this chapter.

Game Concept

Before you get to the game screens and the game logic of the racing game itself, take a quick look at the original concept of the game so you can understand why certain implementations were made and why other parts are missing from the game. Some parts of the game were added later after most features from the concept were implemented. One example of this would be the shadow mapping, which is always a complex part of a game engine because you can spend a lot of time fine-tuning it until it looks right. Other things had to be skipped or were intentionally left out because they were just too complex to implement in such a short time frame. The best example here would be the obstacles on the road (for example, columns) into which the player could crash if he did not drive carefully (see Figure 14-2).

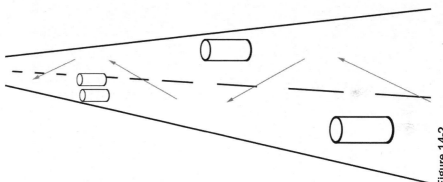

Figure 14-2

The main problem with this idea was to set the obstacle columns effectively. There is no level or track editor for the game as you learned in Chapter 12. All tracks are generated from splines and it would be hard to even set those obstacles as you learned in 3D Studio Max. It would cause even more problems game testing these objects and updating the collision checking system for these obstacles. In an earlier test version I used the road columns that the road stays on (see Figure 14-3) to test out this obstacle idea, but it did not look very convincing and driving on the road was already hard enough. A much better solution was to add destructible objects such as road signs, traffic lights, trash cans, and so on. As you already saw in the last chapter, the physics engine is not capable of handling many different objects. I just checks for any collision between the car and the guard rails and does a couple of physics calculations, and that's it.

After a couple of unit tests I decided to drop the idea and concentrate on the rest of the game. I also added tunnels and an easy way to set palms, signs, lanterns, and so on near the road. I also added a nice technique to automatically add landscape objects to each level near the roads.

The following text is directly from the initial game concept that was made in August 2006 — way before the Racing Game was developed later in 2006. Please be aware that it was written before the first XNA beta came out and I did not know many details about XNA in general. Please also note that the XNA Racing Game was written before XNA 1.0 was released, some of the code was updated at a later point and other code can still be improved. The game was not indented to show you the best way to program a physics engine or as a tutorial on how to use shadow mapping as some of the people in forums have asked or complained about. It is a tutorial and starter kit to get you started writing your own racing game or something similar. I hope the game is still very useful to you and shows you the basic steps required to create a game like this.

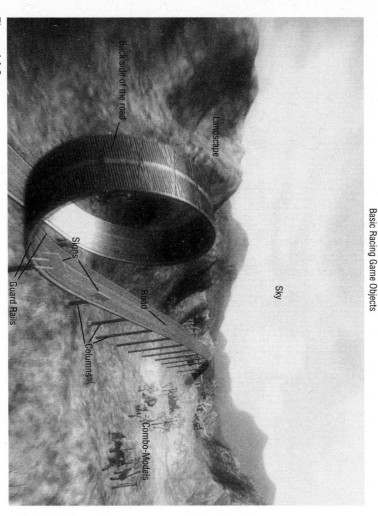

Basic Racing Game Objects

Landscape

Back side of the road

Sky

Signs

Road

Guard Rails

Columns

Combo-Models

Figure 14-3

Chapter 14: Fine-Tuning and "Modding" the Racing Game

Game Idea

The Racing Game is a simple 3D racing game. The player will see his car in the front and can directly control it with an Xbox 360 Controller (Xbox) or the mouse and keyboard (PC). The main goal in the game is to drive as fast as possible to the finish line, circumventing all obstacles in the way. Crashes do not hurt the player, but the car will lose all its speed and the total time for completing the track will be much higher. The player can't lose a game; he just takes a long time to complete a track. There are three tracks with different difficulty settings and a high-score list for each of the tracks. (Note: Neither multiple tracks nor the high-scores or trophies are implemented in this racing game version for this book; please check out the XNA Framework Racing Game Starter Kit for more details and additional features of the game, plus more mods.)

The graphics for this game (see Figure 14-4) are oriented on games such as Trackmania, Grand Tourismo, Need for Speed, and so on. Obviously these games took a very long time to develop and have highly polished graphics, which is not possible in this short time frame, so the main focus for this game is to create a simple and easy-to-learn racing game with just the basic features. The main graphics theme is located in the city (showing streets, some simple buildings, and some trees). The underground is done with the help of a simple 2D graphic, the tracks are auto-generated from a 2D image (using points in certain intervals). For additional difficulty, a height-map is used to create hills and make the track more difficult. (Please note that this idea was abandoned and instead real 3D data is now imported into the game.)

Figure 14-4

In the game, no other cars are around (as in Trackmania), which keeps the code simple and only requires collision checking with objects in the level. The game consists in the basic version of a main menu, three simple single-player tracks, and a highscore list for each of the tracks (time dependent).

More graphics sets (snow, desert, grassland, and so on), more tracks, and maybe even mods or multiplayer game code could be made at a later point (for example, by the XNA community).

Because of the short development time, the project was simplified to the basics of controlling the car and driving through the tracks. A simple physics system is also implemented and collision with static objects in the scene is checked each frame. All other ideas are left out of the basic game. This simplifies the game play and speeds up the learning curve.

The game is viewed from behind, showing the car in the front, the track in the middle, and some more objects and the sky far away. The sky is implemented with a sky cube map.

The XNA Racing Game Starter Kit will be programmed in C# using .NET 2.0 and XNA using XNA Game Studio Express (similar to Visual C# Express with DirectX). A big plus is using the XNA API and managed code in general, which helps you to write very easy-to-read code, which executes powerful functionality such as loading textures, using shaders, or displaying models with just one line of code.

The graphics are all .dds files. All models (Car, Trees, Effects, and so on) are modeled with 3D Studio Max 8 and exported into Microsoft DirectX .x files. Models will not use animations for easier understanding of the underlying code. (Note: As I later found out, XNA does not even support animated models out of the box.)

The game will not use any existing engine or additional complicated framework. Non-game programmers would not be familiar with it and this would only confuse anyone wanting to take a look at the source code. The game consists basically of these parts:

- ☐ Helper classes for texture loading, model loading, game screen handling, managing XNA, handling controls, and so on.

- ☐ Shader class to support rendering models (mainly the car) and the landscape with shader effects. (Note: I quickly found out that I underestimated the amount of landscape objects required to make the road and the landscape look at least somewhat decent.)

- ☐ Pre- and post-screen shader class to help you with rendering the sky and adding effects such as glow, motion blur, and color correction.

- ☐ Main menu class for starting a game, checking the highscores, and for quitting the game.

- ☐ Highscore game screen for showing the highscores and maybe even submitting them to an online server. Highscores are also saved locally, which can be viewed with this class as well. (Note: Because XNA does not support any networking and I wanted to use the same code for the PC and the Xbox 360 version, I left out sending the highscores to an online server.)

- ☐ Mission class to play the game.

That was almost the entire concept and I started coding as soon as I had the first XNA beta in my hands. Of course there were many more problems during the development of the project, but thanks to unit testing and updating the concept from time to time it was not hard to keep track of the general game idea. The hardest parts were definitely getting the landscape and track code working (see Chapter 12), along with the physics engine from Chapter 13. The shadow mapping is probably also not an easy thing for most inexperienced programmers, but I just implemented a shadow mapping engine into another engine a few months back, and by looking at the unfinished racing game I was sure that it would never look very good without implementing some kind of shadows.

Additional Features

If you take a look at the class overview of the whole racing game (see Figure 14-5), it looks quite complex, especially if you think about the short development period. The biggest help was the Rocket Commander project, which allowed me to quickly test out ideas, models, and rendering techniques with the help of its unit tests and code I added early in the development process. Later, when the XNA engine was standing on its own feet, I could move code over and continue testing in the new engine. For example, I found out early that my idea to generate the tracks from 2D images was not very clever and caused more problems than it solved. Implementing the basic tracks was not very hard, but when I needed access to 3D vertices I was happy to have some Managed DirectX code from the Rocket Commander game that allowed me to load .x files and use their vertices to generate an early track. Sadly, XNA does not support accessing or loading the vertices of imported 3D models; you could write you own content importer, but that was too much work because, at the time, I just wanted to test some tracks. I later changed the way tracks are imported and added many features (tunnels, road widths, road objects, palms, and so on). Tracks are now directly exported in 3D Studio Max into the Collada format and then imported in the game engine into a binary format (for quicker loading).

The following features were imported from previous projects (mostly from Rocket Commander):

❑ Helper classes such as the Log class for debugging, the versatile StringHelper class or other important classes such as the RandomHelper, Vector3Helper, or ColorHelper classes.

❑ The graphics engine was written from the ground up, but the basic ideas for handling textures, materials, models, fonts, and lines through special classes, which extend the functionality of XNA classes, was taken from Rocket Commander. Most classes in XNA are much simpler and did not do much at the beginning like the Model class, which just loaded an XNA model and displayed it with a couple lines of code. But later, the model rendering was improved quite a bit for higher performance (which is discussed later in this chapter) and the internal logic for the model class changed completely. Models were no longer rendered directly; instead, the shaders and meshes for each used 3D model were collected and rendered at the end of the frame together with all other meshes that use the same shader, material, and mesh data. This way, the rendering performance was improved by 200–300 percent on the Xbox 360. And thanks to the abstraction to the special model class, none of the code that used models had to be changed — it just got faster!

❑ The game screen logic was stolen 100 percent from Rocket Commander. I really like the idea behind it and it is very simple to implement.

❑ Shaders and other graphical classes such as the ParallaxMapping, PostScreenGlow, PreScreenSkyCubeMapping, and the LensFlare class were imported from Rocket Commander, too, but after a while only the LensFlare and Sky shader classes were left because all the other shaders changed too much. Instead of writing a new shader for every new material, a more general ShaderEffect class was written and all the shaders are now derived from it. This simplified some shaders and made classes such as NormalMapping or ParallaxMapping obsolete because they work now directly from the ShaderEffect class, which can handle all the used shader parameters. The `PostScreenGlow` shader was derived from `PostScreenMenu`, which is a new shader just for the menu.

❑ For unit testing a similar approach was taken, but both NUnit and TestDriven.NET were left out to simplify the development on the Xbox 360 and because TestDriven.NET does not work with the Express editions of Visual Studio anyway.

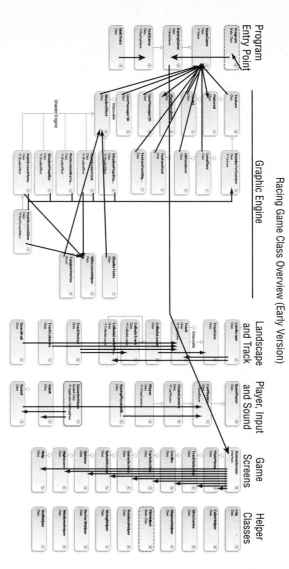

Figure 14-5

There are, of course, several new features in the game, which are not even in the game concept — such as the shadow mapping, which uses the following classes:

❑ `RenderToTexture`: While this class was implemented for the post-screen shaders anyway, it had to be improved to support rendering shadow maps, which require different surface formats for better precision. This means that for normal render targets, you can just use the same format the back buffer uses. This is most likely `R8G8B8A8`, which means that 8 bits are used for all the color channels and 8 bits are reserved because alpha does not make sense for the back buffer, and 32 bit in total is better than 24 bit, which makes it much harder to read pixel data on 32-bit platforms.

Anyway, for shadow maps you need more precision per pixel and you don't really need colors. Each pixel of a shadow map should be just a depth value between 0 and 1 and have as much precision as possible. Good formats are `R32F` or `R16F` if the first one is not available. But these formats have to be initialized differently and the `RenderToTexture` class handles this for you. It also decides based on the options the user selected if the shadow map is 2048 × 2048 in size, or 1024 × 1024 or just 512 × 512 for slower computers. It also supports fallback to a 32-bit color format if both `R32F` and `R16F` are not available.

❑ `ShadowMapBlur`: This class helps you to blur the shadow map. The technique used here is similar to the glow technique for the `PostScreenGlow` shader. It takes the input data and blurs it in two steps. The blur not only makes the shadows much softer and more realistic, but it also fixes certain shadow mapping artifacts, which are just blurred away. This trick was not used in the

Chapter 14: Fine-Tuning and "Modding" the Racing Game

XNA Shooter game because it will not look good if you have a lot of smaller objects in the background and a lot of overlapping shadow areas and non-shadow areas. In this racing game it looks much better; the shadows on the car especially have fewer artifacts and appear much smoother. All the other landscape objects are mostly distant and their shadows do not overlap with other objects. This allows you to use even nicer blur values.

❑ ShadowMapShader: This is the main class for shadows. It initializes all the required render targets, used textures, and the shadow mapping shader, and it handles the ShadowMapBlur class. More about the shadow mapping technique is discussed later in this chapter.

Other game features such as loopings and the landscape rendering engine you saw already in Chapter 12 were also not in the game concept. They just evolved from the early unit tests of the TrackLine and Track classes and they made the game more fun.

The game concept did just state that the main menu should allow starting a mission, viewing the high-scores, and quitting the game. The game ended up with a highly complex game screen namespace (see Figure 14-5), which supports many more game screens than planned. Please note that some of the game screens are not implemented in the code for this chapter (for example, the track or car selection screens); they are only used in the full Racing Game Starter Kit for the XNA Framework. The main reason here is that you have only one track and one car and it would not make much sense to implement those screens if there is nothing to select anyway. You can find a more complex version of the racing game and more information about the game in general at www.xnaracinggame.com, the official website for the game.

Game Screens

The racing game features many different game screens, which are all managed by the RacingGame class by the gameScreens stack variable. This section describes most game screens used in the game and exactly what they do. Most game screen classes are fairly simple, but others are a little bit more complex and feature a unit test, which can be used to learn more about the class. For example, the Credits screen is fairly simple and just displays a background texture, but the main menu is more complex and has all the buttons to get to the other game screens. The Options screen introduces many new controls, which had to be tested, and there is obviously a unit test in this class to help you out with that process.

All game screen classes are derived from the interface IGameScreen (see Figure 14-6), which you probably will remember from the Rocket Commander game in Chapter 8. It is pretty much the same class, but it was made a little bit simpler. You now have only one method left called Render, which takes no parameters and returns a Boolean value. The code is actually the same as you used in the XNA Shooter game. If a game screen Render method call returns true, it means you are done with this class and can return to the previous game screen until you run out of game screens and exit the game. Usually game screens return false because the user does not immediately quit them again after joining a game screen.

Figure 14-6

409

Because of this simple interface, all the game screen classes in the class diagram view look just the same; they all just have a Render method and not much else. Some classes have some private helper methods, but they are mostly very simple. Some of the more complex game screens have unit tests for testing if all elements are aligned correctly and function the way they should. Not even the GameScreen class, which handles the complete game, is that complex. Unlike XNA Shooter or Rocket Commander, all the game code is handled and rendered in the landscape and model classes. The game logic is handled in the Player class, which is a little bit more complex, but you already learned all about the underlying physics of the CarPhysics class and the ChaseCamera class in the last chapter.

Take a look at Figure 14-7 for a basic overview of all the game screens used in this version of the racing game. The most complex class is obviously the Mission class, which handles the game play and game logic. It does not contain all the game code, however; some of it is handled in the player classes and the RacingGame main class also handles a bit of the general game content.

Splash Screen

The splash screen (see Figure 14-8) is implemented in one of the easier classes, the SplashScreen class; it basically just sits around and waits for the user to press Start on his gamepad. Space or Esc on the keyboard or the left mouse button will let the player also continue if he does not have a game pad. The only thing for this class that is even remotely interesting is the code to let the "Press start to continue" text blink.

```
/// <summary>
/// Render splash screen
/// </summary>
public bool Render()
{
    // This starts both menu and in game post screen shader!
    BaseGame.UI.PostScreenMenuShader.Start();
    // Render background and black bar
    BaseGame.UI.RenderMenuBackground();
    BaseGame.UI.RenderBlackBar(352, 61);
    // Show Press Start to continue.
    if ((int)(BaseGame.TotalTime / 0.375f) % 3 != 0)
        BaseGame.UI.Logos.RenderOnScreen(
            BaseGame.CalcRectangleCenteredWithGivenHeight(
                512, 352 + 61 / 2, 26, UIRenderer.PressStartGfxRect),
            UIRenderer.PressStartGfxRect);

    // Show logos
    BaseGame.UI.RenderLogos();
    // Clicking or pressing start will go to the menu
    return Input.MouseLeftButtonJustPressed ||
        Input.KeyboardSpaceJustPressed ||
        Input.KeyboardEscapeJustPressed ||
        Input.GamePadStartPressed;
} // Render()
```

GameScreen Classes in the Racing Game

GameScreen (The game itself)

SplashScreen

MainMenu

Highscores

Options

Help

Credits

Exit

Figure 14-7

Figure 14-8

The `RenderMenuBackgroundTrackBackground` method is a little bit more complex. It is used to show the menu background behind the splash screen, which shows the car driving through one of the tracks. The car is controlled by the computer and the camera just follows it. The code for that is not very complex:

```
// [From RenderMenuBackgroundTrackBackground(), which is called by
// RenderMenuBackground(), both located in the UIRenderer class]
// [Some code to calculate carPos, carMatrix, etc.]
// Put camera behind car
RacingGame.Player.SetCameraPosition(
    carPos + carMatrix.Forward * 9 - carMatrix.Up * 2.3f);
// For rendering rotate car to stay correctly on the road
carMatrix =
    Matrix.CreateRotationX(MathHelper.Pi / 2.0f) *
    Matrix.CreateRotationZ(MathHelper.Pi) *
    carMatrix;
RacingGame.Landscape.Render();
RacingGame.CarModel.RenderCar(
    randomCarNumber, randomCarColor, carMatrix);
```

Thanks to the `Render` method of the `Landscape` class and the `RenderCar` method of the `Model` class, you do not have to worry about rendering the landscape, track, or anything else here. The camera matrix makes sure you look at the correct position and the car advances through the track through the car matrix variable.

All other menu game screens also use the `RenderMenuBackground` method to render the game in the background, but it can be less visible in some game screens because you put darker textures in the front (for example, in the Credits screen it is harder to see the background anymore). It is just a background effect, however; you can see more of the game when you actually start playing it.

Main Menu

The main menu (see Figure 14-9) is a little bit more complex than most other menu screen classes, but even this class is just about 250 lines of code. Every other game screen can be started from here except the Splash screen, which is only shown initially after starting the application. The most important choices are starting the game and viewing the highscores (the first two buttons).

The coolest feature of this class is the menu button animation. Every button gets a float value between 0 and 1, where 0 is the smallest possible button size and 1 is the biggest button size. When you hover over a button with the mouse or select it with the gamepad or keyboard, it gets bigger until it reaches 1.0. When you leave the button, it slowly gets smaller again.

Figure 14-9

The first button is initially set to 1. All other buttons are left at the smallest size (0).

```
/// <summary>
/// Current button sizes for scaling up/down smooth effect.
/// </summary>
float[] currentButtonSizes =
    new float[NumberOfButtons] { 1, 0, 0, 0, 0 };
```

Then in the Render method, the button selection code and scaling of the buttons is handled. To make sure you do not hover over more than one button at the same time, a helper variable is used for the mouse. If no mouse is used to select the menu buttons, this variable will never be used.

```
// Little helper to keep track if mouse is actually over a button.
// Required because buttons are selected even when not hovering over
// them for GamePad support, but we still want the mouse only to
```

```
// be applied when we are actually over the button.
int mouseIsOverButton = -1;
// [a little later in the code ...]
for (int num = 0; num < NumberOfButtons; num++)
{
  // Is this button currently selected?
  bool selected = num == selectedButton;
  // Increase size if selected, decrease otherwise
  currentButtonSizes[num] +=
    (selected ? 1 : -1) * BaseGame.MoveFactorPerSecond * 2;
  if (currentButtonSizes[num] < 0)
    currentButtonSizes[num] = 0;
  if (currentButtonSizes[num] > 1)
    currentButtonSizes[num] = 1;

  // Use this size to build rect
  Rectangle thisRect =
    InterpolateRect(activeRect, inactiveRect, currentButtonSizes[num]);
  Rectangle renderRect = new Rectangle(
    xPos, yPos - (thisRect.Height - inactiveRect.Height) / 2,
    thisRect.Width, thisRect.Height);
  BaseGame.UI.Buttons.RenderOnScreen(renderRect, ButtonRects[num],
    // Make button gray if not selected
    selected ? Color.White : new Color(192, 192, 192));
  // Add border effect if selected
  if (selected)
    BaseGame.UI.Buttons.RenderOnScreen(renderRect,
      UIRenderer.MenuButtonSelectionGfxRect);
  // Also check if the user hovers with the mouse over this button
  if (Input.MouseInBox(renderRect))
    mouseIsOverButton = num;
  // [etc.]
} // for (num)

if (mouseIsOverButton >= 0)
  selectedButton = mouseIsOverButton;
```

Game Screen

The GameScreen class (see Figure 14-10) is the most important game screen because it handles the whole game logic. No game variables are stored here, however, and you do not handle anything exclusive here, but all the important parts (landscape, track, car, objects, HUD, and so on) are still rendered and called from here.

Most of the player variables are stored in the Player class and all the input and physics are handled in the base classes of the Player class (CarPhysics and ChaseCamera). The Player class also makes use of all the game variables. Most variables are displayed in the UI like the current game time on the in-game HUD and they are updated in the HandleGameLogic method of the Player class.

All the Render methods, even the in-game HUD, are located in the UIRenderer helper class for any UI rendering code and the rest is handled and rendered in the landscape and model classes; even the shadow mapping is mostly done there. All the rendering and game handling are called from here, so this class gives you a good overview of what happens in the game. If you write a game modification, start modifying code here. Comment out code here or in the called methods to quickly see what part of the game is affected by that change.

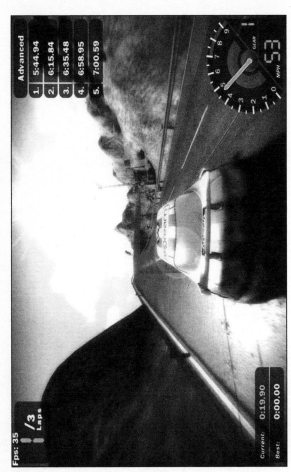

Figure 14-10

The first part of the Render method handles all the shadow mapping rendering, which is not very complex because most of it is handled in the landscape class. You just give the data to the shadow mapping class, which renders everything into the shadow map, which can then be used directly after rendering the 3D objects to shadow the 3D scene. The following code block illustrates the shadow map rendering:

```
/// <summary>
/// Render game screen. Called each frame.
/// </summary>
public bool Render()
{
    if (BaseGame.AllowShadowMapping)
    {
        // Generate shadows
        ShaderEffect.shadowMapping.GenerateShadows(
            delegate
            {
                RacingGame.Landscape.GenerateShadow();
                RacingGame.CarModel.GenerateShadow(
                    RacingGame.Player.CarRenderMatrix);
            });
        // Render shadows
        ShaderEffect.shadowMapping.RenderShadows(
            delegate
            {
                RacingGame.Landscape.UseShadow();
                RacingGame.CarModel.UseShadow(
                    RacingGame.Player.CarRenderMatrix);
            });
    } // if (BaseGame.AllowShadowMapping)
```

Then the post-screen glow shader is started and in game post screen shader and all the 3D game content is rendered. This includes the sky cube map, landscape with the track and all 3D models, and finally the car.

```
// This starts both menu and in game post screen shader!
BaseGame.UI.PostScreenGlowShader.Start();
// Render background sky and lensflare.
BaseGame.UI.RenderGameBackground();
// Render landscape with track and all objects
RacingGame.Landscape.Render();
// Render car with matrix we got from CarPhysics
RacingGame.CarModel.RenderCar(
    RacingGame.currentCarNumber, RacingGame.CarColor,
    RacingGame.Player.CarRenderMatrix);
// And flush all models to be rendered
BaseGame.MeshRenderManager.Render();
```

After the MeshRenderManager has rendered all 3D models, you can add the shadow mapping effect to the 3D scene. The order of the calls here is important because if the 3D models are not rendered before showing the shadows, the shadows will not have the correct effect on them or will not work at all.

```
// Show shadows we calculated above
if (BaseGame.AllowShadowMapping)
{
    ShaderEffect.shadowMapping.ShowShadows();
} // if (BaseGame.AllowShadowMapping)
// Apply post screen shader here before doing the UI
BaseGame.UI.PostScreenGlowShader.Show();
```

And finally, the code for the UI in the game — if you want to get rid of it or change the HUD, here is the place for doing that.

```
// Play motor sound
Sound.UpdateGearSound(RacingGame.Player.Speed,
    RacingGame.Player.Acceleration);
// Show on screen UI for the game.
BaseGame.UI.RenderGameUI(
    (int)RacingGame.Player.GameTimeMilliseconds,
    // Best time and current lap
    (int)RacingGame.Player.BestTimeMs,
    RacingGame.Player.CurrentLap+1,
    RacingGame.Player.Speed * CarPhysics.MeterPerSecToMph,
    // Gear logic with sound (could be improved ^^)
    1+(int)(5*RacingGame.Player.Speed/CarPhysics.MaxSpeed),
    // Motormeter
    0.5f*RacingGame.Player.Speed/CarPhysics.MaxSpeed +
    // This could be improved
    0.5f*RacingGame.Player.Acceleration,
    RacingGame.Landscape.CurrentTrackName,
    Highscore.GetTop5Highscores());
if (Input.KeyboardEscapeJustPressed ||
    Input.GamePadBackJustPressed)
{
    // Stop motor sound
```

```
Sound.StopGearSound();
// Play menu music again
Sound.Play(Sound.Sounds.MenuMusic);
// Return to menu
return true;
} // if (Input.KeyboardEscapeJustPressed)
return false;
} // Render()
```

Highscores

The Highscores screen (see Figure 14-11) is very similar to the highscores of Rocket Commander, but all the online highscores are missing because no network code or web services were implemented yet. Again, the reason for that is the lack of network support in XNA, but it would be possible to implement that just for the PC version.

There are a couple of helper methods in the Highscore class that, for example, help you to determine the current rank in the game while the player is getting points for driving around the track, but most of these methods were already used in earlier games of this book.

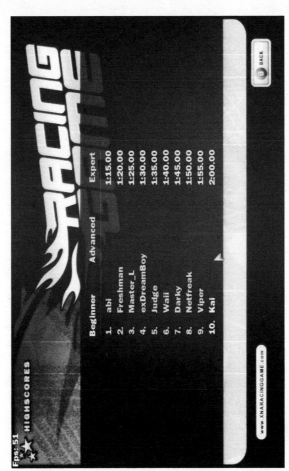

Figure 14-11

The following code is used to render the top ten highscore players on the screen. You will notice that the code is pretty simple thanks to the many helper methods in the UIRenderer class. If you just want to test the highscore game screen, please use the unit test inside the class, which was used to position all the UI elements for this game screen in the same way it was done for most other game screens, too. I also cheated a bit and used TestDriven.NET in Visual Studio 2005 and the new cool feature to re-run tests with a hotkey. This way, I could practically code, press the hotkey, say "oh no," press Escape, and fix the code until the class worked perfectly. In a matter of minutes most UI code was programmed this way.

```
// Go through all highscores
for (int num = 0; num < NumOfHighscores; num++)
{
    // Show player in white if mouse is over line or else use gray color
    Rectangle lineRect = new Rectangle(
        0, yPos, BaseGame.Width, lineHeight);
    Color col = Input.MouseInBox(lineRect) ?
        Color.White : new Color(200, 200, 200);
    // Fill in text for this line
    BaseGame.UI.WriteText(xPos1, yPos, (1 + num) + ".", col);
    BaseGame.UI.WriteText(xPos2, yPos,
        highscores[selectedLevel, num].name, col);
    BaseGame.UI.WriteGameTime(xPos3, yPos,
        highscores[selectedLevel, num].timeMs, Color.Yellow);
    yPos += lineHeight;
} // for (num)
```

The other game screen classes that are left are Options, Help, and Credits. They are all pretty similar to the highscore class and not really exciting. Options has some nice UI features and allows you to enter text with the help of the Input class and to select one of multiple sliders and drag it around with either the mouse or a gamepad. Use the unit test in the Options class to learn more about the features in this class. Both the Help and the Credit classes just display a texture on the screen, very similar to the SplashScreen class you saw earlier.

Finally, the exit button quits the game because there will be no other game screens left after the main menu is closed. All other game screens always return to the main menu (even the SplashScreen class).

Final Unit Testing and Tweaking

You now have all classes together for the game, but you are not done quite yet. We talked a few times about the Player class, but you never saw it called. The reason for this is that XNA separates the update and drawing code. If you look at the Update method of the RacingGame class, you can finally see the call to the Player Update method:

```
/// <summary>
/// Update racing game
/// </summary>
protected override void Update(GameTime time)
{
    // Update game engine
    base.Update(time);

    // Update player and game logic
    player.Update();
} // Update()
```

If you take a look inside the Player class, you might wonder why it is so simple. The Update method does not do much here; it only handles some additional game logic. In the Rocket Commander game, the Player class handled almost the whole game logic and input together with the SpaceCamera class. The game logic in the racing game seems to be much simpler thanks to the separation of all the game logic code into four different classes, which are all connected to each other (see Figure 14-12).

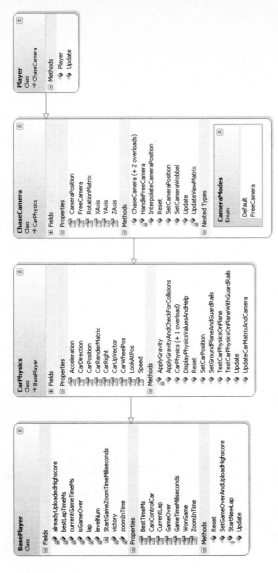

Figure 14-12

- BasePlayer: This is the basic game logic class for the game; it holds all the important variables and helper properties to see if the game is over, how long you played, and if you won the game. The whole purpose of this class is to give the derived classes an easy way to access these data because you are not able to control the car anymore if the game is over or the game has not even started yet because you are still zooming in. Although the BasePlayer class does provide almost anything you need externally (and internally) to know about the current game state, it does not handle much of it. The class will only update the timers; all the rest of the game logic is handled in the derived classes!

```
/// <summary>
/// Update game logic, called every frame. In Rocket
/// Commander we did all the game logic in one big method
/// inside the player class, but it was hard to add new
/// game logic and many small things were also in the
/// GameAsteroidManager. For this game we split everything
/// up into many more classes and every class handles only
/// its own variables. For example this class just handles
/// the game time and zoom in time, for the car speed and
/// physics just go into the CarController class.
/// </summary>
public virtual void Update()
```

```
{
    // Handle zoomInTime at the beginning of a game
    if (zoomInTime > 0)
    {
        // Handle start traffic light object (red, yellow,
        // green)
        RacingGame.Landscape.ReplaceStartLightObject(
            2-(int)(zoomInTime/1000));
        zoomInTime -= BaseGame.ElapsedTimeThisFrameInMs;
        if (zoomInTime < 0)
            zoomInTime = 0;
    } // if (zoomInTime)

    // Don't handle any more game logic if game is over or
    // still zooming in.
    if (CanControlCar == false)
        return;

    // Increase game time
    currentGameTimeMs += BaseGame.ElapsedTimeThisFrameInMs;
} // Update()
```

❑ CarPhysics: This class was already discussed in the previous chapter. It is derived from the BasePlayer class and adds all the physics calculations to the car and the rest of the game. While the Update method updates the internal physics values such as the direction, position, up vector, the car speed, and acceleration, most of the actual physics calculation is done in several helper methods as in the ApplyGravity, ApplyGravityAndCheckForCollisions, and SetGroundPlaneAndGuardRails methods. The UpdateCarMatrixAndCamera helper method is used to obtain car matrix for rendering the car and updating the basic look at position for the camera. For testing the physics, you should use the two unit tests TestCarPhysicsOnPlane and TestCarPhysicsOnPlaneWithGuardRails in this class, especially if you want to change some of the many constants defined in this class such as the car mass, maximum speed, maximum rotation, or acceleration values. You can find more information about this class in Chapter 13.

❑ ChaseCamera is similar to the SpaceCamera class of the Rocket Commander game or the SimpleCamera class of XNA Shooter. The class is not very complex and it does not have to be because it is derived from the CarPhysics class, which provides you with almost everything you need. It supports two camera modes: Default for the game and the menu, and FreeCamera, which is mostly used for unit tests. The view matrix of the BaseGame class is updated here every frame and if you need access to the camera position or the rotation matrix or a rotation axis, this is the place to look. You probably will not need this class very often because most of the important game information like the current car position or game time can be accessed through the properties of the BasePlayer and the CarPhysics classes.

❑ Player is finally the class, which is derived from ChaseCamera and combines all the features of the four classes. If you want to add additional game logic or rules, this is probably the easiest place to do that, but if you don't change the Update methods of the base classes, you will not be able to change much of the behavior of the game. For example, to change the maximum car speed, which is handled directly in the CarPhysics class, it would be easier to change the game logic there, but if you want to add an abort condition or text message after reaching a certain check point or completing a lap, it is probably easier to add that code in the Player class.

Chapter 14: Fine-Tuning and "Modding" the Racing Game

Tweaking the Track

You now know how to change the global game logic rules, but most of the game play and levels is defined directly through the level data. As you already saw in Chapter 12, it is not easy to create the tracks and it doesn't get any easier to import the 3D track data into the game because you need to do the following things (see also Figure 14-13):

1. You need 3D Studio Max to even open one of the tracks and change it. It will probably also work with other 3D modeling programs, but that hasn't been tested yet. In any case, as a game programmer you probably will not have these tools.

2. You have to use a Collada exporter in 3D Studio Max, which is not supported out of the box, and getting one for the latest 3D Studio Max version is not always a piece of cake. For example, at the time of this writing, there is no working Collada exporter for 3D Studio Max 9; you would have to use 3D Studio Max 8 to export the tracks, which again is not compatible with any .max files saved in 3D Studio Max 9. You can see this is getting more complicated even just speaking about it.

3. Import the Collada track data into the game with the help of the unit tests in the TrackImporter class, which will tell you if anything goes wrong, but the unit tests don't give you visual feedback.

4. Test the tracks yourself either by starting and playing the game or using one of the unit tests in the Track or TrackLine classes.

Well, this is not ideal and I will work on an in-game track editor in the future to resolve this issue. Please check the official website for updates of the game and better ways to edit tracks at www.xnaracinggame.com.

Currently you can also create tracks the way they are created for some of the unit tests in the TrackLine class by just defining a couple of 3D points. To "import" such a track you would just write down each of the points of this track in an array of 3D points and then use the array instead of an imported binary track. You can also create tunnels and road width helpers, and set landscape models, but beyond some unit tests this is not the way to go.

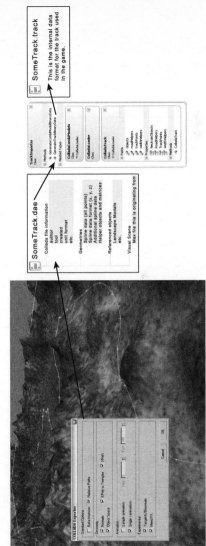

Importing a Racing Game Track into the Game

SomeTrack.max file inside 3D Studio Max

Figure 14-13

421

The TestRenderingTrack unit test shows how to initialize the TrackLine class with a custom array of vectors to create a track. If you just want to quickly play around with some track ideas you might have, I suggest using this unit test first:

```
/// <summary>
/// Test rendering track
/// </summary>
public static void TestRenderingTrack()
{
    TrackLine testTrack = new TrackLine(
        new Vector3[]
        {
            new Vector3(20, 0, 0),
            new Vector3(20, 10, 5),
            new Vector3(20, 20, 10),
            new Vector3(10, 25, 10),
            new Vector3(5, 30, 10),
            new Vector3(-5, 30, 10),
            new Vector3(-10, 25, 10),
            new Vector3(-20, 20, 10),
            new Vector3(-20, 10, 5),
            new Vector3(-20, 0, 0),
            new Vector3(-10, 0, 0),
            new Vector3(-5, 0, 0),
            new Vector3(7, 0, 3),
            new Vector3(10, 0, 10),
            new Vector3(7, 0, 17),
            new Vector3(0, 0, 20),
            new Vector3(-7, 0, 17),
            new Vector3(-10, -2, 10),
            new Vector3(-7, -4, 3),
            new Vector3(5, -6, 0),
            new Vector3(10, -6, 0),
        });

    TestGame.Start(
        delegate
        {
            ShowGroundGrid();
            ShowTrackLines(testTrack);
            ShowUpVectors(testtrack);
        });
} // TestRenderingTrack()
```

Shadow Mapping

The shadow mapping classes, which were discussed earlier in this chapter, are a prime candidate for tweaking. Not only are there many settings and parameters, but there are also several shaders involved, which have to be fine-tuned for both optimal performance and a good visual quality.

The main unit test that was used throughout the development of the shadow mapping techniques in the racing game is the TestShadowMapping method in the ShadowMapShader class (see Figure 14-14). If you press the Shift key (or A on the gamepad), you can see the shadow map and the two blur passes of the ShadowMapBlur shader. You can replace the car with any other 3D model if you would like to test the shadows of other 3D objects.

Earlier in this chapter, you saw in the GameScreen class how to use the ShadowMapShader class. First of all, you call GenerateShadows and RenderShadows on all objects you want to include in the shadow map generation process. Please note that both methods are rendering 3D data and you should only render what is necessary here. The data should be visible from the virtual shadow mapping light, and if the object is just receiving shadows like the plate in Figure 14-14, you don't need to include it into the GenerateShadows method call. Just let the shadows be thrown onto it with the RenderShadows method!

```
if (Input.Keyboard.IsKeyUp(Keys.LeftAlt) &&
    Input.GamePadXPressed == false)
{
    // Generate shadows
    ShaderEffect.shadowMapping.GenerateShadows(
        delegate
        {
            RacingGame.CarModel.GenerateShadow(
                Matrix.CreateRotationZ(0.85f));
        });
    // Render shadows
    ShaderEffect.shadowMapping.RenderShadows(
        delegate
        {
            RacingGame.CarSelectionPlate.UseShadow(
                Matrix.CreateScale(1.5f));
            RacingGame.CarModel.UseShadow(
                Matrix.CreateRotationZ(0.85f));
        });
} // if
```

After the shadow map has been generated, you can start rendering the real 3D content. In this unit test, it is basically the same code as the render delegate for RenderShadows method executes with the additional call to render the game background sky with help of the sky cube mapping shader. This way you can optimize in the actual game which object will be rendered, which ones will generate shadows, and which ones will receive shadows. If you just generate, render, and apply shadows on every single object in the scene your frame rate would go down terribly. Only about 10–20 percent of the visible objects will be included in the shadow map generation in the game code, but for this unit test you just want to test out the shadow mapping on the car and the car selection plate models.

```
if (Input.Keyboard.IsKeyUp(Keys.LeftAlt) &&
    Input.GamePadXPressed == false)
{
    ShaderEffect.shadowMapping.ShowShadows();
} // if
```

With the unit test up and running, you can now tweak the shadow mapping code (after it has been written, of course). Most tweaking variables can be found directly in the ShadowMapShader class, but some of them such as the shadow color for darkening shadowed areas are defined only in the ShadowMap.fx shader file and do not change once the shader is loaded.

423

fps: 135
Press left Shift or A to show all shadow pass textures.
Press Space or B to toggles the car model.
Press Alt or X to skip shadow map rendering.

Figure 14-14

To see the result of each shadow mapping pass, press Shift on your keyboard or the A button on a connected gamepad. The most important render target is the first one, which shows the actual shadow map from the virtual shadow light position. It is displayed in teal because you use a render target surface format of R32F as discussed earlier in this chapter, which just contains the red color channel. All the other color channels are unused and will use the default values of 1.0. If the value in the shadow map is 1.0 (for the farthest possible value) you end up with a completely white color; if you get closer to 0.0 the resulting color will be teal. It is often hard to see the differences in the shadow map. To enhance the values you can multiply it with a fixed constant in the shader and zoom in by moving the virtual shadow light position closer to the look target.

The following variables and constants are the most important ones to tweak; there are a couple more things you can tweak by changing the vertex and pixel shaders in the ShadowMap.fx and PostScreenShadowBlur.fx shaders. Please note that because of the limitations of pixel shader 1.1, most code for shader model 1.1 is pretty much fixed and will not be affected by most of the variables. If you still need support for shader model 1.1 and change some parameters, make sure the shader model 1.1 shader still works. It can be tested by forcing the shader model 1.1 techniques in the shader classes instead of using the techniques ending with 20, which are used for shader model 2.0.

virtualLightDistance and virtualVisibleRange are used to construct the virtual shadow mapping light and especially the LightViewMatrix, which is important for both the shadow map generating and when rendering the shadow map. The virtual light distance is the distance from the shadow mapping look-at position, which is always the current car position, or to be more precise, a position a little bit in front of the car to fit the actual viewing area of the player camera a little bit better. The virtual visible range describes the field of view of the shadow map matrix. The light view matrix can be very different from the view matrix used in the game and it will not be used for any rendering, it is only used for the shadow mapping algorithm.

For example, in the XNA Shooter game, a very distant virtual light position is used and a relatively small virtual visible range results in a small field of view for the shadow mapping matrix, almost orthogonal. This way the shadows are always oriented in the same way, but it gets a little bit harder to tweak a shadow map light with a distant light position. In the racing game, you do not care so much about a closer virtual light distance because when driving around with your car you won't notice the shadows in the distance so much, and the shadows on the car stay pretty much the same because the position of the car in the resulting shadow map is always the same.

nearPlane and farPlane are used to tweak the shadow map depth calculation a little bit. If all the shadow map values have a depth value of 20.0 to 30.0, it would not make sense to use the same near and far plane values as in the game (for example, 1.0 and 500) because the shadow map would then get only 2 percent of the depth buffer precision. For depth buffer values it won't matter so much because you only run into problems if depth values overlap by overlapping geometry, which will not happen very often if the scene is well constructed.

For shadow mapping, on the other hand, you are only looking at depth values that do overlap because you need to test if each pixel in the scene is shadow mapped or not. By using a bad shadow mapping depth buffer precision, the whole shadow mapping looks bad. This is also one of the main reasons there are so many other shadow algorithms available, especially stencil shadows, which are the main competitor of shadow mapping in 3D games. With stencil shadows, a lot of these problems disappear, but they are often a lot harder to handle and they usually involve rendering a lot more geometry, which can slow down any game that already has a lot of polygons.

The racing game mainly uses the farPlane value, which is fairly low (30–50), and then the nearPlane is automatically generated in the shader code. Earlier versions used a nearPlane value, which was more than half of the farPlane value to improve the depth precision, but then any objects near the virtual light would be skipped from the shadow map generation process. For a better tweaked nearPlane value, check out the XNA Shooter game, which also uses better code for the virtual light distance and range values.

```
// Use farplane/10 for the internal near plane, we don't have any
// objects near the light, use this to get much better pecision!
float internalNearPlane = farPlane / 10;
// Linear depth calculation instead of normal depth calculation.
Out.depth = float2(
    (Out.pos.z - internalNearPlane),
    (farPlane - internalNearPlane));
```

texelWidth, texelHeight, and the texOffsetX and texOffsetY values are used to tell the shader about the texel sizes used for the shadow map. These values are calculated in the CalcShadowMapBiasMatrix helper method, which puts all these values into a helper matrix called texScaleBiasMatrix. This is then used by the shader to transform all shadow mapping position values to fit the shadow map better.

```
/// <summary>
/// Calculate the texScaleBiasMatrix for converting proj screen
/// coordinates in the -1..1 range to the shadow depth map
/// texture coordinates.
/// </summary>
```

```
internal void CalcShadowMapBiasMatrix()
{
    texelWidth = 1.0f / (float)shadowMapTexture.Width;
    texelHeight = 1.0f / (float)shadowMapTexture.Height;
    texOffsetX = 0.5f + (0.5f / (float)shadowMapTexture.Width);
    texOffsetY = 0.5f + (0.5f / (float)shadowMapTexture.Height);
    texScaleBiasMatrix = new Matrix(
        0.5f * texExtraScale, 0.0f, 0.0f, 0.0f,
        0.0f, -0.5f * texExtraScale, 0.0f, 0.0f,
        0.0f, 0.0f, texExtraScale, 0.0f,
        texOffsetX, texOffsetY, 0.0f, 1.0f);
} // CalcShadowMapBiasMatrix()
```

The shadowColor constant in the shader is used to darken down the screen color any shadowed areas. Because the shadowMapDepthBias is added to the shadow map generation code to pull the depth values a little bit closer to the viewer.

The shadowColor constant in the shader is used to darken down the screen color any shadowed areas. Because the blur effect used after the shadow map is rendered and thanks to the PCF3x3 (precision closer filtering on a 3 × 3 box, an advanced texel filtering technique, which is often used by GPUs to improve the visual quality of texture filtering) used in PS_UseShadowMap20, the shadow color is interpolated with the surrounding non-shadowed areas. Using completely black shadows (ShadowColor of 0, 0, 0) is often the easiest solution because it fixes many shadow mapping artifacts, but it will not look good if it is bright daylight. In those cases, shadowing does not darken everything to black; there is still ambient color and occlusion lighting left in a realistic 3D scene.

```
// Color for shadowed areas, should be black too, but need
// some alpha value (e.g. 0.5) for blending the color to black.
float4 ShadowColor =
{ 0.25f, 0.26f, 0.27f, 1.0f };
```

depthBias and shadowMapDepthBias are probably the two shadow mapping parameters that were tweaked the most, together with the actual shader code that uses them.

```
// Depth bias, controls how much we remove from the depth
// to fix depth checking artifacts. For ps_1_1 this should
// be a very high value (0.01f), for ps_2_0 it can be very low.
float depthBias = 0.0025f;
// Substract a very low value from shadow map depth to
// move everything a little closer to the camera.
// This is done when the shadow map is rendered before any
// of the depth checking happens, should be a very small value.
float shadowMapDepthBias = -0.0005f;
```

The shadowMapDepthBias is added to the shadow map generation code to pull the depth values a little bit closer to the viewer.

```
// Pixel shader function
float4 PS_GenerateShadowMap20(VB_GenerateShadowMap20 In) : COLOR
{
    // Just set the interpolated depth value.
    float ret = (In.depth.x/In.depth.y) + shadowMapDepthBias;
    return ret;
} // PS_GenerateShadowMap20(.)
```

The depthBias value is a little bit more important because it is used in the shadow depth comparison code of the UseShadowMap20 technique. Without the depthBias, most shadow mapping pixels that are not really shadowed, but are both used to generate and to receive shadows, have such similar values that they often pop in and out of the shadow map comparisons because of depth map precision errors (see Figure 14-15). Please note that the shadow map blur effect hides these artifacts, but the stronger they are, the more apparent they get. Even with a good blur code applied to the shadow map result, it will look wrong in the game, especially when moving the camera around.

```
// Advanced pixel shader for shadow depth calculations in
// ps 2.0. However this shader looks blocky like PCF3x3 and
// should be smoothend out by a good post screen blur
// filter. This advanced shader does a good job faking the
// penumbra and can look very good when adjusted carefully.
float4 PS_UseShadowMap20(VB_UseShadowMap20 In) : COLOR
{
    float depth = (In.depth.x/In.depth.y) - depthBias;
    float2 shadowTex =
        (In.shadowTexCoord.xy / In.shadowTexCoord.w) -
        shadowMapTexelSize / 2.0f;

    float resultDepth = 0;
    for (int i=0; i<10; i++)
        resultDepth += depth > tex2D(ShadowMapSampler20,
            shadowTex+FilterTaps[i]*shadowMapTexelSize) ? 1.0f/10.0f : 0.0f;

    // Multiply the result by the
    // shadowDistanceFadeoutTexture, which fades shadows in
    // and out at the max. shadow distances
    resultDepth *= tex2D(shadowDistanceFadeoutTextureSampler,
        shadowTex).r;

    // We can skip this if its too far away anway (else very
    // far away landscape parts will be darkenend)
    if (depth > 1)
        return 0;
    else
        // And apply shadow color
        return lerp(1, ShadowColor, resultDepth);
} // PS_UseShadowMap20(VB_UseShadowMap20 In)
```

There are probably a lot more things we could discuss about the shadow mapping techniques used in the game and possible improvements — such as using better code to construct the virtual light matrices and tweaking certain parameters even better. You did see some of the most important shader code for the shadow mapping, but there are a lot more tricks in the shader code. Additionally, there are so many shadow mapping techniques and tricks that can be used today, it would probably fill up another book.

Two of the most exciting shadow map techniques today are the perspective shadow mapping light matrix generation techniques. (There are many different variations of it; I wrote some perspective shadow mapping code a year ago and played around with it for some time, but it is really hard to tweak and fine-tune, especially if your game allows many different perspectives.) The other exciting technique is variance shadow mapping, which uses two shadow maps instead of one (or two channels) and allows you to store much higher precision values. I did not have much time to play around with variance shadow mapping. It is a fairly new technique, but early tests showed that you can gain a lot of speed and save memory bandwidth as a result of the much smaller shadow mapping sizes (512×512 looks as good as a 2048×2048 traditional shadow map) and it fixes quite a lot of the shadow mapping problems and artifacts. But again, there are always problems with shadow mapping; some programmers such as the famous John Carmack from id Software dislike it so much, they'd rather implement the more complicated stencil shadows and fight with their issues instead of using shadow mapping.

427

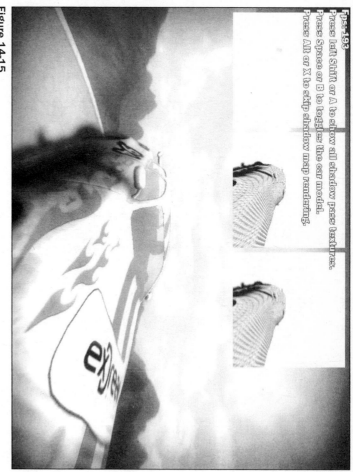

Figure 14-15

Final Testing on Windows

Well, with all that great code lying around some game testing can now be done. Before you start the game and drive around the track trying to beat the highscores, you should make sure that you have checked out most of the unit tests of the game engine (see Figure 14-16).

If you use the unit tests before even testing out the game, you don't have to test any issues with shadow mapping, the physics, the menu, and so on directly in the game. You are going to solve all issues with unit tests instead until they work fine. Then the game will magically run very nicely in the end without you ever testing the game itself; all you did was test smaller unit tests.

Often there are improvements that can be made to the game, or you might want to tweak something directly in the game code. You will find yourself tweaking the game code and fixing bugs in the final testing phase of the game, but you should make sure that you don't spend more time starting the game and testing the issues. For example, if you encounter a bug in some physics calculation or you want to tweak some of the shadow mapping values, you should either use an existing unit test or write a new unit test for the specific issue if it is easier than constantly restarting the game with all its content and submenus. It often just takes a couple of clicks and waiting for the loading and screen transitions, but even that can slow you down.

One common trick I always use at the final stage of any game development project is to change the game screen initialization code. This way, I end up directly in the game instead of the menu where I might have to set some options first. Then I select a level and start a custom game. There is no point in doing that over and over again if you simply want to test some issue inside the game itself.

Some of the Racing Game Unit Tests

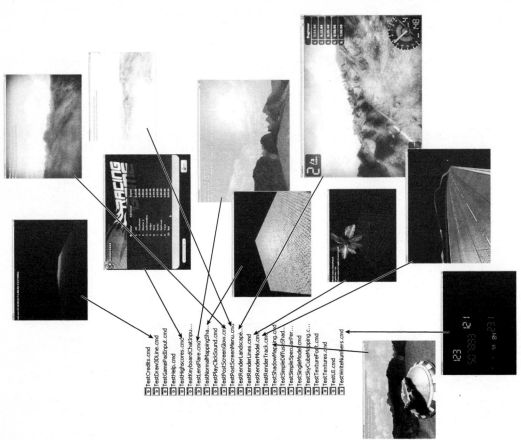

- TestCredits.cmd
- TestDraw3DLine.cmd
- TestGamePadInput.cmd
- TestHighscores.cmd
- TestKeyboardChatInpu...
- TestLensFlare.cmd
- TestNormalMappingSha...
- TestPlayClickSound.cmd
- TestPostScreenGlow.cmd
- TestPostScreenMenu.cmd
- TestRenderLandscape...
- TestRenderLines.cmd
- TestRenderModel.cmd
- TestRenderTrack.cmd
- TestShadowMapping.cmd
- TestSimpleWithoutShad...
- TestSimpleSpecularPer...
- TestSingleModel.cmd
- TestSkyCubeMapping.c...
- TestTextures.cmd
- TestUI.cmd
- TestWriteNumbers.cmd

Figure 14-16

```
// Create main menu at our main entry point
gameScreens.Push(new MainMenu());

// But start with splash screen, if user clicks or presses
// Start, we are back in the main menu.
gameScreens.Push(new SplashScreen());
#if DEBUG
//tst: Directly start the game and load a certain level,
// this code is only used in the debug mode. Remove it when
// you are done with testing! If you press Esc you will
```

429

```
// also quit the game and not just end up in the menu
// again.
gameScreens.Clear();
gameScreens.Push(new GameScreen());
#endif
```

Because all unit tests should work in the debug mode only and you are not even adding the NUnitFramework.dll assembly in the release mode, you should make sure the game runs fine in the release mode, too. Sometimes you also get a little better performance in the release mode, but because most of the performance critical code is probably going to happen inside the XNA Framework, your code will not care if it is run in debug or release mode if it is optimized well enough anyway.

Figure 14-17 shows the racing game in action. There are still things to tweak, but the game runs well and has a good frame rate even in the highest resolution possible on the Xbox 360 (1080p, which is 1920 × 1050). The final fine-tuning, level design, and game testing took an extra week of work, but that was a lot of fun. It is always good to have some people you know play the game, maybe even ones that are not really fans of your game genre. Also make sure the game can be installed easily. No one wants to compile the game himself and find out which assemblies are used the hard way — by dealing with the exceptions. Your installer should contain the compiled game and it should check which frameworks are not installed on a target machine and preferably install them itself. Your game probably needs just the .NET Framework 2.0 (about 30MB), the latest DirectX version (about 50 MB), and the XNA Framework Redistributables (just 2MB). On the Xbox 360 there is currently no deployment method available other than compiling the source code and deploying it with XNA Game Studio Express. For the installer used for this game, I chose NSIS (Nullsoft Installer Script), which allowed me to build the installer in a way that downloads and installs all these frameworks automatically if the user does not have them installed. After that the game can be started and you can play a while and have fun while trying to get the best highscores.

Final Testing on the Xbox 360

You obviously want your game to run on the Xbox 360 as well and the Racing Game was mainly developed especially for the Xbox 360 platform. It makes sense to have a racing game on a console, especially if you have a wheel controller as I do.

As I mentioned so many times before, all the unit tests you write should be tested on both Windows and the Xbox 360 platform, but you will probably forget that from time to time and then at the end of the project when the final test on the Xbox 360 is due you find out, for example, that the shadow mapping is not working the same way as on the PC. Well, time to pull out those unit tests (see Figure 14-16) again and test them on the Xbox 360, one by one, until you find a problem.

Because the racing game was the first project I ever did for the Xbox 360 I made quite a few mistakes that I found out about the first time I was able to run it on the Xbox 360 (the first beta of XNA in August did not support the Xbox 360 platform yet, so I was only able to test XNA on the PC for a while). I discovered that the screen layout in the game and the menu did not fit well on certain TV monitor configurations on the Xbox 360 (we already talked about that earlier in this book) and render targets on the Xbox 360 behave quite differently from the PC.

One of the hardest parts was to get the shadow mapping right on the Xbox 360. There were several issues with resolving the render targets and I used some tricks that are neither allowed nor possible on the Xbox 360, such as using several render targets at the same time and reusing the back buffer information after rendering some render targets.

Figure 14-17

Here is some text from a blog entry from my blog at http://abi.exdream.com early in November 2006 when I talked about this issue while I was visiting the XNA Team in the USA:

Today I worked a lot with the Xbox 360 side of XNA. In the earlier builds I had a lot of problems with testing my starter kit on the Xbox 360, but most of these issues are resolved now. About 99 percent of the game code works the same on the Windows and Xbox 360 platforms, but if you hit that 1 percent it does still get you angry. For example, a couple of the more advanced shadow mapping shaders work fine on the Windows platform, but all kinds of crazy things happen on the Xbox 360 — the game crashes, you see black bars all over the screen, or the output is just not right.

If you are like me and have not worked with the Xbox 360 before, I can tell you that it is not easy getting used to the way the console uses render targets. You have to resolve them with a little helper method in XNA (or in the Xbox 360 SDK) to get the contents copied over to your texture. This is not required on Windows. But even if you take care of that, the shaders might behave a little different. For example, most of my post screen shaders use the background buffer to mix results and sometimes mix them together several times. This works fine on the Windows platform and behaves the same way as it does in DirectX.

But after some discussion with Tom Miller, and Matt and Mitch Walker from the XNA Team and debugging a little, it was clear that the background buffer can have garbage data after rendering into render targets. This was very bad for one of the shaders because it requires two separate images over several passes and then blends them together at the last pass. I used the back buffer to hold one of them and a render target for the other, but that had to be changed in order to run correctly on the Xbox 360. Good thing this was just one shader, in my bigger game engine I have over 100 shaders and it would not be fun to rethink all of the post screen shaders.

Figure 14-18 shows the repositioning code required to make the game look okay on TV monitors attached to the Xbox 360. Because you cannot know what kind of monitor is attached and how much is visible, you can end up displaying more or less of the screen borders, but the values used here look good on all systems I've tested the game on.

The safe region (90 percent visible) is shown as the red border, but even if you see 100 percent of the screen, the game still looks fine. If your TV set is worse and goes below the 90 percent visibility, you will still see all the important information, but some texts might be cut off.

The following code is used to push the UI elements more into the center than for the PC version, which shows all HUD elements near the screen border:

```
// More distance to the screen borders on the Xbox 360 to
// fit better into the safe region. Calculate all
// rectangles for each platform, then they will be used the
// same way on both platforms.
#if XBOX360
// Draw all boxes and background stuff
Rectangle lapsRect = BaseGame.CalcRectangle1600(
  60, 46, LapsGfxRect.Width, LapsGfxRect.Height);
ingame.RenderOnScreen(lapsRect, LapsGfxRect, baseUIColor);
Rectangle timesRect = BaseGame.CalcRectangle1600(
  60, 46, CurrentAndBestGfxRect.Width,
  CurrentAndBestGfxRect.Height);
timesRect.Y = BaseGame.Height - timesRect.Bottom;
ingame.RenderOnScreen(timesRect, CurrentAndBestGfxRect,
  baseUIColor);
// [etc.]
```

Figure 14-18

Additional Ideas

The game runs fine now and if you got through the final testing it is ready to be released. But even after that you might not have enough of it and you still might want to try additional ideas or think about future extensions. I often find myself reusing one of my existing engines just to test out new game ideas. It is just so much easier to use an existing engine you are already familiar with than to start from scratch.

This section is about additional ideas I had before even starting the development of the game and during the development time.

More Cars

Having more car models was one of my earlier wishes, but because I'm not a modeler and none of the modelers I know have much time and think it is "fun" to create a couple more car models for my little racing game, I never got beyond the initial 3D car model that was made specifically for the racing game. It was relatively easy to change the appearance of the car by changing the texture a bit and the starter kit version features three different car textures and some code to recolor the cars dynamically, but they all use the same underlying geometry.

The Speedy Racer Game mod, which is shown at the end of this chapter, will also feature another car model (just a free one from the Internet), but having even more different car types would be fun, especially if you give each car different speeds, acceleration, and braking parameters. For a multiplayer game it would also be more fun to have different cars so every player can choose his favorite car type.

But I guess having as many cars as the commercial racing games you saw in Chapter 12 will cost a lot of money to develop and it also takes a lot of time to get them as good as they are in those games. Let's hope the community will find ways to import new car models, and after a while more game modifications are available.

The car rendering code for the racing game is pretty specific; for example, the Model class uses a customized render method called RenderCar just for rendering the car. If you have more than one car model it would be harder to keep this method up-to-date and it would probably make more sense to implement the cars with the normal Render method.

Online Highscore List

Implementing a call to a web service and getting the top ten online highscores from there is probably not a big problem. You would add such code in the Highscore class and you could even reuse most of the existing code from the Rocket Commander game.

Before you can use web services you will have to add the System.Web.Services assembly to your references list, which is only available on the Windows platform. All the web services code you are going to add to the Highscore class must be disabled on the Xbox 360 platform.

```
Highscore[] onlineHighscores = new Highscore[10];
Thread onlineGetHighscoreThread = null;
/// <summary>
/// Get online highscores
/// </summary>
/// <param name="onlyThisHour">Only this hour</param>
```

```
private void GetOnlineHighscores(bool onlyThisHour)
{
    // Clear all online highscores and wait for a new update!
    for (int num = 0; num < onlineHighscores.Length; num++)
    {
        onlineHighscores[num].name = "-";
        onlineHighscores[num].level = "";
        onlineHighscores[num].points = 0;
    } // for (num)

    // Stop any old threads
    if (onlineGetHighscoreThread != null)
        onlineGetHighscoreThread.Abort();

    // Ask web service for highscore list! Do this asyncronly,
    // it could take a while and we don't want to wait for it to complete.
    onlineGetHighscoreThread = new Thread(new ThreadStart(
        // Anoymous delegates, isn't .NET 2.0 great? ^^
        delegate
        {
            // See notes above
            try
            {
                string ret = new www.xnaracinggame.com.
                    RacingGameService().GetTop10Highscores(onlyThisHour);
                // Now split this up and build the online highscore with it.
                string[] allHighscores = ret.Split(new char[] { ':' });
                for (int num = 0; num < allHighscores.Length &&
                    num < onlineHighscores.Length; num++)
                {
                    string[] oneHighscore =
                        allHighscores[num].Split(new char[] { ':' });
                    onlineHighscores[num] = new Highscore(
                        oneHighscore[0].Trim(), oneHighscore[2],
                        Convert.ToInt32(oneHighscore[1]));
                } // for (num)
            } // try
            catch { } // ignore any exceptions!
        }));
    onlineGetHighscoreThread.Start();
} // GetOnlineHighscores(onlyThisHour)
```

In order for this code to work, you need a web service running at the specified location of the RacingGameService class. Writing the web service itself is rather trivial, but implementing a nice looking website that shows all this data to the visitors is quite a bit of work. Maybe this will be done in the future.

More Shaders and Effects

Having more shaders and effects in a game today is always a good thing, at least from the player's perspective, because games looked cooler and and were more diverse in appearance than a few years ago when many games used similar rendering techniques and looked, at least in that regard, similar.

One thing you could plug in quite easily would be the parallax mapping shader from the Rocket Commander game, but you would also need a height map on all materials where you want to use the parallax shader instead of the standard normal mapping shader.

But adding effects and an effect manager system like for the XNA Shooter game would also be nice (see Figure 14-19). You currently have no effects at all, not even for a car explosion or crashing into something.

For more examples of some good post-screen shaders, go back to Chapter 8. A racing game would greatly benefit from HDR rendering, especially if you change the lighting situations and drive through tunnels (as you actually do in the game).

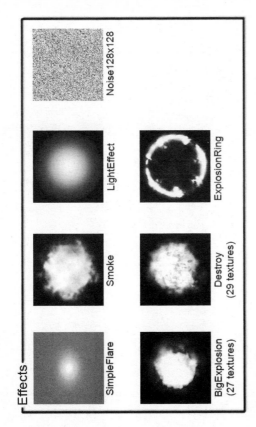

Figure 14-19

The per pixel motion blur effect discussed in Chapter 8 would also be a lot better than the currently implemented whole screen post-processing effect, but it is obviously also a lot harder to implement.

The major thing I would always improve for a racing game mod is to change the color correction factors in the `PostScreenMenu` and `PostScreenGlow` shader classes and the underlying shader code. It will give the whole game a completely different experience without your having to change all of the textures yourself.

More Game Modes

More game modes would also be fun. I'm not really a racing game expert, but maybe it would be fun to implement one or more of the common racing game modes that you can often find in commercial racing games:

❑ **Beat the best time:** This is the mode you have in the racing game currently. It could also be extended to more players, but you would need to add some racing car AI for other players.

❑ **Be the first:** For this game mode you obviously need more than one car and more than one driver. This is the main game mode for most racing games. It is currently not possible because you have no multiplayer and no computer AI code for handling other cars. Even with some AI code you would still need to improve the collision code for the cars because now you would be able to collide with other cars on the track.

- **Practice mode:** Special game mode for some racing games that allow you to train on the tracks before actually going into competition. You can test out tricks and train on certain parts of the track, but this whole game mode makes sense only if you would lose something by training in the competition game mode, which again is not the case in the racing game.

- **Time Trails:** You have to complete the track or certain parts of it in a specified time frame. This way, the game can get a lot harder for beginners because it is usually much harder to beat these times instead of just having to complete the track and beating some highscore or not.

- **Cone Parkour mode or driving lessons mode:** You have to drive around cones placed on the road within a certain time limit and avoid knocking over too many of them. Other parkours could involve driving on certain sides of the road or following the street signs.

- **Tricks:** This is one of the more popular game modes, especially in the street racer games discussed in Chapter 12. Doing tricks means that you have to drift your car, slide through curves, or maybe even jump through certain parts of the track. Games such as Trackmania have other kinds of tricks you have to perform to even complete a track. You do have loopings, but not most of the other advanced mode parts Trackmania has to make it more difficult to complete tracks.

- **Crash mode:** Some games have focused on crashing the car into walls and getting points for it or damaging your car as fast as possible. Sounds like fun for the first couple of times.

- **Add weapons to the cars, or at least add items for special abilities:** Many arcade racing games have this idea implemented and many different game modes can come out of this idea. Items make even more sense in a multiplayer game where everyone is fighting each other and items help you destroy your enemies or push them aside to let you become the first-place player. Popular examples of these games would be Mario Kart, Wacky Wheels, and games such as Micro Machines.

- **Implement your own game ideas or mix existing game ideas into a racing game:** You could even get rid of the racing part altogether and maybe add something completely different. The sky is the limit.

Multiplayer Mode

For most game modes just discussed it would be a lot more fun if you could play the game together with a couple of friends either in your local area network (LAN) or over the Internet. Because networking code is not possible on the Xbox 360, the multiplayer part would only work on the PC right now with XNA.

The main change you would have to do to the game after implementing the basic code for networking is to change the Player class and allow multiple instances of this class. You will also need to handle a list of players and update all the data for each player with help of multiplayer messages. Again, this alone could fill up a book because there are many issues with multiplayer games and many possible ways to implement such code.

As a little example, take a look at Figure 14-20, which shows a couple of such multiplayer network classes working together. The game class holds a list of player objects. Each player receives data from all the other players and adds all received messages to an internal list. Messages are loaded with the help of the Message class and the MessageType enum.

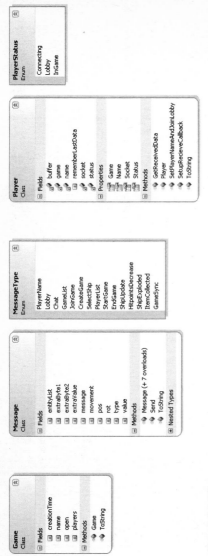

Figure 14-20

Challenge: Write Your Own Mod!

As the final challenge for this book, it is now your task to create your own game modification for the Racing Game. You can implement your own game idea or follow the process of coding the Speedy Racer mod.

As you saw at the very beginning of this chapter, there are quite a lot of mods available for the Rocket Commander game. More than 12 mods were written in 2006 alone and many more game projects were started. I bet even more games and mods were made, but the people involved in that were either too shy to share their games or they did not want to mention that they used the Rocket Commander engine. It is, of course, also possible that I'm just not aware of more game modifications out there, which might be floating around somewhere on the Internet.

The racing game and the XNA Shooter have great potential for modding. Not only are these games less specific than the Rocket Commander game, but they also have more reusable engines, which allows you to create new games more quickly than starting from scratch, even if some of the used technology is not really required for the new game.

If you want to create your own mod and if you already have a certain idea you don't need to read ahead about the Speedy Racer; go ahead and try to implement your own game idea first. In this chapter you learned enough to make incisions into the classes and change whatever you need to make your new game idea work.

You could also take a look at the next few chapters on how to program a multiplayer network game and try to incorporate that into the Racing Game in case you want to add multiplayer capabilities and additional game modes that make more sense if you have more than one player in the game.

437

Example Game: Speedy Racer

The Speedy Racer mod is not completely described here; it is still your challenge to create such a mod yourself, but I will give you everything you need to get started. If you are really lazy and don't want to code your own mod or Speedy Racer yourself right now, you can also just go ahead and install the game from the book CD, but I recommend trying to make the changes to the racing game yourself first before looking at the existing Speedy Racer code.

Step 1: Changing the Car Model

Because the mod had to be created quickly and I could not afford to pay a 3D modeler to make me a nice new car, I searched a little bit on the Internet for 3D models than can be used freely. I found a couple of nice cars, but most of them had too many polygons and others were in strange formats and I found no converters for them. After a while I gave up and just used one of the older 3D models I found earlier. Figure 14-21 shows an early version of this new Speedy Racer Car, which has about 21,000 polygons (compared to the 25,000 polygons of the original car in the Racer Game), but no material data set. I just added some boring red and black materials and the model was good enough to be exported and tested in the game. Later I added normal maps and a little texture mapping to the car model to make it look a little bit better. If you have more time for your project, try to do it better than me.

Figure 14-21

Chapter 14: Fine-Tuning and "Modding" the Racing Game

Step 2: Menu Changes

Changing the menu often involves a lot of textures and was always quite a bit of extra work on the Rocket Commander mods. The Racing Game is no different. Changing the menu did take some time, but only background textures and the used colors were changed; all the code could remain the same. Some of the menu logic was even simplified a little bit to avoid having to re-create certain textures again for the new mod.

If you would like to add more game screens, add more buttons to the main menu, or handle more options, and so on, it would probably help the most if you read the part about the game screens in this chapter again and try to figure out where the best place is to put any new code into the game.

Step 3: New Landscape and Objects

The Speedy Racer mod still uses the same landscape data as the original game, but I changed the landscape shader a little bit to make the game a bit more colorful and I changed everything into the blue color range. The shadow mapping and the post-screen shaders were also changed to make the game look a little bit different. See Chapter 8 for more details about the post-screen shaders and how to change them, especially the color correction shader part in PostScreenMenu.fx and PostScreenGlow.fx.

The following code is from the final post-screen rendering technique of the PostScreenGlow shader. You should be able to easily change the code for other visual effects and resulting colors. A good tip with shaders is always to go crazy first and then settle with more decent values. For example, if you want to test a blue look of the game, try adding 25 or even 50 percent to the blue color value and check the result. Maybe it does not look cool with blue or you like the craziness and settle with a value like 10 percent (which is a lot) for the blue color component. Or try playing around with the contrast values; there are always some variables you can tweak in most used shaders. The main goal of Speedy Racer was not to make it look highly realistic; it just should look different from the original Racing Game.

```
float4 PS_ComposeFinalImage20(
    VB_OutputPos3TexCoords In,
    uniform sampler2D sceneSampler,
    uniform sampler2D blurredSceneSampler) : COLOR
{
    float4 orig = tex2D(sceneSampler, In.texCoord[0]);
    float4 blur = tex2D(blurredSceneSampler, In.texCoord[1]);
    float4 screenBorderFadeout = tex2D(screenBorderFadeoutMapSampler,
        In.texCoord[2]);
    float4 ret =
        0.75f*orig +
        GlowIntensity*blur+
        HighlightIntensity*blur.a;
    ret.rgb *= screenBorderFadeout;
    // Change colors a bit, sub 20% red and add 25% blue (photoshop values)
    // Here the values are -4% and +5%
    ret.rgb = float3(
        ret.r+0.054f/2,
```

```
        ret.g-0.021f/2,
        ret.b-0.035f/2);
    // Change brightness -5% and contrast +10%
    ret.rgb = ret.rgb * 0.975f;
    ret.rgb = (ret.rgb - float3(0.5, 0.5, 0.5)) * 1.05f +
        float3(0.5, 0.5, 0.5);
    return ret;
} // PS_ComposeFinalImage20(...)
```

Step 4: Driving Faster

To drive faster with the car in the game and still have a playable and enjoyable game, you need to make two major changes to the game logic:

Make the roads much wider; this way you can drive faster through them. Also, try to adjust the up vector for straight roads in a way that makes it easier to drive around curves.

The code to change the basic road width can be found in the TrackVertex class of the Track namespace; just change the RoadWidthScale value to something crazy like 50 for testing and then settle for some reasonable value.

```
/// <summary>
/// Minimum, maximum and default road width for our track.
/// </summary>
public const float MinRoadwidth = 0.25f,
    DefaultRoadwidth = 1.0f,
    MaxRoadwidth = 2.0f,
    RoadwidthScale = 13.25f;
// [The constants are then used to generate the left and right track
// vertices ...]
/// <summary>
/// Left side track vertex generation, used for the GuardRail class.
/// </summary>
/// <returns>Track vertex</returns>
public TrackVertex LeftTrackVertex
{
    get
    {
        return new TrackVertex(
            pos - RoadwidthScale * roadwidth * right / 2,
            right, up, dir,
            new Vector2(uv.x, 0),
            roadwidth);
    } // get
} // LeftTrackVertex
// [etc.]
```

Make the car drive much faster. This can be done directly in the CarPhysics class by changing the following code. Constantly use the unit tests of this class to test out the new values. If they look okay, try them in the real game.

```
#region Constants
/// <summary>
```

```
/// Car is 1000 kg
/// </summary>
const float CarMass = 1000;//1000.0f;
/// <summary>
/// Gravity on earth is 9.81 m/s^2
/// </summary>
const float Gravity = 9.81f;
/// <summary>
/// Max speed of our car is 275 mph.
/// While we use mph for the display, we calculate internally with
/// meters per sec since meter is the unit we use for everthing in the
/// game. And it is a much nicer unit than miles or feet.
/// </summary>
public const float MaxSpeed =
    275.0f * MphToMeterPerSec;
/// <summary>
/// Max. acceleration in m/s^2 we can do per second.
/// We have also to define the max and min overall
/// acceleration we can do with our car (very car specfic,
/// but for this game always the same to make it fair).
/// Driving backwards is slower than driving forward.
/// </summary>
const float MaxAccelerationPerSec = 5.0f;
    MaxAcceleration = 10.0f,
    MinAcceleration = -6.0f;
/// <summary>
/// Friction we have on the road each second. If we are
/// driving slow, this slows us down quickly. If we drive
/// really fast, this does not matter so much anymore. The
/// main slowdown will be the air friction.
/// </summary>
const float CarFrictionOnRoad = 17.523456789f;
/// <summary>
/// Air friction that slows us down. This frictions becomes
/// stronger the faster we drive. It makes it also much
/// harder to drive even faster if we already drive at a
/// very fast speed. For slow speeds the air friction does
/// not matter much. This could be extended to include wind
/// and then even at low speeds the air friction would slow
/// us down or even influence our movement. Maybe in a game
/// mod sometime.
/// </summary>
const float AirFrictionPerSpeed = 0.66f;
/// <summary>
/// Max air friction, this way we can have a good air
/// friction for low speeds but we are not limited to
/// 190-210mph, but can drive faster.
/// </summary>
const float MaxAirFriction = AirFrictionPerSpeed * 200.0f;
/// <summary>
/// Break slowdown per second, 1.0 means we need 1 second
/// to do a full break. Slowdown is also limited by max.
/// 100 per sec!
/// Note: This would not make sense in a real world
```

```
/// simulation because stopping the car usually needs more
/// time and is highly dependent on the speed resulting in
/// longer stopping distances. For this game it is easier
/// and more fun to just always brake the same.
/// </summary>
const float BrakeSlowdown = 1.0f;
// [etc.]
```

Step 5: Adding Items and New Sounds

This part was actually the most work. To make the game more fun I added several items (more speed, focus view, road widener, and so on) and new sounds for them. Check out the files in the mod itself for more information about the new items. The code changes were also a bit of work, but not as much work as creating the items themselves and testing them.

Summary

I hope you liked the book so far and learned a little bit from the example games I made. I'm pretty happy with the many example games in the book; I think the more practical approach to writing games will help out beginners more and give more advanced readers a way to quickly skip existing parts and take a look at the more complex things in the game programming world.

The topics in the book cover almost everything you need for learning XNA and game programming in general, but I have hidden each topic under the current game project of the chapter. For example, the physics chapter would still be helpful with some general physics calculations, but linking it to the racing game makes it so much easier to think about the problems that can happen in your game if you add physics. Even if you want to develop a completely different game that uses other physics calculations, you will probably benefit from the approach here because you write some unit tests first, you test out the available physics engines, and you will probably have some early idea about solving your physics problem after reading the chapter because you see some similarities with problems described there.

Here is a short list of the games you encountered in this book thus far and which game programming topics were discussed while developing these games:

- [ ] After Chapter 1, which was only an introduction to the XNA Framework and the first simple game project, you created a Pong game in Chapter 2. Here you learned all the basics for using unit testing properly, planning the whole project, and writing a good game concept. On the technical side you learned how to use sprites, handle the input, play sounds, and do some basic 2D collision testing. The game is playable with multiple players on the same screen and that is as far as you get with multiplayer games in this book.

- [ ] Chapter 3 covered several very important helper classes, but just having some helper classes alone is not really a fun game project so a new game project was created: Breakout, which uses some of the game logic of Pong, but allows you to play against yourself instead of another player or the stupid AI of Pong.

- [ ] Chapter 4 goes through the usefulness of game components and shows how to program one of my all-time favorite classic games: Tetris. Some of the game component classes developed here and in Chapters 5 and 6 survive until the end of this book, but the general idea to do everything with game components was never adopted by any game in this book. It just wouldn't make any sense.

Chapter 14: Fine-Tuning and "Modding" the Racing Game

❑ Part II (Chapters 5–8) focused on developing a basic graphics engine for all the upcoming game projects. Chapter 5 explains how to render models, use unit testing for 3D code, render textures, fonts, and lines on the screen, and finally even do some testing on the Xbox 360. Chapters 6 to 8 focus on shaders, a really big and complex topic, but in every chapter you dive a little deeper into the world of shaders. Chapter 8 finally ends with the great Rocket Commander game, which is now ported to the XNA Framework thanks to the graphics engine that was developed in these chapters.

❑ Part III of the book (Chapters 9–11) is all about improving the game engine. You finally learned how to use XACT properly, how to handle all the game screen classes and the game engine in general, and of course all about the UI and the player input class. To make things a little bit more interesting, the XNA Shooter game was introduced here, which really looks great and is quite a lot of fun to play. Some of the more advanced topics such as shadow mapping are also introduced for the first time, but all the hard stuff is left for Part IV.

❑ Part IV (Chapters 12–14) focuses on the Racing Game, the complex landscape and track generation code and the physics engine used in the game. You also learned a lot about the game screens and game logic in the game and how to test and tweak a relatively big game project like this one. At the end, the cool Speedy Racer mod was written to show you how to create your own mod based on the existing game engine.

❑ Part V (Chapters 15–17) is about Dungeon Quest, a role playing game with multiplayer support. Chapter 15 starts with an explanation of the networking basics and a simple chat application, which also works on Windows even in XNA 1.0 if you like. Then Chapter 16 talks a little bit about role playing games and Chapter 17 finally shows the Dungeon Quest game with some really cool tricks and tips on creating your own full blown role playing game.

This chapter also discussed a lot about the final stages in the game development process, which is sadly not reached by many people because most game projects are canceled before they reach even the alpha stage. Many beginners also stop developing their game because they run into some big problem or they are no longer motivated to keep going, especially if the game project is big. I hope the games in this book can help such people out and give them a handbook on how to write games from start to finish, or at least reuse some existing game engine instead of reinventing the wheel and stopping too early.

The next three chapters, which are new to the second edition of this book, have some amazing game programming tips and tricks in them and if you are interested at all in role playing games, the new chapters will be the most interesting ones for you. Not only is network programming one of the more complex and advanced problems, but creating role playing games is no piece of cake either. The biggest and most expensive games of the world are usually role playing games with a focus on multiplayer support. It is a big job, but someone has to do it.

Part V: Writing Multiplayer Games

Chapter 15: Multiplayer and Xbox Live

Chapter 16: Role-Playing Games

Chapter 17: Dungeon Quest

Multiplayer and Xbox Live

This chapter is about multiplayer game programming and networking concepts. This knowledge will help you no matter which kind of multiplayer game you want to write. It does not matter if it is a role-playing game, strategy game or a first-person shooter; the basic knowledge of writing a networking game or application will be very helpful and you can see that most of the classes can stay the same. You just handle the data differently depending on the game structure and game modes.

This chapter is also all about networking, Xbox Live, and Games for Windows Live. It does not matter what kind of game you want to write; if you want multiplayer support beyond split screens, you will need a powerful networking API. XNA 2.0 happens to deliver just that, but at the time of this writing, it is not publicly available. For that reason, you are going to learn all about networking with the System.Net classes from the .NET Framework. The knowledge is applicable to XNA 2.0 networking. You can save some code by not having to write your own messaging and session management classes because XNA 2.0 already handles all that for you, but it does not hurt to know about how they work. While System.Net provides all the low-level classes you ever need on Windows for network programming; it is not supported on the Xbox 360 via XNA yet. XNA 2.0 uses an own networking API and you can only use this API for any network communication on the Xbox 360. If you just want to write a Windows game, you still can use the XNA 2.0 networking APIs, but you are not limited to it. There are also many other commercial and free networking APIs available and many of them have support for .NET and can be used with your Windows game, but this is beyond the scope of this book.

First, you will learn how to write a very simple chat application via UDP Packets. UDP Packets are also used for the XNA 2.0 networking API, but they are hidden and just used internally. All the classes from this chapter will be the basis for all networking code in the later chapters. While some easy unit tests to send some packets around would usually do the job, a more solid approach is chosen here. You can use the networking classes from this chapter in the next two chapters and the resulting game, which makes it even more important to write a flexible code base and offer the capability to easily extend the messages. More on network messages in a little while after you have learned the basics.

The next chapter develops the concept for the role-playing game and covers important game design decisions. This is not only useful for the game screens and required game classes on top of the existing XNA graphics engine you have so far, but it is also important for designing the game messages. In a multiplayer game you have to think about how all connected players stay in contact and communicate with each other. The next chapter also explains how to add some extra features such as an animation system for models with help of skinning and bone skeletons, and it features an updated UI system for a more complex menu and in-game handling of game events and networking messages.

Chapter 17 finally brings all the new parts together and explains how each part of the Dungeon Quest game fits together. While this book tries to explain as much as possible about the Dungeon Quest game, it is focused on giving you good advice on how to use graphics, sounds and networking in your games. Dungeon Quest is also an open source project that will probably change constantly. More information about Dungeon Quest, the development process, discussions, and new game mods can be found on the official website for the game: www.DungeonQuestGame.com.

What's New in XNA 2.0

Before we get into all the networking theory, let's take a quick look at the features provided by XNA 2.0. As mentioned before, at the time of this writing there is not much information available about the inner workings of XNA 2.0, but from the information available and the first peek previews, we can make some assumptions. Please note that some of this information provided in this section applies to early beta versions of XNA 2.0 and might change in the final XNA 2.0 release.

The ability to do networking was one of the most requested features for XNA when it was released and lacked any support on the Xbox 360 platform. Even on the Windows platform where System.Net is available, almost no XNA games have been written that support any networking. While writing a multiplayer game in itself is a highly complex topic and often goes beyond the responsibility of a good game engine, the total inability to do anything on the Xbox 360 platform made it not very lucrative to write a multiplayer game because it would not run on the Xbox. For a Windows-only game, you could also use Managed DirectX instead of XNA and maybe even the deprecated DirectPlay framework.

DirectPlay was a part of Microsoft's DirectX API, but it was deprecated in 2004. All newer DirectX SDK downloads do not contain the required header files and libraries anymore and on Windows Vista the whole DirectPlay, DirectPlay Voice, and DirectPlay NAT helper dlls were removed, making it even harder (if not impossible) to even use this technology. You might ask yourself why Microsoft no longer supported DirectPlay while all other parts of DirectX were still updated and maintained. There are two reasons for this. Officially, Microsoft was announcing that, in the future, the XNA Framework would bring a new networking API with help of the already existing Xbox Live technology, which could have been ported to Windows PCs. DirectPlay is not supported anymore in Windows Vista, but as already mentioned, the libraries were not even available in newer SDK downloads, even for Windows XP.

The second and probably truer reason for the quick demise of DirectPlay is that no one seriously used it. The framework itself was flawed and it was hard to figure out what it did. Although it worked okay when testing locally, problems arose when the technology was used over the Internet when the connection went bad. Just writing a simple test application or game was okay for DirectPlay, but anything beyond that was hard to maintain and test. While writing multiplayer games is hard, writing the basic networking code is not that complicated, as you will see later in this chapter. It is much harder to find the right model for processing game messages. It usually requires several tries to figure out which protocol is the best for this game, whether the game should be server-client or peer-to-peer and how can you circumvent firewall issues and other networking problems. While DirectPlay supported some simple NAT support and allowed routers that support DirectPlay or UPNP to allow playing games behind firewalls, it usually did not work on most hardware and software configurations and brought more problems than solutions with it.

Many years ago, I started with DirectPlay, too, and wrote some simple chat applications and games with it, but as soon as I tried it out using Sockets directly via the System.Net classes, I never turned back and never again used DirectPlay. The learning curve for Sockets might be a little bit harder, but it is always good to know more about the underlying technology. Once you understand all that, it is not much harder to write your own networking framework yourself — at least if you have the time for it. If you just want to use an existing framework, DirectPlay was fine and quickly hacking together some networking code with System.Net is fine, too.

Overview About Networking in XNA 2.0

Okay, enough talk about the past. XNA 2.0 will hopefully not repeat the same mistakes the DirectPlay framework had before it was declared obsolete. It will certainly help you if you have programmed with DirectPlay, System.Net, or any networking API before because XNA 2.0 will still use the same basic functionality (sessions, players, and messages).

In addition to the other features discussed earlier in this book for XNA 2.0 such as VS 2005 support, improved project management, and more available game components, the main new feature for XNA 2.0 is certainly the ability to write multiplayer games with its new networking API. The new API is easy to use and will help you get started very quickly. As you can see later in this chapter, when you develop all the required classes to make networking work with System.Net, there is quite a bit of ground to cover. When XNA 2.0 is released, the code will be updated, but the old code will still be in the project for comparison. With XNA 2.0, you won't need to write the base classes for session management, handling players, or network messaging. The network code provided in this chapter will also not run on the Xbox 360 yet because it is based on System.Net, a namespace not available on the Xbox 360 side of XNA. When the code is updated and runs directly on the XNA 2.0 Framework, you will be able to use it on the Xbox 360, too.

The code in this chapter tries to be close to the XNA 2.0 networking API, but some information is not revealed yet and even subject to change, so beware of changes. Later in this chapter, I will also talk in more detail about sessions, players, and network messages. If you are not sure what all these words mean, just read ahead — it will get clearer in a few minutes.

XNA 2.0 also allows you to use the existing Xbox LIVE and Windows for Games System Link technology to announce games on these platforms and allow other players to join your game, chat with them in the lobby and use the advanced features of these platforms. Normally you would have to create such lobby and game servers yourself, which is quite a lot of work — they're hard to test and expensive to maintain because you need an always-online server with a lot of bandwidth. Independent developers are usually not ready for this big step and either create just Singleplayer games or provide only very basic multiplayer experiences. With XNA 2.0, it becomes much easier for smaller teams to use these technologies without having to write them yourself. All the session management will be handled for you; you just create a session, and other players will be able to search for it and then join it. You can focus more of your time writing the game and not have to deal with session management yourself much.

Xbox LIVE is beyond the scope of this book and our game Dungeon Quest is not going to use much of it at the moment. At the time of this writing, it supports only a simple web service announcing the currently open games, but maybe it will be extended to support Xbox LIVE at a later point in time. For more information about Xbox LIVE and usage examples from XNA 2.0, you should visit the official Xbox LIVE and XNA websites (`www.Xbox.com`, `http://msdn2.microsoft.com/en-us/xna/default.aspx`, and `http://Creators.Xna.com`).

In addition to providing services to make a session of your game visible to other players around the world, XNA 2.0 also provides base classes to simplify the game flow. There are predefined messages that will notify you of standard events such as if a player joined the game, if the host has left, or if the network connection was interrupted. You don't have to define them all by yourself as we do later in this chapter. One cool feature is Host Migration, which was also present in DirectPlay. Once the host player (the player that created the game) has left, the game usually ends or gets out of sync. In Server-Client games, the host is also the server and when he leaves, all connections will get destroyed, making it impossible for anyone to play with any of the other players. Host Migration will prevent that from happening. A message is sent to another player, who then becomes the new host, and all network communication will now go through him. While this concept sounds great, there are some cautions. It can also go all wrong because of firewall issues and the inability for certain players to connect with each other. Most games do not support this feature because it is hard to test, and it is very hard to make sure it will work all of the time. All I'm saying is that you should not design your game around this feature before testing if it works sufficiently. For example, in a simple chat application, it makes sense to migrate, but a more complex real-time strategy game usually involves a lot of other problems on top of the host migration that can fail (keeping the game in sync after the migration, missing messages or game turns, and so on).

TCP Versus UDP

You have probably heard of these two networking protocols. This section will not explain them in detail; there is plenty of information available on the Internet about the differences, nuances, and uses of these protocols we use every day. In short: XNA and most games use the UDP protocol, whereas most applications such web browsing, e-mail, FTP, file sharing, and so on use the TCP protocol.

Both protocols work with IP addresses and ports; you probably know your computer's local IP address (something like 192.168.0.1) and ports range from 0 to 65536, enabling each application to choose one or more ports. For example, web browsing is usually done on port 80, which is displayed as http:// in the browser; a DNS server translates the domain to an IP and the rest of the URL is then processed by the web server and returned to the user that wants to see the web page.

Figure 15-1 shows the way a TCP connection is initiated. Once the connection is up and running, data can be exchanged between the two parties until one of them closes the connection. This is usually used for Server-Client architectures, where the client connects to the server and requests some information; then the server sends the information back and the interchange is over. You can see this happening every time you request a web site from a web server in your browser; when you connect to a FTP server or even when you get your e-mail.

In games, this approach is also used for game servers, which return the list of available games by request, the number of players online, and so on. Other than that, most first person shooters also use Server-Client architecture — usually not with the TCP protocol, but with UDP instead, which we will discuss in a second. In those games, one player is the server and all other players connect to him. Only the server communicates with the clients; the clients don't know each other's IP addresses and they can only relay messages through the server to each other. TCP is great if you just want to provide some information, handle some requests, and especially if you want to make sure the information actually ends up on the other side before closing the connection.

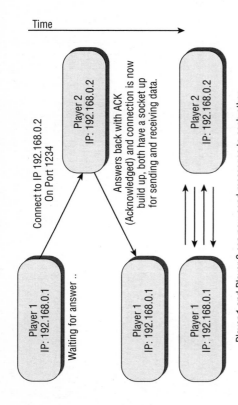

TCP Connections

Time

Player 1
IP: 192.168.0.1

Waiting for answer ..

Player 2
IP: 192.168.0.2

Connect to IP 192.168.0.2
On Port 1234

Player 1
IP: 192.168.0.1

Answers back with ACK
(Acknowledged) and connection is now
build up, both have a socket set up
for sending and receiving data.

Player 1
IP: 192.168.0.1

Player 2
IP: 192.168.0.2

Player 1 and Player 2 can now send messages to each other,
both have to maintain the connection, else it will be disconnected
from the other party as well.

Figure 15-1

However, TCP also has some drawbacks: Each message is confirmed on the other side, which takes longer than just sending the data and even ignoring it if some of it did not arrive. For certain situations, it is much more important to send data fast than to make each message confirm itself on the other end. TCP is not only adding time for this confirmation until a message arrives, but it also makes each network packet bigger, which is not an issue if you are sending just a few big packets around such as when you are surfing and downloading images, HTML pages, and files. But in network games you might want to send out many game messages and player input many times each second and each message involves only a few bytes (for example a new player position). Now you can multiply this by the amount of players you are connected to. Some games support 32 or more players running around at the same time shooting each other; if a Server-Client architecture is used, a server has to send updates to all clients and receive input messages very often to keep the game as realistic as possible. There are also other MMO (massively multiplayer online) games that allow many more players to see each other at the same time, which is even more complex.

While it is a drawback of UDP that you don't know if a message has arrived, it is also a good reason to use it. It's also good that you have less overhead and lag compared to TCP. Sometimes it is not that important if one of ten position–update-messages actually arrives at the other end; the other nine messages will still provide sufficient information and will arrive in very short intervals anyway. The game code can even interpolate the values and it won't matter much if ten or just two messages are sent or received each second; the movement just gets jerkier as fewer messages arrive in case a player has a bad network connection. Luckily, today more players have a better connection than a few years ago when most people were still using dial-up connections with a very limited amount of data that could be sent and received each second.

As you can see in Figure 15-2, UDP is connectionless, which means you just send some data to a specific IP and port and it may or may not arrive. While this sounds horrible, it is actually quite useful for peer-to-peer scenarios, where every player connects with every other player. Only one UDP listener has to be created at each one of the connected computers. The UDP listener can be used to receive messages from all players, even new players that were not in the game previously. You just remember the destination IP and port for each player (usually stored in an IPEndpoint structure) and keep sending data. Many firewalls are also designed in a way that allow UDP Punch Through, which means that even if all UDP ports are blocked by the firewall, and it will prevent another player from connecting to you, once you try to connect to him at the same port, the firewall will notice this and allow incoming UDP packets from the other side. If just one player has a firewall and all other players are reachable, there will not be much of a problem. However, if two players both have a firewall and are blocking each other, this will be a serious problem. One very famous application that uses many firewall punch-through tricks is Skype, which works with many different firewall situations and allows people to connect to each other behind NATs and Firewalls without much trouble. Most games do not use advanced techniques like this and force the player to open up a certain port on their firewall and NAT to allow playing the game or using an application (see Figure 15.3 for an example to set up the Arena Wars or Battle.Net port). The next section of this chapter will talk in more detail about advanced networking problems.

Some games also use the TCP protocol because it is easier to ensure messages actually get across the network to the other player unlike UDP where you never get any confirmation that a message has arrived or not. This means that if you are using UDP and want to make sure a message that is sent to another player actually arrives and is processed you have to implement your own message checking system. For example, an important message — for example, a player is leaving or the game is over because your team won — should not be delivered without any confirmation.

Choosing between TCP and UDP is always a decision you have to make for each game or application. It won't make much sense to use UDP for web browsing because parts or even the whole web site may not arrive at the client. For first person shooters, you usually don't want the TCP overhead and you can live with missing update messages because your game engine interpolates the player positions anyway.

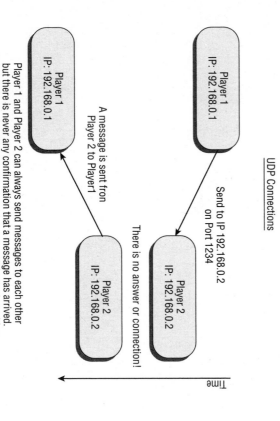

UDP Connections

Send to IP 192.168.0.2
on Port 1234

There is no answer or connection!

A message is sent from
Player 2 to Player1

Time

Player 1 and Player 2 can always send messages to each other
but there is never any confirmation that a message has arrived.
Even an important message like joining a game might get lost either
sending it or when the host sends joined game messages to us.

Figure 15-2

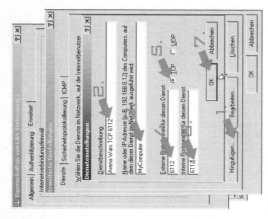

Figure 15-3

Firewalls and Punching Through NATs

Most games use Server-Client network architectures, but many games, especially strategy games, use Peer-To-Peer networking, too. When using Server-Client, each client just connects to the server player; in a Peer-To-Peer model, every player is connected to every other player in the game, which can be quite a lot of connections if many players are in the same game. Applications also use the name Peer-To-Peer, usually for file sharing. In those applications, each user is connected to many other users and not to one server.

The following figures show the problems that can occur when a player tries to connect to another player and what can happen if one or both have a blocking firewall or NAT (that is, Network Address Translator, or what you would usually call your router). These images are from the Arena Wars FAQ and explain how players are connected to each other in the Arena Wars game, which uses Peer-To-Peer and a TCP architecture. Figure 15-4 shows the normal connection process from one player to another when the IP can be reached directly. In addition to the process described here, Arena Wars used some tricks with port guessing for NAT punching and UPnP support. These will automatically configure ports on a NAT firewall. In later game versions, the game server managed all games, similar to role-playing games where the game logic is also calculated on the game server and not on the clients.

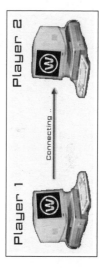

Figure 15-4

Figure 15-5 shows the easiest trick to circumvent firewall problems, if just one specific player has a blocking firewall; nearly all good multiplayer games support this technique. If a player can't be reached, try connecting the other way around. Because all players are connected to the game server that manages chat, channels, and the global games list, each player's IP and port are also known to the game server. The server can initiate a reverse connect if the first connection attempt did not succeed in a certain timeout (for example, 3 seconds). If player 1 is joining an existing game of player 2, but cannot connect, then the host player 2 will try to connect to the new player 1.

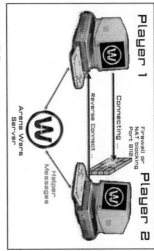

Figure 15-5

While this technique is useful, sometimes it will not help because both players are behind firewalls or NATs, which is especially true for Peer-To-Peer with many players. Figure 15-6 shows this problem; both firewalls are not allowing any incoming connection on Port 6112 to come through. When both players are unreachable, the game should display a message to both players that they cannot reach each other.

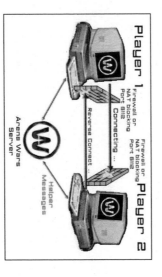

Figure 15-6

Some firewalls allow the so-called NAT Punching trick, but usually it only works with UDP because it is connectionless and it will allow incoming connections on a certain port if the user behind the firewall is simultaneously also sending data out on the same port. The technique also sometimes works with TCP, but it involves more complicated tricks such as guessing the next port the firewall would allow once a port was blocked and then connecting on the new port, but that is very hard to do and does not work on many firewall configurations anyway. Most players today are not used to open ports on their firewall and because many games such as first person shooters and role-playing games use a server-client architecture where the server is always reachable on a public IP, it does not matter if the user has a firewall that blocks incoming connections. All connections are made to the server and will work just fine (unless the user firewall is also blocking all outgoing connections, but then it can't be used for gaming at all). Figure 15-7 shows NAT Punching in action. When you are using UDP, you don't need any extra programming or server messages because the previously implemented reverse connect will also punch through both fire-walls if the other connection attempt happens fast enough or multiple times.

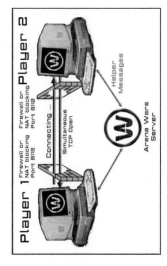

Figure 15-7

XNA 2.0 will probably use some of these techniques and will probably support UPnP, too, because DirectPlay also supported this, but this is one of the areas you can't improve when you are just using the networking API because you need full control before you ever get a `PlayerHasJoinedGame` message. In Dungeon Quest, you will not worry about these problems for now. The game uses the Server-Client architecture and the host player will always have to make sure all other players can connect to him; otherwise, no one will be able to join. Maybe some of the tricks presented here will be implemented into the game at a later point in time, but for now let's focus on getting the networking code up and running!

Network Architecture

This section describes the way networking was implemented into Dungeon Quest. I already discussed most of the techniques and protocols used, so let's take a quick look at the networking classes in Dungeon Quest (see Figure 15-8).

That looks like a lot of classes, but many of them are really short. Most of them can be tested separately. For example, the GameServer handles all the communication with the game list web service and you can test all the available methods with the unit tests at the end of the file. For networking, you should check out the `SessionConnection` class, which is the low-level UDP support class.

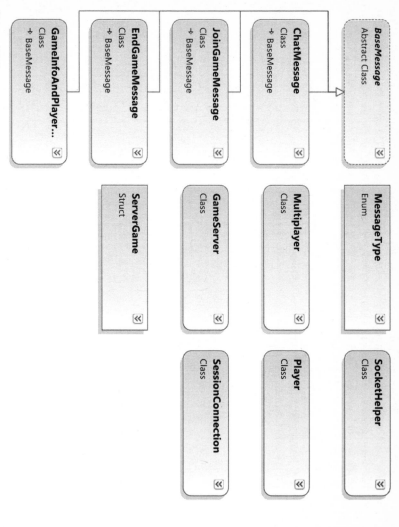

Figure 15-8

Before continuing the discussion about the implementation details, let me give you a short overview about each class, in the order they were developed:

☐ `SessionConnection`: Provides the basic connection abilities through System.Net by using the `UdpClient` class. This class will probably be replaced later by the XNA 2.0 networking API to support the Xbox 360 platform, too.

Derive from this class to provide more detailed networking messages and whatever you need, this class just provides methods to connect to other parties and to send messages! Because UDP is not reliable, there is no guarantee that a message will ever arrive. You will pretty much ignore this fact; if nothing arrives at the other end, it should not matter. Sometimes it can be bad for chat messages or when connecting, because the player will notice such events failing, but the game is designed in a way that all messages are sent repeatedly.

Note that this class is internal; use the `Player` class to instantiate players and connect to them. The `Player` class is also used to store all game states for each connected player plus everything else you need.

☐ `GameServer`: This class could probably be implemented at a later point in time, maybe even after all the other classes are finished. The class provides a Web service we are using for the game server. It provides us with the list of games and allows us to promote our own game online!

The rest of the multiplayer classes would work fine without this, but without it the only way to join game sessions from other players is by entering their IP addresses, which is not very convenient for the players. Not to mention that usually players don't know each others' IP addresses, not even in a local area network and certainly not in the whole wide Internet. Thanks to the GameServer class, you don't have to worry about this; you can retrieve a list of available games with the IP addresses of their hosts. This allows your game to provide a list of games when the user clicks on Multiplayer and everyone can just join a game or create his own game, which is then visible for other players. In addition to public games, private games can also be created, which will not show up on the public games list.

❑ ServerGame: Server game structure used mainly for the GameServer game list, but also for the Multiplayer class to store all global information about the current game. Each game has a game name, an IP to connect to (always using the default port, which is 6112 by the way), a host player name, and the number of players currently in the game. All public games are announced to the server; private games are just in LAN or when someone knows the IP.

To refresh the list of server games, we can press a refresh button in the multiplayer screen; the list is also updated every time we enter the multiplayer screen. Currently, a web service is used to add a new game to the server list and to retrieve the current list of active server games. Webservices will obviously not work on the Xbox 360 and in order to allow players finding multiplayer game sessions on the Xbox 360 the Xbox Live service with the help of XNA 2.0 has to be used. Maybe the game will even support both kinds of server games to provide the widest possible range of players. For example if Xbox Live only works when the player has a subscription, PC players may not want to use this service, they just want to play on the PC.

❑ Multiplayer: Main class to manage all the multiplayer stuff used in this game. The class maintains a list of players, all the chat messages, all game messages, and the state of the game. The Multiplayer class is also used for Singleplayer games, but then only one player is initialized.

This class is the high-level class for most multiplayer functionality required in the game. You can create new games, join existing games, and finally end the multiplayer game once it is over. Additionally, it provides helper methods to send out chat messages and check the connection status in case anything goes wrong. You can easily access all of the known multiplayer parameters such as the game name, the IP of the host, and a list of all players currently in the game. Only the host player manages all these values; clients just send messages to the host, who will resend it to all the other clients.

This class heavily depends on the SessionConnection class as well as the Player class. For the game messages, the BaseMessage class and derived classes are used. More details about the game messages will be discussed shortly.

❑ Player: The player class is used to hold all player information in a multiplayer game. One instance of this class is used for each player in the game holding all his data. The Multiplayer class makes sure all players and the game stay in sync. It is important to note that we just need a player name and the IP and port (represented in the IPEndPoint variable) for each player. Clients only need the player name for each player and the IP and port is only used for the host player to be able to send network messages to each client. Because the game uses a Server-Client architecture we do not have direct connections between any two clients; only connections to the host are maintained. When I say connection here, I mean just holding the IP and port. Because we are using UDP, no actual network connection is maintained.

❑ SocketHelper: Helper class for sending and receiving data through network sockets. This class will not be required at all when using XNA 2.0, it is very specific to System.Net and the way we are using the UDP protocol.

☐ BaseMessage, ChatMessage, JoinGameMessage, etc.: Base networking message for all messages we use in multiplayer mode. There is no real data in the BaseMessage class except the type of the game message; all the data and logic is in the derived classes.

ChatMessage, for example, contains a player name from the one sending the chat message and the chat message text itself. All message classes provide a constructor to initialize the message and they override the Write method to store all data to a stream with help of a BinaryWriter instance. All message classes are written the same way and are very easy to maintain; they are usually 50 lines or less. The MessageType enumeration is used to figure out which message type belongs to which message class. All the message handling is also done in the SessionConnection class, mostly in the OnHandleMessage method, which is called by the OnRetrieve method, which is triggered when we receive network data on the UDP port the class is listening at.

Looks like a long list of classes and yes, it might look a little complex at the first sight, but once you get used to them, they are pretty easy to use. Let's start with some simple networking code and let's figure out how UDP is used to send some bytes over the network.

Sending UDP Data

You can find many tutorials and samples about sending UDP or TCP data from one socket to another, but it is very hard to make the jump from just sending bytes around and actually having a meaningful messaging system behind your network engine. Because some of this information is not relevant for XNA 2.0 programming because you don't have to worry about low level methods in XNA, I will keep this as short as possible.

All of the following code is from the UdpTests class inside the Unit Testing region of the SessionConnection class. As mentioned, the SessionConnection class was the first class created in the Networking namespace. I like to play around a bit with the underlying technology with the help of some unit tests before I go to the more serious code. Please note that for the Dungeon Quest code, a new unit-testing framework with the name xUnit is used, but is very similar to NUnit, which is used in the rest of this book. You probably won't notice it in most unit tests.

There are three methods in the UdpTests class: TestUdpServer, TestUdpClient, and TestUdpServerAndClient. You need three unit tests to test sending messages from the client to the server because you can start only one unit test at a time. No matter if you use VS2005/VS2008 and an add-in like TestDriven.Net or if you call a unit test from the Program Main method, only one method is executed at a time. But for networking you need at least two sockets, one server socket that is listening on a certain IP and port and the client socket that connects to the server and sends data to it (and the other way around, too). TestUdpServerAndClient will just call both methods. Earlier versions did this with threads, but the code is now rewritten to run asynchronously. TestUdpServer will return immediately and start listening on the specified port (which is 6112 again). TestUdpClient will just connect to the server and send some test data to it. The test data is a stream of bytes that is written to the log file on the server side. After waiting 750ms, the unit test will be exited and all sockets will be disposed.

Let's take a look at the TestUdpServer method:

```
/// <summary>
/// The UdpTests class performs some simple UDP connection tests.
/// </summary>
[Test]
```

```
public static void TestUdpServer()
{
    Console.WriteLine("Started server .." );
    try
    {
        // Use UDP sockets
        Socket serverSocket = new Socket(AddressFamily.InterNetwork,
            SocketType.Dgram, ProtocolType.UDP);
        // Assign the any IP of the machine and listen on the specfied port
        IPEndPoint ipEndPoint = new IPEndPoint(IPAddress.Any, Port);
        // Bind this address to the server
        serverSocket.Bind(ipEndPoint);
        IPEndPoint ipeSender = new IPEndPoint(IPAddress.Any, 0);
        // The epSender identifies the incoming clients
        EndPoint epSender = (EndPoint)ipeSender;
        // Start receiving data
        byte[] byteData = new byte[1024];
        serverSocket.BeginReceiveFrom(byteData, 0, byteData.Length,
            SocketFlags.None, ref epSender,
            // Note: This delegate will stay active, but we will leave this method!
            new AsyncCallback(delegate(IAsyncResult ar)
            {
                serverSocket.EndReceiveFrom(ar, ref epSender);
                Log.Write("Received message: " +
                    StringHelper.WriteArrayData(byteData, 8));
            }),
            epSender);
    } // try
    catch (Exception ex)
    {
        Log.Write("Failed to start udp server: " + ex.ToString());
    } // catch
} // TestUdpServer()
```

As you can see, the server is started with a console message to indicate what is going on in the unit test once it gets started. If anything goes wrong, an error message is displayed. Once we receive any network data, we will just display it. Actually, just the first 8 bytes with help of the WriteArrayData helper method inside the receiving delegate.

But before any sending or receiving of data can happen we have to set up the Socket for that purpose first. A socket is initialized by specifying the address family, usually InterNetwork, used for both UDP and TCP. The socket type is usually Dgram and, finally, the protocol type we are using is UDP. There are many different sockets we can create, but using raw sockets is much more complicated and involves writing your own low-level networking layer, which is not something we are interested in here. For most applications, UDP or TCP are just fine.

Next, an IPEndPoint is defined. For the server, only the port is important, which is a constant containing the value 6112. The IP is set to Any meaning that any of the IP addresses this machine is using are listening on the specified port. You might ask yourself why a machine might have multiple IP addresses, but this is very common for servers. Specifying a certain IP here allows you to write services that will only listen on a specific IP. One example would be a web server with multiple IP addresses and each IP address running a different web server instance. For our game engine, we are not interested in that functionality; we are always going to listen on all IPs.

After the socket `Bind` method has been called to assign the `IPEndPoint` to it, you can start listening. The `Bind` method is important, as it will associate the local endpoint to the socket. When using TCP, it has to be called before `Listen` is called because you have to know on which port you are listening for incoming connections. `Bind` does not have to be called when using the `Connect` method because you are already specifying the target IP and port there.

For UDP, you won't use `Listen` or `Connect` because the protocol is connectionless, but the `Bind` method is important if you want to allow other people to connect to you, which is exactly what you want in `TestUdpServer`. Clients won't need to call `Bind`; you can directly send data to a endpoint after creating a UDP socket, that is certainly an advantage of UDP.

Finally, we can listen for data on the UDP port; `epSender` is used to specify where the data is allowed to come from. Again, you can only allow listening from certain IP addresses, but that is usually only important for servers and security; you won't filter out anything. Anyone can send you network messages. Network security is certainly a big topic and might be important for more complex games, but it is beyond the scope of this book.

The `BeginReceiveFrom` method expects a byte array for incoming data. In addition to the `epSender` variable, you also have to specify a method that will be called once data arrives for you. Thanks to .NET 2.0, you can use anonymous delegates, which are quite useful in unit tests. In the delegate itself, which will stay active even after leaving the `TestUdpServer` method, the byte data is just dumped to the log. It is important to call the `EndReceiveFrom` method after receiving data. Typically, you would call `BeginReceiveFrom` again to keep listening for data on the socket, but for this unit test you are just waiting for the first data stream.

Just starting this unit test will not do much yet. The text "Started server . . ." is output and nothing else happens. You need a client sending you some data to get the "Received message:" message in the console. Let's take a look at the `TestUdpClient` unit test for that.

```
/// <summary>
/// Test udp client
/// </summary>
[Test]
public static void TestUdpClient()
{
    try
    {
        Console.WriteLine("Started client .."); 

        // Using UDP sockets
        Socket clientSocket = new Socket(AddressFamily.InterNetwork,
            SocketType.Dgram, ProtocolType.UDP);

        // Server is listening on the specified port and we use localhost here
        EndPoint epServer = (EndPoint)new IPEndPoint(
            IPAddress.Parse("127.0.0.1"), Port);
        byte[] byteData =
            new byte[] { 1, 2, 3, 4, 10, 11, 12, 13, 14, 15, 16 };

        // Send message to the server
        clientSocket.BeginSendTo(byteData, 0, byteData.Length,
            SocketFlags.None, epServer,
            new AsyncCallback(delegate(IAsyncResult ar)
        {
            //Nothing in here yet ..
```

```
        clientSocket.EndSend(ar);
      }),
      null);
    Thread.Sleep(750);
    Console.WriteLine("Ended client .."); 
  } // try
  catch (Exception ex)
  {
    Log.Write("Failed to start udp client: " + ex.ToString());
  } // catch
} // TestUdpClient()
```

The unit test is very similar to `TestUdpServer`. You will later see that the code in the `SessionConnection` class is also almost identical for the host and the clients; the main difference is the way the socket is set up and how we send messages just to the host player or to all clients. As mentioned, we just have to create a socket and the `IPEndPoint` for server that is listening on the specified port. Please note that the IP is hard-coded here; this is not how the game code will connect to the server. The port is still 6112 and once you have `epServer` assigned and the socket up and running, you can start sending data to the server with the `BeginSendTo` method.

`BeginSendTo` looks very similar to `ReceiveDataFrom` and it expects the same parameters, but this time the byte data array is used to send data out, not to receive data. The delegate is then called after the send-ing operation is complete; we will just close the operation with `EndSend`. Check out the `SocketHelper` class on how to handle these things in the real game network code.

After sending the data, the method waits for a while and finally outputs a final message to the console. It is important to wait because the data is sent asynchronously. It will not appear on the server instantly. It is certainly pretty fast when using localhost, but you have to think about sending messages over the Internet, which just takes some time because you don't want to block in any of your methods, but will always use asynchronously methods. Another thing you always have to think about when using UDP sockets is to be aware that a message might not arrive and you might not get any error when sending a UDP message to a not-listening IP. The catch block will usually just catch major network problems or programming errors.

Finally, you can call both unit tests together with the `TestUdpServerAndClient` method:

```
/// <summary>
/// Test udp server and client
/// </summary>
public static void TestUdpServerAndClient()
{
  TestUdpServer();
  TestUdpClient();
} // TestUdpServerAndClient()
```

You should now see the following output indicating that the network message was sent from the client to the server (both running locally on your machine):

```
Started server ..
Started client ..
[09:05:00] Received message: 1, 2, 3, 4, 10, 11, 12, 13
Ended client ..
```

461

Connecting Two Players

While the UdpTests class provides all the low-level functionality you need for writing a network game, it is pretty useless because you don't have any player management yet. Just sending some byte arrays around is not going to cut it. Before I discuss the network messages, you should make sure that you have fully mastered the basic network code to do more high-level and advanced tests.

The SessionConnection class (see Figure 15-9) was written exactly for that purpose — to make it easy to use UDP sockets and so that you don't have to worry about any of the underlying protocols. You could even change the whole game from using UDP to TCP without having to change anything but the SessionConnection class (and maybe add some more helper methods in SocketHelper).

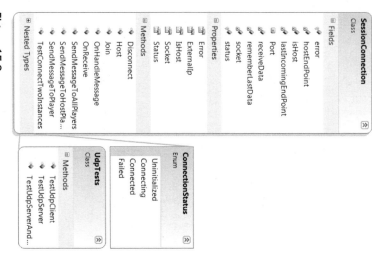

Figure 15-9

There are many internal and private methods in SessionConnection, but there are also some important methods like Host, Join, and OnHandleMessage, which I discuss in a second. In addition to the methods and mostly private fields, several properties allow you to get the used socket, see the status the connection is in, and get any errors that might have occurred. The most important methods are:

❑   Host: This method is similar to TestUdpServer. It will initialize the socket for the host player and start listening for incoming data. The method also accepts the new game name, and you can specify if this is a public game or a private one. Public games are announced on the game server list, which this method also handles for us. All incoming data will be processed in the internal `OnReceive` method, which will process the incoming data and convert it to game messages with the help of the `OnHandleMessage` method that will be discussed in the next section.

❑ `Join`: Pretty much the opposite of `Host`. Like `TestUdpClient`, will connect to a host IP address, but you are not sending a dummy byte array to the server. Instead, the `JoinGameMessage` is sent to the server and you, as the client, are also listening for incoming data with the help of the `BeginReceiveFrom` method and the `OnReceive` event handler.

❑ `Disconnect`: Called when the game is over or you cancel the "start game" screen. A client just disconnects from the server by sending the `EndGame` message first. The host player will remove the player from the player list, which will also happen if sending data to the client is no longer possible. If the host player disconnects, all clients will receive the `EndGame` message and the game will end for all players.

❑ `OnReceive` and `OnHandleMessage`: Called from the `Host` and `Join` method and again inside the `OnReceive` method to continue listing for incoming data once some data was processed. The `OnReceive` method is the low-level helper method and the `OnHandleMessage` method is called once you have the byte data ready and can convert it to a game message.

❑ `SendMessageToPlayer` and `SendMessageToAllPlayers`: These two methods are helpers, which are mainly called from other high-level methods of the `Multiplayer` class to send out data to a specific player (usually to the host player) or to all players (from the server to all clients). Because all of the sending logic is encapsulated in the `BaseMessage` class, these methods are pretty simple and will just handle the player list and check if the player is still valid to send to.

You should now know enough to take a look at the `TestConnectTwoInstances` unit test of the `SessionConnection` class, which will just create two instances of `SessionConnection`, one to host a game and one to connect to the game. Please note that this version of the unit test is just to check whether creating and joining a game session is possible and whether the connection status behaves as you expect it to. In later versions of the game, the unit test will probably support more functionality such as involving the game server and testing results from the public game list, and connecting via DNS names and sending messages. But for now, be happy to just connect two instances of `SessionConnection`. The game itself will have only one `SessionConnection` instance, which is maintained in the `Multiplayer` class. Each player has one session he is connected to; you are just simulating two players in the unit test.

```
/// <summary>
/// Simple test to connect two instances of SessionConnection via all
/// the helper functionality from this class and GameServer.
/// </summary>
[Test]
public static void TestConnectTwoInstances()
{
    // Just create two instances
    SessionConnection connectionOne = new SessionConnection();
    SessionConnection connectionTwo = new SessionConnection();
    // Each connection should know its external Ip
    string ourIp = GameServer.GetOurExternalIp();
    Assert.Equal(ourIp, connectionOne.ExternalIp);
    Assert.Equal(ourIp, connectionTwo.ExternalIp);
    // We are not connected yet
    Assert.Equal(ConnectionStatus.Uninitialized, connectionOne.Status);
    Assert.Equal(ConnectionStatus.Uninitialized, connectionTwo.Status);
```

```
// Connect them to each other, start by creating a new public session
const string TestGameName = "TestConnectTwoInstances's game";
connectionOne.Host(TestGameName, true);
// Host must be in created state now, we should have a game, etc.
Assert.Equal(ConnectionStatus.Connected, connectionOne.Status);
// Change our player name for the client
Player.OurPlayerName = "SecondPlayer";
// Join the session the directy way (via Ip)
connectionTwo.Join(ourIp);
/*hard to test, usually we are already connected because it is fast!
// We should be in connecting state right now
Assert.Equal(ConnectionStatus.Connecting, connectionTwo.Status);
*/
// Wait for a while until we are connected.
Thread.Sleep(500);
// Client must be in created state now, we should have a game, etc.
Assert.Equal(ConnectionStatus.Connected, connectionTwo.Status);
} // TestConnectTwoInstances()
```

First, both connections are created, but until you call either the Host or Join method, the connection is the Uninitialized state and not useable yet. xUnit assertions are written with the Assert.Equal method; in NUnit, we would use Assert.AreEqual, but the functionality is the same. Connection one is then created via the Host method, which will create a new public game, which can also be found on the game server list discussed later in this chapter. Connection one is now connected, but connection two did not do anything yet. Time to connect the client, too; we just have to call the Join method with the host IP address. After you wait a short while, both the host and the client are now connected and could send messages back and forth, but you are not doing this right now. First of all, you have to talk a little bit about designing the network messages.

Network Messages

You can now connect two players with each other, at least in the sense that they can send data between each other. Because the game engine uses UDP they are not really connected, just listening for each other. Please also note that the host player will create new players via the JoinGameMessage class once a client connects. New clients are then added to the player list and also announced to all players in the game.

But just sending bytes around is not really a good way to design a multiplayer game. You need a more meaningful way to tell the other party what is going on. Take a look at the BaseMessage class and the ChatMessage class as an example, both of which will be used later in this chapter to write a chat application. The BaseMessage class is abstract and cannot be used directly, but it contains many useful methods and holds the type of the message, which is described with a big comment block for each possible type in the MessageType enumeration.

```
/// <summary>
/// Message type for communication between clients. The
/// GameServer functionality is not handled with messages,
/// see GameServer.cs for more details!
/// All messages are derived from the BaseMessage class.
/// </summary>
```

```
public enum MessageType
{
    /// <summary>
    /// Simple message sent by new clients to the host if
    /// they want to join the game. The host responds with
    /// GameInfoAndPlayerList or he will kill the connection
    /// if the game is full.
    /// </summary>
    JoinGame,

    /// <summary>
    /// This message is sent by the host player if anyone
    /// joins or leaves this session. The host then sends the
    /// PlayerList message to all players including the new
    /// player and informs everyone about all players
    /// currently in the game. Each player chooses his
    /// character before joining the game. Each player has a
    /// name and ip to allow all others to connect to him.
    /// </summary>
    GameInfoAndPlayerList,

    /// <summary>
    /// Simple chat message, always goes to all players in
    /// the game. Contains both the sending player name and
    /// the chat message.
    /// </summary>
    ChatMessage,

    /// <summary>
    /// End game, sent by the host when the game ends, but
    /// also by a client to indicate he is leaving. Other
    /// than using this message a client or event the host
    /// can also disconnect and then the game is also ended
    /// for the other party.
    /// </summary>
    EndGame,

    //TODO: all the ingame messages!

    /// <summary>
    /// End of enum, just to count how many members we have!
    /// </summary>
    NumOfMessageTypes,
} // enum MessageType
```

These are the message types used for the chat application from this chapter. The game will later support more message types for the in-game communication.

Let's take a look at the BaseMessage class — how the ChatMessage is derived from it and how this all is used to send a message over the network as a byte stream and finally put it back together on the other side. Figure 15-10 shows the BaseMessage class, the MessageType enumeration, and the ChatMessage class. All the other message types also have a class associated to them, but the data in them is the only thing that is different from the ChatMessage class.

The constructor of BaseMessage just assigns the message type and is not very spectacular.

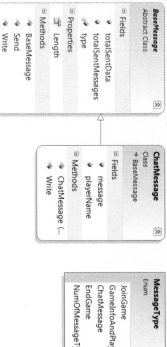

Figure 15-10

```
/// <summary>
/// Init message from given parameters!
/// </summary>
/// <param name="setType">Set type</param>
public BaseMessage(MessageType setType)
{
    type = setType;
} // BaseMessage(setType)
```

Derived classes, however, usually have two constructors, one to create a message from some data that is just set to the data fields and one to create the message from a byte stream received from another player. For example, the ChatMessage constructors just initialize the internal data.

```
/// <summary>
/// Create chat message
/// </summary>
/// <param name="setPlayerName">Set player name</param>
/// <param name="setMessage">Set message</param>
public ChatMessage(string setPlayerName, string setMessage)
    : base(MessageType.ChatMessage)
{
    playerName = setPlayerName;
    message = setMessage;
} // ChatMessage(setPlayerName, setMessage)

/// <summary>
/// Constructor from reader
/// </summary>
/// <param name="reader">Reader</param>
public ChatMessage(BinaryReader reader)
    : base(MessageType.ChatMessage)
{
    playerName = reader.ReadString();
    message = reader.ReadString();
} // ChatMessage(reader)
```

Analog to the constructor, each message class also has a `Write` method, which should be used to write the data in the same manner as it is extracted in the `BinaryReader` constructor. If the class does not have any extra data like the `EndGameMessage` class, both constructors can be empty and the `Write` method does not have to be overwritten at all. Usually, most messages have some data associated to them. The `BaseMessage Write` method is very simple:

```
/// <summary>
/// Write data to writer of a stream, derived classes should override
/// this method to write more data to the stream!
/// </summary>
/// <param name="writer">Writer</param>
public virtual void Write(BinaryWriter writer)
{
    writer.Write((byte)type);
} // Write(writer)
```

Overwritten in the `ChatMessage` class, the `Write` method just calls its base `Write` method and adds additional data to the stream.

```
/// <summary>
/// Write data to writer
/// </summary>
/// <param name="writer">Writer</param>
public override void Write(BinaryWriter writer)
{
    base.Write(writer);
    writer.Write(playerName);
    writer.Write(message);
} // Write(writer)
```

This all makes sense once you try to send out data, which is always done via the `BaseMessage Send` method, which does not have to be overwritten. It will always work thanks to the `Write` method. Here, a byte array is created and sent out to a socket:

```
/// <summary>
/// Helpers to count messages and for statistics.
/// </summary>
public static int totalSentMessages = 0, totalSentData = 0;
/// <summary>
/// Send stuff with help of Write over network via socket.
/// </summary>
/// <param name="socket">Socket</param>
public void Send(EndPoint targetEndPoint, Socket socket)
{
    if (targetEndPoint == null ||
        socket == null)
        return;
    MemoryStream memStream = new MemoryStream();
    BinaryWriter writer = new BinaryWriter(memStream);
    Write(writer);
    SocketHelper.SendData(targetEndPoint, socket, memStream.ToArray());
    totalSentMessages++;
    totalSentData += (int)memStream.Length;
} // Send(socket)
```

Here, a memory stream is created and filled with help of the Write method, which is virtual and will write all the data from the game message out, no matter in which one of the derived BaseMessage classes you are currently in. Then this data is sent out to the target end point and socket with help of the SocketHelper SendData method. The SendData method is not particularly interesting and like most methods in SocketHelper, once you understand it, you will just use it and not worry about the internals anymore. But here is the code for the SendData method anyway:

```
/// <summary>
/// Send data to socket, will build packet with length of message, etc.
/// </summary>
static public void SendData(EndPoint targetEndPoint, Socket socket,
byte[] data)
{
    // Not connected? Then simply don't send!
    if (targetEndPoint == null ||
        socket == null)
        return;

    MemoryStream memStream = new MemoryStream();
    BinaryWriter writer = new BinaryWriter(memStream);
    if (data.Length > 255)
        throw new NotSupportedException(
            "Messages above 255 bytes in length are not supported yet!");
    writer.Write((byte)data.Length);
    writer.Write(data);
    writer.Flush();
    // Begin sending the data to the remote device.
    socket.BeginSendTo(memStream.ToArray(), 0, (int)memStream.Length,
        SocketFlags.None, targetEndPoint, new AsyncCallback(SendCallback),
        socket);
} // SendData(socket, data)/// </summary>
```

The only important thing to mention here is the maximum length of messages, which cannot exceed 255 bytes yet, but you probably won't need to extend this any time soon. If you want to send more data, you can either split up messages or just use something bigger than a byte value for the length of the message. Also note that you need to send the length of the message with the message itself because it can happen that only part of it arrives or multiple messages are sent together and you have to split them up into the single messages they were sent out to you in. This is only possible if you know how long each message is. Other than that, the sending of the data is pretty much the same as you already know from the TestUdpClient unit test.

After incoming data is processed with the OnReceive method in the SessionConnection class, all byte data for one single message is passed to the OnHandleMessage method, which then converts the byte data to a meaningful message and handles it appropriately. Handling the message directly in the SessionConnection class and doing it in one big switch statement is probably not the best way to do it, but it is easy to write and easy to maintain if you don't have too many messages. For more complex network systems and games, you will have to think about refactoring this into a better way of handling the messages. I started with a Run method for each game message class, but it made the code hard to read and it was usually hard to get access to certain session and multiplayer variables from inside the message class. Because of that, I reverted back to the OnHandleMessage method:

```
public void OnHandleMessage(MessageType type, byte[] restData)
{
    MemoryStream memStream = restData != null ?
```

```
new MemoryStream(restData)) : new MemoryStream();
BinaryReader reader = new BinaryReader(memStream);
// Figure out which player has sent this message
Player thisPlayer = null;
if (isHost &&
    lastIncomingEndPoint as IPEndPoint != null)
{
    IPEndPoint playerEndPoint =
        lastIncomingEndPoint as IPEndPoint;
    foreach (Player player in Multiplayer.players)
        if (player.endPoint != null &&
            player.endPoint.Address.ToString() ==
            playerEndPoint.Address.ToString())
            thisPlayer = player;
} // if (isHost)
switch (type)
{
    case MessageType.JoinGame:
        JoinGameMessage joinGameMsg =
            new JoinGameMessage(reader);
        if (Multiplayer.players.Count <
            ServerGame.MaxPlayers)
        {
            // First figure out if there is already a player
            // with this name in the game. If that is so, we
            // have to rename the new player!
            foreach (Player player in Multiplayer.players)
                if (player.name == joinGameMsg.newPlayerName)
                {
                    if (joinGameMsg.newPlayerName.EndsWith("#2"))
                        joinGameMsg.newPlayerName =
                            joinGameMsg.newPlayerName.Replace("#2", "#3");
                    else if(joinGameMsg.newPlayerName.EndsWith("#3"))
                        joinGameMsg.newPlayerName =
                            joinGameMsg.newPlayerName.Replace("#3", "#4");
                    else
                        joinGameMsg.newPlayerName =
                            joinGameMsg.newPlayerName + "#2";
                } // foreach if (player.name)

            // Display player has joined message
            Multiplayer.SendPlayerChatMessage("Server",
                joinGameMsg.newPlayerName +
                " has joined the game.");
            // Add new player to the game
            Multiplayer.players.Add(new Player(
                joinGameMsg.newPlayerName,
                lastIncomingEndPoint));
            Multiplayer.currentGame.PlayersInGame =
                Multiplayer.players.Count;

            // And finally inform all players about the new
            // player!
            SendMessageToAllPlayers(
                new GameInfoAndPlayerListMessage(
```

```
    Multiplayer.currentGame, Multiplayer.players));
} // if (Multiplayer.currentGame.PlayersInGame)
else
{
    // Game is full, do not allow player to join!
    Multiplayer.AddServerMessage(
        joinGameMsg.newPlayerName +
        " can't join, the game is already full!");
    // Just inform the incoming player that this game
    // is not for him!
    SendMessageToPlayer(lastIncomingEndPoint,
        new EndGameMessage());
} // else

break;
case MessageType.EndGame:
[...]
case MessageType.GameInfoAndPlayerList:
[...]
case MessageType.ChatMessage:
    ChatMessage chatMsg = new ChatMessage(reader);
    // If we are the host, resent to all players
    if (isHost)
        Multiplayer.SendPlayerChatMessage(
            chatMsg.playerName, chatMsg.message);

    // Else just display the message, if it is not us
    else if (chatMsg.playerName != Player.OurPlayerName)
        Multiplayer.AddChatMessageFromServer(
            chatMsg.playerName, chatMsg.message);

break;
[... and all the other game messages]
} // switch
} // OnHandleMessage(type, restData)
```

The preceding code shows only two of the four game messages implemented for the chat application later in this chapter. The ChatMessage case is handled quickly without much code and most in-game messages will look similar, where the code in OnHandleMessage will just do some validation and call the appropriate method, mostly from the Multiplayer class. Messages such as JoinGameMessage or EndGameMessage are more complicated because you also handle all the joining issues, naming conflicts, cases when the game is full and managing the player list. But luckily for you, this code has to be written only once. You can extend your chat application to the full Dungeon Quest code in Chapter 17.

If you want to know more about the game message classes, just take a look at them; they are very short and easy to understand. OnHandleMessage will do most of the game logic required to handle each message.

Server Game List

In case you are wondering how the server game list is maintained, this section will describe how the Web service was implemented and tested. If you just want to go ahead and write the chat application, skip over this section. You can still read it later if you want to know how the server games are created and retrieved.

Chapter 15: Multiplayer and Xbox Live

The GameServer class (see Figure 15-11) manages all the online games and handles all the functionality to create games, remove them, and get a list of games from the game server. The unit tests in this class were written first before the web service itself was created. I based the web service on the same one I had written for a website I created a while ago in just one day. See http://XnaProjects.Net for all the XNA games I have created, plus projects from other people in the XNA community. The web service maintains an XML file in the App_Data directory and stores the current list of server games there. Then there are several methods to create, delete, and get server games. Writing web services is not something you will need to know when using XNA, so if you are using Xbox Live, you can safely ignore the web service and the GameServer class, but at the time of this writing, the class is the only way to make sure players can find each other's games on the Internet.

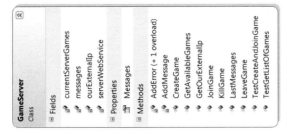

Figure 15-11

The easiest unit test is TestGetListOfGames, which just returns the current list of available public server games. This is also the most called method besides GetExternalIP, which is a helper to get the public IP address for each player that wants to know it for himself. GetAvailableGames is called when you enter the multiplayer screen in your game and also when you click the Refresh button.

```
/// <summary>
/// Test get list of games
/// </summary>
public static void TestGetListOfGames()
{
    Log.Write("List of games from the game server:\n" +
        StringHelper.WriteArrayData(GetAvailableGames()));
    Log.Write("Server messages: " +
        StringHelper.WriteArrayData(messages, "\n"));
} // TestGetListOfGames()
```

The next unit test, `TestCreateAndJoinGame`, is more complex and actually covers the whole `GameServer` class. I'm actually proud of this unit test because it does so many things and because I wrote all of this before even writing a single line of code in the `GameServer` or web service. The unit test goes through all steps of creating a game on the online game server, checking if it exists after creation, then joining the game and checking again if the game was updated, and so on until the server game is finally disposed. The comments in the unit test should be sufficient to understand what is tested and how you can use this class to announce, update, and get server games.

```
/// <summary>
/// Create game, check if it exists on the server game
/// list, let someone join and then finally kill the game
/// before anyone gets any ideas.
/// </summary>
public static void TestCreateAndJoinGame()
{
    // This is a 10-step unit test, which goes through all
    // methods of the web service and makes sure the web
    // service data always behaves the way it should!
    const string TestGameName = "TestGame";
    bool gameExists = false;
    string gameIp = "";
    int numberOfPlayersInGame = 0;
    List<ServerGame> games = new List<ServerGame>();
    try
    {
        // Step 1: Create game
        Assert.True(CreateGame(TestGameName));

        // Step 2: Check if game exists on server list
        games = GetAvailableGames();
        foreach (ServerGame game in games)
            if (game.Name == TestGameName)
            {
                gameExists = true;
                gameIp = game.IpAddress;
                numberOfPlayersInGame = game.PlayersInGame;
                break;
            } // foreach if (game.Name)
        // Make sure it was found
        Assert.True(gameExists);
        // And there must be just 1 player in that game right
        // now!
        Assert.Equal(1, numberOfPlayersInGame);

        // Step 3: Check if the external IP matches
        Assert.Equal(gameIp, GetOurExternalIp());

        // Step 4: Join the game (just for testing), must
        // return true
        Assert.True(JoinGame(gameIp));
```

```
    // Step 5: Check again if the game on the server has
    // now 2 players
    games = GetAvailableGames();
    foreach (ServerGame game in games)
      if (game.Name == TestGameName)
      {
        numberOfPlayersInGame = game.PlayersInGame;
        break;
      } // foreach if (game.Name)
    // There must 2 players in that game right now!
    Assert.Equal(2, numberOfPlayersInGame);

    // Step 6: Leave the game again
    LeaveGame(gameIp);

    // Step 7: Check again if the game on the server has
    // now 1 player again
    games = GetAvailableGames();
    foreach (ServerGame game in games)
      if (game.Name == TestGameName)
      {
        numberOfPlayersInGame = game.PlayersInGame;
        break;
      } // foreach if (game.Name)
    // There must 1 player in the game again!
    Assert.Equal(1, numberOfPlayersInGame);
  } // try
  finally
  {
    // Step 8: Finally kill the game (should always be
    // done!)
    KillGame(gameIp);

    // Step 9: Make sure the game is really gone
    games = GetAvailableGames();
    gameExists = false;
    foreach (ServerGame game in games)
      if (game.Name == TestGameName)
      {
        gameExists = true;
        break;
      } // foreach if (game.Name)
    // Make sure the game is not longer found
    Assert.False(gameExists);

    // Step 10: Output all the server messages that
    // occurred here.
    Log.Write("Server messages: " +
      StringHelper.WriteArrayData(messages, "\n"));
  } // finally
} // TestCreateAndJoinGame()
```

Writing a Chat Application

With all the network classes you've seen so far, you have a solid networking framework, but there is no real use behind it yet. For that reason, and to make sure you understand everything, you need for a full a multiplayer game we are going to write a little chat application in this chapter. If you want to use XNA 2.0 directly and not the classes presented until now in this chapter you should be able to adapt most of the following code without problems. For updated code, take a look at the official Dungeon Quest website: http://DungeonQuestGame.com.

The idea for the chat application is to provide a simple example of how to use the network classes you wrote this far. The code will not all be useless because for the Dungeon Quest game chat functionality will be quite useful. Please note that the chat application will not be very useful on the Xbox 360 because users normally don't have a keyboard attached to the Xbox 360. In addition, the code is currently based on System.Net sockets and would have to be ported to the networking API of XNA 2.0 to compile on the Xbox.

Let's take a look at the required classes to make the chat application work. It will not be as simple as the many console applications for Windows forms tutorials you may find on the Internet. You need your own UI, game screen classes, all the network API you got so far, and finally the chat message class plus the required logic to enter chat text and display all chat messages on the screen.

Game Screens

Figure 15-12 shows all the game screen classes involved in Dungeon Quest and the chat application (only the game screen for the game itself is not linked up yet). Some of the game screens are not used in the chat application, but I wrote all the classes anyway because they will be filled later with the Dungeon Quest game logic. All game screens just have a Run method, which is defined in the IGameScreen interface; there is nothing else a game screen class has to take care of. For example, the options or the Singleplayer screens are still empty at this point. We are going to focus our attention on the MultiplayerScreen and the StartGameScreen classes. The application starts with the SplashScreen class, which will then run the MainMenuScreen class where the player can select one of the other game screens or exit the game. All game screens always return back to the main menu if they are ended.

In the MultiplayerScreen class, all the hosting, joining, and handling of the GameServer games list is handled. The most complex thing here is the UI code, which involves different kind of buttons, a clickable list for the public games with details about each game, the scrollbar and other little features such as the server console log at the bottom of the screen. Because UI was already a big topic earlier in this book, I will not talk in detail about the UI code. In Dungeon Quest, the UI code is far more complex and can handle all kinds of resolutions with all kinds of aspect ratios. The UI is also animated with the help of some simple physics classes and looks much cooler in animation.

For this chapter, we are only interested in the network logic. Let's take a quick look at the Multiplayer screen (see Figure 15-13), which is accessible directly from the main menu. The player can join existing public games here, create his own game, or join private games via an IP. For easier testing, I also added a Refresh button that I left in because it is quite useful to update the list of public games. Please note that only the client can request the game list from the web service. You cannot send it out from the web service; it will only respond to incoming requests.

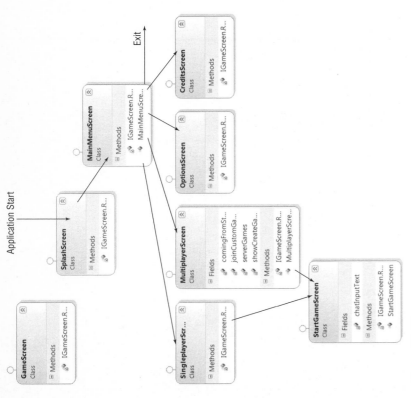

Figure 15-12

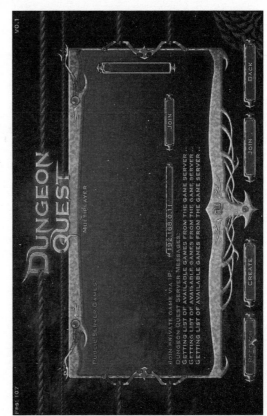

Figure 15-13

After the player has created his own game and is now the host of that new game, or if he joined a game and is only a client, the StartGameScreen is shown. Later this screen will allow the player to choose one of the player characters and then start the game when everyone is ready. Figure 15-14 shows the StartGameScreen in action. The important thing here is the chat text box, which allows you to enter chat messages that will be sent to the host player and then resent to all of the clients, which is the same way game messages are processed. All the joining, hosting, leaving, and player list update code is also handled by this sample application, but it is pretty much not visible for the user except when something goes wrong and an error message is displayed. Usually only short information messages are displayed from the engine such as "Game was created by x." or "Player y has joined the game."

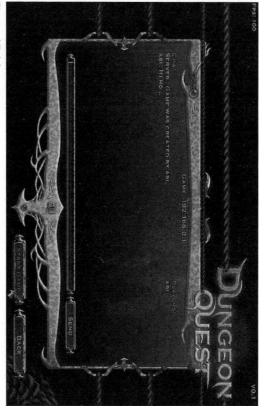

Figure 15-14

Before you continue looking at the internal chat message handling, you should at least check out the Run method of the StartGameScreen class. The MultiplayerScreen class is a little bit more complex, but it should also not be too hard to understand because most of the UI code is separated and handled in the MenuElements class in the UserInterface namespace, which allows you to show lists, buttons, text boxes, and panels with ease. The following code is from the Run method of the StartGameScreen class:

```
/// <summary>
/// Render start game screen, handles the connection
/// process and displays all the players in the game plus
/// the chat messages. Each player can add his own chat
/// messages and will later be allowed to choose one of the
/// four character classes for the game.
/// </summary>
/// <param name="game">Game</param>
void IGameScreen.Run(BaseGame game)
{
    DungeonQuestGame dungeonGame = game as DungeonQuestGame;
    dungeonGame.Menu.RenderMenu(
        MenuElements.LogoPosition.TopRight,
```

```
Multiplayer.currentGame.Name == "" ?
"Trying to connect .." : "Game: " +
Multiplayer.currentGame.Name);
RelativeScreenRect panel = dungeonGame.Menu.SubMenuPanel.SubRect(
  0.025f, 0.05f, 0.95f, 0.965f, false, false);
RelativeScreenRect chatPanel =
  panel.SubRect(0, 0, 0.75f, 0.9f, false, false);
RelativeScreenRect playersPanel =
  panel.SubRect(0.75f, 0.0f, 0.25f, 0.9f, false, false);
RelativeScreenRect chatLinePanel =
  panel.SubRect(0.0f, 0.9f, 1.0f, 0.1f, false, false);

// Show chat messages
int chatLines = (int)Math.Round(
  chatPanel.ScreenHeight / (float)Ui.MenuFont.Height);
int xPos = chatPanel.ScreenXPosition,
  yPos = chatPanel.ScreenYPosition;
Ui.MenuFont.WriteText(xPos, yPos, "Chat:", Color.Orange);
yPos += Ui.MenuFont.Height;
foreach (ChatMessage chatMsg in Multiplayer.GetLastChatMessages(
  chatLines - 1))
{
  Ui.MenuFont.WriteText(xPos, yPos, chatMsg.playerName,
    Color.Yellow);
  Ui.MenuFont.WriteText(xPos +
    Ui.MenuFont.GetTextWidth(chatMsg.playerName),
    yPos, ": " + chatMsg.message);
  yPos += Ui.MenuFont.Height;
} // foreach (chatMsg)

// Show players
xPos = playersPanel.ScreenXPosition;
yPos = playersPanel.ScreenYPosition;
Ui.MenuFont.WriteText(xPos, yPos,
  "Players:", Color.Orange);
yPos += Ui.MenuFont.Height;
foreach (Player player in Multiplayer.players)
{
  Ui.MenuFont.WriteText(xPos, yPos, player.name,
    Color.Yellow);
  yPos += Ui.MenuFont.Height;
} // foreach (player)
// Chatline to submit new chat messages!
if ((dungeonGame.Menu.RenderTextBox(chatLinePanel,
  0.0f, 0.0f, 0.8f, 1.0f, ref chatInputText) ||
  dungeonGame.Menu.RenderButton(chatLinePanel, 0.9f,
  0.5f, 0.2f, "Send", false) &&
  chatInputText.Length > 0)
{
  Multiplayer.SendChatMessage(chatInputText);
  chatInputText = "";
} // if (dungeonGame.Menu.RenderTextBox)
Multiplayer.CheckConnectionStatus();
bool backPressed = dungeonGame.Menu.RenderBottomButton("Back");
```

```
//TODO: only if host!
bool startPressed = dungeonGame.Menu.RenderBottomButton("Start Game");

// Clicking or pressing start will go to the menu
if (backPressed ||
    Input.KeyboardEscapeJustPressed ||
    Input.GamePadBackJustPressed ||
    Input.GamePadBJustPressed)
{
    Multiplayer.EndGame();
    BaseGame.RemoveCurrentGameScreen();
} // if (backPressed)
} // Run(game)
```

Most of the code should be easy to understand, but you probably have not seen the new RelativeScreenRect class yet. It is a new helper class I wrote for Dungeon Quest, which does handle almost all of the 2D graphics and UI in the menu and game. The idea is pretty simple; the screen is one big area, which goes from 0.0 to 1.0 on both axes. Now you can create relative rectangles on this big area such as from 0.5 to 0.75 for x and 0.0 to 0.5 for y. Inside this rectangle, everything again is relative and you can go from 0.0 to 1.0 again on both axes.

Figure 15-15 shows how these relative screen rectangles work. Please note that you can nest them as often as you want and there are many helper methods to create subsections and to handle the percentages. To get the graphics finally on the screen the ScreenPositionX, ScreenPositionY, ScreenWidth and ScreenHeight properties are used, which will always return a pixel position. But you will never actually work with these pixel values; they are only used to render the textures on the screen. Please look at the Test.RenderWithRelativeScreenRect unit test inside the Texture class. It contains six different samples and shows how RelativeScreenRect can be used.

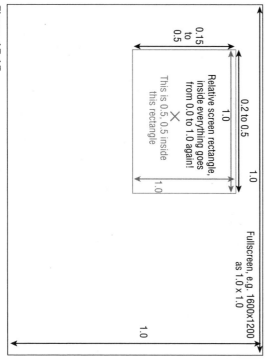

Figure 15-15

If you take a look back to the preceding game screen code, you will notice that most of the code is just displaying some text for the chat messages and player list and rendering the text box and buttons. But there are also some calls to the Multiplayer class, which is where all the interesting network code is located at. At the end of this chapter you will take a look at these methods, but before you do that, let us take another trip to the game messages and see how a chat message actually gets from one player to all other players in the game.

Handling Chat Messages

You now know how the game screen classes are managed and how the player can enter text with help of the MenuElements UI class, which already handles all the text-entering issues with XNA for you. (Take a look at Chapter 9 if you want to see the used code from the Input class.) I also have discussed the way network messages are handled with help of the BaseMessage class and the SessionConnection, which processes all incoming data in the OnReceive and OnHandleMessage methods. You also saw how a received chat message is processed in OnHandleMessage, but there are still pieces missing from the puzzle. You have not seen any methods of the Multiplayer class yet.

In this section, you will go the whole way from entering the chat message via the Input class, and then handling and displaying it with the MenuElements, which is called from the StartGameScreen class and then sent to the SendChatMessage method in the Multiplayer class. From there, the chat message is added to your internal chatMessages array and displayed locally for the user, but it is also sent out to either the host or all client players via the ChatMessage class and especially the Send method, which utilizes the overloaded Write method. The data stream is then sent across the network and handled by the receiving player in the OnRetrieve method, which calls OnHandleMessage with the byte data of the message.

There the data gets converted back to a ChatMessage structure, which is then passed to the same AddChatMessage method the sending player used on his side. After the chat message has been added to the internal chatMessages array, it will be shown on the screen the next time it is drawn in the StartGameScreen via the foreach loop in the middle of the Run method and the GetLastChatMessages method of the Multiplayer class. Wow, this was quite a long way for the data and it is probably not easy to read. Take a look at Figure 15-16 to understand this process a little bit better.

Most of the code to make this work is in the SessionConnection class, which you already saw, and the Multiplayer class, which is fairly high level and easy to understand. Before checking the AddChatMessage method in the Multiplayer class, you should first check out the ChatMessage class itself because this is where you would insert you own messages. The code in the other classes will stay pretty much the same except for the OnHandleMessage and maybe some more helper methods in the Multiplayer class. You should also add new message types to the MessageType enumeration and write a nice long comment there about the things your new message can do for the game.

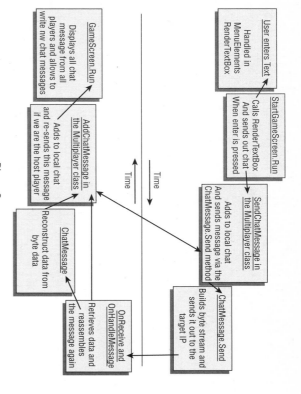

Figure 15-16

The following code is the whole `ChatMessage` class and, as you can see, it is not hard to add new game messages. Change the variables and rewrite the constructors and the `Write` method — that's it. You are done with the new network message.

```
/// <summary>
/// Simple chat message, always goes to all players in the
/// game. Contains both the sending player name and the
/// chat message.
/// </summary>
public class ChatMessage : BaseMessage
{
    #region Variables
    /// <summary>
    /// Player name
    /// </summary>
    public string playerName;
    /// <summary>
    /// Message
    /// </summary>
    public string message;
    #endregion

    #region Constructors
    /// <summary>
```

```
/// Create chat message
/// </summary>
/// <param name="setPlayerName">Set player name</param>
/// <param name="setMessage">Set message</param>
public ChatMessage(string setPlayerName, string setMessage)
    : base(MessageType.ChatMessage)
{
    playerName = setPlayerName;
    message = setMessage;
} // ChatMessage(setPlayerName, setMessage)
/// <summary>
/// Constructor from reader
/// </summary>
/// <param name="reader">Reader</param>
public ChatMessage(BinaryReader reader)
    : base(MessageType.ChatMessage)
{
    playerName = reader.ReadString();
    message = reader.ReadString();
} // ChatMessage(reader)
#endregion

#region Write
/// <summary>
/// Write data to writer
/// </summary>
/// <param name="writer">Writer</param>
public override void Write(BinaryWriter writer)
{
    base.Write(writer);
    writer.Write(playerName);
    writer.Write(message);
} // Write(writer)
#endregion
} // class ChatMessage
```

The `Multiplayer` class finally contains the high-level methods `SendChatMessage` and `AddChatMessage`. The first one is called if you want to send out chat messages and the second one is used to add received chat messages, but also server messages that just contain information for you — for example, when something went wrong or someone joined the game.

```
/// <summary>
/// Add chat message
/// </summary>
/// <param name="text">Text</param>
public static void SendChatMessage(string text)
{
    ChatMessage newChatMsg = new ChatMessage(Player.OurPlayerName, text);
    chatMessages.Add(newChatMsg);
    if (connection.IsHost)
        connection.SendMessageToAllPlayers(newChatMsg);
    else
        connection.SendMessageToHostPlayer(newChatMsg);
```

```
        }   // AddChatMessage(text)

        ///   <summary>
        ///   Add chat message from server
        ///   </summary>
        ///   <param name="playerName">Player name</param>
        ///   <param name="text">Text</param>
        public static void AddChatMessageFromServer(string playerName, string text)
        {
            ChatMessage newChatMsg = new ChatMessage(playerName,
                text);
            chatMessages.Add(newChatMsg);
            // Do not send it out again!
        }   // AddChatMessageFromServer(playerName, text)
```

These two methods (and some more variants) make use of the message classes and the ability to send messages out to the host player or all players depending on whether you are the host player or not. The `SendMessage` methods in the `SessionConnection` class are used to perform this; they call the `Send` method of the message, which is always a different method depending on the underlying implementation in each message class. This will probably be refactored at a later point in time if many game messages behave the same way. You don't want to write the same code over and over again. But because this is currently the only game message you send out directly from the UI or game logic, don't worry about that yet.

The Final Chat Application

Figure 15-17 shows the final chat application with all the UI code Dungeon Quest has so far. You can start the application multiple times and join your own games on your computer. You should make sure to run in windowed mode (check the settings file) to make testing easier. You can of course also test this over a local area network or the Internet.

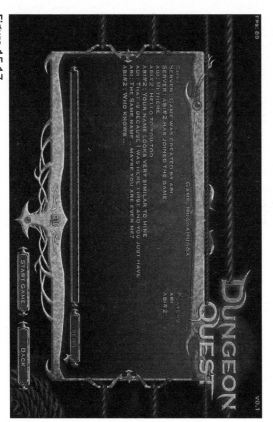

Figure 15-17

Coming up with the networking architecture was not easy and it involved writing more classes than I first thought of, but I think the network engine is now pretty solid and you can use it for your little game Dungeon Quest. Please note that there is no message delivery guarantee built in right now and you did not handle any firewall or NAT issues yet (and probably never will, this would involve writing something more than just a web service as the game server). Maybe XNA 2.0 is powerful and sufficient enough to provide these advanced capabilities, but for now, you should continue writing the Dungeon Quest game. Improving the networking engine can still be done at a later point in time.

Challenge: Write a Multiplayer Application

In this chapter I talked quite a bit about networking techniques. You also wrote a little chat application, but there is no game here yet. Your task is now to write a simple multiplayer application. One good idea is to take the pong game from Chapter 2 and add network support to it. This is not only a great exercise, but it will also make you more familiar with the network classes for the Dungeon Quest game, which will be discussed in the next chapters.

XnaPong (see Figure 15-18) already supports a two-player mode on a local PC or console, and you need to add only one network message to make it work (besides the JoinGameMessage). This message could be called PaddleUpdate and contain the new paddle position for the player. When the game is lagging, the results could be different, so each player should check for his side. When the ball is lost, a BallLost message should be sent out if the game does not stay in synchrony.

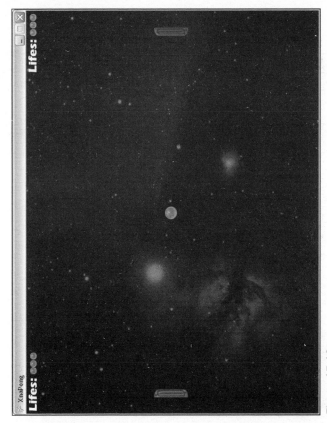

Figure 15-18

Summary

In this chapter you learned a lot about handling network protocols, handling network messages, and what to expect from the networking API of XNA 2.0. The code for Dungeon Quest was updated for XNA 2.0 in late 2007, but the overall network engine remained pretty much the same.

At the beginning of this chapter I covered the advantages of the XNA 2.0 networking API and I continued to talk about choosing between the TCP versus UDP network protocols. TCP is useful for websites, web services, and all kinds of applications where you want to make sure that one single request will return some data without your having to worry about packets getting lost. UDP, on the other hand, is less reliable, but a little bit faster and also easier to set up both in the game engine and also on firewalls in case you want to use some NAT punching tricks.

Then I discussed all classes used for the network engine — most important, the SessionConnection class handles the low-level functionality together with some helper classes such as the SocketHelper and the BaseMessage class and its derived classes. The Multiplayer class, on the other hand, provides a high-level view for the application and provides you with the multiplayer game information, a player list, and whatever data you need for the application — in our case, the chat messages.

At the end of the chapter, the chat application, written with the Dungeon Quest engine, was introduced and explained in detail. This will be the base engine for the Dungeon Quest game, which is built on top of the existing XnaGraphicEngine from Chapter 8 and the Racing Game engine from Chapter 14.

In the next chapter, you learn more about role playing games and some of the design decisions behind the Dungeon Quest game. After going through the design phase and some early unit tests, you will finally reach the last chapter, which is going to explain all game parts of the Dungeon Quest game. The Dungeon Quest game is constantly in development and will be more of a community project, unlike the other XNA projects from this book, which just provide source code and some Modding capabilities. Dungeon Quest is not just developed by me alone. There is a team behind the project that I started, but other people can participate and contribute their ideas making the game even better. These are exciting times for role-playing game lovers and XNA enthusiasts.

Role-Playing Games

This chapter covers role-playing games in general and then explains the concept of the Dungeon Quest game in detail. Not only are the concept and the ranking and leveling system explained, but we will also take a look at the available player characters and enemies in the game. The chapter ends with some general game logic unit tests and a little bit more about the UI, both in the menu and in game.

But before we get back to coding, let's first get into the game concept of Dungeon Quest. The very first version of Dungeon Quest was developed in just four days live at the Game Developer Conference (GDC) 2007, in March 2007. The game was part of a contest hosted by Microsoft called XNA Challenge, where four games were developed in four days by four teams directly in the GDC lobby with all the noise and distractions a big conference like the GDC brings with it. But each team managed to finish their game on time. Our team consisted of one programmer (me) and one artist (a friend of mine, Christoph Rienaecker).

The absolutely insane idea was to create a multiplayer role-playing game from scratch in these four days. While the multiplayer part was pretty hard to do on the Xbox 360 console (we tried split screen support, but it never made it into the game logic, just a unit test was written), the rest of the game went as we wanted. This version of Dungeon Quest (see Figure 16-1) featured a third-person view from behind like many current role-playing games, supported skinned animations, and had five different enemies. A player character with five different animations blended smoothly. Then there is the cave, which consists of half a million polygons and uses a highly complex shader (more complex than Pixel Shader 2.0 would allow) with up to six dynamic point lights. All the game entities have collision detection against a lower polygon version of the cave.

But even with all the cool shaders, animations, and effects, everything was just thrown together as fast as we could. The game is not easily extendable and it does not have any replay value, which most role-playing games have in abundance. Once you have gotten through the cave, opened the door to the second level, and found the treasure at the end of the big hall, the game is over and playing it again will not reveal anything new.

Figure 16-1

For that reason and because we have some better ideas, we've decided to remake Dungeon Quest, but this time we are not going to copy one of the popular Massively Multiplayer Online Role-Playing Games (MMORPGs) game principles. While Dungeon Quest is not really a Massively Multiplayer Online (MMO) game anyway, why try to make it similar in any way. It is highly unrealistic that we will create a complex role-playing game in a few days or weeks that took other teams many years, possibly with hundreds of man-years of work behind them. Instead, we thought of the earlier and simpler role-playing games such as Diablo 1 and 2, and Sacred, but also newer games such as Titan Quest or Dungeon Siege. Writing these games is not a piece of cake either, but we always liked the team-play aspect of these games, even if they were originally designed to be played in singleplayer mode. This is where the new Dungeon Quest game comes in, keeping the basic game simple, but allowing it to be extensible both via the source code and via the editor, which allows you to create more maps and worlds. The fun of this game should come from its replay value and extensibility. In particular, more complex maps and quests should be more fun when playing them with a few teammates.

Types of Role-Playing Games

Before we get to the game concept of Dungeon Quest, let's first take a quick tour of role-playing games. This way we don't have to repeat existing facts about role-playing games in our own concept, but can just say "see game x." One of the first computer role-playing games was Dungeon & Dragons, which was still very similar to tabletop role-playing games.

Computer role-playing games come directly from tabletop games. Unlike most computer game genres, they have their replay-ability and social aspects from these non-computer games from a long time ago before any complex computer games were written. The basic idea is that each player of the game slips into a fictional role, usually in the fantasy setting of some mystical world full of powerful enemies, magic abilities and complex stories. Unlike other board or card games, role-playing games do last much longer and do not simply end after a few rounds. Games can be played over a long time and the world remains persistent, which makes it highly addictive. Such games have a high replay value because the player feels with his character in the game and does not simply win by beating other players in a few moves. Usually, players play together and fight against opponents, which get stronger as the players advance.

Those role-playing board games can also be seen as an interactive story, in which all of the participating players can influence the story, which is the main reason that you can play it again and again because it will always be different. Different players will act differently each time, and rolling the dice provides an element of randomness. When you are just watching a movie or reading a book, it will get boring when you do it again, sometimes even computer games can get very boring when you play them again, but both role-playing games and strategy games usually have great replay value and you can easily change some of the parameters and make the game very different, allowing it to play the game even more or try different variants. It is important to note that tabletop role-playing games still exist and are not replaced by computer games. Tabletop games are still very different from computer games. They are played on a much slower pace, are usually round-based and not real-time. Computer games are usually more action-driven. Both kinds of games have their own fans and there is no reason to continue talking about tabletop or even live role-playing games (also called medieval games) here.

I'm no expert in tabletop role-playing games and I'm not even an expert in most computer role-playing games. I have seen most of them and played the ones I like (e.g., Diablo 2 or Sacred), but I'm not an MMO RPG player because I find it too time consuming. Also, the tasks players have to do in these games to get more points are highly repetitive and can become boring if you do not really care about special items or the in-game currency. But the other people in the Dungeon Quest team are big fans of RPGs and they will try to influence the game as much as they can to make it still enjoyable for these kinds of players.

For this reason I will skip over the old-school tabletop role-playing games and older role-playing computer games such as Ultima, which are more related to these tabletop games. Instead we are going to compare our game with the hack and slash role-playing games and action role-playing games, which influenced many games in the last couple of years. Even games that were originally first-person shooters or strategy games have Mods that allow you to play the game in a role-playing game manner. It is also worth mentioning that some games have elements of role-playing games mixed in; sometimes strategy games have role-playing elements (like WarCraft III), or tactical games (like Silent Storm) have detailed character statistics and ranking similar to role-playing games. Even other games such as the popular GTA (Grand Theft Auto) series embraced RPG elements into their games. The player does not just get points, but he has several abilities, which he can train to become better or to have more health, strength, and so on. For example, in GTA San Andreas the player can train several fighting arts to become better over the course of the game. The player can also train his lung capacity, increase his overall Hitpoints, and so on. While many of today's games include some RPG aspects, they are usually not as complex as RPG-only games.

"Hack and Slash" Role-Playing Games

One of the best known and successful "hack and slash" role-playing games is Diablo 2 (released in 2000), the successor of Diablo (released late in 1996). The first Diablo game was the most successful role-playing game of its time (selling almost 3 million copies), and Diablo 2 was even more successful with 4 million sold copies. When excluding MMORPG games such as World of WarCraft (also from Blizzard like the Diablo games), Diablo is still the most successful role-playing game.

Diablo did not invent role-playing games, but it certainly influenced many other action role-playing games. While players still level up, can choose between different character classes and learn spells, the player does actually fight most of the time in the game against monsters, which spawn in randomly generated levels. The game is played from a top-down perspective (see Figure 16-2) and the player can play the whole game with just his mouse, mainly using the left mouse button to attack, run around, and select spells. But the use of hotkeys and the right mouse button for spells, drinks and accessing in-game menus allows the user to handle his character more efficiently.

Figure 16-2

Because levels are generated randomly, but always have about the same amount of monsters in them for balancing reasons, no playthroughs of the game are alike. The player always enters a unique world, which is different every time he starts with a new character or difficulty setting. This alone, the leveling system and many spells the player can learn, and the huge worlds and many areas the player can conquer give the game a high replay value.

Dungeon Quest wants to be similar to Diablo-style hack and slash games, and do it with 3D graphics and a highly extendable game engine allowing the players to create new maps and worlds instead of playing the same maps over and over again. Dungeon Quest will just have a few spells in the beginning, but we hope that we can add more spells and abilities later if the game is successful. It is also important to notice that Dungeon Quest was created and will continue to be developed in just a matter of weeks and mostly in our free time on weekends, unlike all the other role-playing games mentioned here, which usually took 3–4 years to develop for a large team with up to 100 professional game developers.

Other hack and slash games that are worth mentioning are Sacred, which is very similar to Diablo and was released in 2004. Sacred features five character classes and added two additional characters in its expansion pack. Similar to Diablo, the world is composed of 2D images on the ground, but the player character in Sacred is actually a 3D model unlike Diablo 2, where 2D images are still used. Sacred also allows zooming in and out, has support for a greater set of screen resolutions, and has some additions to the game play.

Chapter 16: Role-Playing Games

You can, for example, compose combos out of several spells and attacks and create a more powerful series of attacks and save Mana this way. But Sacred was in no way as successful as Diablo or other Diablo-like games, mainly because of its high rate of bugs, the bad online mode, and the graphical style, which was not as polished as Diablo 2 even with a better technology and the fact that it has been released 4 years later.

A more successful game is Dungeon Siege, one of the first 3D action role-playing games (see Figure 16-3). It was released in 2002 and later bundled with video cards; in 2005 the successor Dungeon Siege 2 was released and also very successful. Dungeon Siege 1 was getting boring after users had played it over and over again; Dungeon Siege 2 added more variety and had a better replay value. For example, spells were shared and in Dungeon Siege 2 each character class (implemented through specialization instead of choosing a character right away) now got his own unique set of skills, displayed in a skill tree similar to Diablo 2. Not only does Dungeon Siege have a great cooperative play mode, which makes the game more fun in local multiplayer mode with a couple of friends, but even when playing alone, the player can hire up to six characters (depending on the difficulty setting) to fight with him side by side. In addition, the player can buy pets, which fight with him and level up (reaching the next stage for your player character), too. This game element can also be found in many MMO games such as World of WarCraft.

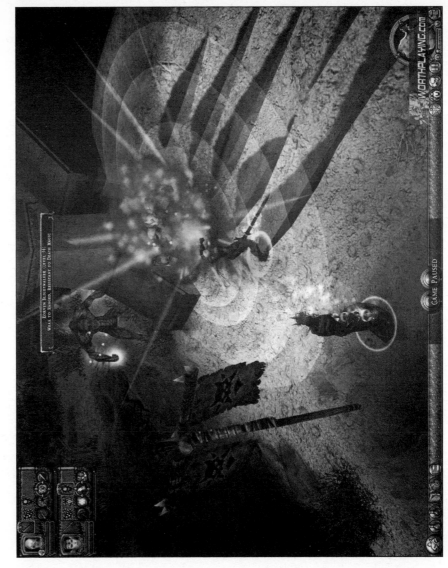

Figure 16-3

489

Part V: Writing Multiplayer Games

The balancing in Dungeon Siege was not as good as in Diablo 2 and the multiplayer Internet mode was only supported through the GameSpy service and not implemented nearly as well as Blizzards own Battle.Net system. For this reason Diablo 2, which is even 5 years older than Dungeon Siege 2, is played a lot more today and continues to have a huge fan-base.

One final hack and slash game I like to mention is Titan Quest (see Figure 16-4), which is more recent than the other games mentioned so far. It was released in 2006 and features nice 3D graphics and has a sophisticated game engine supporting ragdoll physics, day-night cycles, and even a world editor, which are features usually not seen by role-playing games. Another reason that Titan Quest is so successful is that no other good action role-playing games were released at that time and highly anticipated games such as Diablo 3 are not even announced. Sacred also was released at a good time — no real competitors except 4-year-old games were on the market. Titan Quest was received as a hard game by some critics, but aside from that the game was very successful and has an active community behind it. The first versions were a little bit buggy but since regular patches are common for PC role-playing games, most issues were fixed. Through the advanced toolset, editor, and replay-ability the game can be played over and over again without getting boring.

Figure 16-4

Similar to some other smaller role-playing games, the team that developed Titan Quest was initially not that big (just 6 people) and the team at full size (40 people) is still a lot smaller than some of the big players on the market. In my opinion, Titan Quest has the best action role-playing game engine today, especially given the easy-to-use editor. And that is being said by someone who gets quickly bored by role-playing games. I rarely ever complete one and I certainly do not play them over and over again as many of my friends do.

Massively Multiplayer Role-Playing Games

Okay, while I'm talking about not playing role-playing games over and over again, it is time to mention World of WarCraft, the biggest time-waster game currently available. This is actually meant as a compliment to WoW (World of WarCraft), which is based on the popular WarCraft strategy games, at least story-wise. It was released late in 2004 and already has over 9 million subscribers, who pay up to 15 dollars each month to play the game. This is unheard of. Usually MMO games in the past had a couple of hundred thousand subscribers if they were very successful. With Lineage in Asia, a very successful MMO game was created and reached several million subscribers in 2004, more than all other MMO role-playing games combined at that time. But WoW topped that and had reached over 6 million subscribers in less than a year after its initial release. While many people think all of the 9 million subscribers pay 15 dollars each month, this is just not true. The pricing differs greatly from one continent to the next.

For example, in the US and in Europe, the player usually buys the game from the store and gets a one month subscription with the game. But in Asia, especially in China, Korea, or Taiwan, players don't necessarily buy MMO games or even subscribe to them on a monthly basis. Instead, players buy game cards to them and the game is played on an hourly basis. Two-thirds of the players are in Asia, and a lot of them just buy game cards to play 30 hours for 2 or 3 dollars. But even with these hourly players, the game is hugely successful and its user base keeps growing at a steady rate, which is very impressive as MMO games usually fade out after a while. Blizzard also creates new expansion packs every year, making the game more complex by adding more items, characters, spells and game modes. You can also compare WoW to Guild Wars, where the player does not have to pay a monthly subscription. The player can just buy Guild Wars once and play it as often as he wants. The game is quite similar to WoW, features a better graphics engine, but has less content than WoW. Guild Wars does also not have as many characters and classes and levels, but even with its reduced complexity, it is still a very big game that can be played many times. Its buy-once-and-play-as-long-as-you-want model made it highly successful, too. (It has sold over 4 million copies and two expansion packs are already available.)

As you can see from Figure 16-5, WoW does not look much different from other role-playing games; its graphics even seem less compelling and advanced than other games released in 2004 and 2005, when shader-based games were very popular (see Chapter 6 for some examples). WoW does not derive its fun and game play from shader-based graphics effects, but instead from its huge and persistent world and the insane amount of content in the game. Not only can the players choose from eight character classes (four on the Alliance side, four on the Horde side), with the expansion pack, The Burning Crusade, the player can even choose from ten characters (five on each side) WoW allows each character to select one of the nine character classes, which give the player different abilities. Not only does this result in a huge set of possible characters, but each player can also choose which talents are most important for him (do damage, heal, tanking, and so on), which is especially important when playing in groups because a group is a lot stronger when it has all kinds of different characters in them.

The game also includes a lot of Non-Player Characters (NPC), which can talk to the player, give him quests, or possibly even attack the player if hostile. WoW has many major and minor cities, which you can buy and sell merchandise from NPCs, similar to other role-playing games, but there are many more opportunities for the player in WoW. The player can gain experience to level up, get quests or advice from these NPCs. More quests, items, and balance changes are constantly introduced and updated through patches. Even with its old graphics engine that doesn't even support advanced shader effects, the designers manage to give each part of the game world a unique look. A friend of mine told me that they have a team of people just devoted to fine-tuning colors for the light and fog effects in the game so each area has a nice and unique look. WoW is also a great example of how to reuse existing textures many times over and create a new look with different settings and sizes.

Figure 16-5

WoW has great replay value, far greater than other role-playing games, mostly because of its complexity and the many different things a player can focus on. Not everyone plays the game the same way. Some people like the item system and might always be on the search for more powerful items or sets; other players like fighting more, and even other players get the most fun out of the game because they can play with their friends and clans and fight together against big monsters or other groups of players. There are many more things in WoW, such as professions, all the different rules of dropping items, PvP (player versus player) and role-playing enforcing modes, the honor system, and many more things I don't even know about because I'm not a WoW player.

One last thing worth mentioning about WoW is its highly customizable user interface through the Lua scripting language, which allows players to reposition UI elements and even add non-intrusive UI features (mostly chat and interaction related since loading and saving files is not allowed to prevent cheating). The rest of the game is always hosted on game servers and the player cannot modify any of his character settings directly, but only through playing the game online. For this reason, there is also no singleplayer mode available, as in most MMO games. Other games (or also called simulations) such as Second Life allow much more customization and have a completely different audience group, but with the success of WoW, it seems like highly balanced and fine-tuned game play is more liked than user-generated content.

Designing Dungeon Quest

Enough talk about existing games. If you are an experienced role-playing games player you probably know even more about role-playing games than I do. The greatest thing about role-playing games, in my opinion, is the ability to play them in many different styles and with many different characters, which can differ greatly. First-person shooters are usually always the same and once you have played once from start to finish it is not a lot of fun to play them again. Strategy games may not appeal to everyone and other games such as fighting games or race games can be boring to certain people. Role-playing games, on the other hand, allow you to play a very aggressive character or someone sneaky, who deals a lot of damage, but can be hurt easily. Or you might want to be a magician with many powerful spells, or maybe you like to be the one at the front fighting in close combat and getting all the hits while your allies hit the enemies from behind. Role-playing games also have a history of cooperative game play, which is especially nice because we want to create a multiplayer game here. Even getting together with just one other person creates a completely new game feeling and makes you much stronger than playing a role-playing game alone. The complexity of WoW even allows big parties with up to 50 people playing side by side, which can also be a lot of fun.

So the idea is to create a multiplayer, cooperative role-playing game similar to Diablo style hack and slash games. There is also a singleplayer game option, but the game is designed as a multiplayer game, which means that it might not be possible to beat the game easily in singleplayer, especially not with one of the weaker character classes, which will require a lot of hit-and-run tactics. You can advance much faster in the multiplayer mode and the game is also more fun through chat and voice features, which I hope will be added in XNA 2.0.

Let's start with the game design document. The rules for writing game design documents can be found in Chapter 2. This game design document might be more complex, but it was much shorter in the first versions. It just got bigger and bigger as the game grew. It is important to notice that we (the team of Dungeon Quest) first tried to make a simple role-playing game similar to a proof-of-concept game and then added more features later because we still believed in the game idea.

Please note that most of the following information is related to the official game design document for Dungeon Quest, which can also be found online on the official Dungeon Quest Game website at www .DungeonQuestGame.com. Because the game design document was already updated many times at the time of this writing, it does not reflect the first simple idea anymore. It has become more sophisticated and it will continue to evolve in the future. For the most up-to-date information, always refer to the online version of the game design document.

Ideas

The first Dungeon Quest was a simple 3D role-playing game in which the player sees himself running around and collecting weapons and items in front of the screen. The game was written for the Xbox 360 and utilizes the Xbox 360 Controller (Xbox), but it also runs on the PC and also supports mouse and keyboard input. The main goal in the game is to finish all quests and get points for it to level up. Encounters with Goblins, Ogres, and other kind of Monsters will hurt the player, but each time you level up, the health is restored. Additionally there are better weapons and items that can be found in the level after killing monsters that might carry them. For certain quests, the player has to do several actions in a sequence, such as collecting a key first, and then opening a door to proceed. If the player loses all his health, he dies and has to start over. There is just one level in the game, but it features multiple stages and is very big. The game is also easily extensible, allowing players to create their own levels and additions.

While this kind of game can be fun for a short while — it is initially action loaded and does not require much balancing work — it is just not compelling enough to play it again and again. It would be possible to add more story, more moves, more enemies and more effects to the game, but even then it is hard to compete with any existing action role playing games, which have huge graphics-rich worlds with a lot of content, quests, different enemies, and special game rules.

Instead of staying in the 3D action role-playing game genre, we decided that we could also return back to the classic Diablo-style hack and slash role-playing games, which means you have a 2D view from the top and really focus on the game play instead of adding fancy 3D effects, shaders, fog, lens flares, sky cubes, or level of detail models. It would be nice to see such effects in a first person–like game, but when you are viewing the world from above (Iso-Perspective) it is much more important that you can see you player all the time. The controls should be good and the game play is key!

The graphics for this new game are oriented very much on games such as Diablo 2, Titan Quest, and other Iso top-down role-playing games. Obviously, these games took a very long time to develop and have highly polished graphics, which is not possible in this short timeframe, so the main focus for this game is to create a simple and easy-to-learn role-playing game with just the basic features. The main graphics theme is located in the desert — maybe some temple ruins as background themes and some caves to fight boss enemies behind some locked doors later. There are also some extra objects in the level, but while it will be simple to add content, the basic game does feature just the basic amount of required level objects by itself.

In the basic version, the game consists of just the game menu, some options and help, and the game itself. A level selection screen is used to navigate to one of the levels, either one of the default maps or a custom-created level. A high score list is used to store the top players and is transmitted to a Web service in Windows (not possible on the Xbox 360 yet). The new version of Dungeon Quest will feature multiplayer support via split screen and through the new networking API in XNA 2.0, allowing multiple players to play together. In the future, more characters, more graphics sets and levels (outdoor, snow, desert, grassland, and so on), and more game content could be made (Act II and III), but this would require more time and especially balancing.

Scenario

Dungeon Quest features three acts with different graphics styles, but most of the game concept in this chapter will focus on the first act. Similar to most role-playing games, Dungeon Quest is also set in a fantasy environment with typical monsters, which consist of big animals, skeletons, and Orcs as well as

Chapter 16: Role-Playing Games

magical elements in the later acts. If that turns out to be successful, we are going to focus our attention on completing the second and third act.

Dungeon Quest might not always take itself seriously. While we will try our best, the story, animations, and game play might contain some jokes. The graphics will not look as polished as other AAA games anyway, so we might do some fun stuff here, too. More information about the story and Acts I, II, and III can be found in section 3.

For objects in the map, we use mostly simple objects (boxes, stones, lamps, doors, and so son) and the placement of the enemies can be done via the level map editor. The maps are built in a way that allows the player to run through without losing orientation. There is no mini-map support yet, but it might be added later if the maps become too big and it is hard to locate the allied players and quest locations (which can also be done with screen arrows for now).

The game is always viewed from a top-down Iso-Perspective, as in Diablo 2 or Titan Quest (see Figure 16-6). The camera is fixed at a certain angle and cannot be changed in any way except for moving around when the player moves on the screen. The screen is usually filled with the player models, some enemies, and the current level the players are in. There are no advanced fire or water effects, and no support for any sky cube mapping, lens flare effects, or similar because they are not required. There will be a particle system in place used to display hit effects and for several weapons and skills.

Figure 16-6

495

The graphics will be created on-demand to shorten the development time, reducing the artwork to just some concept sketches (which can be seen below in Figure 16-8 and following). More content is produced when it is needed.

Story

After selecting one of the four character classes, the player gets a short introduction into the game via a storyboard (Figure 16-7) and an introduction text that is displayed in ten screens (one paragraph for each screen).

☐ When I woke up this morning I got a letter from my old mentat Andor, who is also a good friend of my father. Both my father and Andor are members of the secret council, which got notice about attacks from dark creatures on the town folk. Not only humans were captured and killed, but even the animals were infested by the darkness.

☐ The letter contains directions to the monastery, where I will learn more. Since this issue is very important I immediately get on my way. My father told me in my childhood stories about him and Andor, where they liberated the Philosopher's Stone from Dragonas castle.

☐ After I reached the monastery, I noticed how much it changed in the last years. When I was younger the monastery was not completed. Today I see a gorgeous and very majestic monastery. But it seems like there are only very few people around the monastery, most of the people from here must be inside because something important is going on.

☐ When I got closer, I saw two guards in dark capes in front of the main entrance of the monastery. They did not move at all. They must already know of my coming. Then the main entrance opened up and a dark figure came out of the brightness from inside. In spite of the dark cloak I quickly recognized Andor, my old mentat. He greets me firmly and tells me about the recent developments. He also tells me about the latest construction efforts of the now completed monastery. I notice that he is very serious and also sorrowful, which is not the way I remembered him.

☐ We walk through several corridors and I see many serious figures, who are looking at me with hope and curiosity. Finally I'm guided through a bigger hall to the main room, where everyone is gathered.

☐ There I see the portal in the center of the room for the first time. My father told me a lot about the portal, but I have not seen it myself until now. The portal was build hundred of years ago, but could not be used because not all of the Philosopher's Stones were found. Now with both the portal and the stone in this monastery, the portal can finally be used for good purposes.

☐ I was interrupted from my thoughts when the high priest behind lifted his right hand with the Philosopher's Stone in it and explained the use of the stone and the portal. A part of the portal is now useable, but all four parts of the stone are required to fully activate the portal and use it against the power of evil that is reigning over the land.

☐ The high priest turns his attention to me and tells me that the time is running out and I should go to the center of the portal. My father and Andor nod in agreement and I feel honored to be chosen for this task. The priest tells me I'm the best man for this job since I know so much about the stones. He activates the portal on the right side with his Philosopher's Stone.

☐ Everything was getting very bright, but I could still hear the people from my world. The high priest shouted in the last second that I only had to get the second part of the stone from the Magi and then return back through the portal.

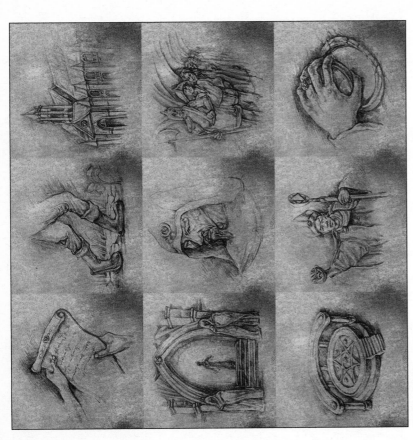

Figure 16-7

After the story is told the player starts in the Dungeon Quest world, but has no idea where he is. It will become more clear how to save the world after completing the first quests. The story continues in the game via dialogs:

"After waking up, you find yourself surrounded by trees on a barren grass landscape. After exploring the surrounding area for a while you can see a couple of houses in the far. There seems to be a small farm out there. Since you have no clue yet what this all is about, it should be worth checking it out."

The player now explores the area and the story continues after clicking on one of the farm people.

"After asking some of the farm people about this world and you find out that you have landed in a known parallel world, but to get back to your own world you have to activate the portal back to your world. The Magi also tell you that in order to activate the portal you have to find the missing Philosopher's Stone yourself first."

Sounds easy, but the problem is that the stones are not just lying around somewhere here, but three powerful legions are protecting them. It is only known that the first legion and its leader are located in the caves nearby. This is where you should start the search, but it will be useful if you first solve some smaller tasks first and get to know the area and its peculiarities.

497

The player can now choose to proceed to the caves or to explore the area a little bit more and some simple quests first. The quests are described in the level editor and are not included here in the story (but they will fit in). One of the first quests will be to help out a boy finding his dog he lost in the woods. After killing wolves, rats and other smaller enemies you will gain experience and returning the dog you get extra experience. Quests also give you tips about the game, the ranking system and weapons.

After solving act one and finding the first stone, more of the story will be told, including where the second stone can be found and more information about this part of the world. Act I is mostly located in the grassland and at the end in the caves. Most enemies in Act I are smaller animals, such as rats, wolves, spiders, bugs, and bears. Act II is mostly located in the caves and dungeons; most enemies here are Orcs and Skeletons, which are much harder to defeat than the enemies in Act I. The players (usually the game should be played in multiplayer mode) should have specialized powers by now, and for most quests, teamplay and different abilities are required. Act III is much darker than the first two parts; it plays on the dark side of this world. There are so many fires and volcanoes burning here, the sun hardly ever reaches the ground. Enemies in this area are magical, inflict major damage, and are immune to certain attacks (different for each enemy type). Each act ends by defeating the leader of this area, who is also protecting one of the runes.

After solving all three acts and bringing all stones back to our world, the high priest can finally it. The ending is unclear; the player will not see whether the portal actually saves the world or not. Instead he will land once again in the parallel world again and has to find his way back. This way, the game can be extended later, allowing more worlds to be included.

Characters

The Character Introduction is shown to the player when starting a new game after the story is told. Each character has a different description. A short version of this text is displayed in the character selection screen from the menu. Please note that the following artworks are all created by some of the team members. The in-game 3D models might also look a little bit different as these are just a guideline for the modeler to create the 3D models. But for this game concept, it is very useful to have a concrete representation of how the team sees each character and monster in the game.

❑   **The Barbarian:** The Barbarian (see Figure 16-8) is a fearless and intense warrior. His roots are nomadic. He was trained to fight from a very young age and all he cares about is fighting honorably. His long lasting and merciless training in the coldest areas of his home world has strengthened him into a dangerous and bold melee fighter. He not only protects his allies, but he actually prefers if the enemies concentrate their attacks on him. He likes when the opponents have to look into his eyes and he would much rather die than flee from a fight, which is also his greatest weakness. The Barbarian might be the strongest of the bunch, but without support, especially by Priests to heal him, he does not stand a chance in the long run.

❑   **The Priest:** The Priest (see Figure 16-9) is a servant of the light and belongs to the grand folk of the elves, who reign over the east part of their world. She has the gift of healing. She can not only heal herself in dangerous situations, but also her allies, even at the very last second. This makes her to the most useful companion for long journeys. She knows her role as a healer exactly and loves it. She is not only resourceful as a supporting character, but her calm and gentle mind does give her allies the strength to continue the fight. She also has several anti-magic abilities, which can make her the most powerful fighter against undead and other magical empowered enemies.

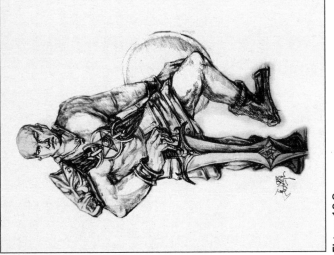

Figure 16-8

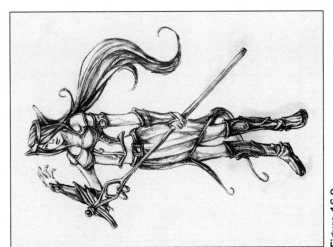

Figure 16-9

☐ **The Mage:** The Mage (see Figure 16-10) has his home everywhere around the world. He is constantly investigating long forgotten creatures and he has collected a seemingly endless amount of knowledge. His actions are always wise and even in his old age he is never afraid of confrontations. He never acts headless and even if his friends want to run into the fight, he can usually convince them not to go directly into traps and to find alternative ways first. His masterful handling of magic gives him incredible power and he does not fear using his great powers. Nevertheless, he has respect for unknown enemies, whose characteristics he seeks to explore first. Despite the fact that the mage always seems calm and deliberate, you should never anger him and force him to act on his anger. Even with all his powerful magic abilities, the mage should not fight on his own as he does not withstand a lot of attacks. He is strong against many weaker enemies, but once other powerful opponents approach him, it is better when someone else gets hit while the mage can choose an appropriate action.

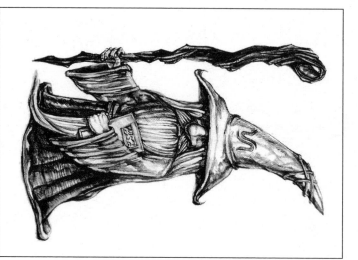

Figure 16-10

☐ **The Hunter:** The Hunter (see Figure 16-11) grew up in the forest and she knows each type of tree and plants, and she knows about every hiding place. She is a master of archery and track reading; she also has an enormous sense of orientation, which helps her and her allies to find the most strategic ways to circumvent dangerous passages. Her perfect handling of the bow makes her the most effective fighter and the deadliest warrior against powerful and strong enemies. You should always have a hunter in your team when fighting against bosses and big enemies. Not only does the hunter hurt enemies from a safe distance, but she is also incredibly agile and can get out of dangerous situations by her superior speed. From a safe distance she can engage against the opponents until they are all down and it is safe to proceed. She feels safe in the woods and areas she has been before, but she also has major drawbacks. First of all, she does not have many magic abilities and is weak against magic attacks. Once she is trapped and cannot escape, she is more helpless than any other character class. For that reason you should always protect the hunter and let her do her work from a distance. While the Mage and the Hunter inflict the most damage, they need protection and these classes are harder to play and master, but without them you will not have enough firepower against the enemies in this world.

Figure 16-11

Enemies

There are many different monsters, enemies, and even non-player characters in most role-playing games; not only can there be many different types, but each type also has several sub-types and can have different settings while still using the same graphics (maybe just changing the color or size of the 3D Model). We are just going to take a look at the first couple of monsters in Act I of Dungeon Quest; be aware that these enemies appear many times and do not only get stronger as the player levels up (monsters also level up to keep the game interesting), but there are also many variations of each monster type. We have developed a shader with up to ten different color settings (similar to the color changing option in the Racing Game from Chapter 14) for each 3D Model, allowing us to create, for example, many different kinds of Spiders with different Hitpoints and attack values.

The enemies in Act I are smaller — mostly small animals and insect-like creatures such as spiders, rats, wolves, bugs, and some skeletons of Act II at the later stages. The Spider King is the boss at the end of Act I. Let's take a look at the six main enemy types in Act I:

☐ **Rat:** First enemy the player will encounter (see Figure 16-12). It is very weak and a melee fighter. Can be ignored at later stages because it does not give you experience. Rats may just hold of you of killing more important enemies. In the beginning, most easily defeated by the Barbarian and Hunter, the other classes have a harder time, but can use their early spells. As with all monsters, rats come in different colors and sizes, the bigger ones are more delicious — err — give more points. Early rats may appear alone, but later they always spawn in groups and can block your way. In those cases, the Mage is the most efficient as he can kill many smaller monsters with his powerful spells easily.

☐ **Wolf:** The wolf (see Figure 16-13) is a fast and furious enemy, which can be dangerous when you are low on Hitpoints as it might hunt you down and kill you before you can recover. The Barbarian has an easy time with wolves, but the other classes might need to use spells or use hit-and-run tactics to escape death, especially when wolves are in bunches. Wolves also can have a Werewolf leader, which is bigger and stronger than wolves and can even revive surrounding killed wolves back to life, which makes it important to kill the Werewolf first.

☐ **Werewolf:** Can appear alone or together with wolves, which he can revive if they fall. Hard to kill and even harder to get around if multiple Werewolves (see Figure 16-14) are together. Ranged characters such as the Hunter or the Mage should concentrate their fire on Werewolves whenever they can and try to kill them one by one to help the melee fighters at the front and to save health drinks for all players, which would have to be used eventually when wolves are revived. It is also important to notice that the Werewolf is the first enemy that can attack over a distance with his fireballs; hit-and-run tactics are recommended.

Figure 16-12

Figure 16-13

Figure 16-14

- **Spider:** Spiders (see Figure 16-15) first appear in Act I when the player enters the first caves. Spiders are not hard to kill, but they appear in bunches and can spit poison, which is both dangerous for Barbarians and for Hunters; once they get hit by the poison, they will slowly lose Hitpoints. Many Spiders are also hard to kill for both the Barbarian and the Hunter because they usually concentrate their fire on just one enemy. Mages have an easier time with spiders, but they should avoid getting hit by them, too. If their spell does not kill a spider quickly enough, bigger spiders may become a problem for the Mages, too. Priests can usually heal themselves and other players quickly enough to prevent major injuries from Spiders and to reverse their Poison effect.

- **Firebug:** The Firebug (see Figure 16-16) can also be found in the caves and is harder to defeat than spiders, but luckily he is very stupid and does not only hurt the players, but also other monsters, which can be used to kill monsters indirectly by navigating cleverly through the caves. The player still gets the experience from kills even if monsters are killed by Firebugs and not himself. Ranged characters should stay away as far as possible from Firebugs or run away from the attack of Firebugs once they start to fire. When not in range, Firebugs will run toward the player and, because of their size and stupidity, usually block each other. But when they are in range, they can hurt many players and monsters at once through their powerful fire-spitting attack.

- **Spider-King:** The Spider-King (see Figure 16-17) is the boss of Act I and he protects the first rune. While the player can decide not to kill certain monsters and he may not want to complete all quests, he always has to defeat the boss of each Act to proceed. The Spider-King is very strong and protected by many smaller spiders surrounding him, which have to be killed first to reach him. The Barbarian and the Hunter do the most damage against him, but they also get hit in the worst way by its poison and spider legs. The Mage and Priest do not inflict enough damage to kill him quickly except for the Ion Cannon of the Priest, which is quite useful against bigger monsters if they do not move away from the attack area. The Spider-King should only be approached by a team of players that has leveled up enough, or else your whole party might be killed off.

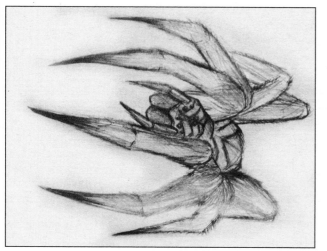

Figure 16-15

Figure 16-16

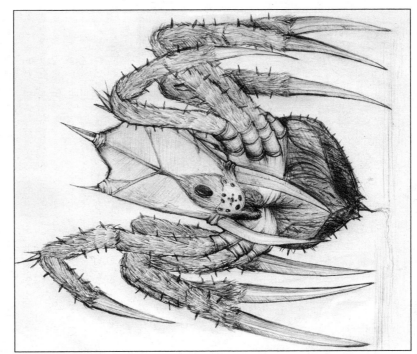

Figure 16-17

Weapons and Items

In role-playing games items are dropped from time to time after killing monsters. These items get more valuable the bigger and harder a monster-kill was. It is also important to notice that these items are dropped randomly. All the item values are also randomly generated and some items might be very rare and unique. In Dungeon Quest, we have highly simplified the weapons, armor, and items into four categories: Weapons, Armors, Rings and Amulets, and Drinks.

Weapons can only be carried by a certain character class; for example, a bow can only be used by Hunters. This way, the weapons in the game become easier to use and players are forced to exchange weapons so each player gets what he needs. If three players all play Mages, then they would have to fight for each staff they find, but it will be very hard for three mages anyway because they all have similar abilities in the end and to successfully play the game and master hard enemies you need the other player characters, too.

Armors are also character-specific in Dungeon Quest. There are several armors, which are attached to the player model (e.g., the Mage gets a new hat, the hunter gets a belt and top, the barbarian gets another armor plate, and so on). We are trying to avoid problems with rendering highly complex closes, which can be exchanged; instead, all armor models are static and will be similar. Each player can carry only one weapon and one armor piece at the same time.

Rings, Amulets, and Drinks, on the other hand, can always be carried and can fill up the inventory. They are not visible in the 3D world, only in the inventory of each player. But because the inventory is very limited (ten slots, but four of them are used by drinks, the weapon, and the armor piece), each player should only use the rings and amulets most useful for him. Later we might also implement the ability to merge rings of the same type to more powerful rings, but players should always exchange rings, which is the only currency currently planned for the game. There is no gold, no shops, and no trading except for rings, which you get after completing quests or killing big monsters.

Figure 16-18 shows some of the weapons that will be dropped by monsters or given through NPCs after completing quests. Except for the Priest and Mage, who can share staffs, all weapons are only usable for one character class. Because weapons and other items might increase spells and abilities it is important to find and use as many items as possible supporting the spells and abilities (see the next section) the player wants to master anyway. For example, using a highly powerful weapon or ring that increases the Amok skill for the Barbarian will not be of as much worth to a Barbarian specializing in the All-Around-Attack than to a Barbarian that actually uses the Amok skill all the time.

Abilities and Spells

As you probably have noticed, a game design document for a role-playing game can become quite extensive and we are not even done yet. The most important part for role-playing games is the ability to level up, learn spells for the player character, and to increase his abilities — making him stronger, faster, or more magical.

Chapter 16: Role-Playing Games

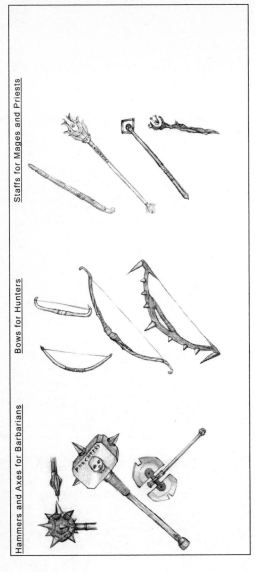

Hammers and Axes for Barbarians Bows for Hunters Staffs for Mages and Priests

Figure 16-18

Again, we decided to cut the many different abilities and spells that can usually be found in role-playing games down to a bare minimum. We do plan to extend these spells in the future, add more of them, and add a typical tree structure, which prevents you from learning powerful late game skills right away. Dungeon Quest currently has only five passive abilities in which players can invest points and three spells for each character class. For each level up, the player gets five points, which he then can invest in abilities or skills. Unlike some other role-playing games, we do not differentiate between abilities and skills. The player can invest all his points into spells if he wants to become more powerful or he can invest them all into abilities to get faster, have more Hitpoints, or become stronger this way.

Abilities

The following abilities are passive skills. The player does not have to do anything to use them, and they are always present without having to use Mana. Everyone can invest skill points here to improve his character. These abilities are shared by all character classes, but some skills make more sense to certain character classes than others. The player has to decide!

- ❑ **Strength:** Increases the amount of damage the player and his weapons do.

- ❑ **Agility:** Increases the attack speed of weapons; also decreases the casting times and gives a little bit of extra speed to the player plus a higher chance to avoid hits from enemies.

- ❑ **Magic:** Increases the total Mana we can have and how fast it regenerates. Obviously, the most important skill for Mages, but because they also have to choose one of their skills and may want to increase the damage they do it is always a tradeoff. Magic is also useful for the priest and even for the other classes.

☐   **Life:** Increases the total Health points the player can have and how fast they regenerate. Most important for any melee fighter or even for the other classes if they do not play together with a Barbarian.

☐   **Dexterity:** Increases the probability to hit the enemy by a few percentage points, which is not that important if you are doing area damage such as the Mage, but it is very important for the Hunter to hit enemies more effectively. Also increases the chance of inflicting critical hits (killing the enemy with 200 percent or more damage).

Spells

Each character class also has its own personal spells. We are trying to keep it simple by limiting the amount of spells for each class to just three skills. This way, we can make the spell effects more beautiful and might leave some room open for additional skills some time later. Figure 16-19 shows an early version of the spell icons that can be seen in the game. The icon graphic will obviously be exchanged with something better looking later, but it is always useful to have dummy textures around in case the graphic artist has something else to do, but the programmer wants to implement a certain feature without having to wait.

Figure 16-19

Barbarian Spells

The Barbarian has mostly attack spells, but also the very useful Shield spell to survive longer in hard battles. Amok, Shield and the All-Around-Attack are the current three spells for the Barbarian, more will be added later through extensible XML files:

☐ **Amok:** Runs quickly toward the enemies and carries out a battle cry to turn the attention of nearby enemies to him. In a short period of time, he also hits a little bit faster and runs faster until the effect wears off. Duration: 5 seconds; Refresh: 10 seconds.

☐ **Shield:** Quite the opposite of Amok, this spell protects the Barbarian for a short period of time and makes him invincible. Other players nearby can also be protected with this spell. Duration: 10 seconds; Refresh: 50 seconds.

☐ **All-Around-Attack:** Barbarian swings around like a mad man, hitting multiple melee enemies at once. Can be highly effective against both a few medium to strong armoured enemies and to masses of nearby enemies because the Barbarian does quite a lot of damage if upgraded properly, but usually just to a single enemy. With this skill, he can hit a lot of enemies at once and, positioned correctly, help him to clear a lot of enemies at once. Duration: 8 seconds; Refresh: 24 seconds.

Priest Spells

The spells of the Priest are mostly passive, but can also be used for attacks. For example, Heal is the most useful spell for the other members in the team, but it can also be used to remove bad spells and to attack unholy enemies. The other two spells are Attack-Aura and Ion-Cannon:

☐ **Heal:** Main skill obviously, especially important to heal Barbarians, which will constantly be hit. Also gives a little Mana and this way is even important for the other classes, including the Mage, who is in constant need of more Mana. Also removes any active bad spells on the target player when it is cast. If it is cast on enemy players, they get hurt and the Priest can absorb Hitpoints and energy. The priest cannot heal himself. Duration: 2.5 seconds; Refresh: 4 seconds.

☐ **Attack-Aura:** Every friendly player in screen range gets stronger as long as this effect stays active. Attributes increase also by the amount of points the Priest has for the Attack-Aura. This can be quite helpful to increase the abilities (passive skills) for a short while to crease damage, dexterity, life, and so on or even to use a weapon that is not yet wearable. Duration: always; updated all 10 seconds; Refresh: 90 seconds.

☐ **Ion Cannon:** The only powerful attack spell for the Priest. The Ion Cannon is shot by a satellite down to the battlefield; hey, wait a second, a satellite in a fantasy RPG? Who cares — magic spells are not much more realistic either. Anyway, the Ion Cannon deals a *huge* amount of damage, especially magic damage (it is a holy Ion Cannon, you know), but it is hard to control because it takes a while until the Ion Cannon unloads its fury and then the enemies can be long gone. Clever enemies will notice the icon cannon, and instead of waiting around and dying, they will approach the player, which can be hard in singleplayer, but useful in multiplayer. Duration: 3 seconds (2 seconds delay, 1 second damage); Refresh: 20 seconds.

Mage Spells

Unlike the other characters the Mage usually uses his spells more often than his weapons. He has both a much faster Mana regeneration rate and his spells can be used quickly over and over again:

☐ **Burning Ground:** Attacks in a straight line, fire spikes are coming from the ground. At each spike, a fire will be spawned at the ground and stay active for a little while. Every enemy that runs though it will get hurt. This is highly effective against smaller enemies that are stupid enough to run from start to finish though the Burning Ground. Duration: 10 seconds; Refresh: 5 seconds.

☐ **Ice:** Slows down the enemy or even freezes him. Does very little damage, but together with allies or other weapon makes it very easy to kill both single enemies and group of enemies. The disadvantage of single big enemies is that the bigger they get the more resistant they are. Duration: 15 seconds; Refresh: 7 seconds.

☐ **Lighting:** Really cool chain lighting effect, which hits multiple enemies, one by one. If just one enemy is around the damage is not very high, but if they are many enemies standing close to each other the lighting skill works best. Duration: 2 seconds; Refresh: 8 seconds

Hunter Spells

The Hunter has only spells to make more damage or to increase the running speed, which are the two most important features for the Hunter. For example, using the Magic Arrow spell can be a lot of fun and highly effective, but without the support of other players the Hunter can die quickly if not cautious.

☐ **Multiple Arrows:** Useful spell to shoot multiple arrows at once to hit either the same enemy many times if he is really close or to hit several enemies from a distance if they are spread out. Duration: 15s; Refresh: 20s.

☐ **Speed Aura:** Lets the Hunter and nearby players (half a screen) run much faster and shoot also a little bit faster. This is not only useful to get quicker to target locations, but it also helps you to run away more easily if something goes wrong. Duration: 25s; Refresh: 60s.

☐ **Magic Arrow:** Basically a rail gun, which when active, will cause any arrow shot to just go through the enemy and hit all enemies behind it. The damage of the arrow is also slightly increased to 150 percent. If you also invest skill points to other skills, especially strength, this can be become a very powerful skill, which also gives an advantage and bonus points to players who can cleverly find ways to shoot many enemies at once from a good angle. Duration: 5 seconds; Refresh: 10 seconds.

Leveling System

We have now covered all the basics for building the foundation of a role-playing system, except that the player should also have the ability to level up after gaining a certain amount of experience points each level. Because the monsters get stronger, the quests get harder, and the awards get bigger all the time in role-playing games, it would not make much sense to allow the player to level up at the same rate. Instead, we want the player to level up relatively fast in the beginning to make the game more fun and let him decide which abilities and skills he wants to invest in and then later he levels up much slower, but can increase the amount of experience he gets with stronger weapons, better skills, and items he got so far.

Figure 16-20 shows a typical experience needed for each level graph used in most role-playing systems. Some games have more complex graphs to make it easier in the beginning and even harder later to level up, or games might cap the maximum number of levels a player can reach. Dungeon Quest does not limit the player; he can get as strong as he wants, but it gets obviously much harder to reach level 50 from level 49 (can be many hours of game play) than it is to reach level 5 from level 4 (which can happen in a matter of minutes). The formula used to calculate the needed experience to level up is a basic exponential function $\exp(x)$, which is written for graphs as $y = e^x$ (in C# written with help of the Math.Pow function), where e is the Euler's number, but we will use a different constant and offset for the formula in Dungeon Quest:

```
const float BaseExperience = 1000.0f;
const float ExperienceFactor = 75.0f;
float experienceNeededForNextLevel = BaseExperience +
    Math.Pow(ExperienceFactor, currentLevel);
```

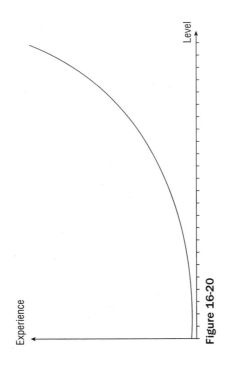

Experience

Level

Figure 16-20

The game engine, which will be discussed in more detail in the next chapter, will manage all the player characters and monsters, which are based on models contained in the AnimatedModel class. The game uses collada XML files to load all static mesh data and animations through bones and skinning information. Then additional meta information is loaded through a special XML file, which exists for each character and monster, where all the animation types, the general character attributes and start values, and other model-related information are stored. Then finally in the game we just use this Character class and let it handle all the underlying rendering of the character or monster itself plus the weapon, armor, and graphics effects it might need in the current animation state. The game extends the Character class with a game entity that also stores the current health, level, damage and other properties that might be important. For example, the skills each contain helper functions about the damage they currently do at their level.

This whole process is visualized in Figure 16-21 with the Barbarian.xml file as the main information center. Our idea was to allow everyone in the team to tweak and modify character and monster values without having to change any code. Not only is all the animation information stored there and information about which model file is used, but we also got the basic skills and attribute information inside this XML data file, which means we could just add more skills in this file or add more animations and no code would have to be changed. The game would just have more skills and animations available to use. Hopefully this concept will make the game highly extensible and allow even those players without any coding experience not only to create new maps, but also tweak and extend the game the way he thinks is best. Later, the players will have the ability to share their settings with other players via the website. More information about extensibility can be found in the Dungeon Quest Game Design Document.

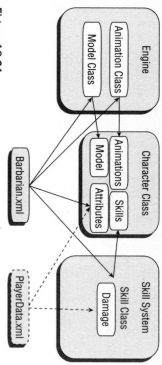

Figure 16-21

In addition to the `Barbarian.xml` file where all the global character information is stored, a `PlayerData.xml` file is also used to store the current process of the player in the game. The level is always regenerated when the player starts a new game with an existing character. The player wants to leave the game and continue where he left last time with his level, all his skills and abilities plus all the weapons and items he has collected. Currently, it is planned that everything will be stored in `PlayerData.xml`, but later versions of the game will support creating different player characters and allowing them to load them before joining a single or multiplayer game. While cheating is certainly possible this way (just edit the XML file), the game was not designed to prevent that anyway.

The game entities can attack each other. Usually the player will attack the monsters and they will fight back. Each entity has a Damage method, which will deal all the damage with the currently selected weapon or spell and trigger all the associated effects, animations, and sounds. Figure 16-22 shows this process with the Barbarian again. The image was created very early in the development process, but it shows the basic functionality of dealing two types of damage:

☐ **Magical** or Elemental, which will decrease the Hitpoints also after subtracting the magical part of the armor, but it also decreases Mana of the entity to a certain degree.

☐ **Physical**, which decreases the Hitpoints of the entity after subtracting the armor the entity has with the armor piece, his abilities and rings combined.

Figure 16-22

The first couple of monsters (rats, wolves, and so on) have only physical Hitpoints and deal only physical damage, whereas enemies at later stages of the game deal more magical damage and also have Mana on their own or might be very resistant against magical attacks. These rules force the player to switch attacks. Just dealing pure physical damage is not going to cut it against heavily armored enemies and just dealing pure magical damage will not hurt magic-resistant monsters. Obviously just having one kind of magical damage is not going to cut it when more monsters are introduced into the game. We will probably split it up into fire, ice, and poison damage types, each with its own resistant values, but for now we are trying to keep it as simple as possible.

To prevent players from cheating all the level and player data would not only have to be stored on the server side, but also all the game logic should happen there to prevent players from modifying the game while it is running (or via the freely available source code, which obviously makes cheating a lot easier). Currently, the multiplayer code only runs on the player's computer; to introduce server-based games we would need to build a game server, which then would have to manage all players and games. This is not only a complex task, but it also costs money to host and maintain such servers, and it gets more expensive as more players want to play the game. If the game gets that popular, we might think about such steps, but at the point we are just concentrating on getting the game done. Extending it later is always an option. It doesn't have to be us who will use the existing technology and build a sever-based game out of it; other teams can certainly do the same and even you as the reader can try to do so if you are interested in such things. The game is available, and the source code and content are free to use. Just give us some credit if you use parts of Dungeon Quest.

Challenge: Improve the Leveling System

In this chapter, we talked a lot about existing role-playing games and you have seen many parts of the game design document, which is actually even longer (you can check it out yourself if you want to read more). Your challenge for this chapter is to improve the leveling system and not only think about better and more complex Hitpoints and damage system, but also on ways you would implement such rules. If you are a role-playing games player, you probably know about some aspects, which I did not mention in this chapter, but that might be important for your role-playing game you might want to develop with the help of Dungeon Quest.

Improvements to the leveling system could be a better experience formula, more abilities and skills the player can invest his points in, or more Hitpoints and damage types, plus armors, resistances, and limiting formulas.

You could also take a look at the game data files to learn more about the game, ways to tweak or extend the capabilities, and ways in which you can implement your better leveling formulas. For example, the following XML data is from an early version of the Barbarian.xml file:

```xml
<?xml version="1.0" encoding="utf-8" ?>
<Character>
  <Animations>
    <Animation Name="Idle" StartFrame="0" EndFrame="99" />
    <Animation Name="Run" StartFrame="121" EndFrame="140" />
    <Animation Name="Attack1" StartFrame="100" EndFrame="120" />
    <Animation Name="Attack2" StartFrame="0" EndFrame="0" />
    <Animation Name="GotHit" StartFrame="0" EndFrame="0" />
    <Animation Name="Death" StartFrame="0" EndFrame="0" />
  </Animations>
  <Sounds>
    <Sound Name="Attack1" Filename="BarbarianAttack1.wav" />
    <Sound Name="Attack2" Filename="BarbarianAttack2.wav" />
    <Sound Name="Hit1" Filename="BarbarianHit1.wav" />
    <Sound Name="Hit2" Filename="BarbarianHit2.wav" />
```

```
        <Sound Name="Run" Filename="BarbarianRun.wav" />
        <Sound Name="Death" Filename="BarbarianDeath.wav" />
    </Sounds>
    <Attributes>
        <Attribute Name="Strength" Base="30" Effectivity="1" />
        <Attribute Name="Agility" Base="15" Effectivity="0.75" />
        <Attribute Name="Magic" Base="5" Effectivity="0.5" />
        <Attribute Name="Life" Base="25" Effectivity="1.0" />
        <Attribute Name="Dexternity" Base="10" Effectivity="0.4" />
    </Attributes>
    <Skills>
        <Skill Name="Amok"
            ManaCost="3"
            Radius="1" RadiusPerLevel="0"
            Damage="2.5" DamageType="Physical"
            Duration="5.0" DurationPerLevel="0.25"
            Cooldown="10.0" CooldownPerLevel="0.55" />
        <Skill Name="Shield"
            ManaCost="15"
            Radius="2" RadiusPerLevel="0.1"
            Damage="0" DamageType="Physical"
            Duration="10.0" DurationPerLevel="0.5"
            Cooldown="40.0" CooldownPerLevel="0.5" />
        <Skill Name="AllAroundAttack"
            ManaCost="15"
            Radius="1.1" RadiusPerLevel="0.1"
            Damage="0.8" DamageType="Physical"
            Duration="10.0" DurationPerLevel="0.5"
            Cooldown="40.0" CooldownPerLevel="0.5" />
    </Skills>
</Character>
```

Summary

In this chapter, you learned quite a bit about role-playing games — what exactly will be used in Dungeon Quest and which parts of the game logic had to be simplified to make it even possible to develop the game in a short timeframe. I think you will agree with me that creating role-playing games is a highly complex task, especially when you have to compare your game with the many successful and complex games out there.

Aside from learning about popular role-playing games such as Dungeons & Dragons, Diablo 2, Dungeon Siege, Titan Quest, and World of WarCraft, this chapter also discussed the major game design parts for Dungeon Quest:

☐ **Idea:** Dungeon Quest is a 3D top-down action role-playing game similar to Diablo 2. It features four player characters and has most of the features of other role-playing games, but many of these features are reduced to shorten the development time.

☐ **Scenario:** Typical fantasy setting, does not take itself seriously all the time; we want to have fun developing the game and the player should enjoy it, too. No reason to compete with any of the existing role-playing games. Main advantage of Dungeon Quest is the ability to extend and for players to learn how to develop role-playing games in general.

❑ **Story:** Player wakes up in the Dungeon Quest world and finds more about it through quests. The basic idea is to collect three runes to create a portal back to your own world.

❑ **Characters:** There are four character classes in the game, but it should be easy to add more classes later — just add more models and settings to the game. The four characters are the Barbarian, the Priest, the Mage, and the Hunter, which are all very different from each other and carry different weapons and have different skills.

❑ **Enemies:** In Act I, there are currently only six enemy types — Rats, Wolves, Werewolves, Spiders, Firebugs, and the Spider King, which appear in groups most of the time and are not hard to combat. The first act is all about leveling up and preparing for the later stages of the game.

❑ **Skills:** All characters share the five base attributes — Strength, Agility, Magic, Life, and Dexterity, but every character class also has three class specific spells. More spells will probably be added at a later point in time, especially after the game gets more than one type of magic damage.

❑ **Leveling system:** The player levels up after reaching a certain amount of experience points, which increases each level exponentially. The player then gets five points, which can be invested to increase his abilities or spells. A more sophisticated system might be implemented in the future, but my guess would be that more content like enemies, spells and characters would be more important first.

The next chapter will go into more detail about the game engine, and it will also make use of all the graphics engine, sound engine, and multiplayer code we have written this far in the book. Because Dungeon Quest is still in development at the time of this writing we will go through many smaller unit tests to create a proof-of-concept-type game at the end of Chapter 17. By the end of Chapter 17, it should be clear how the game is played and in which ways you can extend and tweak the source code and data files.

17

Dungeon Quest

This is the final chapter about Dungeon Quest and also the final chapter of this book. Because of the complexity of a role-playing game such as Dungeon Quest, we are unable to discuss all of its details here. We will, however, cover all the basics to get you started. You can find additional information about the game, get help with the implementation, and obtain recent updates on the official site: www.DungeonQuestGame.com.

The first part of this chapter discusses the game engine and its features. In the previous chapter, I discussed some of the game engine features. While we are still using the XnaGraphicEngine from Part II of this book, and the parts of the engine from the Racing Game from Chapter 14, many parts have been updated or even completely rewritten. For example, all 3D models use the Collada model format now. This makes it much easier to fix exporting errors, to miss textures, and to import animation data. It also allows a greater range of 3D tools to be used to create 3D models for the game. I am also going to discuss the new shaders used for the maps. In addition, I discuss how skinned animation works and how to use multi-pass shaders for the underground and lighting effects. Most of the engine features are shown with help of the in-game editor Dungeon Quest provides to the player.

In the previous chapter, most player characters and enemy types were introduced. In order to allow them to run around, attack players, and be killed, you need some basic AI (artificial intelligence) for them. The AI engine will still be simple, but it gives you the basic foundation for adding AI to your own games. Luckily for us, the AI for role-playing games does not have to be very sophisticated because most enemies should not be intelligent. Zombies, for example, are expected to be dumb. However, if you want to make the game and enemies appear to be more intelligent, you can add the alert-system to the AI engine. Whenever a monster sees one of the players or gets attacked, the monster will cry and alert surrounding monsters to go into attack mode as well. This is especially important for ranged attacks from the Hunter or Mage because otherwise they could simply kill one monster at a time and have it far too easy.

Later in this chapter, I discuss multiplayer support by introducing all the required steps to make the game a good multiplayer game. In Chapter 15, you saw some of the networking code for the lobby and chat screens. Because we are mainly adding more network messages here, I will discuss the opportunities with Xbox Live via XNA 2.0. Networking is only possible via Xbox Live on the Xbox 360 with XNA 2.0, so we have to investigate it a little. At the time of this writing, however, it makes absolutely no sense to use the networking capabilities of XNA 2.0 for a Windows game because it would require all players to be both Xbox Live Gold subscribers and XNA Creators Club subscribers. Both subscriptions cost quite a lot of money each year. I discuss this issue and what it means for XNA developers at the end of this chapter.

The last part of this chapter focuses on the level editor and all its features that enable you to quickly create new maps and play with the 3D models, adding enemies and the lighting effects. Getting used to the Dungeon Quest level editor is the first step in getting to know Dungeon Quests and building your own modifications. I hope that more players and non-programmers will extend the game and make their own modifications than for the Rocket Commander or Racing Game, which did not include an editor and made it hard for non-programmers to modify the game.

Creating the Engine

Because I have written quite a lot of game engines, I had a pretty clear idea on what was required for this game. Even if you have done certain rendering techniques before, it will be hard to apply them in a new game engine. Not only do most of the shaders and vertex formats change from game to game; certain techniques might not even work because of a different rendering pipeline. For example, in Dungeon Quest, a map can have an unlimited amount of point lights, whereas all the previous games of this book had one directional light source. But I worked with point lights in previous projects and wrote shaders for them. After implementing the first two point lights into the Dungeon Quest Editor, I discovered that the editor became complex and slow. To make things even worse, two of my co-workers could not launch the editor because the shader was too complex for their graphic cards, which could not handle pixel shader 2.b or 3.0. Point lights are discussed in a little bit.

Before you dive into the many changes that were made to the engine, let's discuss the goals and features of the Dungeon Quest game engine. In addition to the features discussed in earlier chapters such as the multiplayer support, high score list, and extensible game structure, the following list was written at the concept stage to determine which changes were important for the game engine of Dungeon Quest:

☐ **Written and optimized for XNA Game Studio 2.0:** Dungeon Quest is one of the first games released for XNA 2.0. It was important to me to ensure that Dungeon Quest made it to the top of this list, just as the XNA Racing Game did.

☐ **Open Source:** While all of the other games in this book are also free to use and include the source code, they were mainly used for people to learn about XNA. Dungeon Quest has an extensible structure and features a level editor, which makes it much easier for non-programmers and especially artists to create their own content without having to touch the source code of the game. If a little community around Dungeon Quest evolves around the game on www.DungeonQuestGame.com, everyone in the team will be happy.

☐ **Stunning 3D effects:** These effects are included in game engine feature lists, which means utilizing all the shader effects you have learned about this far in this book. In addition to the post screen shaders from Chapter 8 and the shadow mapping effects from the Racing Game, Dungeon Quest features unlimited point lights with different colors and nice-looking normal maps on both the ground and 3D models.

□ **HDR (High Dynamic Range) Rendering:** All the rendering now happens in HDR, which allows us to use better glowing effects and adjust the scene dynamically with tone mapping. More details about this rendering technique can be found in the RenderToTexture helper class.

□ **Easy to learn game:** The game can be controlled with mouse and keyboard on the PC and with the Xbox 360 Controller on the console. All the other supported new input devices (see Chapter 10) are also supported and can be customized. The game itself allows the player to both point and click or to use direct control with the controller or keyboard. Thanks to the shoot and run ability, the game is more fun to play and gives it a more action-like game feeling.

□ **Interchangeable graphics and 3D models:** Players can not only change the source code, but also put in other graphics or 3D models using the Collada model file format and the dds graphic file format. This makes it easier for people not having much experience in 3D tools to import their works into the game. All game content files are also XMLbased such as the Collada model file format itself, which makes it easy to read, understand and edit, if necessary.

Changes to the Graphic Engine

Figure 17-1 shows the classes of the Dungeon Quest game engine at the time of this writing. There may be additional classes in the future. As you can see, the graphics engine alone is quite complex. There are even more helper classes in the utilities assembly and other external assemblies such as the game server service. In the previous games of this book and all of the XNA games I have written thus far, all the game code, the engine, the utilities, and the helper classes were all contained in one project. But as projects grow bigger, and especially if you want to reuse elements from earlier projects, a separate game engine is very helpful. While writing the game engine, we can always use unit tests to help us direct which part has to be written next and to ensure that everything works as expected.

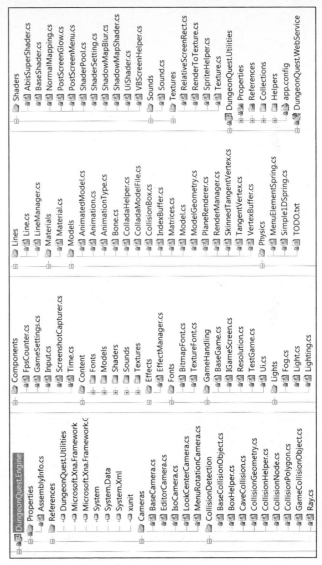

Figure 17-1

519

I will not have enough time to cover all the classes in this book. Most of the underlying code was already covered in previous chapters of this book. Instead, this chapter will cover exciting new features such as rendering many point lights, using HDR (High Dynamic Range) rendering, and handling Collada 3D model files. The following list states briefly what each namespace in the engine does:

☐ **Used assemblies:** In addition to the usual System assemblies, the XNA 2.0 assemblies, and XUnit for unit testing (as described in Chapter 15), the utilities assembly from the Dungeon Quest solution are used. The entire engine lacks game code. Thus, we are only using game content to test some of its features such as rendering Collada models. This way the game engine can easily be used for other projects too, without even having to change a single line of the game engine. Mods for the Rocket Commander game or the Racing Game usually included the whole original game code, which will no longer be necessary for Dungeon Quest engine-based games. You can write something completely different with the game engine or use it as a foundation for your own game engine.

☐ **Cameras:** We learned early in the process of making Dungeon Quest that different unit tests require different cameras. The game requires a different camera than the menu, where we want to have more control and move freely around. The Rocket Commander game, for example, used only one camera but had many switches in it to allow using it for unit testing and the menu, too. This approach, however, is too complex and not generic enough for a game engine. The most important camera classes are IsoCamera and EditorCamera. IsoCamera is used in the game and is bound to the player position. The EditorCamera, for the editor, enables you to freely move around and zoom with the mouse wheel or keyboard Page Up/Page Down keys. Most unit tests use the LookCenterCamera, which focuses the camera at the origin and allows rotating around the object in the 3D origin. This camera was basically used throughout the whole book in all unit tests except when the SpaceCamera for the Rocket Commander game or the ChaseCarCamera for the Racing Game were tested.

☐ **Collision Detection:** Currently, this is still based on the polygon-based collision detecting capabilities from the first Dungeon Quest game. These classes will probably not be used much because most of the collision testing in the new Dungeon Quest game can be done with simple collision boxes (see CollisionBox in the Models namespace).

☐ **Components:** Contains easily reusable game components for simple tasks such as using FPS counters, capturing screenshots, handling Input devices, and storing game settings. Some of these classes were used before, but they are refactored now into game components, which are easier to use in XNA 2.0. More information about game components and their advantages can be found in Chapter 4.

☐ **Content:** The content directory is used to hold all the game content. In the game engine only test models, global UI textures and texture fonts are stored here. These content files provide the basic ability to render text and some simple menu elements on the screen. More important, all of the shaders are located here, too. They can be tested with the shaders in the Shaders namespace.

☐ **Effects:** Not implemented yet, but this namespace will provide classes to add 2D effects (and possibly 3D effects, too) on top of the 3D models for things such as blood splatters, explosions, fire, and additional light effects. XnaShooter uses an extensive effects system. Please check out Chapter 11 to learn more about implementing effects into your game.

☐ **Fonts:** This class was previously used together with materials, render targets, and other texture classes in the Textures namespace. In addition to the TextureFont class being separated from the Texture class and its namespace, the underlying logic is now being implemented in the BitmapFont class. The BitmapFont class handles both rendering existing bitmap fonts and generating new font characters dynamically when required to support other languages

(German, Chinese, and so on). The `TextureFont` class then encapsulates this functionality and makes it easy to use. It also optimizes the rendering process to allow many fonts to be rendered efficiently. Figure 17-2 shows the result of running the `TestRenderFont` unit test of the `TextureFont` class. While all this is exciting and improves font rendering abilities of game engines, explaining it in detail would require at least a full chapter. Both classes in this namespace have a lot of comments and links. I encourage you to check them out if you want to know how all this works and how you can use them for your games, too.

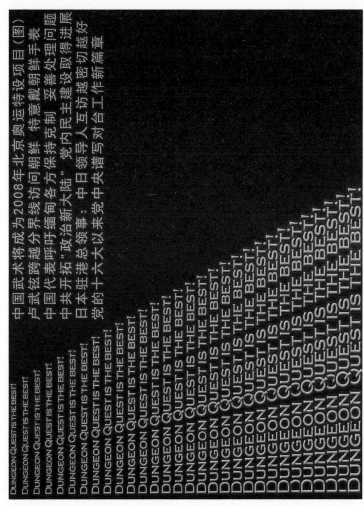

Figure 17-2

❑ **Game Handling:** Provides all the base game capabilities, the `IGameScreen` interface for game and menu screens and all the other resolution, test, and UI helper classes we know from previous projects. The main difference in this engine is the highly reduced `BaseGame` class, which contains only the most basic functionality now and no longer contains all the FPS, time, input, render target and overall state management functionality. The `BaseGame` class is heavily refactored and wherever possible the functionality is extracted to simpler classes such as Resolution, which now handles the screen resolution (screen width and height).

❑ **Lights:** Because Dungeon Quest does not only use a simple directional light and all of the lighting properties were removed from the `BaseGame` class; the `Lighting` class was introduced. It contains a list of lights that are currently active. Each light is encapsulated with the help of the `Light` class, which contains the light position for point lights, light direction for directional lights, the light color and additional parameters for the distance and falloff values. More information about point lights are explained in the next section.

- ❑ **Lines:** The line helper classes from the XNA graphics engine, as introduced in Chapter 3. These offer a few new functions for rendering rectangles and 3D grids, plus the ability to render on top of 3D geometry after the 3D render pass. Use the unit tests in the `LineManager` class to learn more.

- ❑ **Models:** This is the most complex namespace in the engine and it covers everything from the low level 3D model support with classes such as `VertexBuffer`, `IndexBuffer`, and `TangentVertex` to the high level classes to render 3D models with help of `Model` and `AnimatedModel` classes. As discussed in the next section, Collada model files are used and most of the functionality to make this work is contained in the `ColladaModelFile` class. You might ask yourself why so many classes are required when previous game engines in this book just used a handful of classes for rendering 3D models. The main reason for the added complexity comes from the animated model support, skinning, and handling the underlying bone skeleton.

- ❑ **Physics:** While it would be nice to have a complete physics engine (see Chapter 13 for details about many physics engines) support in Dungeon Quest, it was left out right from the beginning. Physics could be used to improve the game and add some realism, but they are not important to make the game run. There are still some simple physic classes left in this namespace, but they are currently only used for simpler physics effects and for the menu, which bounces around with help of the `MenuElementSpring` class. Because the Ageia physics engine is now free to use, it may be implemented in the future for the PC version of the game (Ageia does not work on the Xbox 360 with XNA yet, because it uses native assemblies).

- ❑ **Shaders:** This namespace looks a lot like the shaders namespace of the Racing Game, but the underlying code has changed a bit. Most shaders now have more parameters and have added a new class named `AbisSuperShader`, which contains many different techniques and adds quite a lot of functionality to support all the new Fresnel shader effects, the point lights used in the game engine, and other shader effects for re-coloring, fog, and reflection. Figure 17-3 shows some of the available parameters and techniques of `AbisSuperShader.fx`.

- ❑ **Sounds:** The sound effects and the game music have not changed much. It would probably be best to refactor this into general sound effects used in the engine, and then use and load the game sound effects dynamically in the game itself. However, I have no idea how to do this properly with XACT files. See Chapter 9 to learn more about XACT and sound effects.

- ❑ **Textures:** And finally, these classes are the texture, sprites, and render target helper classes. Nothing has changed in these classes, but a new class `RelativeScreenRect` was added to support relative rendering. Check out the unit tests in the class to learn more about it. Some of the unit tests were discussed in Chapter 16. All the game screens in Dungeon Quest use this new helper class quite a lot.

Using Collada Model Files

I talked a lot about the XNA Content Pipeline and its problems earlier in this book (Chapter 6 and following). For projects like Rocket Commander or even the Racing Game it was sometimes a little bit tedious. You could, however, do everything you needed by loading X files and adding some features to it to fix the tangents, load the correct shader techniques, and so on.

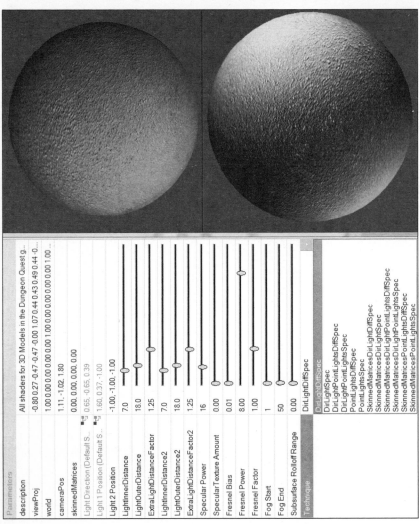

Figure 17-3

However, XNA does not support loading animation data and does not give you a way to display them. You have to do all that work by yourself. This includes static mesh animations (as was used in Rocket Commander), and it includes skeletal animation with bones and skinned meshes. I have created a long blog post to explain all of the following in more detail. Be sure to read it if you are interested in more details about the Collada model format implementation: http://exdream.no-ip.info/blog/2007/02/25/ SkeletalBoneAnimationAndSkinningWithColladaModelsInXNA.aspx.

Before I go into the details, Figure 17-4 shows the most important classes for loading and displaying Collada files. Please note that most of the ColladaModel class from the older Collada project was refactored into the ColladaModelFile class and the rendering now happens mostly in the Model and AnimatedModel classes. The SkinnedTangentVertex class is also new. It contains pretty much the same as the TangentVertex class from Chapter 6. Plus, it has additional fields for blend indices and weights.

The two most important unit tests are contained in the `AnimatedModel` class and are called `TestShowBones` and `TestRenderAnimatedModel`. The `AnimatedModel` class itself provides a constructor and a Render method. Everything else is protected and will be handled automatically for you. The Bone class is used to store all the bones in a flat list, but each entry has a parent and a list of old children bones. This way the list can be used both in a simple for loop, and you can also go through it recursively (which is obviously slower and often more complicated).

Figure 17-4

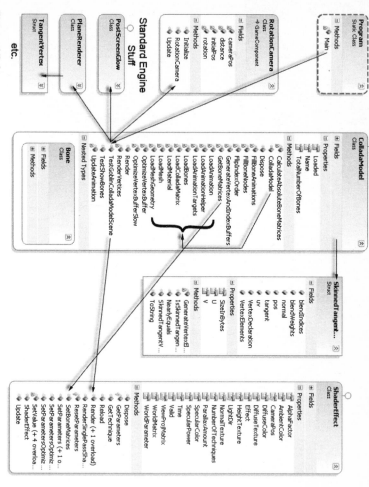

All the mesh data is stored in vertices, which is just a list of `SkinnedTangentVertex` structures. The `SkinnedTangentVertex` structure is very much like the standard `TangentVertex` structure used in Rocket Commander XNA, but it has two new members: `blendIndices` and `blendWeights`. Both are in the form of Vector3, and therefore, can hold three values allowing us to interpolate up to three bone influences for each vertex in the shader. Because you have to re-normalize all bone weights, skipping the least important bone weights is not a big deal. Most test models use mostly two to three influences. Please also note that the vertex shader now has more work to do with all that skinning and you should really optimize it as much as possible. Both the number of vertices to process and the number of vertex shader instructions are important. Both numbers should be as low as possible. The GPU is really fast processing this data. If you do not have animated geometry with bones, there is no reason to let it process all that data (which can make the vertex shader two to three times longer and slower). The underground layer or static meshes without animations do not need to be rendered with a skinned shader technique.

There are several load methods in the ColladaModelFile class and you should be able to figure them out with help of the article on my blog and by reading the comments in the source code. The following code shows how the bones are loaded. The matrices are located in the LoadBones method. Even through the bones are located at the end of the Collada file, you have to load them first because all other loading methods, specifically LoadMeshes and LoadAnimation need the bone tree structure and the over-all bone list to work. All bones are loaded in sequential order because we want to make sure that we can use the animation matrices later in an easy way without having to check the parent order.

```
foreach (XmlNode boneNode in boneNodes)
  if (boneNode.Name == "node" &&
    (XmlHelper.GetXmlAttribute(boneNode,
     "id").Contains("Bone") ||
    XmlHelper.GetXmlAttribute(boneNode,
     "type").Contains("JOINT")))
  {
    // [...] get matrix
    matrix = LoadColladaMatrix(...);
    // Create this node, use the current number of
    // bones as number.
    Bone newBone = new Bone(matrix, parentBone,
      bones.Count,
      XmlHelper.GetXmlAttribute(boneNode, "sid"));
    // Add to our global bones list
    bones.Add(newBone);
    // And to our parent, this way we have a tree and a
    // flat list in the bones list :)
    if (parentBone != null)
      parentBone.children.Add(newBone);
    // Create all children (will do nothing if there
    // are no sub bones)
    FillBoneNodes(newBone, boneNode);
  } // foreach if (boneNode.Name)
```

As you can see, the code uses the new XmlHelper class extensively because the code would look much uglier and complex. You can check out the XmlHelper class in the Dungeon Quest utilities project. For more information about the Collada models, please read through the other load methods in the ColladaModelFile class.

Figure 17-5 shows what the collada skinning test project looks like when you press Ctrl to show all the post screen processing textures. Most shader passes do several things at once and the list of operations (see right side of the image) is longer than the list of used passes. Most of this was just trying to get the best-looking values together quickly. If you are an experienced artist (or know one) you can probably do a much better job.

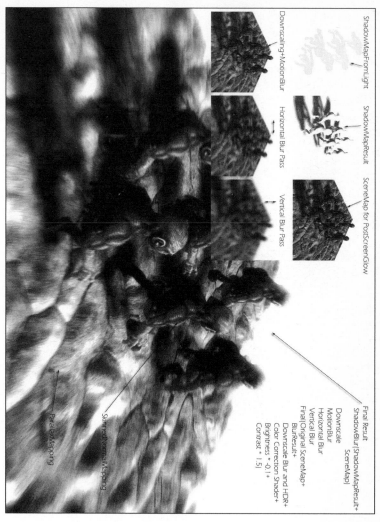

Figure 17-5

Handling Many Point Lights

As described earlier in this chapter, handling a single point light is not hard. However, allowing an unlimited number of point lights for the maps in Dungeon Quests introduced many unforeseen problems. Other game engines either limit the number of lights you can see at a time or use similar multi-pass rendering techniques. And many others use even more advanced rendering techniques such as deferred shading where the whole scene is rendered into several render targets with all the color, position, and normal information in screen space. Then, in the post screen shaders, the lighting calculations happen. While deferred shading is very complex and requires a fast GPU, it allows you to render many point lights and to do other effects in the post processing very cheaply. The game, Stalker, implemented this technique. However, the game engine programmers spent many years to perfect it. We are not going to have that amount of time for this little project.

In order to make the many point lights work without having to rewrite the whole engine and to support the older pixel shader 2.0 hardware, I had to rethink the rendering process completely. Instead of rendering the whole map underground at once, it is now rendered in several shader passes, which is not an easy thing if you have not done that before. It works similarly to post screen shaders (see Chapter 8 for details), but instead of rendering into render target textures, we render results directly on the screen in the first shader pass, and then, apply certain blending modes for the other passes. Figure 17-6 illustrates this technique with the first pass setting the ambient color, the second pass doing one single point light and the final pass applying the diffuse textures. The second pass can be repeated as often as you want to support as many point lights as you need. As you can imagine, rendering the scene many times is obviously a lot slower than just rendering it once. If you are able to reduce the shader complexity, the overall performance can be improved a lot. You also only have to render the visible lights. Even if a map has 100 point lights, we usually just see a few of them in one scene. Often, three or four lights are visible at a time.

Figure 17-6

The geometry for the underground is also very simple (flat polygons, about 20 × 15 visible at a time). The vertex rendering is very fast and can be done many times without a performance impact. On the other hand, the 3D models in Dungeon Quest have a high amount of polygons and it would not be a good idea to render them in several passes. Instead, 3D Models are only affected by the nearest two point lights and are rendered this way. This technique was already introduced in the first version of Dungeon Quest. While the shader is pretty complex, the rendering process is easy to handle. Figure 17-7 shows the Barbarian with two point lights and a directional light source from the unit test TestRenderMultipleAnimatedModels in the AnimatedModel class. You can use the tests in the AnimatedModel class and the Model class itself to check out 3D models and to play around with some of the shader settings. The editor also makes it very easy to test out 3D models.

For the underground shader, each light is rendered in a separate pass. For 3D models, you use only a single-pass shader to reduce the complexity and to minimize the amount of vertices that have to be processed. You still want to have point-light support for 3D Models in the game. The scene will look more realistic if everything is shaded the same way. The ground always covers almost 100 percent of the screen, while 3D models usually reside at a certain location and may not be affected by as many lights. You can often simply use the nearest two or three point lights while still getting a decent result. Figure 17-8 shows an early screenshot of the editor with two point lights. (It supported only two lights at that time; now you can have an unlimited number of lights.) While some unit tests still use a directional light source, the editor and the game just work with the ambient color and the point lights, which gives the game a more dark and mystical look.

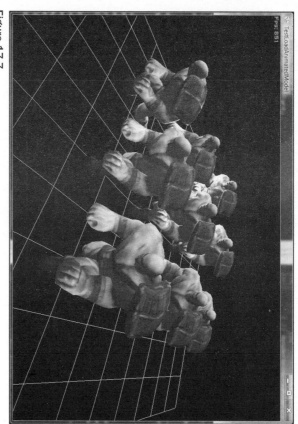

Figure 17-7

Figure 17-8

Chapter 17: Dungeon Quest

The shader for the 3D models is pretty much the same as the normal mapping shader I have used often in this book, especially for the Rocket Commander game and the Racing Game. The main difference is added parameters and new effects such as Fresnel for specular colors and subsurface scattering, and of course the added point lights. Most of these new effects will add only a few instructions to the shader and give the rendering a cool look, as in Figure 17-7, but some additions such as processing every point light in the pixel shader will increase the pixel shader instruction length to a huge amount. Not only does this make the shader a lot slower, but you will also run into problems when you want to support pixel shader 2.0 GPUs, which can do only 64 pixel shader instructions. It is very important to keep the overall shader instructions as low as possible for every point light to allow you to do two or three point light calculations in one shader pass. Playing around with optimization ideas allows you to add more point lights — for example, when just doing the specular calculation for the first point light (the nearest one), you can have enough instructions for another one or two point lights if required. The following code shows the full loop of point lights in the pixel shader of AbisSuperShader.fx:

```
if (usePointLights)
{
    for (int num=0; num<NUMBER_OF_LIGHTS; num++)
    {
        lightVector = In.pointLightVecs[num].xyz;
        // Compute the angle to the light
        float attenuation = In.pointLightVecs[num].w;
        // If this is the first light (player flare),
        // make it much weaker
        float thisBump = saturate(dot(normalVector,
            lightVector)) * attenuation;
        // Apply the light color
        if (num == 0)
        {
            bumpWithColor += thisBump * light1Color;
        else if (num == 1)
            bumpWithColor += thisBump * light2Color;
        else
            bumpWithColor += thisBump * light3Color;

        // Specular factor
        reflectVector = normalize(2 * thisBump *
            normalVector - lightVector);
        float thisSpec = pow(max(dot(reflectVector,
            viewVector), 0), specularPower);
        // We have to multiply with our bump to make sure
        // the other side does not get any specular
        // lighting effects (big problem if we don't do
        // this!)
        spec += thisBump * thisSpec;
    } // for (int num=0; num<NUMBER_OF_LIGHTS; num++)
} // if
```

These lines create approximately eight to ten instructions per point light. Please note that this for-loop will be completely unrolled by the shader compiler because pixel shader 2.0 does not support loops or if statements. The usePointLights variable is also just a condition that is pre-compiled and given to the pixel shader as a uniform parameter, which does not add any instructions or constants to the shader. In the for-loop, there are also several if-else statements, which will be removed by the for-loop unrolling since each unrolled loop uses one of these conditions. You could also write all this code yourself, but having a nice tight for-loop is much easier to handle and every time you want to make a change you don't have to change it at three places. Just modify the content of the loop and let the compiler handle all the work for you.

529

Adding AI

Adding Artificial Intelligence (AI) to a game can be a difficult task. In the games at the beginning of this book, some simpler AI routines were already implemented. For example, in the XNA Pong game it was sufficient to have just a few `if-else` blocks to handle all the AI, and with the help of some constants the difficulty could be tweaked.

Other game types such as strategy games require a much more sophisticated AI, a complex strategy game with a Singleplayer mode will need a solid path-finding algorithm, both micro-management and macro-management abilities for the AI, and finally, triggers for game events and complex build-orders and structure placement logic for building up bases. Earlier strategy games such as Command & Conquer 1 implemented just some of these features. For example, the AI never built any bases in Command & Conquer or Dune II; they were already set by the level editor. Micro-management is the ability to handle units effectively; scout the map, attack, defend, or retreat from a fight when necessary. Micro-management is usually not implemented well in strategy games for the AI because it is both hard to implement and it can cause many issues with players tricking the enemy into doing the same stupid action over and over again. Macro-management is the ability to rebuild armies quickly and to attack when you have enough units. It is not hard to implement and is usually something the AI does better than human players, but macro-management alone will not let the AI win.

Role-playing games might be complex to build but adding AI is not that complicated. The path-finding does not have to be as good as it does for strategy games or 3D action games; you can get away with stupid zombie-like behavior of units just moving straight toward the player. Base-building and macro-management are also non-issues. But even with this reduced complexity, implementing and testing AI code is not a piece of cake. For Dungeon Quest, I am going to keep it as simple as possible.

Path-Finding

I have some experience with path-finding algorithms through the strategy games I have written (e.g., Arena Wars). Algorithms, such as A*-Path-Finding, can make the task easier, but you still have to partition your world into tiles or other objects and then allow all your entities to move in this space according to the A* results. Dungeon Quest does not use an advanced path-finding algorithm at this time and I won't have any time to explain A* in more detail here. If you want to learn more about AI and path-finding algorithms, please check out Steve Rabin's website at www.AIWisdom.com and the *AI Game Programming Wisdom* and *Game Programming Gems* books (both from Charles River Media) he has contributed to. He is an expert in the AI area and gives out a lot of tips and tricks plus provides all the links you need to learn more if you are interested.

Figure 17-9 shows simple path-finding as it is implemented in Dungeon Quest, which was already used for the first version of the game. All it needs is the position, rotation vector, and movement speed for each entity, plus some kind of simple collision detection in order to avoid going through static objects such as houses, trees, stones, or barrels. The player can freely move around; no path finding will be performed. Enemies, on the other hand, do always run toward the player once in attack mode and will engage once in attacking range. If an enemy is trapped in like the one in the lower right of Figure 17-9, it will not be intelligent enough to get out of this situation. The player can ignore such enemies or shoot at them at a distance if possible. Level design should take care of these issues and should not allow enemies to be blocked off often; the game would be too easy and not much fun. It may even seem buggy if the enemies behave stupidly, which can easily be fixed by opening up the level a bit and allowing enemies to reach the player in most situations.

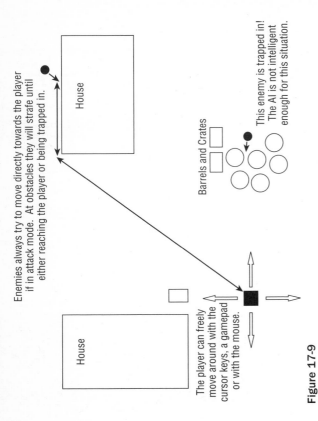

Enemies always try to move directly towards the player if in attack mode. At obstacles they will strafe until either reaching the player or being trapped in.

House

House

The player can freely move around with the cursor keys, a gamepad or with the mouse.

Barrels and Crates

This enemy is trapped in! The AI is not intelligent enough for this situation.

Figure 17-9

Currently enemies can intersect with each other and the player can also move through them and not be trapped in yet, but this part will probably be added as soon as the game testing and balancing happens. Simple sphere-based collision detection between game entities (enemies and players) will be sufficient. The collision checking for the level geometry is currently polygon-based, but if more performance is required, it might be good enough to check for collisions with the help of much simpler bounding boxes.

Alert-System via Cries

One simple idea I had on the GDC when developing the first version of Dungeon Quest in four days was to allow monsters to behave as a collective, not as individuals. We had just added sound effects and it was fun to hit monsters and hear them cry or to go into their visible attack range and let them attack you. The problem was, if you were to run quickly into a room and alert all monsters yourself, the game was very hard. On the other hand, if you just ran slowly into a room and alerted just one monster at a time by slowly advancing, the game was way too easy. We did not like that play testers would abuse the game this way.

To resolve this problem, I added the ability of other monsters to hear the cry of an attacked monster. A monster will also attack and cry if he sees the player in his sight range or if the player directly attacks him. Figure 17-10 illustrates the solution. Once the player brings one of the enemies into attack mode (1), for example by attacking him from a distance (2), the monster cries out. Both the player himself and all surrounding monsters in the cry-range (3) are alerted that this monster is now in attack mode. Monsters outside of the cry-range, which can be different for each monster type, are not affected. But all players that heard the cry are now in attack mode, too, and will engage the player (4), making it more difficult for him to kill the enemies one by one. This technique can be improved by recursively adding cries to the engaging enemies, alerting even more enemies, but this was not required yet; the simple cry-alert-system alone made the game much harder and fairer already.

There are also other AI things implemented in Dungeon Quest, but most of them are currently coded directly in wherever they are needed. In the future, our team plans to add the ability to set triggers and even to add a complex quest system to make the game more fun, but for now we are just on the mission to finish the first version of the game.

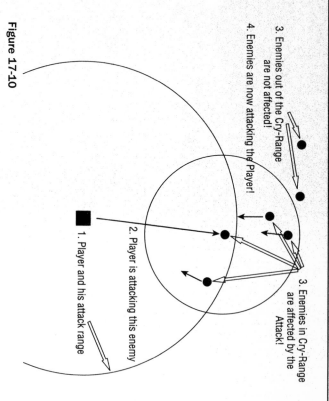

3. Enemies out of the Cry-Range are not affected!

4. Enemies are now attacking the Player!

3. Enemies in Cry-Range are affected by the Attack!

1. Player and his attack range

2. Player is attacking this enemy

Figure 17-10

Multiplayer Support

The basic foundation for the network support was already written in Chapter 15; we just have to add more network messages here to support multiple players. The networking system is not yet completely tested nor advanced enough to handle cases such as players disconnecting, packet loss (which is a big issue when using the UDP protocol) or synchronizing the game state between players.

Currently every player runs the game on his own machine and just simulates all the actions of the other players they send via network messages on their machine. A typical player update network message contains the player position, the current rotation value, and other data such as which attack state the player is in. While such a message is important, it is not critical to the game in most of the cases and since the same message with updated values will be sent out every couple of hundred milliseconds it won't matter if you miss one from time to time. Other messages, such as if a monster loses Hitpoints or dies, or if someone picks up an item, are more important and when such a message gets lost or is not executed on the other multiplayer machines at the same time the game can quickly get out of sync.

Because testing is not yet that advanced, these problems will occur and we are totally aware of them, but currently the main focus is to get it working. Once we find out which messages have to be sent or how we can improve the game synchrony by using other techniques or protocols (see Chapter 15 on TCP versus UDP), the multiplayer engine will be improved and the game will get better and better.

With that warning out of the way, let's take a look at the network messages and the current messaging system. Split-screen support will work the same way — two players are created on one machine and they send messages to each other the same way they would to other computers. This way, split-screen support does not require any additional code yet, but just needs to take care of rendering the two player characters and controlling them locally with game controllers or the keyboard and mouse.

Network Messages

The following values were added to the `MessageType` enumeration in the `DungeonQuest.Networking` namespace:

☐ `JoinGame`: This message type was already introduced in Chapter 15. It is a Simple message sent by new clients to the host to indicate if they want to join the game. The host responds with a `GameInfoAndPlayerList` message or he will kill the connection if the game is full.

☐ `GameInfoAndPlayerList`: This message was also used in Chapter 15 like `ChatMessage` and `EndGame`. The message is sent by the host player if anyone joins or leaves this session. The host then sends the `GameInfoAndPlayerList` message to all players including the new player and informs everyone about all players currently in the game. Each player chooses one of the four player characters (Barbarian, Hunter, Mage, or Priest) before joining the game. By default, the Barbarian is selected; each player can choose any character. Each player has a name and IP to allow all others to connect to him.

☐ `ChatMessage`: Simple chat message, which always goes to all players in the game. Contains both the sending player name and the chat message.

☐ `StartGame`: Start game message, sent by the game host to all players in the game. The game starts immediately. All players have to have their characters chosen before this. This message does also contain a randomizer seed value to make sure all clients generate the same effects and other random level effects, making the game look the same on all computers!

☐ `EndGame`: End game, sent by the host when the game ends, but also by a client to indicate he is leaving. In addition to this message a client or even the host player can also disconnect from all connected players to completely end a game.

☐ `PlayerUpdate`: Player update message, sent from client to server and from server back to all other clients. It contains the position (Vector2) of the character, 1 byte containing the current rotation (0255 to 0-2*PI) and 1 byte containing the current status (bit 0=moving, bit 1=attacking, bit 2=performing spell 1, and so on). We could even optimize that down to 3–5 bytes, but I don't see the necessity of that yet. Each client keeps a list of player positions and adjusts them based on received PlayerUpdate messages. Future versions might even interpolate more smoothly, add predictions, and fix wrong prediction values, as in advanced 3D action shooter game engines.

☐ `HitpointsDecrease`: This message is sent out a lot; it contains an enemy unit-ID and the amount of Hitpoints it lost.

☐ `UnitDied`: This message is sent out when a player kills a monster. The player will get points, and the monster will die on all computers and cannot be killed anymore. Contains an enemy unit id and the player who killed it.

☐ `PlayerDied`: This message is sent when your player character reaches 0 Hitpoints and dies. The player will die on all computers after the server sends this message back to all players. Priest players can revive other players; otherwise players can restart in the city and run to their dead bodies to recover them.

- `ItemCollected`: Have any of the players collected an item? Send to all players to remove item from game world. The item contains the position and the item type. You can't collect the same item again. The game keeps a list of collected items. If the same item is collected again (two players too near and both are trying to collect it), it is ignored.

- `LevelUp`: This message is sent out whenever a player reaches his experience limit and reaches the next level of his player character. This message also contains the new abilities, spells and other player values and is sent again after the player chooses to spend his points. If a player does want to use his ability points at a later time, that works fine, too. All the calculated damage is always based on the player abilities.

- `GameSync`: The final network message, but it is used in debug mode only. It is a helper message for debugging to find out if all players and the server are still in sync. Each player and the host generate this message, which can then be compared. It may be hard to compare because we have no game ticks and we have to see if the `GameSync` message makes sense from the client perspective. Data included in the sync process: All friendly player positions (using server data, not interpolated positions), also all their rotations and states (moving, attacking, etc) All enemy monster positions and states, which must be the same on all machines. All items, if collected or not and their positions. And finally all player level rank values, score, abilities, spells, energy, etc. Maybe other things such as the game time will be included in the future.

The entire set of new network messages is handled the same way as before; each message type has its own simple class derived from the `BaseMessage` class. You can use the usual constructor logic to create a new message by setting all required data yourself or from a network stream via the `BinaryReader` constructor. To send out a message, the `SendMessageToAllPlayers` or `SendMessageToHostPlayer` from the `SessionConnection` class is used.

To illustrate the added network message functionality, the following code shows the method to send out a `UnitDied` message:

```
/// <summary>
/// Send out a UnitDied message
/// </summary>
/// <param name="unitId">Unit id of the enemy that
/// died</param>
public static void SendUnitDiedMessage(int unitId)
{
    // Add us as the player that killed the monster.
    UnitDiedMessage newUnitDiedMsg =
        new UnitDiedMessage(unitId,
        Player.OurPlayerNumber);
    gameMessages.Add(newUnitDiedMsg);
    if (connection.IsHost)
        connection.SendMessageToAllPlayers(newUnitDiedMsg);
    else
        connection.SendMessageToHostPlayer(newUnitDiedMsg);
} // SendUnitDiedMessage(unitId)
```

If you want to learn more about the network code, check out the classes in the `DungeonQuest.Networking` namespace, especially the new message classes and the `Multiplayer` class on the high level, and of course the `SessionConnection` class, which is the low level implementation of our network engine.

Xbox LIVE Support

Until now, we have used only our own networking engine, which was written because XNA Game Studio 2.0 was not available at the time the Dungeon Quest project was started and it was not very clear which networking capabilities were possible through XNA 2.0. XNA 2.0 is still not available at the time of this writing, but there have been some recent announcements, which indicate the direction in which the XNA team is going. While the ability to create networked games is still one of the biggest features of XNA 2.0, it is only possible over the Xbox LIVE and Games for Windows LIVE services.

It is important to state again that our own networking engine in Dungeon Quest is based on the System.Net namespace, which is only available on Windows and not on the Xbox 360. The only way to do any networking on the Xbox 360 with XNA 2.0 is via the build in the networking API.

XNA 2.0 allows you to connect your computer to your Xbox 360 console via the System Link technology, which is just a term used for local networking games. To use XNA on your Xbox 360 console, you will need a XNA Creators Club Membership, which you will probably have anyway when you are developing and testing on the Xbox 360. This makes creating and testing network games not much harder than before. Well, it is harder because testing multiplayer games is always harder than testing Singleplayer games, but you won't need any special or additional hardware or software or licenses.

Everything beyond this scenario is very hard to test and even harder when you try to publish your game. Even if you just want to test the game on two local Xbox 360 consoles, you will need two XNA Creators Club and Xbox LIVE Silver subscriptions. The situation is even worse if you want to test it via the Internet as both you and the other Xbox 360 console or PC will need a full Xbox LIVE Gold subscription and a XNA Creators Club subscription, both of which cost money. You might be able to test your XNA 2.0 game with another XNA developer if he has both of those subscriptions, too, but it is highly unlikely that any player except XNA game developers will have or buy these subscriptions just for playing your game.

I can understand this situation on the Xbox 360. I don't think it is a good solution, because opening up the Xbox 360 to independent developers and making it easy for casual players to download and play XNA games would not only benefit the XNA platform in general, but also give the Xbox 360 console a great extra value. The Xbox 360 would be far ahead of its competition and thanks to the XNA Framework there is not much work required either on the game developer side to write those games or on Microsoft side to publish these games on their Xbox LIVE platform and even make money with them through subscriptions. But no casual gamer, who may even be willing to pay five or ten dollars for a little game, will pay for an Xbox Live Gold subscription and then buy the XNA Creators Club subscription for an additional 99 dollars each year just to play some game, which he probably could get for free on the PC.

What I absolutely cannot understand is why this restriction is also on the Xbox 360. I don't want to use the XNA 2.0 networking API, but are not interested in the Xbox 360 support, you still have to have all the XNA Creators Club and Xbox LIVE Gold subscriptions to write and test your game. And every player that wants to use your game and play with other people will need the same two subscriptions and probably also an Xbox 360 console to even purchase these subscriptions (currently only available on the Xbox 360), which makes no sense if you want to write a PC only game.

For this reason, I'm glad that Dungeon Quest has its own server architecture and the networking engine is already in place. The PC version will stay this way and it is highly unlikely that Microsoft will change its policy soon, which will make Dungeon Quest not a game any Xbox 360 gamer would know about because, as I said before, no one is going to pay for the XNA Creators Club just to play a game. Adding network support for the Xbox 360 version of Dungeon Quest has become a lower priority and it is a little bit depressing after expecting much more from the XNA 2.0 networking API.

Let's take a look at the API anyway. The first release version of the Dungeon Quest Xbox 360 version will include networking support on the Xbox 360 via Xbox LIVE just because it is an interesting platform. Figure 17-11 shows the most important classes of the XNA 2.0 network architecture. As you can see, most classes are high level and the `GamerService` namespace contains all the helper classes you need to implement Xbox LIVE support to your game. Adding this to an existing game might be a little bit of a hassle, but if you are using the existing classes for your gamer profile, you can save a lot of code.

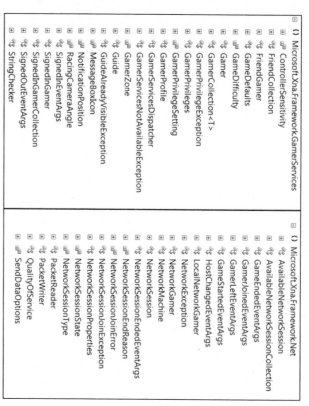

Figure 17-11

To get started, you will need only to instantiate the `NetworkSession` class to manage the connection (similar to the `SessionConnection` class from our network engine) and use the `GamerServiceComponent` class for handling `System.Link` or Xbox LIVE. You can also check out the `creators.xna.com` and `www.ziggyware.com` websites to learn more from tutorials and samples on how to use the networking API. At the time of this writing, much more information is available, but as soon as the XNA 2.0 beta or final version is available at the end of 2007, more tutorials and samples will be available making it easier to learn about the networking API in XNA 2.0.

Basically you will have to do the same things we did in the Multiplayer class of Dungeon Quest; you have to handle players joining and leaving your session, and you have to manage the network messages and in a host-client scenario resending messaging to all other clients if you are the host player. For example, to join a session you can use the `Join` method of the `NetworkSession` class, which awaits `AvailableNetworkSession` as a parameter. To get such a session up and running, you can use the `Guide` helper class, which will display a message on the screen and handle all the choosing, joining, and entering of text logic automatically for you. This is especially important on the Xbox 360 because you don't want to write that all by yourself.

The following code block illustrates the joining process:

```
// First get a list of available LAN games
// SystemLink is for local games, use PlayerMatch and
// Ranked for network games and finding players.
NetworkSessionProperties sessionProperties =
    new NetworkSessionProperties();
AvailableNetworkSessionCollection availableGames =
NetworkSession.Find(NetworkSessionType.SystemLink,
    1, sessionProperties);
// When no games are found, we have to create one
if (availableGames.Count == 0)
    CreateSession();
// Show the available games, please note that only
// three of them can be displayed here. We usually
// expect just one session!
Guide.BeginShowMessageBox(PlayerIndex.One,
    "Join local game",
    "Please select one of the following local games",
    new string[] { "Some Game" }, 0, MessageBoxIcon.None,
    JoinSession, availableGames);
```

If no LAN game is available, you have to create one via the Create method of the NetworkSession class; just specify the SystemLink type there and the number of players you want to allow. For the host player who created the session it is also important to join the session, which is again very similar to the JoinGame and EndGame handlers to allow other players to join the session. If a LAN session was found, you allow the player to join it via the Guide helper class, which shows a big message box on the screen (works both on the Xbox 360 and on Windows). If you have ever played a Xbox LIVE or Windows for Games LIVE game such as Halo before, you probably know what these message boxes look like.

The JoinSession method is actually a callback that will be called once the player selects one of the available games. Please note that you normally would display some real game name, not just "Some Game." The JoinSession method could be implemented in the following way:

```
private void JoinSession(IAsyncResult result)
{
    // Get the list of available games from the
    // AsyncState parameter
    AvailableNetworkSessionCollection games =
        (AvailableNetworkSessionCollection)result.
        AsyncState;
    // Join the session the player has selected
    clientSession = NetworkSession.Join(
    games[Guide.EndShowMessageBox(result).Value]);
    // Now we could use the session to get the names of
    // the other players in it, etc.
} // JoinSession(result)
```

With that code you should be able to connect two computers or your computer and an Xbox 360 together into a session and send data between them, which again is very similar to the way we did it in our own network engine in Dungeon Quest. The session has a collection of local gamers (usually just containing us ourselves) and a collection of remote gamers, which can be used to send binary data around. Instead of using the `BinaryWriter` class, XNA 2.0 uses its own `PacketWriter` class, but the rest of the code is pretty much the same and you still can use all the message logic we have discussed earlier in this chapter.

The following code block sends out a message to all connected remote players in the session:

```
ChatMessage testChatMessage =
    new ChatMessage("us", "Hi Guys");
// Write the message via the PacketWriter to a stream
PacketWriter writer = new PacketWriter();
testChatMessage.Write(writer);
// Now send it to all connected players
foreach (NetworkGamer player in
    clientSession.RemoteGamers)
{
    clientSession.LocalGamers[0].SendData(writer,
        SendDataOptions.ReliableInOrder, player);
} // foreach (player)
```

The `ChatMessage` class can still be constructed and used the same way; we just add another Write method, which now writes all binary data to the `PacketWriter` class. The session player list is then just enumerated and we send the message out to all players via the `SendData` method, which should be received on the other end and can be pulled by updating and checking the session class:

```
clientSession.Update();
if (clientSession.LocalGamers[0].IsDataAvailable)
{
    // Get the data via the reader and construct a
    // message from it!
    PacketReader reader = new PacketReader();
    NetworkGamer remotePlayer;
    clientSession.LocalGamers[0].ReceiveData(
        reader, out remotePlayer);

    // No data? Then skip it
    if (remotePlayer == null)
        return;

    // Since we already now its type in this case, lets
    // rebuild it
    ChatMessage testChatMessage =
        new ChatMessage(reader);
    // Display the chat message, etc.
} // if (IsDataAvailable)
```

Please check out the unit tests in the `Multiplayer` class to see how this all works with the existing network engine of Dungeon Quest. These unit tests can also be useful if you just want to know how to get started quickly. It might be painful to get the first network application up and running for the first time, but once you do, you can always go back to your first solution and extend your network engine from there.

The Dungeon Quest Editor

Last but not least, I want to show you the level editor of Dungeon Quest shortly. It is still a work in progress, but it is possible to create maps for Dungeon Quests quickly and more and more 3D models are added every week. The level editor is implemented with the EditorScreen class, as shown in Figure 17-12. Most work is performed in the Run method, as in most other game screen classes. The five editor modes are defined in the EditorMode enumeration, and there are some helper method and fields for the selected texture type — the current object rotation and light values for setting new lights, for example.

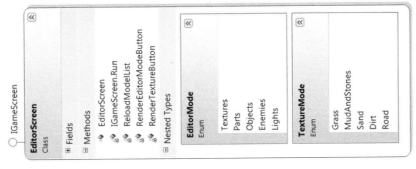

Figure 17-12

The code in the EditorScreen class uses mostly the RelativeScreenRect class and the MenuElements class you saw in Chapter 15. Most of the other code is UI code and the actual functionality of setting new objects; changing the underground textures or adding lights is handled in the Level class and its dependent class. The relationship between the Level class and the other classes in the Levels namespace can be seen in Figure 17-13. The Level class is the high-level class, which contains almost no code, but just calls to the underlying classes and some helper methods to add and remove objects, lights, and enemies.

The LevelGroundRender class, for example, handles all the underground rendering and setting of underground data via the SetGroundData method and the LevelVertex structure to hold all the level vertices.

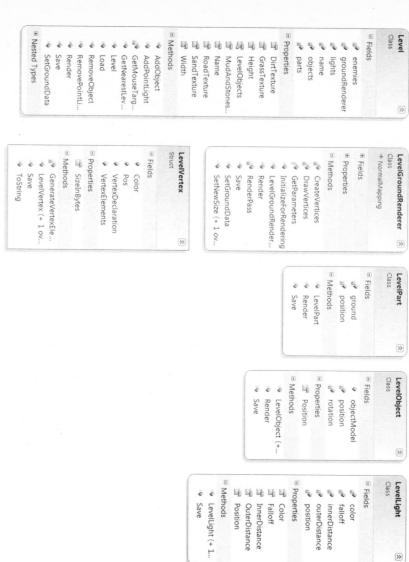

Figure 17-13

The level editor itself allows you to load and save maps and change their size in the upper-left corner. As you can see on Figure 17-14, all the UI from the menu was used for the editor, too, to get it up and running as quickly as possible. The first version of the editor was a Windows-Forms application and it was a lot of work to get the interaction between the Windows-Forms controls and the game engine working. But in the end there were too many problems and the whole concept of having an extra editor outside of the game itself did not seem like such a good idea after all. One day I showed the old editor to a friend who had not seen it before, but did know some of the other games I wrote, which also had editors in them. He immediately asked me why I did not make an in-game editor as before. He associated the Windows program with complex locking programs that are hard to learn and not as much fun as playing games. For that reason and because XNA 2.0 did not make it much easier (at least yet) to use Windows forms, I switched back to an in-game editor. The layout will probably be improved in the future, but for now I'm much quicker in editing levels with the new editor than the clumsy old editor. Hopefully the editor is as much fun for other people as it is to me.

Below the Load and Save buttons, you can see five buttons for the editor modes. In Figure 17-14, the ground mode is selected, which allows you to easily select one of the five underground textures that can be seen on the lower-right side. You can then paint with the selected texture directly on the ground and mix them in any way you like. Each vertex of the underground uses a Vector4 color, which is then used in the pixel shader to mix between the five underground textures (all zero means grass, x to 1.0 means mud, and so on). Because the texture layer is rendered in the last render pass for the underground (see the section "Handling Many Point Lights" from earlier in this chapter) you can mix the underground textures as much as you want, it won't affect the performance unlike adding more and more point lights, which makes the game slower.

Figure 17-14

The next mode in the editor is setting Level Parts, which is mostly used to add blocking objects, walls, and big 3D models composed of multiple smaller models to make it both easier to set them and to automatically align walls for you once you set them. Level parts cannot freely be placed everywhere; they are oriented on a 10 × 10 grid and are also used to partition bigger maps.

Figure 17-15 shows the objects mode, which was already shown earlier in this chapter. This mode allows you to easily set one of the existing 3D models and rotate them around. It is used both for testing new 3D models and to improve the level with static 3D models such as trees, plants, stones, barrels, crates, and farm houses.

Figure 17-15

Enemies can be set the same way; they will be rotated randomly and all enemy models are, in fact, not static models, but animated models, which are rendered and handled in a separate loop in the `Render` method of the `Level` class.

Finally, the lights can be set for the level; this step is very important because the level will be very dark and hard to see without any lights in it. As you can see in Figure 17-16, it is easy to set a bunch of colorful lights. It is much harder to find nice and fitting settings, but once you get a graphic artist interested in tweaking light values in the editor, let her do all the work.

Figure 17-17 shows the `AttackEnemy` unit test from the `Character` class, which shows the final game in a little constructed scene where you can test out the attack logic of the player character. Please check out the unit tests in the `GameLogic` and `Levels` namespaces, especially in the `Level` class and the `Character` class, to learn more about the Dungeon Quest game engine. Additional tutorials and sample code will also be available online on the Dungeon Quest website, where you can also find the most recent game version and source code.

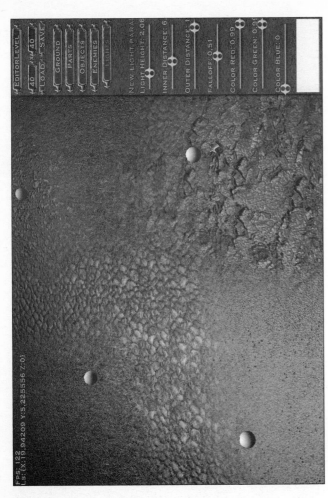

Figure 17-16

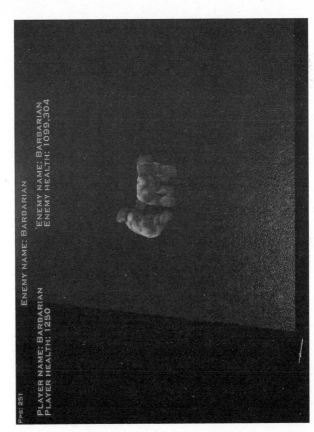

Figure 17-17

Summary

I hope you enjoyed this chapter and the whole book with all the XNA games. I tried to put as much energy as possible into the games and I'm always happy to see the code and 3D models or ideas used in other games or projects.

In this chapter, I have gone through most features of the Dungeon Quest game. The game engine for Dungeon Quest is quite comprehensive and can be used for other game projects, too, without your having to change the engine code. This makes it easier to reuse the code than it was for the Racing Game, for example, which consisted just of one big project with all the files and classes in it. Later, you saw how 3D models are exported as Collada files and rendered with the Dungeon Quest engine, which does now support animated models and makes it much easier to import more models at runtime.

Then we took a look at some rendering techniques of Dungeon Quest. In particular, the multi-pass shaders for the underground and lighting effects are interesting and can be helpful if you ever want to create other multi-pass shaders, which were not required before in this book.

After talking about AI, path-finding, and monster behavior after getting attacked for a while, we have gone back to the multiplayer code, messages, and classes required to make Dungeon Quest a multiplayer game. You also took a look at the new networking classes in XNA 2.0 and I discussed the advantages and disadvantages of using networking via XNA 2.0. For the Xbox 360 console, the XNA 2.0 networking API is the only way to go and while it might be sad that every player needs an XNA Creators Club membership to play any XNA game, it is quite exciting to see your own multiplayer game on the Xbox 360. On the PC side, on the other hand, it does not make much sense to use the XNA 2.0 networking API because you cannot expect that your PC gamers buy an Xbox LIVE Gold membership and also subscribe to the XNA Creators Club for a fee just to play your multiplayer game, which is probably otherwise free to use. It was a good thing that we created our own network engine in Chapter 15. We can still use it on the PC side, and for the Xbox 360 we have multiplayer support via XNA 2.0 and the Xbox LIVE system.

Finally, I discussed all the features of the Dungeon Quest Editor at the end of this chapter. The basic layout of Dungeon Quest is set and the game will improve even after this book is out. I hope Dungeon Quest sounds like an interesting project to you right now and that you will try it out online and play it a bit. It would be nice if readers can participate in the Dungeon Quest project at www.DungeonQuestGame.com.

That's about it for this book. I constantly update my blog and the websites for the games of this book, so if you want to read more material from me, check it out. I'm also always happy to receive any e-mails about new game programmers who are getting started, cool new game projects based on my engines, or more mods for one of the games described in this book.

Resources

This book has covered a lot of ground. I hope you have learned enough to develop better games. The following resources should help you out a little — I've included all the links, books, source code, and games that were mentioned throughout the book.

Links

Here's a list of many important links from the book:

```
http://creators.xna.com
```

XNA Creators Club from Microsoft is where all the XNA Game Studio forums are located. They are the most active XNA forums you will find on the Internet. You can also download the latest XNA version here, check out tutorials and samples, read the FAQ, and see what's new.

```
http://blogs.msdn.com/xna/
```

Bookmark this XNA Team blog to stay up-to-date with the latest news from the XNA team.

```
http://abi.exdream.com
```

This is the official website of the author. You can find more games here, as well as Rocket Commander XNA, the XNA Shooter, and the Racing Game from this book. All of the documentation and video tutorials that I made for the games are also here. Additionally, I suggest checking out the Rocket Commander Video Tutorials, which were pretty popular on Coding4Fun.

`www.rocketcommander.com`

This is the official website for Rocket Commander, which was released at the beginning of 2006. It was written for Managed DirectX originally. A new version running completely on XNA to support the Xbox 360 was released at the end of 2006.

`www.xnaracinggame.com`

This is the official website for the racing game discussed in Chapters 12 to 14 of this book.

`www.dungeonquestgame.com`

The official website for the Dungeon Quest game discussed at the end of this book.

`www.xnashooter.com`

This is the official website for the XNA Shooter game from Chapter 11 of this book. All the other games of this book can also be found on my blog.

`http://xnaresources.com`

A nice XNA-focused site with many links, tutorials, and tips to get you started in the XNA world. There are also several very active forums on this page. Ziggy also sponsors some cool contests from time to time. It also offers the usual community features such as image of the day, and so on.

`www.ziggyware.com`

Another site with lots of news and some really useful tutorials on tile engines. It also contains a lot of game components you might enjoy.

`http://en.wikipedia.org/wiki/Microsoft_XNA`

An entry on Wikipedia about XNA. It is constantly updated and contains many links to other topics. On the bottom of the page are a few useful external links.

`http://martinfowler.com`

Chapter 2 covered unit testing and agile methodologies. If you want to read more about unit testing, I recommend reading this website of Martin Fowler, one of the founders.

`www.nvidia.com`

Home of the Nvidia homepage and many free tools such as the FX Composer, which is used in Chapter 6. You can also learn a lot about graphic card architecture, special rendering techniques, shaders, and so on from the many samples, tutorials, and documentation that can be found in the developers section.

Code Download Structure

You can download all the code from the book. You can also download other important files that were discussed in the book; for example, in Chapter 2, the concept for the first game is discussed. (The information can be found in a PDF file.) To make your life even easier, I've included executables, which let you start the game or sample code. If you don't have .NET, DirectX, or XNA installed, please use one of the game installers because they will automatically install all of the files for you. You can also install everything yourself from the Setup folder.

Here's a list of items that you can download:

☐ **Readme.txt:** Contains additional information about the sample code.

☐ **Setup folder:** This folder contains all the setup for the frameworks used in the game, namely .NET 2.0, the current DirectX version, and the XNA Framework Redistributable, as well as XNA Game Studio Express. If you have not installed anything yet, follow these steps to install these tools:

1. Install Visual C# Express from the Internet Shortcut file in the Setup folder first, which will also install the .NET Framework automatically for you.

2. Install XNA Game Studio Express, which will install the XNA Framework for you also and notify you if you need an updated DirectX version. You can also just use the Internet Shortcut in the Setup folder.

☐ **Executables folder:** This directory contains all the precompiled samples and games from all the chapters. For the source code please look at the Chapter 1–14 directories, where all the other content (help files, concepts, textures, sounds, and so on) is located.

☐ **Games folder:** All games that are presented in the book can be installed through the installers located in this directory. You can also just start the games from the Executables directory, but it often makes more sense to install the games and keep them on your PC.

☐ **Folders for Chapter 1 to Chapter 17:** Contain all the source code and samples from the book including all the content files (textures, sounds, fonts, music, and so on). You might also find several additional files like concepts or links that are used in the chapter.

Please note that you can start all projects in either the Windows mode or in the Xbox 360 mode. Because XNA Game Studio Express does not allow switching the project type dynamically (because different assembly references are used), I have created two project files for all projects in this book. The normal project (.csproj) file is always for the Windows platform output. The projects ending with xbox360.csproj are used to allow you to deploy and test projects directly on the Xbox 360 console. Both projects actually use the exact same source files and if there are any differences they are marked with the XBOX360 keyword in the source code files, which are used as #if XBOX360 #endif blocks.

For more information and updates you can check the official website for this book at www.wiley.com.

You can also check out my blog for more information at http://abi.exdream.com.

Books

On my blog, you will find many books that I have read and reviewed. They are still very useful and fit perfectly with this book. I recommend these books here for the interested reader who wants to learn more about the many topics in the game programming world. If you have problems finding these books, just type the name in Google. The first match will always return the correct book result.

Graphics and Shader Technologies

☐ *Game Programming Gems 5 (and recently 6 and 7):* As with any other *Game Programming Gems* book, this one is no exception; it is just great. You can read it from front to back or use it as a reference if you're looking for solutions to common game programming problems and even programming problems in general. It covers seven sections — general programming, mathematics, AI, physics, graphics, network, and audio. This is the most recommended game programming book series.

☐ *ShaderX:* I read the first three books in this series and use them as a reference whenever I look for cool shader effects. The 4th and 5th volumes are as good as the predecessors. Wolfgang Engel is a good editor and he knows a lot about shaders.

☐ *GPU Gems 2:* This is yet another book series. Good stuff for Nvidia developers, and because most shaders work fine on ATI hardware (except when you tried to write PS3.0 shader when ATI still hadn't any cards for that), it is a good shader book. It covers some nice tricks and can be compared to the *ShaderX* books. Unlike the *Game Programming Gems* or the *ShaderX* books, every page is printed in color. As a result, this is a good colorful picture book where I can show effects to my artists.

☐ *Shaders for Game Programmers and Artists:* This is one of the first shader books that I read, but even for a first book on the topic I think it is too shallow. It jumps right into post-screen shaders that are very advanced in my opinion, and then continues with much easier shaders. The book is all about ATI's Render Monkey tool, which I don't like because the output is unusable (I need fx files). It is still a good shader book and may be helpful for artists, beginners, or people who just want an overview of shader technologies.

☐ *Programming Vertex & Pixel Shaders:* This book is the best and most complete shader programming book for anyone seriously wanting to learn shader technologies. It is a bit harder to read than the previous one. It can also be too mathematical instead of just having fun with shaders. However, it pays off because you learn all the basic shader technologies you will ever need. This is another book by Wolfgang Engel (like the *ShaderX* books, which are more advanced).

AI Programming

☐ *AI Game Engine Programming:* This book goes into a lot of first-person shooter AI problems and discusses useful techniques, not only about AI, but also how to use scripts (Lua), how to write all kinds of state machines, and neural nets. The CD not only contains all the source code and figures, but also a bunch of useful web bookmarks sorted by category. I like that.

☐ *Programming Game AI by Example:* This book is more for beginners and intermediate programmers than the rest of the books here. It is still a great book, but it "only" explains how to get into

AI programming, and as soon as you are ready to go, the book ends. The book starts with math and physics and does a good job explaining them. Then it goes to state-driven design and continues with game agents. It also covers questions about path finding, fuzzy logic, and scripting. It is well written by the founder of www.ai-junkie.com. My only criticism is the fact that it is a good beginner book.Maybe it is good for reference or to steer interns or wannabe AI programmers in the direction to "Go read that."

❑ *AI Game Programming Wisdom I and II:* Similar to *Game Programming Gems,* this series is all about finding skilled professionals writing chapters and articles, which do really help you out. Steve Rabin is the editor. He also edited the *Game Programming Gems* AI sections and he is the creator of www.AIwisdom.com. As with the other two AI books, I haven't read it from front to back (I'm so busy, you know). However, from what I've seen, this is a really helpful resource when doing anything related to AI programming.

General Development and Programming

❑ *Refactoring: Improving the Design of Existing Code:* Someone told me when I read this book on the flight to the PDC two years ago that you could probably dry up a cellar with this book. Maybe he is right. This book is all about crazy design pattern and rules. The first couple of chapters are good to read and the rest is more of a reference. Refactoring is one of the most useful processes today in writing big programs. This very useful book was first released in 1999 and still applies 100%.

❑ *Rapid Development:* This is a good book about software design and keeping schedules, but it is a bit too long and sometimes hard to read (you know I have this problem of reading only half the book and then never finding time to finish it). It was written back in 1996 and the techniques described still apply, but some of the ideas are not as flexible as they could be with all this new technology (for example, when using Agile Methodologies you have to plan differently). Still, it is a very good book and it contains a couple of interesting stories from big products such as MS Word's inability to keep to their schedule.

❑ *Code Complete 2:* This is one of the best books ever for any kind of programmer. It is about describing the process of developing software and it helps you to find out the most efficient ways to manage your projects. It goes into great detail by explaining which data structures, which routines, which loops, or which strategies are the most useful. It is one of the books I would recommend to both new and experienced programmers. This book just helps anyone and should be on every programmer's desk, not just in their book shelves.

❑ *Managing Agile Projects:* What does Agile Projects mean? It is about scaling and customizing your project depending on the customer feedback. That still sounds too vague? Okay, it means that you don't plan every single bit before writing code. Instead, you cut your project into smaller pieces and only plan the overview and then directly start developing. Now you can present a very early version really fast and with the help of feedback (customers or yourself) you can adjust your project instead of wasting time and resources developing something no one wants. You can also shorten specific parts of your project if you see there is no time left or you discover that other parts are more important. Again, this is not possible if you had planned every bit of your project in advance. It is a technique that goes hand-in-hand with unit testing and refactoring (see the *Refactoring: Improving the Design of Existing Code* book above). This book gives a very broad overview and doesn't really talk about coding; it's just methodologies.

❑ *Maximizing .NET Performance:* I'm a performance freak. In the past, I often tried to re-implement existing and working code into assembler code just to see how much faster it could get. Later, I found out that it is often much more important to work at a much higher level and rethink a problem until the solution is good enough to run very fast, even if not optimized to every bit. This is still true. I believe that most performance problems come from bad coding or suboptimal algorithms and not because of the language. However, to even think of good solutions you need some knowledge of what is possible, what is fast, and how certain things affect your performance. This book gives you a very useful inside view of .NET and covers a lot of tricks and tips about .NET performance. It is also a good reference book.

❑ *Code Generation in Microsoft .NET:* I first heard of this topic from the DotNetRocks radio show where the author Kathleen Dollard was the guest a few years ago. She talked about code generation using templates and other tricks. I immediately bought this book. It is mostly written in Visual Basic, but a C# conversion exists, too. It does a good job explaining how to use code generation with the Code Dom, but it does not go into detail about MSIL (which I was more interested in). Anyway, the book is written nicely and I learned a lot from it. The book presents an entire framework for building SQL bindings, stored procedures, and building Win Forms from XML templates. It is also one of the first books on this subject (and maybe still the only one going into the Code Dom instead of MSIL).

Another Useful Title

❑ *Programming in Lua:* This is *the* book for Lua programmers. It is also available for free to download from lua.org. I first read the online version and then bought the book because it is so good. It helps to have a reference. Lua is a very simple script language. But sometimes it is so simple that you just don't know which keyword to use or what to type. Having a few useful code examples every other page is the biggest help. With the aid of this book, I learned Lua in one to two days and could do really useful stuff with it (instead of just writing hello like you do most languages).

Tips and Golden Rules

Here are some tips and "golden rules" you discovered in the book, but they're worth repeating.

Tips

❑ You need an Xbox 360 Live Account on your Xbox 360, which must be connected at all times when you develop and test your XNA games.

❑ Make sure your PC and the Xbox 360 are on the same network and they can "see" each other. You can test ping-ing the Xbox 360 IP from your PC or connecting to your PC as a media center from the Xbox 360.

❑ When you create an encryption key in the Settings of the XNA Game Launcher and it is not accepted by your PC because you perhaps mistyped it or it contained 0 (the number zero) and O letters, which look almost the same, just try it again. You can always create a new encryption key. See Chapter 1 for details.

❑ If you run into compiler errors from the code in this book, make sure you have all required content in the project and all the classes and used variables are defined correctly for graphics, sounds, and music files.

❑ Read the compiler error message and change the code accordingly. Maybe you are trying to use some obsolete method; either replace it with the new method or just comment it out to see how the rest of the code behaves.

❑ If the compiling works, but the program crashes or throws an exception it is most likely that you have some content file missing or that your graphic hardware does not support at least Shader Model 1.1.

❑ It is important to write down your ideas and to develop a small concept. Just one page of concepts can be quite useful.

❑ To solve problems you use a top-down approach. Use unit testing to stay at just the top level without even thinking of the implementation. This way you can quickly adopt ideas from the concept and write them down in unit tests, making it easier to see exactly what methods you have to implement.

❑ Final tips about managing your projects: Think about your problems and divide them into small manageable parts.

❑ Write the tests first and do not think about the implementation. Just write them down like you think the final code should look or like you want to have your game code.

❑ Try to make sure you test as much as possible. For example, the `TestIsInList` method tests both a successful call to `IsInList` and a failure from the `IsInList` call. Spend time with your unit tests, but never more than 50%. You should not have to write 30 checks for a method that has only two lines of code.

❑ Start the test constantly from this point on, even when you think it does not make sense. It will force you to see what has to be done and how far you are in the implementation process. At first the test will not even compile because you haven't implemented anything. Then after implementing empty methods the test should fail because you are not doing anything yet. Later when everything works you'll feel much better.

❑ While you will not test your static unit tests very often, dynamic unit tests can be tested every single time you compile your code (if they all run quick enough). Always try to run all unit tests once a day or once a week to make sure your latest code changes did not add new bugs or errors.

Golden Rules

❑ **Do not use any external dlls if not required.** When using the XNA Game library, Dlls are supported. Most Dlls on the Windows platform will call System Dlls that are not available on the Xbox 360. Even worse, they may call unmanaged Dlls with P-Invoke, which is absolutely not supported on the Xbox 360 for security reasons. Also don't use unsafe code or make any attempts to call external code, access devices, or use unsupported features. It will be a waste of time and you are better off just playing by the rules.

❑ **Don't wait with the testing.** Always test if your code compiles and make sure the game runs on your PC and the Xbox 360 if you want to support it too. Often methods you might get used to may be missing on the Xbox 360. For example, there are no `TryParse` methods in the System.dll on the Xbox 360, and some XNA methods and classes such as the `MouseState` classes are even missing and unsupported.

☐ **Don't load content directly.** On the Windows platform, it is possible to load textures or shaders directly with the help of the `Texture2D` or `CompiledEffect` constructors. These methods are completely missing from the Xbox 360. You can only load content from the content pipeline. If you use code that dynamically loads or reloads textures or shaders, it will only work on your Windows platform. In that case, use the XBOX360 define to exclude the code parts to make the project still compile on the Xbox 360 platform.

☐ **Save games and loading other content.** For save games, you can use the Content namespace and the many available helper classes. To load content you will always have to make sure you use the correct path with the help of `StorageContainer.TitleLocation`, which works on the Windows platform too and just uses your output directory there. Loading from other locations on the Xbox 360 results in Access Denied exceptions for IO operations.

☐ **Test resolutions.** The Xbox 360 supports many different resolutions compared to the PC and you should test at least two to three different resolutions to make sure the game runs fine with it.

☐ **Allow controlling everything with a gamepad.** Most XNA games I've seen made the mistake of only allowing keyboard input or only gamepad input, which means it runs either only on Windows or only if you have an Xbox 360 controller. Always add support for as many input devices as you can think of and that make sense for your game.

☐ **Debug and unit test on the Xbox 360.** Debugging and unit testing is no different on your console; the same rules apply. It might be a little harder to trace errors and log messages, but stepping through code and testing unit tests works great with XNA. Take advantage of that. By the way: Edit-and-continue works only on the Windows platform. You can't do that with Xbox 360 games, which can be annoying, but you will probably do the major part of your development on the Windows platform anyway.

Class Overviews

Finally, I've included the class overviews from four of the more complex games described in the book:

☐ Rocket Commander XNA from Chapter 8 (see Figure A-1)

☐ XNA Shooter from Chapter 11 (see Figure A-2)

☐ The Racing Game from Chapter 14 (see Figure A-3)

☐ And finally the Dungeon Quest game engine from Chapter 17 (see Figure A-4)

Figure A-1

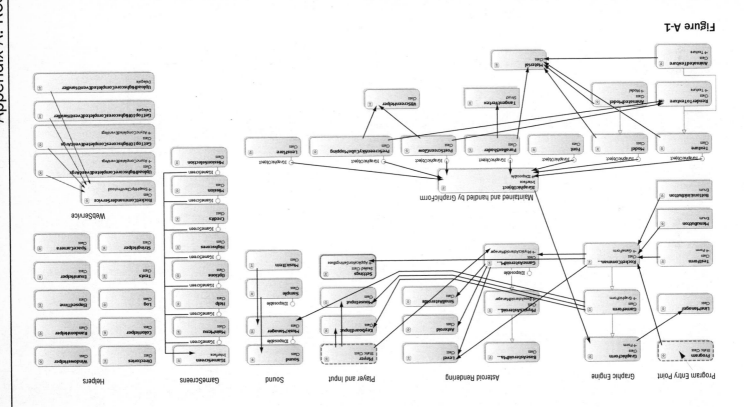

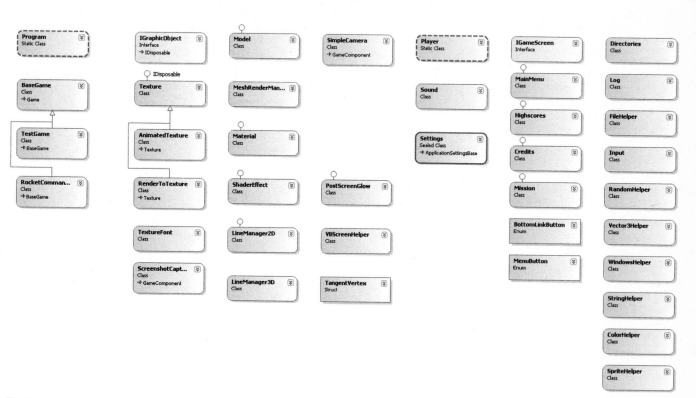

Figure A-2

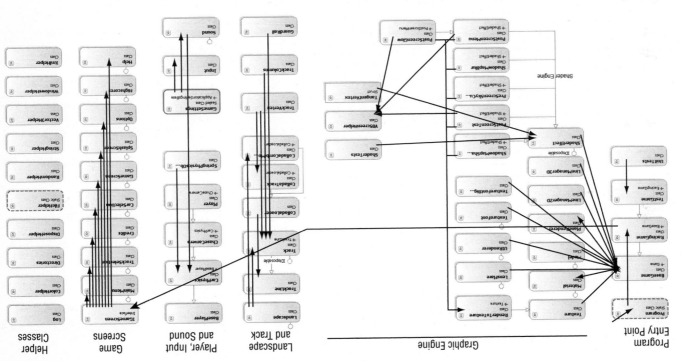

Figure A-3

Racing Game Class Overview (Early Version)

Figure A-4

Index

NUMERALS

3D listener object, 264

3D models, 119–121

file formats, 63

lines, rendering, 123–127

MeshRenderManager, 416

textures, rendering, 121–123

unit testing, 131–135

XnaShooters, 301–303

3D programming, 127–131

A

AddChatMessage method, 479

AddEffect method, 319

AddRandomBlock method, 104

AddSpriteToRender method, 122

Ageia PhysX, 381–382

Agine Methodology, 32–33

AI (Artificial Intelligence), Dungeon Quest, 530

AlphaBlending property, BaseGame, 126

animated textures, XnaShooter, 303–304

AnimatedModel class, 524

AnimatedModel classes, 523

AnimatedModel.cs, 296

AnimatedTexture, 304

annotations, 156

Ants Profiler, 24

ApplyGravity method, 378

ApplyGravityAndCheckForCollisions method, 395

ArrayList class, 76

Assert helper class, 71

Asteroid.cs, 296

Asteroids, 178–182

Automatic, VertexBuffers and, 213

B

background

scrolling, 20

Tetris, rendering, 100–102

textures, displaying, 19

BallSpeedMultiplicator, 46

BaseAsteroidManager.cs, 296

BaseGame class, 81, 307

AlphaBlending property, 126

BaseMessage class, 458, 465

BasicEffect class, 124

BeginReceiveFrom method, 460

BeginSendTo method, 461

Big-Button-Pad, 269

billboards, XnaShooter, 305–308

Billboard class, 306

BlockColors, 104

BlockFalldown sound, Tetris, 99

BlockMove sound, Tetris, 99

BlockRotate sound, Tetris, 99

BlockTypes enum, 104

BlockTypeShapes, 104

.bmp file format, 63

bounding boxes, 51

Breakout game, 80–82

collision tesing, 88–89

Draw method, 86–87, 86–88

Breakout game *(continued)*
drawing, 86–88
game loop, 85–86
improving, 89–90
levels, 83–85
unit testing, 82–83
BreakoutBlockKill.wav, 82
BreakoutGame.png, 82
BreakoutVictory.wav, 82
Bullet Physics Library, 384

C

C#, game development and, 22–23
CalcLandscapePos helper method, 344
CalculateTangentFrames, 196
CalculateTangentMatrix, 185
CalcVectors helper method, 307
Camera class, 137–139
Canyon Commander, 401–403
  cars, more, 433
  concept, 403–404
  effects, 434–435
  final testing
    Windows, 428–430
    Xbox 360, 430–432
  game idea, 405–407
  game screen, logic, 407
  game screens, 409–410
  Highscores, 417–418
  main menu, 413–414
  splash screen, 410–412
  GameScreen class, 414–417
  graphics engine, 407
  Helper classes, 407
  highscores, online, 433–434
  modes, 435–436
  multiplayer mode, 436–437
  RenderToTexture class, 408
  shaders, 407, 434–435

shadow mapping classes, 422–428
  ShadowMapBlur class, 408
  ShadowMapShader class, 409
  tweaking, 421–422
  unit testing, 408, 418–420
  write your own mode, 437–442
car collision, 395–399
car physics, 375
CarPhysics class, 373
ChaseCamera class, 378
ChatMessage, 458
Chatpad device, 269
CheckBallCollisions method, 86
classes
  AnimatedModel, 524
  ArrayList, 76
  BaseGame, 81, 307
  BaseMessage, 465
  BasicEffect, 124
  Billboard, 306
  Camera, 137–139
  CarPhysics, 373
  ChaseCamera, 378
  ColladaCombiModels, 356
  ColladaLoader, 356
  ColladaModelFile, 523
  ColladaTrack, 356
  DrawableGameComponent, 93
  EditorScreen, 539
  EffectManager, 295
  EndGameMessage, 467
  FontToRender, 97
  Game, 92–93
  GameServer, 456
  Highscore, 433
  Input, 267, 268–271
  Item, 325–327
  JoinGameMessage, 464
  Landscape, 342
  LevelGroundRender, 540

LineManager3D, 125
LoadLevel, 343
Log, 68
Material, 190
MeshHelper, 197
Mission, 312
Model, 132
Multiplayer, 457
NextBlock, 105
NumbersFont, 282
ParallaxMapping, 407
PhysicsAsteroidManager, 392–395
player, 457
PostScreenDarkenBorder, 221–224
PostScreenGlow, 407
Projectile, 323–325
RandomHelper, 73–74
RelativeScreenRect, 478
RenderTarget, 219
RenderToTexture, 220–221
RocketCommanderGame, 296
ScreenshotCapturer, 139
ServerGame, 457
SessionConnection, 456, 462
ShaderEffect, 127, 189–200
ShadowMapBlur, 408
ShadowMappingShader, 314
ShadowMapShader, 409
SimpleCamera, 288
SimpleEffect, 147
SkinnedTangentVertex, 523
SocketHelper, 457
Sound, 260–265
SpaceCamera, 289
SplashScreen, 410
SpriteBatch, 35
StartGameScreen, 476
StringHelper, 74–77
TangentVertex, 191
TestGame, 81

TestRenderingTrack, 349
TetrisGame, 93
TetrisGrid, 94
TrackImporter, 355
TrackLine, 349
UdpTests, 458
Vector3Helper, 407
XmlHelper, 356
XnaShooterGame, 296

ClearColor, 214
ClearDepth, 214
CodeRush, 12
Collada, 355
  Dungeon Quest, 522–526
ColladaCombiModels class, 356
ColladaLoader class, 356
ColladaModelFile class, 523
ColladaTrack class, 356
collision detection
  Dungeon Quest, 520
  physics and, 391–392
collision testing, Pong, 47–52
color correction, 228–231
ColorHelper class, 80
Components property, 93
compression, 247
ComputeTangentMatrix method, 186
connecting players, 462–464
content
  accessing, 66–68
  importing, 66–68
content directories, 65–66
  Rocket Commander, 65
content pipeline, 8–9
Content Processor, 18
Content Processor mode, 66
coordinate system, 130
CreateLookAt method, 129
CreateRotation method, 128
CreateScale method, 128

CreateTranslation method, 128

cries of monsters, Dungeon Quest, **531–532**

CutExtension method, 75

D

.dds file format, 63

Default Chase Car Game Camera, 378

deploying games, Xbox 360, 141–142

depthBias, 426

detail in objects, 174–178

directional lights, 156

directories

  content directories, 65–66

  Rocket Commander, 65

DirectSound, 244–245

  .wav files, 245–247

DirectSound device, initializing, 244

Displacement Mapping, 174

Draw( ) method, 7

  Breakout game, 86–87

DrawableGameComponent class, 93

DrawIndexedPrimitives, 168

DrawSprites method, 40, 77–78

Drum Sticks, 270

Dungeon Quest

  abilities, 506–507, 507–508

  AI (Artificial Intelligence), 530

  cameras, 520

  characters, 498–501

  Collada model files, 522–526

  collision detection, 520

  components, 520

  content, 520

  cries of monsters, 531–532

  designing, 493

  editor, 539–543

  effects, 520

  enemies, 501–505

  engine

    creating, 518–519

    graphic, 519–522

  fonts, 520

  game handling, 521

  ideas for, 494

  items, 506

  leveling system, 510–513

  improving, 513–514

  lights, 521, 526–529

  lines, 522

  models, 522

  multiplayer support, 532–533

  network messages, 533–534

  Xbox LIVE, 535–538

  path-finding, 530–531

  physics, 522

  scenario, 494–496

  shaders, 522

  sound, 522

  spells, 506–507, 508

  barbarian, 509

  hunter, 510

  mage, 510

  priest, 509

  story, 496–498

  textures, 522

  used assemblies, 520

  weapons, 506

DXT, 18

DXT compression algorithms, 181

DXT1, 67

dynamic unit tests, 29

E

edge detection shaders, 237–238

EditorScreen class, 539

EffectManager class, 539

EnableDefaultLighting method, 26

EndGame message, 533
EndGameMessage class, 467
engines
  capabilities, 116–117
  physics engines, 372, 379–381
    Ageia PhysX, 381–382
    Bullet Physics Library, 384
    Farseer Physics Engine, 383
    Havok, 382–383
    Newton Game Dynamics, 384
    nV Physics Engine, 384
    ODE (Open Dynamics Engine), 383
    Physics and Math Library, 384
    Tokamak Game Physics, 384
    XPA, 383
  shaders, importing, 164–170
  unit testing, 117–118
entering text, 275–277
EnumHelper class, 79–80
error messages, logging, 68–69
Esc, 17
ExtractFilename method, 75

F

F5, 16
farPlane, 425
Farseer Physics Engine, 383
.fbx file format, 63
FBX Model Importer, 67
Fight sound, Tetris, 99
file formats, textures, 63
filenames, StringHelper class, 75–76
firewalls, 453–455
floatingGrid, 104
FontToRender class, 97
Free Camera Mode, 378
FX Composer, shaders and, 151–153
.fx files
  layout, 153–55
  parameters, 155–157

G

GAC (Global Assembly Cache), 69
Game class, 6, 92–93
  Draw( ) method, 7
  Initialize( ) method, 7
  Update( ) method, 7
Game namespace, 296
GameAsteroidManager.cs, 296
GameInfoAndPlayerList message, 533
GamePadAJustPressed method, 98
gamePadUp, 47
GameScreens namespace, 296
  Help class, 280–281
GameServer class, 456
GameSync message, 534
GenerateLandscapeHeightFile, 342
GenerateTangents method, 197
GenerateVerticesAndObjects helper
  method, 360
GetAnimatedTexture method, 304
GetCue method, 261
GetDirectory method, 75
GetFasterAndMoveDown, 323
GetLastChatMessage method, 479
GetOnlineHighscores method, 434
GetTextWidth method, 96
glass shader, 202
GPU (graphic processing unit), 128
Gran Tourismo, 335
Graphics namespace, 296
graphics, loading, 17
GraphicsDeviceManager, 92
gravitation, 376–379
Guitars, 270

H

hack and slash role-playing games, 487–491
HandleAsteroidCollision method, 394
HandleKeyboardInput method, 276–277

HandleSectorPhysics method, 393

Havok, 382–383

Help.cs, 296

helper classes, 61
  Assert, 71
  Canyon Commander, 407
  ColorHelper class, 80
  EnumHelper class, 79–80
  Input class, 97–99
  RandomHelper class, 73–74
  SpriteHelper class, 77–79
  StringHelper class, 74–77
  TextureFont class, 95–97

Helpers namespace, 77

Highscore class, 433

Highscores screen, 417–418

HitpointsDecrease message, 533

HLSL (High Level Shader Language), 146

Hooke's law, 390

http://abi.exdream.com, 20

http://creators.xna.com, 26

http://en.wikipedia.org/wiki/Microsoft_XNA, 20

http://forums.xna.com, 26

http://martinfowler.com, 33

http://msdn.microsoft.com/directx/xna, 20

http://xnadevelopment.com, 20

http://xnaresources.com, 20

I

IGameScreen, 279–280

importing, shaders to engines, 164–170

In-Game UI, 281–286

Initialize( ) method, 7

input
  Big-Button-Pad, 269
  Chatpad device, 269
  Drum Sticks, 270
  entering text, 275–277
  Guitars, 270
  Tetris, 107–110

Input class, 97–99, 267, 268–271
  mouse rectangles, 272–275
  Update method, 271–272

InvalidOperationException, 244

Item class, 325–327

ItemCollected message, 534

J

JoinGame message type, 533

JoinGameMessage class, 458, 464

JoinSession method, 537

.jpg file format, 63

K

KaktusSeg.dds, 175

KaktusSegNormal.dds, 175

KeyboardSpaceJustPressed property, 98

KeyboardState struct, 275

keyboardStateLastFrame variable, 275

L

landscape, 333, 338–339
  rendering, 340–345
  textures, 339–340
  unit testing, 342

Landscape class, 342

LandscapeGridHeights.png, 339

LandscapeNormalMapping shader, 344

Landscapes namespace, 340

laws of motion, 370–371

left hand coordinate system, 130

LensFlare.cs, 296, 407

Level.cs, 296

LevelGroundRender class, 540

menu sounds, 265
MeshHelper class, 197
MeshRenderManager, 416
messages, network messages, 464–470
methods
AddChatMessage, 479
AddEffect, 319
AddSpriteToRender, 122
ApplyGravity, 378
ApplyGravityAndCheckForCollisions, 395
BeginReceiveFrom, 460
BeginSendTo, 461
CalcLandscapePos, 344
CalcVectors, 307
CheckBallCollisions, 86
ComputeTangentMatrix, 186
CreateLookAt, 129
CreateRotation, 128
CreateScale, 128
CreateTranslation, 128
CutExtension, 75
Draw( ), 7
DrawSprites, 40, 77–78
EnableDefaultLighting, 26
ExtractFilename, 75
GamePadAJustPressed, 98
GenerateTangents, 197
GenerateVerticesAndObjects, 360
GetAnimatedTexture, 304
GetCue, 261
GetDirectory, 75
GetLastChatMessage, 479
GetOnlineHighscores, 434
GetTextWidth, 96
HandleAsteroidCollision, 394
HandleKeyboardInput, 276–277
HandleSectorPhysics, 393
Initialize( ), 7
JoinSession, 537
KeyboardSpaceJustPressed, 98

LevelUp message, 534
lighting
directional lights, 156
Dungeon Quest, 526–529
point lights, 156
spot lights, 156
lightVec variable, 186
LineKill sound, Tetris, 99
LineManager3D class, 125
LineRendering.fx shader, 126, 127
lines, rendering in 3D models, 123–127
links, bookmarks, 21–22
lists, StringHelper class, 76–77
Load method, 352–353
LoadAnimation method, 525
LoadBones method, 525
LoadGraphicsContent method, 7
loading, textures, 36
LoadLevel class, 343
LoadLevel method, 343
LoadMeshes method, 525
Log class, 68
Log.txt file, 68
Log4Net, 68
loopings, 385–387
Lose sound, Tetris, 99

M

MainMenu Run method, 299
MakeScreenshot method, 139
mapping
Displacement Mapping, 174
Normal Mapping, 174
Offset Mapping, 174
Parallax Mapping, 174
marble.dds texture, 163
Material class, 190
MDX (Managed DirectX), 24
menu effects, 231–232

methods *(continued)*

Load method, 352
LoadAnimation, 525
LoadBones, 525
LoadGraphicsContent, 7
LoadLevel, 343
LoadMeshes, 525
MakeScreenshot, 139
OnHandleMessage, 479
OnReceive, 479
Play, 260
ReceiveDataFrom, 461
Render, 125, 132–134
RenderBall( ), 42–43
RenderBillboards, 307
RenderCar, 412
RenderCentered, 87
RenderMenuBackground, 412
RenderModel, 166
RenderOnScreen, 118
RenderPaddles( ), 43
RenderSky, 212
Resolve, 220
ResolveBackBuffer, 139
Select, 304
SendChatMessage, 481
SetParameters, 190
SetRenderTarget, 220
Show, 223
ShowGroundGrid, 350
ShowLives, 42
ShowTrackLines, 351
SpriteBatch, 36
StartLevel, 84
StartMusic, 255
StartNewBall, 47–48
StartTest, 38
TestBackgroundBoxes, 100
TestBallCollisions, 49–50
TestGameSprites( ), 41–42

TestGetAllEnumNames, 79–80
TestMenuSprites, 37, 38
TestNormalMappingShader, 193–194
TestRenderModel, 135
TestSimpleShader, 165
TestSkyCubeMapping, 211–212
TestSounds( ), 54
TestUdpClient, 458
TestUdpServer, 458
tex2D, 163
TryParse, 56
Update( ), 7
UpdateVertexBuffer, 125
Write( ), 69
WriteArrayData, 80
WriteText, 96
XnaTexture, 220

Mission class, 312
MissionSelection.cs, 296
Model class, 132
motion blur, 227–228
mouse, Xbox 360, 268
mouse rectangles, 272–275
moveFactorPerSecond, 20, 50
MoveTypes enum, 107–108
multiplayer application, writing, 483
Multiplayer class, 457, 470
multiplayer games, role-playing, 491–493
multiplayer support, Dungeon Quest, 532–533
network messages, 533–534
Xbox LIVE, 535–538
music, file format, 63

N

NATs (Network Address Translators), 453–455
nearPlane, 425
Need for Speed, 335–336

.NET 2.0 Framework, 12

networks
architecture, 455–458
chat application
chat messages, 479–482
final application, 482–483
game screens, 474–479
connecting two players, 462–464
messages, 464–470
multiplayer support, Dungeon Quest, 533–534
server game list, 470–473

Newton Game Dynamics, 384
Newton's laws of motion, 370–371
NextBlock class, 105
NextBlock game component, 104, 111
Normal Mapping
pixels, 176
shaders, 174
textures, 175
unit testing, ShaderEffect Class, 193–195
NormalMapCompressor, 180
normalVector, 187
NumbersFont class, 282
NumbersFont.png texture, 282
NumOfBlockTypes, 104
NUnit Framework, 70–71
NUnit GUI, 71–72
nV Physics Engine, 384

O

objects, detail, 174–178
ODE (Open Dynamics Engine), 383
Offset Mapping, 174, 201–202
OnHandleMessage method, 479
OnReceive method, 479
Options.cs, 296
oscilloscope, Pong and, 29

P

Parallax Mapping, 174, 201–202, 204
ParallaxMapping class, 407
ParallaxMapping.fx shader, 119, 180
ParallaxShader.cs, 296
parameters
.fx files, 155–157
shaders, 166–167
path-finding, Dungeon Quest, 530–531
physics, 369–370
car collision, 395–398
car physics, 375
collision detection, 391–392
Dungeon Quest, 522
gravitation, 376–379
loopings, 385–387
spring physics, 388–391
Physics and Math Library, 384
physics engines, 372, 379–381
Ageia PhysX, 381–382
Bullet Physics Library, 384
Farseer Physics Engine, 383
Havok, 382–383
Newton Game Dynamics, 384
nV Physics Engine, 384
ODE (Open Dynamics Engine), 383
Physics and Math Library, 384
Tokamak Game Physics, 384
XPA, 383
PhysicsAsteroidmanager class, 392–395
PhysicsAsteroidManager.cs, 296
Pixel Shader, 173
pixel shader, 162–164, 187–189
pixels, Normal Mapping, 176
planning, 30–31
initial difficulties, 33–34
Pong, 31–32
Play method, 260
PlayCue, 261

player class, 457
player input, Pong, 44–47
PlayerDied message, 533
players, connecting, 462–464
PlayerUpdate message, 533
.png file format, 63
point lights, 156
Pong
 ball, adding, 41–44
 collision testing, 47–52
 improving, 57
 original, 29
 paddles, adding, 41–44
 planning, 31–32
 player input, 44–47
 initial difficulties, 33–34
 sound, 53–55
 sprites, 35–36
 TestSingleplayerGame, 47
 textures, 34
 troubleshooting, 58–59
 unit testing, 37–74
 writing, 214–217
PongBallHit.wav, 35, 53
PongBallLost.wav, 35, 53
post-screen shaders
 implementation
 PostScreenDarkenBorder class, 221–224
 RenderToTexture class, 220–221
 unit testing, 224–225
 sky cube mapping, 208–213
PostScreenDarkenBorder class, 221–224
PostScreenDarkenBorder.fx, 214
PostScreenGlow, 225
PostScreenGlow class, 407
postScreenShader variable, 222
PostScreenShadowBlur.fx shader, 424
PreScreenSkyCubeMapping.cs, 296, 407
PreScreenSkyCubeMapping.fx, 210
Principia Mathematica, 371

Projectile class, 323–325
ProjectionMatrix, 129
projects, new, 15
properties, Components, 93

Q
quitting program, 17

R
racing simulations, 334–335
 Gran Tourismo, 335
 Need for Speed, 335–336
 Trackmania, 336–337
RandomHelper class, 73–74
ReceiveDataFrom method, 461
reflection, 203
Reflector, 6
RelativeScreenRect class, 478
remDownPressed, 47
Render method, 125, 132–134
RenderBall( ) method, 42–43
RenderBillboards method, 307
RenderCar method, 412
RenderCentered method, 87
rendering
 lines, 3D models, 123–127
 shaders and, 167–168
 textures, 3D models, 121–123
RenderLandscapeBackground, 313
RenderMenuBackground method, 412
RenderModel method, 166
RenderOnScreen method, 118
RenderPaddles( ) method, 43
RenderSky method, 212
RenderTarget class, 219
RenderToTexture class, 220–221
Resolve method, 220
ResolveBackBuffer method, 139

ResourceName annotation, 157

Rocket Commander

directories, 65

MDX, 234–235

PhysicsAsteroidManager class, 392–395

Rocket Motor sound, 263

screenshots, 235–237

threads, 235

XNA and, 232–234

Rocket.dds, 119

RocketCommanderGame class, 296

RocketCommanderXna namespace, 297

RocketHeight.dds, 119

RocketNormal.dds, 119

role-playing games, 485

types, 486–487

hack and slash, 487–491

multiplayer, 491–493

Shader Model, 173

ShaderEffect class, 127, 189–191

Normal Mapping unit test, 193–195

tangent data, custom processor and, 195–199

TangentVertex class, 191–193

shaders, 145. See also Pixel Shader

Canyon Commander, 407

compiling, 165–166

Dungeon Quest, 522

edge detection, 237–238

example games, 148–149

.fx files, layout, 153–55

glass shader, 202

history of, 146–147

importing to engine, 164–170

LandscapeNormalMapping, 344

LineRendering.fx, 126, 127

Normal Mapping shaders, 174

offset mapping, 201–202

overview, 182–185

parallax mapping, 201–202

ParallaxMapping.fx, 119

parameters, 166–167

pixel shader, 162–164, 187–189

post-screen shaders

implementation, 220–225

sky cube mapping, 208–213

writing, 214–217

reflection, 203

rendering with, 167–168

testing, 169–170

vertex formats, 167

vertex input, format, 158–159

vertex shader, 159–161, 185–186

matrices, 185–186

water, 203

Shaders namespace, 296

shadowColor, 426

ShadowMapBlur class, 408

S

ScreenBorderFadeout.dds, 215

ScreenHeight property, 478

ScreenPositionX property, 478

ScreenPositionY property, 478

screens, 277

background, 278

Help, 280–281

In-Game UI, 281–286

ScreenshotCapturer class, 139

ScreenWidth property, 478

scrolling, background, 20

scrollPosition, 20

Select method, 304

SendChatMessage method, 481

server, game list, 470–473

ServerGame class, 457

SessionConnection class, 456, 462

SetParameters method, 190

SetRenderTarget method, 220

shadowMapDepthBias, 426
ShadowMappingShader class, 314
ShadowMapShader class, 409
shipRotation, calculating, 318
Show method, 223
ShowGroundGrid method, 350
ShowLives method, 42
ShowTrackLines method, 351
SimpleCamera class, 288
SimpleEffect class, 147
SimpleShader.fx, 150
    file layout, 153–55
    FX Composer, 151–153
SizeType parameter, 220
SkinnedTangentVertex class, 523
skyCube variable, 222
SmallAsteroid.cs, 296
SocketHelper class, 457
sound
    compression, XACT, 252–254
    Dungeon Quest, 522
    file format, 63
    menu sounds, 265
    Pong, 53–55
    XACT and, 243
        cues, 256–257
    XnaShooter, 297–298
Sound Bank, 54
Sound class, Play method, 260
Sound Cues, 54
space camera, 289–292
SpaceBackground.dds texture, 36
SpaceCamera class, 289
SpaceCamera.cs, 296
SpeedOfSound variable, 249
SplashScreen class, 410
spot lights, 156
spring physics, 388–391
SpriteBatch class, 35
SpriteBatch methods, 36
SpriteHelper class, 77–79

sprites, Pong, 35–36
StartGame message, 533
StartGameScreen class, 533
StartGameScreen class, 476
StartLevel method, 84
StartMusic method, 255
StartNewBall method, 47–48
StartTest method, 38
static unit tests, 29
StreamWriter, 68
StringHelper class, 74–77

T

tangent data, ShaderEffect class,
    195–199
TangentVertex class, 191
TCP, UDP and, 450–453
TestAsteroidPhysicsSmallScene unit
    test, 392
TestBackgroundBoxes method, 100
TestBallCollisions, 49–50, 83
TestCarPhysicsOnPlane unit test, 376
TestCarPhysicsOnPlaneWithGuardRails
    unit test, 375
TestCreateAndJoinGame unit test, 472
TestDriven.NET, 12, 24, 70–71
TestFallingBlockAndLineKill unit test,
    105, 110
TestGame class, 81
TestGameSprites method, 41–42
TestGameSprites test, 83
TestGameSprites( ) method, 41
TestGetAllEnumNames( ) method, 79–80
TestGetListOfGames unit test, 471
testing
    shaders, 169–170
    unit testing, 37–74
TestMenuSprites method, 37, 38
testModel variable, 222
TestNormalMappingShader method,
    193–194
TestPlaySounds unit test, 298

TestRenderAnimatedModel unit test, 524

TestRenderingTrack class, 349

TestRenderLandscape unit test, 342

TestRenderLandscapeBackground unit test, 313

TestRenderLines unit test, 124

TestRenderModel method, 135

TestRotatingBlock unit test, 110

TestShowBones unit test, 524

TestSimpleShader method, 165

TestSingleplayerGame, 47

TestSingleplayerGame unit test, 55

TestSkyCubeMapping method, 211–212

TestSounds, 83

TestSounds( ) method, 54

TestUdpClient method, 458

TestUdpServer method, 458

Tetris

  background, rendering, 100–102

  block types, 102–105

  BlockFalldown sound, 99

  BlockMove sound, 99

  BlockRotate sound, 99

  blocks, gravity, 105–107

  Fight sound, 99

  input handling, 107–110

  LineKill sound, 99

  Lose sound, 99

  NextBlock game component, 111

  TestFallingBlockAndLineKill unit test, 105

  Victory sound, 99

TetrisGame class, 93

TetrisGrid class, 94

tex2D method, 163

texelHeight, 425

texelWidth, 425

texOffsetX, 425

texOffsetY, 425

text, entering, 275–277

TextureFont class, 95–97, 96

  implementation, 96–97

textures

  background, displaying, 19

  Dungeon Quest, 522

  file formats, 63

  landscapes, 339–340

  loading, 18, 36

    imported, 18

  Normal Mapping, 175

  Pong, 34

  rendering, 3D models, 121–123

  SpaceBackground.dds, 36

  XnaShooter, 300–301

    animated, 303–304

.tga file format, 63

threads, Rocket Commander and, 235

Tokamak Game Physics, 384

track, vertices, 358–363

TrackImporter class, 355

TrackLine class, 349

Trackmania, 336–337

tracks

  importing data, 356–358

  interpolating splines, 352–354

  unit testing, 349–352

Tracks namespace, 340

TransformPosition, 184

troubleshooting, 27–28

  Pong, 58–59

TryParse method, 56

U

UDP

  sending data, 458–461

  TCP and, 450–453

UdpTests class, 458

unit testing, 37–74, 69–70

  3D models, 131–135

  Breakout, 82–83

  Canyon Commander, 408, 418–420

  engines, 117–118

unit testing (*continued*)
landscape, 342
NUnit Framework, 70–71
post-screen shaders, 224–225
rules for, 73
starting unit tests, 71–72
TestDriven.Net, 70–71
TestRenderLines, 124
tracks, 349–352
UnitDied message, 533, 534
Update( ) method, 7
Input class, 271–272
UpdateVertexBuffer method, 125
usePointLights variable, 529
user interface
In-Game UI, 281–286
XnaShooter, 298–300

V
VBScreenHelper, 212
Vector3Helper class, 407
vertex formats, 167
vertex input format, 158–159
vertex shaders, 159–161
matrices, 185–186
problems with, 177
VertexBuffers, 213
VertexPositionColor, 125
VertexOutput_Specular20 structure, 187
VertexOutput structure, 158
VertexInput structure, 160
VertexElement method, parameters, 193
VertexPositionNormalTexture, 158, 167
vertices, track, 358–363
Victory sound, Tetris, 99
viewVec variable, 186
virtualLightDistance, 424
virtualVisibleRange, 424
Visual Studio 2005 Professional, 12–13

W
water, 203
.wav files, 53, 245–247
Wave Bank, 54
websites
http://abi.exdream.com, 20
http://creators.xna.com, 26
http://en.wikipedia.org/wiki/
Microsoft_XNA, 20
http://forums.xna.com, 26
http://martinfowler.com, 33
http://msdn.microsoft.com/directx/xna, 20
http://xnadevelopment.com, 20
http://xnaresources.com, 20
www.AIWisdom.com, 530
www.DungeonQuestGame.com, 517
www.riemers.net, 20
www.thezbuffer.com, 20
www.ziggyware.com, 20
WorldMatrix, 128
worldToTangentSpace matrix, 186
worldViewProj matrix, 155
Write( ) method, 69
WriteArrayData method, 76, 80
WriteOnly, VertexBuffers, 213
WriteText method, 96
www.AIWisdom.com, 530
www.DungeonQuestGame.com, 517
www.riemers.net, 20
www.thezbuffer.com, 20
www.ziggyware.com, 20

X
.x model files, 63
X Model Importer, 67
X3Audio, 264
X3AudioListener, 264
X3DAudio, 264
X3DAudioListener, 264

XACT, 53
compression, 252–254
project creation, 249–250
sound and, 243
  cues, 256–257
Sound Bank, 54
sound banks, 254–256
Sound Cues, 54
Wave Bank, 54
wave bank, creation, 250–251
XACT Audio Project, .xap files, 63
XNA and, 248
  changes in XNA 2.0, 259–260
.xap file format, 63, 248
XAudio, 259
Xbox 360
configuration, 13–15
console debugging, 142
debugging, 56
deploying games, 141–142
dlls, external, 56
Dungeon Quest, 535–538
game component, writing, 143
gamepads, 56
loading content directly, 56
mouse functionality, 268
save games, 56
test resolutions, 56
testing, 56
unit testing, 56
Xbox Live Service, 13
XNA Game Launcher, downloading, 140–141
XmlHelper class, 356
XNA 2.0, 25–27
networking, 449–450
new features, 448–449
TCP and UDP, 450–453
XNA Content Pipeline, 5, 8–9, 23–24
advantages, 64–65
disadvantages, 64–65
management, 62–63

XNA Framework, 3–4
application model, 5–8
DirectX and, 3–4
Xbox 360, 13–15
XNA Game Application Model, 5
XNA Game Launcher, downloading, 140–141
XNA Game Studio Express, 4–5
installation, 10–12
requirements, 10
XNA Graphic Engine, 5
XNA Racing Game, 333, 337–338.
  See also Canyon Commander
XNA Shooter, 295
3D effects, 319–320
asteroids, 303
Corvette, 301
Firebird, 303
game logic, 317–319
Item class, 325–327
OwnShip, 301
Projectile class, 323–325
Rocket-Frigate, 303
Small-Transporter, 302
unit class, 320–323
XnaGraphicEngine, 155
XnaShooter, 296
3D models, 301–303
billboards, 305–308
landscape rendering, 308–315
sounds, 297–298
textures, 300–301
  animated, 303–304
user interface, 298–300
XnaShooter namespace, 297
XnaShooter.xap, 297
XnaShooterGame class, 296
XnaShooterGameMusic, 254
XnaTexture method, 220
XPA physics engine, 383

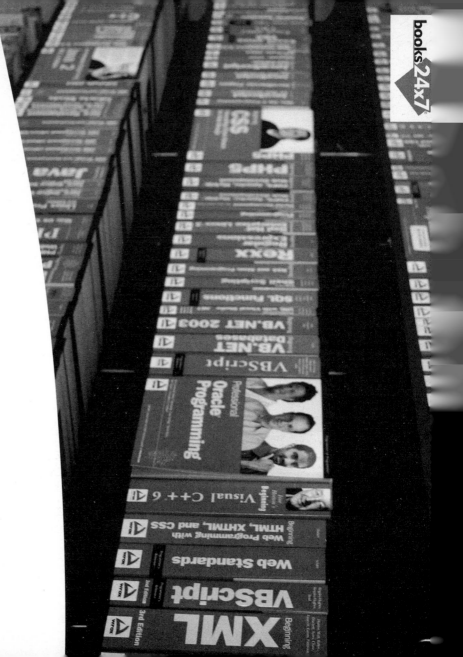